What's Critical Abo
Realism?

What's Critical About Critical Realism? Essays in Reconstructive Social Theory draws together five major essays that are situated at the intersection of philosophy and sociology. The book opens with a lengthy introduction to critical realism in which the author presents a general overview of Bhaskar's work and lays the groundwork for 'metacritical realism', a comprehensive social theory that is grounded in a positive humanist anthropology that points beyond the dire straits of critical theory and seeks reconstructive alternatives to the crisis. Throughout the book, critical realism is used to explore and interweave various themes that are at the forefront of contemporary social theory: the hermeneutics of internal conversations; the constitution of collective subjectivities and social movements; the generative structuralism of Pierre Bourdieu; the development of capitalism, biotechnologies and posthumanism.

The book as a whole is unified through a continuous reference to Bhaskar's philosophy of science, Habermas's communicative theory of society and Bourdieu's theory of practices. Alternating between exegesis and theory construction, it connects critical realism to critical theory, hermeneutics to pragmatism, and structuralism to posthumanism. The result of this ongoing dialogue between British critical realism, French historical epistemology, German critical theory and American pragmatism is the outline of the contours of a general social theory of personal, cultural and social change in late capitalist societies.

As suits a collection of essays in social theory, this book will address a broad audience of sociologists, philosophers, social psychologists and anthropologists who are interested in contemporary social theory at the cutting edge. Academics and advanced students who relate to critical realism and critical theory, epistemology and philosophy of the social sciences, hermeneutics and pragmatism, or anyone else who follows the work of Roy Bhaskar, Pierre Bourdieu, Bruno Latour or Margaret Archer will find a keen interest in some of the theoretical questions the book raises.

Frederic Vandenberghe is Professor of Sociology at the Institute of Social and Political Studies (IESP), which is part of the State University of Rio de Janeiro in Brazil. Personal webpage: http://frederic.iesp.uerj.br.

Ontological explorations

Other titles in this series:

From One 'Empire' to the Next
Radha D'Souza

Science for Humanism
The recovery of human agency
Charles R. Varela

Philosophical Problems of Sustainability
Taking sustainability forward with a critical realist approach
Jenneth Parker

Dialectic and Difference
Dialectical critical realism and the grounds of justice
Alan Norrie

Interdisciplinarity and Climate Change
Transforming knowledge and practice for our global future
Edited by Roy Bhaskar, Cheryl Frank, Karl Georg Høyer, Petter Naess and Jenneth Parker

Conversations about Reflexivity
Edited by Margaret S. Archer

Relational Sociology
A new paradigm for the social sciences
Pierpaolo Donati

Sociological Realism
Edited by Andrea M. Maccarini, Emmanuele Morandi and Riccardo Prandini

The Economics of Science: A Critical Realist Overview
Volume 1: Illustrations and philosophical preliminaries
David Tyfield

The Economics of Science: A Critical Realist Overview
Volume 2: Towards a synthesis of political economy and science and technology studies
David Tyfield

Ontology Revisited
Metaphysics in social and political philosophy
Ruth Groff

Childhoods, Real and Imagined
Volume 1: an introduction to critical realism and childhood studies
Priscilla Alderson

Naturalizing Critical Realist Social Ontology
Tuukka Kaidesoja

What's Critical About Critical Realism?
Essays in reconstructive social theory
Frederic Vandenberghe

What's Critical About Critical Realism?

Essays in reconstructive social theory

Frederic Vandenberghe

Routledge
Taylor & Francis Group
LONDON AND NEW YORK

First published 2014
by Routledge
2 Park Square, Milton Park, Abingdon, Oxfordshire OX14 4RN

and by Routledge
711 Third Avenue, New York, NY 10017

First issued in paperback 2014

Routledge is an imprint of the Taylor & Francis Group, an informa business

British Library Cataloguing in Publication Data
A catalogue record for this book is available from the British Library

Library of Congress Cataloging-in-Publication Data
Vandenberghe, Frédéric
What's critical about critical realism?: essays in reconstructive social theory / Frederic Vandenberghe.
pages cm. – (Ontological explorations)
Includes bibliographical references and index.
1. Critical realism. 2. Sociology–Philosophy. 3. Bhaskar, Roy, Bourdieu, Pierre. I. Title.
B835.V28 2014
149'.2–dc23

2013004358

ISBN 978-0-415-69601-2 (hbk)
ISBN 978-1-138-79857-1 (pbk)
ISBN 978-0-203-79850-8 (ebk)

Typeset in Times New Roman
by Wearset Ltd, Boldon, Tyne and Wear

Contents

Preface

> What is lost from the standpoint of would-be science is regained from the standpoint of humanity.
>
> Dewey, *Reconstruction in Philosophy*

There are, basically, two modes of theorising in the social sciences. The first mode is systematic. It is exemplified by the work of Talcott Parsons, Pierre Bourdieu and Margaret Archer, among others. Having developed their basic intuitions relatively early in their careers, their work consists largely of an ongoing elaboration of the 'mother-scheme' through further clarification of its stellar concepts and integration into a coherent and comprehensive analytical framework. Once the system is in place, it is parsed in new materials that demonstrate how the theoretical apparatus functions, how it compares with its rivals and how it is able to throw new light on old issues. As a result, every new book is, at it were, a new chapter of a single book.

The second mode is more eclectic. It is exemplified by the work of Karl Mannheim, Jeffrey Alexander and Luc Boltanski. These authors do not start with an analytic framework that, like the outmoded deductive systems of transcendental philosophy, needs to be played out over and again to strengthen its foundations and extend its reach till it eventually covers the whole world. Instead, they latch on to a particular topic, work their way through the materials and try to systematise them as well as they can as they proceed from one theme and one bookshelf to the next. The system is not a priori, but a posteriori. The coherence is not given, but searched for every time anew.

My work clearly belongs to the second category. While all the chapters in this book aim at maximal coherence, they are not integrated in an overarching system of thought. There's a theoretical habitus at work in each of the chapters, but like any generative structure that remains relatively invariant in its transformations, the habitus itself only shows forth in its actualisations. By virtue of their size and the complexity of their arguments, as well as the enormous amount of reading materials they try to synthesise, each of the chapters represents a short book in itself – five books into one, as it were – and explores at length a given theme: critical and metacritical realism in the introduction, the pragmatics of internal conversations in Chapter 1, the structuration of collective subjectivities in Chapter 2, the rationalist epistemology of Bourdieu's social theory in Chapter 3 and biocapitalism and posthumanism in Chapter 4. The book as a whole is unified by a continuous reference to Roy Bhaskar's philosophy of science and Jürgen Habermas' theory of communicative action. It takes the form of a sustained dialogue between critical realism, critical theory and contemporary social theory. The dialogue I propose is meant as a constructive and friendly one. I do not mean to make the theories weaker, but, in and through communication, I want to bolster them and make them stronger. By bringing new perspectives (hermeneutics, pragmatism and phenomenology) into the discussion, I have tried to update and renew the synergy between social theory and philosophy that marked the first formulations of critical realism. I have also sought to give critical realism a stronger grounding in phenomenology and a tighter integration with hermeneutics and critical theory. I have done so with the conviction that the philosophical questions of sociology should not be 'outsourced' to professional philosophers. Rather, social theorists should have the courage to work out and think through their own ontology, epistemology, axiology and anthropology.

The fact that I have hesitated about the title is testimony of the fact that various themes and motifs recur throughout the book. The initial title I had proposed was *Bhaskar, etc.: Essays in Realist Social Theory*. Although the title had the advantage of paying due homage to the founder and figurehead of critical realism, it severely restricted the audience to a mere handful of readers. To make things worse, a first reviewer of the book proposal thought that, given my lack of sympathy for the dialectical turn within critical realism, my reference to and pun on *Plato, etc.* was perhaps not the most appropriate; a second reviewer objected that a large part of the book is more about the 'etc'. than about Bhaskar himself. So, while writing the introduction to the book, I varied another of Bhaskar's titles and substituted the first title for a second one: *Reclaiming Humanity*, because it expresses my unwavering allegiance to the creed of post-secular humanism and also squarely situates my social theoretical reflections on critical realism within the German tradition of the *Geisteswissenschaften* (from Dilthey and Gadamer to Ricoeur and Habermas). Indeed, if anything characterises my soft-line approach to critical realism and gives it a distinctive tone, it is, I think, its indebtedness to hermeneutics, phenomenology and critical theory. The title may have been apt, but various friends I consulted on the issue didn't find it snappy enough. So I thought again and I finally decided upon *What's Critical about Critical Realism? Essays in Reconstructive Social Theory*. I call my essays in realist social theory 'reconstructive' not only because I reconstruct the theories of Bhaskar, etc., adding my own little ideas to their big ones, but also because the adjective points beyond critique and thereby opens the path of metacritical realism.

The book is composed of five massive texts which, with the exception of the introduction, were all written in a frenzy. While the chapter on Bourdieu and the one on collective subjectivities have been published before, the remaining pieces have not, at least not in their entirety.[1] The lengthy introduction to the book presents a general overview of the entire philosophical system of critical realism and lays also the groundwork for 'metacritical realism', a comprehensive perspective that fuses first-wave critical realism and the philosophy of meta-Reality into a general social theory of personal, cultural and social transformation. Incorporating hermeneutics into critical realism, metacritical realism fully endorses Bhaskar's critique of positivism and utilitarianism, but moves beyond critique and deconstruction to reconstruction. To lay the groundwork of such a reconstructive approach to social theory, I present a metatheoretical analysis of the basic positions within social theory, suggest that hermeneutics is really an idealist version of critical realism and propose critical hermeneutics as a meaningful alternative to critical naturalism. Grounded in a positive anthropology that emphasises and interlinks culture, communication and giving into an anti-utilitarian theory of action, metacritical realism strives to overcome the negativism of critical theory and to open up new vistas beyond the crisis and capitalism. I confess that I have become tired of the litany of denunciations that sails under the flag of critical theory (Frankfurt School) and critical sociology (Bourdieu). Why install oneself in the darkness of the basement if one can bask in the sun and the light on the balcony? Instead of focusing on the structures of domination and alienation that block the horizon, I reverse the perspective and explore how personal crisis can lead to re-narrations of oneself, how existential questions about what one wants to do *with* one's life carry over into questions about what one wants to do *in* life and show how, thanks to new internetworked technologies, a new convivial world is coming into existence.

More meditative in style, the first chapter on internal speech focuses more intently on existential issues, but does so from the vantage point of the 'linguistic turn' within the human sciences. It suggests that we do not merely have conversations with ourselves, but that we *are* these conversations. In an ongoing dialogue with Margaret Archer, I bring the internal conversations back into communication with continental hermeneutics and American pragmatism. Drawing on Gadamer, I open the discussion with the argument that we cannot start a conversation. To the extent that we are always already in a collective conversation, we can only continue it. To overcome the anti-humanism of hermeneutics, I next try to 'graft' pragmatism onto hermeneutics. Through a rereading of John Dewey, Georg Herbert Mead and Charles Horton Cooley, I bring back the question of alterity into the internal conversation and reinterpret the latter as a form of 'intrasubjective intersubjectivity'. In the spirit of symbolic interactionism, I foreground linguistically mediated interaction and analyse the role reflexivity plays for the coordination of social actions into a common action. In dialogue with William James, I conclude the chapter with some reflections on multiple selves and the problem of intrasubjective collective action.

If the first chapter is an ongoing dialogue with Margaret Archer, the second one is really an exchange with Rom Harré. I take up the question of the ontology of the social world once again, but this time I focus on the formation of collectives (categories, classes, communities, groups, networks, etc.) and outline a realist theory of 'collective subjectivities'. The question that drives my reflections on the causal powers of collectives is how abstract categories (like the Proletariat, the Church, England, etc.) that exist 'on paper' can be organised into a concrete network of people that can act 'with will and consciousness' in the real world. As the Proletariat is out of fashion these days, I focus on internetworked social movements like the Global Justice Movement who act in the name of humanity. The analysis I propose is a sequential one. Within a single dialectical process, I distinguish three constitutive moments. In a first moment, thanks to symbolic identification, the collective becomes a symbolic community that conceives of itself as a We; in a second moment, thanks to technological mediation, the symbolic community becomes a quasi-group that can be mobilised; in a third and last moment, thanks to political representation, the quasi-group becomes an organised group that can represent its members in their absence. I start with the phenomenology of the dyad, move to imagined communities, discuss social movements and finish the essay with spokespersons that represent in person the collective at large.

There is no doubt about it: Pierre Bourdieu is the major theorist of the second half of the twentieth century. In Chapter 3 I submit the epistemological foundations of his critical sociology to a realist investigation. Rather than starting with the concept of 'habitus', as is usually done, I systematically reconstruct his social theory by an in-depth analysis of the relational logic which permeates his whole work. I trace out his debt to Bachelard's rationalism and Cassirer's relationalism, examine his epistemological writings of the 1960s and make the case that Bourdieu's sociological metascience represents a rationalist version of Bhaskar's critical realism. Following the discussion of Bachelard and Cassirer, I show how Bourdieu's epistemological assumptions are reflected in his primary theoretical constructs of 'habitus' and 'field'. To concretise their discussion, I finally analyse the reinterpretation of Weber in his theory of the field of religion and of the young Mannheim in his theory of the scientific field.

The final chapter is called 'Posthumanism, or the cultural logic of global neo-capitalism'. It deals with contemporary developments in biotechnologies and is more polemical in tone and intent. Written in the spirit of the Frankfurt School, it offers a rather bleak and pessimist picture of the ontology of the present. The main thesis that drives my critical analysis is that posthumanism is the ideological expression of contemporary network capitalism. Through a materialist and humanist reading of some of the main theories (Leroi-Gourhan, Serres, Simondon, but above all Deleuze and Guattari) that form the background of the work of Bruno Latour and have been integrated in actor–network theory, I argue that the posthumanist attempts to theoretically deconstruct the opposition between the human, the animal and the machine countenance the technological modifications and commodifications of human nature by the bio-industries of neo-capitalism.

The chapters in the book are so many stations in a personal and intellectual trajectory that has brought me from the heart of Europe via North America to Brazil. One can read the book forwards – from the hyperbole of metacritical realism to the hypercritique of biocapitalism – or backwards. I have not tried to paper over the tensions between the melancholy of the last chapter and the hope of the opening chapters. The two are not unconnected, however. It is precisely because I was aware that my analysis of biocapitalism had driven me into a wall that I desperately started to look for a way out. Eventually, I found it on a new continent, a new country, a new community: *Brazil, land of the future*.

The pieces that compose the book were written over a period of 15 years and bear the imprint of the academic institutions where I have worked. My mind works better when it is 'provoked' by its surroundings. The text on Bourdieu was written in 1998 at Brunel, the University of West London, as a response to the constructivist ethos of my colleagues from Sciences Studies. I thank Steve Woolgar, Mike Lynch and Dick Pels for their stimulation and defiance. The text on posthumanism was written in 2002 at the University for Humanist Studies, a small experimental university in the Netherlands that is committed to the normative project of making the world more humane. Without the enduring companionship of Harry Kunneman, Marc de Leeuw and Fernando Suárez Müller, I would not be the 'humie' I have become. I acknowledge with gratitude the generous support of the Dutch NWO (Nederlandse Organisatie voor Wetenschappelijk Onderzoek) during the period 1998–2002. The piece on 'collective subjectivities' was written in 2005 at the University of Yale. I thank Seyla Benhabib, Jeffrey Alexander, Phil Gorski and Ron Eyerman for the moral support and the spirited discussions during my stay as a visiting professor at the Economics, Politics and Ethics Program. The texts on internal conversations and metacritical realism were both written at the Institute for Social and Political Studies in Rio de Janeiro and exude the enthusiasm and vitality of the place. I am grateful to my colleagues, but even more to my students at IESP-UERJ for the trust they have invested in me and the warm welcome they have given to my intellectual project. Like teaching, supervision is also research through other means. At Sociofilo, the research lab I direct, we practise the cooperation we preach in earnest and with humility. *Obrigado* to the Fellows for making this dream possible! As for the other academic colleagues, their contributions to the individual chapters are acknowledged at the beginning of each chapter. Wholeheartedly, I thank Roy Bhaskar for his unwavering support. I have been a critical realist since the late 1980s, but I had never met Roy in person. When the IACR came to Brazil in 2009 we finally met and I immediately joined the Brotherhood. I am also grateful to Margaret Archer, whom I first met in Bielefeld in 1994, for inspiration, discussion and friendship, and to Cynthia Hamlin for the weekly workshop on Skype. Thanks to Mervyn Hartwig and Nick Wilson for their constructive review. Praise to Alan Jarvis, the editor at Routledge, for extending the deadline again and again. And thanks to Martín Sánchez-Jankowski for inviting me over to the Institute for the Study of Societal Issues in Berkeley, where I am finishing this preface.

Note

1 Parts of the introduction have been published before in the *Journal for Critical Realism* (2009, 8, 2, pp. 203–232) and in Archer, M. and Maccarini, A., eds (2013) *Engaging*

with the World: Agency, Institutions, Historical Formations. Parts of Chapter 1 have appeared in Archer, M., ed. (2010) *Conversations about Reflexivity*. Chapters 2 and 3 were published in *Sociological Theory* (1999, 17, 1, pp. 32–67 and 2007, 25, 4, pp. 295–324). Parts of Chapter 4 were published in *Sociétés* (2005, 24–25, pp. 55–132), *Journal for the Theory of Social Behaviour* (33, 4, pp. 461–475), *Tijdschrift voor Humanistiek* (2004, 18, 5, pp. 82–93) and *Philosophy and Social Criticism* (2008, 34, 8, pp. 877–903).

Introduction

Metacritical realism – a proposal[1]

'There is no alternative to ontology.'

Bhaskar, *From Science to Emancipation*, p. 16

This book is written in the conviction that the historical mission of contemporary social theory consists of the double reconnection of sociology to philosophy and philosophy to sociology. While classical sociology consciously (dis)continued the tradition of moral and political philosophy through different means – even in its rupture, however, it paid homage to it – contemporary sociology has become so professional and inward looking that it has become a specialised language game on its own. Inspecting its categories, one would hardly notice that the world is facing the biggest crisis in a century! With its diagnoses of the pathologies of modernity, critical theory (broadly understood – it includes the whole gamut of social theories from Marx to Negri, Weber to Foucault, Lukács to Zizek, Adorno to Bourdieu and Horkheimer to Honneth[2]) has certainly maintained the continuity with moral and political philosophy, but at the price of increasing negativism. As if one could only get to the moral high ground by writing off everything that does not revolutionise the world in a single stroke! Unconvinced by the litany of denunciations of domination and oppression that has become the hallmark of critical theory, I have grown increasingly tired of hypercritiques of the present (though Chapter 4 on posthumanism is still very much part of that same genre of 'melancholy science'). Not that I want to deny that the current state of the world is rather worrisome and depressing. But painting black on grey is not helpful either. The techno-capitalist world has indeed become an 'iron cage', as Max Weber intimated in the final pages of *The Protestant Ethic*, but precisely because we are going through 'dark times' once again, we desperately need to open a little window on the world and let in some light and colours to illuminate our caged existence.[3] Nor do I contest that moral revolt is a precondition of collective action or that moral indignation can fuel social change, but instead of mobilising the *passions tristes* (anger, resentment and fear), why not mobilise the *passions joyeuses* (awe, empathy and generosity)? Why not try theorising from the heart (rather than the stomach) and philosophising with the open hand (rather than the closed fist)? Is it just disingenuous to suggest we can move from the hermeneutics of suspicion to a propedeutics of liberation?

To mark the transition from critique and deconstruction to reconstruction, I want to introduce 'metacritical realism' as an alternative that points beyond the dire straits of critical theory and opens new vistas on the world – beyond critique and, possibly, also beyond realism. In the same way as Bhaskar coined the term critical realism through elision of the terms of 'transcendental realism' and 'critical naturalism', I submit the term metacritical realism as a contraction of 'critical realism' and the 'philosophy of meta-Reality'. Although this contraction squeezes out the middle period (or second wave) of critical realism, the ambiguity of the new term has, however, another advantage: it does not only introduce the 'newly arisen superior tone in philosophy' that comes with the spiritual turn, but it also allows me to reconnect my own understanding of metacritique to Bhaskar's. I understand metacritique as a critique of the metatheoretical foundations of sociology that takes its cues from Talcott Parsons, Jeffrey Alexander and Jürgen Habermas and have used it to systematically reconstruct the theories of alienation, rationalisation and reification in German sociology (Vandenberghe, 2009). Bhaskar envisions it as a radicalisation of immanent critique that traces back the inner aporias to the social grounds that cause it and seeks to upend and solve all the antinomies of Western philosophy by pointing to their practical resolution. The two are perfectly compatible in my opinion. After all, if metacritical realism wants to move beyond the 'pathos of victimisation' of the first generation of critical theory, it does not want to relinquish the moral seriousness of the second generation. To the contrary, metacritical realism stands clearly poised between Bhaskar and Habermas. Through cross-fertilisation it seeks to enrich the former with the legacy of critical hermeneutics and the latter with the requirements of depth ontology. Critical realism is more incisive on epistemo-ontological questions; critical theory has stronger credentials in normative issues. When both strengths are joined together and work in tandem, the promises of metacritical realism can be realised.

This introduction sets itself three major tasks: (1) to present a systematic reconstruction of critical realism; (2) to outline the rudiments of metacritical realism; and (3) to search for constructive alternatives to the crisis. As a tribute to Roy Bhaskar, I will first present a systematic reconstruction of critical realism and follow the deployment of the philosophical system through its 'three waves'. As I think that Bhaskar's world-historical contribution to Western philosophy consists, above all, of its definitive critique of positivism, I will give more attention to the first wave of critical realism than to the other two (dialectical critical realism and the philosophy of meta-Reality). In continuous dialogue with 'neo-classical' sociology, I will show how Habermas, Giddens, Bourdieu and Luhmann converge with critical realism in their rejection of positivism. Arguing against the so-called 'Studies', I will present hermeneutics as an idealist version of critical realism and introduce 'critical hermeneutics' as a realist alternative to post-structuralism and posthumanism. As I follow the successive deployment of critical realism through its various incarnations, I will progressively depart from hard-line critical realism and gently question the distinction between the transitive and the intransitive dimension of knowledge.

In the second part of this introduction, I will move beyond critical realism and propose metacritical realism as a comprehensive social theory that is grounded in a positive humanist anthropology. To flesh out what I mean by metacritical realism, I will initiate the second part of this introduction with a metatheoretical discussion of some of the central problems of social theory. I will argue that in social theory everything hinges on the articulation of hermeneutics with a generous theory of action and I will strongly recommend a junction between the realist movement and the anti-utilitarian movement in the social sciences, which takes its cues from Marcel Mauss' famous article on the gift and transforms it into a transformative general social theory of action, social order and social change.

Finally, in the third and last part, I will move from social to sociological theory. I will sketch out an idealist theory of human development and interpret capitalism as a 'historical block' that obstructs the logical passage to ever higher levels of consciousness. I will analyse the current economic and political crisis as a harbinger of the second post-modernity. Although everything indicates that the future will be rather grim, I will nevertheless argue that post-capitalism is on the cards, not at a structural level though, but at the existential, cultural and communal levels of society. While the first and second tasks presuppose that one defeats positivism and utilitarianism, the third task is even more formidable and proposes that one rises above capitalism.

The three waves of critical realism

What's critical about critical realism?

Critical realism is not the invention of one man, Bhaskar, but his demolition of positivism is so rigorous, radical and powerful that it makes one wonder how standard accounts of science have been able to keep the best minds captive for such a long time. As a radical critique of positivist and postmodernist philosophies of science, critical realism offers an alternative philosophy for both the natural and the social sciences that foregrounds ontological questions. Inverting Kant's idealism, while maintaining its method of presuppositional analysis, it puts transcendental philosophy 'back on its feet'. Critical realism revindicates ontology as a theory of being, distinct from epistemology, and defends the strong thesis that the theory of being cannot be reduced to the theory of knowledge. Although essences and existences can only be known 'to us' under certain descriptions, they nevertheless exist independently from 'our' descriptions. Showing by transcendental arguments that ontology cannot be reduced to epistemology, it develops a non-anthropocentric ontology for the natural sciences and a humanist praxeology for the social sciences.

As a militant anti-positivist, I first became interested in critical realism because it offered the hammer I was looking for to crush the numbers. Through an analysis of scientific experiments, it shows that positivism is not even adequate for the natural sciences. If that is the case and Popper got it all wrong, as I think he has, then one would have to come up with very strong arguments indeed to make the positivist position in the social sciences minimally plausible.[4] The rejection of the positivist model of explanation does not mean, however, that in the social sciences there's only space for interpretation. Standard critiques of positivism are parasitical on positivism. They simply invert positivism and assault it where it is weakest, but they do not confront and defeat it on its own terrain. Even when positivism itself is openly contested, like in the famous controversy about positivism of the 1960s (Adorno *et al.*, 1969), which opposed critical theorists (Adorno, Habermas) to critical rationalists (Popper, Albert), the disputants typically accepted an essentially Humean account of natural law and of natural scientific theories. By introducing a new conception of causality and breaking with the empiricist misconception of the experimental sciences, scientific realism defeats empiricist realism on its own terrain and offers a coherent transcendental-dialectical approach of reality that points beyond the '*Erklären-Verstehen* controversy'. Thereby, it brings the *Positivismusstreit* to a proper end. Coming after neo-Kantianism (Weber), neo-positivism (Popper), neo-Wittgensteinian philosophy (Winch) and critical theory (Habermas), critical realism is the grand finale that finishes the positivist struggle and defeats positivism

Like Jürgen Habermas' (1968) and Karl-Otto Apel's (1981, II) approach, critical realism is transcendental – it thinks through the conditions of possibility or necessity of scientific knowledge to make ontological claims about the world. It is also dialectical – it continues the Hegelian tradition by analytic means and seeks to reconstruct Marxism. But Bhaskar is more radical in his critique of positivism, because unlike his German colleagues, he does not only question the limits of positivism and the reification of the social world it induces when it overreaches its limits, but he also questions the very validity of positivism in the natural sciences.

Critical realism enters the 'science wars' by fighting two fronts. This is not a 'war of position', it is a 'war of movement' that is being waged at the same time against the empiricist-positivist misconception of the sciences and against conventionalist, constructivist and relativist conceptions that are rooted in idealism and drift towards super-idealism. Against the naturalism that seeks a unified conception of the sciences along positivist lines, hermeneutics, structuralism and deconstruction have insisted that nature is socially and linguistically constructed.[5] This is the case, because facts are always and inevitably 'overdetermined' by theory, while theories are always 'underdetermined' by facts.

The 'underdetermination thesis' states that for every fact there are always a variety of theoretical explanations that are compossible with it and, if one fiddles enough with the *ceteribus paribus* clausula, it is always possible to 'save the phenomena' (Duhem-Quine). The social enters into this picture to narrow down the multiplicity of possible theories and to create order by reducing the complexity to more manageable proportions. As in Leibnitz, the social assumes the role of God and reduces the number of compossible worlds to one – the best of all possible worlds. Which theories are ultimately selected depends, among other things, on the *Weltanschauung* that is compatible with the theory and the distribution of the relations of power within the scientific field.

If the 'underdetermination thesis' fills the gap between theory and facts by introducing the social, the 'overdetermination thesis' eliminates the gap altogether and socialises the whole apparatus of science, from the basic categories to the technologies of observation. To show that facts are theory-laden, let us imagine Johannes Kepler and Tycho Brache sitting next to each other on the hill watching the dawn (Hanson, 1958). Did they see the same thing? No, they didn't. Kepler regards the sun as fixed and sees the world dropping away beyond the rim, whereas Tycho, who follows Ptolemaius, considers the earth as fixed and sees the sun rising at the horizon. Facts don't speak for themselves. As they are always categorised and schematised by one or another theory, philosophy or cosmology that is socio-historically determined, there is no observation that is not an interpretation and no interpretation that does not involve an imaginary representation of reality.

What one observes is paradigmatically induced and paradigms change over time. So, when Thomas Kuhn writes that after a scientific revolution 'the scientist afterwards works in another world' (Kuhn, 1962: 121), he is only stating the obvious, but without caution. What has changed is the life-world, his or her world, the 'world' if you want, but not the world in itself. It was there before the scientist arrived on the scene and will, presumably, still be there when the last human being expires (in a couple of millennia from now if we are lucky, a couple of centuries or decades if we are not).

Whoever suggests that the world changes with every paradigm change is drifting into super-idealism and flirting with irrationalism. Without the assumption that different theories offer alternative accounts of the *same* world, no science is possible. At the limit, we arrive at the patently absurd proposition that there are as many worlds as there are theories and as many worlds as there are theorists, and as everybody is a theorist, as many worlds as there are individuals. (But if one is talking about life-worlds, the latter proposition makes a lot of sense. We could even invert it and say that every individual is a world, a monad.)

Critical realism wholeheartedly accepts epistemological relativism, but to avoid the irrationalism of the multiplication of worlds, it introduces a categorical distinction between the *intransitive* or ontological dimension of reality and its *transitive* or epistemic dimension. The intransitive dimension refers to entities in the world which are real and exist independently of what we think (externalism), while the transitive dimension refers to things which are real but whose existence is dependent on what we think (internalism).[6] Thanks to this crucially important distinction between the theory-independence of the world (intransitive dimension) and the socio-historical variability of scientific knowledge (transitive dimension), critical realism is able to avoid the 'epistemic fallacy' which reduces ontology to epistemology and defines being in terms of knowledge. Thanks to this double focus, critical realism manages to combine and reconcile ontological realism, epistemological relativism and judgemental rationality.[7] It is thus uniquely compatible with a sociology of science and technology, while avoiding the excesses of radical (de)constructivism.

Critical realism does not only destroy and deconstruct; as a propaedeutic to the sciences, it also constructs and reconstructs. It acts, as Bhaskar says, quoting Locke, as 'the under-labourer, and occasionally as the midwife, of science' (1975: 10). It clears the rubble, removes the idols (Bacon), ideologies (Marx) and other 'epistemological obstacles' (Bachelard) that block a better understanding of scientific practices. In addition, it cuts the umbilical cord with the reigning philosophy of science and develops a comprehensive alternative that is animated by an interest in emancipation and Enlightenment (in the Occidental and Oriental senses of the term). As a philosophy *for* science (and against ideologies that threaten it), critical realism offers solid ontological foundations, not just for the natural sciences, but also for the social sciences. With Bachelard, we could say that critical realism 'gives the sciences the philosophy it deserves'.

In the natural sciences, critical realism leads to a total eclipse of positivism. In the social sciences, it leads to a consequent reformulation of Marxism that is able to overcome the old debate of the 1960s about the epistemological *coupure* that, allegedly, separates the young Dr Marx from the mature analyst of *Das Kapital* (Althusser, 1965). Instead of opposing (Hegelian) humanist and structuralist (Spinozist) readings of Marx, Bhaskar develops a strong relational conception of social structure that derives from a realist reading of Althusser, but that sacrifices neither structure to agency nor science to emancipation. Like all good Marxists who know their Aristotle and their Hegel, Bhaskar conceives of Marxism as a practical philosophy of emancipation and proposes a transformational model of social action that overcomes the opposition between agency and structure in dialectical fashion. As a self-confessed socialist, our social theorist also wonders 'how we switch the social process from a primarily reproductive to a primarily transformative mode' (Bhaskar, 1989: 8).

Although Bhaskar's praxeology has some notable affinities with Giddens' structuration theory, it avoids some of its central problems, which are, as I will argue further on, mainly related to the theorem of the 'duality of structure' and the omission of the phenomenon of emergence. Thanks to a sustained emphasis on the phenomenon of emergence (Bhaskar, 1982) and an implicit re-introduction of the dualism of agency and structure (Archer, 1996), critical realism offers a stratified ontology that is able to take into account the alienating autonomy of social systems without denying the power agents have to change society, culture and themselves. As this stratified ontology reduces neither social systems to social structures nor social structures to agency, it avoids the double reduction that characterises the fallacy of 'central conflation' (Archer, 1988: 72–100; 1995: 87–134). Although I think critical realism needs a stronger phenomenological grounding and also a stronger integration with hermeneutics than Harré, Bhaskar or Archer, who are steeped in the Anglo-Saxon philosophy of action and ordinary language, have offered so far, I am quite confident that it offers the best foundations for a solid critical theory of society that tries to integrate the critique of reification and the promise of emancipation into a single framework.

The realist groundswell

Bhaskar Roy is a man of many trades with many lives. Born during the Second World War in England of an Indian father and an English mother, both of whom were theosophists, he went to Oxford to study philosophy, political sciences and economics. Having started a PhD under the supervision of Romano Harré, which was rejected by the Oxford Dons, he went on to develop the philosophical system of transcendental realism at the end of the 1960s when, concerned with the problem of underdevelopment in the Third World, he came to the conclusion that economics is autistic and without relevance for the real world and for real people. Like his illustrious predecessors who opened up whole new vistas and were driven by a mission statement and a strong conviction that they would be able not only to solve the problems of philosophy, but also of humanity, Bhaskar is a man of grandiose ambitions and innumerous projects. More than once he has announced books (or series of books) with over-ambitious titles that were never published – at least not as yet: *Philosophical Underlabouring; Critical History of Western Philosophy*; *Philosophy and the Eclipse of Reason*; *Hume, Kant, Hegel, Marx*; *Philosophical Ideologies*; *Dialectical Social Theory*; *The Philosophy of Money*; *Transcendence and Totality*; *Between East and West*; *Re-enchanting Reality*; *Living meta-Reality*; *Work In: A Manual.*

His trajectory reminds me somehow of the one of Auguste Comte and Charles Sanders Peirce. Like Comte, he started out with a strong belief in science and ended up in the mystical waters beyond religion. Like Peirce, he is a bit of a genius (he wrote his first book when he was 20), but as he advanced in his reflections and deepened his ideas, his writings and his language became more and more idiosyncratic, obscure and esoteric. He abuses neologisms, TLA's (three letter acronyms) and semi-formalised arguments with *N*-dimensional graphic representations, which may well constitute, as in the case of Peirce, his 'natural language of self-communication' (*apud* Colapietro, 1989, xiv). Aware of the problem, he has added glossaries to his books, but as they are packed with internal references they are not always very helpful to make full sense of Bhaskarese.[8]

As an evolving system of thought that dialectically proceeds from 'thinking being' to 'being being', critical realism is a philosophical groundswell that has created a permanent, long-lasting shift in the way the world is conceived of. I call it a groundswell, because of the ground (critical realism is a depth ontology) and also because within the swell, we can distinguish three waves: critical realism (first wave), dialectical critical realism (second wave) and the philosophy of meta-Reality (third wave). The first and strongest wave can be subdivided in turn in three moments: transcendental realism (1), critical naturalism (2) and explanatory critique (3). As my discussion is not straightforward, but interspersed with multiple considerations that serve to maintain the connection between critical realism and social theory, I will indicate the sequences in the text in square brackets.

[First-wave critical realism – first moment: transcendental realism]

In a first, foundational moment, which coincides with the simultaneous publication of a *Realist Theory of Science* by Bhaskar (1975/1978) and *Causal Powers* by Rom Harré and E.H. Madden (1975), Bhaskar extends Harré's pathbreaking critique of the Humean concept of law with a conceptual investigation of the conditions of possibility of scientific practices. As a philosopher he treats the self-same world as the natural sciences, but transcendentally, i.e. from the perspective of what such scientific practices necessarily presuppose about the world prior to any empirical investigation, and asks the crucial question: 'What must the world be like for science to be possible?' (Bhaskar, 1975: 23). The answer to this question deserves to be called ontology.[9]

As an investigation into the ontology of natural kinds, transcendental realism submits the world of the positivists to a critical scrutiny and, thinking through the presuppositions of scientific experiments, it concludes that the familiar hypothetico-deductive model of Mill, Popper and Hempel is ill-conceived. By focusing on the empirical invariance between observable events (if *x*, then *y*), positivists have reduced the world to a world of atomic facts – a flat, predictable world of events without structure that looks like a cosmic table on which billiard balls (preferably white and red) collide with each other without necessity, without internal connection, without being embedded within a gravitational field.

Following von Wright's (1971) analysis of the causal intervention of the scientist in scientific experiments, Bhaskar demonstrates that scientific practices only make sense if one assumes that the world is an open system in which a multiplicity of factors operates at the same time.[10] To artificially close the system, experiments are set up. Allowing for meticulous control of all the factors and antecedent conditions (which are otherwise smuggled into the *ceteris paribus* clause, which, uncontrolled, creates havoc), experiments make causal explanation and prediction possible. Restricting significantly the validity of the D–N model, Bhaskar (1975: 103) affirms that 'it is only under conditions of closure that given the antecedent, the deduction of the consequent event is possible, so that the conditions for the Popper–Hempel theory of explanation are satisfied'.

Unlike positivists, who, following Hume, think of laws as constant conjunction or empirical invariance between contingently related observable events (two billiard balls that collide) and assume that laws can be observed in nature, critical realists know that the constant conjunction of events are rare in nature and that they are made to happen through artificial closure of the system. By making abstraction of the causal intervention of the scientist in experiments, positivists unknowingly identify the laws of nature that they observe in experimental circumstances with the laws in nature. Consequently, they generalise their findings beyond the experimental setting and do not realise that by identifying causal laws with constant conjunctions of events that are artificially produced they are led to the absurd conclusion that scientists cause and even change the laws of nature!

There is an 'ontological difference' between scientific laws and sequences of events. While the latter are man-made and belong to the transitive dimension of reality, the former belong to the intransitive dimension of reality and exist independently of human beings. If experimental activity is to be rendered intelligible, one must radically 'exhume' the sciences and conceive of laws as statements about 'causal powers' (Harré) or 'tendencies' (Bhaskar) of underlying or overarching generative mechanisms (like a gravitational field) which the scientist does not produce, but which operate in nature and whose presumed existence explains the conjunctions of events the scientist actually observes and registers in the laboratory as a *necessary* one.

Although these generative mechanisms themselves may be invisible or may only become visible through the use of sense-extending technology (Bachelard's 'phenomenotechnics'), their existence is nevertheless presupposed in scientific practice to explain the observable conjunction between events. Affirming the existence of generative mechanisms that internally bind causes and effects together does not lead back to metaphysics (nor to psychedelics – the *virtus dormitiva* of opium, according to Molière's famous doctor).

As a matter of fact, a good deal of theory construction in the natural sciences consists in building models of generative mechanisms and in setting up tests to find out what their structure is and how they function (Harré, 1970). Events are not to be thought of as producing other events without intermediary mechanism that establishes an ontological tie that binds cause and effects together, not contingently, but necessarily so. By virtue of the internal structure of the thing, the thing has the disposition it has to act in a certain way, and hence it must produce the effect it does produce, in favourable conditions and in the absence of constraints. As Mao (1966: 235) said: 'The fundamental cause of the development of a thing is not external, but internal.' The contingent conjunction of acid and litmus paper does not explain why the blue acid paper turns red. It is because litmus paper is sensitive to acid that, under suitable conditions, it turns red when it is conjoined to acid solution. By virtue of its intrinsic nature, because of its inner structure, litmus paper changes colour when it is dipped in proper acid. In science one observes an empirical regularity, invents a plausible explanation for it and then checks the reality of the entities and processes postulated in the explanation.

Unlike positivists, who unduly privilege empirical experiences, critical realism is a modal ontology that gives priority to potentiality over actuality and to actuality over experience. Foregrounding the causal powers of entities and processes, it stresses that tendencies of generative mechanisms may be real, yet unexercised, exercised, yet unactualised and actualised independently of human perception or detection. A causal power can be exercised over and again or not be exercised at all. Although exercised, its power may be neutralised by other countervailing powers (chlorine gas turns blue litmus paper white), so that actually nothing results and factually nothing happens. And when something happens, it may well happen without anyone noticing it, like in Berkeley's famous riddle about the tree that falls in the forest. In any case, the experimental situation in which the real (the potential), the actual (the factual) and the empirical (the observable) coincide is an exceptional one and should not be taken as the rule.

Science never ends. When a hypothetical generative mechanism that explains the relation between phenomena as a necessary one is identified, confirmed and described, the hypothesis turns into a fact that needs not only further exploration, but also further explanation. Indeed, the *explicans* of today becomes the *explicandum* of tomorrow. Scientists look further and delve deeper to find a more basic, underlying generative mechanism that explains the emergence of the phenomena. Because of the phenomenon of emergence, reality is stratified and science has not only a horizontal, but also a vertical carriage. 'Science is (vertically) in motion in a world (horizontally) in motion' (Bhaskar, 1986: 40). Like a miner, science always delves deeper and deeper, moving from one stratum of reality to the next (vertical dimension), discovering on each stratum a multiplicity of generative mechanisms that explain the relation between events (horizontal dimension). And at the very bottom, science discovers the ground of all beings and unveils the mystery of being itself: *Aletheia.*[11] Not everything that is or can be can be the object of the sciences.

Anti-positivism and neo-classical social theory

Bhaskar may be a professional philosopher, but he has mainly been read by social theorists, first in the UK and then all over the world. Apart from a few incursions beyond the Anglo-Saxon world (like in Italy or Québec, for instance), French, German or Latin-American philosophers generally ignore his work, not because they disagree, but simply because it has not reached them. Unlike their colleagues from the philosophy department, sociologists, geographers, political economists and social psychologists with a Marxist background and a keen interest in social theory quickly realised the import of critical realism for the social sciences. By the mid-1980s, the first wave of critical realism had received a very favourable reception. High-quality books with a realist imprint were published by Ted Benton (1977), Russell Keat and John Urry (1982), William Outhwaite (1987), Derek Layder (1990) and Andrew Sayer (1992). At the intersection of philosophy, sociology and politics, social theorists were probing the philosophical foundations of sociology and cognate disciplines, assailing the 'orthodox consensus' (evolutionism + functionalism + positivism) of post-war sociology and reassessing the merits of structuration theory. Thanks to the good services of Anthony Giddens, social theory had meanwhile emerged as a relatively autonomous subfield within British sociology, while elsewhere, galvanised by ethnomethodology, structuralism and systems theory, new ambitious theoretical syntheses were published almost simultaneously. By now the story of the 'new theoretical movement' (Alexander, 1988) and its attempt to overcome the opposition of agency and structure has become a hackneyed one, but back in the 1980s when Pierre Bourdieu, Anthony Giddens, Jürgen Habermas and Niklas Luhmann were writing their main works, sociology was ebullient.

It is in this context of theoretical effervescence that the favourable reception of first-wave critical realism by social theorists has to be understood. When the intellectual climate changed in the late 1960s, the American hegemony over professional sociology slowly came to its end. Within the social sciences, Talcott Parsons' sophisticated synthesis of neo-Kantian idealism and empiricist positivism (Münch, 1982) lost a good deal of its attraction and was successfully being recast as a form of establishment conservatism. Although this political character-assassination of the prime mover of American post-war sociology was wrong-headed, the axis of power shifted away from the Ivy Leagues to Europe and the West Coast of the United States. Standard versions of the recent history of sociology tend to emphasise how the demise of structural functionalism was brought about by an unlikely coalition of Californian action theorists, like Blumer, Goffman and Garfinkel, who sapped the praxeological presuppositions of systems theory, and European conflict theorists, like Touraine, Lockwood and Marcuse, who unmasked the broad-based axiological consensus as a massive mystification that obscures the class contradictions of capitalist societies. What is less often remarked, however, is that the main social theorists who challenged mainstream sociology did so through a sophisticated critique of positivism. They did rebut the deductive-nomological model not just in the social, but also in the natural sciences.

Through incorporation of the neo-Wittgensteinian argument that observations are embedded in a network of 'models and analogies' (Hesse) that conceptually structure its perception and 'iconic metaphors' (Harré) that are isomorphic to reality, Anthony Giddens (1974, 1976: ch. 4, 1977: ch. 1) advances the 'double hermeneutic' as a main point of his attack of positivism and regularity determinism: to make sense of facts, scientists interpret them not only in the light of explicitly formulated theories, but also by means of implicit theories of common sense that pre-structure the data. In knowledge societies, the latter are increasingly permeated by fragments of scientific theories, with the result that the boundary between common sense and the sciences becomes rather porous. Between science and common sense, traffic goes both ways. This is even more the case with the human sciences, whose concepts emanate from the life-world and, eventually, return to it, forming and transforming the social world which they pretend to describe. Positivism, with its emphasis on 'sense data', obfuscates the theory-ladenness of observations, while its built-in regularity determinism neglects the active role theories play in the constitution of the world. The idea that one could make predictions in an open multi-level system is, as Popper knew all too well, preposterous. It transforms a lack of reflexivity into a parade of scientificity.

Like Giddens, but coming from a different tradition in the philosophy of science (neo-Kantianism, pragmatism and dialectics), Jürgen Habermas (1969a, 1969b, 1974) assails positivism for its incapacity to theorise the role of theories and theorists in its own terms. Intervening in the second round of the famous

Positivismusstreit that opposed the critical theory of the Frankfurt School to the critical rationalism of Popper and Hans Albert, Habermas argues that communication among scientists is the blind spot of critical rationalism. Presupposed in practice, yet denied in theory, it leads to a 'performative contradiction' ('a T/P inconsistency', as Bhaskar would say). By adopting a scientistic perspective on science, Habermas charges, Popper has actually bisected reason and immunised his own theory against experience and common sense. In spite of its insistence on problem solving and the elimination of errors, the deductive-nomological model does not have the proper conceptual resources to understand scientific activity. As soon as scientists start to experiment, falsification is falsified; as soon as they start to talk among themselves, positivism is overcome.

Both Giddens' and Habermas' critique of positivism introduce arguments from the human sciences into the philosophy of the natural sciences, but do not question positivism's pertinence to the natural sciences. If they assail positivism, they do so from a humanist position. What they object to is the overreach of naturalism. The positivist affirmation of the unity of sciences misrecognises the fundamental differences between the natural and the social world. To counter the colonisation of the human sciences by the natural sciences, they want to clearly indicate the ontological limits of naturalism. This project of hermeneutically informed philosophy of sciences is sound. Provided it avoids the relativism that comes when hermeneutics slides over into a deconstruction that denies the referent, it is, I think, compatible with critical realism's triple defence of ontological depth, epistemic relativism and judgemental rationalism. Later on, when we will look at the contributions of critical realism to social theory, and then again in the second part of this introduction, I will explicitly defend hermeneutics as a form of realism, albeit an idealist one, and argue that it is necessary to vanquish utilitarianism in the social sciences.

But for now, what we want to really overcome is positivism, and to do so one has to contest it on its own terrain and show, once and for all, that the deductive-nomological model doesn't even hold in the natural sciences. That is exactly what Pierre Bourdieu, whose work will be analysed at length in Chapter 3, argues. Like Althusser and Foucault, he stands squarely in the rationalist tradition of Bachelard, Canguilhem and Cavaillès. Unlike Giddens and Habermas, however, he is neither a humanist nor a hermeneutician. He does not attack positivism because of its naturalism. Like Bhaskar, whose work he overlooked, he wants to reclaim naturalism from usurpation by the positivists. Both positivists and humanists are united by a false representation of the natural sciences. Once this mystification is unveiled, a naturalist scientific sociology becomes possible. According to Bourdieu, who, follows Bachelard and Cassirer on this point, the task of the sciences is a double one: to propose a rational model of 'generative structures' that produce the phenomena, and to develop 'phenomenotechnologies' of observation that make them visible. That holds for both the natural and the social sciences. Like his or her counterpart in the hard sciences, the social scientist has to effectuate an 'epistemological rupture' with common sense and develop complex models of the underlying structures that generate social practices.

Readers of Bourdieu know that he always explains social practices by reference to the field and the habitus of the agents and that he uses the techniques of 'correspondence analysis' to represent their location in society. While the field is constructed as a structural space of objective relations between social positions, the habitus is understood as a system of mental and corporal dispositions to act in accordance with one's social position. Together, field and habitus constitute the generative mechanisms outside and inside the persons that are needed to scientifically explain their practices. Provided one puts rationalism 'back on its feet', all this is quite compatible with critical realism in my opinion. Bourdieu is indeed a realist when it comes to society, but one with strong conventionalist tendencies (strangely enough, though, when it comes to collective subjectivities, he is an outright constructivist and nominalist). To avoid the 'epistemic fallacy', which considers reality as an emanation or instantiation of a theoretical construct, and transform critical sociology into a genuinely realist endeavour, one only needs to carefully parse the relations between his rationalist theory of science and his materialist understanding of the social world. Contra Bourdieu, one should insist that causal mechanisms are not materialised models of reality; rather, with Bhaskar, one should affirm the reverse and consider theoretical models as fallible attempts to capture the reality out there.

The complexity theory of Niklas Luhmann offers perhaps the most serious challenge to critical realism. While the hermeneutics of Giddens and Habermas are compatible with critical realism's conjunction of ontological depth and epistemic relativism, Luhmann's constructivist epistemology is only so as long as one does not introduce an observer into the system.[12] As long as one remains on the first level of observation, one might even be led to think that Luhmann's version of systems theory is more realist than Parsons'. After all, when he affirms that systems of all sorts exist in reality and that they themselves (rather than the scientists) establish the distinction between system and environment that constitutes them as systems, one seems indeed to be on firm ground. Unlike Parsons, whose analytical realism follows Kant and Weber, Luhmann (1981: 244ff., 378ff., *passim*) argues that before being observed by scientific observers systems observe themselves and they are also recognised as systems by other systems in their environment.

As soon as one brings in the scientific observer, however, the ground begins to wobble. The scientific point of view on reality is only one point of view on reality among others. Frogs and elephants constitute their world in their own way and even for us, humans, the scientific perspective is not the only one. The world can also be observed from a religious, literary, juridical, educational or economic point of view. Like other perspectives, the scientific point of view belongs to the world and does not merely disclose it; rather, it adds itself to the world. An external observer cannot observe the world. Following complexity theory, Luhmann argues that the world can only be observed from within the world as a point of view on that world. There's no observation that does not construct the world as 'its world'. This holds not only for frogs and elephants, but also for social theorists, including realists.

From the scientific point of view, the world appears as it is – a complex set of generative mechanisms endowed with causal powers. Realism is the regional ontology of science. It is the natural worldview of scientists who observe the world and what happens in it. But here comes the rub: realists and scientists 'see what they see, but cannot see what they cannot see [sic]' (Luhmann, 1990: 85). Indeed, the problem is not that they do not see. Like everybody else, realists and scientists also have a blind spot in their field of vision. This blind spot is a condition of the possibility of seeing. The problem is, rather, that they cannot see that they cannot see. They see *what*, but it takes a second-order observer to see *how* these observations are constituted as first-order observations. Operationally, realism is the failure to allow for variation. It does rule out the auto-reflexive loop that analyses the conditions of science as its consequences. From the point of view of second-order cybernetics, it is the philosophy of a science that protects its foundations. From a constructivist point of view, the transcendental presuppositions of realism are confirmed as presuppositions of the sciences. Without them, the sciences could not operate. What appears obvious and necessary to the sciences appears, however, to an outside observer as highly improbable, variable and pretty contingent. The world as we know it is neither necessary nor impossible. It is as it is, or better, as it appears to be from a certain perspective. Like the human species, science is an accident. Everything could have been different. Without a transcendental observer of all observers, realism is, at best, a contingent attempt to reduce contingency, and, at worst, a lack of reflexivity that transforms its own weakness into strength. Like the snake that bites its own tail, critical realism and radical constructivism are caught in a loop. On the first level of observation, realism is confirmed; on the second, it is reconstructed as a presupposition of the scientific point of view, which is, however, relativised as a contingent point of view. Steeped as it is in the hard sciences, radical constructivism cannot be written off as anti-science. That is why its provocations constitute perhaps the most serious challenge to critical realism.

Anti-realism and the 'Studies'

At the same time as our neo-classical sociologists presented their general theories of the social world, postmodernism stumbled on the scene and became the intellectual fad of the *fin de siècle*. Postmodernism defies definition. It includes authors like Lyotard, Baudrillard and Foucault, though the latter explicitly distanced himself from it. The roots of postmodernism lie in the intellectual crisis of Western Marxism. As a symptom of its time, it expresses a general disbelief in philosophies of history that promise a radiant future, yet are complicit in the perpetuation of the present. Postmodernism eschews any reference to underlying 'causal mechanisms' that produce phenomena, 'deep structures' that control events or 'grand narratives' that drive history. Avoiding depth and promoting superficiality, it fastens on the surface of things and texts – things-as-texts – and lingers there. Despite its repeated denunciation of all authoritative discourses, it relies heavily on a series of anti-philosophical injunctions that go against the spirit of critical realism: 'Thou shall not spin grand historical narratives, construct big societal pictures, entertain high utopian ideals, or think deep philosophical thoughts' (Hoy and McCarthy, 1994: 218; see also Vandenberghe, 2006).

With the benefit of hindsight, we can now understand postmodernism, which came forth as a movement in architecture and the arts (Connor, 1989), as a systematic attempt to bring aesthetic issues of representation into philosophy in general and epistemology in particular. When this aesthetic motif, which considers every representation as a possible version of reality, is extended to the sciences, ontology becomes an exercise in 'decorative philosophy'[13]: no longer a presupposition of science, reality becomes the 'pro-ject' and 'pro-duct' of its re/presentations. Like the arts, scientific discourses (texts without authors) are said to 'perform' the realities they purportedly describe. Underneath the discourse, outside the text, between the lines, there is nothing, according to postmodernists, but text. Nothing but texts, discourses and signs that proliferate and disseminate. Discourses and texts without referents, but full of referrals and references to other texts. Deconstructed and destroyed, reality (without quotation marks or, as Butler has it, with 'invisible quotation marks') is textualised and reappears as 'reality'. According to aftermodernists, reality is, at best, a *Ding an sich* to which we have no access; at worst, a reification of discourse that presents itself as nature and, thereby, prohibits the proliferation of other discourses and the realisation of other worlds.

At this point, where realism is rejected as a restraining order on the margins of creativity, the aesthetic becomes political. For postmodernists, every scientific and philosophical statement has to be read and decoded as a political one. Though it may not always be a conscious statement by the authors themselves, it is nevertheless seized upon by the campus radical to show off his progressivism and her political correctness. In the politicised, textual readings of 'reality', there is always a political subtext to be found in the margins that is repressed and that allows one to reread the core of the text against the grain. All too often, postmodernists' politicised readings of scientific practice have led to confusion between the political and philosophical registers – as if political correctness could overrule epistemic correctness! When scientific texts are read like any other genre, the distinction between science and literature collapses. From the point of view of critical realism, the confusion of registers and genres typically inverts epistemology and ontology. Instead of considering alternative visions of reality as different visions of the same reality, the elementary distinction between descriptions of the real and what they refer to is deconstructed, with the result that interpretations are cut loose from reality and relativism is set free to luxuriate. Not only does postmodernism dispense of a correspondence theory, it also explicitly excludes discursive theories of truth. Without a commitment to dialogue, discussion and consensus, the 'fusion of horizons' that marks every genuine attempt at understanding is foreclosed. Between different language communities, there is no bridgehead. Only difference, incommunicability and incommensurability. If Habermas and Giddens introduced hermeneutics into the sciences to delimit the remit of the natural sciences, postmodernists universalise hermeneutics beyond their limits, with the result that the natural sciences are now seen as a branch of the humanities.

Notwithstanding appearances, the 'post' of postmodernism, poststructuralism and other post-isms is not so much a temporal as a spatial marker. The prefix indicates what happens to 'French theory' (Cusset, 2005) when it crosses the Atlantic and decorative philosophy enters American departments of comparative literature. When the same process of dislocation occurs in the social sciences, the various post-isms of philosophy sire a rhapsody of post-disciplinary investigations of the power–discourse nexus – the so-called 'Studies' that enter in direct competition with the social sciences and may even throw them into disarray (as evidenced by the crisis of anthropology). The impact of Gramsci's cultural Marxism and Foucault's genealogy on the 'Studies' could hardly be underestimated.[14] Whether it is cultural-, gender-, race- or any other of the 'Studies' (e.g. subaltern, diasporic, postcolonial) that is a spinoff of post-ism, the variety of decorative sociologies and anthropologies have become quite ingenious in exploring and exposing the hidden connections between discourses, power and practices. This combination of structuralist emphasis on discourses, Foucaldian genealogy and Wittgensteinian practices has become so common by now that one might well portray it as the New Orthodox Consensus – with poststructuralism replacing positivism, deconstruction functionalism and contingency evolutionism. Through a generalisation and concatenation of the 'suspicious' readings of Marx, Nietzsche and Freud (or Althusser, Foucault and Lacan), discourses, texts and images are traced back to the base reality of violence they express as much as they conceal. This is how ideology functions: representations of reality within language do not so much repress as produce both the knowing subjects and the objects of knowledge as objects that are 'hailed' by discourses that bring them into existence and subjected to the subtle workings of governmentality and power. The whole point of the interpretative exercise of the 'Studies' seems to consist in an exposure of how class, gender and/or race appear and intersect in the cracks and crevices of the discourse. Once the subtext of power is un/covered, the author will usually hint at other voices that are waiting to be released from the margins of the text. Through identification with the excluded other that presses against the text, the analyst pretends to subvert its core and, thereby, hasten the demise of the Enlightenment.

In spite of their anti-philosophical stance and their wholesale attack on Western logocentrism, the 'Studies' have, however, something important to contribute to social theory. Provided they overcome their eclecticism and enter into a genuine dialogue with social theory, they could legitimately claim to continue the honourable tradition of critical theory – with the philosophical sophistication of the first generation of the Frankfurt School, the moral commitment of the second one and the commitment to sociological analysis of the third.[15] The impulse to liberate the Other of Reason and move beyond the traps of identity-thinking is not necessarily regressive. There is a genuine ethical voice there that should be heard and listened to (Honneth, 2000: 133–170). In the same way as Derrida's and Levinas' invocations of alterity resonate with Adorno's remembrances of mimesis, Judith Butler's (2005) later work on the narratives of the self usefully entangles some of the intricacies of Honneth's theory of recognition. Similarly, with its sensibility for voices from the periphery, the 'Studies' point to some of the obvious blinders of old European thought. Living in Brazil, I have often wondered if the theories that are imported from the centre do not hinder rather than help to understand life in the former colonies. Colonisation of the life-world (Habermas)? Here it is the life-world that corrupts and colonises the system. Routines and reproduction of the system (Giddens)? Here the actors have to continuously improvise to adapt to the system and keep it going. Discipline and punish (Foucault)? Here the prisons do not have cells for individual inmates but, reproducing the violence of the outside world within its walls, they are largely replicas of the former slave quarters. To make theories work, one has to systematically read them against the grain, twist and tear them apart and then piece them together again in a different fashion. Instead of arguing for 'Southern Theory' as a postcolonial alternative to metropolitan theory (Connell, 2007), one might as well take metropolitan theory to the global South and critically engage it on new terrain, where its limitations will be uncovered at the same time as they are overcome in a refurbished theory that is made to measure. Thus understood, postcolonial social theory is not a genre of investigation that offers an alternative to theories from the centre, but an attempt to apply metropolitan theories to make sense of local situations that the standard theories could not even imagine.

Constructivism and Science Studies

Like the other 'Studies', Science Studies sprang forth as an attempt to reconduct discourses, texts and representations to its historical, social and cultural determinations.[16] To radicalise the Mannheimian project of the sociology of knowledge to scientific knowledge as such, the 'Strong Programme' of the Edinburgh School proposed to investigate the 'existential determination' of scientific thought without any restrictions. While Karl Mannheim had largely exempted the exact sciences, as well as mathematics, geometry and even 'pure economics' (!) from his inquiry (Mannheim, 1974: 43), allegedly because truths like $2 \times 2 = 4$ are simply the Truth and, therefore, not subject to socio-historical variation, David Bloor (1976) recommended a causal, impartial, symmetrical and reflexive approach to truth and error. The social determination of science does not only hold for ideological deviations; even the Truth itself is socially produced and constructed.

Once the genie of relativism was out of the bottle, British Science Studies went into a frenzy. In their race to the bottom, a variety of Schools – the Bath School with Harry Collins and Trevor Pinch, the York School around Michael Mulkay, the Brunel School around Steve Woolgar – started to mushroom during the 1980s. One way or another, all were influenced by Garfinkel's ethnomethodology and each one aspired to be more radical than the other. Upping the ante, they were 'playing chicken' (Pickering, 1992). Trying out all positions – from the social construction of scientific facts and the social destruction of technological artefacts to literary deconstruction and stylistic experimentation – the main business of Science Studies consisted largely in the application of some well-tried methods of social, cultural and historical contextualisation of scientific practice that demonstrated how the 'over- and underdetermination theses' worked in any concrete case. Let's take an empirical example: a dead man lying on the dusty ground with a bullet in his head (Grint and Woolgar, 1992: 153–167). Although everything indicates that he's been killed by a gun, one can always question the fact and deconstruct it *ad libidum*, argue that it is not guns or roses, but people, that kill, question the meaning of the gun, as well as the expertise of the police and the coroner, invoke different conceptions of death in other cultures, and so on. The fiddling with the facts deconstructs the distinction between the physical and the social. It mollifies the bullet, which, in spite of all the hard evidence, never hits its target.

Notwithstanding the intense competition and occasional mudslinging, all protagonists were united in their rejection of the normative injunctions of the philosophy of science. Through a well-ordered series of concerted displacements, they moved the cursor of scientific investigation from prescription to description, internalism to externalism, logics to dynamics, theory to practices, as well as from the transcendental to the historical, the global to the local, the macro to the micro, the rational to the irrational, and far beyond. If they had a mission, it was to debunk any prescriptive philosophy of science and to empirically demonstrate that Logic, Reason, Reality, Truth, Progress and so on hardly accounted for the scientific practices. One might thus as well do without them.

Accusing each other of lack of nerve, they entered the laboratory to study science as it was being made and showed that scientists, like cooks and the rest of us, were only muddling through, inventing theories, massaging the data, fabricating their facts, constructing networks, trafficking influence, using rhetoric and presenting the result as scientific truth. Eventually, when every layer of science was questioned and removed, when the whole of science was exposed as a social construction of sorts, the provocations of the social studies of sciences were becoming tedious, repetitive and compulsive, like an old clown's act.[17]

Had it not been for the talents and the charms of Bruno Latour, a French postmodern socio-anthropologist with a theological background, STS would have settled as a normal science of science. Sometimes derided as a charlatan, Latour has not only renovated Science Studies, however, but drawing on a host of authors, like Deleuze and Tarde, but also others like Greimas, Serres, Simondon and Leroi-Gourhan who are hardly known outside of France, he has also worked out actor–network theory (ANT) into an ambitious, expansive and provocative general theory of society. Although I disagree with most of his philosophical positions, I esteem his contributions and respect his work. I would advice any realist to read his work and to seriously engage with it.[18]

To keep it short, I will summarise his work in three points:

1 *Science is social* (Latour, 1988). In a 'technography' of a scientific laboratory in California, Latour and Woolgar showed how scientific facts are literally constructed and fabricated by scientists. Working with 'inscription devices' that re-present nature on paper and reduce reality to a flat surface, scientists were busy transforming rats and chemicals into a series of blots, graphs and figures that could be integrated in their articles. As their vision of nature became generally accepted by colleagues, who quoted the article, the scientific representation of nature was progressively hardened and transformed into a scientific fact ('blackboxed'). When the square quotes around 'nature' were eventually removed, nature ended up appearing as something that was not made but discovered by the scientist. In spite of the radical constructivist assumptions, one should not conclude too quickly, however, that Latour is anti-science. His work on scientific inscriptions aims to show how scientists construct nature as a scientific fact through a 'cascade of representations' that describes nature more and more accurately. Nor should one conclude that he is anti-realist. Sure, he always blasts off as a constructivist, but usually ends up a realist of sorts. Therefore, my advice is to read his books like one reads *One Thousand and One Nights* – from back to front, starting with the last page and reading his account as a savvy 'phenomenotechnological' description of the material constitution of scientific facts.

2 *Society is natural* (Latour, 1996). Scientific facts are socially constructed but cannot be reduced to the social because the social is also made up of objects mobilised to construct it. For too long sociologists have analysed society as a commonwealth of humans (subjects), without understanding that society is impossible without non-humans (objects) that stabilise social relations and keep society together. Thanks to common objects (walls, doors, tables, televisions, etc.), the social order does not have to be continuously renegotiated and constantly remade *in situ*. Non-humans do not only replace and stand in for humans – e.g. the traffic light replaces a policeman and the automatic door a porter – but they can be considered as actors in their own right. Drawing on Greimas' structural semiotics, Latour and Callon introduce the notion of 'actant' to refer to any actor, human or non human – God, scientists, microbes, scallops, etc. – that intervenes in the construction of society as a heterogeneous network of humans and non-humans. If one quietly puts aside the anti-humanist provocations of Latour, his point about the materialisation of society is well taken and can easily be incorporated into sociological analysis. As a matter of fact, it is enough to follow the networks and see how they are part and parcel of larger systems that govern their structure, determining what is possible and what is not, to bring back the theory of associations within the fold of materialist social theory (Vandenberghe, 2002).

3 *Nature and society are co-constructed in and through socio-technical networks that associate humans and non-humans into a seamless web* (Callon

and Latour, 1981). Nature and society are not given, but always in the making; neither is a cause, both are a result and emerge out of the network that continuously transforms and performs reality. Mutually constitutive of each other, nature and society are co-produced and constituted in and through the heterogeneous network that associates humans and non-humans. Redefining sociology as the science of associations, ANT analyses how micro-actors become macro-actors by enrolling humans and non-humans alike in an expanding rhizomatic network. At this point the sociology of science takes a political turn and science is analysed as politics by other means. Natural scientists (like Pasteur) who represent nature or social scientists (like Bourdieu) who represent society, speak in the name of others and give them a voice. Speaking in their name, they 'translate' their interests, associate them to their project, integrate them in a collective and progressively compose the world as an expanding network among networks that potentially covers the whole world. The problem with this alternative theory of globalisation is that it systematically eliminates differentials of power the actors have to change the world. With its advocacy of a 'flat ontology' and its denial of a stratified world, it inevitably reduces the real to the actual and the actual to the empirical. As a result of this move, it becomes impossible to analyse the capitalist world system as a system with a centre, a semi-periphery and a periphery. For Latour, everything is in flux and in process. There is no being, only becoming; no structure, only relations; no system, only networks; no society, only associations.

Posthumanism and late capitalism

In the last chapter of the book I will present posthumanism as the ultimate consummation of postmodernism. Whatever postmodernism is, and however one wants to define it, it always operates through the erasure of binary oppositions. Having deconstructed the distinctions between depth and surface, reality and representation, ontology and epistemology, discourse and power, text and context, it assails the opposition between the human and the non-human as the last bastion of foundationalism. Decentring the subject, redefining it as a position within language and scattering it over a series of discourses, deconstruction aimed to remove the Cartesian subject from the theatre of knowledge. Posthumanism radicalises the anti-humanism of poststructuralism and negates the species-subject. Instead of humanism, it commends a rejuvenated vitalism. Like Nietzsche, posthumanists like Deleuze and Latour want to overcome the human. To undercut it, they plunge it back into life and open it up to anomalous becoming. The human is not a being, but an anonymous becoming that comes from the depth of life and is bound to return to it. Posthumanists are set to deny human essence and contest its existence. As far as they are concerned, there is no ontological invariant that allows one to define human nature. The distinction between the human and the animal species is a specious one. For sure, the human is an animal. Genetically speaking, humans and animals are all part of the same pool.

Were it not for some moral taboos, biotechnology could alter the boundaries between the species and engineer a being that is neither human nor animal, but infra-, trans- or superhuman. Similarly, they claim that the distinction between the human and the machine is now outdated. With the advances in cybertechnology, the machine becomes every day more human, while the human becomes more machine-like. We are all bound to become 'cyborgs'. Given that posthumanists have abandoned the very idea of a human essence that can be alienated, the question is whether the new socio-technical assemblages are to be celebrated as a triumph of mind over matter or, more soberly, registered as a mere fact of life of high-tech societies.

Within contemporary philosophy and the human sciences, we can distinguish various strands of posthumanism. They are not exclusive and may intermingle. They hover between an essayistic neo-vitalism and a scientistic supermechanicism. Whereas neo-vitalists like Latour and Sloterdijk are joyous, playful and ironic, supermechanicists like Luhmann and Serres are stern, sombre and cynical. One way or another, they all go back to Nietzsche and, like him, thrive on provocations.

The first strand is eminently French and interconnects Leibniz's monadology with Nietzsche's vitalism. Heavily influenced by Gabriel Tarde, Gilles Deleuze is, no doubt, the central figure behind a good deal of today's excursions into posthuman assemblages. Deleuze's ontology of becoming is a vitalist ontology of pulsating fluxes and vibrating currents of all sorts at the molecular level that occasionally intermingle, but usually bifurcate and go their own haphazard way. The whole movement is one of creative chaosmosis in which all compossible worlds are actualised and come into existence at the same time. The anarcho-communist Antonio Negri and the anthropo-sociologist Bruno Latour, both Deleuzians, are perhaps the best-known representatives of neo-vitalism in contemporary social theory.[19]

In Germany, where *Lebensphilosophie* and its irrationalism have been discredited by history, the Nietzschean connection passes through Heidegger and, at times, also through Derrida. At the boundary between philosophy, comparative literature and media studies, *Medienphilosophie* (Hartmann, 2002) has emerged as a new field of reflection and speculation on the various mediations and medialogics of thought, from language and writing to television and the new digital media. Of the various authors that are associated with the new interdiscipline (Kittler, Sandbothe, Vogel, etc.), Peter Sloterdijk, the talented polywriter and co-host of a philosophical show on German television, is the most exuberant and vociferous. In a provocative essay on Heidegger's *Letter on Humanism* that set off a nasty polemics by proxy with Habermas, Sloterdijk (1999) suggested that, with the closing of the age of writing, the domestication, cultivation and breeding (*Züchtung*) of the human animal no longer occurs through the medium of writing, but by other, more powerful anthropotechnics of selection, including biotechnology.[20]

Elsewhere, cybernetics, the scientific study of 'control and communication in the animal and the machine' (Wiener), has evolved into a science of complex self-organising systems. Through incorporation of new developments in mathematics, physics, biology, computer science, etc., cybernetics is now also applied in the human sciences. In spite of the exceeding difficulty of the theories behind the prose, concepts such as complexity, fluidity, autopoiesis, fractals and chaos have become fashionable, not just among managers, but also among sociologists and economists. Although complexity theory is not necessarily incompatible with humanism – see the multi-volume work on Method of Edgar Morin and the morphogenetic perspective of Margaret Archer – the conceptualisation of societies as self-regulating systems tends to eliminate the human subject or, what amounts to the same thing, to integrate it as an integral part of the functioning of systems. The systems theory of Niklas Luhmann, who has assimilated the whole of cybernetics into his work, is posthumanist through and through: humans are not even part of the system. Only communications belong to it. Humans belong to the environment. They do not communicate. Only communications communicate.

If posthumanism were only a passing fashion, it wouldn't be preoccupying. Like installations in contemporary art shows, it would hold up a mirror to society. As far as I am concerned, the problem is not with technology as such, but with the way bio-, cyber- and nanotechnologies are coupled with, and tied to, post-industrial capitalism. The age of pure science is over (Pestre, 2003). Nowadays, all the hard sciences are applied sciences that follow the so-called 'Mode 2' of knowledge production which is problem-focused and pragmatic. The corporations have entered academia and sponsor R&D. The concept of the 'technosciences' was coined to indicate that the sciences are now, from their very inception, conceived of as applied sciences. Big science is big business. Against this background of the technological modification and industrial commodification of life, posthumanism is not a *Spielerei*. What decorative philosophers deconstruct in theory, the technosciences reconstruct in practice. That is why I have entitled the long chapter on Bruno Latour, which is, in fact, a chapter on reification in the age of the technological reproduction of Man, 'Posthumanism or the cultural logic of global neo-capitalism'.

Critical naturalism or critical hermeneutics?

[First-wave critical realism – second moment: critical naturalism]

So far, we have basically analysed the anti-positivism of neo-classical sociology and the anti-realism of postmodern 'Studies' against the background of critical realism. We have shown how both parties introduce sociological arguments into their critique of the positivist account of natural sciences. Assuming that critical realism offers a unique philosophical platform for the successful synthesis of ontological depth, epistemic relativism and judgemental rationalism that is able to integrate the strengths of naturalism, hermeneutics and discourse ethics, we now will move from the natural to the social sciences. The invaluable contribution of critical realism to the social sciences consists in having established beyond reasonable doubt that positivism is not the only philosophy of the natural sciences. If positivism does not hold in the natural sciences, then, of course, one wonders how it could possibly prevail in the social sciences. Defeated in the natural sciences, it becomes simply untenable in the social sciences! Not because they are pseudo-sciences, but because of the very nature of the social world itself. Those who are still of the opinion that the social sciences are too immature to be scientific have, I am afraid, understood neither the nature of science nor that of society. Against scientism, I will defend hermeneutics and against naturalism, I will argue for humanism. Following Bhaskar's transition from transcendental realism to critical naturalism and explanatory critique, corresponding respectively to the first, second and third moment in the groundswell of first-wave critical realism, I will now explore the ontological limits of the naturalist approach in the social sciences. At the risk of belabouring the obvious, I cannot stress enough that societies are always, necessarily and inevitably, social constructions. Unlike mountains, trees and humming birds, which grow naturally, societies are man-made. They are social products. Ontologically, all social facts presuppose social acts and practices as condition of their possibility. It is analytical to social action that it depends on the intentions, reasons, motives, meanings, causes, representations, descriptions or, in short, concepts of the actors who bring it about. Hence, social structures are practice- and concept-dependent, though they are usually most dependent on concepts of actors (including scientists) in the past, not today.

In the social world, the descriptions of the social world are reflexively and constitutively tied to its reproduction and transformation. This is true for the scientific descriptions, which as Giddens says, 'circle in and out' of the sciences, and also, *a fortiori*, for the common sense descriptions and symbolic representations of the world that ordinary actors use in their everyday life.[21] As scientific concepts slip over into common sense, the social sciences are complicit in the constitution of the social world they describe. In this sense, every competent actor may be said to be a social theorist. Consequently, the distinction between the transitive and the intransitive dimension of knowledge collapses. Because the transitive is in the transitive, the hermeneutic dimension of social knowledge cannot and should not be underplayed.

Hermeneutics is more than a method of understanding. It is the very ontological condition of life in society as such (Gadamer, 1999: I). It is only because the world is always already pre-interpreted, pre-understood and pre-structured by the background of a shared context of meaning that human action is possible. The world is disclosed to us as a meaningful one that always already makes sense. Yet, in another sense, the world is disclosed through us. As actors, we give meaning to the world. Between the actors and the world, cultural understandings always intervene as a mediating element that discloses the world as a properly human world that is shared by others. This collective constitution of the world as a common one is what makes social action possible. Thanks to the sedimentation of experiences in cultural forms, actors are not only able to pre-reflexively understand objects, themselves and others – the three principal elements that make up the situation – but also to reflexively endow their actions with meaning and intentionally act in concert. Together, the macro-social background of shared meanings and the micro-intentional foreground of social practices form a functional unit. The intentions of the individual and collective actors are embedded in a contexture of meanings that form the background of their intentional actions; their actions reactivate the contexture of meaning and keep the 'hermeneutic circle' dynamic and alive. The hermeneutics of culture and the phenomenology of intentional action complement each other like whole and part, background and figure, spirit and soul. While phenomenology is a kind of a hermeneutics in the first-person singular, hermeneutics is a phenomenology in the first person plural. In any case, the world of symbolic representations and intentional meanings can only be accessed from the perspective of the participant. The linguistic turn within philosophy and the human sciences implies, therefore, a hermeneutic turn. *Pace* Rorty, the linguistic turn marks, in truth, a return to ontology. Critical realism cannot and should not neglect hermeneutics. Hermeneutics is not incompatible with realism. Although postmodernism has co-opted hermeneutics and pushed it into a nominalist direction, unlike poststructuralism, hermeneutics is a form of realism. As I will argue later on, and more extensively in the next chapter, it represents its idealist counterpart and should be fully incorporated within critical realism not as its other, but as its necessary complement.

The social sciences are part and parcel of the human sciences. Yet, they are also more than human sciences. To the extent that social acts have crystallised into 'pseudo-natural' social formations that are grounded in, yet irreducible to individual and collective acts, we need, however, to temper our bold affirmation and speak of a 'quasi-intransitive' dimension of social knowledge. After all, when social scientists get to work, they come up against a society whose existence does not depend on their analysis. Following Searle (1995), we could say that society is an 'ontologically objective fact'. Unlike 'ontologically subjective facts', which only exist in the mind of individual observers, society is extramental and presupposes a collective subject, a 'We', endowed with collective intentionality as a precondition of its being observable and analysable. Social structures are, for sure, sedimentations of past intentional activities, but, endowed with autonomy and inertia, they are independent not only of the descriptions of the social analyst, but also of the current practices of ordinary actors. Most of the social knowledge that actors mobilise in their daily life is itself an inheritance of the past (Archer, 1988). The past is sedimented in the present in the same way as the present is conditioned by the past. This dialectic between the past and the present, whereby the past acts as a condition for practices in the present that contribute, intentionally or not, to the reproduction and/or transformation of existing arrangements, is, ideally, a lively one. In complex societies this dialectic seems, however, to have come to a relative standstill. Contemporary social systems are dangerously out of control. Social structures that hardly anyone wants continue to rule the existence of 99 per cent of the population. If the past and the present were synchronous, we would not be in the sorry situation we are in today. With the good will of all, like in a dream, everything could be changed overnight.

Unfortunately, this is not going to happen.

The main reason for this inertia is to be found in the 'emergence' of relatively autonomous social systems with more complex and differentiated higher-level structures that arise from the organisation and interaction of simpler, lower-level component parts, with the former being irreducible to the latter.[22] A product of social practices, both individual and collective, the emergence of social systems is not a project. Rather, it is an unintended, unavoidable and, at times, even a perverse consequence at a macro-(societal) level of a myriad of anonymous ordinary social practices. In the modern world, the autonomy of the social and technological systems and their subsystems may become pathological, both alienated from its purpose and alienating for those who are subject to them (Vandenberghe, 2009). Impervious to their wishes, thwarting their projects, individuals face society like a 'pseudo-natural' world they do not understand and cannot change, which imposes its constraints on them from without and regulates their behaviour from within. When social facts are like pseudo-natural facts, they have to be treated as things, not because they really are things – they are not; 'things are', as Sartre (1960: 246) once said, 'social facts' – but because when societies become inhuman, the negation of the limits of hermeneutics becomes counterproductive, verging on the ideological. In tandem with humanism, which seeks to reactivate the dialectics between agency and structure, naturalism is not only perfectly legitimate in the social sciences, it is also necessary.

The emergent structural, systemic quality of complex societies warrants Bhaskar's invocation of 'critical naturalism'. In order not to forget the praxeological nature of society, I would, however, rather follow humanists, like Habermas, Apel and Ricoeur, and call for a 'critical hermeneutics'.[23] This hermeneutics is a critical one, not only because it recognises in the autonomy of the social world its own ontological limits, but also because it believes, as a matter of principle, that a conscious reactivation of the practices that constitute the social world can make it more human (and, in this sense, less natural).

In an attempt to bring emergence into hermeneutics and hermeneutics into critical realism, I will present a chiasmatic reading of Giddens' structuration theory (Giddens, 1976, 1979, 1984) and Bhaskar's transformational model of social action (Bhaskar, 1979, 1986). With Bhaskar, I will argue that the concept of emergence is necessary if one wants to account for the structural 'disembedding' of social systems and *a fortiori* for their alienation; conversely, with Giddens I will stress the importance of symbolism for praxis. Extending both Bhaskar's and Giddens' takes on the agency–structure problem, I will also try to shift the focus from individual to collective action. Anticipating the gist of Chapter 2, I will argue that collective subjectivities intentionally intervene in society to reproduce or change it and that they are the levers that make society move to a higher level of development. The result of this double correction of Giddens should be something akin to a realist theory of restructuration.

Critical realism and structuration theory

At first, when Bhaskar (1979) explored the possibility of naturalism in the human sciences, there seemed to be a host of family resemblances between his transformational model of social action and Giddens' structuration theory. Giddens was aware of critical realism and sympathised with it; similarly, Bhaskar had read Giddens, and the synergy between philosophy and social theory seemed quite promising. In an attempt to marry the structuralism of Saussure to the theory of practices of Wittgenstein, Britain's most famous sociologist developed the theory of structuration as an ambitious theory of social practices that would be able to overcome the gap between the micro-analysis of situations of action and the macro-historical analysis of societies via the mediation of culture.[24] Purged of its paraphernalia, structuration theory is nothing but a conceptual framework that integrates practices, culture and social systems, with culture (which, rather confusingly, Giddens referred to as 'structures') acting as mediator that fastens praxis to the practices that reproduce and transform social systems.[25] The dialectical sequence can be analytically decomposed in two phases. The first moment explores the connections between culture and praxis. In their everyday life, social agents spontaneously draw on culture to give meaning to their actions, orient themselves in the social world, interact with others and coordinate their actions. These actions and interactions do not only presuppose culture as the medium that regulates their practices, but they also reproduce and transform it. Culture is, therefore, as the theorem of the duality of structure states, 'both medium and consequence' (Giddens, 1984: 25) of ordinary practices.

In a second moment, the same practices are said to tie the ongoing flow of day-to-day experience to the *longue durée* of institutional time. Fastening short stretches of action in situations of co-presence to the reproduction or transformation across generations of the main social systems of modern societies, such as capitalism, bureaucracy, class and other classical topics of sociology, the practices of everyday life are the zip that interlocks agency and structure into a single mo(ve)ment. So, to make up a contemporary example, when people go to the bank to pay their mortgage or to invest in private pension funds, they draw on the cultural stock of knowledge that any competent member of society has at hand and that allows them to make their financial transactions. Although their actions are intentional and actors know what they are doing, their actions have, however, the unintended but inevitable consequence of reproducing financial capitalism. At the aggregate level, their actions may even trigger a systemic breakdown. Until further notice, capitalism remains the unacknowledged yet omnipresent condition of most of our ordinary practices. In this way, via culture, which regulates and structures social practices, the latter are joined to historical social systems which, at an aggregated level, are the outcome of the practices.

The distinction between social and sociological theory, with the former referring to fundamental ontological processes that characterise all human societies and the latter to more historically circumscribed processes, structures and mechanisms that are proper to modern and postmodern societies, is not watertight. But it allows us to pinpoint a rift in Giddens' work between his ontology of practices and his historical sociology. The major flaw of structuration theory is to be found in the fact that it does not acknowledge the phenomenon of emergence. Its ontology of practices is an ontology of processes without emergence and, ironically, also without structure. Ultimately, for Giddens, the social world is an ongoing process of individual and collective social practices without beginning or end. Although his writings on the sociology of early and late modernity presuppose an account of emergence, Giddens does not admit it, neither ontologically nor historically. Ontologically, practices cannot be disjointed from culture (structure) or social structures (systems). The fact that he speaks of the 'duality of structure' is symptomatic in this regard of a 'central conflation' (Archer, 1988, 1995) of agency and culture or structure. Surely, social systems, social structures and cultures presuppose social practices. Without practices, they would cease to exist. But when they emerge at the collective level as the unintended result of intentional social practices, they have distinct irreducible causal properties – characteristic ways of being and becoming which they possess in virtue of their intrinsic structure and which generate or prevent, enable or constrain the agency of individuals and collectives. If these emergent properties of social structures (cultures and systems) were reducible to, and could be explained by, reference to the causal properties of individuals and collectives, the social sciences would be redundant. Although social systems are, ultimately, the product of individual and collective agency, the former cannot be reduced to the latter. Moreover, to avoid that structuration theory collapses into methodological individualism, one should not just analyse the constitution of society, but also that of collective subjectivities. Instead of asserting with Giddens that social systems are just diluted collectives (as in Domingues, 1995), I will argue with critical realism that collective subjectivities intervene in society to change or reproduce it and investigate their structuration into an intentional group that can act with consciousness and will.

In accordance with Amitai Etzioni's (1968) seminal theory of societal control and guidance, I assume that collectivities can set goals, commit themselves to their realisation and pursue them. It is not only individuals who have a self; societies also have one. To the extent that they institutionalise their awareness on a collective level and develop specialised mechanisms of self-observation, they have a societal consciousness too. Consciousness is a prerequisite of self-steering, but to exercise their causal powers and have an actual impact on society, collectives also need to establish control networks that can supervise and organise the units of the system into a potent whole. Like individuals, macroscopic collectives can be active – i.e. aware of themselves and their surroundings – committed to certain normative goals and values and capable of self-transformation and societal guidance. To become truly active and have a macroscopic effect on societies of which they are part and which they try to change, collectivities need both a high degree of 'social integration' and of 'systemic control' (Etzioni, 1968: 94–130). To enhance their integration, they need to sustain the normative bonds that tie their members into a self-conscious category and muster consensus; and to augment the control of their environment, they need to organise the relations between the units of which they are composed into an active network that can control, coordinate and implement the decisions of the collective without too much coercion or manipulation of its members.

> From the viewpoint of a theory of societal guidance, a societal unit may have varying combinations of both cohesive relations and control networks. An active unit has a greater amount of both elements. Cohesive networks lack the capacity for self-control and, hence, are passive. Organizations without a cohesive base have at best a deficient ability to build consensus. They can serve as coercive or utilitarian organizations, but not as effective tools of societal and political action, which require strong normative elements.
>
> (Etzioni, 1968: 108)

By means of a theory of ordinary practices, structuration theory integrates structuralism and hermeneutics. To the extent that structuralism and hermeneutics represent idealist forms of realism, Giddens' ontology of practices is indeed a realist one. As such, it is well suited to account for the symbolic and normative elements that keep society together. As a hermeneutically informed theory of symbolic practices that are culturally regulated, it befits investigations that underscore the dialectical interplay between culture and agency. The insistence on common culture as a web of symbolic representations and imaginary significations that orient practices from within is essential if one wants to avoid the utilitarian reduction of action to a form of strategic behaviour. As a general social theory with ontological pretensions, its sensitising concepts apply to any community or society without institutionalised societal control. Between practices and culture there is duality, though, at times, individuals and collectives may stand back to reflexively analyse the structure of culture in order to change it; they may even create specific organisations to institutionalise reflexivity and steer societies to a common end. Yet, between action and social systems, there is dualism, disjuncture and solution of continuity (Mouzelis, 1989).

Indeed, if we reanalyse structuration theory not from an ontological and synchronic perspective, but from the diachronic and historical perspective that characterises all sociological theory from Marx, Weber and Durkheim onwards to Habermas, Luhmann and Michel Freitag, we can see that Giddens' description of a society that functions 'like a language' is valid for primitive societies 'without politics' and 'without history' – hence, without active 'societal guidance' (Etzioni) – that are studied by anthropologists.[26] As soon as those societies become aware of themselves through an idealised projection of their symbolic representation, first in myths, but later also in the form of religions and political ideologies, dualism sets in and culture becomes an explicit object of thematisation, theorisation and formalisation. With the emergence of the state, societies produce their own mediations and regulations in the form of legitimate political institutions that reflexively steer and coordinate social practices. When capitalism liberates the market from traditional norms that contained and limited its expansion, the economy emerges as a relatively autonomous subsystem that is 'disembedded' from the life-world and follows its own laws. When the transition from traditional to modern societies is accomplished, the 'beautiful totality' is sundered once and for all. The dualism between culture and agency is now amplified with a dualism between agency and social structure. This disjuncture between the life-world and the system is, no doubt, part of the modern condition (Habermas, 1981, II: 229–293). The dedifferentiation of society is no longer a collective option. The autonomy of the system is the price we have to pay for the increasing complexity of modern societies. But it now has radicalised to the point that systems are out of control and no longer subject to societal guidance; unchecked, it may well lead to a catastrophic tipping point. According to the experts, we have at most a century or two to go before the whole ecosystem collapses. The critical point I want to make is that when the autonomy of social and technological systems becomes pathological, societies becomes reified and actors alienated. To acknowledge the existence of social pathologies of alienation, manifest in feelings of meaninglessness and powerlessness that are induced by the alienating autonomy of social systems, one has, however, to recognise beforehand the existence of the phenomenon of emergence. As structuration theory denies dualism and emergence, it cannot acknowledge their pathological forms either and incapacitates its own critical potential.

Critical theory all too often assumes that a redescriptive analysis and normative denunciation of the forces of domination, oppression and alienation that damage life is able to fuel moral indignation and social change. The recognition that the whole system is off-track may, however, lead to fatalism, acquiescence and demobilisation (as happens when students are introduced to the *Dialectic of Enlightenment*) or worse, cynicism, enlightened false consciousness and remobilisation of critical insights for the perpetuation of the self-same system (as happens when *Distinction* is taught in courses of marketing or *Empire* is appropriated by management consultants). To avoid defeatism, the objective analysis of the structures of domination has to be anchored in a hermeneutic investigation of the culture of liberation and the politics of emancipation. It is only when the dialectical interchange between the system, culture and practices remains a lively one that a critical hermeneutics that seeks to promote social, cultural and self-transformation becomes conceivable. Such a generalised morphogenesis whereby society, culture and personality are all changed at once coincides with the emergence of conscious, intentional and capable subjectivities at a collective level that are driven by principles, values and ideas and that can bring about both a change in society and of society at large. Although there is no single collective subjectivity as yet to replace the function of the Glorious Proletariat, a realist analysis of collective subjectivities should at least offer an outline of the constitution of collective action at all levels of society – from local interactions between individuals (e.g. two or more individuals walking together) and groups (e.g. two or more social movements working together) to the global organisation of humanity into a intentional community of fate. In Chapter 2 I will provide such an analysis of the structuration of collectives and investigate the cultural, technological and political mediations that transform a bunch of individuals into a conscious whole, into a We, that can intervene in society to change it and make it move again.

The transformative model of social action

[Critical realism – third moment: explanatory critique]

Bhaskar's extension of the naturalist model of explanation to the social sciences underscores the phenomenon of emergence. With a strong interest in Marxism, Bhaskar (1979) was from the outset convinced that the challenge of the social sciences was to integrate a realist account of societies with a praxeological account of human action. Whereas his transcendental realism provided a philosophical clarification of the ontological assumptions of the natural sciences that remained neutral in regards to substantive investigations in the fields of physics, chemistry and biology, his critical naturalism was rather more partisan. Instead of merely exploring the ontological presuppositions of the social sciences, asking himself: 'What must society/agency be like for social sciences to be possible?', he tied the fate of critical naturalism to Marxism. Not only did he take up a determinate position in the field of social theory, developing the transformational model of social action (TMSA) as a dialectical resolution (*Aufhebung*) of Durkheimian theories of structure and Weberian theories of action, but, within Marxism itself, he clearly favoured the Althusserian readings of Marx that had become hegemonic within the *New Left Review*, while avoiding its anti-Hegelian drift towards poststructuralism and deconstruction. Given that Althusser's structuralism basically came up with a Marxist elaboration of Gaston Bachelard's rationalist reconstruction of scientific practices – the same one that inspired Bourdieu's theory of sociological knowledge, as we will see in Chapter 3 – this is hardly surprising. Like all Marxists with a Hegelian bent, from Korsch and Lukács to Sartre and Colletti, he sought, however, to inject a theory of praxis into historical materialism and develop a dialectical theory of social and political transformation.

Interestingly, his realist theory of science allowed him to do what others had failed to do, namely to avoid the stalemate between the 'two Marxisms' (Gouldner, 1980) and to work out a social theory that combines the scientific rigour of the late Marx with the humanist fervour of the young Marx. Given that only few authors were able to successfully overcome the opposition between Spinozian and Hegelian readings of Marx that up till today separate post-(Althusserian) structuralism from (post-Lukácsian) critical theory, this is quite a feature indeed.[27]

A general social theory should always, one way or another, theorise and interrelate social structures, culture structures and human practices into a unitary conceptual framework. Without a solid concept of structure and social systems, social theory becomes idealistic and loses its critical edge (as is the case with structuration theory); without an adequate conception of culture and symbolism, it becomes mechanistic and deterministic (as is the case with Althusser); without a convincing theory of practices, social and cultural structures are reified into anonymous processes without subjects. Bhaskar's TMSA works with a Marxist conception of social structure, a neo-Wittgensteinian conception of culture and a humanist conception of practices. Above all, concerned with the dialectical linkages between social and cultural structures on the one hand and transformative practices on the other, the exact connections between social structure, culture and practices remain somewhat sketchy. They will be parsed out in more detail by Margaret Archer (1988, 1995).

Like Bourdieu's concept of the field, Bhaskar's concept of social structure is rigorously realist, relational and materialist. It is realist, because structures are understood as transfactual generative mechanisms with emergent causal powers that condition practices. It is also relational, because structures are defined not as substances, but as systems of relations that hold between internally related social positions that individuals occupy and that, together, compose the social system. And, finally, it is also materialist, because structures are not identical to culture, as is the case in structuration theory, but to the 'generalized master–slave relations' (Bhaskar, 1993: 330–335; 1994: 229–230) that characterise systems of domination and exploitation of capitalist societies. As a system of objective relations between social positions, social structure is both a (largely unacknowledged) pre-condition and a (largely unintended) consequence of the intentional social practices of social actors. Although social structures presuppose social practices for their reproduction, TMSA advocates a collectivist and emergentist position: social structures cannot be reduced to individual and collective practices that sustain them; analytically, they always precede them as their *causa formalis*.

When it comes to culture, critical realism is on the same track as structuration theory, with the notable difference, however, that it explicitly acknowledges the phenomenon of emergence not only with regard to social structures, but also with regard to culture structures.[28] Like Giddens, Bhaskar largely seeks to integrate a structuralist conception of culture as a system of relations between signs, with a typical neo-Wittgensteinian insistence on rules, concepts and reasons of action. Although Bhaskar does mention the German tradition of Dilthey, Heidegger and Gadamer, his realist approach to culture is not so much inspired by the German tradition of hermeneutics as by the twin analytic tradition of ordinary language philosophy (Wittgenstein, Austin, Harré) and the philosophy of action (Winch, Louch, Taylor) that come with it. Like in structuration theory, the connection between social structure and practices is mediated in TMSA by the culture structures that provide the actors with a public repertoire of personal motives and reasons to act. For any critical theory worthy of its name, the reference to culture as a symbolic structure of significations that constitutes the world as a meaningful one is essential. Without symbolism, praxis is impossible.

Reasons are central to intentional human agency; in the social world they act as causes (Bernstein, 1971: 160–180). Causes link agency to social structures and they do so via reasons. This link of intentions to reasons, reasons to causes and causes to structures is what makes critical naturalism possible. This is naturalism, because like natural structures, material and ideal structures act as generative causal mechanisms. Yet, as it recognises that in the social world individual and collective actors are the only efficient causes and that structures operate only by virtue of intentional action, it is also rather critical of naturalism. Given the internal relation between reasons and causes, one might as well consider critical naturalism a form of critical hermeneutics. This presupposes, however, that one more intently probes the rapprochement between critical realism, hermeneutics and interpretative sociology. Although Bhaskar recognises that the causal effect of social structures is always mediated by culture and emphasises that social structures never constrain or enable actors from without, but only ever from within, like most authors in the Marxist tradition, he still tends to conceive of culture as a kind of superstructural reflection of the material basis of society and to neglect the relative autonomy of culture. As a result, the transformative power of symbolic representations of reality is underemphasised and culture is apprehended as, and reduced to, a form of 'symbolic power', i.e. an ideological force that reflects the existing world as it is and contributes to its reproduction by presenting it as a natural and normal condition. In this case, everything happens as if social structure directly determined the social practices that reproduce society. Instead of following their real interests, actors behave like agents who act according to reasons that society has induced in them, giving them the impression that they move freely, whereas, in fact, their reasons for acting are systematically deformed through the perlocutionary force of persuasion that makes them move against their interests.[29]

Mystified actors usually do not have the conscious intention to reproduce society. When Ms. Craveheart goes shopping and tries on a new dress, she wants to look good and feel good, but at an aggregated level, the reproduction of a society of consumption with its crass commercialism is nevertheless the inevitable and unintended consequence of her regular visit to the shopping mall. Similarly, when our colleagues go to academic bookshops and come out with a couple of books from Verso, they may do so because they want to change society, yet the inevitable outcome of their purchase is the reproduction of intellectual private property. By calling his model a transformative one, Bhaskar obviously wants to give culture its due, but like all Marxists, he thinks that social change is only possible when the workings of the whole machinery of social reproduction is scientifically exposed as an unnecessary one that can be changed by the actors themselves. By holding critical knowledge as a critical factor that can break the doxic spell of reproduction, Bhaskar contests the neutrality of social scientific descriptions of social structure. His explanatory critique (Bhaskar, 1986), which consists of the third and last moment of the first wave of critical realism, formalises the traditional workings of ideology critique in such a way that if one can show that a social structure of domination necessarily generates a false consciousness, induces wrong beliefs and makes actors accept reasons that go against their real interests, and if one can show, moreover, that the beliefs are wrong, the reasons manipulated and the interests misunderstood, then, *ceteris paribus*, one can immediately pass from fact to values, justify the transformation of the social structures and call for the absenting of domination as a categorical imperative of freedom.

Dialectics, alienation and reconnection

[Second wave: dialectical critical realism]

Dialectic: The Pulse of Freedom, the tract that ushers in the second wave of critical realism, is a massive, challenging and, ultimately, as Alan Norrie (2010: 7) says, a rather 'annoying book'. Conceived of as an ambitious philosophical system that continues and completes the Hegelian–Marxist tradition, it offers a completely new way of thinking the relation between being and becoming that foregrounds the productivity of 'the not' (absence, difference, negativity) – *die nichtende Nichtung des Nichts* (the annihilating annihilation of nothing), as I'm almost tempted to say with Heidegger to stress the active, processual and dialectical nature of negativity. If first-wave critical realism attacked positivist and postmodernist philosophies of science for their 'ontological actualism' (the denial of ontological depth) and their committing of the 'epistemic fallacy' (the reduction of questions about being to questions of knowing), second-wave critical realism deepens its critique of inherited philosophies with a sustained assailment of the 'ontological monovalence' (the denial of negativity, difference and contingency) that characterises identity thinking.[30] Instead of recognising the importance of absences, voids and gaps in reality that lead to productive tensions and rifts that make change possible, Western philosophy abhors the void and refuses to 'think the not'. Its denial of causality and difference as a fixture of reality is bound to ignore the causality of absence.

What dialectical critical realism (DCR) aims to do is to systematically introduce the dialectic into critical realism ('dialecticising realism') and critical realism into the dialectic tradition ('realising the dialectic') with the intention to offer a sustained metacritique of Western philosophy, from Parmenides to Plato, Descartes to Hume, Kant to Hegel and Habermas to Derrida (Norrie, 2010). As a metacritique of the whole Western tradition, DCR diagnoses recurrent fault lines in the canon, traces them back to splits in society and indicates ways to overcome the antinomies both in thought and in practice. Although I do not wish to question that Bhaskar's dialectical project is a coherent one, I doubt that I can explain it in an elegant and convincing way to the reader.[31] I will therefore limit myself to a brief presentation of its main articulations, show how the 'four-planar cube of existence' further develops TMSA and promises an alternative conception of alienation that allows not only for linkages to critical theory, but also opens the way to the philosophy of meta-Reality.

DCR presents itself as a systematic philosophy of natural, social, cultural and personal becoming that deepens the analysis of causality and makes it move by following through four phases, which Bhaskar dubs the 'MELD-circuit' (abstracting from the numerals, the acronym refers to the sequence of moments that leads from structure and process to totality and praxis): in a first phase, the so-called prime Moment (1M), critical realism is reaffirmed as a theory of causal structures that, far from denying non-identity, affirms it in a series of dualisms (such as the transitive/intransitive dimension, emergence, etc.). Moving from the prime Moment to the second Edge (2E), Bhaskar introduces the category of absences that bring movement into the system and the structures. At this level of real negativity, where being is conceived of as a becoming and becoming as a 'begoing', that is as an absenting of what is there, stable structures are transformed into dynamic spatio-temporal processes. Insisting on the openness and incompleteness of history, Bhaskar takes on Hegel's and Marx's dialectics. Instead of assuming that there is only one system and that all relations within the system are internal ones, Bhaskar 'diffracts' the dialectic and conceives of the world as a multiplicity of open and incomplete systems that may interact, complement or contradict each other, but whose trajectory is undetermined and unpredictable. His refusal of any onto-teleo-theology in which contradictions drive the system to its completion and end is followed at the third Level (3L) by an inquiry that investigates the alienating tensions, contradictions and splits that detotalise reality and fracture the world into a jumble of contingently connected parts. Where there should be unity and connection, there is dualism, separation and alienation. Social structures become independent of the practices that gave rise to them, take on a life of their own and may even turn against their creators. Bhaskar fully acknowledges the phenomenon of emergence and associates it to the concept of absence. Intriguingly, he asserts that a social structure may survive '(i) without any human agency and even despite any human agency, (ii) in virtue of our inaction, (iii) in virtue of our compliance and/or (iv) in virtue of the indirectness of the human agency which reproduces it' (Bhaskar, 1993: 158).

Generalising Hegel's famous investigation of the master–slave relation in Hegel's *Phenomenology of the Spirit* and Marx's analysis of alienation in the *Parisian Manuscripts*, our dialectician argues that in capitalism the alienation of essential human powers and capabilities manifests itself on the four planes of being and is experienced as a form of existential disconnection from nature, others, society and the self. When the human being is disconnected from nature, a Cartesian split ensues. We do not feel part of nature, but treating it as a 'standing reserve' we engage in material transactions with the environment in an instrumental mode. When we are alienated from our fellows, both intra- and intersubjectively, we experience the other as a threat, retreat from the social world and may even come to lose our social skills altogether. When we are alienated from society and no longer feel part of it, we experience it as a meaningless, hostile entity we cannot change and want to destroy, through violence if necessary. When we as human beings are no longer able to connect to ourselves, we feel lost and fragmented. Having lost our narrative or the purpose of our life, we lose our personal power and capability not only to change ourselves, but at the limit even to act and bring change in our environment, our social relationships and society.

The third Level (3L) does not only uncover disconnections and alienations, however; it also explores the possibility of intra- and interconnection between the parts and the whole. The central category here is the one of 'internal' (or necessary) relations that tie the parts to the whole and the whole to the parts. When the parts cannot be defined without reference to the other parts that make up the whole and to the whole itself, holistic causality obtains. Dialecticians know that nature, others, society and the self form a living unity. They do not merely presuppose each other; they represent different aspects of the same reality that are enfolded into each other.[32] When this unity is not just theorised and thought, but felt and experienced as a living connection, alienation is overcome, first at the individual, but then also increasingly at the collective level. Social structures dissolve into processes, culture is transformed, and so are the practices. Transformative social action is itself transformed by the dialectical changes that re-connection at all planes of human existence bring into the world.

When the structures of domination, repression and alienation are analysed from the point of view of a practical philosophy that aims to reanimate the dialectics between agency and structure, self and other, nature and society, the pulse of freedom reaches the fourth Dimension (4D). At this point, we encounter the transformative model of social action of critical naturalism as a special case of a more general dialectic of freedom. When freedom comes to the fore as both presupposition and end of action, the causality of intentional agency is, finally, liberated. DCR turns into a philosophy of praxis that releases agents from structures of domination, promotes autonomy and promises happiness to each and every one. When the agents become conscious of the social and cultural structures that alienate them and come to understand that the reification of social structures is the consequence of their actions and non-actions, ethics and politics fuse into the utopian attempt to finally realise the eudaemonic project of the good society in which 'the free flourishing of each is the condition of the free flourishing of all' (Bhaskar, 1993: 202, 284).

The dialectical movement from 1M to 4D (and beyond) can be construed as a continuous development of causation. From the causal power of generative mechanisms at 1M (as a *reprise* of first-wave critical realism) and spatio-temporal or geo-historical causality at 2E (as a revisit of Hegel's and Marx's travails of the Spirit) via the liability of alienation and the holistic causality at 3L (as a reflection on external and internal relations that brake or make a totality) and, from there, on to the transformative power of collective agency and the utopian politics of universal eudemonia at 4D (as the grand finale of the Socratic quest of the good society).

When morphostasis and its cycles of endless social reproduction, cultural reflection and personal repetition give way to morphogenesis and its dialectical spirals of social movement, cultural change and personal transformation, the four planes of the cube of social existence shift out into the cosmos and dialectics begets a fifth Aspect (5A) – the spiritual aspect in which the self connects to everything and everything is enfolded in the cosmic envelope. This spiritual enhancement of DCR is not to be found in *Dialectic* or *Plato, etc.*; it is the main subject of the philosophy of meta-Reality.

Being being

[Third-wave critical realism: the philosophy of meta-reality]

Since the dawn of the millennium, critical realism has taken a spiritual turn and entered its third wave. Passing from the transcendental to the transcendent, the erratic founder of critical realism started to invoke the healing powers of love and the oceanic experience of oneness. Taken aback by this spiritual turn, most of the dialectical realists refused his New Age Marxism as a spiritual deviation. The old Marxists and the young Hegelians were waiting for the Proletariat, not for Buddha, Sankara or Krishnamurti! When Bhaskar published *Between East and West* in 2000 and narrated the life of his former incarnations (he crossed the Red sea with Moses, joined Pythagoras' community, was baptised by Saint John . . .), their dismay was at least as impressive as their surprise. Used to the rhetoric of class struggle, convinced that revolutions always have to be violent, they hardly knew what to do with Bhaskar's 'realist embrace' of innerworldly mysticism and spiritual soma-aesthetic practices, like yoga, reiki and tree-hugging that accompanied his philosophy of mindfulness. So they rejected it and stuck to their guns.

Second-wave critical realism was not without the visionary thing – if anything, the convoluted, overambitious and increasingly hasty nature of Bhaskar's writings that followed the dialectical turn were testimony of the fact that he thought he was on to something unheard of. It was still largely a cognitive and academic endeavour, however. In spite of its pretensions to solve all the problems of Western philosophy, the pathos and impetus of DCR was mainly political. While critical realism was born as a philosophy of science that focused on ontological issues, it ended as an analytical philosophy in grand Hegelian style that thought through the notion of causality and reconnected it to ontology. As a successor to critical realism, the philosophy of meta-Reality (PMR) does not so much attempt to think being to overcome the contradictions of Western philosophy. True to the wisdom of ancient India, it tries to overcome dual thinking and displaces the emphasis from thinking to 'being being' (Bhaskar, 2002c: xx, 224). Being being, becoming being, becoming who one is and realising one's *dharma* by reconnecting/grounding oneself to the deepest level of reality in which all beings are connected and everything is one, that is the ultimate commandment of PMR.

According to Bhaskar, all that exists depends on an ultimatum – an ultimate or basic level of the universe which is ingredient or immanent in all others levels of reality and sustains it. With the idea that all beings partake of this ultimate reality and that they all have a specific ground-state that connects them to a cosmic envelope (which corresponds to what David Bohm (1980), who is also influenced by Krishnamurti, calls the 'en-folded'), the unity or non-duality of the whole universe is guaranteed. Like everything else, we, humans, also have our own 'ground-state'. When we are in this state of watchful passivity and connect to our inner being, we become aware that there's something that transcends us of which we are part. Ingredient in every human being, this transcendence is immanent. It binds not only humans, but all that exists into a potentially self-conscious unity. Like in Schelling, everything in the world, including matter, is implicitly conscious and has consciousness enfolded in its core. When this implicit consciousness awakens and becomes explicit in me, by implication, every object in the universe is enfolded in my consciousness. When I become conscious of the whole universe enfolded within me (= God), I am in my ground-state of being and without effort I connect to the 'cosmic envelope' (which is increasingly becoming conscious of itself). I see the world in a different way, I feel the other in a more intense way and having changed the way I am, I also act in a different way – with love, care and compassion. Through a hyperconscious link I am connected to you, the fish in the oceans and the stars in the sky. The consciousness of this immanent transcendence is as much consciousness-of-as-in-transcendence. As such, it transcends thought and duality. Indeed, it is not sufficient to think this unity. One also has to feel and experience it, be its witness and practise it, through meditation, yoga, use of drugs or other mind-expanding techniques that connect the inside to the outside, the soul to the world, knowing to being.

The philosophy of meta-Reality does not annul critical realism, but it seriously questions it and transcends it. 'Realism about transcendence necessitates transcendence of duality, realism and even thought itself' (Bhaskar, 2002a: 166). Bhaskar affirms that critical realism remains the best philosophy available for the ordinary world of science and everyday life. But from the higher perspective of a deeper, subtler and more encompassing reality, this world is only a 'demi-world', an illusion that is covered by the veil of Maya. This illusion is real (causally efficacious and real in its consequences), but false nevertheless. To the extent that critical realism remains wedded to its analysis, it offers a valid account of a false world – the world we live in and will have one day to get rid of. As the true philosophy of a false world, critical realism has to be overcome – whether it will be overcome or not, is, however, not a theoretical question, but an eminently practical one. One really has to work at it. It is only when we come to understand that this demi-world is sustained by another world of non-duality that we can decide to cut the lifeline that reproduces it and transform it from within and from without. That, however, presupposes that we stop to 'I-dentify' with our ego and come to realise our true, alethic, self instead.

From the vantage point of PMR, the basic premises of critical realism turn out to be false: ultimately, the distinction between the intransitive and the transitive dimension of knowledge has to go.[33] The whole distinction smacks of duality. As if we could, by a mere act of will, separate out the intransitive from the transitive dimension. The whole distinction itself is, definitely, a transitive one. In the same way as I am in the stars and the stars are in me, the transitive is in the intransitive, and the intransitive in the transitive. At the ground-level, we are in/transitive – in trance and in transition beyond dualism. We only get to the Truth when we are in the Truth. Beyond consciousness and beyond thought, we become who we are, truthful to our inner being. When we are in the truth, reality simply disintegrates. There is no longer an I or an Ego that tries to understand a world. No longer *res intensa* nor *extensa*. Reality disintegrates into a dance of particles. The I is dissolved and scatters into a rain of diamonds. Everything is in flux. Everyone is in peace. The rest is silence.

The turn to spirituality does not necessarily mean that critical realism turns away from society. On the contrary, by connecting one Enlightenment to the other, Bhaskar claims to have radicalised the project of emancipation of the *Aufklärung* with a humanist project of universal self-transformation. His mysticism is practical and innerworldly. We have to withdraw from the world in order to change it. The enlightened are in the world, but not of the world, to vary another Weberian formula. The realisation of the good society is only possible if we liberate ourselves from structures of oppression and alienation. The ultimate cause of all suffering is the alienation of our true selves. When we disconnect from the world to connect to the deeper level of *Dasein*, we become free and stop feeding the system that alienates us. We start to change the heteronomous system when we cut off the supply lines on which it depends. Bhaskar argues that, as a matter of fact, we are already essentially free. The structures of oppression and exploitation only persist because people are not conscious of what binds them; the system depends partially on free, spontaneous, creative, generous, loving activity. The Marxists will no doubt balk at his suggestion that the base of society is, ultimately, spiritual, not material: 'There's a spiritual substructure within society, an infrastructure without which society could not function' (Bhaskar, 2012: 191). They will also be baffled by his affirmation that war is sustained by love (solidarity of the soldiers at the front) and exploitation by creativity. 'It is love which sustains all the negative emotions and all the forms of oppression and violence. Similarly, it is creativity which keeps exploitation going.... The further you dig, the more you will find that it subsists upon a level of joy, bliss, love and creativity' (Bhaskar, 2002a: 41).

We have now come full circle. First-wave critical realism started out as an attempt to reclaim reality from the conventionalist and the super-idealist philosophies of science (from Kuhn to Rorty and postmodernism). Second-wave realism deepened critical realism and tried to anchor the transitive into the intransitive dimension of knowledge, the former appearing now as a manifestation and realisation of the truth of the latter. While the second wave deepened critical realism, the third wave elevated it into another dimension altogether. From realism via dialectics to idealism and beyond, that is the trajectory we have followed in this introduction. Whereas realism was initially a materialist philosophy of science that insisted on the existence of a reality that exists independent of our thoughts, PMR is definitely more idealist (and, perhaps, even surrealist) in its suggestion that the truth is beyond thought, duality and reality. The position of Bhaskar's ultimate philosophy is ontologically idealist, whereas initially it was materialist. Whether transcendent idealism really threatens transcendental realism is a moot point.[34] In any case, unlike critical realism, which remains intently focused on the sciences, PMR seeks a source of knowledge beyond the sciences and is concerned with the deeper truth of reality itself that all sciences necessarily presuppose, but that can hardly be captured in scientific propositions: *a-letheia* – the lived experience of truth beyond the oblivion of Being and the veil of Maya. From scientific experiments with nature to the ecstatic experience of oneness in nature, and from this 'oceanic feeling' back to the dialectics of social change and the hermeneutics of self-transformation, this is the way of meta-critical realism.

Metatheory, metacritique and metacritical realism

A humanist anthropology

Metacritical realism moves beyond realism, and also beyond critique. The espousal of an integral philosophy of truth does not necessarily transform critical realism into 'New Age abacadabra', as Hartwig (2001: 149) charges. Bhaskar's 'position of innocence' is definitely not without risk (including financial ones – two spiritual charlatans ran away with his savings!) I believe, however, that his anti-Weberian call for a 're-enchantment of the world' is compatible with progressive humanism (though not with the aggressive Enlightenment fundamentalism that has gained prominence in the West since 9/11). To make his 'esoteric sociology of everyday life' palatable to those who, like Weber, have 'no ear for religion' or, like Habermas (2012b: 111, 126) can only access religion 'in the highly sublimated form of aesthetic experience', one might as well rephrase and repack it as a form of 'atheistic mysticism' of which religious mysticism happens to be only a particular variant and not even the most interesting one. The deep egosyntonic connection with the body, the self, others and the cosmos can not only be felt in spiritual practices (praying and meditation); one can also have 'peak experiences' (plateau experiences) when one is totally engaged in existential soul-to-soul communication with the other or fully immersed in intense bodily activities (sport, dancing and sex), contemplates the sublime beauty of nature or is exposed to great art, gets carried away by the muse or experiments with recreational drugs (like MDMA or LSD). I, for one, occasionally feel ecstatic and have my little epiphanies when I am running along the beach of Rio de Janeiro or when the text I am writing is running away with me. Others get their kicks from cycling, singing in a choir or listening to the *Goldberg Variations*.

The experience of wholeness is not necessarily a religious one, though all experiences of self-transcendence have a spiritual dimension. What is important here is the deep contact with 'little transcendences' and the fact that those occasional encounters with the transpersonal can have a genuinely transformative and lasting impact on one's self, one's worldview and one's view of the self in the world. Again, when I'm running on my beach, I am no longer a Cartesian Ego disconnected from my own body and my surroundings. Rather, like Merleau-Ponty, instead of facing the world from without, I am at one with myself and the world. Reconnected to my body, the ocean, the breeze and the sun, I am enclosed by something more encompassing of which I am part. Advancing rhythmically as the horizon slowly recedes, I am a living midpoint at the intersection of the earth and the sky, the beach and the city, myself and the others.

The experience of 'flow' and the attendant positive psychology is not without implications for one's connection with, and conception of, humankind (Csikszentmihalyi, 1990). Whatever humanism is, it seems to me that, at the end of the day, its basic creed boils down to a positive anthropology and the falsely ingenuous affirmation that, generically speaking, Man is good.[35] In spite of everything, humanism reflexively chooses to believe that humans are also driven by sublime ideals, high moral principles and binding values – not just by interests, power and sex – and that, together, humans are capable of learning from their mistakes. This belief in the inherent goodness of Man and the perfectibility of Mankind is a belief of the second order. Humanism does not ignore that Man is capable of the worst. It knows that the 'naked ape' can be as violent as a chimpanzee or as lovely and affectionate as a bonobo (De Waal, 2005). Similarly, it acknowledges that the *Homo faber* who turns a piece of wood into a flute is also the one who transforms the other into an instrument. It is fully cognisant that the *Homo simbolicus* does not only invent Gods and angels, but also spins political utopias and ideologies that culminate in death camps. However, if humanism reflexively opts for a positive anthropology, it does so in the conviction that the other option is simply worse. Without trust in the essential capabilities of Man, without the belief that human behaviour is also inspired by ideas and ideals, moved by moral sentiments, driven by love, generosity and enthusiasm, nothing constructive is possible. At best, one can put in place strong institutions that domesticate the beast and control the violent impulses so as to avert the worst; alternatively, one can find cynical delight in one's own lucidity and denounce the whole human spectacle as a theatre of vanities in which the strong and the clever will always have the upper hand. After all, isn't history written from the perspective of the winners, as Benjamin (Franklin) famously said?

Without an ethical commitment to 'reflexive innocence', the primacy of practise cannot be upheld. Without reference to the symbolic, the normative and the expressive capabilities of humans, without reference to categories, norms and sentiments that orient action 'from within', the latter is necessarily reduced to its instrumental, strategic and utilitarian dimensions.[36] Against critical realists (in the political sense), like Machiavelli, Hobbes and Carl Schmitt, who believe that action is always driven by the basest impulses (power, money and sex), I will adopt an idealist position and foreground the principles of generosity, reciprocity and sociability that make human life not only possible, but also valuable. Indeed, inspired by Marcel Mauss' famous essay on the gift and the Anti-Utilitarian Movement in the Social Sciences,[37] I will try to forge linkages between German critical theory, British critical realism and French anti-utilitarianism. The main intent behind such a rapprochement of the lifework of Habermas, Bhaskar and Alain Caillé is to explore the contours of a hermeneutically inspired theory of action, order and social change that is grounded in a generous and regenerative anthropology that does not conceive of Man as *Homo economicus* – 'a machine, enhanced with a calculator' (Mauss, 1950: 272) – but rather as *Homo reciprocus*. Contra Hobbes and his desolate vision of humanity as a pack of wolves, I imagine the human being as a sympathetic animal of sorts. By conceiving of human beings as communicative, cooperative and creative creatures who are inspired by the highest ideals of civilisation to search, together with others, for constructive alternatives in the present that point beyond the utilitarian imaginary, I hope to be able to sketch out the contours of a metacritical, reconstructive and realist theory that fuses the positive anthropology of humanism, the ethical concern of critical theory and the politics of the gift into a general (and generous) social theory of common action.

Metacritique$_{1,2,3 \text{ and } 4}$

Before we get to action, let us return to Bhaskar and articulate his dialectical concept of metacritique to our metatheoretical critique of rational choice and the Frankfurt School (Vandenberghe, 2009). Bhaskar's whole enterprise can be construed as an ongoing reflection on, and deepening of, critique in all its different forms. The first wave of critical realism can be understood as a sequential exploration of the transcendental, immanent and explanatory forms of critique. The second wave lays the groundwork for a dialectical metacritique of the philosophical discourse of modernity, while the third moves beyond critique to a joyous affirmation of Eastern wisdom and non-duality that contains an implicit critique of critical realism itself.

In Bhaskar's conceptual universe, metacritique comes in two (and, perhaps, even in three) forms (Bhaskar, 1993: 354–365): metacritique$_1$ isolates an absence in a text, theory or practice, indicating an incompleteness, inconsistency or tension that is not contingent, but of a systematic nature. The pinpointing of a 'performative contradiction' within positivism, which denies in theory the communication it presupposes and practises is an example of the first type of metacritique. If metacritique$_1$ identifies the omission of a concept or category in a theory as a symptom of a systematic error in the theoretical construction, metacritique$_2$ traces this error back to its historical roots and to the underlying structures of oppression and domination in society. Thus, radicalising Horkheimer's classic critique of traditional theory, Bhaskar (1986: ch. 3) explains the theory/practise inconsistency of positivism through a reconceptualisation of the latter as an ideology of science that obfuscates the possibility of practise, an inconsistency that can only be overcome in practise through a radical transformation of society. In this way, metacritique$_2$ operates as a bridge between the theory under scrutiny and the practices that help to reproduce it.

Bhaskar has not explicitly presented his philosophy of meta-Reality as a metacritique of his own philosophy. I think, however, that it can be understood as a third type of metacritique that overrules the prominence of science in critical realism by bringing in alternative experiences of nature, society and self that reconnect theory to practice. By showing that the subject/object split and the attendant distinction between the transitive and intransitive is engulfed by a deeper and subtler reality that encompasses both the subject and the object of knowledge and constitutes their 'pre-ontological ground', metacritique$_3$ overcomes the dual worldview of modern science to which critical realism remains largely indebted. Reconnecting with the subterranean 'Orphic' tradition of Western thought that discovers the mystery of existence in appearances (Hadot, 2004), the philosophy of meta-Reality does not reflect on scientific experiments. As a testimony of Bhaskar's 'personal experiments with truth', it calls for a qualitatively different experience of reality altogether.

Now that I have introduced metacritique$_3$ and linked it to alternative ways of being-in-the-world that disclose the world in different ways, letting in some rays of light in the iron cage of modern existence, I can present my own understanding of metacritique and draw some of the conceptual connections between critical realism, hermeneutics and the anti-utilitarian theory of action. To the extent that critical realism tends to bypass hermeneutics and that my whole endeavour aims to bring the constitutive role of language to the fore, it can, perhaps, be considered a fourth form of metacritique.

Grounded in a humanist anthropology that conceives of the human being as an *animal simbolicum reciprocum*, metacritique$_4$ respects religious and spiritual experiences, but tries to reformulate them in secular idiom that systematically 'linguistifies the sacred'.[38] In any case, by metacritique, I mean to refer to a 'Habermaussian' (!) critique of the metatheoretical presuppositions of Frankfurt-style critical theory which finds its clues and its inspiration in a transformed theory of transformative practice that insists on the importance of symbolism for the disclosure of reality as a human one, as well as for the conceptualisation of social action. The voluntarism that expresses itself in a slight exaggeration of the transformative power of human agency is a countermeasure that aims to overcome the one-dimensionality of a critical theory of society that is transfixed with the denunciation of the alienating structures of domination and oppression. This transformative power of the agent (power$_1$, understood with Giddens as the 'capacity to act otherwise' that agents have by virtue of being human) is presupposed yet at the same time denied by a hypercritical theory of society that foregrounds the powers of oppression and domination (power$_2$, understood with Bhaskar as 'generalized master–slave relations').

To unhinge the infernal cycle of social reproduction and shift from a theory of domination to a theory of emancipation, it is essential not to reduce culture to 'ideology' or 'symbolic violence'. Rather, culture should be conceived of as a causal power in its own right. Composed of symbolic representations of reality, normative invocations of principles and values, and artistic expressions that transfigure reality, culture is the totality of symbolic forms that disclose the world as a meaningful one and regulates the actions of individuals and collectives 'from within' by pre-structuring their universe and pre-selecting possible courses of action. The insistence on culture as the totality of symbolic forms that always and inevitably mediates the relation between human beings and their *Umwelt*, disclosing nature, society and personality as a human environment, is essential for any theory of action that refuses to reduce action to instrumental and strategic action that is determined 'from without' by the alienating constraints of an (almost) inhuman world. If the mediation by symbolic forms is discounted, human action becomes a mere reaction to material conditions. Assuming that the end is given, which at its most basic coincides with mere survival and self-conservation, the means can be rationally determined by a simple calculus of optimisation. In the absence of rational deliberation about the end themselves, not much choice is left. At the limit, there is only one correct way to the end. However intelligent or instrumentally rational behaviour may be, without reference to culture as a formative precondition that guides it from within, it is not action at all; it constitutes an adaptation to the material environment that is directly determined by it.

Culture not only makes worlds; by virtue of the fact that it transposes the actor in a different world than the existing one, it also breaks them and makes the actors conscious of alternatives. It is true that with its emphasis on cultural transmission and tradition hermeneutics is a rather conservative force. But in the same way as one should not assume a priori that culture always functions as a form of symbolic violence, one should not affirm too quickly that it is always reproductive. To avert reproduction and reclaim hermeneutics for a humanist theory of cultural, social and personal change, I will 'graft' it in the first chapter on to pragmatism and symbolic interactionism. But the same point can be made via Habermas: as a mediation between actors, language is structured in such a way that the system of personal pronouns allows actors to transpose themselves in the position of the other. The symbolically mediated exchange of perspectives forces the actors to 'decentre' themselves and look at the same world from a different perspective. Even if one does not necessarily accept the shortcut between *logos* and reason that universal pragmatics establishes, the internal connection between culture, language and reflexivity is, I think, a consensual one.

The affinity that exists between a hermeneutic theory of culture and a phenomenological theory of intentional action is grounded in the hermeneutic circle that relates culture and meanings, as well as the collective and the personal, as whole to part. The causal power of symbolical forms is, however, a paradoxical one. The very mediation by symbols that discloses the world has the effect of making them vanish. When the formative power of culture is activated, the mediations become translucid and transparent: the world is disclosed as it *is*. This is, no doubt, what phenomenology meant with its resounding call to 'return to the things themselves'. *Zu den Sachen selbst!*[39] Given that the symbolic mediations all point to the selfsame world, eventually, when the mediations are themselves mediated and brought into communication through conversation, the horizons of understanding 'fuse' and we get access to the world beyond symbols … to the world itself. Note that we do so not in spite of, but thanks to the very mediations. This is, I surmise, the deeper meaning of truth as *Aletheia*.[40] The veils of oblivion are lifted and, thanks to and through the symbols, we are in the in/transitive truth. Truth is not something that symbols bring into the world, but something that belongs to the world. We should therefore not say that symbols reveal the truth, but that the truth reveals itself to us thanks to, and through, the disclosing power of language.

When the deeper meaning of Being is thus revealed to us, the distinction between the transitive and the intransitive collapses. This does not mean that the real is reduced to the ideal and that there is nothing outside language. As an idealist version of realism, hermeneutics does not deny the existence of the real. To the contrary, if it insists on the mystery of Being that always shines through in language, that language always presupposes as its ultimate ground, yet that it can hardly grasp, it is precisely to affirm the limits of language. Language does not refer to itself, but to the world. By pointing to something essential beyond language, hermeneutics thereby confirms our finitude. Even if it undercuts the distinction between the transitive and the intransitive dimension of knowledge, hermeneutics is indeed compatible with critical realism. Unlike the latter, however, it has a larger and more poetic conception of knowledge (including of nature) that remains anchored in common sense and transcends science to return to the things themselves: the smell of wet grass, the sound of breaking waves, the vanishing bicycle on the horizon, the disarming tears on her face....

The space of social theory

If I have initiated the discussion with culture, rather than action, it is because I am convinced that sociology is only possible on holist, collectivist and emergentist footings. Modern societies may be individualist, but if one does not assume that individuals share basic meanings, norms and values, one cannot properly answer the question of questions that every self-respecting social theorist has to resolve: How is society possible? How can one transform a bunch of atomised individuals into an organised whole? How can individuals coordinate their actions and act together? With Hegel, Durkheim, Parsons and many others, I assume that Tocqueville (1961: II, 20) was basically right: 'Without common ideas, there is no common action, and in the absence of common action, men still do exist but not a social body.' Even if modern societies ideologically negate and deny holistic principles, those still remain active in practise and continue to regulate and motivate individuals who establish the social synthesis themselves. By saying that individuals are connected to each other through the mediation of culture (Hegel's objective spirit, Durkheim's *conscience collective*, Parsons' general norms and binding values), I do not wish to deny, like the glad girl Pollyanna, that material structures impinge on behaviour or that individuals are driven by interests, power and sex. To the contrary, it is precisely because utilitarianism forms the axiological horizon of the present that it is so important to open up other vistas and affirm, in spite of everything, the presence of the Spirit as a third element (beyond the material and the individual) that interconnects individuals into a *koinon kosmon* and makes common action possible.

With its notion of society as a well-ordered arrangement between socialised individuals, sociology entails a normative project. Indeed, sociology is not just a science. It continues the tradition of moral and political philosophy through empirical research (Chanial, 2011). Society is not just an object of knowledge; from the very beginning, it was also conceived of as a moral and political project that seeks to empirically demonstrate that the integration of individuals into a whole is the work and the realisation of the individuals themselves.[41] 'They make society', as Marx famously said in *The Eighteenth Brumaire*, 'but not in conditions they have themselves freely chosen.' Sociology's scientific-normative project is twofold: in spite of everything, it wants to make individuals conscious of what keeps them together; and through consciousness raising, it also wants to contribute to the advent and realisation of the society of individuals. Notwithstanding occasional nostalgia for traditional communities, it is in no way opposed to the project of modernity. Like Hegel, sociology inscribes the project of individual autonomy in its object and subscribes to the value of freedom, but only to the extent that the 'freedom of each' is a condition of the 'self-realisation of all' in a common project (Bhaskar, 1994: 141–160).[42] Its individualism is, therefore, conditional and other-directed; it is a moral one that conceives of the individual not as an atom, but as part and parcel of something encompassing that transcends individual interests and integrates them through collective action into a common project.

A critical theory cannot remain content with the denunciation of utilitarianism. It has not only to investigate the structures of domination, but also to indicate possibilities of emancipation. If it is to be more than a continuously rehearsed lamentation on alienation and reification, it has to move 'from negative to positive anti-utilitarianism' (Caillé, 2000: 41–44) and elaborate an alternative axiology that shows that individuals continue to orient themselves to higher ends and to fashion society accordingly. Positive anti-utilitarianism offers essentially an alternative to visions of social life that privilege the axiomatics of economic interests ('truck, barter and exchange'), political struggle (the 'will to power') and sexual conquest (the 'survival of the fittest') over any other motivation that cannot be reduced to self-interest. Unlike neo-classical economics and its reductionist allies (evolutionary psychology, sociobiology and cognitive neurology), positive anti-utilitarianism discovers the anthropological foundations of social life in the opening towards the other and the transcendence of the self in reciprocity. In the gift, or any other activities like dialogue, communication and recognition that are similarly oriented towards the other and animated by the spirit of generosity that keeps society going, it discovers one of the principal motifs and motors of social life – 'one of the rocks on which our societies are built' (Mauss, 1950: 148), to quote Durkheim's nephew once again. It does not ignore the predominance of interests in contemporary life at all; rather, like the founding fathers of anthropology and sociology, it combats and transcends the narrow confines of marginal utility to investigate what keeps society together and what drives it apart.

In an attempt to join critical hermeneutics to humanist anthropology, I want to defend the primacy of symbolic, normative and expressive practice and argue that in social theory everything hinges on the concept of action. Contradicting the most pessimist affirmations of critical theory, according to which in modern industrial-capitalist societies material structures of domination trump and repress the causal power of ideal structures, I would like to argue that critical theory only arrives at this desolate conclusion because it has refrained from properly connecting agency to culture. This holds for both the German (Webero-Marxist) tradition of the Frankfurt School and for the French (Durkheimo-Marxist) tradition of structuralism and post-structuralism. From a metatheoretical point of view, which analyses the ultimate presuppositions of social theory and investigates the way questions of action are systematically interconnected to questions of order and of social change, it is exactly the reverse: it is because they have conceived of action too narrowly and reduced it to instrumental or strategic action, excluding the ideals, norms and values that meaningfully orient action, that they fell back into a reified universe in which material structures determine action from without.

To make my case, I will draw on the transcendental 'space of possibilities' of the social sciences that every social theory presupposes. If a theory of society is to genuinely be a general one and give a coherent answer to the central questions of the social sciences – namely the essence and the forms of social action, their relations to social order and the possibility of social change – it has to ideally take into account all of its possibilities and permutations. Through dialogue and communication between positions and counterpositions, it has to systematically navigate its way through the space, transcend its own limitations and strive towards generality and synthesis (Alexander, 1982–1983).

The space of possibilities is obtained by simple crosscutting of what I consider the two main axes of opposition that divide and unite the social sciences. While the first axis opposes materialism to idealism, the second one opposes individualism to holism.

As comprehensive worldviews, materialism and idealism are in tension with each other. Each pretends to be able to incorporate, partially or totally, the other. Similarly, individualism (atomism) and holism (emergentism) are not simply theories, but fundamental options to approach the social world, stressing either that only individuals are real or, to the contrary, insisting that the interactions between individuals lead to the emergence of society as a complex, irreducible stratum of reality. By calling it a space of possibilities, I want to suggest that sociology is, ultimately, an *ars combinatoria*, a complex way of combining simple elements into a number of ever new, but structurally limited combinations, permutations and complexions. In the social sciences, everything happens

	Individualism (individual)	Holism (society)
Idealism (culture)	(A) Weber	(C) Durkheim
Materialism (nature)	(B) Rational choice	(D) Marx

Figure I.1 The space of social theory.

as if one had to reformulate well-tested philosophical positions (materialism + atomism = empiricism; idealism + collectivism = rationalism; etc.) in sociological language and to associate each of them with the name of a 'founding figure' to be able to submit them to empirical investigation.

Interestingly, the two axes seem to coincide with the basic oppositions that have structured anthropology and sociology from the very beginning. Indeed, with Lévi-Strauss, one can consider the whole of anthropology an ongoing reflection on the distinction between nature and culture. As an anthropology of the modern world, sociology for its part dwelled on the opposition between individual and society. My contention is that the social sciences are unified by the two antinomies (nature/culture and individual/society) and that any general social theory has to work its way through both of the antinomies. If the social sciences are unified by their oppositions, they are, however, divided by the way they resolve the metatheoretical dilemma (Viveiros de Castro, 2002: 295–316): either society and culture are conceived of as being continuous with their conceptual opposites (reductionist solution) or as being discontinuous with them (emergentist solution). The individual–society connection is only successfully resolved if culture is introduced as the symbolic mediator that regulates individual and collective actions from within and thereby allows for the reproduction and transformation of society. If culture is reduced to an epiphenomenon of material structures within the individuals (cognitive psychology) or society (historical materialism), the symbolical dimension of action thanks to which individuals and groups are integrated into society disappears and action is reduced to instrumental-strategic behaviour.

The elimination of culture from social analysis has a paradoxical result: while it reduces society to a bunch of strategising individuals and groups that struggle for material interests, utilitarianism does not lead to freedom, however, but to its exact opposite:

> The person becomes 'just another brick in the wall'. The individual has to behave rationally with regard to its self-interest, but if he does so, he carries out a systemic logic that is not his and that cannot take into account collateral damages.
>
> (Willke, 2001: 13)

Society comes back with a vengeance as 'second nature' that imposes its social order from without, be it as an 'invisible hand' that coordinates their actions through the mechanism of prices (market) or as a 'visible punch' that does the same by threatening them with the force of the law (government). Constrained by the material conditions, actors have only one choice, which amounts to no choice: to adapt themselves to their environment. To act rationally, they have to concentrate on the means and make abstraction of their ends, values and norms. Unless culture is explicitly brought into the analysis as medium and mediator, the individual and society are bound to confront each other not as a part and whole, but in the alienated form of *res cogitans* and *res extensa*.

As a scientific reflection of modern societies on themselves, sociology offers a reflexive self-description of modern societies (Luhmann, 1984). As such, it is the equivalent of psychoanalysis on a collective scale. The late arrival of sociology in the system of sciences is reflected in its theories, its concepts and its semantics.[43] Inseparable from the advent of modernity, the self-description of societies is part of the self-conception of sociology. It is therefore no wonder that the modern project is already inscribed in sociology's object. Given that sociology defines modern societies (and thus also itself!) in contrast with primitive, traditional and transitional societies, a certain degree of evolutionism is inevitable. This bias is most evident when sociology reflects on the nature, the culture and the cosmologies of pre-modern societies. What anthropologists call cosmologies is, in fact, the life-world of peoples who have not lost the connection with their natural and supra-natural environments. For them nature is not inert, but alive and ablaze with spirits and voices. Their relations with plants, animals and gods are not instrumental, but sensual, expressive and communicative. Anthropological concepts like animism, totemism and fetishism are far from neutral. Thanks to their full immersion in the field, contemporary anthropologists like Tim Ingold, Philippe Descola or Eduardo Viveiros de Castro are still capable, however vicariously, of evoking and transmitting the lived experiences of the natives with the natural and the supernatural. As a child of its time, sociology finds it difficult, if not impossible, to describe pre-modern experiences of nature without ascribing them temporally to the past. The 'denial of coevalness' is as it were written into its grammar.[44] Unlike them, we, moderns, do not communicate with spirits. For us, nature is material, unanimated stuff, standing reserve. To better understand the cosmology of the natives, anthropologists have proposed a methodological suspension of 'our' scientific worldview. Notwithstanding postcolonialism, I have not come across anything similar to 'reverse anthropology' in sociology. If we were to suspend our judgement of their natural worldview, would we not come to the conclusion that naturalism is our totemism and scientism our fetishism? Even when sociologists, like Ulrich Beck or Donna Haraway, for instance, try to politicise the sciences, they do not question the scientific understanding of nature or propose to substitute experiments with nature for pre-scientific experiences of nature. Nor do I for that matter. If I have opposed anthropology to sociology, it is only to point out that sociology hardly has access to alternative experiences of nature and that it cannot evoke them without incurring the bias of either scientific disbelief or New Age credulity. I could have made the same point against critical realism with Heidegger's poetics of nature.

Critical realism and classical sociology

Metatheoretical analysis is not end an end in itself. As propaedeutics to general theory construction, it enjoins the theorist to systematically compare and contrast theoretical positions within the field as he or she works his or her way from action to order and change. The spirit of metatheoretical comparison is not agonistic, but dialogic. The point of metatheory is not to evince adversarial positions in the field, but to embrace their point of view and construct theory in such a way that it is able to overcome its own limitations in a more encompassing dialogical and dialectical framework. With due apologies for didactic simplifications, I will consider the founding fathers of sociology as so many stand-ins and personifications of complex research traditions.

Dutifully filling in the quadrants of the space of social theory (cf. *supra* Figure I.1), we can associate Weber to the subjectivist tradition (idealism plus individualism), Durkheim to the idealist and Marx to the materialist branch of the collectivist tradition. In spite of their inner complexity, which accounts for hesitations, drifts and tensions in their work, it is rather striking that all of our classical figures take direct aim at the crass utilitarianism (conjunction of materialism and individualism) that has become the hallmark of classical and neo-classical economics, from Adam Smith to Hayek and the contemporary bankers of Wall Street. In the same way as the main figures of neo-classical sociology (Bourdieu, Giddens, Habermas and Luhmann) took issue, as we have seen, with positivism as a philosophy of science, classical sociologists developed their position in direct confrontation with utilitarianism, proposing their own view as a correction and systematic alternative to the axiomatic of 'rational choice' (Shilling and Mellor, 2001; Laval, 2002). In their struggle against the economic vision of social life, each of them insisted in his own way on the symbolic dimension of social life: as a young Hegelian, Marx developed a dialectical philosophy of praxis; as a neo-Kantian, Weber proposed his interpretative sociology as a science of culture; while Durkheim, who should always be read in conjunction with Marcel Mauss, never tired of insisting that social facts are moral facts. If one were to introduce Talcott Parsons and Pierre Bourdieu as genuinely classical figures, as I bet future generations of sociologists will, one would arrive at the same conclusions, namely that their work is an ongoing battle against (Parsons) and with (Bourdieu) rational choice.

Each of the classical figures represents and personifies a possible strategy to counter the hegemony of utilitarianism. In spite of their opposition to rational choice, both Marx and Weber share one of the presuppositions of rational choice. This complicity makes them vulnerable to drifting and co-optation by *the rat's* (sic). As Durkheim refuses both individualism and materialism, he is the champion of anti-utilitarianism and our figure of choice. To make him more sympathetic and progressive, one should, however, always read him through Mauss, who often corrects his sharp edges without openly saying so (Caillé, 2000: 27–44). To strengthen his position, one should, ideally, also try to bolster his defences through a systematic exploration of the counterpositions, arguing with Weber and Marx against Durkheim and Mauss. Not to make them weaker, but to uncover their hidden angles through triangulation and, thereby, to make them stronger.

The reader will recall that I constructed the metatheoretical space of possibilities by combining the conceptual pairs nature/culture (anthropology) and individual/society (sociology) in a two-dimensional square that integrates anthropology and sociology in a single universe of discourse. To bring the founding figures of sociology into dialogue with critical realism and the latter with hermeneutics, I will now bring the opposition between subject and object (philosophy) as a third polarity into the picture. The question of how a subject can possibly have knowledge of an object outside of itself can be answered by looking for the conditions of knowledge either on the object side (realism/nominalism) or on the subject side (rationalism/empiricism). One way or another, philosophy has to join both ends of the spectrum and work its way through the basic oppositions that unite and divide it. Those oppositions are basic ones, because philosophy is the basic discipline that founds the others and because they undergird the oppositions of anthropology and sociology. Indeed, the contrasting pairs of anthropology and sociology are structurally homologous to the double pair that structures philosophy. How one resolves the antinomies of philosophy ultimately decides how one resolves the other ones.

Thanks to the third dimension, we can bring back critical realism into the discussion. In the social sciences, critical realism is a proxy of Marxism. In a rare synthesis of sociology and socialism, historical materialism purports to be scientific and utopian, as well as structural and historical. As a scientific analysis of the dynamics of structural relations between capital and labour that define a social formation, it typically fuses a materialist understanding of social structures as antagonistic relations between social positions with a praxeological analysis of social production and social change that is driven by normative ideals. Although Marxism successfully overcomes the opposition between materialism and idealism in a dialectical theory of practices, it stands and falls with its materialism.

If Marx is a dialectical and materialist thinker, Durkheim is an idealist and rationalist one. All too often Durkheim is still understood as a positivist. This understanding is, however, largely a misunderstanding (which, incidentally, was shared by Durkheim himself). Thanks to critical realism, we can now appreciate that Durkheim was, first and foremost, a realist and rationalist. While his insistence that social facts are *sui generis*, emergent from yet irreducible to psychological facts, makes him a realist, his affirmation that the sociologist has to break with common sense and construct a scientific concept of the facts defines him as a rationalist. The combination of realism and rationalism eventuates in structuralism, which I consider an idealist version of critical realism. But haven't I said before that hermeneutics represents an idealist version of critical realism? Yes, I have, and as a matter of fact, both hermeneutics and structuralism are compatible in my opinion with critical realism. What distinguishes structuralism from hermeneutics is neither its realism (deep structures) nor its idealism (culture), but the position of exteriority of the analyst: when social facts, which are, as we know, essentially moral facts made up of collective representations, are analysed from without, i.e. from the point of view of an external observer, they become things as it were; when they are analysed from within, i.e. from the point of view of the participant, they become symbols.[45] Either one treats social facts as things whose regularity has to be explained by reference to causal structures, or one treats them as symbols whose meaning has to be interpreted so as to disclose the realities to which they refer.

As a structuralist, Durkheim opted for the first position; with his call for an interpretative sociology, Weber chose the second position, while Marcel Mauss, who shifted the analysis from social to symbolic representations of reality, stands in the middle. Thanks to his symbolism, we can connect Durkheim to Weber and dislodge the Webero-Marxist and Durkheimo-Marxist syntheses of critical theory. As a neo-Kantian, Max Weber conceives of sociology as a *Kulturwissenschaft* that is part of the humanities and that practises the method of *Verstehen* to get access to cultural meanings that inform intentional social action; as a disenchanted Nietzschean, he is a nominalist and a staunch defender of ontological individualism. If we weaken his Nietzscheanism and strengthen his neo-Kantianism, we can perhaps attempt an articulation between Durkheim's collectivism and Weber's interpretativism, pushing both in the direction of 'post-Hegelian neo-Kantianism' that defines Dilthey's hermeneutic reconstruction of the social and historical sciences as *Geisteswissenschaften* (Dilthey, 1958).[46] With Weber and the neo-Kantians, we can insist that culture can only be disclosed from within through participation in its symbolic forms. Thanks to spontaneous activation of culture, the world becomes a meaningful one in which actors can proceed and act together; with Durkheim we can underscore that the meanings of action are not individual ones. Social action always already presupposes collective culture structures that furnish the actors with pre-interpretations of the world that schematise their representation of reality.[47]

At this point, we can also bring Marx back into the discussion and reformulate his notion of ideology as a symbolic misrepresentation of reality that is socially necessary and historically variable. By tying it more intently to symbolic representations, the nature of ideology as a passive reflection and refraction of the material infrastructure can be overcome. Just like utopias, ideologies are active forces of world-making. The causal power of culture as a 'structuring structure' that symbolically (mis)represents reality presupposes intentional action by individual or collective actors to be activated. The inner connection between culture and agency does, however, not transform actors into mere conducts of the collective. Even when culture functions as a factor that legitimises reality through a systematic distortion of its representation and thereby contributes to the reproduction of society, it forms and transforms the actors by making them conscious and reflexive.

By the mere fact that symbolism transfigures the given, there is always a possible rift between reality and its representation. By offering alternative conceptions of reality or by throwing new light on existing ones, culture opens up new possibilities among which the actors can, in principle, choose. In practise, such a choice is, of course, not always possible. Material interests may restrain the margins of action, directly by making action too costly or indirectly through cultural pre-selection. Similarly, individuals may be willing, but unable, to act, or able, but unwilling, or both unable and unwilling. In any case, material interests never directly determine individual or collective practices.

The relation between social structure and intentional action is always, necessarily and inevitably, mediated by culture (Kögler, 1997). Standing in between social structure and social practices, culture is a mediator that is shaped by the social conditions (that impose a certain structure on culture as a symbolic form that mis/represents reality) and shapes social practices (by providing symbolic representations of reality on which actors draw to make sense of it). Whether culture is conceived of as a reflection and refraction of the social structure (as in Marx and Durkheim) or as the totality of symbolic representations of reality that make intentional and meaningful action possible (as in Dilthey and Weber), I venture, in the last instance is determined by one's philosophical anthropology. If one is a humanist, one will turn to action and culture and see how one can make structures move; if one is an anti-humanist, one will start with structure and work one's way down to culture and practices to see how the latter are moved by the former.

Every general social theory has to find its own articulation between social structure, culture and agency. With Marx, Bourdieu and Bhaskar, I generically conceive of social structure as a material system of internal relations between social positions that define a social formation; following Durkheim, Mauss and Dilthey, I define culture not so much as a system of relations between ideas, but as the totality of symbolic forms that transform the world into a meaningful one that forms the diffuse background of intentional action; with Habermas, Mauss and the whole anti-utilitarian tradition, I think of human action not as an instrumental-strategic way of intervening in the world to change it or adapt oneself to it, but first and foremost as a symbolic, communicative and cooperative way of being in the world with and for others that is inspired by humanist ideas and ideals, moved by moral sentiments, driven by enthusiasm, generosity and sociability.

Do I need to repeat here that my sentimentalism is principally reflexive, that I am fully aware that society at large is not an *ashram* and that the world is going to the dogs? Instead of qualifying my anti-utilitarianism, I would rather resume the project of critical hermeneutics and indicate how social structures impact on culture and inhibit the spontaneous release of positive energies and joyous passions that drive norms and values to their realisation. The dominance of utilitarianism in everyday life interferes with the structures of the life-world through a pre-structuring of the cultural environment of action that perverts the intentions of the actors. Such an insidious pre-structuring of the possibilities of action may even happen unbeknownst to the actors themselves, who intentionally and consciously pursue their life-course in practical situations of everyday life. What I am thinking of is the whole gamut of social actions that appear superficially as generous and genuine acts of other-directedness, but that are, in fact, either staged or misunderstood by the actors themselves, as real instances of communication, cooperation and giving.

At one end of pseudo-communication, pseudo-cooperation and pseudo-giving, we find the skilled performances of impression managers who ply their spiritual wares while pretending to be genuinely concerned with the well-being of others. The crass commercialism of New Age gurus without scruples, like Bhagwan Shree Rajneesh (aka Osho) and Da Free John (aka Adi Da), or of New Left revolutionaries who insist on flying first-class (like Marcuse, allegedly because of the length of his legs), are only the crassest examples of bad faith. At the other end of systematically deformed communication, cooperation and giving, we find the self-delusion of people in good faith who think they are really communicating, cooperating and giving, but are, in fact, incapable of doing so. Instead of listening, they talk; instead of cooperating with others, they order and boss them around; instead of giving, accepting and returning the gift, they take, refuse and break the cycle of reciprocity that animates sociability and keeps society going.

With this reference to those who, consciously or not, go against the spirit of the gift and always keep more than they contribute, I am already reformulating Marx's theory of exploitation in terms of a theory that fuses Mauss' theory of the gift with Habermas' (1971) theory of systematically deformed communication. From the point of view of a Maussian theory that stresses 'fair trade', while bypassing Marx's obsolete theory of surplus value, exploitation is nothing else but a social situation in which the gift is systematically skewed to the detriment of a given class and to the benefit of another: a dominant class always takes more than it deserves without reciprocity, while the dominated class gives more without return and, possibly, also without counting. To justify the deviation from the universal maxim, as formulated by the beautiful Maori proverb: 'Give as much as you take and everything will be alright' (Mauss, 1950: 265), the norm of reciprocity can be refunctionalised and transformed into an ideology that hides and justifies the inequality of the transaction under the benevolent veil of pseudo-giving, pseudo-generosity and pseudo-cooperation. To avoid the trap of moralism, an anti-utilitarian theory of the gift should, however, not indulge in 'social physionomics' (Adorno) that aggrandises particular cases to find the totality in the details. To better understand given cases of exploitation, one should explain them with systematic reference to the social logics of domination that characterise contemporary societies of control. Perhaps a revisit of Negri's theory of 'immaterial labour', as I will present it in the final chapter, might go some way to show how power and money systematically, yet insidiously, colonise the various spheres of life, subverting the logics of reciprocity in a staging of communality (as happens in spiritual workshops, professional coaching, pastoral care, clinical psychoanalysis and, last but not least, reality shows on TV).

The 'new orthodox consensus'

The articulation between Marx, Durkheim and Weber I propose tries to fuse critical realism and critical hermeneutics into an anti-positivist and anti-utilitarian social theory. As such, it goes against the grain of the 'new orthodox consensus' that has taken hold of the human sciences since the 1990s. To the extent that it is inseparable from the onmarch of the 'Studies' into the social sciences and its wholesale denunciation of academic complicity with the powers of domination and exclusion, I might, in fact, as well have called it the 'heterodox consensus'. Inspired by Foucault, Derrida and Lacan, among others, who have proposed to radically 'decentre' and 'deconstruct' the subject, so-called 'French theory' (an amalgam and artefact of American import) typically investigates the interplay of power, discourse and identity. Although its subject is ultimately identity, at its most radical it dispenses of the subject and analyses it as an object, effect and consequence of power/discourses that produce the subject. All things considered, the real subject of their investigations is power, not the person on, through and against whom it is exercised. By showing how the workings of power articulate discourses from within and fashion subjects from without through a series of 'representations' that propose and project the subject positions that produce the identities, the heterodox consensus integrates power and discourses into a critical theory of discursive practices.

The continuous invocation of discursive practices should not hide, however, that the integration of a genealogical theory of power, a structuralist theory of discourses and a psychoanalytic analysis of subject formation that poststructuralism proposes is anything but a theory of action. A theory of action presupposes a reflexive subject, not an agent who is subjected to an endless power/discourse circuit. As they do not adopt the perspective of the participant, but systematically analyse the discourses from without, poststructuralist theories of discursive practices lack the phenomenological emphasis on subjectivity, reflexivity and intentionality that define theories of action. In spite of the fact that the 'Studies' refuse to be tied down to any discipline, let alone to sociology, I think their basic stance essentially amalgamates Durkheim, Marx and Nietzsche: discourses (representations of reality within language) produce practices that reproduce and/or subvert the structures of power and domination. In this formula, Durkheim's rationalism is, however, largely substituted and undercut by a militant deconstruction of metaphysics that is inspired by Nietzsche, while his determinism is not tempered by a Weberian theory of action, but rather reinforced by a generalised suspicion of structures of power and domination that oppress manifestations at the margins by making them unthinkable through 'foreclosure'. Indeed, the discourses produce the practices, not the agents. The latter are not efficient causes. They are produced in discourse as a consequence of the discursive practices.

The early work of Judith Butler, the 'mistress of suspicion', is symptomatic in that regard. For her, the subject which is presupposed by action is understood to be an effect of subjection to power.[48] The formation of the subject and the subjection to power are one and the same thing. 'Power not only acts on a subject', says Butler (1997: 13), 'but in a transitive sense, enacts the subject into being.' This is the case because the power to which the subject is subjected is, according to Butler, also unconsciously desired by the subject. In the affirmation that the individual is the subject of power, the genitive has to be understood both in its objective and subjective sense. Like in Adorno, the objective has, however, clear priority over the subjective. Power not only produces the subject, but also the illusion of subjectivity. Like in Nietzsche and Foucault, it is exactly when the subject affirms his/her subjectivity against power that power is at its most subtle and efficacious. Indeed, the interiority, reflexivity and autonomy of the subject do not belong to the subject, but in a transitive sense to power: 'At some point, a reversal and concealment occurs, and power emerges as what belongs exclusively to the subject (making the subject appear as if it belonged to no prior operation of power)' (Butler, 1997: 15). But if there's no real subject other than power – if there's 'no being behind the doing', 'no doer beyond the deed', as she says elsewhere with a reference to Nietzsche (Butler, 1999: 34, 195) – then there can't be real action either. There's agency, for sure, but it arrives on the scene as an unintentional consequence of power, as a failure of reproduction. In the same way as every repetition is an attempt to change that fails, every change is an attempt to reproduce that fails. Caught in between repetition and change, the agent always emerges as a consequence of power, while the actor that agency presupposes is performatively produced by power and discourse as a cause.

Although the circuit of power, discourses and practices seems reminiscent of the much-rehearsed agency–structure debate in social theory, the practitioners of the 'Studies' are hardly concerned with a careful parsing of the linkages between individual and society, agency and structure or practices and culture. As a matter of fact, postmodernists and poststructuralists have largely displaced the problematic of the micro–macro link. Instead of latching on to the individual–society polarity, they privilege the nature–culture debate of the anthropologists, but to the extent that they treat it philosophically in terms of a wholesale rejection of foundationalism (humanism in all its different guises: rationalism, logocentrism, essentialism, etc.), the opposition between realism and constructivism (or humanism and relativism) gets centre stage. A host of new themes and fashionable topics as identity, gender and ethnicity, recognition, difference and multiplicity or intersection, performance and resistance have come to the fore as a result. What unites the congeries of cultural, gender, ethnic, postcolonial and other 'Studies' is the grand refusal of an underlying or overarching hegemonic structure or system that finds its ground and its unity in a stable extra-discursive foundation. What interests them is not so much the identity that keeps the whole hegemonic structure together, but the differences that escape from it and subvert its closure.

It has now become a fixture of introductions to sociology to present the recent history of the discipline in terms of antinomy between agency and structure or action and order – as if sociologists had to wait for Jeffrey Alexander, Pierre Bourdieu or Tony Giddens to look for a dialectical theory of practices that solves the conundrum! This canonical history is not only uninspiring and repetitive; it is also misleading. Whoever looks at the Californian 'micro-revolution of the 1960s' without the blinders of the agency–structure debate will notice that Goffman, Garfinkel and Harvey Sacks, the champions of situational analysis, were obsessed with the question of order. For them, the challenge consisted of demonstrating the orderly nature of everyday life. Waiting for the bus, driving down the motorway, looking in the microscope, all these ordinary activities are orderly – i.e. observable and reportable, analysable and predictable or, in short, 'accountable' (Lynch, 1993: 14–15) as concerted activities in concrete situations. Similarly, they did not oppose agency to structure, but found structure at every level of society and, more particularly, at the nano-level of agency.

As a matter of fact, instead of opposing agency to structure, one might as well oppose action to practice and distinguish the various micro-sociologies according to whether they look at the actor from within or from without, whether they adopt the first-person perspective of the participant or the third-person perspective of the observer, whether they try to interpret social behaviour or whether they merely describe it. While the sociology of action is an interpretative sociology that can legitimately claim to go back to the opening paragraph of *Economy and Society*,[49] the sociology of practice is a descriptive sociology that finds its main inspiration not in Weber or Marx, but in Durkheim. Coming from phenomenology and pragmatism, practice theoreticians creatively read Durkheim (or 'misread' him, as the late Garfinkel instructed his fellow members of the gang) and projected his structuralist analysis of social facts to the micro-level.

In between a phenomenological sociology of action that investigates the motives, meanings and typifications of actors and stresses intentionality and reflexivity, on the one hand, and a micro-structuralist sociology of practices that describes ordered sequences of situated doings by anonymous agents who routinely do what they do without much thinking, on the other hand, one finds a sociology of interaction that analyses how actors define the situations they find themselves in to coordinate their actions with others who find themselves in the same situation. This interactionist sociology of action, which can be traced back to Georg Simmel, Marcel Mauss or G.H. Mead, can go either way. When it stresses the connection between agency and culture and conceives of language as the symbolic medium that allows Ego and Alter to coordinate their actions and act together, it rejoins the phenomenological-hermeneutic theory of action of Weber, Schütz and Parsons. However, when it focuses more on the situation of action than on the actors themselves to analyse how agents are faced with situational constraints that form a micro-system that rigorously conditions their practices, it joins the theory of practices of Goffman, Garfinkel and Wittgenstein.

Given that the 'Studies' and the situational sociologies share the point of view of the external observer, it is no wonder that rapprochements between both strands of analysis have been attempted by some of the main stars in the intellectual firmament. In spite of some initial confusion between 'performativity' and 'performance', Butler has now fully incorporated Goffman's histrionics into her queer theory of resistance. As a rhizomatic offshoot of Science Studies, Latour has fused the poststructuralist insistence on dissemination of texts with the hyperempiricism of Garfinkel into a neo-materialist narration of the expansion of socio-technical networks through the world, while Laclau has integrated Wittgenstein into his theory of hegemonic articulations, arguing, for instance, rather implausibly, that the building of a house is also a discursive practice of sorts. I only mention those 'fusions' of the structural and the situational to underscore that it is not enough to invoke discourses and practices to have a genuine theory of action. What matters is not scale or size, but how one conceives of the actor, meaning and culture and, as I will show in the next section, how one links that to personal, cultural and social change. No general social theory is possible if one does not, one way or another, think through the whole field of possibilities and work towards a synthetic position that overcomes the unilateralism of Marx, Weber and Durkheim by bringing them, and their followers, into a dialogue of sorts.

Crisis, convivialism and postcapitalism

Dynamic representation of the field

The metatheoretical space of possibilities (see Figure I.1) is only an analytic device. By mapping out the articulations between the basic oppositions of philosophy (subject–object), anthropology (nature–culture) and sociology (individual–society), it indicates the necessary constitutive elements that every social theory with general pretensions, at whatever level of analysis and whatever its paradigm, has to take into account and integrate in a coherent framework: intentional consciousness (quadrant A: individualism–idealism), material things and bodies (quadrant B: individualism–materialism), culture (quadrant C: holism–idealism) and social structure (quadrant D: holism–materialism). Theories that absent an element or that are built on a single quadrant will not pass the metacritical test of multidimensionality. That does not mean that all theories have to give equal weight to all the quadrants. As a metacritical realist, I have privileged antipositivist, culturalist and anti-utilitarian approaches to social action, social order and social change. I have entered the space of possibilities via the upper-right quadrant (holism plus idealism), I have outlined the contours of a humanist, hermeneutically informed and phenomenologically inspired anti-utilitarian theory of action in a common world.

To transform the space of possibilities into a systematic device for the investigation and diagnosis of the existing social order and the possibilities of change, one has to recast the general analytics of the social world as a morphogenetic dialectics. To apply the scheme to contemporary societies and make it move, one has to move, I suggest, from dialogic metatheory to developmental metahistory. To find out how the basic elements are configured and, thus, whether societies tend towards morphostasis or, rather, towards morphogenesis, one needs, basically, to introduce the temporal dimension of human development and interlink the elements of the space into an 'integral field' (Arnsperger, 2009: 43–57, 72, 86).[50] The idea behind the integral field is that individual consciousnesses, material bodies, cultures and social structures are not contingently, but systematically related to each other in specific configurations that define a variety of social formations through the ages. Through an evolutionary sequence of morphogenetic cycles of human development, individuals, cultures, societies and humanity as such can attain higher levels of consciousness, from the pre-personal and pre-modern (subconscious, instinctive and mythical) via the personal and modern (self-conscious, rational and scientific) to the transpersonal and postmodern (postmaterial, spiritual, integral). While the developmental logics of personal, cultural and social unfolding point to the attainment of integral consciousness of universal 'Oneness' of all that exists and is gathered in the 'cosmic envelope' (Bhaskar), nothing guarantees that the end state of full-spectrum consciousness will be attained. Just as persons, cultures and societies may be arrested in their development, humanity may fail to realise its potential, regress and never reach its pleroma.

In accordance with the principle of 'ecumenical secularism', which stipulates that encompassing doctrines have to be reformulated in terms that are acceptable to (post-) secular humanists,[51] I would like to rephrase the cosmic philosophy of higher consciousness of the likes of Plotinus, Sri Auribindo and Teilhard de Chardin or, closer to us, Ken Wilber and Roy Bhaskar, with reference to Habermas' developmental moral philosophy and Caillé's spirited defence of 'convivialism' as a successor ideology for our times. With his distinction between 'developmental logics' and 'factual dynamics', Habermas' (1976) proposal to reconstruct historical materialism in such a way that collective processes of learning through discursive testing of validity claims would allow human societies to move steadily forwards to ever higher levels of cognitive, moral and expressive consciousness, from the pre- to the post-conventional stage and beyond, was threading along similar paths. For sure, in the 1970s he still considered spirituality and religion as bourgeois forms of false consciousness that would be progressively rationalised away as people would reflexively question and discursively test its validity claims. Notwithstanding its adherence to an idealist philosophy of reflexivity, the idea that history presupposes hierarchically ordered levels of moral development, both at the individual, collective and planetary level – as a condition of human survival, let alone further development toward a cosmopolitan world order – would not be unconscionable to secular humanists (who waver somewhat uncomfortably between New Age spirituality and Enlightenment fundamentalism).

The problem with Habermas' evolutionary sketch of teleologically oriented learning processes that, supposedly, lead to the emergence of a rational democratic society is, ultimately, I think, a motivational one. Even if we were to assume for a moment that the utopia of a fully deliberative democracy in which political decisions would result from rational consensus formation that counterfactually expresses the assent of all those who are concerned by the decisions, even if such a society were to come into existence, in the absence of a substantive conception of the 'good life', nothing excludes that this well-ordered society might provide justice, though – and here's the rub – without happiness. Indeed, a social order may be just and well ordered, while being alienated and promoting inauthentic forms of life (Arnsperger, 2005: 79). To the extent that it offers a formal procedure, but no substantive content, and provides a discursive foundation, but no normative horizon, a rational society whose members are related to each other as anonymous citizens endowed with a series of basic rights, may fail to sufficiently motivate its members to engage in, and give themselves over to, a common project that is at once social, political, cultural and personal.

In a short but powerful draft of a manifesto, Alain Caillé (2011b) has recently proposed 'convivialism' as a successor to the secular ideologies of communism, socialism, liberalism and anarchism.[52] Unlike Wilber, he does not waffle about 'Oneness', but invokes the principle of common humanity. Unlike Habermas, he does not privilege consensus, but conjures difference and plurality. Caillé sets off with social division, conflict and violence and conceives of social order not as a negation and denial of conflict, but as a continuously renewed attempt to manage the divisions and live with them: how can individuals live together with one another in relative peace, 'opposing themselves to each other, without massacring each other' (Mauss: 1950: 278)? That is the central question that convivial societies have to satisfactorily resolve. For the former assistant of Claude Lefort, democracy is the answer. It is not a procedure, but a way of life; not a means, but an end in itself.

Through engagement in cooperative practices, the associations of the lifeworld transpose Mauss' triple obligation of the gift – 'to give, to receive and to return the gift' – from the interpersonal to the political domain of civil society. Beyond the positivism of utilitarianism and the negativism of anti-capitalism, convivialism proposes a post-materialist vision of a possible future without continuous growth (*décroissance*) that finds its intrinsic motivation in the mere pleasure of coming together and acting in concert for a common purpose. The common purpose, nowadays, is to protect the generative principles of sociability that make decent life in a democratic society possible and to animate and invigorate social actions that contribute to the qualitative growth of the 'commons' and the preservation of the 'good life' on earth.

Now that we have sketched the contours of 'the good life with and for the others in just institutions and a sustainable environment' (Ricoeur, 1990: 202),[53] we can revert to the present. With a modicum of developmental psychology, evolutionary sociology and reflexive philosophy of history, capitalism can be understood as a social formation that systematically arrests further development towards post-material convivial democratic societies. With its mechanical linkages between the base and the superstructure, historical materialism is, perhaps, the philosophy of history that best captures the world-historical obstruction of capitalism. Going back to the metatheoretical space, but interpreting it now as a metahistorical field of morphogenesis, we can characterise capitalism as a social formation that systematically reduces the human being to quadrant B: a sensing body with needs and interests that faces a (pseudo-)natural social environment which it tries to control instrumentally and to which it tries to adapt itself strategically to survive.

Folding back the quadrants of the metatheoretical space into one, the behavioural space of the psycho-somatic, capitalism is the social system that suppresses the cultural meanings of existence that transcend self-interest and produces the *Homo economicus* that its utilitarian vision of the world presupposes (Arnsperger, 2005, 2009).[54] It is true that capitalism ignores neither culture or meaning. Nor does it neglect communication, cooperation or giving. To the contrary, it knows all too well that the human being is more than a producer and a consumer of commodities, but by systematically interpreting human existence in the utilitarian language of a rational choice between preferences, it reduces all possible goods (things and ideas) to commodities that can be possessed and exchanged. By occupying the body and the mind, its non-culture of utilitarianism produces the subjects that produce the goods and live to consume them as commodities. Thus, it tends not only to occupy the whole space of experience, but also to arrest the development of persons, cultures, societies and humanity as such to a higher level of 'conscientious consciousness', i.e. awareness, connectedness and togetherness. With its insistence on private property, accumulation, work, competition, innovation, consumption and continuous growth, capitalism is a self-perpetuating system of alienation that commodifies, instrumentalises and colonises the spirit and the soul, as well as the mind and the body. As Arnsperger (2009: 111) says in his existential critique of capitalism: 'We are capitalist bodies and minds, in a capitalist culture and a capitalist economic and political system, with a capitalist consciousness of ourselves.' From an anthropological point of view, capitalism is a catastrophe; from an existential and spiritual point of view, it is a calamity; and to the extent that it needs and feeds on economic growth to sustain itself, from an ecological point of view, it is a real disaster too.

The second post-modernity

As I am writing (June 2012), the world-system seems to be moving slowly but surely towards systemic collapse. It will probably not end with a spectacular bang, but with the whispers of an unending series of social upheavals and pragmatic political adaptations in the very centre of the world-system. Precisely because the current juncture is a critical one, I deem it necessary to give metacritical realism a chance and propose an anascopic reading (a bottom-up and rather upbeat reading as opposed to a top-down, katascopic and catastrophic one) that hesitatingly explores the possibility of personal, cultural and structural change in dark times of transition. Having suggested that it makes sense to move beyond critique and beyond realism, I will now argue that we can also move beyond capitalism, not at all levels of existence, though, but in personal life, at work and in internetworked peer-to-peer communities.

At the structural levels of the world-system, the future seems blocked. It is still too early to know for sure whether the global economic crisis really spells the beginning of the end of the world-system (Wallerstein), the final demise of the West (Spengler) or merely the tumultuous transition to a new regime of accumulation beyond 'financialisation' (Boyer). Recovery and return to 'business as usual' is a possibility, but given that the crisis is a dramatic moment within a longer-term geopolitical shift from the West to the East and to a lesser extent also from the North to the South, it seems rather unlikely at this stage. Whatever new system may come into place to succeed 30 years of market fundamentalism, or neo-liberalism, most probably it will not be a post-capitalist one!

As yet we do not have a satisfying social scientific interpretation of the current juncture.[55] We are in the midst of a global shift and, like most of my colleagues, I am in the fog. What is, perhaps, most surprising (and rather preoccupying) is that, unlike economics and anthropology, sociology is not even in crisis.[56] Our grand theories of late modernity, post-Fordism and post-industrialism are only valid till 2007. Not that they are wrong, but the analyses of Wallerstein, Habermas, Giddens, Beck, Castells, Boltanski and Cie have to be updated, if not reformulated altogether. Seen from the vantage point of the semi-periphery of the world-system (but note how semi-peripheric countries like Brazil and India, not to mention China, have quickly become 'pericentric'), they also seem rather Eurocentric and, in this sense, rather 'provincial'.

To focus the mind on the present and underscore its uncertainties, I will call the current juncture the 'second post-modernity'.[57] Almost 30 years ago, in a much-noted report to the government of Québec, François Lyotard proclaimed the advent of a postmodern condition. Foregrounding the breakdown of totalising philosophies of history that promise emancipation, he defined the new epoch in cultural terms: 'Simplified to the extreme, we consider postmodern the incredulity towards grand narratives' (Lyotard, 1979: 7). It may seem ironic that the epochal debate on post-ism of the 1980s was quickly replaced in the 1990s by the even grander narrative of globalisation. If postmodernism refers to the 'cultural logic' of advanced industrial-capitalist societies, globalisation stresses the 'structural logic' of the expansion of industrial capitalism across the globe.

With hindsight, we can now understand that postmodernism was a swansong of the West and that the cracking of the cultural code of modernity was only the opening phase of a protracted process of global systemic breakdown. This time the shift is 'for real'. It is not just the culture of modernity that is fragmenting and diffracting. Second post-modernity means that the very structures of the global system are being undone in real time. Chaos may spread from the centre to the periphery of the world-system, reorganise geo-politics and spread from the economic and political subsystems to all spheres of social, cultural and personal life. As I will argue in the final chapter of the book, the ecological, military, technological, economic, political, cultural and personal risks of the world-society are so daunting that the very survival of the human species is at stake. Humanity may fail to rise up to the challenges and regress to a stationary state of civilisation full of strife, conflict and pathologies. 'The old is dying & the new cannot be born. In this interregnum there arises a great diversity of morbid symptoms' (Gramsci, 1971: 276).

Legitimation Crisis *revisited*

Recently, Jürgen Habermas (2012a), the last remaining intellectual in the grand European tradition, published an essay on the crisis. His analysis of the 'democratic deficit' of the EU is not uninteresting, but as a whole *The Constitution of Europe* represents, as the French say, a *fuite en avant* – a leap of faith from a factual to a transfactual European Union that would lead the way to a transnational democracy on the world scale. Somewhat disappointed by his Kantian cosmopolitanism, I returned to *Legitimation Crisis* (Habermas, 1973). To my great surprise, I found the book absolutely relevant, highly pertinent and, above all, timely and actual – with one proviso: Habermas could simply not imagine at the time that the welfare state would ever vanish. In a modest attempt to update it, I will therefore use it as a template to investigate the dynamics of the present downturn as its effects ripple from the economic and the political subsystem of society to the socio-cultural life-world.[58]

The current downshift reveals a systemic contradiction at the heart of post-industrial capitalism. Thriving capitalism depends on continuous growth. Yet, at the same time as growth is economically necessary (no growth, no gain, no jobs, no welfare), it is ecologically impossible. Ignoring the 'negationists' on the loony fringes of science, we can safely state that the occurrence of irreversible climate change is now a proven fact. Michel Freitag's (2008: 367–401) question, 'How long can we sustain sustainable development?' is, indeed, a rather haunting one. Growth may be unsustainable in the medium to long run; in the short run, the return of economic growth seems anything but imperative. Since the Fordist–Keynesian regime of growth entered a crisis in the 1970s, it has been superseded by a post-Fordist, post-industrial, flexible mode of accumulation that runs on neo-liberal principles, as ensconced in the so-called 'Washington Consensus'. Compared with the very few crises that occurred during the 'Golden Thirties' (1945–1973), the recurrence of financial downturns (1973–1982, 1992–1994, 1997, 1998, 2000–2001, 2008–2012) in various parts of the world since the 1970s indicates that the crunch is a structural one.

The 'subprime crisis' that exploded in 2007 in the United States and the current sovereign debt crisis in the Eurozone are one and the same crisis. To understand its dynamics, we need to revert to the 1970s and consider with 'regulation theorists' (like Harvey, 2010 and Boyer, 2011) how capitalism has found in 'financialisation' an illusory solution to the problem of 'overaccumulation of capital' (Marx's declining rate of profit). On Marx's analysis, capitalists always have to produce surpluses in the form of profit, reinvest a part of that surplus in expansion and find ever new profitable outlets. Even as real wages stagnated, a low profit margin regime arose in almost all lines of conventional industrial production in the 1970s. To enhance profitability and stimulate it artificially, the surplus money was invested in highly speculative financial markets. Attracting 'the best and the brightest' to Wall Street and the City of London, highly complex financial instruments (such as derivatives, hedge-funds and credit default swaps) were invented. The stock market became a 'global casino' in which astronomical amounts of free-floating capital, disconnected from the real economy and amounting to many multiples of the global GDP, were circulating without much regulation or taxation. During the 1980s financial markets were increasingly liberalised, deregulated and, since the 'Big Bang' of 1986, also globalised and unified, acting as a single unit in real time. The 'regime of accumulation pulled by financialisation' was a highly lucrative one, but to overcome the problem of 'underconsumption' (Marx's failure of capital realisation) in deindustrialising countries in the Western hemisphere, credit cards and mortgages were massively dispensed to American customers with modest incomes without proper checking of their credit worthiness. For a decade, they went on a shopping spree, incurring huge debts in the process. The financial whiz kids dreamed up the idea that their debts could actually be sold and that insecure mortgages that were cut and mixed with secure ones could be traded as assets and sold to a multiplicity of financial institutions along the chain. When the 'subprime crisis' exploded in 2007, soon to be followed by an even more severe 'credit default swap crisis' in 2008, they woke up and their dream turned into a nightmare from which they are still trying to wake. The destruction of wealth is colossal. I still remember reading the *International Herald Tribune* on 1 January 2010 with disbelief: worldwide, the shares of your average investor had lost 30 per cent of their value. Since then, we slowly got used to staggering figures, hundreds of billions that evaporated overnight and tens of trillions of dollars spent on bailouts or deposited in 'firewalls' that are supposed to protect the system from collapse.

To save the economic system from complete meltdown, the American government bailed out the banks, while China shored up the American Fed with its huge reserves of up to $3 trillion. Capitalism was 'saved' by the state, but in a typical capitalist fashion: the profits were privatised, the losses socialised. Following the election of President Obama, it seemed for a while (2008–2010) as if massive stimulus had brought the state back and pushed the whole economy in a more Keynesian direction. By 2011 the epicentre of the downshift had, however, not only moved from the United States to Europe, but also from the economic to the political system: the crisis within the financial system centred on the banks had morphed into a fiscal crisis of the state. Confronted with intractable sovereign debt and banking crises, the 'PIGS' (a derogatory reference to Portugal, Ireland, Italy, Greece and Spain) were forced by the troika of lenders (EU, ECB and IMF) to an extremely severe cure of austerity that placed them at the same time under the humiliating tutelage of their creditors. Neo-liberalism came back with a vengeance. Without democratic consultation and without any ideological justification, the European Council, which consists in theory of the heads of state, but which was, de facto, headed in tandem by Merkel and Sarkozy (dubbed 'Merkozy' by the popular press), imposed a never-ending series of merciless budget cuts that revoke the whole post-war arrangement of the European welfare state.

Unresolved, the economic crisis is displaced to the political system (Habermas, 1973: 68–70, 87–96). Overburdened, the political system becomes properly ungovernable. The stakes are high, but without leadership no economic solution is in sight. The future is dim, yet highly uncertain and unpredictable. Nationalism or cosmopolitanism? Democracy or technocracy? Austerity or growth? Eurobonds or further quantitative easing by the ECB? Greek and possibly also British exit or fiscal and budgetary union within the Eurozone? United States of Europe or collapse of the Eurozone? Disintegration of the European Union and worldwide depression? It's still too early to judge, but anything can happen.

From systemic crisis to social pathologies

When the economic and political systems become overburdened, disoriented and disorganised, the crisis of the system slowly evolves into a full-blown 'legitimation crisis'. The state apparatus is faced simultaneously with the difficult task of having to stimulate growth under austerity and to avoid the suspicion of kowtowing to the financial markets.

> On the one hand, it is supposed to raise the requisite amount of taxes so rationally that crisis-ridden disturbances of growth can be avoided. On the other hand, the selective raising of taxes, the discernible pattern of priorities in their use, and the administrative performances themselves must be so constituted that the need for legitimation can be satisfied as it arises.
>
> (Habermas, 1973: 88–89)

If it fails in the first task, with the result that the risk of systemic disintegration spreads from the economic to the political subsystem, a 'rationality crisis' arises. If it fails in the latter task and cannot maintain a semblance of fairness, the turbulence spreads from the system to civil society. As social unrest escalates, the government faces a deficit of legitimacy.

Notwithstanding austerity (or, more likely, because of it), the economy remains anaemic and without growth. The people suffer. Some of them have lost their savings, their houses, their jobs, their pensions; taxes go up and social provisions go down; among the younger people, with unemployment rising to over 50 per cent for those under 24 – 56 per cent in Spain and 59 per cent in Greece, a whole generation once again seems sacrificed. Public services are privatised. In England, the university fees now run up to £13,000 per year. Never mind the intimate connection between construction boosts and housing bubbles, speculation on real estate continues unabated in the great metropolises (in Rio de Janeiro the prices have tripled in the last two years). Housing becomes unaffordable even for those who still have good jobs.

Civil society protests against the injustice it perceives. The people no longer believe that the system is fair. They know a 'class war' is going on – though it is not a 'class struggle' in the Marxist sense – and that capital is winning it. According to a popular slogan, widely used by the Occupy Movement, 99 per cent is getting poorer while the 1 per cent of the wealthy at the top of the pyramid is getting richer, stacking their money offshore and avoiding taxes. Millionaires are running as presidential candidates. The masses are convinced that they are paying for the banks. Conspiracy theories about the organised stripping of national assets by banks run wild. Profoundly scandalised by the material excesses of the rich, the citizens also resent the moral corruption of their politicians (epitomised by Berlusconi). The multitude loses faith in the political system and withdraws its support from the established political parties. Only in Europe, 16 incumbent governments have been punished in elections since the onset of the crisis. The political field gets dangerously polarised between xenophobic parties on the extreme right (Front National in France, Partij voor de Vrijheid in the Nederlands, Jobik in Hungary, Chrysi Avgi in Greece) and populist parties on the far left (Parti de Gauche in France, Socialistische Partij in the Netherlands, Syriza in Greece). The centre cannot hold. In the United States, the politics are so dysfunctional that bipartisan politics are nigh impossible, as became all too obvious in 2011 when, following a principled refusal by Tea Party Republicans to raise the debt ceiling, Standard & Poor's downgraded the credit rating of the US government bond for the first time in the country's history.

From diffuse anger in public spaces to organised violence against immigrants, from rising levels of despair and depression to a spike in suicide levels, all indicators show that when the 'markets' rule unchecked by the countervailing mechanism of 'redistribution', the structures of 'reciprocity' of the life-world come under strain too (Polanyi, 1957). Anomic manifestations abound and there arises, to quote Gramsci once again 'a great diversity of morbid symptoms'.

When 'the system' is perceived as basically unfair and revolting, society faces a serious identity crisis. Habermas calls it a 'motivation crisis', but in accordance with Honneth's (2000: 11–69) reformulation of the tasks of social philosophy, one might as well change medical metaphors and refer to the lived crises (loss of meaning, freedom and community) as 'social pathologies'. Alienated from society, the citizens turn their back on it, refuse to further play their role in the system or are otherwise unable to function. Meaning becomes a scarce resource. Once it is lacking, it cannot be artificially regenerated by systemic means. It can neither be purchased by money nor mandated by power. Disappointed and disaffected, angry and demoralised, without a genuine project that gives meaning to their lives, the citizens may withdraw to the private sphere of the family (if they have one), join churches and sects (if they still have any faith), engage in deviant behaviour (drug use and petty crime), recoil to the virtual world (computer games and internet surfing) and lead a pre-suicidal existence at the margins of social life.

The withdrawal from society and the principled rejection of its norms and values does not need to be destructive, however. In Merton's (1968: 185–214) famous typology of the individual modes of adaptation to anomic strain, ritualism, retreatism and deviance are not the only possibilities. Alienation may lead to political contention and rebellion. Similarly, anomy may trigger a quest for autonomy. Now, as before, the members of society may mobilise against the assault on the welfare state unleashed by the capitalist downturn. To protect themselves against the wholesale destruction of a form of life, they may propose radical alternatives to the system. This creative response coming from the depths of civil society is a normal and healthy reaction to the destruction of organic life by self-regulating markets that are disembedded from society. It corresponds to the second moment of Karl Polanyi's (1953) 'double movement': when the market expands to incorporate the real commodities, society responds to stall further incorporation of the 'fictive commodities' (nature, labour, money) under the laws of the market.[59] As a creative and innovative response to the commodification of labour (people), land (nature) and money (purchasing power) that render social bonds, despoil the commons and destroy livelihoods, internetworked protest movements, like 15-M in Spain ('*los indignados*') and '#Occupy Wall Street', invent new autonomous forms of collective action that aim to 'reclaim life' and 'regenerate the commons'.

Without formal leadership or any clearly defined political programme, self-organising movements protest against social inequality and economic injustice and demand, as Judith Butler says in her public support to the movement, 'the impossible':

> *If hope is an impossible demand, then we demand the impossible.* If the right to shelter, food and employment are impossible demands than we demand the impossible. If it is impossible to demand that those who profit from the recession redistribute their wealth and cease their greed than yes we demand the impossible.[60]

In their joyous anarchic protests against the global powers of finance capitalism, the 'newest social movements' do not only innovate the repertoires of political contention, with their new leaderless modes of spontaneous organisation (with general assemblies, affinity groups, spokescouncils and other innovative methodologies of 'government by consensus'), they also reinvent and rejuvenate the cooperatives, the commons and direct democracy. With direct appeals to 'moral sentiments' (empathy and solidarity, but also indignation and rage) and the 'principles of reciprocity', the blogosphere of the extraparliamentary opposition to the system offers counterhegemonic analyses to the crisis that hardly reach the dominant media. They may even propose seemingly ingenuous solutions, such as the following one, which merits consideration: Why not organise a Jubilee, cancel all outstanding debts in one stroke and start all over again?[61]

Beyond capitalism?

Now that we are reaching the end of our lengthy introduction to metacritical realism, I want to tie some of the strands of my argument together and explore the possibilities of a post-capitalist future. Unlike some Marxist comrades, I am of the opinion that the theory of the 'final breakdown' (*Zusammenbruch*) of capitalism broke down a long time ago. The horizon is blocked and I am not expecting a happy end to the crisis soon. Whatever future awaits us, it will not be a socialist, let alone a communist one. It will get worse before it gets better. And yet, if I dare to speak of post-capitalism (rather than posthumanism, as I do in the final chapter of the book), it is not at the structural or systemic level of the world society, but below in the life-world at the personal, professional and communal levels of social existence. Indeed, while I find it hard to imagine how the whole world-system might evolve beyond capitalism – sure, it might crash or otherwise destroy itself through self-inflicted catastrophes like climate change, technological drift or nuclear war – I think post-capitalism already exists not just as a regulative ideal, but as a daily practice in personal life, some professional spheres and internetworked communities.

Just looking around me, in academia and elsewhere, I see a lot of people who, at least, try to live in accordance with the principles they espouse, the norms they adhere to and the values they believe in. They may not be completely unselfish or other-regarding (who is?), but as metareflexive individuals they seem to have made a conscious existential choice to live the 'good life'. Even if they make a good living and assume managerial responsibilities in all sorts of organisations, they are 'beyond power and money'. The fact that they are highly successful professionals and espouse post-material values as well should not be written off as another instance of 'bourgeois-bohemianism'. It should rather be considered an integral part of the 'long march through the institutions'. If one wants to change the world, one has to be in the world – 'In the world, but not of the world' (Romans, 12.2). The strategy of changing the institutions from within is not revolutionary. It is radically reformist. In many cases, notably those that are related to the global governance of the risk society, the practice of 'radical entrism' (Trotsky) has been shown to be much more effective than the Grand Refusal (Vandenberghe, 2011).

The world cannot be changed overnight, but assuming that we want to change it, we might as well depart from where we are. As Bhaskar says somewhere: 'The only thing we can change here and now is ourselves.' Through the conscious application of principles and values we believe in, as 'existential militants' (Arnsperger, 2009), we can contribute to the humanisation of the life-world and expand the reach of post-capitalism, so that when the system eventually comes crashing down, if it ever does, there will be an alternative system in place, underneath the existing one, providing the living infrastructure of the post-capitalist convivial societies of the future.

If one were to start with an analysis of the economic, technological and political systems of the second postmodernity, it would be difficult, if not impossible, to develop a dynamic analysis of social change that avoids the pathos of victimisation of the Frankfurt School (hypercritique, moralism and nostalgia) or the pitfalls of lucidity of Luhmann's systems theory (hypertheory, nihilism and irony). I will therefore reverse the perspective. In a preliminary sketch of a theory of personal, cultural and social morphogenesis that needs further development I will work my way from the bottom up and make my point concerning a possible progression towards post-capitalism in three small but cumulative steps. In continuous dialogue with the work of Margaret Archer on the modes of reflexivity, Harry Kunneman on normative professionalism and Michel Bauwens on peer-to-peer production, I will start with existential questions at the individual level and follow these through at the institutional and systemic levels of society.

Metareflexivity and the noetic imperative

It is not only capitalism that is in crisis. Individuals are increasingly so too. The fact that 10–25 per cent of the individuals of developed societies are suffering from severe existential crises is indicative of a growing psychological, social and spiritual misery. The classical neuroses of yesterday have increasingly given way to depressions, compulsive-obsessive disorders and panic attacks. Researchers have recently discovered that the groundwater in England is polluted by antidepressants! France is the country with the highest consumption of tranquilisers and sleeping pills in the world. Medication may offer some relief and help individuals to function normally, while making them dependent on the pharmaceutical industry.[62] It does not provide meaning to life, though. The meaning of life cannot be bought; it has to be sought, actively and desperately. It takes a whole life to find out what one really wants do with one's life and who one really is. And at the end, in the middle or right from the very beginning, one may still arrive at the conclusion that one failed. As Paul Valéry (1943: 55) said in a pithy phrase: '*La mort dure toute une vie.*'

In France, the sociology of individualism has become a niche within the discipline.[63] Following a trend that was initiated in the United States with the work of Christopher Lash, David Riesman and Richard Sennett in the 1970s, continued in Germany with Ulrich Beck in the 1980s and reached the UK with Anthony Giddens and Zygmunt Bauman in the 1990s, the 'individualisation thesis' is now an obligatory topos in Paris. It definitely is a sign of the times. Is it because society and its institutions have disintegrated that individuals no longer feel part of a whole? Or is it because they are no longer inscribed in a collective that society has become a society of individuals without a common project?[64] In between those who propose a rather depressing picture (like Ehrenberg, Castel and Gauchet), identifying individualisation with the privatisation and atomisation of existence, and those who propose a more constructive analysis (like Dubet, Martucelli and de Singly) of the human condition in second postmodernity, I will consider existential crises from a morphogenetic and narrative perspective as dramatic, but increasingly common moments of incapacitation that force individuals to reflect on their ways of being and, if possible, to consciously change the direction of their life-course and revolutionise themselves. To quote a popular mystagogue:

> 'You have to change your life!' [Rilke] – this is the formulation of the imperative that transcends the alternative between hypothetic and categorical imperative. It is the absolute imperative – the metanoetic commandment as such. It is the call for a revolution in the second person singular. It determines life as an intermediary stage between higher and lower forms.
>
> (Sloterdijk, 2009: 47)

Although nothing, absolutely nothing, guarantees that a given individual will be able to overcome the challenges he or she faces, every existential crisis demands a reflexive reorganisation of the metanarrative of one's life.

Usually described as breakups or breakdowns, existential crises may lead to peaks of personal growth, plateaus of stagnation or the abyss of despair. It's only in retrospect, when the worst is over, that movement can be discerned. It can go from utter despondency (with its own cycles of never-ending repetition) via slow recovery to progressive reorientation of one's whole life. Relapses are always possible. During the storm there is only confusion, disorientation and pain. Nothing moves. The narratives of one's life come to a standstill. There is a question, but no answer. Developmentally speaking, nervous breakdowns, panic attacks, burnouts, etc. are reflexive moments of transition between two regimes of reflexivity and consciousness. The transitions are fluid, the changes molecular. Small, almost imperceptible changes of mood and mind may suddenly unblock a situation and lead to new insights – or old relapses. Existentially speaking, crises are 'ex-stases' in which the present is 'unhinged' from the past and the future.[65] From within, an existence may 'pro-ject' itself into another time and space. Possibilities of transcendence may open up – or not. Crisis may lead an existence from facticity to authenticity – or, as the case may be, back from authenticity to facticity and fracture. Sociologically speaking, the accumulation of existential crises and the need to radically revise one's metanarratives carry over from the personal and social spheres of life, possibly leading to generalised morphostasis in which everything changes at the same time.

Phrased in terms of Margaret Archer's (2003) typology of internal conversations, my hypothesis is a triple one: first, metareflexivity itself comes in three forms (meta-communicative, meta-autonomous and meta-metareflexivity); second, every form of metareflexivity is the result of an attempt to overcome fracture and crisis; third, at an aggregate level, as a higher number of individuals practice metareflexivity in daily life, the metanoetic imperative has a synergetic impact on personality, culture and society. Although the existential quest for meaning does not necessarily imply social and political engagement, as demonstrated by 'authenticity junkies' who actively disengage from politics to cultivate their beautiful bodies and souls, there nevertheless is a conceptual connection between the search for the 'good life' and the realisation of the 'good society' that needs to be philosophically grounded, sociologically theorised and empirically investigated. In any case, the search for personal transformation and the research of institutional change have to go hand in hand, both intellectually and existentially.

What happens when revolutionaries who want to change everything but themselves go through an intense process of personal deconstruction? What happens to the grand narratives when their internal conversations no longer work and their self-narratives come to a grinding standstill? These are not just rhetorical questions, but ones that are amenable to concrete empirical research on the internal conversations they have with themselves (and with others within themselves). Whether or not the individuals are able to envisage another life and how they re-orient their life-stories in and through internal conversations and external communication are empirical questions. The conversations may be internal and personal, but as I will show in the next chapter, they draw on collective cultural (intellectual, normative, spiritual) resources that are public and that constitute the linkage between the past and the present, the part and the whole, the personal and the social, the existential and the political.

One of the tasks of a developmental existential sociology is to trace the relations between reflexivity, normativity and humanity that point beyond capitalism towards ever higher levels of 'conscientious consciousness', at individual, institutional and planetary levels. This task is a sociological one, not because sociology is the master discipline that needs to be defended at any price against psychology (as in Comte, Durkheim and Lahire) and philosophy (as in Weber, Elias and Bourdieu), but rather because society is investigated through the kind of humanity that it engenders or fails to bring into existence, while the individuals are analysed as conscious social actors who draw on traditions to change themselves through personal reflection and thereby also bring social change into the world. The sociological perspective is both metacritical and metahistorical. The revolutionaries have only changed the world; the point is to change the revolutionaries! Changing the revolutionaries means interpreting them differently and coming to realise that the world is already full of 'existential militants' who ask themselves continuously what they want to do not only *with* their life, but also *in* their life, with and for others, in their work and other institutional spheres, to bring change into the world. Varying an apocryphal remark of Gandhi, I'd say that they themselves strive to be the change they want to see in the world.

Contemporary sociology tends to operate with a worldview in which there is hardly anything between the individual and society at large. Without a common culture and a common project that integrates individuals into a whole, everything happens as if society had already evaporated, with the result that individual bodies directly confront the world-system. Together, the institutional deficit in sociology and the eclipse of societal mediations lead to a kind of sociological Cartesianism. Consequently, the *Homo clausus*, that hyper-reflexive Occidental Man who from within is closed off from the others and the surrounding world, becomes the default vision of the human being.[66] Once the individual (body) has been split off from the system (mind), without intersubjectivities, collective bodies or institutional mediations in between, it is indeed hard to join them together again. The stand-off between globalisation and individualisation – or rationalisation and subjectivation (Touraine, 1992) – goes some way to explain the increasingly desperate calls for a global social movement that would bring radical social change without having to transform all the intermediary social institutions. As an alternative to radical theories of globalisation and social contestation, I would like to argue that social change starts in everyday life: every time one hesitates and stops to consciously think through the possibilities the situation offers for oneself and others, the institutions in which one finds oneself are also changed. On this point, I agree with Gabriel Tarde, a genius of sorts and a dreamer who banked on molecular change: 'This hesitation, this little internal battle that reproduces itself at each moment within the life of people, is the infinitesimal and infinitely fruitful opposition of history; it introduces in sociology a quiet and profound revolution' (Tarde, 1999: 80). So, to radically change the world, one has to start with oneself and change the institutions one is part of, insufflating new life into the old institutional orders of cooperation (family and friends, the work sphere, the associations of civil society, etc.) that govern everyday life. To investigate the contemporary importance of institutions, I will now turn to the work of Axel Honneth and then return to Talcott Parsons.

The new spirit of critical theory

In an ambitious attempt to actualise Hegel's *Philosophy of Right*, Axel Honneth (2011) has recently proposed to rewrite the theory of justice as normatively reconstructed social analysis (*Gerechtigkeitstheorie als Gesellschaftsanalyse*). Against normative theories of justice that fix their gaze on normative principles that are universally valid, yet disconnected from social life and social analysis, he wants to bring back the objective Spirit into social theory (and *vice versa*) in the guise of a critical theory of social institutions. Against philosophers in the Kantian tradition, like John Rawls and Jürgen Habermas, who 'invent' abstract, formal and transfactual norms, Honneth wants to go back to Hegel, though not to his dialectics and certainly not to his conception of the state.

In continuous dialogue with (and against) Habermas, his mentor, he reconstructs the philosophical discourse of modernity around the idea of freedom.[67] The very idea of freedom defines modernity; its history can be read as a progressive deployment of the idea, first as 'negative freedom' (as in contract theories of Hobbes and Locke), then as 'reflexive freedom' (as in theories of self-realisation and self-determination of Rousseau and Kant) and, finally, as 'social freedom' too (in the speculative sociologies of the old Hegel and the young Marx). Penetrating all spheres of social life, liberty launches modernity on a world-historical trajectory. The idea of freedom is, thus, not an extramundane ideal. To the extent that it is incorporated in the existing institutions of society and the customary social practices, the value of freedom is already, at least in part, 'realised'. The Spirit lives in society and animates all of its parts.

Honneth's neo-Hegelian theory of *Sittlichkeit* as institutionalised morality is not a conflict, but a consensus theory of society. To highlight its pneumatic element, I will call it a 'conspiracy theory' (from *con-spirare*): as the Spirit gently 'breathes' through all the institutions of society (the family, civil society and the public sphere), infuses its attendant practices (love, work and communication) and inspires the social actors in their daily life, the social conditions that make the freedom of all possible progressively come into existence. No wonder that with his insistence on shared values and norms, the leading figure of the third generation of the Frankfurt School encounters the sociologies of Durkheim and Parsons (rather than Marx or Weber) on his way. Unlike Talcott Parsons, Honneth does not propose an affirmative reading of the present, however, but a critical and corrective one. By means of an idealtypical 'normative reconstruction' of the guiding values that are already real, but not yet fully actualised, he aims to develop a critical theory that practises an 'immanent critique' of society. Instead of holding society to an ideal standard of justice that it cannot satisfy, as allegedly happens in 'transcendent critiques' of modernity, an immanent critique judges existing social institutions on its own terms.[68] It takes the ideals at their word and enjoins the institutions and its members to fully realise the ideals they proudly proclaim.

Such a philosophical reconstruction of the social grounds of critique skilfully avoids some of the pitfalls of a pure theory of justice that hangs in the air, but, like Rawls', has no feet on the ground. From a sociological point of view, it remains nevertheless problematic. The problem is not to be found in its idealism, which I actually share, but rather in its lack of realism. By conceiving of society as a complex of normatively regulated systems of action, Honneth is unable to properly conceptualise the daunting systemic problems that trouble second post-modernity. Not unlike structuration theory, Honneth's refurbished theory of 'relational institutions' refuses to acknowledge structural emergence and dualism. Given that it does not recognise the phenomenon of emergence, it cannot theorise the problem of reification either.[69]

For a critical theory that returns to Hegel to revise Marx, or, as Habermas says on the back cover of Honneth's book, 'that takes the historical step back from Marx to Hegel in order to restore the programme "from Hegel to Marx" ', the fact that the alienating autonomy of social, economic and technological systems cannot be properly analysed is, definitely, a major drawback. The current conjunction of economic and ecological crises demonstrates all too dramatically that complex systems are dangerously out of control; it illustrates almost graphically how their breakdown brings havoc to the communicative and cooperative infrastructures of reciprocity. In his attempt to correct the Luhmannian overemphasis on the structural 'decoupling' (Habermas) or 'disembedding' (Polanyi) of the autonomous systems from the life-world, I am afraid Honneth has bent the stick too far to the other side. The rejection of the functionalist notion of a 'system free of norms' that follows its own autopoietic laws, impervious to the wishes of the subjects that it is supposed to serve, reduces society to a complex of relational institutions in which the struggle for recognition prevails. What remains when one removes the system is the life-world – which is now being impaired by the very system it fails to account for.

The defunctionalisation of critical theory has two critical consequences: First of all, it makes it difficult, if not impossible, to theorise the civilisational challenges of the second modernity: whole systems are quickly spinning out of control and slowly destroying themselves in real time – as if they were committing suicide not with a single pistol shot, but more akin to a patient with lung cancer who, against his better knowledge, continues smoking.[70] At the same time as it underestimates the global challenges of the risk society – and this is my second critique – it overestimates the demoralisation of societies. Instead of actively searching for current actualisations of the value of freedom, the latter is seen as being increasingly hollowed out. Deanimated and demoralised, societies run wild and go off track.[71] As social life becomes more savage and rough, the struggles for recognition lose their vitality and are increasingly transposed from the public to the private sphere, where they ravage the subjects from within. Reverting to a Frankfurt-style *Verfallsgeschichte* (history of decay) of social freedom since the 1980s, it consequently ends up presenting a rather bleak picture of the spheres of work and the public (and an all-too-rosy one of the family).[72]

A theory of society without self-regulating systems is only half-way to a critical theory. One cannot expect from a normative theory that shrinks society to its life-world, reducing the latter to a series of expanding circles of recognition, and conceives of the economy as a moral economy that it will offer a satisfying critical account of self-regulating and predatory financial systems that are despoiling communities and fleecing individuals. As the removal of the notion of the 'system' from its conceptual toolbox is not compensated by an accentuated attention to the recrudescence of social struggles either, the theoretical optimism of Left Hegelianism is largely cancelled out by its pessimistic readings of contemporary regressions in most spheres of life.

As a reconstructive alternative, I will invert the cursors of optimism and pessimism. To resume my reflections on post-capitalism, I will now return to some of Talcott Parsons' writings of the early and middle period on the moral importance of professions and advance the notions of 'good work' and 'normative professionalism' to argue that existential questions about what to do *with* one's life have an impact on what one does *in* life. The struggle against the system finds its ultimate roots in the communicative infrastructures of the life-world, but to properly institutionalise the normative principles, norms and values in concrete social practices that can trigger social change, they need to be mediated by intermediary institutions that span the gap between the life-world and the system. The thesis I would like to explore is that the 'professions' form this mediation and that they are the locus of interchange where system and the life-world intersect and, as such, the fulcrum of personal and societal change. In case a catchphrase is needed, I would say that the next big social movement might well be a professional one.

Back to Parsons

In his first explorations of ideas on the role of norms, which would later be formalised in his revision of the *Gemeinschaft–Gesellschaft* or socialism–capitalism polarity and result in a combinatorial analysis of 'pattern variables', Parsons goes against the grain of the economics of work and the sociology of organisations.[73] Over and against rational choice approaches to business and formal analyses of government, he brings the professions to the fore of his investigation and demonstrates the role of norms, values and moral sentiments in 'interstitial' institutions, like hospitals, schools, universities and churches that straddle the distinction system and life-world. Unlike business people who are mainly motivated by material interests and bureaucrats who blindly follow administrative rules and procedures, learned professionals, such as medical doctors, teachers, professors, psychoanalysts, therapists, counsellors and the clergy, are not motivated by money or driven by self-interest in the first place. It is only seemingly paradoxical that it is, as Parsons (1951: 473) says, 'to their self-interest to act contrary to their own self-interest – in an immediate situation, of course, not "in the long run"'.[74] Although they obviously 'make money' and share with business-people the insistence on rationality (universalism, functional specificity, achievement, affective neutrality), professionals who offer their services have a strong deontology, as well as an ethos that stresses disinterestedness and orientation to the collectivity. Although the medical profession tends to become more and more commercialised (private care) and bureaucratised (the NHS), the ideal typical doctor–patient relation is still largely governed by the norms of universalism (modern medical practice is not based on magic, but on science and technology), functional specificity (the doctor, even the general practitioner, is a specialist), affective neutrality (the doctor is not supposed to enter into a particular, personal, let alone sexual, relationship with the patient) and collectivism (medicine is not purely capitalistic: the doctor is concerned with the well-being of the patient, he or she does not advertise or exploit the helplessness of those who have put their trust in medicine). If the normative principles that structure the practices of the professionals represent the objective side of institutions, motivations to act in accordance with the culturally prescribed norms represent its subjective corollary. Interestingly, Parsons suggests that recognition by others and the satisfaction of having lived up to the ideals of the professions offer intrinsic rewards of good practices, while moral sentiments like guilt, shame and loss of respect constitute the sanctions of bad practices. 'The loss of respect on the part by those from whom it is expected is one of the severest possible blows to the state of satisfaction of the individual' (Parsons, 1954: 58).

It is, however, not only the 'introjection' (Freud) or 'internalisation' (Parsons) of norms and social control that leads professionals to act in accordance with the norms and values of their profession. The communicative content of their work ('people work') and the success of the services they offer ('diagnosis', 'teaching', 'counselling', 'preaching') demand that they practise their profession not as a 'trade', but as an 'art', and treat their 'clients' neither as 'customers' nor as 'cases', but as people who need to be attended and talked to, listened to and cared for, cured and helped or otherwise accompanied if they are to progress from one state to another – from sickness to health in the case of the patient, from ignorance to autonomy for the student, from sin to salvation for the members of the parish.

America's most famous sociologist may have written most extensively about the relation between medical doctors and patients. I think that as a trained (albeit not practising) psychoanalyst in the Freudian tradition, he derived his deepest intuitions concerning the very nature of professional services from the dialogical encounter between analyst and patient that defines the 'talking cure'. The professional norms (universalism, functional specificity, collectivity orientation and, yes, also affective neutrality) serve to enable the analyst to penetrate sufficiently deeply into the private affairs of the patient and bring repressed materials to the surface. The asymmetry of the *dispositif* of the couch – a kind of panoptic funnel that allows the 'shrink' to peer into the deepest recesses of the patient's mind while revealing nothing about his or her personal life – as well as the principled refusal of the analyst to enter into reciprocity with the patient on an emotional level, refusing, for instance, to meet the latter outside of the therapeutic encounter are justified by good clinical reasons. The control of the channels of communication is meant to stimulate dialogue and communication. Like a priest or a teacher, a good therapist cares about each of his or her patients and is genuinely concerned about their well-being. Unlike psychiatrists who prescribe quick remedial fixes (anti-depressants, anxiolitics, etc.) for long-standing problems of mental health, psychoanalysts do not directly treat the symptoms, but they do so indirectly by entering into a trusting and caring, yet controlled, relation with the patient. Without ever reducing the analysand to a mind or a body, but considering him or her always as a complex psycho-somatic, socio-psychic and pneumatic entity in intense, yet often problematic relations with significant others (family, friends, colleagues, bosses, etc.), the success of the therapy depends on the strength of the mutual commitment to, as well as the depth of the engagement of both parts in the clinical encounter between two human beings. What Parsons says about good medical practice, namely that 'a very important part of it is in fact "unconscious psychotherapy"' (Parsons, 1951: 462, 487) can, *mutatis mutandis*, be generalised to all the professions, including ours.

The academic ethos and the spirit of professionalism

Indeed, like medicine and psychotherapy, science is still in theory, if not always in practice, governed by an ethos, i.e. 'an affectively toned complex of values and norms ... expressed in the form of prescriptions, proscriptions, preferences and permissions ... held to be binding on the man of science' (Merton, 1973: 258–259, 268–269). In his famous yet controversial enumeration of the four interlinked normative imperatives of science, namely communism, universalism, disinterestedness and organised scepticism – or CUDOS, as it is sometimes referred to in the literature – Robert K. Merton underscores, like Parsons, but without his anti-Marxist bias, the collective orientation of a self-regulating scientific community that values collectivist property, defends public communication and primes the sharing of knowledge.[75] The fact that the norms are flagrantly violated and that one can easily oppose an effective anti-norm to every proclaimed one does not mean that the axiology of scientific research is only ideology. In accordance with the principles of immanent critique, one should rather reaffirm the validity of the norms and reinforce the demand of their effective realisation in practice.

Like any other institution, the *Cité de la science* is a commonwealth, a well-ordered community of values that finds its justification in principles of justice. The principles of science, medicine, psychoanalysis, education, etc. need not only to be continuously justified in public discourse and discussed in practical situations, they also need to be publicly proclaimed, so that scientists can be held accountable when they put their own self-interest above that of the community.

I take it that as professional scientists, our vocation is a triple one: to do research, to teach and to supervise. To accomplish these activities well demands more than the possession of knowledge. It requires passion and determination, as well as commitment and dedication. It is hard work. As Weber stressed over and again, science is not a vacation! Good work requires 'good character', but as honourable work in which one can take pride, it is also intrinsically satisfying and self-rewarding. Perhaps the surest way to bring out the academic ethos and the corresponding virtues is to think about an 'imaginary colleague' and his moral lapses: he pretends to value research, but publishes much more than he should; consequently, he looks down on teaching, fails to prepare for the lectures, yet inflicts tons of obligatory readings on the students on a weekly basis; he supervises scores of students but without giving them due care (and when he pays attention, he violates the principle of 'affective neutrality').

In a courageous reflection on 'academic ethics in a preposterous environment', Susan Haack (2013) contrasts the cardinal virtues of seriousness that makes for good and honourable work with the main vices of floppiness in research:

> Industry contrasts, obviously enough, with laziness, a disposition to slack off or cut corners [...]; judgment with an inability to discriminate worthwhile work from the flimsy, the fashionable, the flashy, and the obfuscatory, or serious people from lightweights, charlatans, and clever self-promoters; integrity with a disposition to fudge, obfuscate, or mislead other people, or conveniently to deceive yourself, when it is to your advantage to do so [...]; impartiality with bias, i.e., undiscriminating enthusiasm for, or hostility to, this or that line, or these or those people, etc.; independence with a disposition to conform your interests, your opinions, your line, your approach, etc., to social pressure; consideration with a blindness to, or lack of concern for, others' concerns and priorities.[76]
>
> (Haack, 213: 255)

When it comes to teaching, the same virtues are required according to Professor Haack. Most often, it is a matter of setting the example: not giving the same course again and again, but revising and updating it on a regular basis; dutifully preparing the lectures, carefully choosing the appropriate reading materials, ensuring the material is available in the library and, yes, also reading the texts once again so as to be able to stimulate and facilitate group discussions; presenting the theories, concepts and ideas systematically and clearly, demonstrating solid scholarship without intimidating the students, while exhibiting sound judgement; instilling enthusiasm, encouraging participation, but without imposing it in an authoritarian fashion; responding adequately to the students' questions and being candid about the limits of one's knowledge; being fair in the grading of course work (without grade inflation) and just in the comments one feeds back, etc.

Like research and teaching, supervision only works if one is clear about its finality: to accompany the student to intellectual maturity. The student is not there for the professor's sake – *ad maiorem magistri gloriam* – but, rather, the other way round. Instead of indulging in vanity, one should conscientiously cultivate humility and teach it by example. Similarly, the supervisor should not impose his or her own pet theories and concepts on the students and suggest they work them out and exemplify them in case studies. Our work is *maieutic*. We do not inculcate, but we listen and help the supervisee to deliver the best work he or she is capable of. Like all vocations, supervision presupposes that one 'gives oneself' – one's time, attention, encouragement, knowledge, experience, but also (within limits) one's person. There is no *mysterium* to the *magisterium*. It is, as Parsons well knew, at least in part, based on the psychological mechanisms of transference and counter-transference. The supervisor is both father or mother and brother or sister, while being neither. She or he should be aware that students often go through serious existential crises during the MA or PhD and show the necessary compassion. She or he should definitely not assume that if the supervisee does not produce, she or he went fishing in the Peak District with his or her mates. Most often the opposite is the case: students who get stuck in their writing are not slackers; they are compulsive readers and perfectionists who spend long and lonely hours in front of an empty computer screen. Perhaps the language of the ancient guilds may serve to highlight the 'mission of supervision': to teach the journeyman the craft of science and help the apprentice to produce a masterpiece that will allow him or her to eventually become a fully accredited member of the confraternity of intellectual workers. In a short but thoughtful reflection on 'how to supervise a PhD', Raewyn Connell (1985) reveals some 'tricks of the trade' that may serve to establish a professional relationship of supervision and, thereby, help the apprentice on his or her long journey to complete mastery: it is not good enough to say 'come in and see me any time'; one should really schedule regular meetings, make brief notes on what topics have been covered, discuss the plan of research (what literature will be read, what interviews done, etc.) and the structure of the thesis (outline of chapters and thesis as a whole), etc. In any case, here as in the other 'fiduciary relationships' that presuppose a conscientious use of the symbolic media of influence and persuasion to be fully efficacious, the whole point is to convert institutional power of the professional into a force that nurtures, motivates and empowers those in whose name and for whose benefit it is exercised.

Normative professionalism

Talcott Parsons was mainly concerned about liberal professions (doctors, psychoanalysts, lawyers, professors), but his conclusions can easily be 'democratised' and extended to lower-level professionals (nurses, social workers, secondary school teachers, police agents, prison officers) who work in public or private–public organisations and are directly and continuously in contact with ordinary people. In the last 30 years, following the decline of social-welfare regimes and the concomitant rise of advanced liberal modes of 'governmentality' (Rose, 1999), which will be analysed in more detail in the final chapter of the book, the social professions have been submitted to unrelenting pressures from above to become more rational and efficient, market-driven and customer-centred. As a reaction to the technocratic imposition of 'new public management' in the social sector, with its continuous reorganisations, new rules and procedures, implantations of permanent evaluation through performance indicators, quality controls and audits, etc., that directly interfere with their everyday practices and distract from 'real work', professionals in the field are rediscovering the importance of 'good and honourable work' and becoming more vocal about their normative professional commitments.

At the University for Humanistics (UvH), a small experimental university in the Netherlands that forms humanist counsellors, the interdiscipline of 'humanistics' is taught as an applied normative science that investigates existential questions and promotes processes of humanisation.[77] Over and against the insistence on 'technical professionalisation', my former colleagues from the UvH have developed the notion of 'normative professionalisation' with the intent to investigate and stimulate systematic reflection on the norms and the values, as well as the attitudes and virtues, that are espoused by professionals in health care, social work, education and other soft sectors of society (Kunneman, 1996: 241–260). The guiding idea is that professionals who work in 'interstitial' organisations between the system and the life-world are simultaneously confronted with strategic and communicative demands. On a daily basis, they struggle with tensions between the various levels that impact their decisions (systemic imperatives, organisational cultures, professional practices and personal life). In every concrete case, they have to decide whether they will follow systemic-strategic or, rather, communicative-narrative injunctions. By doing so, they themselves draw the boundaries between the life-world and system. Having arrived at the conclusion that the systemic injunctions detract from their real work, making it often impossible to give their clients the time, attention and care they need, they increasingly start to question the system and the culture of the organisation, while affirming their personal commitment to 'good practices'. Through continuous discussions with like-minded colleagues who are equally committed to 'good work', they become more vocal in their demands for an effective transformation of the organisational culture. By means of reflection on what works well in practice ('reflection-in-action') and explicit formulation of the norms and values, rules and procedures that institutionalise the practices ('reflection-on-action'), while allowing the organisation to realise its mission, the 'directed transformation' of the organisation into a 'learning system' makes morphogenetic change at all levels possible.

Following the example of my Dutch colleagues, I have democratised Parsons' analysis of the 'learned professions'. Now I want to radicalise it and connect it to our former discussion of metareflexivity, existential militantism and post-capitalism. Considered as living representatives of uncompromising idealism, metareflexive persons are concerned with existential questions and engaged in a never-ending quest of the 'good life'. For them the personal quest of 'the true, good and beautiful life' is inseparable from a collective search for a 'just, good and decent society' in which the flourishing of each is a precondition of the flourishing of all. Driven by principles, values and norms they personally believe in, they are 'beyond power and money'. For them money and power are not ends, but means and media they may activate to realise higher ends and ultimate values. As post-materialists endowed with a higher 'conscientious consciousness', their world is a post-capitalist one, based on caring and sharing, reciprocity and solidarity. They are neither for sale nor corruptible. With their eyes fixed on the higher ends of authentic self-realisation with and for others, they are not afraid of downwards mobility. They are more interested in values than in prices and in goods than in commodities. As critics of government and market, as well as of authoritarian institutions like the Church, we may expect that they are not only trying to realise what they believe in and aim for in personal life, but also in the organisations where they work. As a working hypothesis that needs empirical verification, I assume that a good part of the so-called 'social entrepreneurs' who consider work as the surest means to realise their ideals and contribute to the common good, are metareflexive individuals. What moves them is not in the first place the accumulation of profit, but the idea of working together in a common project that benefits the community at large. Unlike corporate governance of private enterprises that benefits the shareholders who have invested their money in a capitalist venture, the cooperative management of social enterprises privileges the stakeholders who are giving themselves to the common project. With the focus steady on the integral vision of 'a good life, with and for others in just institutions, responsible organisations and a sustainable world society' (Kunneman, 2006: 334), the anti-systemic entrepreneurs of social enterprises and the social professionals in private–public organisations are at the forefront of the emergent morphogenetic society. Real social change will come when the ethics of professional communities will be joined to the politics of civil society. Working together in positive synergy, they are the forces that are driving societies worldwide in the direction of cooperative convivialism.

Intentional communities

In a famous passage of the *Critique of Pure Reason*, which significantly influenced Georg Simmel's sociology of the forms of association, Kant (1983: 242–248) speculates on how elements that are in contact and interaction with each other can mutually influence each other so as to constitute a real unity and form a community with a higher level of complexity. He notices, however, that in German the word of community (*Gemeinschaft*) has a double meaning and conveys two related notions which Latin carefully distinguishes: 'It can either mean *communio* or *commercium*' (A 213). Under the latter, Kant understands a dynamic connection between elements that mutually influence each other without, however, intentionally working together towards the realisation of what is common; when this dynamic connection between elements is the result of a conscious intention to work together, the objective community (*commercium*) in space becomes a subjective community (*communio*) that persists over time. What distinguishes the latter from the former is consciousness:

> In the mind, all phenomena, as contents of a possible experience, must exist in community (*communio*) of apperception or consciousness, and in so far as it is requisite that objects be represented as coexistent and connected, in

> so far must they reciprocally determine the position in time of each other and thereby constitute a whole.
>
> (A 214)

In other words, thanks to the intervention of a collective consciousness that operates the 'synthesis of apperception', the individuals enter into interaction with each other and coordinate their action so as to form of 'collective subject' – a 'We' whose members are intentionally united in and through a common project that they seek to realise *together*.

Of course, by the mere fact of being human and, thus, presumably, endowed with the capacity for reason and understanding, individuals are always already members of the largest imaginable community: humanity is an a-priori and unlimited community of communication that counterfactually includes each and every human being on earth. The community that is formed by mutual consciousness and puts individuals into interaction is, by definition, much smaller. Unlike humanity, which is based on 'presupposition', the community is formed by 'identification' (Tietz, 2002: 54). Through identification with a collective that transcends and encompasses them, the members of a community delimit those who belong to a particular social space and historical time. The extension of the community is variable, but with Kant we can assume that the community is always larger than the individual and smaller than humanity.

In accordance with the stress I have put on the causal power of culture and the normative aspects of collective consciousness, and also as a correction to Chapter 2, which is largely written in cognitivist key, I will assume that the members of a collective become a community thanks to the conscious adoption of principles, norms and values that give them their particular identity. It is because they identify with the normative principles that underlie a convivial society in which giving, sharing and caring is the norm that individuals form an 'intentional community'. I use the term 'intentional community' as a sociological alternative to 'collective intentionality', a term used by analytical philosophers like Searle, Tuomela and Bratman, who develop ontologies of the social from the bottom up. Typically, they start with a bunch of individuals and conceptually analyse, often with painstaking detail, how, by following conventional rules ('taking X for Y', in Searle's parlance), they are able to coordinate their plans of action and come to form a 'We'. From a sociological point of view, however, we have to assume that the individuals are always already socialised. They are not socialised because they follow rules, but they follow rules because they are socialised. In any case, one cannot explain the emergence of the social with reference to collective intentionality. The latter does not constitute the former, but presupposes it as a condition of its possibility.

The term intentional community does not only thoroughly socialise the intentional practices; by introducing a moral community of alternative values and goals that constitute the identity of the members who intentionally participate in it, it also politicises it. Indeed, in alternative circles of sociability, the term 'intentional communities' is used to refer to various types of residential communities (*Wohngemeinschaften*, *kibbutzim*, *ashrams*, ecovillages, transition towns, etc.) whose members adhere to a common *Weltanschauung*, share responsibilities and resources and consciously follow a post-capitalist lifestyle. Those alternative communities are usually small-scale. Constituted in direct opposition to the society that surrounds them, their members voluntarily withdraw from the latter and decide to live and work together on a collectively owned plot of land or house in accordance with the political, moral, ecological and spiritual values they believe in. The question now is whether we can extend the analysis of communes of individuals who engage in small-scale social experiments to situations in which the members are not co-present and do not directly interact with one another. Can we expand the notion of intentional community to virtual communities and conceive of utopian communities on a large scale? I think we can and to make my case I will follow the guidance of Michel Bauwens, the founder of the P2P Foundation, and explore how commons-based, computer-mediated, peer-to-peer communication, production and governance can help to bring them into existence.[78]

Peer-to-peer communication basically refers to radically decentralised, distributed modes of organising collectives on and off the internet in which loosely connected individuals voluntarily cooperate and collaborate ('share') in a common project that is neither market-based nor controlled by a hierarchy, but totally open and oriented towards the benefit of the community. The salient feature of peer-to-peer activities is that they are based on so-called 'Commons' which everyone can use and which no single person or organisation can appropriate or control. The origins of the politically conscious P2P community go back to the collaborative practices of open-source software developers, who built an alternative, non-proprietary, type of licence (the GNU General Public License) that authorises the free use of software code on the condition that users who copy, distribute and modify the code make the resultant software freely available to others.[79]

By now, however, P2P movements have left the narrow enclave of software developers. The struggle against the 'enclosure' of the commons by means of patents, intellectual property rights and similar exclusion mechanisms or, more positively formulated, the struggle for the free production, distribution and consumption of information, knowledge and culture has spawned a myriad of loosely interconnected, internetworked communities that have transformed the model of open distributed networks without obligatory hubs into a template for the collaborative construction of a non-hierarchical, non-proprietary, inclusive society that is based on peer-to-peer production, governance and property (Bauwens, 2005). While most of those creative initiatives still largely escape the radars of academia, I think they are quite significant. When the spirit of the counterculture and the new computer technologies meet, the old cooperatives are reinvented and rejuvenated. Thanks to the internet, thousands of local projects that are scattered across the globe are now interconnected and synchronised in real time. The creative non-market economy is no longer at the periphery; it has moved to the very core of the advanced information societies. Software, science, culture, film, music, news, etc. are now produced by decentralised networks that operate at the boundary of capitalism and communism. With P2P production also comes a new mode of democratic governance in which power is transparently distributed and exercised by the participants themselves. Premised on participation rather than representation, everyone can potentially cooperate in a collective project, propose new initiatives and, if necessary, bring them to public discussion and deliberation in the forum. All decisions that are collectively binding are, as a matter of principle, taken by consensus (though, in practice, one may also encounter 'benevolent dictators' who govern the digital commons). If no consensus can be reached, the project can 'fork' and a new collective can be formed to pursue a new project. Collaborative internetworked initiatives (like Wikipedia) have proven to be more efficient than market-based giants (like Encyclopaedia Britannica); car manufacturing has reached the stage where global open-source design can effectively be joined to local production (like in Wikispeed); a new digital currency (Bitcoin) that is managed by a global network without central authority enables instant payments to anyone anywhere in the world. These are just some indications that a new mode of production and governance has emerged in the middle of the most developed economies of the world. The cooperative modes of production and governance are more productive than their capitalist and governmental counterparts, because they are driven by intrinsic motivations (passion and ideals) and not by external ones (interest and power).

Let me illustrate just two initiatives I have recently encountered in the form of vignettes. The first is a global platform that is well-known by young people. It is called 'Couchsurfing'[80] and puts travellers in contact with potential hosts all over the world. By means of a simple interface, it allows locals to put the cosmopolitan principle of hospitality into practice. Whoever has a couch, a spare mattress or an extra room and is willing to offer free accommodation to travellers can sign up. I have done so in Rio de Janeiro. I have not only met wonderful people from various walks of life and made new friends in the process, but I have also gained the conviction that new technologies give us now the possibility to create with a few clicks new communities of principles and values. The idea is far from new, but now we have the technology to implement it. As a visitor phrased it: 'We are hippies with technology.' The system works and is largely self-correcting. Participants who have not properly understood the spirit of the thing – the 'spirit of the gift', as Mauss would say – and are just looking for a free ride or a free lunch will either be converted to the norm of reciprocity or they will receive negative evaluations on the webpage of the community. Meanwhile, 'Be welcome',[81] a new platform that is run according to the protocols of the peer-to-peer community, has emerged as an alternative to 'Couchsurfing' (which is, by the way, registered and certified as a legitimate 'B corporation' that works not for profit, but for the benefit of the community). The idea of bringing people together to share experiences via hosting is similar, but the architecture of the site is set up in such a way that everybody can contribute in an open and transparent fashion to the design of the community.

My second vignette is a local one and refers to a local coffee bar in the centre of Rio de Janeiro. It's called 'Curto Cafe' (and has a page on Facebook).[82] It was created by a couple of young idealists–activists–entrepreneurs who wanted to produce and distribute the best coffee in the world based on peer-to-peer principles. They have reconstructed the whole 'commodity chain' that links producers and consumers according to the collaborative principles of open production. Cutting out the middle man and pooling their resources via 'crowd funding', they have, in effect, almost completely decommodified the business. In order to socialise their knowledge, they have also set up a webpage where one can follow the coffee through the whole chain in real time. The first time I met them, they surprised me with their ingenuity. 'Give a hug and get a coffee for free.' When I asked Vinicius, a self-described 'netweaver', how they survived and how many people lived from the enterprise, he smiled and explained to me that I asked the wrong question and that money was the last of their interests. When I later met the founders of the collective, they told me that they dealt in coffee because the product was so simple that it allowed them to test *in vivo* a new way of connecting people and doing business while controlling all the variables. There are many more examples like these. Singly, they may not add up to much. Taken together, the many projects that are seeing the day point to the emergence of a more convivial society, within the womb of the old one, that runs on post-capitalist principles. For the time being, the Commoners have to be pragmatic. To survive in a capitalist environment and make a living, they move in and out of the formal economy, working part-time for profit while dreaming of a new arrangement in which everybody would get a basic income and, thus, be able to contribute full-time to the realisation of their principles, values and ideals.

P2P communities are ideologically neutral and motivationally agnostic. What matters to them are the practices that weave the expanding network of cooperation into a whole, not the political theories behind them. While most are inspired by social, ecological and spiritual worldviews that underscore the importance of sharing and giving and most would probably also subscribe to progressive social and political agendas that are historically associated with the Left, there's also a rather vocal faction of anarcho-capitalists and libertarians who consider the distributed networks, first and foremost, as an extension of the market and an alternative to the state. Moreover, it should also be conceded that people who decide to join the 'Commons' in order to contribute to a well-defined collective project do not necessarily do so because they are moved and motivated by the Spirit of the gift. They can join them out of enlightened interest. They are even allowed to use the Commons without ever contributing to it.

If I have, however, insisted on the transformative potential of internetworked collectives, it is because I am convinced that metareflexive individuals who are, as Harry Kunneman says, trying to live 'the good life with and for others in responsible organisation and a sustainable environment' are also at the forefront of the new political, moral and spiritual economy of the information society. If I have adduced computer-mediated, commons-based, P2P networks to expand the reach of intentional communities beyond local boundaries, it is because I think that the revolution today is happening on the internet. Not so much because computers are transforming society and culture as we know it, but because the little screens of our computers are windows through which we can see the joyous proliferation of a myriad of loosely interconnected subterranean communities that are working together to bring a new convivial and post-capitalist society into existence. Those intentional communities are the harbingers of a new civilisation. We are on the threshold of a new phase transition, comparable perhaps to the one that led from feudalism to capitalism. Whether they will prevail remains to be seen. Now, as before, there are no metaphysical guarantees. But under the old world, there's another world that is not only possible, but actual and real.

Notes

1 An outline of this proposal was first presented at the 'Bhaskar Seminar' at the University College of London in February 2011. I thank Roy for his suggestion to work out my talk as a general introduction to the book, as well as for his hospitality and generosity. He may not agree with all the details, but I trust we are one when it comes to the greater picture of the universe. I am also grateful to Alain Caillé, Harry Kunneman, Michel Bauwens and Margaret Archer for inspiring and uplifting walks on the bridges of Rome, the polders of Culemborg, the beaches of Rio de Janeiro and in the French Alps. They will find echoes of our ongoing conversations in the text. I have presented a first version of this introduction in the 'Colaboratorio' at IESP-UERJ. Thanks to Gabriel Peters, Glauber Lemos, Diogo Corrêa and Priscila Coutinho for critical interjections and suggestions, though there could have been more of it.

2 On the shelves of fashionable bookshops (like the one at Tate Modern), one finds under the category of Critical Theory books by Adorno, Agamben, Badiou, Baudrillard, Castoriadis, Debord, Deleuze, Derrida, Elias, Foucault, Geertz, Habermas, Jameson, Kristeva, Lacan, Lefebvre, etc.

3 In his dialectical introduction to the positivist debate, Adorno (1969: 33) uses the same image: 'Thought that comes to terms with the non-thought that belongs to its own meaning, explodes the logic of non-contradiction. The prison has windows.' But as a crypto-Platonist, Adorno looks at the prison from the point of view of paradise and describes it as hell, whereas my window aims to let some fresh air into the prison house of critical theory.

4 Popper may well be the most overvalued philosopher of the twentieth century. His neo-positivism did a lot of damage in the natural sciences. As he had to admit that the 'covering law-model' does not really apply to the social sciences, he developed an alternative model of explanation for the human sciences, and introduced the situational logics of rational choice as second best in the human sciences. Positivism plus rational choice – one could hardly do worse! For a more sustained critique of Popperianism, see Vandenberghe (2010); for a realist critique of rational choice, see Archer and Tritter (2000).

5 Let's quote a representative statement:

> It has thus become increasingly apparent that physical 'reality', no less than social 'reality', is at bottom a social and linguistic construct; that scientific 'knowledge', far from being objective, reflects and encodes the dominant ideologies and power relations of the culture that produced it; that the truth claims of science are inherently theory-laden and self-referential; and consequently that the discourse of scientific community, for all its undeniable value, cannot assert a privileged epistemological status with respect to counter-hegemonic narratives, emanating from dissident and marginalised communities.
>
> (Sokal, 1996: 217)

This statement on 'transformative hermeneutics' is certainly representative of mainstream postmodernism, but as it was written by an insincere self-proclaimed realist and only meant to expose the field of STS as institutionalised fraud, it triggered the 'science wars'.

6 Interestingly, in his reflections on the object of the history of science, Canguilhem makes a similar distinction between the natural or intransitive object and the scientific or transitive object:

> The history of the sciences is the history of an object that is, that has a history, whereas science is science of an object that is not and has no history.... This natural object, outside of every discourse with regard to it, is, of course, not the scientific object.
>
> (Canguilhem, 1989: 16)

While historical epistemology has distinguished the two dimensions of knowledge, it lacks, however, the transcendental philosophy that integrates the sciences and the history of sciences into a unified framework.

7 In his scathing, book-length critique of Rorty, which I strongly recommend to any genuine pragmatist, Bhaskar (1991) argues that the American ironist has combined the error of positivism and postmodernism in a single philosophy. As he remains wedded to a positivist account of natural sciences, he has only added a Nietzschean army of metaphors to a Humean–Hempelian ontological base. By reducing the world to a language game (in fact, a game of language), he has replicated the Kantian resolution of the third antinomy: we are rigorously determined as material bodies, but as edifying philosophers we are free subjects who can redescribe the world at will.

8 See also the important and useful *Dictionary of Critical Realism*, edited and largely written by Mervyn Hartwig (2007).

9 There is a distinction between philosophical ontology and specific scientific ontologies ('ontics'). The transcendental argument only says that given that science occurs, the world must be structured in a certain way. The philosopher only affirms *that* certain entities exist in the world and that they do so independently of science, even if they can only be known through science; she does not say *what* these entities are, but wisely leaves the domain of ontics to the scientist. Quarks, superstrings and charms are not her business.

10 Karl-Otto Apel (1979) also used von Wright's interventionist theory of causality as a launching path of a sustained immanent critique of the determinism of the nomologico-deductive model. Updating Apel's remarkable philosophical reconstruction, critical realism can be considered as the fifth and final phase of the protracted *Erklären-Verstehen* controversy.

11 For an erudite exploration of the metaphor of the mystical veil that covers nature, from Heraclites to Heidegger, see Hadot (2004).

12 Note that the observer is not an individual, but a social network of communications. The most concise presentation of Luhmann's sociological take on second-order cybernetics is to be found in chapter 2 of his book on the scientific system (Luhmann, 1990: 68–102). For a brilliant reflexive analysis of 'observing systems', see Fuchs (2001: chs 1 ('Theory after essentialism') and 7 ('Realism explained')).

13 The phrase 'decorative philosophy' is adapted from Rojek and Turner's (2000) incisive critique of 'decorative sociology', by which they mean to refer to 'a branch of modernist aesthetics which is devoted to a politicised, textual reading of society and culture'.

14 Gramsci was, of course, the central reference of Stuart Hall, as well as of Ernesto Laclau and Chantale Mouffe. While Hall is the founding figure of British Cultural Studies (which morphed into postmodernism when it arrived in the United States), *Hegemony and Socialist Strategy*, which formalises the logic of inclusion/exclusion, is considered a classic of poststructuralism. Whatever remains of the original Cultural

Studies has now fused with Governmentality Studies. Indian Subaltern Studies also took its cues from Gramsci, but when it started to mingle with the postcolonialism of Said and arrived in New York City, it took a decisive postmodern turn.

15 In case one really wants to reconnect 'French theory' to the Frankfurt School, one might as well consider Bourdieu as the legitimate, though unrecognised heir of Adorno.

16 In the following, I focus mainly on studies in SSK (Sociology of Scientific Knowledge) and STS (Science and Technology Studies), leaving aside HPS (History and Philosophy of Science) and HST (History of Science and Technology). The best overview of the early science studies, from Merton to Latour, is given by Michael Lynch (1993). Since the 1990s, SSK has lost its bite and settled in the wealthy suburbs of research.

17 'Death and Furniture' (Edwards *et al.* 1995) is, perhaps, the most brilliant and hilarious example of the length to which radical constructivists are willing to go in their critique of realism and their defence of relativism. To refute bottom-line arguments against relativism that place limits on what may be treated as socially constructed, the authors analyse and deconstruct 'Furniture' ('Bang! Bang on the table!' and other invocations of furniture that seek to prove a reality that cannot be denied) and 'Death' (the Holocaust, misery, poverty and other horrors that should not be denied) as two conventional rhetorical tropes in epistemology and politics. While the invocation of 'Furniture' obliterates the work of representation, the mention of 'Death' silences discussion.

18 Disclosure: I was involved in a debate with Latour (*Revue du MAUSS*, 2001, no. 17) and have published a book in French that mentions his name in the subtitle. For a representative and didactic introduction to his work, I recommend *Cogitamus* by Latour (2010) himself.

19 Interestingly, Manuel de Landa (2002), who has worked out Deleuze's rhizomatics into assemblage theory, is sympathetic to critical realism. He approvingly quotes Bhaskar and Archer and integrates some of their ideas (mind-independent existence of reality) and concepts (emergence, morphogenesis) into his Lego-block philosophy of people, communities and organisations. Explicitly, he proposes his complexity theory of the becoming of entities at all scales as an ontology for use by the social sciences.

20 Meanwhile, Sloterdijk (1998–2004) has worked out his mediological/spherological reflections on 'Being and Space' into a philosophical soap opera in three massive volumes with hundreds of intriguing pictures. The first volume of the trilogy deals with 'Bubbles', the second with 'Globes' and the third with 'Foam'. For a powerful critique, see Suárez Müller (2007).

21 The notion of 'double hermeneutics' was coined by Giddens (1982: 1–17) to thematise the two-way circulation of concepts between the ordinary language of lay-actors and the specialised dialects of professional scientists. As a matter of fact, I think it is a quadruple hermeneutics: the common sense interpretations of the analyst are not only parasitic on the common sense interpretations of the actors (double hermeneutics); but as the latter are embedded in symbolic interpretations that are part of culture – one interprets what is already interpreted and understands what is already understood – and the former are formulated with reference to the corpus status of the discipline, our interpretations are of the fourth order (*pace* Schütz not of the second order).

22 Sawyer's (2005) account of emergence in sociology, psychology and economics is, by far, the most sophisticated and comprehensive account available. The book establishes a dialogue between critical realism and third-wave cybernetics, and also discusses cognitive and computational sciences.

23 On critical hermeneutics, see Thompson (1981), Kögler (1992) and Hoy and McCarthy (1994).

24 In his outline of a theory of practice, Bourdieu (1972) was working towards a similar synthesis of Lévi-Strauss and Wittgenstein. Both Bourdieu and Giddens were looking

for a dialectical synthesis of agency and structure, but whereas the former proposes a neo-objectivist theory that always privileges the field and the habitus over practices, the latter puts forward a neo-subjectivist theory that does not foreground reproduction, but the agent's capacity to act otherwise.

25 The idea of structure as medium and mediator was adumbrated by Lévi-Strauss (1962: 173): 'Between praxis and practices, a mediator always intervenes. Thanks to the operation of a conceptual scheme, a material and a form, both of which are deprived of independent existence, come into being as structures, that is to say as beings that are at once empirical and intelligible.'

26 The diachronical reading of structuration theory I present is largely indebted to the unfinished oeuvre of the late Michel Freitag (1986). His systematic theory of the modes of regulation of practices and of the reproduction of society can easily compare with Giddens' structuration and incorporate it; like Bhaskar's theory, which he knew and appreciated, his is realist, dialectical and critical. For a systematic reconstruction and critical discussion of Freitag's dialectical sociology, see Vandenberghe (2001).

27 The whole division of Western Marxism between a 'scientific' and a 'humanist' strand predates Althusser's attempt to introduce an 'epistemological rupture' between the young philosopher of the *Parisian Manuscripts* and the economist Marx would become after 1845. I think it can be reconducted to Gramsci and Lukács, with an ironic twist, however: the Gramscian wing (to which Althusser belongs) has meanwhile converged with poststructuralism and deconstruction, while the humanist wing (to which the Frankfurt School belongs) has found its champion in Habermas' defence of rationalism. The posthumous publication of Althusser's texts of the 1980s, like the one he wrote on the 'subterranean currents of the materialism of the encounter' (Althusser, 1994), offer a testimony of the epochal transition from structural Marxism to a post-structuralist position that is more indebted to Spinoza, Nietzsche and Artaud than Marx, Engels and Lenin. Although poststructuralism and critical theory are now in dialogue – usually with Adorno's philosophy of non-identity as bridgehead – it may be of interest to note that in my studies of the Frankfurt School, from Lukács to Habermas, I have hardly encountered any reference to Gramsci.

28 The question of whether the concept of emergence only applies to material structures is a difficult one. While Archer (1988, 1995) explicitly mentions structural and cultural emergent powers, Sawyer (2005: 29, 59, 62) seems to limit it to material structures. On this point I will follow Archer's morphogenetic approach. Given that she succeeded in convincing Bhaskar that the main difference between TMSA and structuration theory consists of the acknowledgement of emergentism and dualism, I will assume that critical realism defends emergence both for social and culture structures.

29 Bhaskar's invocation of 'real interests' is rather problematic. Not only because it presupposes that the theorist knows better than the agents themselves what interests are true or false, but also because of the utilitarian baggage that comes with any theory of rational choice.

30 Bhaskar's critique of monovalence offers a new take on the critique of identity thinking that has become part and parcel of contemporary critiques of Hegel (Adorno), Marx (Castoriadis) and Husserl (Levinas), not to mention postmodernism (Lyotard), poststructuralism (Laclau) and deconstruction (Derrida).

31 For a more comprehensive and sympathetic reading of *Dialectic*, see Norrie (2010), Hartwig (2007) and articles in the *Journal of Critical Realism* that discuss some of the intricacies of TCR. Personally, I found the clearest exposition of second-wave realism in Hartwig's interviews with Bhaskar (2010: 117–144).

32 In a philosophy of internal relations, all parts are interrelated and each of them can only be defined with reference to the other parts that make up the totality. This is not just dialectics. In the next chapter we will see that the American pragmatists espoused similar ideas: the self is in nature, the other and society; nature, society and the other are in the self, etc.

33 Although it is not entirely clear to me whether the philosophy of meta-Reality actually complements or substitutes for critical realism, it is evident that if one follows all the waves one ends up slightly puzzled. What should we do with the intransitive? Should we bring the intransitive into the transitive (first wave), the transitive into the intransitive (second wave) or transcend the distinction altogether (third wave)? Please observe that I do not deconstruct the ontological difference. My argument is that Bhaskar does. As critical realism moves from the natural to the social to the spiritual, it progressively relaxes and, eventually, jettisons the distinction.

34 Mervyn Hartwig (2001), a hard-line second waver, has pointed out inconsistencies between critical realism and the philosophy of meta-Reality. By moving beyond himself, Bhaskar has allegedly fallen back into absolute idealism ('the possibility of idealism'), committed the epistemic fallacy ('confusing the logical possibility in the transitive with real possibility in the intransitive dimension'), abandoned TMSA (defending creation *ex nihilo*, allowing for 'disemergence') and betrayed the Glorious Proletariat (as if one could change the world by changing oneself, a typical petty bourgeois thought, if we may believe Hartwig).

35 The qualifier 'generically speaking' is more than a concession to political correctness. It is an invocation of, and subscription to, the normative philosophical anthropology of the young Hegelians, including most emphatically Marx's analysis of the essential qualities and capabilities of the *Gattungswesen* in the *Parisian Manuscripts* of 1844.

36 The distinction between internal regulation by meanings, norms and values and external control by force is often used, but rarely explicitly theorised by Weber (see, however, Weber, 1971: 681–682). I will clarify it later in the text.

37 Alain Caillé, a social and political theorist, is the main figure and driving force of the MAUSS, an acronym of *Mouvement Anti-Utilitariste dans les Sciences Sociales*, and its organ, the *Revue du MAUSS*. His most recent and most brilliant reformulation of the essay of the gift is to be found in Caillé (2009).

38 For an exercise in such a profane translation, I refer the reader to my attempt to systematically reformulate the theology of donation as an anthropology of the gift (Vandenberghe, 2008a).

39 *Von den bloßen Worten … zu den Sachen selbst! From mere words … to the things themselves!* The slogan may be Husserl's (1993, II/1: 7), but as he never got to the concrete and remained stuck till the very end in the solipsism of his transcendental meditations, the reference is to Heidegger's (1993: 27ff.) realist-hermeneutic re-appropriation of his mentor's catchphrase.

40 Heidegger has written on *aletheia* at different stages of his career. He mentions it already in the famous paragraph 44 that closes off the first part of *Sein und Zeit* and works it out in 'Aletheia' (Heidegger, 1954: 263–288), a rather difficult text on an obscure fragment by Heraclitus. I prefer by far his amazing essay on the origin of the work of art (Heidegger, 1994: 1–74). Bhaskar for his part has introduced *aletheia* in dialectical critical realism to refer to the real reasons, grounds or causes of things (intransitive dimension), as different and perhaps even opposed to the truth of propositions (transitive dimension), possible by virtue of the ontological stratification of the world and attainable by virtue of the dynamic character of science (Bhaskar, 1993: 394; 1994: 241; see also Groff, 2000).

41 Questioning the very notion of society as a functional interconnection of socialised individuals into a normative social order, François Dubet (2009: 7–47) does not hesitate to qualify sociology as a liberal-communitarian social philosophy, not to say a theology of society. With the invention of society, sociologists do not only become the founders of a discipline, but also the priests of a society in which they believe and want to bring into existence.

42 In his normative reconstruction of a theory of justice that takes the form of a theory of society, Axel Honneth (2011) follows the deployment of the idea of freedom in

modern philosophy (from negative freedom of Hobbes and Locke via the reflexive freedom of Kant, Rawls and Habermas to the social freedom of Hegel and Marx). What he says about critical theory also holds for sociology: 'No social ethics, no critique of society can nowadays transcend the intellectual horizon that came into existence two hundred years ago by coupling a representation of justice to the idea of autonomy' (Honneth, 2011: 37).

43 The socio-historical analysis of the semantics of Old Europe is part and parcel of Luhmann's comprehensive system theory. The four volumes of his *Gesellschaftsstruktur und Semantik*, subtitled *Studies in the Sociology of Knowledge of Modern Societies* (Luhmann, 1993–1999), are the sociological pendant of Koselleck's conceptual history (*Begriffsgeschichte*). For an impressive analysis of the historical development of the main concepts of the social sciences, see Luhmann (1993–1999, II: 195–268 (social order); III: 149–259 (individual); IV: 9–30 (nature), 31–54 (culture)).

44 In his critique of allochronic discourse in anthropology, Johannes Fabian (2002: 31) defines the 'denial of coevalness' as 'a persistent and systematic tendency to place the referent(s) of anthropology in a Time other than the present of the producer of anthropological discourse'.

45 The introduction of the distinction between the external/etic and internal/emic perspectives is meant as a correction of the metatheoretical space I presented and used in *A Philosophical History of German Sociology* to reconstruct critical theory, from Marx to Habermas.

46 The bizarre, but splendorous category of 'post-Hegelian neo-Kantianism' is Ricoeur's (1986: 279).

47 As a methodological corollary to the metatheoretical discussion, I would argue that social scientific categories are not analytic but synthetic ones. With Hegel, Dilthey and Peirce, one should systematically tie concept formation in the social sciences to symbolic representations of reality and common sense constructions, conceiving of the former as systematisations of the latter. This position goes not only against Weber's nominalist conception of ideal types as analytic constructions that the scientist arbitrarily imposes on reality, but also against Durkheim's rationalist justification of an epistemological rupture with pre-notions of common sense. With his Hegelian insistence on the socio-logics of the concept, Marx corrects both Durkheim's scientism and Weber's relativism through immanent critique.

48 For an interesting philosophical debate between Judith Butler, Seyla Benhabib, Drucilla Cornell and Nancy Fraser on the place of subjectivity in feminism and critical theory, see Benhabib *et al.* (1995). See also Stuart Hall's (2000) fascinating but frustrated attempt to find the subject that identifies *in persona* with the identifications that culture provides.

49 §1 'Sociology … is the science which attempts the interpretative understanding of social action in order thereby to arrive at a causal explanation of its course and effects' (Weber, 1972: 1).

50 The idea of the 'integral field' comes from the holistic philosopher Ken Wilber (see Wilber (1997) for a synopsis of his integral philosophy, and Carlson (2008) for a welcome critique of the religious, neo-liberal and neo-conservative elements that have recently infiltrated his writings). According to Wilber, everything that exists is a *holon*, a whole that is simultaneously part of some other whole. Each *holon* inherently has an interior and an exterior and may also be considered as a particular or as a collective. Defending a synthetic or integral perspective on human existence and evolution – the so-called AQAL ('All-Quadrant, All-Level') Approach – Wilber crosscuts the internal/external and individual/collective dimensions of analysis and suggests that any non-reductionistic analysis has to 'simultrack' four perspectives valid for any *holon* (psychoanalysis, hermeneutics, Marxism and behaviourism) with four corresponding validity claims (subjective truthfulness, cultural justness, functional fit and objective truth).

51 Philosophical translation 'linguistifies' sacred content into a secular language that can be understood and, thus, also criticised by those who do not belong to any religious community. The philosophical task of linguistification is 'to discover in religious traditions the unsettled semantic potentials and to translate them by its own conceptual means in a general language that is accessible beyond determinate religious communities – and, thus, to open the discursive game to public reason' (Habermas, 2012b: 17).

52 The draft of the manifesto was preceded by a series of dialogues on the convivial society (Caillé, 2011a) between Alain Caillé, Serge Latouche (a radical theorist of post-development), Patrick Viveret (the main figure behind alternative indicators of wealth) and announced the publication of the real convivialist manifesto (Caillé *et al.*, 2013), signed by Edgar Morin, Jean Pierre Dupuy, Yann Moulier-Boutang and myself, among others.

53 Ricoeur's original formulation of the 'visée de la vie bonne avec et pour les autres dans des institutions justes' did not contain the reference to a sustainable environment.

54 In the same way as utilitarian theories of action privilege the calculus of interest and the material environment, neglecting the noetic synergy between intentional acts of consciousness and culture, they conceive of the human being as a psycho-somatic assemblage of body (soma) and mind (psyché), discarding the connection between the spirit (pneuma) and the soul (animus).

55 See, however, the first of the three volumes edited by Craig Calhoun and Georgi Derluguian (2011) for a coordinated attempt by social scientists on the Left to make sense of the present. The chapters by Arrighi, Harvey, Fraser and Castells are particularly illuminating.

56 The only spat in the discipline concerned the question of 'methodological nationalism' (Chernillo, 2007). Forty years after the concept was coined by Herminio Martins, it is coming back with a vengeance, not to question a discipline that stands and falls with the nation-state, but to rebut the unfinished project of a 'post-national' European community of citizens.

57 I owe the term to my friend and mentor Harry Kunneman. Together, we are writing a text on the issue.

58 Like Habermas' work, the following analysis of the crisis is centred on Europe and the United States. In Brazil, the economy is doing relatively well, with previously unseen levels of employment and steady growth, artificially spiked by the World Cup of 2014 and the Olympic Games of 2016.

59 For a brilliant attempt to theorise the 'second great transition' that is inspired by Polanyi and Habermas, see Fraser (2011).

60 A video of her intervention, amplified by the 'human micro', at Washington Square in New York is posted on YouTube (www.youtube.com/watch?v=rYfLZsb9by4).

61 For the idea of a conditionally unconditional forgiving of debt, see the site of Jubilee Economics (http://jubilee-economics.org).

62 The medicalisation of large swaths of the population is ensconced in the *Diagnostic and Statistical Manual of Mental Disorders* (DSM), published by the American Psychiatric Association (DSM V is due in 2013). By means of a systematic disaggregation of mental disorders into a myriad of pathological symptoms and syndromes, the DSM transforms the subject who needs therapy into a 'case' that needs treatment. In the same way as psychiatry no longer treats the patient, but his or her symptoms, the DSM does not so much classify the pathologies as the drugs that can be used to combat them.

63 See Martuccelli and de Singly (2009) for an overview and Corcuff *et al.* (2010) for a representative sample of the French sociology of individualism.

64 The work of Alain Touraine is symptomatic of this societal change. From the working-class movement of the 1950–1960s to the new social movements of the 1970–1980s as instanciations of the 'historical Subject' with a mission to change and

redirect society through conflict and struggle. And then, from there, to the 'end of Society' and the emergence of personal Subjects who struggle with themselves to change themselves and to become subjects of their own existence.

65 When I invoke existentialism, I mean to refer to the German branch. Unlike French existentialism (Sartre, Camus), which is rather heroic in its lonely struggle with nihilism (Sisyphus), German existentialism (especially Karl Jaspers) offers a humanist, personalist and developmental approach to human existence. It is through 'loving conflict' with the other that the subject advances from the experience of 'limit situations' (death, illness and suffering) to authentic existence with and for the other.

66 To the *homo clausus*, Norbert Elias (1987) opposes the *homines aperti* of the past who are overflowing with affect and have not interiorised the *Selbstzwang* (self-discipline) that comes with the intensification of interhuman relations that defines modern figurations. If his evolutionism had not blinded him to cultural variations of humanity, he might have conceived of the *Homo cordialis* (aka *Homo brasilis)*, as immortalised by Sérgio Buarque de Holanda (2000: 1044–1055), not as a remnant of the past, but as a contemporary of the independent, unencumbered and lonely atom of the European Enlightenment.

67 Jeffrey Alexander does not directly refer to Hegel's 'posthistoire', but his ideas concerning the civil sphere are quite similar to Honneth's. For a review of *The Civil Sphere*, see Vandenberghe (2008b). If Honneth and Alexander present a positive version of the 'interpenetration' of the normative and the social system, Michel Freitag's (2012) rant on the desymbolisation, despiritualisation and decivilisation of postmodern societies represents a hypercritical counterproject to the Parsonian versions on both sides the Atlantic.

68 For a classic account of transcendent and immanent critiques, from Marx to Habermas, that avoids caricature of the transcendent version that has become the stock-in-trade of contemporary social philosophy, see Benhabib (1986).

69 Honneth's (2005) essay on reification prefigured the 'defunctionalisation' of critical theory. Revisiting the old idea of *Verdinglichung* in the new paradigm of intersubjective recognition, Honneth threw Lukács' interpretation of Marx's chapter on the fetishism of commodities overboard (which was overdue anyway), but, unfortunately, with the bathwater of subject philosophy, he also threw away the possibility of a structural, functionalist and systemic critique of capitalism.

70 I owe this striking metaphor of systemic suicide to Diogo Corrêia.

71 As if he wanted to compensate his neglect of the struggles for recognition in his reconstructive genealogy of liberty, Honneth (2013) has recently presented a conflict-interpretation of Parsons' 'conspiracy theory'. Instead of an overlapping consensus on values, he notes a hardening of societies and a return to anomic conflicts about interests.

72 For a powerful critique of the pacific assumptions of the psychology of attachment that belie Honneth's analysis of intimate relations, see Butler (2008). Butler's psychoanalytic critique is indebted to Kojève's terribly influential rendering of the famous passage on the violent struggle for recognition between the master and the slave. In passing, I note that Honneth has never given any due attention to that passage from the *Phenomenology of the Spirit*. The close commentary on the *Phenomenology* he has recently proposed breaks off just before the passage! Cf. Honneth (2010: 15–32).

73 Parsons' 'applied theoretical research' on the professions will find its culmination in chapter 10 of *The Social System* (on the role of medical doctors). Other important texts on the norms and values of the professions can be found in Parsons (1954: 34–50, 50–69, 143–176, 370–386; 1970: 292–324, 325–385.

74 Or, in Alain Caillé's memorable phrasing: 'All things considered, in the long run, the best strategy is to give' (personal communication, 1994). For a confirmation and debunking of the 'interest of disinterest', see Bourdieu's (1994: 175–217) chapter on the 'economics of the offertory'.

75 In his pioneering studies on the reward system of science, Merton (1973: part 4) corrects his analysis of the academic ethos with a more realist portrayal of the *Homo academicus* and his never-ending struggles for recognition. His amazing article on 'the ambivalence of scientists' (Merton, 1973: 383–412), which closes off a sequence of investigations on disputes over priority of scientific discovery, does not only indicate that vanity and egotism are occupational hazards within science; it has smoothing and therapeutic virtues too.

76 With many thanks to professor Haack not just for writing the text, but also for discussing it with me and my students during her first visit to Rio de Janeiro. The text is now also available online (see papers.ssm.com/sol13/papers.cfm?abstract_id=2135732).

77 The research project on normative professionalisation is directed by Harry Kunneman, to whom I owe much more than is acknowledged in the text. For further information about the University for Humanistics, see www.uvh.nl.

78 The Foundation for Peer to Peer Alternatives (www.p2pfoundation.net) is a global think-tank that studies, documents and promotes Commons-based, participatory peer-to-peer practices on the internet and in the real world. On its Wiki, the reader will find a complete encyclopaedia with almost 20,000 texts on collaborative production, open governance and common property; its daily updated blog is also well worth following. For a primer on some of the main concepts of P2P Theory, see http://p2pfoundation.net/Category:P2P_Theory. For a thorough introduction to the new political and moral economy of the information age, see also Benkler (2006).

79 For the history of both the General Public Licence, developed by Richard Stallman and amended by Linus Torvald, and the Creative Commons licences, developed by Lawrence Lessig, which authorises the sharing of creative works that copyright law does not allow, see Bollier (2009).

80 See www.couchsurfing.com.

81 See www.bewelcome.com.

82 See https://www.facebook.com/curtocafe.

Bibliography

Adorno, T.W. 1969. 'Einleitung', pp. 7–79 in Adorno, T.W. *et al.*: *Der Postivismusstreit in der deutschen Soziologie*. Darmstadt: Luchterhand.

Adorno, T.W. *et al.* 1969. *Der Positivismusstreit in der deutschen Soziologie*. Neuwied: Luchterhand.

Alexander, J.C. 1982–1983. *Theoretical Logic in Sociology*, 4 vols. Berkeley, CA: University of California Press.

Alexander, J.C. 1988. 'The new theoretical movement', pp. 77–101 in Smelser, N. (ed.), *Handbook of Sociology*. London: Sage.

Alexander, J.C. 2006. *The Civil Sphere*. Oxford: Oxford University Press.

Althusser, L. 1965. *Pour Marx*. Paris: Maspero.

Althusser, L. 1994. 'Le courant souterrain du matérialisme de la rencontre', pp. 539–579 in *Écrits philosophiques et politiques*, vol. 1. Paris: Stock/Imec.

Apel, K.O. 1979. *Die Erklären-Verstehen Kontroverse in transzendental-pragmatischer Sicht*. Frankfurt am Main: Suhrkamp.

Apel, K.O. 1981. *Transformation der Philosophie*, 2 Bde. Frankfurt am Main: Suhrkamp.

Archer, M. 1988. *Culture and Agency; The Place of Culture in Social Theory*. Cambridge: Cambridge University Press.

Archer, M. 1995. *Realist Social Theory: The Morphogenetic Approach*. Cambridge: Cambridge University Press.

Archer, M. 2003. *Structure, Agency and the Internal Conversation.* Cambridge: Cambridge University Press.

Archer, M. and Tritter, J. 2000. *Rational Choice Theory: Resisting Colonization.* London: Routledge.

Arnsperger, C. 2005. *Critique de l'existence capitaliste: Pour une éthique existentielle de l'économie.* Paris: Cerf.

Arnsperger, C. 2009. *Éthique de l'existence post-capitaliste: Pour un militantisme existentiel.* Paris: Cerf.

Bauwens, M. 2005. 'The political economy of peer production', *1000 Days of Theory* (retrieved on 12 December 2012 from www.ctheory.net/articles.aspx?id=499).

Benhabib, S. 1986. *Critique, Norm and Utopia: A Study of the Foundations of Critical Theory.* New York: Columbia University Press.

Benhabib, S. *et al.* 1995. *Feminist Contentions: A Philosophical Exchange.* London: Routledge.

Benkler, Y. 2006. *The Wealth of Networks. How Social Production Transforms Markets and Freedom.* New Haven, CT: Yale University Press.

Benton, T. 1977. *Philosophical Foundations of the Three Sociologies.* London: Routledge.

Bernstein, R. 1971. *Praxis and Action.* Philadelphia, PA: University of Pennsylvania Press.

Bhaskar, R. 1975. *A Realist Theory of Science.* Second edition 1979, Brighton: Harvester.

Bhaskar, R. 1979. *The Possibility of Naturalism.* Second edition 1989, Brighton: Harvester.

Bhaskar, R. 1982. 'Emergence, explanation, emancipation', in Secord, P. (ed.), *Explaining Human Behaviour: Consciousness, Human Action and Social Structure.* London: Sage.

Bhaskar, R. 1986. *Scientific Realism and Human Emancipation.* London: Verso.

Bhaskar, R. 1989. *Reclaiming Reality: A Critical Introduction to Contemporary Philosophy.* London: Verso.

Bhaskar, R. 1991. *Philosophy and the Idea of Freedom.* Oxford: Blackwell.

Bhaskar, R. 1993. *Dialectics: The Pulse of Freedom.* London: Verso.

Bhaskar, R. 1994. *Plato etc.: The Problems of Philosophy and their Resolution.* London: Verso.

Bhaskar, R. 2000. *From East to West: Odyssey of a Soul.* London: Routledge.

Bhaskar, R. 2002a. *Reflections on meta-Reality: Transcendence, Emancipation and Everyday Life.* New Delhi: Sage.

Bhaskar, R. 2002b. *From Science to Emancipation: Alienation and the Actuality of Enlightenment.* New Delhi: Sage.

Bhaskar, R. 2002c. *The Philosophy of meta-Reality. Vol. 1: meta-Reality: Creativity, Love and Freedom.* New Delhi: Sage.

Bhaskar, R. and Hartwig, M. 2010. *The Formation of Critical Realism: A Personal Perspective.* London: Routledge.

Bhaskar, R. and Hartwig, M. 2012. 'Beyond east and west', pp. 186–202 in Hartwig, M. and Morgan, J. (eds), *Critical Realism and Spirituality.* London: Routledge.

Bloor, D. 1976. *Knowledge and Social Imagery.* London: Routledge.

Bohm, D. 1980. *Wholeness and the Implicate Order.* London: Routledge.

Bollier, D. 2009. *Viral Spiral: How the Commoners Built a Digital Republic of their Own.* New York: New Press.

Bourdieu, P. 1972. *Esquisse d'une théorie de la pratique.* Genève: Droz.

Bourdieu, P. 1994. *Raisons pratiques. Sur la théorie de l'action.* Paris: Seuil.

Boyer, R. 2011. *Les financiers détruiront-ils le capitalisme?* Paris: Economics.

Butler, J. 1990. *Gender Trouble: Feminism and the Subversion of Identity.* London: Routledge.

Butler, J. 1997. *The Psychic Life of Power: Theories in Subjection.* Stanford, CA: Stanford University Press.

Butler, J. 2005. *Giving an Account of Oneself.* New York: Fordham University.

Butler, J. 2008. 'Taking another's view: ambivalent implications', pp. 97–119 in Honneth, H.: *Reification. A New Look at an Old Idea* (Tanner Lectures). Oxford: Oxford University Press.

Caillé, A. 1989. *Critique de la raison utilitaire.* Paris: La découverte.

Caillé, A. 2000. *Anthropologie du don.* Paris: Desclée de Brouwer.

Caillé, A. 2009. *Théorie anti-utilitariste de l'action: Fragments d'une sociologie générale.* Paris: La Découverte.

Caillé, A. 2011a. *De la convivialité: Dialogues sur la société conviviale à venir.* Paris: La Découverte.

Caillé, A. 2011b. *Pour un manifeste du convivialisme.* Lormont: Le bord de l'eau.

Caillé, A. 2013. *Manifeste Convivialiste: Déclaration d'Interdépendance.* Lormont: Le bord de l'eau.

Calhoun, C. and Derluguian, G. 2011. *Business as Usual: The Roots of the Global Financial Meltdown.* New York: NYU Press.

Callon, M. and Latour, B. 1981. 'Unscrewing the big leviathan; or how actors macrostructure reality, and how sociologist help them to do so', pp. 277–303 in Knorr, K. and Cicourel, A. (eds), *Advances in Social Theory and Methodology.* London: Routledge.

Canguilhem, G. 1989. *Etudes d'histoire et de philosophie des sciences.* Paris: Vrin.

Carlson, R. 2008. 'Integral ideology: an ideological genealogy of integral theory and practice' (retrieved on 12 April 2012 www.integralworld.net/carlson.html).

Chanial, P. 2011. *La sociologie comme philosophie pholitique, et réciproquement.* Paris: La Découverte.

Chernillo, D. 2007. *A Social Theory of the Nation State: The Political Forms of Modernity beyond Methodological Nationalism.* London: Routledge.

Colapietro, V. 1989. *Peirce's Approach to the Self: A Semiotic Perspective on Human Subjectivity.* New York: SUNY.

Connell, R.W. 1985. 'How to supervise a PhD', *Vestes: Australian Universities Review,* 28, 2, pp. 38–41.

Connell, R. 2007. *Southern Theory: The Global Dynamics of Knowledge in Social Science.* Cambridge: Polity Press.

Connor, J. 1989. *Postmodernist Culture: An Introduction to Theories of the Contemporary.* Oxford: Blackwell.

Corcuff, P., Le Bart, C. and de Singly, F. 2010. *L'individu aujourd'hui: Débats sociologiques et contrepoints philosophiques.* Rennes: Presses universitaires de Rennes.

Csikszentmihalyi, M. 1990). *Flow: The Psychology of Optimal Experience.* New York: Harper and Row.

Cusset, F. 2005. *French Theory: Foucault, Derrida, Deleuze et cie – et les mutations de la vie intellectuelle aux Etats-Unis.* Paris: La Découverte.

de Landa, M. 2002. *A New Philosophy of Society: Assemblage Theory and Social Complexity.* New York: Continuum.

de Waal, F. 2005. *Our Inner Ape.* New York: Riverhart Books.

Dilthey, W. 1958. *Der Aufbau der geschichtlichen Welt in den Geisteswissenschaften*, in *Gesammelte Schriften*, vol. VII. Göttingen: Vandenhoeck & Ruprecht.

Domingues, M. 1995. *Sociological Theory and Collective Subjectivity*. London: Macmillan.

Dubet, F. 2009. *Le travail des sociétés*. Paris: Seuil.

Edwards, D., Ashmore, M. and Potter, J. 1995. 'Death and furniture: the rhetoric, politics and theology of bottom line arguments against relativism', *History of the Human Sciences*, 8, 2, pp. 25–49.

Elias, N. 1987. *Die Gesellschaft der Individuen*. Frankfurt: Suhrkamp.

Etzioni, A. 1968. *The Active Society: A Theory of Societal and Political Processes*. New York: Free Press.

Fabian, J. 2002. *Time and the Other: How Anthropology Makes its Object*. New York: Columbia University Press.

Fraser, N. 2011. 'Marketization, social protection, emancipation: toward a neo-Polanyian conception of capitalist crisis', pp. 137–158 in Calhoun, C. and Derluguian, G. 2011. *Business as Usual: The Roots of the Global Financial Meltdown*. New York: NYU Press.

Freitag, M. 1986. *Dialectique et société. Vol. 1: Introduction à une théorie générale du symbolique. Vol. 2: Culture, pouvoir, controle: les modes de reproduction formelle de la société*. Lausanne: L'âge d'homme.

Freitag, M. 2008. *L'impasse de la globalisation: Une histoire sociologique et philosophique du capitalisme*. Montréal: Ecosociété.

Freitag, M. 2012. *L'abîme de la liberté*. Montréal: Editions Liber.

Fuchs, S. 2001. *Against Essentialism: A Theory of Culture and Society*. Cambridge, MA: Harvard University Press.

Gadamer, H.G. 1999. *Hermeneutik I. Wahrheit und Methode*, in *Gesammelte Werke, Band. 2*. Tübingen: Mohr.

Giddens, A. (ed.) 1974. *Positivism and Sociology*. London: Heinemann.

Giddens, A. 1976. *New Rules of Sociological Method: A Positive Critique of Interpretative Sociologies*. London: Hutchinson.

Giddens, A. 1977. *Studies in Social and Political Theory*. London: Hutchinson.

Giddens, A. 1979. *Central Problems in Social Theory*. London: Macmillan.

Giddens, A. 1982. *Profiles and Critiques in Social Theory*. London: Macmillan.

Giddens, A. 1984. *The Constitution of Society: Outline of the Theory of Structuration*. Cambridge: Polity.

Gouldner, A. 1980. *The Two Marxisms: Contradictions and Anomalies in the Development of Theory*. London: Macmillan.

Gramsci, A. 1971. *Selections from the Prison Notebooks*. New York: International.

Grint, K. and Woolgar, S. 1992. *The Machine at Work. Technology, Work and Organization*. Cambridge: Polity Press.

Groff, R. 2000. 'The truth of the matter: Roy Bhaskar's critical realism and the concept of alethic truth', *Philosophy of the Social Sciences*, 30, 3, pp. 407–436.

Haack, S. 2013. 'Out of step: academic ethics in a preposterous environment', in *Putting Philosophy to Work: Inquiry and Its Place in Culture* (expanded edition). Amherst: Prometheus Books.

Habermas, J. 1968. *Erkenntnis und Interesse*. Frankfurt am Main: Suhrkamp.

Habermas, J. 1969a. 'Analytische Wissenschaftstheorie und Dialektik: Ein Nachtrag zur Kontroverse zwischen Popper und Adorno', pp. 155–191 in Adorno, T.W. *et al.*: *Der Positivismusstreit in der deutschen Soziologie*. Neuwied: Luchterhand.

Habermas, J. 1969b. 'Gegen einen positivistisch halbierten Rationalismus', pp. 235–266 in Adorno, T.W. *et al.*: *Der Positivismusstreit in der deutschen Soziologie*. Neuwied: Luchterhand.

Habermas, J. 1971. 'Der Universalitätsanspruch der Hermeneutik', pp. 120–159 in Apel, K.O. (ed.), *Hermeneutik und Ideologiekritik*. Frankfurt am Main: Suhrkamp.

Habermas, J. 1973. *Legitimationsprobleme im Spätkapitalismus*. Frankfurt am Main: Suhrkamp.

Habermas, J. 1974. 'Dogmatismus, Vernunft und Entscheidung. Zu Theorie und Praxis in der verwissenschaftlichten Zivilisation', pp. 231–257 in *Theorie und Praxis*. Frankfurt am Main: Suhrkamp.

Habermas, J. 1976. *Zur Rekonstruktion des historischen Materialismus*. Frankfurt am Main: Suhrkamp.

Habermas, J. 1981. *Theorie des kommunikativen Handelns*. Frankfurt am Main: Suhrkamp.

Habermas, J. 2012a. *Zur Verfassung Europas: Ein Essay*. Berlin: Suhrkamp.

Habermas, J. 2012b. *Nachmetaphysisches Denken II. Aufsätze und Repliken*. Berlin: Suhrkamp.

Hadot, P. 2004. *Le Voile d'Isis. Essai sur l'histoire de l'idée de nature*. Paris, Gallimard.

Hall, S. 2000. 'Introduction: who needs "identity"?', pp. 1–17 in Hall, S. and du Gay, P. (eds), *Questions of Cultural Identity*. London: Sage.

Hanson, N. 1958. *Patterns of Discovery*. Cambridge: Cambridge University Press.

Harré, R. 1970. *The Principles of Scientific Thinking*. London: Macmillan.

Harré, R. and Madden, E.H. 1975. *Causal Powers*. Oxford: Blackwell.

Harré, R. and Secord, P. 1972. *The Explanation of Social Behaviour*. Oxford: Blackwell.

Hartmann, F. 2002. 'Medienphilosophische Theorien', pp. 290–320 in Weber, S. (ed.), *Medien- und Kommunikationstheorien: Paradigmen, Theoriespektrum, Komparatistik*. Konstanz: UVK.

Hartwig, M. 2001. 'New left, new age, new paradigm? Roy Bhaskar's *From East to West*', *Journal for the Theory of Social Behaviour*, 31, 2, pp. 139–165.

Hartwig, M. 2007. *Dictionary of Critical Realism*. London: Routledge.

Harvey, D. 2010. *The Enigma of Capital and the Crises of Capitalism*. Oxford: Oxford University Press.

Heidegger, M. 1954. *Vorträge und Aufsätze – Gesamtausgabe Band 7*. Frankfurt am Main: Vittorio Klostermann.

Heidegger, M. 1993. *Sein und Zeit*. Frankfurt am Main. Vittorio Klosterman.

Heidegger, M. 1994. *Holzwege*. Frankfurt am Main: V. Klostermann.

Holanda, S.B. 2000. *Raízes do Brasil*, in *Interpretes do Brasil, vol. 3*. Rio de Janeiro: Novo Aguilar.

Honneth, A. 2000. *Das Andere der Gerechtigkeit. Aufsätzen zur praktischen Philosophie*. Frankfurt am Main: Suhrkamp.

Honneth, A. 2005. *Verdinglichung: Eine anerkennungstheoretische Studie*. Frankfurt am Main: Suhrkamp.

Honneth, A. 2010. *Das Ich im Wir: Studien zur Anerkennungstheorie*. Frankfurt am Main: Suhrkamp.

Honneth, A. 2011. *Das Recht der Freiheit: Grundriβ einder demokratischen Sittlichkeit*. Frankfurt am Main: Suhrkamp.

Honneth, A. 2013. 'Verwilderungen des sozialen Konflikts: Anerkennungskämpfe zu Beginn des 21. Jahrhunderts'., pp. 17–40 in Honneth, A., Lindemann, O. and Voswinkel, S. (eds), *Strukturwandel der Anerkennung: Paradoxien Sozialer Integration in der Gegenwart*. Frankfurt am Main: Campus.

Hoy, D. and McCarthy, T. 1994. *Critical Theory*. Oxford: Blackwell.

Husserl, E. 1993. *Logische Untersuchungen. Zweiter Band: Untersuchungen zur Phänomenologie und Theorie der Erkenntnis*. Tübingen: Max Niemeyer Verlag.

Kant, I. 1983. *Kritik der reinen Vernunft* in *Werke, Band 3*. Darmstadt: WBG.

Keat, R. and Urry, J. 1982. *Social Theory as Science*. London: Routledge.

Kögler, H. 1992. *Die Macht des Dialogs: Kritische Hermeneutik nach Gadamer, Foucault, und Rorty*. Stuttgart: Metzler Verlag.

Kögler, H. 1997. 'Reconceptualizing reflexive sociology', *Social Epistemology*, 11, 2, pp. 223–250.

Kuhn, T. 1962. *The Structure of Scientific Revolutions*. Chicago, IL: University of Chicago Press

Kunneman, H. 1996. *Van theemutscultuur naar walkman-ego: Contouren van postmoderne individualiteit*. Meppel: Boom.

Kunneman, H. 2006. Viable alternatives for commercialized science: the case of humanistics', pp. 307–336 in Radder, H. (ed.), *The Commodification of Academic Research: Critical Perspectives*. Pittsburgh, PA: University of Pittsburgh Press.

Latour, B. 1988. 'Drawing things together', pp. 19–68 in Lynch, M. and Woolgar, S. (eds), *Representations in Scientific Practice*, Cambridge, MA: MIT.

Latour, B. 1996. 'On interobjectivity', *Mind, Culture, and Activity*, 3, 4, pp. 228–245.

Latour, B. 2010. *Cogitamus: Six lettres sur les humanités scientifiques*. Paris: La Découverte.

Laval, C. 2002. *L'ambition sociologique: Saint-Simon, Comte, Tocqueville, Marx, Durkheim, Weber*. Paris: La Découverte.

Layder, D. 1990. *The Realist Image in Social Science*. London: Macmillan.

Lévi-Strauss, C. 1962. *La pensée sauvage*. Paris: Plon.

Luhmann, N. 1981. *Soziale Systeme: Grundriss einer algemeinen Theorie*. Frankfurt am Main: Suhrkamp.

Luhmann, N. 1990. *Die Wissenschaft der Gesellschaft*. Frankfurt am Main: Suhrkamp.

Luhmann, N. 1994. 'The self-description of society: crisis fashion and sociological theory', *International Journal of Comparative Sociology*, 25, pp. 59–72.

Luhmann, N. 1993–1999. *Gesellschaftsstruktur und Semantik: Studien zur Wissenssoziologie der modernen Gesellschaft*, 4 vols. Frankfurt am Main: Suhrkamp.

Luhmann, N. 1998. *Die Gesellschaft der Gesellschaft*. Frankfurt am main: Suhrkamp.

Lynch, M. 1993. *Scientific Practice and Ordinary Action: Ethnomethodology and Social Studies of Science*. Cambridge: Cambridge University Press.

Lyotard, J.F. 1979. *La condition postmoderne*. Paris: Minuit.

Mannheim, K. 1974. *Ideology and Utopia: An Introduction to the Sociology of Knowledge*. London: Routledge.

Mao Tse Tung 1966. *Citations du Président Mao Tse-Toung*. Peking.

Martuccelli, D. and de Singly, F. 2009. *Les sociologies de l'individu*. Paris: Armand Colin.

Mauss, M. 1950. 'Essai sur le don', pp. 143–279 in *Sociologie et anthropologie*. Paris: PUF.

Merton, R. 1968. *Social Theory and Social Structure*. Glencoe, IL: Free Press.

Merton, R. 1973. *The Sociology of Science: Theoretical and Empirical Investigations*. Chicago, IL: Chicago University Press.

Mouzelis, N. 1989. 'Restructuring structuration theory', *Sociological Review*, 37, 4, pp. 613–635.

Münch, R. 1982. *Theorie des Handelns: Zur Rekonstruktion der Beitrage von Talcott Parsons, Emile Durkheim, und Max Weber*. Frankfurt am Main: Suhrkamp.

Norrie, A. 2010. *Dialectic and Difference: Dialectical Critical Realism and the Grounds of Justice*. London: Routledge.
Outhwaite, W. 1987. *New Philosophies of Social Science: Realism, Hermeneutics and Critical Theory*. London: Macmillan.
Parsons, T. 1951. *The Social System*. New York: Free Press.
Parsons, T. 1954. *Essays in Sociological Theory*. Revised edition. New York: Free Press.
Parsons, T. 1970. *Social Structure and Personality*. New York: Free Press.
Pestre, D. 2003. *Science, Argent et Politique*. Paris: INRA Editions.
Pickering, A. 1992. *Science as Practice and Culture*. Chicago, IL: Chicago University Press.
Polanyi, K. 1957. *The Great Transformation: The Political and Economic Origins of our Time*. Boston, MA: Beacon Press.
Ricoeur, P. 1986. *Du texte à l'action: Essais d'herméneutique II*. Paris: Seuil.
Ricoeur, P. 1990. *Soi-même comme un autre*. Paris: Seuil.
Ricoeur, P. 1995. *Réflexion faite: Autobiographie intellectuelle*. Paris: Editions Esprit.
Rojek, C. and Turner, B. 2000. 'Decorative sociology: towards a critique of the cultural turn', *The Sociological Review*, 48, 4, pp. 629–648.
Rose, N. 1999. *The Powers of Freedom: Reframing Political Thought*. Cambridge; Cambridge University Press.
Sartre, J.P. 1960. *Critique de la raison dialectique*. Paris: Gallimard.
Sawyer, R.K. 2005. *Social Emergence: Societies as Complex Systems*. Cambridge: Cambridge University Press.
Sayer, A. 1992. *Method in Social Science: A Realist Approach*. London: Routledge.
Searle, J. 1995. *The Construction of Social Reality*. New York: Simon and Schuster.
Shilling, C. and Mellor, P. 2001. *The Sociological Ambition: Elementary Forms of Social and Moral Life*. London: Sage.
Sloterdijk, P. 1998–2004. *Sphären. Band I: Blasen, Mikrosphärologie. Band II: Globen, Makrosphärologie. Band III: Schäume, Plurale Sphärologie*. Frankfurt am Main: Suhrkamp.
Sloterdijk, P. 1999. *Regeln für den Menschenpark: Ein Antwortschreiben zu Heideggers Brief über den Humanismus*. Frankfurt am Main: Suhrkamp.
Sloterdijk, P. 2009. *Du mußt dein Leben ändern*. Frankfurt am Main: Suhrkamp.
Sloterdijk, P. 2011. *Du mußt dein Leben ändern*. Frankfurt am Main: Suhrkamp.
Sokal, A. 1996. 'Transgressing the boundaries: towards a transformative hermeneutics of quantum gravity', *Social Text*, 46–47, pp. 217–252.
Suárez Müller, F. 2007. 'Die Weideraufstehung des Neffen Rameaus in Sphärenprojeckt Peter Sloterdijks', pp. 225–258 in Goebel, B. and Suárez Müller, F. (eds), *Kritik der Postmodernen Vernunft: Über Derrida, Foucault un andere Zeitgenössiche Denker*. Darmstadt: WBG.
Tarde, G. 1999. *Les lois sociales*, pp. 41–138 in *Oeuvres, vol. IV*. Paris: Les empêcheurs de penser en rond.
Thompson, J. 1981. *Critical Hermeneutics: A Study in the Thought of Paul Ricoeur and Jürgen Habermas*. Cambridge: Cambridge University Press.
Tietz, U. 2002. *Die Grenzen des Wir: Eine Theorie der Gemeinschaft*. Frankfurt am Main: Suhrkamp.
Tocqueville, A. 1961. *De la démocratie en Amérique*. Paris: Gallimard.
Touraine, A. 1992. *Critique de la modernité*. Paris: Fayard.
Valéry, P. 1943. *Tel Quel*. Paris: Gallimard.
Vandenberghe, F. 2001. 'Théorie critique ou critique théorique de l'asociété. Dialogue

constructif entre Freitag, Gauchet, Habermas et quelques autres', in *Cahiers de recherche du Groupe Interuniversitaire d'Etude de la* Postmodernité, 54, pp. 1–80.

Vandenberghe, F. 2002. 'Reconstructing humants. a humanist critique of actant–network theory', *Theory, Culture and Society*, 19, 5/6, pp. 51–67.

Vandenberghe, F. 2006a. *Complexités du posthumanisme. Trois essais dialectiques sur La sociologie de Bruno Latour*. Paris: L'Harmattan.

Vandenberghe, F. 2006b. 'L'aftérologie et le décalogue de la déconstruction', *X-Alta*, 9, pp. 195–206.

Vandenberghe, F. 2008a. 'Entre la voix et la croix, le don et la donation', pp. 213–246 in Archer, M. and Donati, P. (eds), *Pursuing the Common Good: How Solidarity and Subsidiarity Can Work Together. The Proceedings of the 14th. Plenary Session of the Pontifical Academy of Social Sciences*. Vatican City: The Pontifical Academy of the Social Sciences.

Vandenberghe, F. 2008b. 'The cultural transformation of the public sphere: a sociological inquiry into a category of American society' (Review Essay of J.C. Alexander: *The Civil Sphere*), *Constellations*, 15, 3, pp. 422–434.

Vandenberghe, F. 2009. 'Realism in one country?', *Journal of Critical Realism*, 8, 2, pp. 203–232.

Vandenberghe, F. 2010. 'Falsification falsified. a swansong for Lord Karl', pp. 73–77 in Valentini, C. (ed.), *On Objective Knowledge in Social Sciences and Humanities: Karl Popper and Beyond*. Florence: European University Institute.

Vandenberghe, F. 2011. 'The state of cosmopolitanism', *Cridis Working Paper* (UCL), no. 30.

Viveiros de Castro, E. 2002. *A inconstância da alma selvagem*. São Paulo: Cosac Naify.

von Wright, G.H. 1971. *Explanation and Understanding*. Ithaca, NY: Cornell University Press.

Weber, M. 1972. *Wirtschaft und Gesellschaft*. Tübingen: Mohr.

Wilber, K. 1997. 'An integral theory of consciousness', *Journal of Consciousness Studies*, 4, 1, pp. 71–92.

Willke, H. 2001. *Atopia: Studien zur atopischen Gesellschaft*. Frankfurt am Main: Suhrkamp.

1 The internal conversations that we are[1]

For Nobbie

The conversation that we are is a never ending conversation.

Gadamer, X, 140[2]

In medias res

Where shall I start? With the beginning or the end? With practices or with discourses? With myself or with the others? To ask a question is to answer it. As the answer is always an answer to some question, the conversation is essentially dialogical, even when it appears as an internal monologue.[3] And even when we are writing texts, we're always talking to others. Whether these others are our predecessors, contemporaries or successors, to use Schütz's typifications, whether they are past writers, future readers, or a bit of both, as is the case with the author who reads what he writes while he thinks, they are always somehow there as members of a virtual, potentially universal audience we are addressing in thought when we are writing.[4] Consequently, our texts are not really texts, but contributions to an ongoing conversation that we inherit from our predecessors, address to our contemporaries and transmit to our successors.

We are always already in the midst of a conversation. We are as much in the conversation as the conversation is in us. I'll therefore start in the middle. *In medias res*. Etymologically, the thing (*res*) is, in fact, not a thing, but a cause (*causa*), something which is at stake in the conversation.[5] What is at stake in the conversation is the truth, but the truth is still open. When one is convinced that one possesses the truth, one does not really engage in conversation. One talks to the other, not with the other, and one talks to the other to convince him or her of one's own truth.[6] Unlike speech, which is an oral presentation by one person directed to other persons, dialogue seeks a common ground and allows people with different views on a topic to learn from each other.

Needless to say, I'm not in possession of the truth. Nor do I have lessons to give. I'm engaged in a quest and I'm on my way. My research is, literally, a *search*. I raised a question – Where shall I start? – and I'm looking for an answer. The dialectics of question and answer is the undertow of conversation and the way that leads to a common ground. People who talk to each other seek a common ground. By doing so, they not only enter into communication, but also into community. Conversation implies, by definition, the presence of another. Even when I talk to myself and think in silence, I speak to myself as another. As thinking is dialogical through and through, Peirce's 'tuism' – which he defined for the *Century Dictionary* as 'The doctrine that all thought is addressed to a second person, or to one's future self as to a second person' (*apud* Wiley, 2006a: 40) – is, in fact, a truism.[7]

Conversamus ergo sumus

Muddling through, searching for an answer to the question that has been raised, I discover that I cannot really start the conversation. I can only continue it in thought or in writing. In the beginning was the word. Whatever I say, the word does not belong to me, but to language. Language is always already there. It is the beginning that has never started. It is a fundamental insight of hermeneutics that language is the medium of thinking and that thinking is a conversation one has with another. We are always already in the midst of words and thoughts as well as of others. Conversations take place in language. As Gadamer (I: 450) says: 'Language is essentially the language of conversation.' Or, again, with due emphasis on intersubjectivity: 'Language is really where conversation is, in being together with others' (X: 25). And with even more force (II: 144, 206, 364): 'Language is only ever in conversation' (*Sprache ist immer nur im Gespräch*).

Language is not only the medium of conversation, it is also its product ('duality of language'). That language is both the ever-present precondition of conversation and the continually reproduced consequence of intentional practices is not a paradox; rather, it is inherent to the hermeneutic circle.[8] The circle that interrelates conversation and language as part and whole, process and product, *ergon* and *energeia* is an ontological structural feature of the human condition. By virtue of language, thanks to it, we become human. Conversation always already presupposes language and draws on it, while the conversation inevitably fashions and transforms not only language, but also the subject who speaks to others (including him- or herself) about something in the world (in which she or he is included). We always inherit traditions and incessantly participate in the past, which we can reproduce or transform, but which we cannot create *ex nihilo*. As a matter of fact, we belong as much to history as history belongs to us. There is nothing reactionary in saying that even revolutionaries stand in traditions and are bound to continue them – rebellion against tradition being one possible way of expressing it.[9] To avoid the mustiness of conservatism, it should also be noted at this point that while conversations take place in language and presuppose tradition, the latter is dialogical and plural, with central, semi-peripheral and peripheral subtraditions that have porous boundaries and are in constant interaction with each other.

The 'uniduality' of language points to a generalised semiosis not just of the self, but of the world as such (Colapietro, 1989). The world is always already pre-interpreted by language and comes to itself, presents itself to us in language as an open and infinite totality. Language is constitutive of everything that exists for Man. That does not mean that everything is language or that there's nothing outside of language, but rather the reverse. Everything that is thought, felt or otherwise experienced can, in principle, though not in fact, be expressed in language. Language is everything and everything is always already enclosed in language. Whatever is said is always bound, backwards and forwards, by what is not said. The experience of being speechless only confirms that one is seeking the right word to express what one wants to say even if, for the time being, it remains unspeakable. As Wittgenstein says in a letter to Engelmann: 'If only you do not try to say what is unspeakable then *nothing* gets lost. But the unspeakable will be – unspeakably – contained in what has been spoken!' (Engelmann, 1967: 6, transl. modified).[10]

Between inchoate feelings and well formed sentences, there's no solution of continuity. If it cannot be expressed in prose, it can perhaps be expressed in the language of poetry or painting. Even silence speaks, and as the saying goes, it speaks for itself. Language is the medium in which being is wrapped, thought expressed and reality revealed to us as a human reality that makes sense (at least most of the time).

Language is a window that opens onto the world and the bridge that brings us into communication and community. By privileging language, solipsism is overcome from the start. If, *per impossibile*, I were the only individual in the universe, I would not have a language. Not insulation, but conversation is the basic law of human existence.[11] The openness towards the other is what distinguishes Gadamer's hermeneutic dialectics from Heidegger's existential analytics of *Dasein*. Every time I talk to someone, I get out of myself to find the other and using his or her language as a medium of communication, I enter into a dialogue with him or her. Whether we come to an agreement or not, we are always looking for a common ground that we share. In any case, I'm not alone in the world, the world is not constituted by me, the other is not a figment of my imagination. 'Let us not pretend to doubt in philosophy what we do not doubt in our hearts' (Peirce, 1931–1958: 5, 265). *Conversamus, ergo sumus.*[12]

Knowing of the third kind

My contribution to the conversation will be a minor one. I only want to change a word. In fact, a verb, as we shall see later. But by changing a word, one changes the subject. My subject is sociology and the subject of sociology is human beings who, *together*, form a society and by doing so are formed by it and become not only what, but also who they are. Sociology belongs, by nature, to the human sciences. Standing in between the natural sciences (which are descriptive and explanatory) and the humanities (which are interpretative and normative), they partake a bit of both. As such, they develop a third kind of knowledge.[13] It is not theoretical knowledge ('know that', in Ryle's terminology), nor is it merely a craft, a habit, a skill ('know how'). As a reflexive form of common knowledge, yes, as a methodical extension and systematisation of common sense (*sensus communis*) that is shared by all who speak the same language (Habermas, 1973: 178–233), the new sciences represent knowledge of the third type. Perhaps we could call it 'know with' or, in more Peircean vein, knowledge of 'withness'.

The ambit of the human sciences encompasses nature, culture and the practices that interconnect both.[14] Between nature and culture, analysing both the processes of human alienation that transform culture into pseudo-nature, which is devoid of meaning and to which one has no access from within, and the processes of humanisation through which the social world is constituted as a common world of shared meanings that one has to appropriate to become oneself, that is where sociology stands. In the middle, because it investigates the morphogenetic processes of exteriorisation, alienation and internalisation of meaning (Berger and Luckmann, 1966) that constitute the social world as a man-made world that is always on the verge of spinning out of control and of becoming alienated from its origin and its end. But also somehow above it, because it turns into an object of investigation that of which it is itself a part.

In the tradition of Hegel, and closer to us of Dilthey, Gadamer and Habermas, we could say that sociology deals with exteriorisations and internalisations of the Objective Spirit. Indeed, the Spirit is not only at work in the subject that thinks and feels, talks and acts, but also in institutions, organisations and systems of actions, such as the economy, the state, law or society, which are exteriorisations of the Spirit and, hence, subject to understanding.[15] Retranslating the term *Geisteswissenschaften* into English (which the translator Schiel introduced in 1854 to render John Stuart Mill's moral sciences), we can now say that sociology is a spiritual, moral and political science in the humanist tradition and define it as the science that describes, interprets and explains social life in terms of the objective Spirit with the aim and the intent to preserve or restore the living dialectics between the individual and society that ideally allows for the flourishing of both.

Following Ricoeur (1986: 263–288), I take the freedom to transpose practical reason to the collective level and relate it to the struggle against the alienated and alienating objectivation of the Spirit into reified social systems that stifle action by ridding it of all meaning. At the risk of losing the normative dimension of sociology and its connection with practical reason, which reanimates the dialectics between agency and society, but in order not to overburden the discipline with the metaphysical baggage of absolute idealism, we could also, following post-Hegelian neo-Kantians (like Lask, Simmel and Cassirer) and post-Hegelian pragmatists (like Peirce, Dewey and Mead), define sociology as a cultural science that deals with the web of meanings that constitute the world as a human world and summon the subject to realise its inner potential. Believing that 'Man is an animal suspended in webs of meaning' (Cassirer), I conceive therefore of sociology not only as a science in search of causal powers (Bhaskar), but also as interpretative ones in search of meaning (Geertz).[16]

Alethic truth[17]

By focusing on structure to the detriment of culture, critical realists (with the exception perhaps of William Outhwaite) have not paid sufficient attention to language.[18] Language is real and has to be conceived of as a 'causal power' that constitutes the world as a meaningful one in which we find ourselves at home and that we can never fully surpass. The Marxian legacy and the concomitant fear of committing the 'linguistic fallacy', which reduces the world to language, action to performance and the subject to an ever-shifting patchwork of discursive identifications, has led critical realism to underestimate the causal power of language. Although the distrust of structuralism, poststructuralism, deconstruction, psychoanalysis, archaeology, genealogy and other de/constructivist approaches, like Rorty's neo-pragmatism, that do not recognise anything outside of the text, is in part justified, it tends to throw out the baby of hermeneutics with the bathwater of poststructuralism.[19]

Unlike poststructuralism, hermeneutics does not, however, reduce the sign to a play of signifiers without reference. It does not collapse the intransitive into the transitive dimension. Language after all does not speak about itself, but about being and beings – whether this being is a fellow human being, a stone on the road or a flickering flame in the darkness of night. What comes to language, what is expressed and 'presents itself' in language is 'the world itself' (Gadamer, I: 453). Thanks to language, we can get glimpses of the world itself beyond language, even if this world always and inevitably appears to us as an adumbration of the world in itself. If anything, language points beyond itself to alethic truth and, by doing so, it makes us aware of our own finitude. Significantly, Hermes, the messenger of the gods, is associated in Greek mythology with the function of translating the message from the Olympians into a form that human intelligence can understand.

The world itself can be shown and known. It can be experienced as an open totality, but it cannot be scientifically objectified as such without loss. One gets access to it through participation, not through objectification. Unlike structuralism, hermeneutics does not analyse language from the external perspective of the observer, but it conceives it first and foremost as a symbol that has to be disclosed from within through participation. Instead of searching for codes within language from without, it searches horizons within life from within the life-world.[20] As a way of getting access to meaning from within, hermeneutics is a kind of phenomenology in the plural in which the 'We' always has precedence over the 'I' (not to mention Husserl's transcendental ego). Like phenomenology, it is concerned with the constitution of meaning, but unlike phenomenology, which analyses meaning from the micro-perspective of the subject who intentionally gives meaning to his action, hermeneutics is a macro-perspective that interprets, understands and explicates the meanings that the subjects intend as a form of participation in the webs of meanings in which they are suspended and which reveal the world as a familiar one that always already makes sense.

Extending a Weberian metaphor, we could say that phenomenology is more interested in the spider that weaves the web, whereas hermeneutics is more concerned with the web that is woven. If phenomenology adopts the perspective of the participant of the first person singular, hermeneutics deepens and enlarges this perspective by replacing it into the encompassing framework of symbolic meanings that is common to all the subjects who share a common language (by extension, to everyone who speaks a language). With its insistence on ontology, understood as the invisible but real totality of symbols, signs and meanings that constitute the world for us, humans, as a meaningful one, hermeneutics is compatible with critical realism. Metaphysically speaking, language, symbols and concepts are the primal stuff of the world and not simply a fixture that human beings impose on it. As a matter of fact, with its insistence on culture, hermeneutics represents the idealist version of realism. As such, it complements and completes the more materialist version that foregrounds structure.

The mediation of meditation

In accordance with the main tenets of critical realism, I would like to defend the thesis that we do not merely have conversations with ourselves, but that we *are* these conversations. By changing the verb, I intend to bring back the conversation into language and conceive of the self as a hermeneutic and semiotic self – as a self-interpreting animal that is suspended in the conversational webs of language, that communicates with others within oneself. By foregrounding language and intersubjectivity, I do not only aim to continue the great Socratic tradition of dialogue, but I also want to bring critical realism, pragmatism, hermeneutics and phenomenology into an ongoing conversation.

Grafting pragmatism onto hermeneutics

Freely paraphrasing Hans Georg Gadamer, in conversation with him as it were, we were on our way, looking for an answer to a question that had been raised before by others. We arrived at the hermeneutic insight that, through language, the conversation is in us as much as we are in the conversation. Or, to quote the old master himself: 'The conversation that we are is a never ending conversation' (X, 140).[21] In his analysis of C.S. Peirce's semiotics of the self, Vincent Colapietro arrived at a similar conclusion. 'From the perspective of semiotic', he says,

> we are always already in the midst of others as well as of meanings; indeed, otherness and meaning are given together in our experiences of ourselves as beings embedded in a network of relations – more specifically, enmeshed in the 'semiotic web'.
>
> (Colapietro, 1989: 27–28)

This convergence and continuity between hermeneutics and pragmatism is, I hope, an indication that we are on the right path. But with its firm insistence on human subjectivity, reflexivity and consciousness as a phase within action, pragmatism offers a welcome correction to the anti-humanism Gadamer inherited from Heidegger.[22] The existential analytics of *Dasein* is indeed conceived of as a *Fundamentalontologie*, and definitely not as a philosophical anthropology. Although the ontological primacy of the whole over the parts is well taken, one has often the impression that in philosophical hermeneutics it is language that is speaking in conversation rather than the subjects themselves. To foreclose the vanishing of the subject, I will therefore follow pragmatism's lead and think through not only how subjects use language to make sense of their world, their action and their life, but how they are also themselves 'processes and products of semiosis' who become who they are thanks to the internal conversations they have with others as well as with themselves.

Following the maxim of pragmaticism – 'Consider what effects, that might conceivably have practical bearings, we can conceive the object of our conception to have' (Peirce, 1931–1958: 5, 2) – we will wade down the stream of consciousness from the antecedent conditions of thought (*terminus a quo*) to their consequences for action in the real world (*terminus ad quem*). To move from hermeneutics to pragmatics implies two movements: first, from the external conversations we have with others to the inner conversation we have with our selves and, then, back from the inner conversations we have *in foro interno* to the external conversations (communications) that take place in everyday life and in the public sphere. To explore the 'concomitant complementarities' between hermeneutics and pragmatism I will have to execute a delicate operation and 'graft' a pragmatic sociology of internal speech onto a phenomenological hermeneutics of language as the medium of conversation. With its focus on interiority, pragmatism extends the spirit of hermeneutics deep into subjectivity, into the self, into the soul. The natural confluence of the spirit of hermeneutics into the soul of pragmatism avoids from the start the traps of solipsism and the quagmires of psychologism.[23] Indeed, if the self is constituted by language in conversation with one's self and others, individual thinking cannot be the starting point for doubting the existence of the other. As Dewey had correctly understood: 'Failure to recognise that this world of inner experience is dependent upon an extension of language which is a social product and operation led to the subjectivistic, solipsistic, and egotistic strain in modern thought' (*apud* Rochberg-Halton, 1986: 34).

While hermeneutics proposes language as *arché* and conversation as its medium, pragmatism conceives of the self as its product and the good society as its *telos*. The synthesis of hermeneutics and pragmatism I am proposing has various advantages: i) it avoids the Cartesianism of transcendental phenomenology; ii) it solidly grounds pragmatism in holism and overcomes the individualism of W. James and H. Blumer; iii) it corrects the political conservatism of German hermeneutics (Heidegger) with the progressivism of the American social reform movement (Dewey); and last but not least, iv) it opens the way to a 'psychological sociology' (Durkheim) of intrasubjective social communication that would at the same time be an 'interspiritual psychology' (Tarde).

Back to sociological theory

Following the lead of Peirce, Dewey, Mead and Cooley, prominent social theorists (Wiley, 1994; Archer, 2003; Collins, 2004) have finally opened the 'black box' of the mind and started to empirically investigate the internal dialogue people have with themselves – they have discovered it is a 'chatterbox', full of voices![24] In an ongoing dialogue with them, passing the theme through many and varied voices like in a polyphony, I will now move from philosophy to sociology and investigate what the internal conversations can do for us.

As sociologists, we're always concerned with the 'mic/mac' issue. Whether this question has been imposed on us by chroniclers of the discipline (above all Giddens and Alexander) or not, the fact is that, one way or another, we're all thinking about how we could satisfactorily link agency to structure (Giddens), the life-world to the system (Habermas) and the field to the habitus (Bourdieu). Well after the debate had degenerated into the tedium of high scholasticism, Margaret Archer (2003), the *doyenne* of critical realism, introduced the theme of internal conversations into her challenge of the 'neo-orthodox consensus' (structuralism plus language games).[25] Through a systematic integration of a few central concepts ('analytic dualism', the 'morphogenetic sequence', the 'stratification of society') and theorists (Lockwood, Buckley, Bhaskar), she has convincingly shown (at least in my opinion) that structuration theory collapses structure (culture, structure and social systems) into agency – instead of linking agency to structure, it is 'sinking' the distinction (Archer, 1988: xii), as she pithily puts it. Owing to a double compression of agency and structure into practices, Giddens committed the 'fallacy of central conflation' and was, therefore, unable to conceive of either the emergence of a relatively autonomous cultural system from interactions (Archer, 1988) or the supervenience of social structure on the latter (Archer, 1995).

The consequent defence of analytical dualism – a device that freezes the frame and allows for a sequential analysis of the interchange between 'people' (interaction) and 'parts' (systems) – is the other side of her systematic refutation of the theorem of the duality of structure. Instead of collapsing systems into interactions, it upholds the distinction between levels in order to analyse their interplay. The emphasis on emergence and dualism does not deny that social and cultural systems are ultimately man-made (no action: no structure nor system), but the restructuration of structuration theory offers better mileage to think through the inertia of the social world, diagnose its attendant social and psychosocial pathologies (from alienation and anomie to depression and panic disorder), and explore possible remedies (Honneth, 2000: 11–69). What we are concerned about is whole forms of life that have gone awry. As a result of 'heavy', almost unchangeable structures that have sedimented over time and that no one has foreseen and that no one really wants (global capitalism, technological drift, climate change, etc.), the social world is not a dream that one can change overnight; it is rather like history according to James Joyce: 'a nightmare from which we are trying to awake'.

By upholding the distinction between system and life-world, 'parts' and 'people', Archer can do what Giddens cannot do – namely to properly theorise alienation (rather than smuggle it back in via the backdoor). Indeed, with Mouzelis (1991: 25–47) and Archer, I am convinced that the emergence of autonomous and alienating 'figurational structures' can only be properly conceptualised if agents are not seen as continuously reproducing or transforming the society they are making. To think through the phenomenon of alienation critically, the emergence of objective structures that follow their own laws and that cannot be reduced to the practices that constitute them, has to be acknowledged openly. Without 'syntagmatic dualism' (Mouzelis), alienation or *Entfremdung*, to speak like the Marxist philosophers, cannot be conceptualised, let alone remedied. Moreover, it should also be noted that agents can only reflect on the structural and cultural conditions of their actions if they can distance themselves cognitively from them, be it to analyse them in a more theoretical manner or with the practical intent to change them. To question the rules and claim the resources presupposes reflexivity, not the immediacy that marks routine activity. Without 'paradigmatic dualism' (Mouzelis), *Verfremdung* (Brecht) or the reflexive estrangement of one's culture and society to analyse it or to change it 'with will and consciousness', cannot be properly theorised.[26] Dualism and reflexivity are connected, because it is only if the distinction between structure and agency is maintained that one can acknowledge that agents have the capability to reflexively examine their projects and their feasibility, given the objective circumstances in which they find themselves and which they have not freely chosen.

Now that reflexivity has been brought into the analysis, we can return to the theme of internal conversations. To expose what conversation analysis can do for us, sociologists, I will leave Giddens' jargon behind and move on to an analysis of the greatest sociologist of the second half of the twentieth century: Pierre Bourdieu (with whom Archer studied in Paris in the 1970s). As his brand of critical sociology is only too well known by now, no introduction is needed. Whoever has seriously meditated on the intra-related concepts of field, habitus and capital knows that the Achilles' heel of the system is lodged in the short shrift it gives to reflexivity (Kögler, 1997; Lahire, 1998; Mouzelis, 2008). In Bourdieu, everything happens as if the subjects were somehow hypnotised into action. Actors are embodied agents rather than conscious 'subjects' (a word the French sociologist studiously avoids). In spite of the fact that habits are part and parcel of the pragmatist conceptual toolbox – James, but also and above all Dewey who conceived of it as a 'dynamic force' (2002: 43)[27] – the habitus functions as the *malin génie* of frictionless reproduction of the social world. Indeed, in Bourdieu the latter occurs in spite of the subject, thanks to his or her non-reflexivity. To break the circle of reproduction – in fact, it is a circus in which all display the tricks they have learned to play – it is enough to introduce the internal conversations people have with themselves in between the field and the habitus.[28] Through reflection and deliberation, the agents ponder what they want to do not only in their lives, but *with* their lives, and the differential answers they give to these existential questions have implications for the reproduction and transformation of society. Archer's central thesis – let's call it the 'thesis of the mediation of meditation' – can now be formulated: reflexivity is exercised through people holding conversations with themselves in which they clarify, organise and systematise their 'ultimate concerns' (Tillich) in an existential and personal project to which they commit themselves. To find out who they are and what their 'mission' is in this life, people have to decide 'what they care about' (Frankfurt, 1988: 80–94), and they do so through an inner dialogue with themselves and significant others.[29] It is this meditation of the actors on what really matters to them and what they are willing to forego, or to invest in order to realise what they care about and have 'devoted' themselves to, that constitutes the mediatory mechanism which links the causal powers of structure to agency.

Social structures and cultural systems exercise their causal powers by structuring the situation of action through constraints and enablements, but to the extent that the activation of those causal powers depends on the existential projects that the actors forge *in foro interno* (no projects: no constraints or enablements), actors can be said to actively mediate their own social and cultural conditioning. Provided we transform Karl Popper's 'three-world theory' (Popper, 1979) into a 'four-world theory' that takes into account the emergence of social systems without reducing them to practices, it may be used to clarify the topology of the mediation of meditation. World 1 (*physicalia*, i.e. the physical realm of natural objects), world 3 (*intelligibilia*, i.e. the cultural realm of relations between ideas and theories) and world 4 (*sociabilia*, i.e the social realm of relations between positions and roles) are objectively given.[30] They exist independently of 'world 2' (the psychological world of states of consciousness and objects of thought), but nature, culture and society are only linked to each other via internal speech, which belongs to 'world 2'.

In accordance with the 'four-world theory', we can conceive of situations of action as concrete contexts in which actors try to realise their personal projects within the framework of natural, cultural and social circumstances that constitute both the means of achieving their aims and constraints on that achievement. It is important to note that there's always an interrelation between the personal projects of the subjects and the culture of which they are part (world 3/world 2), as well as between the projects and the facts of both the physical (world 2/world 1) and the social (world 2/world 4) context. It follows from this that neither the natural nor the cultural nor the social elements of the situation can directly determine the course of action; they can only do so mediately by constraining or enabling the projects. As courses of action are produced through the actor's reflexive deliberations about how they could possibly integrate their 'ultimate concerns' into sustainable life-projects that are feasible in the given circumstances, the constraints and enablements of the situation need to be activated by the actors themselves if they are to exercise their causal powers. Although Archer is conscious of the connection between culture (which she refers to as the 'Universal Library of Mankind') society and internal conversations, I'm afraid that in her valiant struggle against de/constructivism, she has significantly underemphasised the importance of language. Gently, I would therefore like to invite her to take the 'linguistic turn', which is, in fact, as we shall see, a return to alterity and intersubjectivity.

Experience and nature

Parts and wholes

Now that the meditations and ruminations of the actors have been introduced into the mic/mac debate as a mechanism of mediation that activates the causal powers of the people – 'the power to dream/to rule, to wrestle the world from fools' (Patti Smith) – the next step consists of opening the 'black box' of the mind in order to investigate the connection between language, self and society. At the intersection of the spirit and the soul, Margaret Archer encounters the tradition of pragmatism and engages with it. The works of Charles Sanders Peirce, William James and George Herbert Mead lead her to a progressive break with the paradigm of perception and observation of the external world (to which not only positivists, but also Edmund Husserl remained captive).

Instead of moving outwards, she now moves inwards into introspection, into the self, into the soul.[31] As always, she factors in time. Drawing on Wiley's (1994, 2006a) 'trialogical' synthesis of Peirce and Mead, she schematises the conversations into a cycle of morphogenetic sequences wherein the conversational 'I' speaks to itself in the specious present by projecting itself backwards and forwards into time: the conversational self (the 'I' at T2) interprets the past self (the 'me' at T1) to the future self (the 'you' at T3).[32] The upshot of this imaginary meeting of selves is a working consensus in which the conversational self tries to align context, concern and projects into a possible train of action. Eventually, when the self has rehearsed several possible ways of action in fantasy, it 'makes up its mind', and 'action gears into the outer world' (Schütz, 1962: 20, 67, *passim*).[33]

Sociologists and social psychologists will, no doubt, recognise the input of symbolic interactionism. At this point, it should be noted, however, that Margaret Archer is highly critical of Mead (Blumer is only mentioned in a footnote).[34] In a rather severe assessment of the man and his work, she charges Mead for his 'oversocialised' conception of the inner wo/man: 'Mead is an almost uncompromising externalist.... It is not a dialogue with oneself; it is a conversation with society.... A domain of mental privacy has been lost through its social colonization' (Archer, 2003: 78, 79, 82). Thinking with George Herbert against Margaret, one could, however, easily reverse the charge and say, with due apologies: 'Archer is an almost uncompromising internalist. The internal conversation is not a conversation with others, let alone communication in and about society. A domain of public communication has been lost through introspection of the soul.' Even the more sympathetic critics have noticed 'a solipsistic tendency' in her work (Sannino, 2008: 276) that systematically underemphasises 'interactions' (Mouzelis, 2008: 199–213) and 'transactions between interdependent actors' (Dépelteau, 2008) and pointed to 'the problem of intersubjectivity' (Gronow, 2008).

Fortunately, to bring back intersubjectivity and language into the conversation, one does not need to pass through Husserl, Gadamer, Apel or Habermas – though it helps.[35] All the elements one needs to make the case that internal communication is hermeneutic (mediated by language) and semiotic (mediated by signs), dialogical (conversation between I and Me) and intersubjective (conversation with significant others within oneself) are already available in pragmatism itself. Unlike hermeneutics, which foregrounds the eternity of Being, pragmatism is first and foremost a practical and praxeological philosophy of Becoming (and, thus, of time). As a post-Darwinian and post-Hegelian philosophy of evolution, it conceives of the universe not as an 'iron block-universe' (Dewey) that can be captured in a 'kodak fixation' (Dewey, 1973: I, 211), but as a world that is still in the making, 'brimming with indeterminacy, waiting to be completed and rationalized' (Shalin, 1986: 10).[36]

According to pragmatism, the world is definitely not a thing – all *energeia*, it is work in process/progress. It is always in flux, while all things in the universe are in relation, interaction or transaction with each other. It may be somewhat exaggerated to say that pragmatism offers a secularised version of process theology and a socialist version of Einstein's relativism. The fact is that the genuine pragmatist is a humanist like the ultimate Comte, a solidarist like Mauss and Durkheim, and a relativist like Simmel.[37] Where Descartes only saw an opposition between the mind (*res cogitans*) and the body (*res extensa*), pragmatism roots the spirit and the mind in the organism itself. While it places the organism in its immediate environment, it conceives at the same time of the mind as part of a larger evolving cosmic whole that has become fully conscious in the human being. From the ultra-small to the extra-large, pragmatism considers the universe as a complex spiral of concentric circles that open onto the universe and into the self. As everything enfolds everything, one can either enter the spiral from the bottom or slide down in circular movements from the top to the bottom. The direction does not really matter. What matters is the circular causality that interconnects parts and wholes into a living totality.[38] Like in a hologram, the part is in the whole, the whole is in the part; or more emphatically: the part *is* the whole.[39] As both are relative to each other, one might as well say, without contradiction, that the part is an 'aspect' of the whole as the reverse. As far as pragmatism is concerned, they are the same, only considered from a different angle. With its emphasis on becoming and wholeness, it is only consequent when pragmatism describes the implicate order as a dynamic one in which each 'aspect' is seen as a 'phase' within an evolving totality.

The semiotic circle

Inspired by Darwin's narration of the organic connections he perceived between different life-forms, pragmatism consciously replaces the subject–object relativity with a dynamic integration of the organism into the environment. Instead of opposing the former to the latter, it integrates both in a single movement. 'The organism is', as John Dewey (1973: I, 65) says, 'in and of the world'. It is both an agent and a patient. Whatever influences the changes of other things is itself changed in the process. What is mind and what is matter is relative. Matter and mind are 'two sides or "aspects" of the same thing' (Dewey (1973: I, 299), like the convex and the concave or the inside and the outside. They are integrated into a whole in and through experience. Thanks to experience, the world and the mind are inscribed into each through a recursive loop that co-produces both: 'The world is in the mind, which is in the world' (Morin, 1994: 201).

For pragmatism, experience is the font and origin of everything. 'Experience is *of* as well as *in* nature. It is not experience which is experienced but nature' (Dewey, 1973: I, 252) – stones, plants, animals, energies, fluxes, diseases, etc. Things that interact in certain ways and resist are real and are experienced as such. They are encountered in real life as constraints on action or as enablements, as things that the organism has to adapt to, struggle with, circumvent or otherwise take into account in its ongoing engagement with the world.

Initially, the organism encounters the world as a problem that raises a question. The situation in which it finds itself is confused and confusing, indeterminate and chaotic. To find its bearings in this 'big, blooming, buzzing confusion' (James), the organism has to transform 'an indeterminate situation into a determinately unified one' (Dewey, 1973: I). At its most general level, this ordering of the world occurs in and through inquiry:

> Inquiry is the controlled or directed transformation of an indeterminate situation into one that is so determinate in its constituent distinctions and relations as to convert the elements of the original situation into a unified whole.
>
> (Dewey, 1973: I)[40]

Consequently, when the situation is defined as orderly and coherent, the question is answered, the problem is solved and action spontaneously ensues.

> Suppose it is a question of knowledge of water.... It occurs as a stimulus to action and as the source of certain undergoings. It is something to react to – to drink, to wash with, to put fire out with, and also something that reacts unexpectedly to our reactions.... In this two-fold way, water or anything else enters into experience'.
>
> (Dewey, 1973: I)

Interestingly, the experience of the organism is itself an organic experience that integrates the various phases of the act into a functional whole.

Experience in its vital form is an effort to adapt to the environment by changing it. It is characterised by 'pro-jection', by reaching forward into the unknown to make it known. As connection with the future is a salient trait, experience opens up new possibilities by seeking new directions. Within experience, sensation, emotion, cognition, volition and conation form a living unity. 'This unity is neither emotional, practical, nor intellectual, for these terms name distinctions that reflection can make within it' (Dewey, 1973: II, 556). The root of all knowledge is to be found not in knowledge itself, but in action, not for the sake of knowledge, but for the sake of action itself. All thinking is grounded in practice and returns to practice. Knowledge and consciousness have to be conceived of as phases within a single teleological act that intervenes in the world to change it, to adapt the world to the organism and the organism to the world.

In his revolutionary article on 'The Reflex Arc Concept in Psychology' – an essential piece if one wants to understand Mead – Dewey (1973: I, 136–147) criticises the mechanistic conception of action that underlies all forms of behaviourism – from Thorndike to Watson and Skinner to contemporary rational choice theory. The problem with behaviourism is that it breaks the 'flow' of action into an arc made up of broken segments. Instead of conceiving action as a continuous 'circuit' – let's say, to maintain the continuity with hermeneutics, as a 'semiotic circle' in which the parts are organically coordinated into a living whole – it decomposes action into a mechanical sequence of causes and effects. It is the well-known and much decried stimulus–response model of Pavlov's dogs and Homans' pigeons. What behaviourism does not understand is that the response does not follow the stimulus; it is rather the reverse: the response determines the stimulus. 'The so-called response is not merely *to* the stimulus, it is *into* it' (138). This is the case because the stimulus has to be understood as a functional moment or phase within a process of ongoing adaptation and coordination. What is at one moment a guiding response (dependent variable) may at the next moment become a guiding stimulus (independent variable). When, due to problems of coordination, the act cannot be properly completed and consummated, reflection intervenes in between the stimulus and the response. Inhibited by the conflict in the coordination of the different phases of the act – impulse, perception, manipulation and consummation (Mead, 1931) – the organism bends back on itself to think the situation through and contemplate alternative paths of action.

In between the stimulus and response, consciousness or 'mind', as Mead (1934) will say, intervenes as a phase within an ongoing teleological sequence. The dog hears the noise, because it listens with wide open ears when the master arrives; the bird sees the worm in the apple, because it looks for it; the monkey grasps the banana, because it touches and feels that it is within reach of its left upper arm. 'There is simply a continuously ordered sequence of acts, all adapted in themselves and in the order of their sequence, to reach a certain objective end, the reproduction of the species, the preservation of life, locomotion to a certain place. The end has got thoroughly organized into the means' (Dewey, 1973: I, 143).[41]

Interactive monadology

Up till now, we have spoken about organisms and the sequential organisation of experience into a whole whose members 'conspire' and 'cooperate' towards a common end. Following Dewey's post-Darwinian philosophy of the act, we have mentioned animals and, implicitly, we have included humans into the animal realm. What characterises pragmatism, however, is that it socialises nature and conceives of nature itself as a form of cosmic cooperation that is animated by universal sympathy in which everything vibrates and resonates, communicates and converses with everything. Metaphysically speaking, nature itself is, ultimately, as a commentator put it, 'a biocosmic emergent dialogue' (Rochberg-Halton, 1993: xii).

Although this dialogical perspective on nature is not completely absent in the thought of John Dewey, who generally privileges the instrumental and consummatory engagement of organisms with the objects in their environment, it only fully comes into the open in George Herbert Mead's work.[42] Indeed, unlike his friend, Mead puts practical intersubjectivity at the front and centre of all his reflections and folds instrumental action into communicative action (Joas, 1980). Indeed, picking up the thread of romantic theories of sympathy (*Einfühlung*) that conceive of nature as an animated field of resonance, he not only affirms that natural objects themselves are constituted by the social process of interaction, but he goes further and, seemingly, conceives of nature itself as a kind of society.[43]

In what are perhaps the most speculative pages of his oeuvre (PP: 119–139; 1934: 178–186; 1938: 426–432), he boldly extends his theory of role-taking to nature and proposes a perspectival switch, suggesting that we, humans, take the role of inanimate objects when we interact with them and manipulate them to our own ends.[44] To understand how Mead got to this theory, one has to know the basics of his philosophical anthropology. What distinguishes the human being from lower animals is the capacity to manipulate objects by hand and language. 'Speech and the hand go together in the development of the social human being' (MSS: 237). The upright posture of *Homo sapiens/demens* has liberated the hands from employment in locomotion for manipulation. The dynamic interdependence between manipulation (hand) and perception (eye) into a functional *Gestaltkreis* is not unconnected from communication (mouth). Together, the capability of manipulation of what is at hand (*zuhanden*), the perception of what is distant (*vorhanden*) and the capability of changing perspectives, which is grounded in language, offer the physiological-functional basis of the evolutionary process of hominisation.[45] In his *Philosophy of the Act*, Mead (PA: 3–25, *passim*) argues at length that the coordination of hand and speech, which allow respectively for the manipulation of objects at hand and in thought, has considerably increased the possibilities of action. With the intercalation of a manipulatory phase in between the perception of distant objects and the gratification of consummation, the act becomes an intelligent one. In the absence of the manipulatory phase, as is, allegedly, the case with lower animals, the reaction to the stimulus is direct. Without the intervention of plans, thoughts and ideas, human beings would be at the mercy of the environment like animals.

Mead's characterisation of animal behaviour is, no doubt, unfair, but I think his description of human interactions between subject and object in terms of role taking is less objectionable than might appear at first.[46] In imagination, we anticipate what we will do when we come into contact with the thing – let's suppose it's a stone. We anticipate that it will resist as we 'finger' it and project an 'inside' into it. Our effort to manipulate it by hand finds a response in its resistance ('pushiness' or 'objectity', as Whitehead and Latour would respectively say), and, presumably, as well in the resistance our hand offers to it. The object may be inanimate, but it is not unresponsive. We experience this resistance as a response coming from within the stone itself. Mead affirms: 'The physical object has an interior in the same sense that the social object, or the other, has an interior' (PA: 430). Taking the role of the object, we feel ourselves pressing back against the stone as objects with which we identify. In this quasi-dialogue with the object, we are transformed in turn. Like in Husserl's Fifth Cartesian Meditation (§51), through 'pairing' of the object's inside with our own outside, we become an object among objects, a body among bodies. 'We can become objects to ourselves at the same time that they can become objects to us' (Mead, 1932: 136). Through the exchange of perspective, we identify with the material object and, projecting our own interiority into it, we do not only anthropomorphise and socialise nature, but we also discover at the same time our own materiality. Of course, Mead does not claim that objects are subjects, actants or entelechies endowed with intentionality and consciousness, but rather the reverse: subjects are objects to themselves. His argument is a genetic one: before we become objects to ourselves, we have to be objects for others. Similarly, to become subjects to ourselves, we need others. In imagination, we need to see ourselves as they see us, anticipating in thought, how they will respond to us in interaction.

Objectivity presupposes subjectivity; materiality supposes sociality; and sociality presumes intersubjectivity. Neither the object nor the subject is first. Both emerge in the relation and presuppose sociality as their condition of possibility. At the limit, nature is the integral of perspectives one can possibly adopt on things. The perspective on things emerges out of contact with the things one manipulates, while science is only the methodological extension, formalisation and systematisation of the organism's commerce with nature (Habermas, 1973: 116–178). To the extent that the integration of the multiplicity of perspectives occurs in and through effective communication in 'the open community of scientists', which corresponds to Peirce's 'unlimited community of communication' (Apel), pragmatism can indeed be considered as a semiotic reformulation of Leibniz's monadology.

As in Leibniz, all perspectives are ultimately integrated, interrelated and unified in reality itself. The multiverse is a universe. When one thinks the totality of all things on the one hand and the totality of all possible perspectives on the other hand, then one thinks at both ends the same world. The interrelation of all perspectives in which the whole appears coincides with the world itself. The convergence and coordination of perspectives is, however, no longer conceived of as the work of God, but of Man. By virtue of the fact that the human being is a speaking animal (*zoon logon echon*), it is endowed with the capacity of language. Allowing each and every one to adopt a universal perspective on singular things, it is the medium that enables the rational integration and coordination of perspectives that corresponds, presumably, to the Truth itself – for the time being, because the truth itself is always in flux.

> Different minds may set out with the most antagonistic views, but the progress of investigation carries them by a force outside of themselves to one and the same conclusion.... The opinion which is fated to be ultimately agreed to by all who investigate, is what we mean by the truth, and the object represented in this opinion is the real. That is the way I would explain reality.
>
> (Peirce, 1938–1958: 5, 407)

Unlike Leibniz's, Mead's monadology is not only an intersubjective one; it is also an interactive one. Monads have windows and doors. The other is not merely existent, as in phenomenology, but articulatory and communicative – 'it talks and expresses its intentions, values, judgments and consolations' (Perinbanayagam, 1975: 503). The subjects are in contact, conversation and communication with each other and with themselves, either directly in face-to-face contact or indirectly, via media of communication (language, but also money, power or influence). They are connected to each other and to society through language.[47] What distinguishes human beings from animals and unanimated things is not that they are interrelated – after all, everything in the universe is – but that they are conscious not only of being so but also of doing so when they establish the connections among themselves.

The interconnection of minds and consciousness into a common whole is an active and ongoing process that is mediated by language. Using all kind of signs, from insignificant gestures to genuine symbols, subjects can evoke in themselves implicitly the same response which these signs evoke in others. Although the process of mediation presupposes the imagination of a community, it does not take place in imagination, but in action, imagination being only a 'phase' within collective action. As a mechanism of symbolic representation of the dynamic relations between parts and wholes, language plays a crucial role in the mediation between individual and society. It allows the members of society who share a common discourse not only to 'pro-ject' a common world, but also, and perhaps more importantly, to act in common and coordinate their actions. As H. Gerth and C. Wright Mills (1954: 82) write in their important but forgotten book on the psychology of institutions: 'A community of discourse thus normally coincides with a community of coordinated activities. For the prime function of language is to co-ordinate social conduct.' As a common fund of symbolic representations that each of the interactants has in mind when they enter into communication with each other, language is indeed what makes society possible.

Society, self and mind

Collective subjectivities

Like Peirce and Dewey, George Herbert Mead is a holist, a collectivist and a socialist of sorts. Influenced in his early youth by Hegel, he develops a dialectical social theory in which individual minds are interconnected with each other and brought into society thanks to and through a continuous conversation between the individual Mind and the collective Spirit. Like Dilthey, with whom he took courses in Berlin on ethics and the history of philosophy, he leaves no doubt about the ontological priority of language and society over the individual: 'The whole (society) is prior to the part (the individual), not the part to the whole; and the part is explained in terms of the whole' (MSS: 7).

Mead's reflections on sociology and social psychology are dialectical exercises in mereology (the science of parts and wholes). Societies are cooperative wholes, made up of interactions between elements which are not only parts, but which are wholes themselves. Like groups, individuals are associations of parts that are in interaction, conversation and communication with each other to coordinate their actions into a whole, but as parts of a whole they are themselves wholes, made up of various parts that are in interaction and communication with each other. The conclusion of these mereological considerations on communication and conversation between and within parts of all kinds is that, as humans, we are only the end point of an evolution where the conversation becomes conscious of itself (the mind) and of its evolution (science). Speculative as ever, Mead affirms that the appearance of consciousness (of the first and second order) at the individual and collective levels is 'only the culmination of that sociality which is found throughout the universe' (PP: 86).

The movement from cosmology to sociology and social psychology is inwards – from the whole to the parts, from the external to the internal, from communication to imagination. Given the temporal and logical pre-existence of the social process to the self-conscious individual that arises in it, the analysis of the constitution of society has to precede the analysis of the constitution of the self. The constitution of the self is, after all, only a phase within the constitution of society. Consequently, the book that made Mead famous should really have been entitled *Society, Self and Mind.*

All considered, symbolic interactionism is first and foremost a theory of linguistically mediated collective action. Its subject is society, understood as a 'collective subjectivity' that makes society.[48] Like all idealists, Mead neglects the systemic environments in which symbolically mediated interactions take place and tends to reduce society at large to an ongoing sequence of interactions of interactions, associations of associations or organisations of organisations – we might as well say that collective subjectivities do not only make society, they *are* society. Society is, ultimately, a subjective collectivity in the making that is becoming conscious of itself and coincides, at the limit, with humanity as such.

Against this humanist background, one can better understand why Mead continuously insists on the necessity to adopt the perspective of the 'generalised other', which he identifies, in a first moment, with the 'whole community' and, in a second moment, with the 'universe of discourse'. By taking the perspective of the 'generalised other', the individual interprets his own action in relation with the action of the other members of society and understands it as a contribution to collective action – a contribution that may well determine the direction of society.[49]

The logic behind this social capability of the individuals to engage in concerted action and to interweave their action into a collective act is definitely organicist and functionalist – almost Durkheimian in its understanding of the division of labour as a form of social cooperation.[50] In the same way as the individual player of an organised game is able to collaborate with the other members of the team by understanding his own position in the total field of collective action, any member of a given community is, in principle, able not only to understand his function, but also to organise his own behaviour in function of a larger whole of which he is part. As knowledge of the whole is 'distributed' over the agents in such a way that each member knows not only what the others know, but has also almost complete knowledge of what each member of the community knows, the agents use that collective knowledge to help solve a common problem of action or to realise a common plan.[51] When knowledge is really distributed, the whole act is present as a stimulus in the conduct of all who participate in the collective act. The result of cooperation is a collective product that all have in mind and to which each has consciously contributed his part. 'It may be as different from the sum of what the individuals could have thought out in separation as a ship built by a hundred men is from a hundred boats each built by one man' (Cooley, 1983: 21).[52]

For Mead, society is not a substance, but a verb that is conjugated in the first-person plural. Each of the individuals is engaged in a complex series of organised acts that are moving towards a common end and that are continuously monitored in the process. The integration of all the individual acts into a common process is controlled in the movement, through continuous exchange of mutual perspectives, by the anticipation of the realisation of the final cause.

Let us take a micro-example – a team of surgeons performing an operation *together*. A number of professionals are directly involved in the performance on and around the operation table. All attention is focused on a small part of the patient's body and each member of the working team is closely monitoring the acts of the surgeon and her assistants, while keeping an eye on the medical machinery. As a social object, the body means different things to all the individuals involved, including the patient (and his family). An assistant hands the scalpel to the surgeon. She takes it without looking and nods, while another assistant gets ready to remove the blood that will start to ooze in a few seconds. Each anticipates the acts of the others and organises their own response to the call of the other, their action in common is a single collective act that is moving towards a common end (which, for reasons of decency, I prefer not to call the 'final cause').

Let us now take another bloody example, but a macro one – war. However destructive the aim, it can only be brought off through the cooperation of all. As Kenneth Burke wrote:

> Millions of cooperative acts go into the preparation of one single act. Modern war characteristically requires a myriad of constructive acts for each destructive one; before each culminating blast there must be a vast network of interlocking operations, directed communally.
>
> (Quoted by Perinbanayagam, 2003: 76).

What holds for one community also holds for the next community. In pragmatism, society is conceived of as a multiplicity of interacting communities, each made up in turn of multiple primary and secondary groups (cities, neighbourhoods, peer groups, families, etc.). Through identification and disidentification with the societies, communities and subcommunities one is a member of, collective subjectivities wax and wane. At any given moment, any denizen can join one of the multiple communities she or he belongs to in order to contribute to its functionings, making it stronger in the process, or defect from it, weakening it. By literally taking another role, I can not only change my social identity, but I can also join a group and cooperate in the actualisation of its potential. As I'm writing this text in my office, some of my social identities (e.g. member of staff of my university, member of the 'reflexivity forum', hermeneutician and would-be pragmatist) are activated, while others (e.g. Belgian expat, Carioca, amateur of fine chocolates) are deactivated. I would have liked to go to the World Social Forum in Belém do Pará in Brazil to join its activities, but time constraints and the fact that I had to finish this chapter made it impossible, at least this time. In any case, the possibility of simultaneous identifications that make and break collective subjectivities opens up a third way between nominalism and realism. Collectives are real to the extent that their potential is actualised; to the extent that it remains virtual they are nominal. But nothing precludes that a potential group, like the Glorious Proletariat of yore, regains force as a world historical actor or that a powerful actor, like Wall Street, becomes demoralised and weakened. I will return to that issue in the next chapter.

The standpoint of social behaviourism

I have often wondered about the reference to the 'standpoint of social behaviorism' that appears in the subtitle of *Mind, Self and Society*. As a friend of John B. Watson, Mead may have spent many a Sunday with him in his laboratory in Chicago watching him performing his experiments on rats and monkeys. But that did not stop him from criticising his friend's conclusions for being, literally, 'mindless'.[53] Nevertheless, the reference to a behaviourist standpoint theory remains a puzzling one. I can only make sense of it in terms of the distinction between covert/internal/potential and overt/external/actual behaviour, which 'gears into the external world and alters it', as Schütz would say. Whereas overt behaviour is observable, covert behaviour is not. Mead did not deny the existence of the mind, far from it, but he had serious doubts about the scientific use of the method of sympathetic introspection. To understand the meaning of human action, one does not need to enter into the mind of others to find out what they think. Instead of working from an elusive inside to an expressive outside, one should rather work from the visible (or audible) outside – the act – to the invisible (or inaudible) inside and consider the minding as a phase within the organisation of a publicly observable act. 'The act, then, and not the tract, is the fundamental datum in both social and individual psychology' (MSS: 8). It is not some psychic state that is the object of pragmatic inquiry, but the act in its totality and its sociality, as it is expressed in language. 'There's no private language', as Wittgensteinians are wont to repeat. Language is common and it is public. The meanings which are processed privately *in foro interno* are public meanings. Thinking is a moment of the organisation of the collective act and should be understood as such. 'We want to approach language not from the standpoint of inner meanings to be expressed, but in its larger context of cooperation in the group taking place by means of signals and gestures. Meaning appears within that process' (MSS: 6), and in good pragmatic fashion, it appears as its consequence as a publicly observable act that gears into the outer world.

The meaning is in the open, it is articulated within language as discourse. Instead of trying to get at deep meanings and inner states of the individual, one should understand inner conversations not only as internalisations of public communication, but also as public modes of description of inner thought that configure action as collective action (Cefaï, 1998: 246–261). In other words, the reasons and motives of actors that give meaning to their actions should be understood as 'vocabularies of motives' (Mills, 1940, Gerth and Mills, 1954: 112–129) or, as your local ethnomethologist would have it, as 'accounts' of action that are out there, not in the head of the actors. As Garfinkel (1990: 6) once said: 'There's nothing in the head of interest to us, but brains.'[54]

Interestingly, semiotics and hermeneutics converge once again. When we understand a text, or action as a 'quasi-text' (Ricoeur, 1986: 205–236), it is not a matter of penetrating into the spiritual activities of the author; it is simply a question of grasping the meaning or sense (*Sinn*) of the text. As Gadamer says with the force of conviction: 'The meaning of hermeneutical inquiry is to disclose the miracle of understanding texts or utterances and not the mysterious communication of souls. Understanding is participation in the common aim' (Gadamer, I: 297). The question is, undoubtedly, an important one. In external as well as in internal communication, something comes into language. What we want to understand is not so much what is behind the text (the mind), but rather what is in front of it – the reference, what language talks about, the world

To understand what someone says does not mean to transpose oneself in the mind of the other to re-live her experiences, but to understand what she meant. Although the meaning is intersubjective – it is what the conversation is about – it is objective, and in this sense independent of the speakers. When the conversation is a successful one, the speakers come to a common understanding and a consensus on the issue. What matters is the thing (*die Sache*) one is thinking about in conversation – the thought not the thinker.[55] And in any case, to understand the thinker, whether it is oneself or another who's doing the thinking, one has to make a detour through signs (Peirce) and symbols (Gadamer). As Ricoeur (1986: 33) says – but one can find similar ideas in Peirce and Mead – 'There's no understanding of self that is not mediated by signs, symbols and texts'. In hermeneutics and semiotics, the way to the self is a long, winding and arduous one. Self-reflection is not direct, but mediated and broken by a triple detour through language, false consciousness and unconscious desires and, last but not least, the other (Ricoeur, 1969: 7–28).

This methodological position explains Mead's (1964a) reticence with regards to Cooley's introspective sociology of the larger mind, which he otherwise admired. When Cooley proposed to write an 'autobiography of society', Mead thought the object was too hazy, not to say mystical, to be submitted to scientific investigation. Indeed, for Cooley, society is in the last instance an 'imagined community' of fellows that exists in our own mind:

> The human mind is social, society is mental.... Society exists in my mind. It exists in your mind as a similar group, and so in every mind.... Persons and society must, then, be studied primarily in the imagination.... I conclude, therefore, that the imaginations people have of one another are the *solid facts* of society, and that to observe and interpret these must be a chief aim of sociology.
>
> (Cooley, 1964: 81, 119–121)

Although Mead was quite taken by Cooley's sentimental vision of a society of selves that are in continuous communication and conversation with each other, he objected that this conception was mental, not scientific:

> The locus of society is not in the mind, in the sense in which Cooley uses the term, and the approach to it is not by introspection, though what goes on in the inner forum of our experience is essential to meaningful communication.
>
> (Mead, 1964a: xxxvi)

Indeed, although we need to imagine society in thought if we are to coordinate our actions in the real world, society is extra-mental. It is, as Searle (1995: 7–9) would say, an 'objectively real fact' that exists *extra nos et praeter nos*.

Fellowship in thought

The other does not belong to the same field as my self. The other is not constituted by me, but, as Sartre says somewhere, encountered. She exists in the real world and is not a figment of my imagination. I have internal dialogues with her, I imagine her in the theatre of my mind, but that is only to rehearse our respective roles in the collective action we are going to engage in together.

Mead insisted that the complex cooperative processes and activities of organised human society are possible only in so far as every individual involved in them can take the general attitudes of all other such individuals, understand his own activities as a contribution to the organised social whole that emerges out of these interactions and, last but not least, can direct his own behaviour accordingly. The use of significant symbols that carry the same functional meaning for all the individuals involved is a presupposition of the integration of actions of individuals, who may not even know each other, but who speak the same language, into common action.

Thanks to language, an individual can think through his own activities with respect to those of others. In imagination, anyone can enter into the perspective of others who are not actually present and transcend the immediacy of the environment. Talking to oneself in solitary thought, taking the role of the others towards oneself, one can expand one's world in one's mind. The individual does not only take on the roles and attitudes of the others, however, but thanks to the mediation and schematisation of language, also their world. 'You cannot convey a language as a pure abstraction; you inevitably in some degree convey also the life that lies behind it' (MSS: 283). Indeed, 'to imagine a language is to imagine a form of life' (Wittgenstein, 1954: § 19). Thanks to and through communication, an entire world can thus be 'appresented' to any member of the community.

Like Gadamer, Mead assumes that one is not bound by the horizon of one's own language. The limits of one's language are indeed the limits of one's world, but, *pace* Wittgenstein, limits can be transcended through interpersonal dialogue and intercultural communication. In the same way as the individual can transcend his own local social group, the latter accordingly can transcend itself through language.

> There are, of course, different universes of discourse, but back of all, to the extent that they are potentially comprehensible to each other, lies the logicians' universe of discourse with a set of constants and propositional functions, and anyone using them will belong to that same universe of discourse. It is this which gives a potential universality to the process of communication.
>
> (MSS: 269)

Mead emphasises the intellectual side and conceives of communication first and foremost as a cognitive meeting of minds, and not as an emotional one. Although he mentions sympathy at times, there is, as Axel Honneth (1992: 128) has correctly noticed, no place for love in his system of thought. To find the bonds of love and the ties of sympathy that transform the cold meeting of minds into a general outflowing of hearts, we have to turn to Charles Cooley, that gentle man who brings common humanity into the internal conversation. Continuing the venerable tradition of theories of moral sentiments, from the Cambridge Platonists and the Scottish moralists to the contemporary ethics of care, he focuses explicitly on the affective preconditions of communication that motivate one to exchange perspectives and enter into the world of the other. Like Adam Smith, Cooley conceives of sympathy or fellow feeling as the capacity, yes even the propensity, of the imagination to transport one into the situation of the other and to experience vicariously what the other feels. But unlike Adam Smith, he extracts the individual from the situation of interaction. As a result, he underplays the mutuality of the exchange of perspectives, reducing thereby sympathy to empathy.

In Adam Smith, like in Mead – who overstates his case: 'If there's no response on the part of the other, there cannot be any sympathy' (MSS: 299) – the mutuality of role taking comes better to the fore. The following quotation about the impartial but benevolent spectators who sympathise with a person who suffers fully honours the *syn* of sympathy and the *cum* of conversation:

> As they are continuously placing themselves in his situation, and thence conceiving of emotions similar to what he feels; so he is as constantly placing himself in theirs. As they are constantly considering what they themselves would feel, if they actually were the sufferers, so he is constantly led to imagine in what manner he would be affected if he was only one of the spectators of his own situation. As their sympathy makes them look at it, in some measure, with his eyes, so his sympathy makes him look at it, in some measure with theirs, especially when in their presence and acting under their observation'.
>
> (Smith, 1976: 22)

But before I proceed with my analysis of Mead, let's return to Cooley's one-sided analysis of sympathy. By projecting or, to use the language of contemporary folk psychology, by 'simulating' ourselves into the position of the other, we enter into a 'fellowship in thought' (Cooley, 1983). We look for what we have in common – a common mood, *Stimmung* or feeling that we share – and this commonality unites us in thought. 'The outgoing of the mind into the thought of the other is always, it would seem, an excursion in search of the congenial' (Cooley, 1964: 156).

When we have found what we have in common, we enter not so much in the mind of the other as the other enters into our heart. By opening our heart, we can listen with care to what she says and understand what moves her. It is through sympathetic introspection into the other that we enter into the sentiments of the other. Taking the role of the other, we feel the other's joys and sorrows. Through fellow feeling, our moral sentiments are stimulated and our moral imagination is enhanced at the same time as it is enlarged. Spontaneously, through simulation of ourselves into the position of the other and imaginary identification with him or her, we recognise the other as a fellow human being and welcome him or her in 'the hospitality of the mind' (Cooley, 1964: 146).

While Mead spoke of communication that makes cooperation possible, Cooley talks of communion that fuses minds into a harmonious whole:

> By communion minds are fused into a sympathetic whole, each part of which tends to share the life of all the rest, so that kindness is a common joy, and harshness common pain.... Everything that tends to bring mankind together in larger wholes of sympathy and understanding tends to enlarge the reach of kindly feeling.
>
> (Cooley, 1983: 40, 191)

Of course, initially, the individual is only a member of a given group, community or society. He's in direct contact with his family and neighbours, friends and colleagues, but only indirectly with the friends of his friends, his fellow citizens and other human beings in any part of the world. Nevertheless, through an act of 'sympathetic identification' with concrete others who are not present 'in person', to speak like the phenomenologists, he can vicariously feel what they feel and how they feel by visualising the situation that afflicts them in the eye of his mind. If he can open his mind through language, he can open his heart through sympathy. Extending the boundaries of the world to include those he only knows indirectly, via the media, for instance, he can create in his mind an 'imagined community' and enter into its perspective to adopt the universal stand of an impartial but benevolent spectator, who judges and condemns injustice as unnecessary suffering.[56]

The criterion of judgement is pathocentric, not logocentric, though it must be conceded that the universalist ethics that are founded in reason presuppose that sense of common humanity that makes us not merely human, but humane. Although Cooley's texts are suffused by human warmth and he speaks like a sentimental humanist about the 'dawning of sympathetic renewal' (Cooley, 1964: 158), his sociology of the larger mind exudes the atmosphere of a small American town like Ann Arbor. The man who coined the concept of the 'primary group' effectively limits the reach of affective solidarity to the community. Like love, and out of necessity, sympathy must be selective. 'It is well for a man to open out and take in as much of life as he can organise into a consistent whole', says Cooley (1964: 147), 'but to go beyond that is not desirable.' Unlike Mead, Cooley is not a true cosmopolitan, but a communitarian.[57] From this point of view, Mead's universalism, which is grounded in language, is more generous, even if it lacks the spontaneity, affect and imagination of Cooley. Provided that the common glow of moral sentiments is infused into the community of discourse, we might follow Philip Rieff (1964: xx) and reinterpret 'the categorical imperative not as sublime ethical doctrine but as routine psychological dynamics'.[58]

Intrasubjective intersubjectivity

The self and its other

Reading Mead backwards – from society to the self rather than the other way round – we have analysed the constitution of society as a 'collective subjectivity'. The time has now come to investigate the constitution of the self and the mind, which are at the very heart of his social psychology, *from within*. Mead's main thesis is well known: the mind and the self are social through and through. As personal properties, they emerge out of social life and are linguistically mediated. When it comes to the reflexive capacities of Man, Mead is indeed a social constructivist – and so am I – but he also allows for the existence of non- and pre-reflexive spheres. As a pragmatist he does not deny that prior to an awareness of self and prior to the mind, there is 'the world that is there' (Miller, 1973: 88–102). Neither does he affirm that the world out there arises out of consciousness. It is rather the reverse: consciousness emerges out of, as well as in, our engagement with the world that is there and it is constituted by social interaction and communication with others.

Although we are concerned with the self we have to start with the mind, for the self presupposes thinking. To explain how the mind emerges, Mead has recourse to the gesture and starts his investigation of thinking with Wundt's 'conversation of gestures'. He opens his analysis with the legendary fight between two dogs, but quickly moves on to linguistically mediated communication between humans. The obvious aim of this move is to connect the mind to symbolism and self-consciousness to language. When 'significant symbols' are brought in, the conversation of gestures becomes a meaningful one. Taking each other's role, each of the actors projects himself into the position of the other. Adopting his attitude, he does not only see himself as the other sees him, but he also hears himself as the other hears him. The crucial point is that thanks to the symbolisation of gestures, each actor can arouse in himself the response he's calling out in the other. 'The importance, then, of the vocal stimulus lies in this fact that the individual can hear what he says and in hearing what he says is tending to respond as the other person responds' (MSS: 69–70). As the meaning is a shared one, the interlocutors can understand each other.

To understand each other, the actors have, however, to make the detour via the 'general other' and adopt the perspective of any ordinary language user. Through mutual adjustment of the expectations to one another, they can then, eventually, coordinate their actions. But before they act jointly, there's thinking, and according to Mead, who follows Cooley on this point, thinking is essentially an internalised, implicit and covert conversation the individual has with himself by means of symbols: 'Since higher thought involves language, it always is a kind of imaginary conversation' (Cooley, 1964: 92). 'The internalization of the external conversations of gestures which we carry on with other individuals in the social process is the essence of thinking' (MSS: 47). Thinking may be internal and take place in the individual's mind; it is nevertheless essentially a social phenomenon that finds its origin in communication. The individual is the locus of thought, but the contents of his thought are public. The meanings are not his, but they are common to all subjects who speak the language. Similarly, the symbols he uses are part of the process of communication and belong to a relational field. Out of this field mind arises: 'Out of language emerges the field of mind' (MSS: 47).

In the same way as the thought presupposes language, the self presupposes the other: 'We must be others if we are to be ourselves' (PP: 194).[59] There's no subjectivity without intersubjectivity and, we may add, no intersubjectivity without language. In vaguely Hegelian fashion, Mead defines the self (*ipse*) reflexively as a subject who experiences himself as an object.[60] The subject who minds the other becomes an object to himself. He's both subject and object – or as Adam Smith (1976: 113) has it, both a spectator and an agent – and he knows that he is.[61] He becomes reflexive and conscious of himself as another, thanks to the other (and not owing to the other, as is the case in Sartre's existentialism where the gaze of the other transforms the subject into an object that is under surveillance). By placing himself into the perspective of the other, he becomes an object to himself, but without, however, objectifying or reifying himself in such a way that his subjectivity gets lost (Kögler, 2009). The subject experiences himself as a self only through the mediation of others. Rimbaud's famous dictum (in his letter to Izambard, known as the 'letter of the visionary') – 'Je est un autre/I is another' – thus also holds for the self. To become a self, the subject has to see himself from the external standpoint of another self or, more generally, from any other self who has been fully socialised and can adopt the perspective of the 'participant observer' in the field of social action.

It is important to underscore that the subject does not have an immediate consciousness or unmediated awareness of himself. It is only by imagining what the other thinks of him, by anticipating the response he is going to evoke in the other, that he calls out in himself the response of the other. Through socialisation, the subject is able to get outside of himself not just into the perspective of the concrete other (dad and mum, Peter and Paula), but of a 'general other', any other who knows not only the rules of the game (like an observer), but who also knows how to play it (like a participant). Language is crucial here, because it is largely through the mediation of language that the subject is socialised in such a way that he can enter into the perspective of the generalised other and understand himself as any other understands him. When the response of the general other is thus into the subject – as the stimulus is into the response, according to Dewey – the subject becomes an object to himself and sees his self reflected in the mirror society holds up to him. 'Each to each a looking glass/reflects the other that doth pass' (Cooley, 1964: 184).[62] Contrary to what edifying pragmatists may think, our essence is indeed a 'glassy one' (Rorty, 1979: 42–45). Our self reflects in the other like in a mirror (but beware of analogies, as the images continually change, so does the mirror itself). We become who we are through reflection (like in a mirror) and conversation (like in speech). The point of *Bildung* (or edification) is not only to keep the conversation going, as Rorty has it, but also to find our own subjective truth. It is (partly) out of an image that society holds up to us that each develops a more or less coherent sense of self. To the extent that self is not a given, but a task, we can amend Freud's famous dictum: where the Other was, I shall become.

The self, however, is not a unitary thing. Neither thing, nor unitary, it refers, in fact, to a duality within the subject. 'Two souls, alas, do dwell within his breast.' Insisting once more on the dynamic nature of everything, Mead conceives of the self as a process of alternation between two phases or poles, which he calls, respectively, the 'I' and the 'Me'.[63] The I is linked to spontaneity and creativity, whereas the Me is the organised set of attitudes of the community within the self. Like the impartial spectator, the Me is the 'great inmate of the breast' (Smith, 1976: 130, 134, 262). If the Me represents society as it appears in the mind's eye or, to switch from vision to voice, in the conversation one has with oneself, the I stands for the spontaneous, impulsive reaction toward the collective. The I is aware of the Me and responds to it with varying degrees of creativity. When the I is fully awake and potent, it brings novelty into the conversation. When it is completely knackered, it basically repeats the lines it knows. In reacting creatively to the community, the I changes it, for the better or for the worse. 'The I appears in our experience in memory. It is only when we have spoken that we know what we have said' (MSS: 196). We all know from experience that however much we may rehearse an anticipated conversation in thought, the conversation we will actually have will be different from the one we imagined. It may even derail and go off track, leaving us astonished and the other flabbergasted by what we have just said. 'Did I say that? Where did that come from?' is a common expression of surprise when one realises that the I 'acted out'. 'If the "I" speaks, the "Me" hears' (Mead, 1964b: 143) (but who listens?). And then, retrospectively, when I can look back on myself, I can see that by activating a train of memory in my mind, I have made a new connection between ideas and brought some novelty into the world, which can then be stored and integrated in the Me (my own personal one, but also, through communication, the collective one) as a fund on which I can draw next time when I resume the conversation and try out a new line ('What about morphing this train of memory into a trail? rail? station?', says I to myself).

Conversations on the great society

With the dialogical alternation between the I and the Me, Mead has introduced a transformative dialectics of the self into his semiotic theory of self-reflexivity. In the conversation of the self, everything happens as if the American pragmatist had somehow transposed the dynamics between 'langue' and 'parole' of French semiology into the self. If the I has the capability to reflect on the stand of society and to critically respond to it, the demon of stable social reproduction within the self is silenced from the start. But to become truly critical, innovative and creative, the dialogue has to become properly dialectical. This happens when the dialogue becomes conscious of itself – as in dialogue on dialogue, reflection on reflection, thinking about thinking, *noêsis noesêos* – and the self transcends its own society to project itself in the direction of an ideal society of free, autonomous and self-determining subjects. When dialogue shifts out into dialectics, the dialogue becomes transgressive and integrates the *telos* of universal communication into its own functionings. I like to think that this is what Mead had in mind when, in the final pages of the book, he drew moral and political conclusions and invoked 'the attainment of a universal human society' as 'the ultimate goal of human social progress' (MSS: 310).

From this utopian perspective of a fully reflexive self, formed by a continuous dialogue between a creative I and a future Me, we can overcome the conventional conception of an 'oversocialised self' that has all the trappings not of a person, but of a personage who spends his or her life playing the role society has allocated to him or her.[64] The fully reflexive self incorporates not so much the histrionic figure of the actor (the *prosopeion* of the Greeks and the *persona* of the Romans, meaning the mask) who acts out society's script with a modicum of originality as the one of the director who integrates the different phases of the self into a more or less coherent, harmonious personal project that is at once individual and social, singular and universal. The subject is not 'subjected' to society (the *hypokeimenon* as *subjectum*); she or he is a subject or a person in the emphatic sense of the term – someone who is at the same time fully human, fully social and fully her- or himself.[65]

In Mead as in Dewey, the personal quest for the 'good life' is intrinsically connected to, and inseparable from, 'the search for the great community' (Dewey, 1954: 143–184). In a just and democratic society, the self-determination of the people and the self-realisation of the person are two sides (external/internal) of the same coin. Like in a virtuous circle, there's a continuous morphogenesis between the external and the internal dialectics. In a vibrant democracy, society becomes conscious of itself as a collective subject that determines itself, while its subjects are equally self-conscious as autonomous, yet interdependent subjects: 'There then arises a community in which everyone can be both subject and sovereign, sovereign in so far as he asserts his own rights and recognizes them in others, and subject in that he obeys the laws which he himself makes' (MSS: 287, note 17).

The self-identity of the fully reflexive person of the 'great community' is not conventional, but 'post-conventional' (in the sense that Kohlberg and Habermas have given to this concept). Rather than adopting the perspective of the existing society that judges acts through 'formal-rational' application of the law, she or he imagines an ideal and 'unlimited community of communication' of which she or he is a member and appeals to this higher court to contest the judgement of first instance. 'All intelligent political criticism is comparative' (Dewey, 1954: 110) – the critic sets up a larger community that transcends the specific order of which she or he is part and, taking the attitude of this ideal community, she or he anticipates its realisation in thought and judges the existing society in the name of Reason or, if one prefers, of one's own conscience.

Through the invocation of a higher and larger self, 'practical reason is both socialized and temporalized' (Habermas, 1992: 224) – socialised because the projection of a hypothetical kingdom of ends has to be validated and recognised by one's contemporaries (potentially by all; counterfactually, it even includes predecessors and successors); and temporalised because the idealised form of communication is not only projected into a future, but presupposed as an existing moment of transcendence that grounds critique. Now, to the extent that this future society within one's breast has to be recognised by one's fellows as a legitimate one, individualism and universalism go hand in hand. Entering into the perspective of a larger community that coincides at the limit with the fulfilment of humanity as such, the individual projects and presents a future Me that has to be recognised and validated by the others.[66] Given that this virtual identity is inevitably part of the individual's current identity; given, moreover, that the individual has to get out of himself to take on the perspective of a supposed 'impartial spectator' – 'this demigod within the breast' (Smith, 1976: 131); given, finally, that the individual has to adopt this perspective in the first person – 'never as a mere representative, but always in *propria persona* (Habermas, 1992: 231) – the Me is encouraged to remain him- or herself, even when she or he adopts the perspective of society. As the spectator, thus, necessarily coincides with the actor, socialisation is in no way opposed to individualisation, but most emphatically includes it. To the extent that the individual is socialised into freedom, we can thus conclude that the self is truly dialectical: '"I" that is "We" and "We" that is "I"' (Hegel, 1986: 145).

Imaginary conversations of the impartial spectator

In the same way as socialisation and individualisation are complementary phases within a dynamic process, external communication and internal conversation have to be considered not in opposition to, but in continuity with each other. To show that the internal conversation continues external communication and is destined to return to it to strengthen it, let me refer to the debate between Jürgen Habermas and John Rawls. To maintain the drift of the argument, I will give a pragmatic spin to it and connect it to the theory of moral sentiments. *A Theory of Justice* by John Rawls (1972) is, without doubt, one of the most important books of the second half of the twentieth century. In spite of the fact that every page and footnote of the book has been submitted over and again to analysis and commentary, the book is mostly read as a liberal-Leftist version of rational choice. Consequently, its connections with Adam Smith's theory of sympathy have been overlooked.[67] The guiding idea of the theory of justice is simple: a society would be just if it redistributed the rights and the duties in such a way that every one of its members would subscribe to the principle of fairness without reserve, because it would guarantee the rights and liberties of all, while accepting the social inequalities only to the extent that it compensates the least advantaged.

The theory of justice is a strong theory of the social contract. The main device of this contract theory is the so-called 'original position' (Rawls, 1972: 1–53, esp. 17ff.) in which each would be invited to adopt the perspective of a reasonable yet sympathetic spectator before signing the contract that seals the alliance between the members. Thus, each would imagine him- or herself in the position of the other and when each had adopted the perspective of all the others *seriatim* (each in turn), she or he would hypothetically arrive at the principles of justice for the basic structure of a well-ordered society. Of course, this mechanism of serial identification of all with each and every one can only function on the condition that all make abstraction of their own personal and social situation to retain only what is common to all human beings without distinction. In other words, in imagining oneself in the situation of the other in order to ascend to the superior and encompassing position of the impartial spectator, each is placed under a 'veil of ignorance'. As one would not know if the other were rich or poor, black or white, male or female, we can assume that the principles the members would hypothetically adopt to order their society would be just, not in spite of the anonymous character of the other, but rather because of it.

In Rawls, the justification and validation of the principles of the social contract are the result of the simulated internal conversations the impartial spectator has with his fellow citizens. The spectator sets up an 'inner forum' (MT: 375, 401) in which he confers with himself:

> He asks and answers questions. He develops his ideas and arranges and organizes those ideas as he might do in a conversation with somebody else.... It has not yet become public. But it is part of an act which does become public. We will say that he is thinking out what he is going to say in an important situation, an argument which he is going to present in court, a speech in the legislature. That process which goes on inside of him is only the beginning of the process which is finally carried on in an assembly.
>
> (MT: 402)[68]

In setting up this internal forum within himself everything happens as if the sympathetic spectator, comfortably seated on his couch after a long day of work, had called before his mind any person of his acquaintance and invited him or her into his internal conversation in the evening.[69] In his mind he entreated his friends and acquaintances to sit next to him, discoursing with them on the principles that would be the object of the original agreement. Having left his dear friends, while enclosing them in the depths of his heart, he continued the imaginary conversation by inviting the friends of his friends to the dialogue. Eventually, through an eidetic variation of the friends of his friends, he arrived at a generic and faceless, but well-informed, concerned and caring citizen who would 'look at the system from the standpoint of the least advantaged representative man' (Rawls, 1972: 151).[70]

Through the clever device of representation of the original position, Rawls has thus created a public space in his innermost heart (*in foro interno*, as Kant would say). Habermas objected to the privacy of the internal conversations of his friend. Inviting his American colleague to a public debate, the German philosopher gently convinced his colleague *in actu* of the necessity of continuing the internal conversation with an external communication among equals that takes place in the public sphere.[71] It is by public communication, not just by internal conversation, that speakers progressively arrive at the common and impartial view of the 'Great Judge' (Smith, 1976: 262) or, more affectionately, the 'Great Companion' (James, 1950: I, 316). By inviting not only their friends who share their views, but also the neighbours who don't share them to *voice* their opinions in public, the citizens persuade one another, by means of the force of the better argument, of what is just or wrong.

According to Habermas, moral and political principles become objective and universal through the public use of speech and reason. Indeed, thanks to communication, the citizens can have mutual knowledge of the positions of the others and, thereby, arrive, through overlap of the common content that is publicly communicated and commonly shared, at a consensus on the very principles that order a just society. By transforming the internal conversations that the sympathetic observer has with himself and all the others into a real communication among participants of an external conversation, we move at the same time (in a single breath as it were) from the private (Rawls) to the public (Habermas) use of speech. There's thus an ongoing dialectic – or a 'double morphogenesis', as Archer would say – between internal and external conversations. When the communication is over, the participants can continue the debate internally, and after mature reflection, they can then join again the external conversation. As the internal conversations are constitutive of who we are, individually and collectively, the reconstruction of society cannot be separated from the reconstruction of the human mind. To change society we have to change ourselves, and as the only thing we can change right now is ourselves, why not start social reconstruction with an internal revolution? After all, that is how mankind evolves to higher stages of development. 'Or in short, social reconstruction and self or personality reconstruction are the two sides of a single process – the process of human evolution' (MSS: 309).

Multiple selves

In passing, I have already alluded to the fact that I am a constructivist when it comes to reflexivity and the self. I don't think that realism in sociology is incompatible with constructivism in psychology.[72] I do indeed believe that we construct ourselves in and through internal conversations. We do not merely have such conversations with ourselves and others; to the extent that we constitute ourselves through discourse, we *are* these conversations. Of course, we do not exactly construct ourselves like houses, but we are building sites nevertheless. By describing the self as a 'fabrication' I do not aim to dismiss it, nor do I join the ranks of once-fashionable postmodernists. On the contrary, it as a humanist and archeo-modernist that I welcome the constructivist emphasis on self-empowerment and the capability for self transformation and self-realisation in and through language and conversation.

If hard-line realists find constructivism objectionable, I suspect that they will even be less inclined to accept my next proposal. We have already seen that the self is multiple. It includes an I and a Me. Being a declinative, the self not only incorporates an I and a Me, which I address as a You ('Tuism'); it also includes the whole gamut of persons and things it reflexively refers to as a pronoun. The I would not be a self if it could not distance itself from itself and refer to itself as You, She or He or It and position itself with reference to a We, a You and a They. As all these persons are, one way or another, enclosed in ourselves, I propose to take the reference to 'ourselves' literally and think of it in the plural. Although very few people suffer from 'dissociative identity disorder' (formerly known as multiple personality disorder) and most of us succeed most of the time in keeping our alter egos in a functioning whole, I would nevertheless like to defend the thesis that we are all multiples.[73] For sure, I wouldn't go as far as Pirandello and suggest that, like Moscarda, we are 'one, nobody and a hundred thousand'.[74] I am not that mad, but I would nevertheless like to explore the thesis of the multiple self as a reasonable one.

Mead affirms: 'A multiple personality is in a certain sense normal' (MSS, 142). To make sense of this statement, as well as of what I take to be his real vision of the person, I'll have recourse, in a first moment, to William James and, in a second one, to Bakhtin. In *The Principles of Psychology* (especially the phenomenal chapter 10 on the consciousness of the self), James brilliantly develops a pragmatist theory of the self. The self is not a thing, but a complex process (or 'function') of unification that integrates the objects that appear in the 'stream of thought' into a whole. It does so by making a basic distinction between the inside and the outside. What does not belong to the self, and is in this sense alien to it, is left outside – it is 'not me'; what belongs to it is inside – it is 'Me'. Like Luhmann, James conceives of the self as a complex autopoietic system that splits the whole universe into two halves. Each of us makes a selection that is particular to him or her. 'My experience is what I agree to attend to. Without selective interest, experience is an utter chaos' (James, 1950: I, 402). When the others hold up a mirror to us in which 'we see oursel's as ithers see us', to quote the Scottish poet Robert Burns, we also make a careful selection of the representations. Those we identify with go up into the self; the others are left out. Based on the selective process of attribution that each of us makes on an ongoing basis, the Self emerges at the totality of contents of the universe that we are tempted to call by the name of me:

> *In its widest possible sense, a man's Self is the sum total of all that he* can *call his*, not only his body and his psychic powers, but his clothes and his house, his wife and children, his ancestors and friends, his reputation and works, his lands and horses, and yacht and bank account.
>
> (James, 1950: I, 291)

As this powerful and frequently cited quotation suggests, people and things in the environment belong to the self, as far as they are felt as 'mine'. In trying to systematise the contents of the self, James first distinguishes between the I and the Me, by which he means, respectively, the self as subject (or agent) and the self as object (or spectator).[75] The latter is further subdivided into three hierarchically ordered 'constituents', with the 'spiritual Me' at the top, the 'social Me' in the middle and the 'material Me' at the bottom.[76] With Paranjpe (1998: 78), we can schematically represent this conceptual framework as follows:

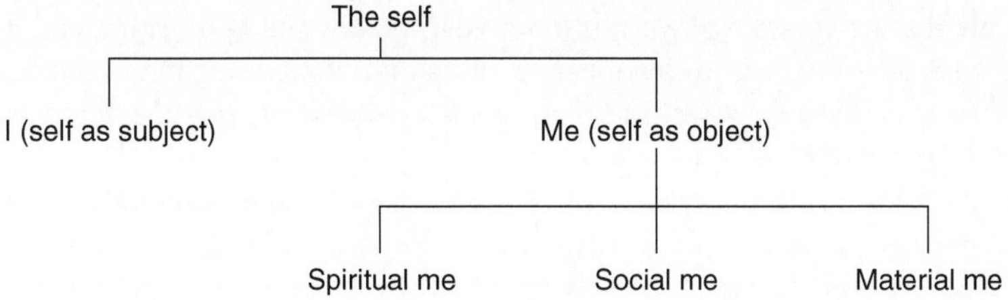

The material Me (or material self) includes the body, clothes, homes and other possessions I am attached to (e.g. my nose, my glasses, my car, my office, my books). My body is the archetype of things I possess. All that is part of the material self is, in fact, felt as an extension of my body. Things have a meaning and a use. The objects I encounter in my surroundings are rather variegated. They can be gifts, works of art, consumer goods, commodities, tools, utilities, instruments, technologies, whatever. Whatever they are, they are invariably and inevitably signs and, therefore, social.[77] The social Me or social self involves the many social roles we play. James does not only argue that we have as many social selves as we have roles, but, most interestingly, he ties roles to recognition, affirming that we have as many selves as there are groups we care about. 'Properly speaking, a man has as many social selves as there are individuals who recognize him and carry an image of him in their mind' (James, 1950: I, 294). The desire to be recognised by others is strong, so strong that it is a vital need. Non-recognition (owing to indifference and invisibility, or even worse, outright hostility and rejection) may be so painful that it mortifies the self. Although the person is not identical to his social persona, any attack on the latter will be felt by the former: 'To wound any one of these his images is to wound him' (James, 1950: I, 294). Sometimes a person's social selves may be at variance with one another, even painfully so, as any academic with a deadline and a lover (not to mention kids!) will be able to confirm – 'So many books, so little time.' One's role-set is not necessarily consistent. We all have our internal contradictions. To maintain the appearances – 'our face' or the 'face of the other', as Goffman would say – we routinely 'backstage' parts of our social self. Between verbally articulated positions and extra-discursive postures incongruities do occur, like in the following cases:

> When the sworn-to-chastity and committed-to-moral-uplift clergy abuse their charges, the misalignment between their preaching and action is painfully obvious. The same goes for police using their night sticks for purposes unspecified in their manuals, judges whose court behavior makes a mockery of the notion of judicious temperament, teachers whose emotional littering vitiates the emotional intelligence they seek to impart to their students.
>
> (Shalin, 2007: 212)

One cannot please everyone, and certainly not all at the same time. One cannot even please oneself and be all the things one would love to be:

> Not that I would not, if I could, be both handsome and fat and well dressed, and a great athlete, and make a million a year, be a wit, a bon-vivant, and a lady-killer, as well as a philosopher; a philanthropist, statesman, warrior, and African explorer, as well as a 'tone-poet' and saint. But the thing is simply impossible.
>
> (James, 1950: I, 309)

Choosing is losing. As we cannot actualise all possible selves, we have to set up a list of possible characters we could live with, review the list carefully, arrange its items 'in an hierarchical scale according to their worth' (James, 1950: I, 314) and, finally, pick out the one on which to stake our salvation. The self that is compossible with the highest value of the person and that would be 'worthy of approving recognition' by an ideal judge, such as God, if he exists, or any other imaginary 'Great Companion' who incorporates humanity in exemplary fashion, corresponds to the real self.[78]

With the introduction of a higher, ideal spectator who ranks and evaluates the representations the actor has of himself impartially, yet sympathetically, we arrive at the spiritual Me, which constitutes the apex of the Self. Unlike the material and the social selves, which refer to evanescent objects that appear in the stream of thought as it were from outside, the spiritual self looks at the process of reflection from within and identifies within thinking the thinker it wants to be. Representing the higher aspirations of the ego that the subject admires and identifies with, the spiritual self refers to the inner core of the person. If we conceive of the self as a spiral of concentric circles that form as it were a citadel, the spiritual self is 'a sanctuary within the citadel' of inner life (James, 1950: I, 297, 303) from which all volitive acts seem to emanate.[79] Although it appears within thought as the inner sanctum, it is not thought, but felt: 'When it is found, it is felt' (James, 1950: I, 299). And when it is attacked, it hurts badly, so badly, one would be willing to give, or even take, one's life for it.

Armed with this trinity (one person, three selves), we can now return to Mead's sociogenesis of the self to counter the argument that he 'oversocialises' the self. As a matter of fact, he doesn't, but by failing to distinguish explicitly between the spiritual and the social self, he has not sufficiently made clear the connection between his social psychology and his moral psychology. Whereas the former suggests that we have as many selves as the situation of interaction requires and that we can change our roles like we change our shirts and socks,[80] the latter indicates that the self can only become a coherent one if the individual integrates all of his or her roles into an exemplary and authentic life project that is at once universal and singular, moral and personal.

With James, we have distinguished three main selves which may each, in turn, contain many sub-selves that do not necessarily cohere. These three selves are not substances, however, but aspects within a single process of 'selving' within the person. My possessions, my roles, my aspirations are all part of a complex process that can be analysed from different angles. When I speak about my body, my profession and my vocation, I'm not speaking of different existences, but of different perspectives on the same thing – my existence, my life, me. People evolve. They age, mature and, eventually, die. My bodily Me is not what it used to be. I'm getting a bit of a stomach these days and my hair starts greying. My social Me is expanding as I'm learning new roles. By moving continents I have made new friendships, while other ones are deteriorating. My spiritual Me has undergone significant changes too. I have become a mystical atheist. Over the years a lot of changes have taken place. Like a boat that is changed plank by plank, I have refurbished myself. What, if anything, has remained the same through all these major changes in every aspect of my self?

The question of unity within diversity or sameness through change is a thorny one. James called the philosophical question of identity – is there 'a Self of all the other selves' (James, 1950: I, 297) that remains invariant through changes? – 'the most puzzling puzzle' (James, 1950: I, 330) with which psychology has to deal.[81] Needless to say that I do not pretend to solve this puzzle that has occupied the best minds for millennia (Taylor, 1989; Paranjpe, 1998). Instead of a solution, I propose to rephrase it as a problem of collective subjectivities, but now the problem of coordination appears, as Elster (1985: 16) says, as 'an intrapersonal, inter-temporal problem of collective action'. Within the person, the problem of coordination can best be thought of as a problem of orchestration between various voices within the internal conversation. Like in a polyphonic orchestra the point is not to silence the independent melodic voices, but to integrate them into an evolving texture so that each new voice fits into a harmonious whole. In accordance with the mereological considerations of pragmatism, one might even think of music with double or multiple choirs that may be separated from each other, as can be observed in performances of sixteenth-century music or, closer to us, in Britten's *War Requiem*.

The metaphor of the polyphonic novel was proposed by the Russian philosopher and semiotician Mikhail Bakhtin in *Problems of Dostoevsky's Poetics*.[82] In this work he rebuts critics who characterised Dostoevsky's method as a Hegelian narrative in which two positions strive for ascendency only to be merged in a synthesis at the end. Inspired by Cassirer's philosophy of symbolic forms, Bakhtin transforms the plurality of cultural forms into a plurality of voices that are in continuous dialogue with each other. He develops the idea that in Dostoevsky's works there's no single, authoritative author at work who plans everything rigidly and in detail (like in the Soviet Union), but that the author gives significant leeway to the characters of his novels. Raskolnikov, Stavrogrin, Ivan Karamazov and the Great Inquisitor are independent, relatively autonomous figures, each with their own character and their own view on the world that unfolds as the heroes present their own unique perspective on the world. Each has a personal life and a personal view of the world. Instead of a multitude of characters and fates within a unified objective world, as is the case in Tolstoy,

Dostoevsky gives voice to a plurality of consciousnesses and worlds. In this polyphony of voices, the voice of the narrator resides beside the voices of the characters and has no greater authority than any other of the voices. Voices intersect and interact dialogically, and as in hermeneutics, they mutually illuminate biases and limitations of the positions they represent.

If we use this polyphonic model to make sense of the internal conversations we have with ourselves, we can understand the self as a choir in which a multiplicity of voices resonate and intermingle. Within the conversation, different voices pop up. They may well be fragments we have picked up from newspapers, books or conversations with others. Coming from different sources, places, times, traditions and generations, the voices are necessarily heterogeneous. Voices can speak through other voices ('ventriloquation') or in different idioms. I swear in French, count in Dutch and when I prepare my classes which I teach in Portuguese, I take notes in English, even if the author is German.

The voices I confer with in dialogue represent alternative perspectives on the world and myself that are adopted by other people (friends, family, colleagues, opinion makers, etc.). The intrasubjective conversation is an intersubjective and dialogical one. The I listens to the interlocutors, which may be aliases of himself or represent different selves of others, asks them questions or gives them answers. Playing through the same theme, like love, competition or suicide, to name but a few, in a multiplicity of voices that represent different positions on the same issue and illuminate it from various angles, the I engages in a dialogue with itself. This dialogue is an ongoing one. While nothing guarantees that the voices come to a consensus – they may very well be incompatible or contradictory – the questions they raise and the various answers they give explain why the intrasubjective intersubjective conversations only come to an end when we die. When we die, they die with us, though others may continue their conversation with us. It is only when we are forgotten by all that our conversation goes out like a candle.[83]

Coda

Instead of a conclusion, let me end with a confession: I have not written the text I intended to write. I wanted to offer some disguised autobiographic meditations on the teleosis of the self – from fracture to full reflexivity and beyond – but ended up grafting pragmatism onto hermeneutics. Instead of developing a transformative hermeneutics of the self, I have only worked out a methodological preamble to it. As this chapter is already far too long, I will keep my internal conversations internal and not make them public for now. One day, in a sequel to this text, I will offer an onto-teleo-theological reading of internal conversations and articulate it in a dialectical sequence of three successive moments. The first moment is ontological. Following Heidegger's and Gadamer's turn to language, I will argue that, like interpretation, conversation is not simply a method to get access to the self, but a way of being that is constitutive of the self. With

Ricoeur and Macintyre, I will sketch out the narrative conception of the self as a mid-way that allows one to steer a course between the exalted self-sufficiency of the Cartesian cogito and its deliberate fracturing that follows the Nietzschean assault on the self. The second moment is teleological. Inspired by Karl Jaspers' *Existenzphilosophie*, I will try to develop an ethics of existence in the form of a developmental moral psychology. To do so, I will not hesitate to reorganise Archer's four distinctive modes of internal speech into a teleological sequence that starts with the fracturing of the self in times of existential crisis and ends with the fully metareflexive self who is in control of its own destiny. The third moment is theological. I will make some of the theological concepts that were smuggled into the internal conversation explicit and suggest that the internal conversation is really an inner conversion of the self. Translating the doctrine of the salvation of the soul into secular language, I will sketch out the contours of a humanist ethics of authenticity in which we become who we are by pursuing 'the good life with and for others in just institutions' (Ricoeur, 1990: 202).

Notes

1 Like in old-fashioned letters, I extend the memorable conversations I had with the honourable members of the Reflexivity Forum in Warwick and in the shadow of Kenilworth Castle into print. Once you're into the conversation, it is indeed hard to get out of it.... Like in all virtuous circles, the point is, however, to enter it properly and to transform the circle into a spiral that points beyond itself to what sustains it: gratitude. I especially would like to thank Margaret Archer, Andrew Sayer, Norbert Wiley, Vincent Colapietro and Pierpaolo Donati for inspiration. I also would like to acknowledge various types of support – material (texts), intellectual (ideas), moral (advice) and emotional (care) – from various persons, notably Fernando Suárez Müller, Harry Kunneman, Hubert Hermans, Marc de Leeuw, Hans Herbert Kögler, Nikos Mouzelis, Gabriel Peters, Thiago Pontes, Rachel Herdy, Cynthia Hamlin, Jennifer Greenleaves, Marguerite Labrunie and Tatiana Rotondora.

2 All references to Gadamer come from the *Gesammelte Werke*. The first number refers to the volume, the second to the page.

3 That thinking is dialogical and takes the form of a conversation is perhaps the central idea of Gadamer's hermeneutics. It is not only at the heart of his habilitation on Plato's dialectical ethics (V: 5–163, esp. 15–48), but also of his communicative elaboration of Heidegger's lonely metaphysics – from *Sein zum Tode* (being unto death) to *Sein zum Texte* (being unto text) – into a theory of being that foregrounds language. 'From dialectics back to dialogue and back to conversation' (II: 368) – that is indeed Gadamer's way into the question concerning being. By thinking through the Socratic dialectics of question and answer, he has expanded Plato's definition of thought as internal conversation of the soul with itself into a full blown philosophy of language as the medium for understanding ourselves, the world and what is beyond language. On conversation (*Gespräch*), see Gadamer, I: 383ff., II: 6ff., 58ff., 151ff., 207ff., 500ff., X, 104ff., 267ff.

4 Perelman and Olbrecht-Tyteca (1992: §7) remind us that the philosopher always addresses himself to a 'universal audience' and argues in the hope of getting its approval for his arguments. This approval is not a factual one, however, but a counterfactual one that is assumed as soon as one starts writing. Even the agreement that there's no consensus to be had on the only issues that really matter – What can I hope? How shall I live? What should I do? – counts as a consensus of sorts.

5 *In medias res* is a literary and artistic technique where the narrative starts in the middle of the story instead of from its beginning. Here I take *res* in its original sense. In Roman law it does not refer to the thing, but to the cause, to that which is in litigation:

> The primitive meaning of *res* oscillates between the ideas of litigation, the litigious situation, and the object that gives rise to contention.... Fundamentally, the 'thing' is the 'cause'.... If *res* is the object, it is first and foremost a debated object, subject to a difference of opinion, a common object that brings together two opposing protagonists into a single relation.
>
> (Thomas, 1980: 416–417)

6 As always, the identity politics of the personal pronouns raise intractable problems: should I refer to the subject as he or she, use the neutral or try to express my own (unstable) identity into my text? Even if I often use the generic masculine to refer to subjects, persons, individuals and actors, I trust no one will infer that I think that women have no subjectivity, personality, individuality or agency!

7 In this chapter I explore convergences between hermeneutics and pragmatism to bring the conversation back into language. To make the point that every conversation is part of a larger conversation, that conversation is always dialogical and that access to reality is always mediated by symbols and signs, I draw on Gadamer and Peirce, but similar arguments can be found in Bakhtin's sociological philosophy of language (which I only recently discovered). Cf. Bakhtin (1977, esp. ch. 6).

8 Whereas Anthony Giddens formulated the theorem of the 'duality of structure' that became the hallmark of structuration theory through a skilful neo-Wittgensteinian interpretation of the relation of co-implication of *langue* and *parole* in Saussure's *Cours de linguistique générale*, I'm trying to arrive at a similar position through a reading of Gadamer's dialogical interpretation of the hermeneutic circle in Heidegger's *Sein und Zeit* (Gadamer, 1999: I, 270ff.; II, 57–66). In the original formulation of structuration theory, the echoes of his encounter with Gadamer's hermeneutic dialectics can still be heard: 'Considered as a structure – and this is crucial – natural language is a condition of the generation of speech acts and the achievement of dialogue, but also the unintended consequence of the production of speech and the accomplishment of dialogue' (Giddens, 1976: 127).

9 The debate between Habermas and Gadamer obscures what the former inherited (*traditur*) from the latter and what he later did to refashion it – to insert speech act theory with its validity claims into language as an operator of Reason. This debate was as much about the relation between tradition and critique – about the place of the tradition of critique within humanism – as it was about the relation between philosophy and the social sciences. While Habermas is definitely a hermeneutician, Gadamer is not a sociologist. As he said in a letter to Richard Bernstein: 'Admittedly, to make me into a sociologist is something no one will succeed in doing, not even myself' (Bernstein, 1983: 265).

10 *Avant la lettre*: I do not ignore nor do I aim to belittle the pre-, the non- and the post-linguistic. But before I concede the point, I want to defend the argument and think it through till the end. Gestures (Mead), sensations and emotions (James), laughing and crying (Plessner), ethnomethods (Garfinkel), habits (Merleau-Ponty), operations and calculations (Piaget), etc. – all these embodied and expressive phenomena are pre-linguistic (or 'pre-predicative', to use more phenomenological language), but that does not mean that they cannot enter the internal conversation or that they cannot be expressed in language. As a matter of fact, by thinking, and *a fortiori* by speaking about them, their tacit dimension is brought into the open.

11 Compare and contrast with William James (1950: I, 226): 'Absolute insulation, irreducible pluralism, is the law.'

12 Cartesian conversations on intersubjective monadology: following K.O. Apel and V. Hösle (rather than Habermas and Mead), Suárez Müller (2004: 48–57) radicalises the

linguistic turn within the tradition of absolute idealism and conceives of internal dialogue as the ultimate foundation (*Letztbegründung*) of thought. Unlike Descartes, he does not smuggle the ego into the cogito, but starts from thinking as a precondition of doubting, affirms that thinking is dialogical and concludes that universal sympathy is the telos of dialogue. But even if we accept that the absolute is thinking, that thinking is dialogical and that dialogue presupposes and projects an infinite community of conversation, if the charge of solipsism is to be avoided, it still has to be shown that this never-ending dialogue is not only intrasubjective, but truly intersubjective. The other is within me without me.

13 In an attempt to put the interdiscipline of 'humanistics' (applied humanist studies) on new foundations, Harry Kunneman (2005) has introduced existential reflection on processes of learning as a third mode of knowledge, somewhere in between pure academic blue-sky research (mode 1) and applied interest-driven research (mode 2). To the extent that the social sciences are committed to the advancement of norms, values and beliefs that further the process of humanisation, they are part of the third mode of knowledge production.

14 The social sciences deal with nature in two respects: to the extent that nature is human (is nature 'for us' and therefore culture) or, inversely, to the extent that culture has crystallised into 'second nature' (alienated culture as pseudo-nature). With nature and culture at opposite ends, the social sciences deal both with the humanisation of nature and the degradation of culture into pseudo-inert facticity. They do not merely analyse these processes, but as normative and practical sciences that consciously continue the humanist tradition, they are animated by the desire to reactivate the practices that keep the dialectics between nature and culture going. As I have analysed the dehumanisation of the social world at length elsewhere (Vandenberghe, 2009), I will focus in this chapter on the relation between culture and practices.

15 As Dilthey (1958: VII, 148) says in his foundation of *Geisteswissenschaften*:

> The range of the human sciences is determined by the objectification of life in the external world. The human spirit can only understand what it has created.... Everything on which man has actively impressed his stamp forms the object of the human sciences.

16 I have amended Geertz's (1973: 5) quotation – 'Man is an animal suspended in webs which he has himself spun' (which he actually borrowed from Cassirer, but without saying so) – by leaving out the Weberian emphasis on action and the subjectivism it implies. Although culture is indeed man-made, one might as well reverse the formula and say that culture transforms the animal into a human being and that, therefore, it makes Man.

17 Giving a dialectical twist to his own thought, Bhaskar (1993: 394) has introduced alethic truth into critical realism. Referring to the real reasons, grounds or reasons of things, alethic truth can be understood as the ontologically deep truth of things (as different and perhaps even opposed to the truth of propositions). At the deepest level, this truth exists independently of its verification by science, though all science necessarily and inevitably presupposes it. In more mystical vein, Heidegger's *aletheia* will reappear in Bhaskar's (2002) ultimate philosophy of meta-Reality as the 'cosmic envelope' one can access and identify with in and through meditation on the unity of being.

18 Following Gadamer, I speak of language as both background and horizon of communication and experience, but language is only a proxy for the 'objective spirit' of the Hegelians, the 'symbolic forms' of the neo Kantians, the 'forms of life' of the neo-Wittgensteinians or the 'life-world' of the phenomenologists.

19 Provided one does not abandon the 'emic' perspective that discloses the realm of meaning from within – as opposed to the 'etic' perspective that objectifies meaning structures in a 'packet of relations' (Lévi-Strauss), hermeneutics and structuralism are

not always and not necessarily exclusive. In his important contribution to the theory of interpretation of *Weltanschauung*, the young Mannheim (1964: 91–154) tried to integrate the three strata of meaning (objective-structural, subjective-expressive and documentary-hermeneutic) into a phenomenologically inspired and hermeneutically sensitive historicist sociology of culture. Closer to us, Ricoeur's (1969) impressive detour through structuralism, semiotics, Marxism and psychoanalysis, has convincingly shown that one can use the 'etic' perspective to better understand meaning. As he put it, forcefully and elegantly: 'To explain more is to understand better' (Ricoeur, 1986: 25).

20 The fact that the philosopher-sociologist brings in her own horizons when she investigates the textures of meaning raises interesting questions about the hermeneutics of hermeneutics. Human investigators reveal the sense and reference of the word not simply by lifting the obscuring veil, but by making it transparent through language. Heidegger's infamous *Destruktion* (aka deconstruction) does not destroy; it clears the sedimentations of language and removes the 'tissue of ideas' (Husserl) in order to return 'to the things themselves' (*zu den sachen selbst*).

21 Heidegger was the first to call attention to Hölderlin's famous passage on 'the dialogue that we are' (Grondin, 1997). But unlike Gadamer, Heidegger followed Hölderlin in understanding this dialogue as a conversation that goes on not between mortals, but between mortals and the Gods.

22 What matters to Heidegger is not Man, but Being and what comes into being by Man. What Heidegger (1964) says about thinking in his *Letter on Humanism* also holds for language:

> Thinking is, in sum, the thinking of Being. The genitive has a double sense. The thinking is of Being in so far as thinking that partakes of Being belongs to Being. Thinking is at the same time the thinking of Beings in so far as it belongs and listens to Being (34).... Not Man but Being is essential (84).... What matters is to put *humanitas* at the service of the truth of Being, but without the humanism in a metaphysical sense (138).

23 Anti-Cartesian as ever, Peirce excludes solipsism as a mere metaphysical afterthought to communication: 'But when a person finds himself in the society of other, he is just as sure of their existence as of his own, though he may entertain a metaphysical theory that they are all hypostatically the same ego' (Peirce 1931–1958: 6, 436, *apud* Colapietro, 1989: 79).

24 In terms of intellectual filiations the sequence goes as follows: Colapietro *genuit* Wiley *genuit* Archer *et* Collins. Colapietro worked out Peirce's semiotics of the self, Wiley proposed a synthesis of Peirce and Mead, Archer picked it up from Wiley in her struggle against Giddens and so did Collins in his attempt to integrate Mead and Goffman in a Durkheimian micro-sociology. Personally, I discovered the fascinating theme of internal conversations via Archer, but coming from critical theory, I had already been prepared for it by Craig Calhoun's (1995: 50) offhand observation that Habermas had neglected intrapersonal dialogue. As Nobbie Wiley has been exploring the continent of internal speech for 20 years on his own and has gone deeper into the recesses of the mind than any of us, he deserves at least an honourable mention (cf. *Theory. The Newsletter of the Research Committee on Sociological Theory of the ISA*, Spring/Summer, 2008).

25 For a more extended presentation of Archer's morphogenetic social theory, see Archer (2011), as well as my review of the first four volumes of 'The Archers' (Vandenberghe, 2005). For a more personal overview of the two decades it took her to develop the morphogenetic approach, see Archer (2007b).

26 The category of reflexivity is so rich and so confusing that I simply prefer to abstain from it (see, however, Vandenberghe, 2006b). I have the impression that Archer has transformed the French verb *réfléchir* (to think) into a concept. In her critique of

reflexive modernisation theory (Lash, Giddens, but above all Beck and his German colleagues (Bonβ, Lau, Holzer) who creatively use the systemic concept of reflexivity to thematise 'the dialectical suicide of whole systems' (Beck and Holzer, 2004: 165)), she dismisses the Luhmannian notion of systemic reflexivity – 'no real meaning can be attached to systemic reflexivity' (Archer 2007a: 30) – but like Donati (2011) I think she does it to her own peril.

27 'Habit means a special sensitiveness or accessibility to certain classes of stimuli, standing predilections and aversions, rather than bare recurrence of specific acts. It means will' (Dewey, 2002: 42). In William James, the habits are rather more sturdy. His philosophy of habits is, in the first instance, 'a chapter in physics' (James, 1950: I, 105). Approvingly, he quotes the Duke of Wellington: 'Habit a second nature! Habit is ten times nature' (James, 1950: I, 120).

28 In my own take on Bourdieu (see Chapter 3, p. 213), I had collocated Blumer's 'self-interaction' and Habermas' 'rational communication' in between the field and the habitus, but I concur that internal conversations is more elegant and powerful. To unhinge Bourdieu's system, one could also bring in a little existential crisis and see what that does to reproduction. I thank Gabriel Peters for this astute observation.

29 Although faith is, undoubtedly, the ultimate concern, it should be noticed that the internal conversations and the sequence that interlink concerns, projects and practices into a personal *modus vivendi* do not necessarily lead to heaven. 'There's nothing idealistic here, because "concerns" can be ignoble, "projects" illegal and "practices" illegitimate' (Archer, 2007b: 42). It would be interesting, though definitely not uplifting, to empirically track the internal conversations of the youngsters from the *favelas* in Brazil who have been enrolled by the *narcotrafico* and transformed into 'soldiers' who attack to defend their turf and kill in order not to die. In-depth interviews with members of the boardrooms of the failing banks (who, among themselves, refer to their clients as 'muppets') would also confirm that a reflexive life is not necessarily virtuous.

30 Popper wavers between Plato and Mannheim. His 'world 3' contains both eternal entities that the mind 'discovers' (e.g. like perfect numbers (6, 28, 496, 8128, etc.) and socio-historical items that it 'invents' (like his own critical rationalism and his unfalsifiable theory of falsification). It should be noted that to the extent that the self is genuinely a hermeneutic and dialectical one that emerges in and through internal conversations, it belongs itself to world 3 (I thank Fernando Suárez Müller for this observation).

31 By turning inwards, Archer consciously avoids the linguistic turn. Unlike Apel (1973: II, 178–219) and Habermas (1991: 9–33), she does not consider Peirce's semiotic transformation of Kant's transcendental philosophy as a first step of the critique of the philosophy of consciousness – a first step that seeks to reintegrate consciousness within language and to understand the internal conversation as an intrasubjective extension of intersubjective communication.

32 In 'Choosing among projects of action', Alfred Schütz (1962: 67–96), who was heavily influenced by pragmatism (James and Dewey), also described the temporalities involved in the act of 'fancying and projecting' of open possibilities of action in the future perfect tense (*modo futuro exacti*). The actor projects himself in fantasy into the future when the anticipated project will already have been accomplished. 'Projecting, as we have seen, is retrospection anticipated in fantasy' (Schütz, 1962: 87).

33 When the self gives its *fiat*, the projected action is executed and thought 'gears into the outer world and alters it'. Twenty years later, I still vividly remember when I first read the Austrian's distinction between 'overt' action or work and 'covert' action, the latter being described as a 'mere performance' of mental operations that can be revoked and annulled at any time. The distinction between action 'by commission' and 'by omission' ('purposive refraining from action') is also pertinent, but, of course,

unlike Archer, Schütz was not thinking about life-projects and life-courses, but about stretches of action and doxic modifications of the pragmatic attitude.

34 Archer is highly critical not just of the linguistic turn in philosophy, but also of the micro-revolution in sociology. Like Colin Campbell, whose trenchant critique of 'international situationalism' she fully endorses, she seems convinced that, notwithstanding all the waffle about the meaning of action, the preoccupation with the situation of action explains why 'there is no action theory in contemporary sociology' (Campbell, 1996: 36). In order to correct some of the excesses of the inheritors of Schütz, Goffman and Garfinkel, she has, however, bent the stick the other way: intra-action and subjectivity are overemphasised, while interaction and intersubjectivity are underemphasised (even within the self). Although I understand why Archer and Campbell want a concept of the self that allows for unmediated experiences of reality, as in 'teaching oneself to swim' (interaction with nature), 'a solo mountaineer learning hand and footholds' (developing practical skills) or 'solitary contemplative prayer' (communion with God) (Archer, 2006: 322), I think a crash course in science studies should be sufficient to effortlessly deconstruct all of the adduced examples.

35 Theunissen's *Der Andere* is still, by far, the best book on intersubjectivity and dialogue within the phenomenological tradition (from Husserl, Heidegger and Sartre to Buber, Löwith and Jaspers).

36 Unlike neo-Darwinism, pragmatism is not a dog-eat-dog philosophy; in spite of the American business ethics that sometimes resonates in some of its most famous maxims (the meaning of the 'cash value' of action, the stress on 'expediency', the necessity to 'adapt' and 'innovate', etc.), it is not utilitarian either. No doubt their Darwinism is better approached via *The Expression of Emotions in Man and Animals* than in *The Evolution of Species*. Towards the end of his life, Peirce did not hesitate to write about evolutionary love ('agapasm'), Mead is all about cooperation, Dewey about solidarity and participatory democracy, while Cooley, that kindred spirit, waxes lyrical about sympathy and community.

37 'In the beginning was the relation…' (Buber). According to Donati (1991: 66, 80), this is 'the most general presupposition in the metaphysical environment of sociological theory'. I have explored Simmel's interactionist and structuralist theories of the relation elsewhere (Vandenberghe, 2002). It would be worthwhile to compare directly Dewey, Simmel and Mauss (without having to pass through the first Chicago School or via Durkheim), but this can obviously not be done here.

38 In the social sciences, the 'mereological' connections between parts and wholes have recently been theorised to great effect by Marilyn Strathern (1991, 1996) to analyse the contextualising interpretation of complex phenomena. In her anthropology of Melanesia, she shows that elements can be part of different systems that are internally related to each other via part–whole relations that can be described differently from different angles and thereby redescribed as something else.

39 Pragmatism's post-Darwinian philosophy is a form of vitalist monadology. Like Leibniz, the pragmatist believes that there are no gaps in nature (Peirce's 'synechism'), that everything is alive (vitalism) and that the universe is full of organisms (behaviorism) and relations (relativism). Or, to quote Leibniz himself: 'Each portion of matter may be conceived as like a garden full of plants and like a pond full of fishes. But each branch of every plant, each member of every animal, each drop of its liquid parts is also some such garden or pond' (*Monadology*, §67).

40 For a more fine-grained phenomenological exploration of the mental activities that go into ordinary inquiries of everyday life, see Schütz's analysis of 'relevances' and 'typicalities' (Schütz and Luckmann, 1973: I, 182–241).

41 For a remarkable pragmatic analysis of the inversion of ends and means within the context of action, where the ends appear as the result (at the end) of a continuous process of adaptation and reorientation of action, see Joas (1992: 218–244).

42 See, however, Dewey's important chapter on communication in *Experience and*

Nature (Dewey, 1925: 165–207). All references to Mead's books will be abbreviated as follows: PP (*The Philosophy of the Present*, 1932); MSS (*Mind, Self and Society*, 1934); MT (*Movements of Thought in the Nineteenth Century*, 1936) and PA (*The Philosophy of the Act*, 1938).

43 Or, as Gabriel Tarde (1999: I, 58) would say: 'Everything is a society, every fact is a social fact.' Of late, Latour has rediscovered Tarde. One of the great merits of actor–network theory (ANT) is that it has brought the materiality/sociality of things back into sociology (cf. Pels *et al.*, 2002). But whereas Latour does not hesitate to ascribe agency to objects, he does not sufficiently take into account the materiality and affectivity of the human subject. What is lacking in his 'interobjectivity' is precisely ... 'intersubjectivity'. Like ethnomethodology, ANT remains stuck in the phenomenalism of the philosophy of observation and does not make the transition to a proper phenomenology of things (Vandenberghe, 2006a). For a sociological account of liminal sociality that takes into account the affective nature of our effective engagement with things, see Knorr-Cetina (1997).

44 Sociologists tend to stick to their guns and limit their understanding of Mead to his theory of the mind, self and society, to use the famous title in which his lectures on social psychology were collected. If they would read on, they would discover that this 'process sociology' is the epitome of his cosmology, metaphysics, ethics, his philosophy of the act, his theory of time and space, etc. For a good account of the larger picture of his mind by one of his former students, see Miller (1973).

45 The capability to exchange perspectives and take the attitude of the other is a universal one that is built into every language. It is grounded in the pragmatics of personal pronouns that differentiates the I, the You and the It, as well as the milieu of activity they are directed at – the It being related to technical manipulation and scientific objectification, the You to intersubjective relations with the other and the I to the expression of the self and the symbolisation of thoughts. As Jean-Marc Ferry (1991: I, 82) states in his intriguing reconstruction of universal grammar:

> To communicate among themselves, the subjects differentiate their objects into addressees that belong to the category of the third person and those that belong to the second person. As speakers, they themselves belong to the first person. It is only by knowing it that they are subjects.

46 In the wake of Jane Goodall, Thelma Lowell, Frank de Waal and others have applied techniques of participant observation to animals. The new ethology has shown that animals (monkeys, elephants, dolphins, crows) are more like us: conscious, intelligent, creative, reflexive, communicative, sensible, playful, funny, compassionate and fair. With Mead, but against him, we could say that animals have a self, a mind and a society.

47 As the relations between the elements that make up the whole are internal ones, one can dialectically reverse the formulations: subjects are connected to each other through society; society is connected to language through the subjects; language is connected to the subjects through society, etc.

48 From a realist perspective, it is obvious that symbolic interactionism has difficulties in grasping the more structural and systemic aspects of society. Instead of granting to materialists and structuralists that collective subjectivities intervene in society, it identifies society with collective subjectivity, i.e. with a 'subjectivity of higher order', to speak like Husserl and Peirce. For an attempt to conceptualise societies and collective subjectivities in more realist terms, see Chapter 2.

49 By conceiving of the mechanism of role taking as a moment in the coordination of action, Mead has given a cognitivist and pragmatic interpretation of sympathy and kindred moral sentiments, but without openly saying so. In the Scottish tradition of moral philosophy, role taking is linked to judgement: we see ourselves through the eyes of the other, observe ourselves in imagination as the other sees us and judge accordingly. As the moralist Adam Smith says:

> We either approve or disapprove of our own conduct, according as we feel that, when we place ourselves in the situation of another man, and view it, as it were, with his eyes and from his station. We endeavour to examine our own conduct as we imagine any other fair and impartial spectator would examine it.
>
> (Smith, 1976: 109–110)

As can be gathered from this quotation, Mead's 'generalised other' is only an alias of Smith's 'impartial spectator'.

50 Mead's universal communitarianism chimes all too well with Durkheim's republican individualism. Both converge in a functionalist reinterpretation of Kant: 'The categorical imperative of moral conscience is taking the following form: Prepare yourself to ultimately accomplish a determinate function' (Durkheim, 1986: 7).

51 For an outstanding presentation of 'distributed knowledge' (Norman, Hutchins, Kirsch, Conein) by one of the leading figures of the new French pragmatist sociology, see Quéré (1997).

52 More than Mead, John Dewey (1954) is fully aware of the 'heterogony of ends' and the quagmire of unintended consequences of cooperative actions on a collective scale. His spirited invocation of the public and defence of representative democracy is nothing else but a call for conscious social control of the indirect, extensive and obnoxious consequences of joint action at the institutional level.

53 Reintroducing thought between the stimulus and the response, Mead (1934: 106) pointed to the question of reflexivity to hoist Watson on his own petard:

> You can explain the child's fear of the white rat by conditioning its reflexes, but you cannot explain the conduct of Mr. Watson in conditioning that stated reflex by means of a set of conditioned reflexes, unless you set up a super-Watson to condition his reflexes.

Instead of setting up a super-Watson, one could also entertain the hypothesis that the rats were playing dumb, while actually conditioning the behaviour of the experimenter!

54 Inspired by Wittgenstein, Bakhtin, Volosinov or Vygotsky, the most interesting constructivist psychologists (like Rom Harré, Kenneth Gergen, John Shotter, Hubert Hermans) who focus on discourse and dialogue have arrived at similar conclusions. Namely that one has to study cognition where it lives, in discourse. Wielding Ockham's razor, Rom Harré (1992: 6) goes too far, however, when he simply decapitates the subject and eliminates the mind:

> Not only is there no one thing that is thinking, in many cases there is clearly only the overt discursive activity. The myth of the mind has come perhaps from the observation that one soon learns to do privately (behind one's face, so to speak) what one first learned to do publicly.

55 Personal experience confirms this conclusion. As I was intensively thinking and writing about internal conversations to write this chapter, I was out of myself – 'into the text', as I said to my friends to apologise for my being unavailable for external conversations. When I went to see my psychoanalyst to get my narratives straight, I had nothing personal to say, so we talked about the self in social psychology.

56 Due to lack of space, I cannot go into consideration of the relation between sympathy, distant suffering and the 'politics of pity'. See Boltanski (1993) on the latter. For a well-known account of the role of the printed media in the constitution of 'imagined communities' (like classes and nations), see also Anderson (1983) and the next chapter. Anderson does not refer to Cooley, Mead or any other of the pragmatists. I'd like to think that if he had done so he would have been able to envision collective subjects beyond the nation-state.

57 In *The Cosmopolitan Self*, which is perhaps the best book on Mead, Mitchell Aboulafia (2001) shows that Mead's account of social development of the self combines

universalism, pluralism and individualism, and culminates in the enlarged *sensus communis* that marks the cosmopolitan mind.

58 While Cooley's argument about sympathy allows one to significantly soften the coldness of Kant's universalism, which treats everyone equally with equanimity and without distinction, it does not, however, personalise ethics. Unlike the ethics of care, Cooley is not concerned with the 'concrete other', but with the common humanity we all share. The movement is inwardly going out from the concrete other towards humanity, not the other way round, to the one we encounter not in our mind, but in real life. On the opposition between the general and the concrete other, see Benhabib's (1992) pointed intervention in the Kohlberg-Gilligan controversy.

59 Unlike people, who can exist by themselves (by the mere grace of God), selves are dialectical. The self presupposes, by definition, a non-self or other, either within or without oneself. Analytically speaking, the self cannot be a loner. As the relation between self and the other is an internal one, the self presupposes the other as the other presupposes the self. Both are mutually constituted in and through the relation. The self, the other and the relation itself that constitutes them are one – three in one, one in three, like in the Trinity.

60 Cf. Hegel (1986: 145): 'When a self-consciousness is the object, the object is as much I as object.' The self or *ipse* in Latin (*das Selbst* in German, *le soi* in French, *o si mesmo* in Portuguese) is a reflexive pronoun in the third person with the particularity that it is capable of referring to all personal pronouns. Following Ricoeur (1990: 11–14, 137–166), I conceive of self-identity not in terms of formal or substantial sameness (*idem*), but as a reflexive, dialogical and narrative process of selfhood (*ipse*) that interweaves continuity and change through continuous, lifelong conversation between the self and the other, within or without oneself. Although I cannot develop the point here, I'd like to defend a narrative conception of self-identity:

> Narration is what 'emplots' and directs the internal conversation. To properly understand how personal identity is formed, one has to understand that the internal conversation takes the form of a narration, while the narration itself has to be understood as a conversation that is intrasubjectively intersubjective. One has not only conversations with 'oneself as another' (Ricoeur), but also with 'the other as oneself' (Mead). It is through an internal conversation with oneself that one communicates with the other. Even if one narrates one's self, the other remains present as an 'inner witness' of the personal identity to which I commit myself and for which I am morally accountable and ultimately responsible.
>
> (Vandenberghe, 2005: 233)

61 What Mead analyses in a cognitive way is described by A. Smith (1976: 113) in an affective and moral key:

> When I endeavour to examine my own conduct, I divide myself, as it were, in two persons. The first is the spectator, whose sentiments with regard to my own conduct I endeavour to enter into, by placing myself in his situation, and by considering how it would appear to me, when seen from that particular point of view. The second is the agent, the person whom I properly call myself, and of whose conduct, under the character of a spectator, I was endeavouring to form some opinion. The first is the judge; the second the 'person judged of'.

62 Although Cooley must have known *The Theory of Moral Sentiments*, he never cites it. Not even the passage where Adam Smith (1976: 110) explicitly speaks about the reflected or looking-glass self:

> Bring him into society, and he is immediately provided with a mirror which he wanted before. It is placed in the countenance and behavior of those he lives

> with.... This the only looking glass by which we can, in some measure, with the eyes of other people, scrutinise the propriety of our own conduct.
>
> (Smith, 1976: 110, 112)

For a comparative analysis of the role of mirrors in Cooley's, Mead's and Lacan's developmental psychology, see Wiley (2003).

63 Some commentators of Mead have interpreted the I and the Me as avatars of Freud's Id and Superego. More sophisticated readers have recognised the transcendental Ego of Kant in the I and the Alter Ego of Freud in the Me. Later on, I will clarify my own reading with reference to Adam Smith and William James.

64 In *Structure, Agency and the Internal Conversations*, Archer proposes such a 'Durksonian' reading of Mead (Mead as a mixture of Durkheim and Parsons). Neither fully autonomous nor fully reflexive, the self appears as a rather conservative force without much individuality – more of a communicative than an autonomous or a metareflexive self, to use her categories. In opposition to this view, I'd like to argue that Mead's dialectical self is fully reflexive. (Taking up a suggestion of Douglas Porpora, I intend to develop the category of full reflexivity – meta/meta, including meta/communicative and meta/autonomous in a subsequent text.) To make my case, I'll rely on Habermas' (1992: 187–241) remarkable essay on Mead's theory of subjectivity (which is, actually, much better than his chapter on Durkheim and Mead in *The Theory of Communicative Action*).

65 One can generalise Carl Schmitt's (1990: 49–66) observation, according to which all main concepts of modern political sciences are secularised theological concepts, to the social sciences in general. The notions of person, subject and individual all have a theological prehistory. With its suggestion that the person is essentially pre-social, the notion of the person is often used polemically by ultraconservative forces to restrict individual choice (see the Church on abortion and euthanasia). With de Beauvoir, I'd say that one is not born, but becomes a person (or ceases to be one).

66 Drawing on the *Critique of Judgment*, Alessandro Ferrara (1998) has introduced the Kantian concept of 'reflexive judgement' into moral philosophy and developed an ambitious theory of reflexive authenticity that integrates the singularity of the self with the universal acclaim of its exemplarity. He not only advocates authenticity as a normative ideal, but also holds that authenticity, understood as 'exemplary congruency of an individual, collective or symbolic identity with itself', provides us with a new ideal of universal validity that shifts the emphasis away from the generalisable towards the exemplary and the authentic. Just like well-formed works of art, authentic identities inspire in us a sense of admiration.

67 As far as I can see, only feminist philosophers like Susan Moller Okin (1989) and Seyla Benhabib (1992: 148–177) have seen the connection between Rawls and Adam Smith, reason and feeling, justice and benevolence, fairness and care. Coincidentally, in sociology, Rawls' daughter, who is a collaborator of Garfinkel, has introduced the notion of sympathy into Goffman's interaction order and Sacks' conversation analysis (Rawls, 1988).

68 In his collective psychology of reasoning, Halbwachs uses a similar metaphor as Mead and arrives at similar conclusions – but whereas the movement in Mead is outwards, the movement in Halbwachs (1938: 357) is inwards: 'Our thought is often as a deliberation room where arguments, ideas or abstractions that we largely owe to others meet: so that it is the others who debate in us, defend theses, formulate propositions which are only the echo of the outside in our mind.'

69 In a delightful passage, Cooley quotes Goethe's thought experiment, who speaks of himself in the third person:

> Accustomed to pass his time most pleasantly in society, he changed even solitary thought into social converse, and this in the following manner: He had the habit, when he was alone, of calling before his mind any person of his acquaintance.

> This person he entreated to sit down, walked up and down by him, remained standing before him and discoursed with him on the subject he had in mind.
>
> (Cooley, 1964: 91; see also Wiley, 1994: 54–55).

70 There are some faint echoes in Rawls of the gospel (esp. Matthew (25:5) who summons the faithful to help 'the least of these') and liberation theology with its 'preferential option for the poor' (second conference of the episcopate of Latin America, Medellin, 1968). For a more extended elaboration of the ascent from the 'concrete other' to the anonymous and faceless *socius*, see Vandenberghe (2008).

71 See the debate between two of the greatest political philosophers of the twentieth century in *Journal of Philosophy*, 1995, 93, 3, and the 'Habermas-Rawls blogspot' for a continuous actualisation.

72 In a debate with Rom Harré, Margaret Archer (2006) criticises his 'position theory' for 'oversocialising' the self. I for my part have criticised him for 'overpsychologising' society (Vandenberghe, 2007). At the time I hadn't really engaged with the new social psychology – that social psychology that does not so much investigate how the individual behaves in groups, but rather how groups behave in the individual. Having glanced at some of the more interesting and more philosophical representatives of discursive psychology (Shotter, 1993; Gergen, 1999) and cross-cultural psychology (Paranjpe, 1998; Hermans, 2001) who study dialogue and conversation, I tend to concur that the self is by and large a conversational reality – with the hermeneutic proviso that language is precisely what allows the self to reveal its essential powers and to become the 'Alethic Self' (Bhaskar) that it really is.

73 For a humane and compassionate account of multiple personality disorder, see Hacking (1995), especially chapter 2 where he analyses how it feels to be a multiple ('But how does it feel? Miserable, scary, that's how it feels' (p. 35)). Within a single person, multiple personalities (so called alters) with their own complex and unique behaviour patterns and social relationships may come out at various times and determine the behaviour of the person. Dr Jekyll and Mr Hyde are popular representations of such alternation of personalities. The alters of a single individual may differ not only in age, but also in race, sexual inclination and even sex. A person who is visibly masculine may, when an alter is in control, claim to be feminine. A woman who wants to have nothing to do with sex has an alter who does it with her husband. For an analysis of the internal conversations of schizophrenics, who are different from multiples, see Lysaker and Lysaker (2002).

74 In *One, Nobody and a Hundred Thousand*, Pirandello narrates the story of a man who follows through the project of systematically 'deconstructing' each and every one of the social selves that others expect him to play. The novel ends tragically with the internment of the protagonist. For a fine sociological analysis of this Garfinkelian novel that explains action as result of the interaction between a multiplicity of internal dispositions and a plurality of internal contexts (practices = dispositions + contexts), see Lahire (2005: 230–248).

75 Like Mead, James is talking about the empirical or phenomenal self and not about the noumenal one. What he analyses at this stage (pp. 291–328) are the objects of thought as they appear in the stream of consciousness. He's concerned with the *cogitatum* or the *noema*, to speak like Husserl, but as the Ego is not submitted to a transcendental reduction, it is neither a priori, nor pure, but empirical. It is only at a later stage (pp. 329–371), which will not concern us, that he will introduce the pure ego as a kind of changeless non-phenomenal 'Arch-Ego' that accompanies all the thoughts and unifies them synthetically.

76 With some good will one can recognise the three types of sign of Peircian semiotics: the spiritual Me as symbol, the social Me as index and the material Me as icon of the Self. For a provocative analysis of the triangulation of the symbolic-discursive, the somatic-affective and the behavioural-performative dimensions of the self with a special emphasis on misalignments between these dimensions, see Shalin (2007).

77 For a good pragmatic analysis of the meanings of things, see Csikszentmihalyi and Rochberg-Halton (1981) on domestic symbols and the self.

78 Scheler's (1958) essay on 'exemplars and leaders' remains unsurpassed. Unlike Weber, who is obsessed with strong leaders, Scheler enlarges and deepens the perspective on leadership by considering spiritual leaders (like Jesus or the Buddha), cultural geniuses (like Socrates and Goethe), political and military leaders (like Caesar and Napoleon) and successful entrepreneurs (like Henry Ford or Richard Branson). For an analysis of Scheler's material ethics, allow me to refer to Vandenberghe (2006c).

79 Sentimental as ever, Cooley extends James' metaphor of the citadel, fusing it with Peirce's image of bounty and treasures. Allowing for two-way traffic between the self and the universe, he affirms that the gates to the other can be opened through love:

> The self, from this point of view, might be regarded as a sort of citadel of the mind, fortified without and containing selected treasures within, while love is an undivided share in the rest of the universe. In a healthy mind each contributes to the growth of the other. What we love intensely for a long time we are likely to bring within the citadel, and to assert as part of ourself.
>
> (Cooley, 1964: 187–188)

80 Lahire quotes a statement on the infinite fragmentation of the self in everyday life by Jean-Claude Kaufmann, who has produced beautiful ethnographies on the management of laundry by nascent couples, but ended up writing pop and pulp sociology for the masses:

> The individual who leaves his dirty clothes in a heap in the room is not the same one who in the morning puts the same heap in the washing machine. He does not touch things in the same way, with the same ideas in his head. He is really another person, in another system of thought and action, changed by the different perception of the same objects.
>
> (Lahire, 1998: 25, note 7)

81 In the history of philosophy two positions are recurrent: either one follows Hume and Nietzsche or Descartes and Kant. Either one denies the existence of a self: nothing remains the same (Hume); the self has to be overcome (Nietzsche). Or, alternatively, one affirms its existence: 'I think, therefore I am' (Descartes); the transcendental Ego accompanies all of my perceptions (Kant). The opposition between Hume and Descartes is paralleled in Indian philosophy by the Buddhist denial and the Upanisadic affirmation of the Self. As a midway between these two extreme positions – the exalted subject of Descartes and the wounded ego of Nietzsche – Ricoeur (1990) has proposed to think of narrative identity in terms of a dialectics between *idem* and *ipse*.

82 As I haven't properly studied Bakhtin as yet, I freely draw in the following paragraph on Hermans (2001).

83 As Michael Jackson (2009: 53) says in a thoughtful anthropological reflection on life, death and the afterlife:

> Our lives belong to others as well to ourselves. Just as the stars at night are set in imperceptible galaxies, so our lives flicker and fail in the dark streams of history, fate, and genealogy. One might say that we each are given three lives. First is our conscious incarnation, occupying most of the space between life and death. Second is our existence in the hearts and minds of others – a life that precedes the moment of our birth and extends beyond our death for as long as we are remembered. Finally, there is our afterlife as a barely recognised name, a persona, a figure in myth. And this existence begins with the death of the last person who knew us in life.

Bibliography

Aboulafia, M. 2001. *The Cosmopolitan Self: George Herbert Mead and Continental Philosophy*. Urbana, IL: Illinois university Press.

Anderson, B. 1983. *Imagined Communities: Reflections on the Origin and Spread of Nationalism*. London: Verso.

Apel, K.O. 1973. *Transformation der Philosophie. Bd. 1: Bd. 1. Sprachanalytik, Semiotik, Hermeneutik. Bd. 2: Das a priori der Kommunikationsgemeinschaft*. Frankfurt am Main: Suhrkamp.

Archer, M. 1988. *Culture and Agency: The Place of Culture in Social Theory*. Cambridge: Cambridge University Press.

Archer, M. 1995. *Realist Social Theory: The Morphogenetic Approach*. Cambridge: Cambridge University Press.

Archer, M. 2003. *Structure, Agency and the Internal Conversation*. Cambridge: Cambridge University Press.

Archer, M. 2006. 'The concept of the person as the gift of society', pp. 313–322 in Malinvaud, E. and Glendon, M. (eds), *Conceptualization of the Person in the Social Sciences*. Vatican City: Pontifical Academy of Social Sciences.

Archer, M. 2007a. *Making our Way through the World: Human Reflexivity and Social Mobility*. Cambridge: Cambridge University Press.

Archer, M. 2007b. 'The trajectory of the morphogenetic approach: an account in the first-person', *Sociologia: Problemas e práticas*, 54, 35–47.

Archer, M. 2011. 'Morphogenesis: realism's explanatory framework', pp. 59-94 in Maccarini, A., Morandi, E. and Prandini, R. (eds), *Sociological Realism*. London: Routledge.

Bakhtin, M. 1977. *Le Marxisme et la philosophie du langage: Essai d'application de la méthode sociologique en linguistique*. Paris: Minuit.

Beck, U. and Holzer, B. 2004. 'Reflexivität und reflexion', in Beck, U. and Lau, C. (eds), *Entgrenzung und Entscheidung: Was ist neu an der Theorie reflexiver Modernisierung?* Frankfurt am Main: Suhrkamp.

Benhabib, S. 1992. *Situating the Self: Gender, Community and Postmodernism in Contemporary Ethics*. London: Routledge.

Berger, P. and Luckmann, T. 1966. *The Social Construction of Reality*. London: Penguin.

Bernstein, R. 1983. *Beyond Objectivism and Relativism: Science, Hermeneutics and Praxis*. Philadelphia, PA: University of Pennsylvania Press.

Bhaskar, R. 1993. *Dialectic: The Pulse of Freedom*. London: Verso.

Bhaskar, R. 2002. *Reflections on Meta-Reality: Transcendence, Emancipation and Everyday Life*. New Delhi: Sage.

Boltanski, L. 1993. *La souffrance à distance*. Paris: Metaillié.

Calhoun, C. 1995. *Critical Social Theory: Culture, History and the Challenge of Difference*. Oxford: Blackwell.

Campbell, C. 1996. *The Myth of Social Action*. Cambridge: Cambridge University Press.

Cefaï, D. 1998. *Phénoménologie et sciences sociales: Alfred Schutz. Naissance d'une anthropologie philosophique*. Genève: Droz.

Colapietro, V. 1989. *Peirce's Approach to the Self: A Semiotic Perspective on Human Subjectivity*. Albany, NY: SUNY.

Collins, R. 2004. *Interaction Ritual Chains*. Princeton, NJ: Princeton University Press.

Cooley, C. 1964. *Human Nature and the Social Order*. New York: Schocken Books.

Cooley, C. 1983. *Social Organization: A Study of the Larger Mind*. New Brunswick, NJ: Transaction Books.

Csikszentmihalyi, M. and Rochberg-Halton, E. 1981. *The Meaning of Things: Domestic Symbols and the Self.* Cambridge: Cambridge University Press.

Dépelteau, F. 2008. 'Relational thinking: a critique of co-deterministic theories of structure and agency', *Sociological Theory*, 26, 1, pp. 51–73.

Dewey, J. 1925. *Experience and Nature*. Chicago, IL: Open Court.

Dewey, J. 1954. *The Public and its Problems*. Athens, OH: Ohio University Press.

Dewey, J. 1973. *The Philosophy of John Dewey. Vol. 1: The Structure of Experience. Vol. 2: The Lived Experience*. New York: Putnam.

Dewey, J. 2002. *Human Nature and Conduct*. New York: Dover.

Dilthey, W. 1958. *Der Aufbau der geschichtlichen Welt in den Geisteswissenschaften*, in *Gesammelte Schriften, vol. VII*. Göttingen: Vandenhoeck & Ruprecht.

Donati, P. 1991. *Teoria relazionale della società*. Milano: Franco Angeli.

Donati, P. 2011. 'Critical realism as viewed by relational sociology', pp. 122–146 in Maccarini, A., Morandi, E. and Prandini, R. (eds), *Sociological Realism*. London: Routledge.

Durkheim, E. 1986. *De la division du travail social*. Paris: P.U.F.

Elster, J. (ed.) 1985. *The Multiple Self.* Cambridge: Cambridge University Press.

Engelman, P. 1967. *Letters from Ludwig Wittgenstein: With a Memoir*. Oxford: Blackwell.

Ferrara, A. 1998. *Reflective Authenticity: Rethinking the Project of Modernity*. London: Routledge.

Ferry, J.M. 1991. *Les puissances de l'expérience. Vol. 1: Le sujet et le verbe*. Paris: Cerf.

Frankfurt, H. 1988. *The Importance of What We Care About*. Cambridge: Cambridge University Press.

Fuchs, S. 2001. *Against Essentialism: A Theory of Culture and Society*. Cambridge, MA: Harvard University Press.

Gadamer, H.G. 1999. *Gesammelte Werke*, 10 vols. Tübingen: Mohr.

Garfinkel, H. 1990. 'A conception of, and experiments with, "trust" as a condition of stable, concerted actions', in Coulter, J. (ed.), *Ethnomethodological Sociology*. Aldershot: Ashgate Publishing.

Geertz, C. 1973. *The Interpretation of Cultures*. New York: Basic Books.

Gergen, K. 1999. *An Invitation to Social Construction*. London: Sage.

Gerth, H. and Wright Mills, C. 1954. *Character and Social Structure: The Psychology of Social Institutions*. London: Routledge.

Giddens, A. 1976. *New Rules of Sociological Method: A Positive Critique of Interpretative Sociologies*. London: Hutchinson.

Grondin, J. 1997. 'Gadamer on humanism', pp. 157–170 in Hahn, L. (ed.), *Library of Living Philosophers, Volume XXIV: The Philosophy of Hans-Georg Gadamer*. Chicago, IL: Open Court.

Gronow, A. 2008. 'The over- or the undersocialized conception of man? Practice theory and the problem of intersubjectivity', *Sociology*, 42, 2, pp. 243–259.

Habermas, J. 1973. *Erkenntnis und Interesse*. Frankfurt am Main: Suhrkamp.

Habermas, J. 1991. *Texte und Kontexte*. Frankfurt am Main: Suhrkamp.

Habermas, J. 1992. *Nachmetaphysisches Denken. Philosophische Aufsätze*. Frankfurt am Main: Suhrkamp.

Hacking, I. 1995. *Rewriting the Soul: Multiple Personality and the Sciences of Memory*. Princeton, NJ: Princeton University Press.

Halbwachs, M. 1938. 'La psychologie collective du raisonnement', *Zeitschrift für Sozialforschung*, 7, 3, pp. 357–375.

Harré, R. 1992. 'The second cognitive revolution', *American Behavioral Scientist*, 36, 1, pp. 5–7.

Hegel, W.F. 1986. *Phänomenologie des Geistes*, in *Werke, Band 3*. Frankfurt am Main: Suhrkamp.

Heidegger, M. 1964. *Lettre sur l'humanisme/Über den Humanismus*. Paris: Aubier.

Hermans, H. 2001. 'The dialogical self: toward a theory of personal and cultural positioning', *Culture and Psychology*, 7, 3, pp. 243–281.

Honneth, A. 1992. *Kampf um Anerkennung: Zur moralischen Grammatik sozialer Konflikte*. Frankfurt am Main: Suhrkamp.

Honneth, A. 2000. *Das Andere der Gerechtigkeit: Aufsätze zur praktischen Philosophie*. Frankfurt am Main: Suhrkamp.

Jackson, M. 2009. *The Palm at the End of the Mind: Relatedness, Religiosity, and the Real*. Durham, NC: Duke University Press.

James, W. 1950. *The Principles of Psychology*, 2 vols. New York: Dover Publications.

Joas, H. 1980. *Praktische Intersubjektivität: Die Entwicklung des Werkes von Georg Herbert Mead*. Frankfurt am Main: Suhrkamp.

Joas, H. 1992. *Die Kreativität des Handelns*. Frankfurt am Main: Suhrkamp.

Knorr Cetina, K. 1997. 'Sociality with objects: social relations in postsocial knowledge societies', *Theory, Culture & Society*, 14, pp. 1–30.

Kögler, H. 1997. 'Alienation as epistemological source: reflexivity and social background after Mannheim and Bourdieu', *Social Epistemology*, 11, 2, pp. 141–164.

Kögler, H.H. 2009. 'Agency and the other: on the intersubjective roots of self-identity', *New Ideas in Psychology*, 30, 1, pp. 47–64.

Kunneman, H. 2005. *Voorbij het dikke-ik*. Amsterdam: Humanistics University Press.

Lahire, B. 1998. *L'homme pluriel: Les ressorts de l' action*. Paris: Nathan.

Lahire, B. 2005. *L'esprit sociologique*. Paris: La Découverte.

Lysaker, P. and Lysaker, J. 2002. 'Narrative structure in psychosis: schizophrenia and disruptions in the dialogical self', *Theory and Psychology*, 12, 2, pp. 207–220.

Mannheim, K. 1964. 'Beiträge zur Theorie der Weltanschauungs-Interpretation', pp. 91–154 in *Wissenssoziologie*. Neuwied: Luchterhand.

Mead, G.H. 1932. *The Philosophy of the Present*. Chicago, IL: Chicago University Press.

Mead, G.H. 1934. *Mind, Self and Society from the Standpoint of a Social Behaviorist*. Chicago, IL: Chicago University Press.

Mead, G.H. 1936. *Movements of Thought in the Nineteenth Century*. Chicago, IL: Chicago University Press.

Mead, G.H. 1938. *The Philosophy of the Act*. Chicago, IL: Chicago University Press.

Mead, G.H. 1964a. 'Foreword: Cooley's contribution to American social thought' pp. ix–xxxviii in Cooley, C.H.: *Human Nature and the Social Order*. New York: Schocken Books.

Mead, G.H. 1964b. *Selected Writings*. New York: Bobbs-Merrill.

Miller, D. 1973. *Georg Herbert Mead: Self, Language and the World*. Chicago, IL: Chicago University Press.

Mills, C.W. 1940. 'Situated actions and vocabularies of motives', *American Sociological Review*, 5, pp. 904–913.

Moller Okin, S. 1989. 'Reason and feeling in thinking about justice', *Ethics*, 99, 2, pp. 229–249.

Morin, E. 1994. *La complexité humaine*. Paris: Flammarion.

Mouzelis, N. 1991. *Back to Sociological Theory: The Construction of Social Orders*. London: Macmillan.

Mouzelis, N. 2008. *Modern and Postmodern Social Theorizing: Bridging the Divide*. Cambridge: Cambridge University Press.

Paranjpe, A. 1998. *Self and Identity in Modern Psychology and Indian Thought*. Hingham: Kluwer.

Peirce, C.S. 1931–1958. *Collected Papers*, 8 vols. Cambridge, MA: Harvard University Press.

Pels, D., Hetherington, K. and Vandenberghe, F. (eds) 2002. *Sociality/Materiality: The Status of the Object in Social Science*. Special issue of *Theory, Culture & Society*, 19, 5/6.

Perelman, C. and Olbrecht-Tyteca, N. 1992. *Traité de l'argumentation: La nouvelle rhétorique*. Brussels: Editions de l'ULB.

Perinbanayagam, R. 1975. 'The significance of others in the thought of Alfred Schütz, G.H. Mead and C.H. Cooley', *Sociological Quarterly*, 18, pp. 500–521.

Perinbanayagam, R. 2003. 'Telic reflections: interactional processes, as such', *Symbolic Interaction*, 26, 1, 67–83.

Popper, K.R. 1979. *Objective Knowledge: An Evolutionary Approach*. Oxford: Clarendon Press.

Quéré, L. 1997. 'La situation toujours negligée?', *Réseaux*, 85, pp. 163–192.

Rawls, A. 1988. 'The interaction order *sui generis*: Goffman's contribution to social theory', *Sociological Theory*, 5, pp. 136–149.

Rawls, J. 1972. *A Theory of Justice*. Oxford: Oxford University Press.

Ricoeur, P. 1969. *Le conflit des interpretations: Essais d'herméneutique*. Paris: Seuil.

Ricoeur, P. 1986. *Du texte à l'action: Essais d'herméneutique II*. Paris: Seuil.

Ricoeur, P. 1990. *Soi-même comme un autre*. Paris: Seuil.

Rieff, P. 1964. 'Introduction', pp. ix–xx in Cooley, C.: *Human Nature and the Social Order*. New York: Schocken Books.

Rochberg-Halton, E. 1986. *Meaning and Modernity: Social Theory in the Pragmatic Attitude*. Chicago, IL: Chicago University Press.

Rochberg-Halton, E. 1993. *Meaning and Modernity: Social Theory in the Pragmatic Attitude*. Chicago: Chicago University Press.

Rorty, R. 1979. *Philosophy and the Mirror of Nature*. Princeton, NJ: Princeton University Press.

Sannino, A. 2008. 'Experiencing conversations: bridging the gap between discourse and activity', *Journal for the Theory of Social Behaviour*, 38, 3, pp. 267–291.

Scheler, M. 1958. 'Vorbilder und führer', pp. 255–344 in *Gesammelte Werke, Band 10*. Bern: Franke Verlag.

Schmitt, C. 1990. *Politische Theologie: Vier Kapitel zur Lehre der Souveränität*. Berlin: Duncker & Humblot.

Schütz, A. 1962. *Collected Papers I: The Problem of Social Reality*. The Hague: M. Nijhoff.

Schütz, A. and Luckmann, T. 1973. *Structures of the Life-world*. Evanston, IL: Northwestern University Press.

Searle, J. 1995. *The Construction of Social Reality*. New York: Simon & Schuster.

Shalin, D. 1986. 'Pramatism and social interactionism', *American Sociological Review*, 51, pp. 9–30.

Shalin, D. 2007. 'Signing in the flesh: notes on pragmatist hermeneutics', *Sociological Theory*, 25, 3, pp. 193–224.

Smith, A. 1976. *The Theory of Moral Sentiments*. Indianapolis, IN: Liberty Fund.

Shotter, J. 1993. *Conversational Realities: Constructing Life through Language*. London: Sage.

Strathern, M. 1991. *Partial Connections*. London: Rowman and Littlefield.

Strathern, M. 1996. *The Relation*. Cambridge: Prickly Pear.

Suárez Müller, F. 2004. *Skepsis und Geschichte: Das Werk Foucaults im Lichte des absoluten Idealismus*. Würzburg: Königshausen & Neumann.

Tarde, G. 1999. *Oeuvres de Gabriel Tarde. Vol. 1: Monadologie et sociologie*. Le Plessis-Robinson: Institut Synthélabo.

Taylor, C. 1989. *Sources of the Self: The Making of the Modern Identity*. Cambridge, MA: Harvard University Press.

Theunissen, M. 1977. *Der Andere: Studien zur Sozialontologie der Gegenwart*. Berlin: Walter de Gruyter.

Thomas, Y. 1980. 'Res, chose et patrimoine' (Note sur le rapport sujet-objet en droit romain), *Archives de philosophie du droit*, 25, pp. 413–426.

Vandenberghe, F. 2002. 'Relativisme, relationnisme, structuralisme', *Simmel Studies*, 12, 1, pp. 41–84.

Vandenberghe, F. 2005. 'The Archers: a tale of folk (final episode?)', *European Journal of Social Theory*, 8, 2, pp. 227–237.

Vandenberghe, F. 2006a. *Complexités du posthumanisme: Trois essais dialectique sur la sociologie de Bruno Latour*. Paris: L'Harmattan.

Vandenberghe, F. 2006b. 'Réflexivité et modernité', pp. 975–977 in Savidan, P. and Mesure, S. (eds), *Dictionnaire des sciences humaines*. Paris: P.U.F.

Vandenberghe, F. 2006c. 'L'archéologie du valoir: Amour, don et valeurs dans la philosophie de Max Scheler', *Revue du MAUSS*, 27, pp. 138–175.

Vandenberghe, F. 2007. 'Une ontologie réaliste pour la sociologie: système, morphogénèse et collectifs', *Social Science Information/Information sur les sciences sociales*, 46, 3, pp. 487–542.

Vandenberghe, F. 2008. 'Entre la voix et la croix, le don et la donation', pp. 213–246 in Archer, M. and Donati, P. (eds), *Pursuing the Common Good: How Solidarity and Subsidiarity Can Work Together*. Vatican City: Pontifical Academy of Social Sciences.

Vandenberghe, F. 2009. *A Philosophical History of German Sociology*. London: Routledge.

Wiley, N. 1994. *The Semiotic Self*. Chicago, IL: Chicago University Press.

Wiley, N. 2003. 'The self as self-fulfilling prophecy', *Symbolic Interaction*, 26, 4, pp. 501–513.

Wiley, N. 2006a. 'Peirce and the founding of American sociology', *Journal of Classical Sociology*, 6, 1, pp. 23–50.

Wiley, N. 2006b. 'Inner speech as a language: a Saussurean inquiry', *Journal for the Theory of Social Behaviour*, 36, 3, pp. 319–341.

Wittgenstein, L. 1953. *Logical Investigations*. London: Macmillan.

Woolgar, S. (ed.) 1988. *Knowledge and Reflexivity: New Frontiers in the Sociology of Knowledge*. London: Sage.

2 A realist theory of collective subjectivities[1]

> Let it be a network of voices.... A network of voices that not only speak, but also struggle and resist for humanity.
>
> Subcomandante Marcos

Unlike philosophy, which is not a science and is literally, 'without object', as Althusser (1974: 18) once said, sociology is a science with an object of its own: *the social*. Science of the social or science of society, that's how sociology has always been defined to demark it from its neighbouring disciplines, especially philosophy, which is neither scientific nor empirical, and psychology, which does not deal with society, but with the individual *qua* individual. One could think that in spite of all the philosophical, theoretical, methodological and ideological divergences that differentiate the different currents, schools and chapels of sociology, each and every sociologist would subscribe *qua* sociologist to the junction that Durkheim establishes between the relative autonomy of sociology and the relative autonomy of its object. Sociology is possible as a (relatively) independent science by virtue of the fact that social facts exist (relatively) independently from our consciousness and can thus not be deduced from, or reduced to, psychological facts. Unlike psychology, sociology studies social facts, i.e. social actions, relations, representations, institutions, organisations and systems that possess 'this particular property of existing outside of individual consciousness' (Durkheim, 1977: 4) – not of every consciousness nor of the consciousness of all, of course, but of yours and mine (*existentia extra nos et praeter nos*).

The quarrel of the universals

The mark of the social

So far, sociologists have, however, failed to come to any agreement concerning the ontological status of society. As soon as one starts to ask more precise questions about the distinctive properties that mark the essence of the social, sociologists immediately distance themselves from Durkheim's metaphysics for fear of committing the fallacy of reification. The critique of reification that is so often addressed to Durkheim is partly justified in my opinion, but the source is not so much to be found in his militant sociologism as in his extravagant scientism. What is problematic is not his realist conception of social facts, but the empiricism that accompanies it (and conflicts with his identification of social with moral facts). Social facts are sense data, but not in the sense that empiricists have understood it. One does not observe society like a train that enters a station, but rather one feels it in the flesh, vaguely or intensely, as a qualitative and diffuse sensation (Sandelands, 1994). By insisting on the constraint and exteriority of social facts, Durkheim has foregrounded their facticity and backgrounded their sociality. It should be noted that social facts share these properties with the objects of the natural sciences, by virtue of which they become appropriate objects of a 'scientific' sociology. Durkheim has therefore failed to specify the mark of the social (Greenwood, 1997: 1–2).

What is the mark of the social? What are the distinctive properties of the social? Is the social a domain *sui generis*, with its own consistence, laws and regularities, or are we dealing here with an aggregation of individual facts without emergence and supervenience? Does the social exist outside of the mind, independently of our representations, actions and intentions, or is its existence merely conventional? Do institutions, classes, groups and other collectives exist? Do they have causal power and can they act? Or are they only social representations that orient the action of the agents, but that as such do not exist in reality? These are, admittedly, difficult and tricky metasociological questions. Although they may fall beyond the remit of sociology, narrowly conceived, they are nevertheless fundamental: they *found* sociology. The answers one can give to these foundational questions are empirically underdetermined and philosophically overdetermined.

Realism, nominalism, conceptualism

Sociology continues the philosophical tradition by other means and inherits some of its oppositions, antinomies and amphibolies. As soon as we start thinking about the existence of society, we encounter the same ontological oppositions, epistemological divisions and ideological cleavages of yore. When sociologists ponder whether society is a 'subsistent reality in itself' or rather 'a simple conception of the mind' (Porphyrius, quoted in de Libera, 1996: 35), they ask exactly the same question Porphyrius asked in the *Isagoge* that sparked the late medieval 'quarrel of the universals' – in reality a quarrel about the concept of the universal in Aristotle's *Categories*. Contemporary debates between Bhaskar and Harré, Collins and Mayhew or Boudon and Bourdieu, to name a few examples, seem like a replay of the debates of the eleventh and twelfth century in which Porphyry and Boethius, Al-Farabi and Averroes, Abailard and Ockham disputed whether the universal, *casu quo* the collective, is actually a thing (*res*), a concept (*vox*) or perhaps even just a gentle breath (*flatus vocis*), as Roscelin claimed in his doctrine of voices. Slightly transfigured, the ancient opposition between nominalism and realism reappears periodically in sociology in the form of an opposition between collectivism and individualism.[2] Like philosophy's long history, sociology's short history is punctuated by alternating waves of nominalism, realism and conceptualism. Currently, sociology seems to be going once again through a phase of accentuated nominalism – with Randall Collins as the reincarnation of Wilhelm of Ockham, Garfinkel as a new Johannes Buridan and Bruno Latour as a postmodern version of Abailard. In any case, the tugging between the collectivism of the Durkheimians and the individualism of the Weberians explains the course sociology is steering between the Scylla of reification and the Charybdis of reduction.

In the wake of philosophical realism, collectivism confirms the ordinary realism of common sense and affirms that social facts exist in the social world in the same way as the *universalia* do in the transsubjective one. Countering this ontological proposition, radical individualists reject the existence of collectives *in rerum natura, extra nos* and *praeter nos*, arguing that only individuals are real.[3] Between the extremes of realism and nominalism, methodological individualists rejoin the positions of the ancient conceptualists (Sorokin, 1957: 324–327). In the same way as the conceptualists came to accept that *universalia* exist in the mind as concepts, methodological individualists deny that collective entities exist in the transsubjective world, but, reducing social facts to mental representations of social effects, they concede the former exist as 'representations in the minds of individual persons of something actually existing' (Weber, 1964: 7).

The compromise formation

In sociology, the three ontological positions reappear among the different fractions of the discipline as regional sub-ontologies that often function as symbolic markers of more or less articulated theoretical currents. Generally, the empirical sociologist in the field is a realist who ignores him- or herself. Whether she or he investigates stratification or business organisations, the integration of immigrants or religion, discrimination in school or competition in sports, most of the time, she or he will follow common sense and take it for granted that the objects of research really exist in the world 'out there'. It is true that sociologists are supposed to effectuate an 'epistemological rupture' that breaks with common sense and to construct their concepts as theoretically infused scientific concepts, but (Bourdieusians, poststructuralists and postmodernists aside) when they are in the field, they hardly seem preoccupied with epistemological reflections. In any case, one cannot do research on an object and submit it at the same time to a reflection on the conditions of possibility of its knowledge. This is best left as an afterthought for 'nocturnal epistemology', as Bachelard suggested.

While empirical sociology is massively but implicitly realist, philosophical reflection on sociology on the other hand clearly veers towards nominalism, confirming as it were Peirce's suspicion that the whole of modern philosophy is nominalist. Indeed, whether it is Kantian and rationalist, analytic and scientific, existential and constructivist, deconstructivist or straight out postmodernist, across the board, contemporary epistemological reflection tends to dissolve the objects of thought in the thought of the object, and to accept as real only the activities of consciousness (in the sense of *Geist* for the idealist versions; and of mind in the materialist ones).

Overwhelmed on one side by the ordinary realism of common sense that multiplies the entities and, on the other, by the reflexive inquiry of the philosopher who seeks to explain or interpret them away, sociological theory is ontologically 'hung up'. Oscillating between the temptations of reification and reduction, it tends to privilege the epistemological vector over the ontological one and typically proposes the following compromise formation: ontological individualism (Weber) plus methodological collectivism (Durkheim) (Archer, 1995).[4] Weberian by conviction, Durkheimian by convention, the average theorist adopts a conceptualist, conventionalist and sceptical version of Durkheim's sociology. The philosopher Pierre Livet – but one could easily adduce other examples – has described the essence of the compromise formation in the following terms: 'Starting from the point of view of the individual, we can next integrate his or her representations and hypotheses about the collective. But instead of having to assume that the collective is a real and overarching entity, more or less interiorised by the individual, the collective is only 'presumed'. It always has a virtual status. The collective can thus remain a counterfact, a fiction' (Livet, 1994: 18).

Critical realism and collective subjectivities

The affirmation that social facts do not exist, but that everything happens as if (*als ob*) they existed, leads to an aporia. To get out of the conundrum, I offer some advice: sociologists should defend the project of sociology and affirm the relative autonomy of its object. What is required is ontological boldness: social facts really *do exist*. To be understood by analytic philosophers and sociologists, let me be clear: I contend that as sociologists we cannot do without collective predicates, but these predicates do not merely refer to 'collective representations', but to collective entities (structures, systems, mechanisms, collectives, etc.) that exist relatively independently of individual beliefs and actions and possess emergent and irreducible causal powers. The position of ontological collectivism to which I am committed is inspired by 'critical realism', but extends it to the new domain of collective subjectivities. By 'critical realism', a denomination that arose by elision of the terms 'transcendental realism' and 'critical naturalism', I mean to refer to the British-based anti-positivist movement in philosophy and the human sciences led by Roy Bhaskar. Critical realism is a version of entity realism. It focuses on ontology and is above all concerned with the reality of entities, generative mechanisms, deep structures and causal powers. Having presented critical realism in the introduction to this book, I can safely limit myself here to a short sketch of three of its main tenets that are relevant for a realist analysis of collectives.

First, in the same way that Bhaskar assumes nature exists independently of the conceptions, descriptions and representations that the scientist may have of it, I assume that collective subjectivities exist independently of the conceptions that the analyst has of it, though obviously not of the conceptions that agents have of it. In other words, like Bhaskar, I distinguish between the 'intransitive' or ontological dimension of knowledge and the 'transitive' or epistemic dimension of science, and refuse the 'epistemic fallacy' that systematically collapses the intransitive dimension of knowledge into its transitive dimension, thereby reducing reality to a representation of reality.

Second, following Bhaskar's dispositional ontology, I conceive of the world as a set of real, transfactual and causally efficacious structures and generative mechanisms that possess causal power. Causal powers should be analysed as tendencies and potentialities. By virtue of their intrinsic structure, things possess causal powers. When the causal power of the thing is actualised, it can enter into action and function as a generative mechanism that produces certain effects that are empirically observable in the life-world. In the social world, social systems, collectives and individuals have emergent causal properties.

Finally, like Bhaskar, I analyse the world as a stratified reality, comprised of the strata of nature, life, psyche and society, whereby each higher stratum emerges out of the lower stratum and possesses its own irreducible causal powers (Sawyer, 2003). The highest stratum of reality, society, is itself composed of five dialectically interrelated and loosely coupled emergent orders (the social, cultural, institutional, interactional and individual orders) and exists at three different levels of reality, namely micro, meso and macro (Vandenberghe, 2007a). At the highest level of society, we find the social order and the cultural order. Co-constitutive of one another, both are conceived of in relational terms as systems of paradigmatic relations between social positions (social order) or ideas, values and expressions (cultural order) that condition, but do not determine, the lower orders of reality that mediate and actualise the causal powers of the system in the life-world. At the meso-level we find the institutional order: society exists as a set of institutions, i.e. repeated actions and interactions that are symbolically regulated and strategically coordinated. Organisations and corporations, created to realise a specific end in the most efficacious way, are a subtype of institutions. Finally, at the micro-level of society, society exists both as a representation (the individual order) and as an intentional association of individuals who interact and are interconnected through a mental connection (the interaction order). Although I have presented the orders in a descending order, from extra large to small, they can also be analysed in an ascending one (with emergence, upwards and downwards causation, multiple feedback loops, etc.). Society, culture, institutions, interactions and individuals are mutually constitutive and ultimately grounded in a hermeneutic ontology of *praxis* that generates the social world.[5]

Taxonomic collectives, structured groups and networks

The structuration of collectives

I assert that collectives exist in the same way as society does, though – and this is important, although I cannot develop it here – *in* society, and that they have causal powers.[6] In my opinion, it does not make much sense to oppose abstract categories to concrete groups. Instead of contraposing categories or 'taxonomic collectives' to 'structured groups', suggesting as Rom Harré (1981) and others do that the former stand for theoretical macro-sociological fictions that do not exist, while the latter are real empirical institutional or interactional entities, I will argue: (1) that categories should be understood as potential groups that can organise themselves to realise their causal power; (2) that they are constituted and manifest themselves in the life-world; and (3) that we should investigate this passage from *potentia* to *actus* – the *passage à l'acte* – as an enfolding praxeological process of 'structuration' whereby social categories are progressively organised into groups (Giddens, 1980: 105–117).[7]

Like birds, collectives come in many stripes and colours, from peoples, nations, races, genders, classes, parties and status groups to humanity as such (and perhaps even beyond to interstellar cosmic associations of spirits). My entry into the question is via class and social movements, with a special focus on activist groups.[8] Although I will refrain from talking about the Proletariat, its very existence is at stake in this chapter, as well as that of new social movements and other presumptive successors of the working-class movements of the nineteenth century.

From a realist perspective, the ontology of collectives appears as a generic theory of collective action that distinguishes itself from other theories of collective action in that it attributes causal power to collective actors and conceives of them as transfactual generative mechanisms that can be active or not, but whose inaction can nevertheless produce social movement. In his theory of collective subjectivity, José Maurício Domingues formulates the rippling effect of collectives in the following terms: 'With their own, collective causality, collective subjectivities create movement in social life (regardless of being mobile or not), producing stability and triggering change' (Domingues, 1995: 137). Even without being active or mobilised, by virtue of their mere being, collectives have a real influence on the life-world in at least two ways. First, the mere fact that they exist already has an effect on other collectives – by registering their virtual existence they are obliged to consider them and take them into account. Second, as potential collectives, they offer anticipatory sketches and glimpses of groups in formation.

Sociological 'personnages'

The realist idea that collectives exist in society as generative mechanisms that possess causal powers, which, even at a virtual state, can produce social movement in the life-world, clashes fundamentally with nominalist, analytic, constructivist and deconstructivist theories on both sides of the Atlantic that seek to explain and interpret collectives away, or otherwise deny their existence, by reducing the collective to a representation of the collective. Convinced that collectives can only exist as groups, communities or networks at the micro- and meso-levels of society, they accuse realists who introduce causal entities at the macro-level of reality of hypostasising their theoretical constructs. They confound 'the logic of the things' with 'the things of logic' (Marx, 1976: 216) – the charge that Marx directed against Hegel is now turned once again, by Bourdieu, for instance, against the realists.[9] According to constructivists, collectives, starting with classes only refer to theoretical and hypothetical entities. As ideal types, they represent conceptual utopias that do not exist as such in reality. The sociologist who constructs classes as analytical categories should no more be allowed to take his concepts for reality than his desires. It is not because actors take classes for real in their 'folk sociologies' that sociologists should do so as well and cast them as actors in their theories. Rather than reinforcing the personification of categories that characterise common sense with a reification of groups in social analysis, sociologists should be methodological nominalists and eliminate collectives from their analytical toolbox. In an impressive critique of the tendency to reify categories into groups, Rogers Brubaker warns his colleagues against the fallacy of 'groupism': 'the tendency to take discrete, sharply differentiated, internally homogeneous and externally bounded groups as basic constituents of social life, chief protagonists of social conflicts, and fundamental units of social analysis' (Brubaker, 2002: 164).

Analytic categories are not empirical and common sense concepts are not scientific. Categories should under no account be hypostatised and reified, transformed into living characters that act on the stage of history. Those theoretical collectives that regroup 'pre-grouped' social actors who occupy a similar social position within a social structure and whose involuntary placement explains why they tend to 'resemble and assemble' in groups to defend their interests, share their ideas or express their identities, exist only 'on paper' (Bourdieu, 1984a: 4). The result of this reification is a highly personified collective, endowed with causal properties, that acts and operates in society like a supra-individual. In fact, those macro-collectives that people the world are only meta-individuals that haunt the sociologist and perform their tricks on the theatre of his mind. The sociologist who mistakes the word for the world makes a massive 'category mistake', and falls back into some kind of conceptual mythology (with Gods, spirits and spooks – hence a 'hauntology', to borrow one of Derrida's more felicitous *bons mots)*. After all, 'England', 'the United States of America', 'the Proletariat', 'the anti-globalisation movement' – all these propositional subjects are only grammatical fictions, cast in the same mould as 'the bald king of France' (Russell) or the 'University of Cambridge' (Ryle).[10]

Categories and groups

In a landmark essay on the philosophical aspects of the micro–macro problem, Rom Harré (1981; see also Harré, 1979: 83–97, 139–143; 1997), the mentor and former supervisor of Roy Bhaskar, questions the ontological status of macro-sociological collectives. In order to show that these are logical constructs that only exist in discourse and that their usage is, consequently, purely rhetorical and ideological, he introduces a clear and crisp distinction between 'taxonomic collectives' (or categories) and 'relational and structured groups' (or interpersonal networks). The former refer to 'a set of individuals who form a group because each member has a property that is like that of each other member', whereas the latter are 'constituted by a structure of relations by which individuals come to have their defining properties' (Harré, 1981: 147). To the extent that the relations between the members of a taxonomic collective are logical relations (and not interactional or institutional ones), the taxonomic collectives exist only, according to Harré, in the mind of the classifier who subsumes them under the same category. The presumed similarities in beliefs, dispositions, actions, etc. that allow one to classify individuals in the same category, such as the Sunni Muslims, the Belgian expatriates, or the Proletariat, are abstractions that are constituted by an observer, and only exist in his mind. Between the destitute shop keeper in Fairfield who gets home late in the evening and the distinguished professor of Yale University who wakes up at 10 o' clock in the morning, there's no relation at all, even if they are both female, both Americans and happen to live around New Haven. The same observation holds for the metalworker in Chicago, the sacked electrician who worked for General Motors in Detroit and the exploited manual labourer in New York. There is no relation whatsoever between them, even if, presumably, they are all members of the exploited working class and, therefore, also of the Proletariat.

With structured groups, like football clubs, academic departments, local support groups, combat commandos and other tightly bounded networks, the situation is entirely different. Connected through a common culture, shared norms of interaction, institutional rules and regulations and perhaps even legal conventions, the members of a structured group have real relations with one another. Our distinguished professor, for example, has real relations with the colleagues, secretarial staff and students at the department where she teaches. If she were to oversleep (once again), she could ask one of her colleagues to replace her or ask another to represent her at the faculty meeting. In certain collectives, the relations can be so regular and regulated, dense and systematic, that even a sceptic like Harré would be willing to grant them causal power and consider them as genuine supra-individual entities and, who knows – perhaps even as quasi-persons with a life and a mind of their own.

Social network analysis

Harré's analysis is very insightful, but not helpful. If we want to understand how collectives are structured, we have to overcome the 'anti-categorical imperative' (Emirbayer and Goodwin, 1994: 1414) and analyse the interplay between categories and groups. As it stands, the distinction between taxonomic collectives, categories and classes, on the one hand, and structural groups, communities and networks, on the other, is overdrawn. My critique of Harré is twofold. First, he has confounded relational groups and networks, reducing the latter to the former; and second, he overlooks the fact that people belong to networks as well as categories, and that categories refer, in fact, to potential groups.

In spite of the fact that Harré insists on the interpersonal relations that make up the network, he does not draw on social network analysis and implicitly seems to assume that groups are small-scale, multiplex, densely knit and tightly bounded unities, more akin to families, neighbourhoods, orchestras, political parties or contractually based businesses than to long-distance relationships, diasporas, transnational social movements or global corporations. If each group is necessarily a network, not every network is, however, a group. Following 'social network analysis', as developed first in British anthropology by the Manchester School of social anthropology and later also in American sociology by the disciples of Harrison White, we can define networks generically as a set of ties linking social system members (sometimes called 'nodes' to avoid identification with individuals) *across* social categories and bounded groups.[11] The definition of the network as a set of interconnected nodes leaves open the morphology of the network, the nature of its ties and its boundaries. While network analysis insists on the structural interrelations that make up the network, it does not predefine its structure, which can be regular like a crystal, schizoid like a rhizome or complex like a cloud. Similarly, it does not predetermine the boundaries and the nature of the ties, but conceives of networks as open structures that can expand, integrating new nodes as they spread out through space. Connections can be local or global, single-stranded or multiplex, densely or sparsely knit, tightly or loosely bounded.

Consequently, from the perspective of network analysis, the group appears as only a special type of social network, one that is densely knit (most people are directly connected) and tightly bounded (most relations stay within the same set of people). If one studies a group, for instance a bunch of colleagues at the departmental New Year's party, as a network and follows the ties that connect the members, wherever they go, one will quickly transcend the boundaries of the group and discover non-local ties that spread across the world. It is a small world indeed, and if we may believe Stanley Milgram (Milgram, 1967), it only takes five intermediaries to deliver a folder from Kansas to the wife of a divinity student in Cambridge, Massachusetts, or from Nebraska to a stockbroker in Sharon, Massachusetts. The topology of social networks is such that it links any two nodes in the entire world by paths of five indirect ties between acquaintances.

Networks not only cut across bounded groups, but they also cut across social categories. Although this might seem at first a concession to Harré, we can, however, also interpret it to further open up and loosen his concept of groups, and to interconnect different groups into an expanding network. Categorical membership can be considered as a proxy measure and an indication of a potential structured relationship between nodes. The nodes in the network are not necessarily individuals, but can be groups of all sorts, from cliques (people who all know each other) and clusters (people whose ties are relatively dense, but do not constitute a clique) to corporations, nation-states and federations. Studies on interlocking directorates have shown the 'strength of weak ties' (Granovetter, 1973) that allows the interconnection of different networks. Nodes are indeed generally interconnected through individuals who belong to multiple social circles. When nodes are interconnected through ties that link members of different categories, the members become thereby potentially linked in a loose network. This will be more important at a later stage in the argument, but I introduce it here to point to the possibility of 'reticulation' between groups that cuts across categories through the discursive 'articulation' of their differences.[12]

Triple morphogenesis

Harré asks a real question. But the opposition he establishes between groups and categories is too neat, and also too static, to be entirely satisfactory. What is needed is a more dialectical and dynamic approach that is able to track the immanent development of the categories (in the Hegelian sense of the term) and their transformation into groups. Taxonomic collectives and structured groups are not necessarily opposed to each other and do not always exclude each other, but they form a continuum: under certain conditions, which we will have to analyse, taxonomic collectives can be organised into structured groups and form organised networks that become more and more real as they structure themselves, realising their potential in the process (from *dynamis* to *energeia*). To avoid the constructivist impression that taxonomic collectives do not exist in reality and that they are always and inevitably reifications that 'float in the head of actors', as Max Weber (1964: 7) said, we should probably reformulate the issue and maintain that collectives are real, that they exist as virtual groups whose causal power manifests itself progressively as they are structured in groups that can produce social movement, sending ripples through the whole of society. To avoid the reification of collectives, we should, however, follow the constructivists and insist that they are not given as finished entities, but as social products that are always socially and locally constructed in concrete situations of action; that they are not things, but processes; not reifications, but realisations and concretisations of abstract categories. I offer those grammatical precisions not only to avoid 'category mistakes', but also to indicate that a realist ontology of collectives could easily integrate the performative ontologies of the constructivists, such as Randall Collins' (2004) theory of interaction ritual chains or Bruno Latour's (2005) actor–network theory, for instance, in a processual and dynamic analysis of the progressive structuration of collectives. Collectives can be more or less structured. They can wax and wane. Although I claim that collectives are real, I do not wish to deny that 'groupness' is variable. Like Brubaker and Cooper (2000: 28), I consider 'groupness' not as given, but as an 'emergent property of particular structural or conjunctural settings'.

In the remainder of this chapter I will theorise the structuration of collectives as a *triple morphogenetic process. Symbolic identification, technological mediation and political representation will be presented as so many 'moments' that dialectically transform and structure the collective into a symbolic community, the symbolic community into a quasi-group that can be mobilised, and the quasi-group into an organised group that can represent its members in their absence.*

What we will thus analyse through an investigation of these three ('trialectical') moments of the structuration of collectives are the conditions of collective action, not the action in common as such.[13]

Categorisation, identification and the constitution of the symbolic community

Persons of a higher order

So far I have suggested that one should not oppose taxonomic collectives to structured groups. One should try instead to dissolve the opposition and integrate categories and networks into a more dynamic dialectical scheme that can analyse how collectives are actually constituted as a symbolic community through the mutual implication of performative descriptions of the collective in the first-person plural and structural description of the collective in the third-person plural. In this realist-constructivist perspective, collectives lead a double existence. First, they exist objectively and virtually as categories that comprise members of a set because of the position that they occupy in the social structure and, second, they exist subjectively and intentionally as a symbolic community in which the members are directly interconnected through a mental or a spiritual link.[14] If taxonomic collectives are constituted by alter-phenomenological categorisations of an observer who offers a structural description of the collective from the perspective of the third person, groups are constituted through an auto-phenomenological categorisation, i.e. a self-identification, by the members themselves. Unlike the former, the latter is not brought in from without to the collective, but it is applied by the members of the group themselves to the group, as well as to the members of the group, who are thereby constituted into an 'us'. The 'us' is a *Gesamtperson*, a social supra-individual subjectivity or personality that is intentionally and polythetically constituted as a living collective and experienced as such by all the members of the group.

Following the phenomenological description that Edmund Husserl (1973: II, 165–230) has given of the phenomena of intra- and intersubjectivity, we can say that the group is intentionally constituted by the members of the group as a 'person of higher order', thanks to communication.[15] The communication that takes place between the members of a group follows upon the constitution of intersubjectivity by the transcendental ego. It presupposes the noetic and noematic syntheses of the transcendental ego, yet at the same time, it really overcomes the solipsism of the lonely monad through the establishment of a real, effective, interspiritual and intercorporal relation between the subjects that takes place in the life-world. The other is not constituted as an *alter ego*, but encountered as a *socius* with whom one can interact in real time. As intersubjective communication is intramundane, and not intrasubjective, Husserl's analysis is perfectly compatible with Habermas' theory of communicative action. In communication, Ego and Alter 'give one another the spiritual hand' (Husserl, 1973: II, 168), and really enter into contact with one another. Taking an active interest in one another, the actors not only have a mutual consciousness of their reciprocity, but the acts of the one also directly affect the other and become interlocked; the actors can unify their wills and mutually coordinate their actions into a single collective action. The whole operation, the collective work, is 'my operation'; yet at the same time it is also his or her operation, specifically 'in a foundational and superior sense', because when we consciously, knowingly and mutually, coordinate our actions in a single operative chain, my action supports her action and becomes complementary to it. As my intentions, plans and actions mesh with hers, we come to common action and form a collective subjectivity with collective intentionality. The result of our action in common is a common achievement, which we jointly and intentionally accomplish *together*.

If we now move up from the communication between two people to the association of minds and wills of several people, we can easily transfer Husserl's communicative, proto-Habermasian analysis of the unification of wills and the social coordination of action by Ego and Alter into a collective subjectivity, to structured groups.[16] Through communication, the mind of persons are united in a 'common stream of consciousness' (Husserl, 1973: II, 203). A supra-individual consciousness is formed. This consciousness lives in each and every person who participates in the group. It flows through them, yet at the same time it emanates from them. As a complex unity, this quasi-Durkheimian collective consciousness results from a collective act of unification. Founded upon the individual unifications, the collective act of unification is a synthetic act that polythetically integrates the individual syntheses into a superior unity that operates like a personal consciousness. 'This common subjectivity', says Husserl, 'is a subjectivity with multiple heads, a form of the *ego-alteri*' (Husserl, 1973: II, 218). Distributed over all the persons that participate in the joint or shared action by mutually and spontaneously aligning their intentional actions into one single common action, this supra-personal consciousness seemingly forms the unique intentional correlate of the psychic community, even if each person necessarily conserves a certain amount of independence and the individual consciousnesses only partially coincide and overlap with the supra-individual consciousness of the collective.

Interaction rituals

Husserl's theory of intentional collective consciousness is essentially a cognitive one. In spite of its Durkheimian resonances, it discounts the fact that the emergence of persons of a higher order is not based only on a rational and conscious agreement between minds. Active communication is grounded in the mutual attunement of the participants and presupposes passive syntheses of a more diffuse, emotional nature that precede the cognitions in the order of foundation. Like cognitions, emotions are inter-subjective, relational and transactional phenomena (Emirbayer and Goldberg, 2005: 483–493). Emotions arise not solely inside the heads and hearts of individuals (as 'states of mind'), but also and primarily *between* actors. As transactional transient phenomena, they are passively constituted and emerge in and out of the situation of interaction. Following Durkheim and Goffman, we can conceive of communication as an 'interaction ritual chain' (Collins, 2004) that can be decomposed in the following ingredients: Two or more people are physically assembled in the same locale, so that they affect each other in a situation of co-presence, whether it is in the foreground of their conscious attention ('active synthesis') or not ('passive synthesis'). The situation of physical co-presence is spatially bounded and participants have a sense of who is taking part in the communication and who is excluded. The participants focus their attention to a common object or activity and, unified by a common intentional consciousness that is directed towards the same *noema*, they communicate this focus to each other so that each and every one becomes aware of each other's focus of attention.

Moreover, they also share a common mood of emotional experience and are attuned to each other through synchronisation of bodily movements, rhythmic entrainment and mutual arousal of sentiments. The experience of heightened mutual awareness and common emotional attunement can occasionally be so intense that it transforms communication into a form of 'communion, i.e. a fusion of all particular sentiments into one common sentiment' (Durkheim, 1960: 329) that emanates from the collective, supersedes all the participants and flows through each and every one of them. This experience of 'collective effervescence' gives subsequently rise to sacred group emblems and other cathected markers of identity, like totems, flags and leaders, but also slogans and words, that express, condense, embody, store and prolong the transient feeling of unity in a material or ideational object that symbolises the collective, even when the members are not assembled. Through a consequent micro-translation and secularisation of Durkheim's sociology of religion in terms of situated ritual interactions, the communicative situation can thus be approached and analysed as a ritual process that produces collective subjectivities through mutually focused attention, the synchronisation of motion and the sharing of emotions, which generate a sense of belonging and symbols of group membership.

Plural subjects

The introduction of emotive and kinaesthetic components into Husserl's phenomenology of intersubjectivity allows us to understand the constitution of the group not just as a unifying community of minds, but also of hearts and bodies. A sense of belonging is essential for the constitution of a group, but so is its delimitation with regard to other groups. To show that the constitution of a group is coterminous with its identification against a third party, I now turn to Margaret Gilbert's analytical theory of 'plural subjects' (Gilbert, 1989; 1990).[17] In her attempt to clarify common sense notions as 'community', 'group', 'we', 'common action', etc., the British philosopher submits ordinary common activities as 'walking together', 'dancing together' or 'travelling together' to a detailed conceptual investigation. It takes at least two to 'walk together', but simply walking next to one another or in one another's company won't do. It is necessary that each of the walkers overtly expresses to the other his intention to walk with her and that the walkers jointly agree to form an 'ambulant we' unified by the common goal of walking together in the company of each other. In spite of the fact that walking together is an eminently kinaesthetic experience, Gilbert makes abstraction of intercorporality and considers the unification of wills and consciousnesses that marks joint action as the crucible of society. This assimilation of sociability (*Geselligkeit*) and society (*Gesellschaft*) is problematic, however. Henry David Thoreau was perhaps a better sociologist when he suggested in an epigram that it takes three to form a society: 'I have three chairs in my house: one for solitude; two for company; three for society' (quoted by Collins, 2004: 376, note 8). Indeed, Gilbert does not only tend to reduce society to a *pas de deux*, but she also forgets that dyads (or triads, quartets and quintets for that matter) always already have their location in society. This typical individualist abstraction of social structure and culture at the systemic levels of society explains why she can consider the joint action of 'walking together' as a paradigmatic social phenomenon that offers a model for society at large. Following in the footsteps of Georg Simmel – who knew better and had such a strong 'sense' of social structures that even Durkheim acceded to him – Gilbert thinks that the phenomenon of 'walking together' marvellously illustrates what Simmel might have meant when he said that 'the consciousness of constituting with the others a unity' is the necessary and sufficient condition of society.[18] Reducing society to a collective, the collective to an association, the association to a dyad and the dyad to a 'we', Gilbert formalises Simmel's proto-phenomenological analysis of association (*Vergesellschaftung*), and offers the following formula as a stenographic notation of her analysis of 'plural subjects' that make up a collective: 'Human beings X, Y and Z constitute a collectivity (social group) if and only if each correctly thinks of himself and the other, taken together, as 'us*' or 'we*' (Gilbert, 1989: 147).[19]

Us vs. them

The semantics of the 'we' may successfully elucidate the grammatical conditions of the intentional constitution of the collective through self-identification of the members of a group to the group. It remains, however, rather limited. Gilbert does not see that the 'we' always presupposes a 'you'. Collectives are always related to other collectives.[20] A collective constitutes itself as a symbolic community by distinguishing itself from another community from which it tries to differentiate itself. In order to constitute itself as a more or less unified 'we', the 'us' presupposes a differentiation from a 'them'. In other words: no identity without difference – and to avoid the suggestion that identities are unified, stable and homogenous, composed of a single rather than several – sometimes conflicting – identities, we might perhaps add with Freud that there is no identity without identification and no identification without differentiation.

To the extent that the constitution of the identity of a 'we' presupposes its differentiation with respect to another 'us', the categorisation of the 'others' is mutually implicated in the identification of the 'we'. It follows, as Stuart Hall (1996a: 3; 1996b: 608) has correctly noted, that identification is a construction, a process that remains always incomplete, that is 'always "in process"'. To consolidate the process of construction of the collective as an auto-phenomenological group, identification needs an 'other', an 'outside' that is 'constitutive' of the group's identity. Identities are never completely unified, however. They are decentred and dislocated, made up of different strands that are provisionally 'stitched' or 'sutured' together through the 'articulation' of differences into a common cultural identity (Laclau and Mouffe, 1985). As they construct themselves by reference to representation of a difference, of an 'other', of a 'constitutive outside' that is always already inside the collective and affects its identity from within, the symbolic frontiers between the groups are necessarily leaky (even if the borders are closing fast). To arrive at a closure that, by definition, can only be provisory, identities are continuously constructed, deconstructed and reconstructed. Even if I do not wish to endorse at this point poststructuralist and postmodern theories of identity and difference, I wholeheartedly accept its ontological conclusions (and given the recent upsurge of rampant Islamophobia, also their political conclusions).

The opposition between 'us' and 'them' is not identical to the opposition between friend and foe, and should not be identified with it. Whereas the distinction between 'us' and 'them' remains relatively porous, the distinction between friend and foe rigidifies the categorisations and transforms diacritical cultural markers of relative difference (nation, language, ethnicity, race, religion) into absolute oppositions of kind. In *The Concept of the Political*, Carl Schmitt insists that the enemy is 'in a very intensive sense existentially another', a stranger who is 'naturally and essentially different' (Schmitt, 1933: 8).[21] The Schmittian binary functions as a conceptual war machine. As the enemy cannot be assimilated by the group, he has to be expulsed and eliminated, and if necessary, exterminated. The designation of the other as an enemy realises the most extreme degree of unity and separation, and of association and dissociation. When the group closes the ranks from within and unifies itself against the external enemy, the boundaries harden and lose their fluidity to the point that they can no longer be crossed by individuals on either side of the boundary.

The crucial question is not only whether collectives always have to be constituted against other collectives, but whether antagonism is inevitable.[22] Although the political logic of sovereignty somehow forces communities to define themselves as a *demos* by distinguishing between 'us' and 'them', *Wir und die Anderen* – that much should perhaps be granted to Schmitt[23] – the normative question is really how identity and difference can be articulated into open and flexible collectives that do not a priori exclude the inclusion of outsiders within its bounds. Zooming in on the boundaries and opening up the imaginary line that separates communities, we can investigate the social construction of the boundaries and find out how are they are opened or closed, and how they can be crossed. To avoid the closure of the collective and circumvent the fatal implications of Carl Schmitt's ultra-politics, two intellectual strategies seem to be available. One can either redraw boundaries ('boundary shifting') or, alternatively, maintain boundaries, but allow for interchange of personnel across the boundary ('boundary crossing').[24]

Boundary politics

The first strategy comes in two versions, a universalist one and a more differentialist one.[25] Habermas' (1997) procedural cosmopolitanism and his spirited defence of 'constitutional patriotism' probably provides the best-known contemporary example of the modernist strategy of universalist reconstruction. It aims to include the other as a citizen into the community through a progressive enlargement of the bounds of the collectivity. In her remarkable book on the rights of aliens, Seyla Benhabib (2004) has recently applied the discourse theoretical principle of justification D (according to which all those who are concerned or affected by the consequences of the adoption of a norm should have a say in its formulation) to issues of immigration. The problem is that immigrants, who are by definition non-citizens, are initially excluded from the social covenant. Concerned about the inclusion of the other into the polity, Benhabib has suggested that the tension between the exclusionary logic of politics (sovereignty) and the inclusive logics of morality (human rights) can be negotiated through 'democratic iterations' whereby the collective periodically reconstitutes and redefines itself so as to enable the extension of the democratic voice to new members of the polity who were excluded at the time of the initial articulation of the identity. Through 'democratic iterations', the alien others are progressively included in the polity, while the acknowledgement of the other as other becomes a feature of the common identity of the people.

If the strategy of universalist reconstruction aims to transform strangers into friends, sojourners into residents and citizens, the strategy of differentialist deconstruction of the boundary aims to convert enemies into adversaries who share a common allegiance to the principles of liberal democracy, but struggle to affirm their differences against their opponents without the possibility of ever coming to a rational consensus. The deconstructive strategy is perhaps best represented by Laclau and Mouffe's (1985) influential formalisation of the differential logic that animates postmodern identity politics. In spite of the difficulty of the prose, the basic message of the neo-Gramscian poststructuralists is relatively simple: every order is political and based on some form of exclusion of the other. There are, however, always other possibilities that have been repressed through hegemony and that can be reactivated through counter-hegemonic practices of articulation. To reactivate these repressed possibilities, the extant hegemonic identity has to be deconstructed by democratic struggles. Deconstruction problematises the unity of the 'us' and the otherness of the 'other' by questioning the radical separation between the two that makes the opposition possible in the first place. Deconstruction does not destroy the boundary between insiders and outsiders, but it dislocates it. It decomposes and recomposes, disarticulates and rearticulates identities. As lines of connections are multiplied and alliances are shifted, identities are continuously made and unmade.

Thinking 'with Schmitt against Schmitt', Mouffe (1999a: 6; 1999b: 52, note 2) revisits his sulphuric writings and revises them for the context of pluralist societies.[26] Challenging Schmitt's insistence on the homogeneity of the demos, she argues that there are no fixed identities and no absolute enemies either. In a pluralistic society, there are only adversaries who clash to affirm their differences and forge new identities. The constitution of the collective is agonistic, based on democratic struggles, not antagonistic and existential, as in Schmitt's decisionism. As the collective is continuously redefined through hegemonic and counter-hegemonic struggles, the boundaries become arbitrary and contingent. The 'frontier is an internal one', not an external one. At the end of the day, it's no longer clear who is in and who is out.[27]

If the strategies of re- and deconstruction blur the boundaries, the strategy of personnel interchange maintains them, but allows members of different categories to cross the boundaries and change identities. This strategy is adopted by the social anthropologist Frederik Barth (1969, 1994) in his path-breaking fieldwork on boundary maintenance and the social organisation of cultural difference among the Swat Pathans. Working in the European tradition, Barth is a social, not a cultural, anthropologist. He analyses the social organisation of cultural difference and regards identity as a feature of social organisation rather than a nebulous expression of culture. The basic premise of his approach is that ethnic groups are dialectically constituted and socially constructed through practices of auto-phenomenological identification and alter-phenomenological categorisation – 'self-ascription' and 'ascription of others' in his terms. It is not so much the group that defines the symbolic boundaries, but it is the ascriptive practices of social boundary making that define the social groups. Instead of focusing on the cultural stuff that the boundary encloses, we should focus on the boundary and the processes of boundary making that defines the group. Barth does not deny that boundaries can shift and change. He also recognises that the cultural characteristics of members may be transformed. But he insists that in spite of all the practices of articulation, the dichotomisation between insiders and outsiders, strangers and familiars, kin and akin, is somehow bound to stay. What can change, however, are the personnel and their identities. The interchange of personnel leaves the categories intact (though it affects their numbers), but recategorises aliens into members, strangers into friends. The boundary between the in- and the out-group remains in place, but outsiders are allowed to cross the boundaries and are eventually accepted and identified as members of the in-group. By changing their identity, they can 'pass' and become full members of the community.

Dialectics of identification and categorisation

Now that we have given an overview of the different theoretical-cum-political strategies that aim to overcome the Schmittian closure of the collective and keep its boundaries porous, we can return to Rom Harré's distinction between taxonomic collectives and structured groups. We know that the philosopher from Oxford opposes categories to groups, but I believe that if we follow through Barth's insights about the constitutive implication of self- and other-ascription, identification and categorisation, we can dialectically dissolve the opposition between categories and groups. Identity formation is 'joint work' (Barth, 1994: 16). Groups are not only constituted by identification as an 'us' posited against a 'them', but they are also, and perhaps as importantly, constituted as a group *by* the categorisations of the others (in the etymological sense of 'public accusations', though we should not exclude a priori more affirmative ascriptions). The auto-phenomenological identification of the collective by the members of the group and the alter-phenomenological categorisation of the collective by an external observer do not exclude each other. Both processes of identification of collectives are dialectically implicated in the double morphogenesis of collectives as groups and categories:

> First, categorisation – external definition – is basic to internal definition. The process of defining 'us' demands that 'they' should be contrasted with 'us'. Group identification is likely to proceed, at least in part, through categorising others, positively or negatively. Second, external definition – by others of us – effects our internal definition(s), not least because it will influence how they orient their behavior towards us.
>
> (Jenkins, 2000: 9)

The implication of this course of argumentation is that collectives become groups by being constituted as categories, and that taxonomic categories refer to potential groups that can transform themselves, or be transformed through pressure from without, into structured and organised groups, endowed with a collective consciousness and a will to act that is distributed over the members of the group.

Technological mediation, imagined communities and the construction of the quasi-group

Mediations of the collective

To constitute itself as a structured and unified group, capable of collective action, more is needed than a collective identity. It's not enough for the members of the group to identify with the in-group and to differentiate themselves from the members of the out-group. Two other conditions have to be satisfied: first, the presumed members of a potential group have to be able to enter into contact with one another and to form a virtual communicative network and, second, they have to be represented by a spokesperson who speaks in their name and actualises the collective as an organised group that exists in space and persists over time. For collectives to pass from potentiality to actuality and exercise their causal powers, they have to 'structure' or, as Domingues (1995, 2000) says, 'centre' themselves.[28] The self-identification of the members is a necessary but insufficient condition of the structuration of collectives. A collective that wants to act and intervene in the life-world to change the system (or oppose its transformation), needs the intervention of a 'technological mediation' that transforms the symbolic community into a quasi-group, as well as of a 'political representation' that transforms the quasi-group into an organised group.[29]

Following Régis Debray's (1991) grandiloquent attempt to found 'mediology' as an encyclopaedic science that studies the socio-logistics of cultural transmission and political organisation, I conceive of technological mediation and political representation as two sides of a single process of mediation that organises people and things, humans and non-humans, to speak like the followers of Michele Serres, into a heterogeneous association. Mediation has two sides – a logistical side that has to do with the technological organisation of matter and a strategic side that relates to the organisation of people into a network (Debray 2000; see also Vandenberghe, 2007b). To diffuse a message through society and organise the members of a category into a 'triple I group' that successfully defends its 'ideas, identities and interests', one must not only ensure the material and technological conditions of the transmission of ideas through society, but also organise and mobilise the members into a tightly knit corporate group that can represent the multitude and act 'like one man'. Unlike media and communication studies, mediation studies is not transfixed on newspapers, colour televisions and the internet, but analyses all the possible vectors of transmission that allow for the transport of messages through space and across generations – from roads and canals, ports and portals to monuments and documents. Without waves of sound, vocal chords and the larynx, there's no voice and thus no oral communication; without the bikes of the suffragettes, feminist ideas would probably not have spread through the English countryside. But even if the material world is technologically organised in such a way that individuals can be successfully interconnected in a network of communication – and thanks to the modern technologies of information and communication (TICs) people can nowadays communicate 'without propinquity', i.e. without being physically co-present – one still has to organise the individuals into active political groups, like parties, unions and cells, schools, academies and institutes, or sects, chapels and churches, that can represent all the individuals who adhere to the ideals, identities or interests of the group and speak in the name of the larger collective. In any case, *symbolic identification, technological mediation and political representation are the three moments of the structuration of the collective that propel the progressive actualisation of the causal power of the collective.*[30] *Symbolic community, mobilisable quasi-group and organised group, those are the three avatars of the collective that correspond to the three moments of its structuration.*[31]

Mass-mediations

To form a structured and unified group, the collective needs a cultural (national, ethnic, linguistic, class, etc.) identity that symbolises and represents the unity of the group. Poststructuralists, postmodernists and psychoanalysts know that the identity of the group is largely imaginary: it presupposes a symbolic representation of the group within language that projects the unity of the group outside of itself and allows it thereby to overcome its 'lack' and resolve its differences through an imaginary identification with the totality (Hall, 1996b). In modernity, the symbolic representation of the collective is almost invariably fragmented and fractured. It is composed of collages and montages of multiple alter-phenomenological descriptions that offer multiple auto-phenomenological descriptions of a potential identity with which the group could identify itself and constitute itself as a symbolic community. Nowadays, symbolic representations of groups are predominantly carried, expressed and diffused by mass media in the form of commercial images, cultural products and ideological discourses. The discursive practices of mass media propose 'subject positions' that project cultural identities onto collective screens that function as Lacano-Althusserian mirrors in which collectives are represented and addressed, 'hailed', to recognise and articulate themselves as collective subjects.

Mass media are not only machineries of symbolic representation, however. They are also machineries of socio-technical mediation that interconnect the members of a symbolic community, who would never be integrated into a potential quasi-group without their intervention, into a network (Calhoun, 1991, 1992). As technologies of representation and mediation, the technologies of information and communication are technological vectors that 'project articulations of actions across time and space' (Glaeser, 2005: 25–26), allowing thereby for the 'distanciation' (Giddens) and 'compression' (Harvey) of time and space. Disembedding the relations of co-presence, the media recompose and distribute the interpersonal relations in such a way that persons who are separated in time and space can nevertheless enter into contact with each other, virtually or actually, indirectly or directly, and form a virtual social network that can, if needed, be activated and mobilised to defend common interests, collective identities or shared ideas. Even if people do not encounter each other directly or communicate face to face, they know that, thanks to various media, they could do so if they wished. In line with the realist conception of society, we could say that it is the relations between the social positions that condition and make possible the emergence of collectives, understood as generative mechanisms that produce social movement. But to appear in the life-world as structured quasi-groups that can be mobilised to reproduce or transform the structure and the culture of society in accordance with the interests, identities and ideas that correspond to their social positions, the collectives first have to constitute themselves as symbolic communities whose members are virtually interconnected by the media.[32]

Media function like 'generalised symbolic media' (Parsons–Luhmann). In theory, they allow us to think together 'social integration' and 'systemic integration' (Lockwood, 1964). As conveyer belts that link the global system to the local life-worlds, they are the ideal tools to construct systematic linkages between systemic relations between social positions and ideas on the one hand, and interpersonal or intergroupal relations on the other. To the extent that they mediate interpersonal relations and allow people and groups that are not physically co-present, but who share convergent interests, identities and ideas by virtue of the position they occupy in the system, to enter into contact and communication, media essentially function as socio-technical systems of social integration that allow the actors to coordinate their action by means of communication, even outside of situations of interaction.

Imagined communities

Borrowing a concept that had quite an impact on the emerging field of cultural studies, we could say with Benedict Anderson (1983) that media produce and project 'imagined communities'. Imagined communities are not imaginary communities like the ones that analytic philosophers like to invent, but taxonomic collectives that refer to possible communities composed of people who share a common diacritical characteristic that differentiates them from other communities. In his reflections on the origins and the diffusion of nationalism, Anderson makes it quite clear from the beginning that imagined communities, such as nations – but one can easily extend the concept to classes, ethnic groups, sexual minorities and other political and cultural groupings – are not groups, but quasi-groups. 'The community is imagined', he says, 'because the members of even the smallest nation will never know most of their fellow-members, meet them, or even hear of them, yet in the minds of each lives the image of their communion' (Anderson, 1983: 6). Reinforcing his point, he immediately adds, 'In fact, all communities larger than primordial villages of face-to-face contact (and perhaps even these) are imagined' (Anderson, 1983: 6).

Anderson finds the model of the social construction of nations in the constructions of classes; not in the working classes, however, but in the bourgeoisie: 'In world-historical terms bourgeoisies were the first classes to achieve solidarities on an essentially imagined basis' (Anderson, 1983: 77). It is thanks to the images and the discourses that were published in newspapers and journals that the bourgeois have been able to visualise the existence of thousands and thousands of property owners like themselves. Thanks to the printing press, potential relations, say between a factory-owner in Manchester and one in Rochester or Leeds could be imagined. Later, when the owners of property would organise themselves into the Confederation of British Industry in order to defend their vested interests, the relations they had anticipated in imagination would, in effect, be realised. If I invoke this historical example, it is to make two theoretical points: first, the passage from categories to structured groups presupposes the establishment of imagined relations between people; and, second, the relations between people do not have to be direct, they can be indirect and mediated by technologies of communication, information and transportation, from the voice to the taxi and the mobile phone to the plane.

Relations between people are always mediated by a technical interface, which is itself the result of the metabolism of man with nature, and has its own history. Mingling the material, social and cultural aspects of the transmission of ideas, identities and interests, Régis Debray (1991) has introduced the notion of 'mediasphere' to analyse the ecological interchanges between the medium and its environment over the ages. Media are not just technological vectors of cultural transmission; they impose a certain worldview, configure a certain way of thinking, condition the possible forms of sociability and shape the politics of the age. Each epoch has its own dominant medium, which conditions the form of the dominant ideologies, practices and institutions of its time. The medium is the messenger, and the messenger is the message (to unpack McLuhan's famous one-liner). The invention of the printing press (medium) in the fifteenth century shifted the locus of power from the church to the intellectuals (messenger) and this tectonic shift led to the emergence of the public sphere in the seventeenth and eighteenth centuries; similarly, the invention of the television (medium) in the first half of the twentieth century shifted the locus of power from the intellectuals to the journalists (messenger) in the second half of the century, with the decline of the public sphere (*Öffentlichkeit)* and the emergence of publicity as a consequence (message). The invention of writing, the printing press, and closer to us, the radio, the television and the internet have dramatically altered intellectual life, public opinion and politics. Debray discusses at length the 'logosphere', the 'graphosphere' and the 'videosphere', but has little to say about the 'hypersphere' – which may be due to the fact that he doesn't use the computer and still writes his books by hand.

Networks all the way down

As the internet has made possible new forms of loose association that allow for the coordination of collective action on a global scale, the hypersphere deserves, however, more attention.[33] Computer-mediated communication (CMC) has not only enabled the transmission of information and communication across technological, social and geographical boundaries at the speed of light and given rise to new kinds of identities and communities, but, and perhaps more importantly for the topic at hand, mobile phones, streaming technologies, the internet and wireless networks have also stimulated the emergence of a global network of networks that interconnects NGOs and INGOs, advocacy networks, social movements, grass-roots organisations, churches, unions, intellectuals and journalists into globally oriented social movements that have led to episodic mass mobilisations of resistance (Bennett, 2003, 2005; Langman, 2005).

'Seattle', or the organised response to the Multilateral Agreement on Investment that aimed to subordinate the politics of the nation-states all over world to mercantile interests of transnational grand capital, proves, if necessary, that under the pressure of circumstances computer-mediated communication can diffuse militant discourses and action plans that make the interconnection of activists who are dispersed all over the world possible. The 'battle of Seattle' was not a spontaneous event, but the highly organised and highly publicised end-sequence of months of intense internetworking among a multiplicity of (national) social movements and (transnational) networks at different scales and levels.

High-level spectacular protests like Seattle, or those that now accompany the 'summits' of the world leaders, catch the attention of mass media and the imagination of sympathisers around the world. Metaphorically speaking, such protests at the summits are like a well attended rave party that occurs on the top of a mountain under a sunlit rainbow flag (that embodies, expresses and symbolises the 'unity in diversity' of the collective movement). Underneath the flag, but still above the clouds, we find a much larger configuration of more dispersed and less publicised practices. While thousands of activists and loony ravers were battling in Seattle and appearing on TV, concurrent mass demonstrations were taking place in more than 50 cities all over the world, from London to New Delhi and Seoul to Manila.

Further down the mountain, underneath the clouds, we find the camps and the tents of the social movement organisations, the SMOs of resource mobilisation theory (Zald and McCarthy, 1987) that have organised the demonstrations (and the counter-demonstrations that take place simultaneously on the other flank of the mountain).[34] This is the level of the 'social movement industry' that organises the campaigns, recruits the 'adherents' (sympathisers) and mobilises the 'constituents' (activists) into action. That is where we find a great variety of organisations and activist networks that mobilise and control resources, especially money, time and labour, but also the social capital of connections they can activate, and their spokespersons (see *infra*). It's also where the linkages with other social movements, groups, associations and networks of all stripes are established through continuous practices of 'reticulation' and 'articulation' between the activists. Unlike the old social movements of the past, like the worker's movement, the new social movements of the present form a heterogeneous group, a kind of rainbow coalition that cuts across categories (the workers, the farmers, the indigenous, the lesbians, etc.) and boundaries (local, national, transnational, global). Members often belong to different networks. Cross-linkages between groups at different levels and negotiations between their spokespersons form the structural basis of global coalitions. When the networks are interlinked in coalitions and the collective action of the coalitions is in turn coordinated at a higher level, a 'scale shift' occurs (Tarrow, 2005: 99–140). Social movements today are loosely integrated in an expanding network of networks, glued together by the multiple belongings of its members and the articulatory practices of its spokespersons.[35]

Finally, at the base of the mountain, we find the millions, if not billions, of sympathisers and adherents who believe in the goals of the movement and support their actions.[36] They have not joined the protests, at least not this time, but as a critical mass, they constitute a reservoir of capillary forces the movement can tap into and that can be occasionally mobilised to defend the general interests, ideas or identities that the movement vicariously represents. Dispersed like a rhizome, the adherents form a 'submerged network' (Melucci, 1989: 70–73) in everyday life that can occasionally emerge from the underground and form a dense 'group in fusion' (Malraux–Sartre) to confront a public authority on a given issue and defend the interests, ideas and identities of the movement.

Following Sartre (1960: 381–431), 'groups in fusion' can be conceived of more generally as practical and intentional communities that are mobilised around the collective project of common struggle against the 'pratico-inert' structures of domination.

Humanity in action

The linking of the base and the summit is greatly facilitated by CMC. In the same way as the press of the eighteenth century was instrumental in overcoming the episodic and localised character of popular protest and facilitated the formation of coalitions on a national scale (Tarrow, 1994: 48–61), the mass media of the twentieth century, and above all the television, made a massive synchronisation of minds possible and played a major role in the formation of global imagined communities, like McLuhan's global village, which includes all inhabitants of the planet in a self-conscious community of fate. If television makes the synchronisation of minds possible, the internet allows for the efficient coordination of collective actions across space. Electronic networks link individuals to movements, and also movements to each other. E-mail lists, for instance, allow for an instantaneous interconnection of minds ('online') that may occasionally lead to a massive congregation of bodies ('offline') in a protest demonstration. 'It is the capacity to move easily between on- and offline relationships that makes the scale shift to transnational activism possible' (Bennett, 2005: 205).

Compared with the more centralised movements of the past, internetworked social movements display a remarkable degree of organisational flexibility and structural fluidity. At the very extreme, they may even dispense with leadership altogether, although probably not with spokespersonship. Negri and Hardt, the talented spokespersons of the anarcho-communist factions of the direct action networks, have suggested that the new struggles of the multitude take the form of distributed, or full matrix, networks that are at once fluid, collective and individualistic, and do not display a hierarchical command organisation:

> There's no center and all nodes can communicate directly with each other.... The distributed network might be imagined like a swarm of ants or bees – a seemingly amorphous multiplicity that can strike at a single point from all sides or disperse in the environment so as to become almost invisible.
>
> (Hardt and Negri, 2004: 57)

Based on communication between nodes without hub or centre, the swarm intelligence of the multitude can be characterised as polycephalous (though not exactly in the sense that Husserl meant when he said that collective intentionality of the personality of the higher order was multi-headed).

The new media contribute to the organisation of different social movements (anti-capitalist, ecopax, feminist, gay and lesbian, etc.) and help them to gather in a single but loosely connected global social movement that counterfactually represents humanity and vicariously advocates its interests (Brunkhorst, 2002). From this point of view, the so-called anti-globalisation movement of the twenty-first century appears as the legitimate successor of the working-class movement of the nineteenth century, and perhaps even of the Proletariat as the 'identical subject–object' of history. Although it speaks in many voices and possesses many heads, it may well represent the contemporary incarnation of the *Weltgeist*. It is no longer seated on a white horse that triumphantly enters the city of Iena; it now manifests (itself) in the streets of Seattle, Davos and Genoa and makes episodic appearances at the World Social Forum in Porto Allegre, Mumbai, Caracas and Nairobi. Interconnecting all the individuals who feel concerned by the state of the world (the planet) in a hidden, dispersed and virtual network that can occasionally centre, actualise and manifest itself as a 'group in fusion', the global network of networks works as a powerful medium that can liquidate the 'seriality' of the collective and interconnect the individuals in an action group, conscious of itself and capable of common collective action, now or in the future. The 'collective effervescence' that marks groups in fusion engenders a strong feeling of unity that energises its members. The emotional energy, stored in sacred symbols, objects and slogans, but also in the memory of a shared experience, can be reactivated and released when the situation demands it, motivating the members to gather again, if necessary. 'We are here now, we were there then, and we will be together in the future. We are a movement' (Eyerman, 2006: 196). This chapter was written in 2005. Since then the Zeitgeist has moved on and 'newer' social movements, like Occupy and the Indignados, inspired by the Arab Spring, have emerged on the world scene.

Political representation and spokespersonship

Catnets and spokes

If the representation and visualisation of the collective by the members of the group transforms the collective into a symbolic community, the technological mediation that potentially connects the members of a community in a latent and dispersed network transforms the latter into a serial quasi-group that can at times manifest itself as a group in fusion. Symbolic representation and technological mediation are two necessary, albeit insufficient moments of the structuration of collectives. To become a real 'triple I group' with interests, ideas and an identity that persist over time, the quasi-group needs a more or less permanent organisational structure that transforms the mobilised group into a mobilisable group that can act 'as one man' and make decisions that commits the group as a group.

By organising itself, the group stabilises, canalises and externalises permanently the fused energies in a social institution that keeps the causal power of the group on standby and guarantees, almost at every moment, the possibility of a future collective praxis directed against the reified structures of society. 'Against the seriality that threatens to dissolve it', Sartre (1960: 440) suggests, 'the collective has to create an artificial inertia that protects it against the threat of the pratico-inert.' This artificial inertia that protects against inertia is the organisation. Sartre thinks of the organisation as an entity, but it can also be conceived of as a process that increases the common identity of the collective at the same time as it unifies its structure. Organisation (dis)solves Harré's problem: it effectively transforms categories of people who share some common characteristic into networks of people who are linked to each other, directly or indirectly, by a specific kind of interpersonal bond. Taking up a suggestion of Harrison White, Charles Tilly (1978: 62–64) has introduced the exotic concept of 'catnets' into research on social movements to refer to the set of individuals comprising both a category and a network. Catnets are strong when they combine a high degree of common identity ('high on catness') with a high degree of interconnectedness ('high on netness').

I have already analysed the social construction of categorical identities that wed the collective into a symbolic community (high catness), as well as the technological mediations that allow for the coordination of dispersed actions into a quasi-group (low to medium netness). I now want to conclude this article with some final considerations on the role of the spokesperson in the organisation of collective (high netness). The notion of spokespersonship does not serve to rescue the Leninist vanguard-party, representing the interests of 'a class that cannot represent itself and has therefore to be represented' (Marx, 1960: 198), but is meant as a modest theoretical contribution to resource mobilisation theory.[37] Borrowing freely some ideas from Pierre Bourdieu and Bruno Latour on the role of spokespersonship (Pels, 2000), I would like to defend the thesis that the transformation of the quasi-group into a tightly organised 'triple I group' that exists empirically as an institution, organisation or corporation at the meso- and macro-levels of society is the result of the work of political representation of the collective by 'the spoke'.[38]

The voice of the network

The power of the spokesperson is largely metonymic, as Keck and Sikkink (1998: 207) have correctly observed: 'The network-as-actor derives a great deal of its effectiveness from the network-as-structure.' The spokesperson condenses the network. Speaking in its name, she – let's assume, for once, it's a black woman – gives it a voice. Networks are communicative structures. Although they need a minimum of consensus to coordinate the actions of their different members (or 'nodes' – members can also be groups), they should not be thought of as old-fashioned Habermasian jukeboxes with only one tune on record. Communication does not exclude, but presupposes and includes the articulation of differences in a search for a common language and position. The critical pursuit of 'what is identical in seeming diversity of form and of what is distinct and even opposed in apparent uniformity' ensues in 'formulae of unity and federation' that 'organize and interconnect closely what is similar' (Gramsci, 1971: 190–191). Much of what goes on within networks concerns the formation of a workable consensus through the articulation of differences and similarities. When a divergent position between the members emerges, the discussion aims to enlarge the framework so as to progressively encompass the point of view of the dissenter into a new consensus. In research on social movements, such interpretative practices that interactively link divergent positions into congruent and complementary positions that overcome the 'differend' (Lyotard's *différend*) and can, consequently, be defended and assumed by all of the constituents, are called 'frame alignment' (Snow *et al.*, 1986).[39]

To 'frame' an issue, an event or an experience differently is to categorically define, redefine, refine or smooth it in such a way that the elements eventually 'con-spire', breathe and hang together, in a relatively unified and meaningful fashion that can be accepted as a working consensus by the protagonists without compromising their moral standing or draining their emotional energy. 'Frame bridging' (linkage of two or more ideologically congruent, but structurally unconnected frames, such as deforestation and regional development, for instance) and 'frame extension' (extension of boundaries of primary framework to 'hook up' different issues – such as ecology and feminism – and encompass other constituencies) are the principal routes that lead to the realignment of the protagonists. Processes of negotiation and articulation that aim to realign the protagonists and their discourses do not only take place within networks, but also between networks, that are thereby welded into a new 'bloc', i.e. 'a unity of opposites and of distincts', to speak like Gramsci (1971: 137).

Spokespeople that represent, formulate and translate the positions of their respective networks often have to articulate and negotiate, reframe and rephrase their position before they come to agree on a common platform of action. As collating devices, the discourses of human rights or, more recently, those on global justice, have been quite instrumental as 'master frameworks' that are sufficiently broad to gather different movements championing women, gays and lesbians, the disabled, ethnic minorities, indigenous movements and exploited workers of the 'third world' under a single umbrella and to align them into a rainbow coalition that speaks with one voice. 'The "voice" of the network is not the sum of the network components, but the product of an interaction of voices (and different from any single voice of a network member)' (Keck and Sikkink, 1998: 207).

Compared with the old and new social movements of the last century, the transnational networks of today are much more heterogeneous, flexible and fluid in their infrastructure ('distributed networks') and much more open, inclusive and tolerant in their identities ('unity in diversity'). Differences are now accepted and fostered, reframed as an asset and no longer as a liability. They are also more democratic, individualistic and anarchistic. Contrasting the first generation of transnational activism described by Keck and Sikkink (1998) with second-generation direct activism, Lance Bennet argues that loose activist networks that adopt self-organising CMC technologies advocate multiple issues and flexible identities 'not only challenge previous organisational forms of transnational activism. These networks also challenge social movement theories that focus on brokered coalitions, ideological framing, and collective movement identities fashioned around national politics' (Bennet, 2005: 213). However much they mistrust authority and distrust leadership, they cannot, however, I contend, avoid spokespersonship altogether. Spokespersonship is inescapable, but it can be democratised so as to allow for more flexible forms of consensus building. Communication is not just a procedure (as in Habermas) for arriving at a consensus; it is also an art and a technique. Activist networks have now devised a whole gamut of innovative techniques and instruments, such as spokescouncils, breakouts, fishbowls and vibe-watchers, for example, that facilitate consensus formation without stifling dissenting voices.[40] Although spokespersons are now multiplied and can speak with many voices, they still have to aim for the moral high ground and aspire to a form of consensus that is more than of particular interest.

Performing the collective

Representation is largely metonymic, condensing the network into the person who embodies it. It also has a strong performative effect that adds its own symbolic power to the power of the group.[41] The very act of representation is also an act of transubstantiation – by invoking the group, the spokesperson seeks to evoke it and bring it into existence. Representing the group, standing for it and acting in its name, the spokesperson calls it into being. When she addresses the members of the group, all attention is focused on her and, aware of the common focus, the members are unified by a common intentional consciousness and a shared experience of togetherness. Occasionally, when the spokesperson is charismatic enough to energise the members, communication can become effusive and may even take an ecstatic form. When this occurs, 'It is no longer a simple individual who speaks, but a group that is embodied and personified' (Durkheim, 1960: 301). As a living symbol of the group, the spokesperson embodies the unity of the group and condenses its energies in material form. When she speaks in the absence of the members of the group, she represents them, acting and speaking in and on their behalf. As an official representative of the group, the spokesperson produces and realises the group that delegates and authorises her to represent in the form of institutions, organisations and corporations that exist in space and last over time. The spokesperson who represents the group 'in person', as phenomenologists like to say, acts as a mediator between the members of the group and the group: in their absence, she acts and speaks in their name and makes them present; by representing them, she 'presentifies' the group (if you allow me this Heideggerianism). By delegation, she makes the collective visible, almost tangible, and asserts and defends its ideas, interests and identities in public. This representation of the group by its representative gives a permanent visibility to the group and actually brings it into existence, not just for the members of the group, but also for those in other groups.

Following Luc Boltanski's (1982) important analysis of the formation of the category of the 'cadres' (executives), we can use the polysemy of the notion of representation fruitfully to theorise the power of delegation. The visibility of a collective, like the 'cadres' or other groups that are designated by a single substantive, is the end result of a long and patient work of objectivation that finally channels the mental, social, and legal representations of the group into its political representation by delegation:

> [The cadres] are the product of a social effort of representation which is applied not only in the realm of mental representations (categories of thought and schemes for perceiving the social world) and in that of social representations (in the sense which American social psychology gives to the concept of 'display'), but also in the realm of political representation in the sense of 'delegation', whereby a group equips itself with official spokesmen authorised to speak and act on its behalf, to embody in the struggle with other groups and other classes.
>
> (Boltanski, 1984: 484)[42]

Thanks to the delegation of the speaker, who personalises the collective and represents it politically and legally in situations of interaction, the collective manifests and realises itself not only *in rerum natura* as a supra-individual, but also as a personified entity that is not just a collective fiction existing only somewhere in the heads of individuals. Authorised by the members of the group she represents, the spokesperson objectivates the group and transforms it into an organisation or a corporation (the *universitas personarum* of Roman law). Legally recognised by the state that recognises the organisation as a moral person, the organisation becomes an authorised social agent that can act as a supra-individual person.

If collectives exist *in potentia* at the macro-level, organisations exist *in actu* at the meso-level. Offices, secretaries, desks, telephones, mailboxes, official paper with letterhead, mailing lists of members, regular meetings, regulated discussions, and so on – just like the spokeswoman herself, all those material indices of the organised group are available for inspection and can be seen and inspected on the spot. Nobody, not even the radical positivist or grant-funded empiricist, would deny its existence – which does not mean, of course, that its legitimacy has to be accepted at face value. As a representative of the collective, the spokesperson acts in micro-situations, but mandated by the organised collective, her actions can indeed have considerable impact on the macro-level. The spokesperson is therefore a 'mega-actor' (Mouzelis, 1995: 16–18), i.e. a corporate individual who can mobilise important organisational resources and whose decisions on the spot transcend the local situations of action, affect the organisation and can even transform the social system. It is because the speaker is an intermediary between the group and its members that she can function as a mediator between the micro- and the macro-level of society. As a personification of the causal power of the collective, she embodies and represents the organisation of the collective and, speaking in its name, she represents, realises and performatively reifies the collective. It already existed potentially and virtually, but now, thanks to her actions, the potential is actualised. Appearing in society as an organised community that can be mobilised occasionally and can mobilise its members as a group in fusion, the collective now appears 'as if' it had always existed as a corporate body capable of collective common action.

Bourdieu: vox populi

In his 'realist-constructivist' theory of the social construction of classes, Pierre Bourdieu (1984a, 1987) underscores the constitutive role of spokespersonship. The spokesperson intervenes as a living hyphen that allows him to connect the realist theory of classes, understood as theoretical or taxonomic categories that exist 'on paper', to a more constructivist analysis that conceives of classes as practical groups that exist and manifest themselves in society. Speaking in the name of the group, the words of the spokesperson have the magic quality of invocations that 'perform' the collective and bring it into existence, not as an analytic category, constructed by the observer ('class-in-itself'), but as an empirical group, intentionally constituted by the actors ('class-for-itself') and recognised by other organised groups that realises, actualises and exercises the collective power of the group. Even if the analytic categories are founded in reality, they still need the intervention of the spokesperson to actualise their potential, realise the theory and transform the collective into an effective historical force, capable of intervening in the world 'with will and consciousness' (Marx).[43] 'In other words', says Bourdieu, summing up his analysis with a reference to the work of his former assistant on the cadres (Boltanski, 1982), 'one could show for other categories as well, such as the Proletariat or the professors, that to leave the serial existence behind and get access to collective existence, there's no other way, but to pass through the spokesperson' (Bourdieu, 1984b: 50).

If Bourdieu has correctly perceived that the spokesperson uses the power of delegation to represent the group and render it visible by mobilising it, it should, however, also be noted that his analyses are significantly weakened, epistemologically, by a manifest scepticism and, politically, by a latent populism. Bourdieu's scepticism is manifest in the fact that he never considers collectives, such as the nation, the people or the proletariat, as hypothetical actors, but always as hypostatised ones. To subvert and correct this nominalist strain in his work, his constructivist analyses need to be reframed in a realist perspective. This does not mean that one should take the collectives at face value and introduce them into the analysis without critique. To the contrary, one should analyse the conditions of their possibility and investigate the mediations of their actuality. The latent populism of Bourdieu expresses itself in his deconstructive critique of the fetishism of political delegation (Bourdieu, 1984b), and in some of his interventions in the public sphere (Bourdieu, 2002a: 81ff., 159ff.).[44] In the tradition of Roberto Michels and other elite theorists on the left and the right, he seems to think that complex and effective forms of organisations that are set up to mobilise the people will give the spokespersons new interests to advance and defend, and that these will necessarily enter into conflict with the interests they were supposed to represent and defend in the first place ('iron law of oligarchy'). The forced alternative he sees between the 'demission in abstention' and the 'dispossession by delegation' shows that he considers delegation as a political alienation of the silent majority by the spokesperson. Instead of giving a voice to those who are deprived of it, the spokesperson takes their vote, their voice and their silence. Thereby, she or he not only deprives the members of the group of their voice, but privatises their voice and uses it publicly to advance his or her own interests. As a result of his principled mistrust of representation and delegation, Bourdieu is led to consider the spokesperson as an impostor, usurper and ventriloquist who does not speak in the name of the members of the group, but in their place:

> A whole series of symbolic effects that appear everyday in politics rely on this sort of ventriloquism of the usurper, which consists in making those talk in whose name one is talking, making those talk in whose name one is authorized to speak, making the people talk in whose name one is authorized to speak.
>
> (Bourdieu, 1984b: 52)

To thwart the distrust of representative democracy and the concomitant populism, one should analyse the role of the representative and the delegate from the discourse theoretical perspective of deliberative democracy (Habermas, 1992). One should not so much analyse the conditions of impossibility of democratic representation of power, but the procedural conditions of possibility of the institution of a legitimate power that would not confiscate the voice of the people, but would express it counterfactually and advocatorily by putting itself at the service of the general interest. By reframing Bourdieu's analysis of the spokesperson in a realist and radically democratic perspective, one could show how the spokesperson consults the members, how they come to a consensus that 'articulates' the collective will, and how this discursive practice does not only legitimate the spokesperson, but also contributes performatively to the political organisation of the collective that seeks to democratically reform society and eliminate the structures of domination that do not so much express as repress the general interest of the adherents.[45]

Latour: vox rerum

Radicalising the nominalism that undergirds the populist critique of political fetishism, Bruno Latour adds his Machiavellism to Bourdieu's Nietzscheanism and exposes his former supervisor as an impostor who exercises an effect of domination by advancing himself as the spokesperson of the dominated – 'I am the spokesperson, the herald of an oppressed collective that cannot speak' (Bourdieu, 2002b: 232). When Bourdieu defines 'the invisible forces that manipulate the actors' and does that in the name of science and 'in the place of the actors', he speaks as a scientist and, giving a voice to the hidden structures of domination, he assumes the privilege of knowledge and silences thereby the ignorant from the height of his chair (Latour, 1998). In this ultra-Bourdieusian perspective, critical sociology is unmasked as a perfidious continuation of the politics of domination that continues the class struggle within theory to advance its own interests and extend its power over the academic world and beyond.

For Foucaldians, Latourians and other Deleuzians, knowledge and power are the same thing, viewed from a different perspective. When the scientists speak in the name of nature or society, it is to enrol them in an expanding actor-network, which grows in size and eventually becomes a powerful macro-social actor that extends its empire over the world. From this strategic viewpoint, science is the continuation of politics by other means, as Althusser said with regard to Lenin. When scientists transport their allies, human and non-human, in their laboratories and manipulate them, they do so to simplify reality and represent it scientifically in the form of numbers, graphs, statistics, words, etc., which they later insert into their articles and books. Once the tridimensional entities of the world out there are transposed, transformed, flattened, simplified and represented in texts, the world is, in effect, 'reduced to paper' (Latour, 2002: 242).

The scientist who speaks in the name of science can articulate the word to the world. Giving a voice to humans and non-humans, she or he represents them, scientifically and politically. Through science, the scientist becomes the spokesperson of humans and non-humans, and continues the political task of the construction of the collective – except that the collective is now deemed a socio-technical network that experimentally associates humans and non humans – the so-called 'actants' – in a heterogeneous post-human socio-natural community and collectivity. As Latour says in *Politics of Nature*, preening himself for having deconstructed all the oppositions between science and politics, facts and values, nature and society, technology and sociology, by mixing and fixing humans and non-humans in a socio-technical network: 'We have discovered what science and politics have in common: mixing the entities of the collective in order to articulate them and make them speak' (Latour, 1999: 132).

In the same way as one should redeploy Bourdieu's analysis in a realist and democratic perspective, one could 'refunctionalise' ANT in a realist and humanist framework and employ it in a critical theory of advancing globalisation in late modernity (Vandenberghe, 2002). When one analyses ANT from the perspective of critical realism, one understands that it really is an empiricist theory that freely associates humans and non-humans into socio-technical networks. Conceiving of society as an association and concatenation of actants, it eliminates the systemic levels of society and reduces society to a syntagmatic relation between actants (together Thoreau and his chair now form an association of sorts). *A la limite*, I am prepared to concede to Latour that socio-technical networks can be conceived of as collective subjects that construct associations and produce organisations, but one should nevertheless not forget that the networks that perform and transform society are lodged within society. Instead of reducing society to a network that exists at the meso-level and is constructed at the micro-level, one should reinsert the network in society and show that the empirical relations between actants are always conditioned and 'overdetermined' by the overarching structural and cultural relations of society at the systemic level. Provided one does not flatten society and reduce it to an interactional or institutional order, one can envelop the performative analysis of the socio-technical construction of society in a realist dialectical analysis of the structuration of collectives in organised groups.

If we calmly leave aside the provocations of the fanciful, vitalist and post-humanist actant–rhizome ontology that Latour proposes, we can accept the idea that social integration is impossible without objects that frame and stabilise human interactions as an important contribution to sociology. The same holds at the meso-level for the organisation of collectives. To structure the collective into an organised group, represented and mobilised by a spokesperson, one has indeed to associate humans and non-humans in institutions, organisations and corporations. The collective needs a spokesperson and, nowadays, a mobile phone and access to the internet are minimum requirements for every spokesperson. But that does not transform the spokesperson into an associate of Nokia, Microsoft or Linux. What is determinant (in the last instance) are the relations between social positions and ideas, not the relations between actants. They are contingent and their form depends on the structure of the overarching system that contains them and that they seek to reproduce or, as the case may be, to reform and transform.

Conclusion: history and sociology

Unlike philosophy, sociology cannot write history with capital letters *modo futuri exacti*. Sociology can no doubt propose developmental ideal types of universal history (see Max Weber, for example), but it cannot introduce a collective subjectivity – be it the Proletariat or humanity itself – as the 'identical subject–object' (Lukács) that embodies the *logos* of History and realises its *telos*. A dialectical philosophy of history comprehends sociology and totalises its results in an encompassing vision that spells out the internal logics of the development of reason that drives history forwards to its full realisation (conceived of not just as a regulative ideal, but as a living *logos* that is immanent in reality). Sociology cannot be that speculative and has to limit itself to research. Its task is *Forschung* (research) not *Darstellung* (dialectical presentation of research), but it can nevertheless offer its modest contribution by analysing how collective subjectivities are actually constituted.

In this chapter I have presented a realist theory of collective subjectivities that spans the gap between categories and networks. Categories are conceived of as virtual and potential groups. The structuration of collectives that releases and realises their causal powers has been analysed as a triple morphogenetic process that comprises three 'moments' (symbolic identification, socio-technical mediation and political representation) and produces the three avatars of the collective (the symbolic community, the mobilisable quasi-group and the organised group). At the end of this analysis, groups that counterfactually represent humanity and are represented by their spokespersons who vicariously advocate their interests in the real world appear on the scene of history as collective actors. Philosophers may now resume their work and speculate on the ends of history, but whether collectives realise those ends or not, does not depend on them. As Marx said, it is not the philosophers who make history, but the actors themselves, and they do it in circumstances which they have not chosen.

Notes

1 Like any other work, this text is the product of a collective subjectivity. I have presented different versions of this text at the Institut Marc Bloch in Berlin, at the Castle Colloquium at Yale University and also at the Seminar of the Groupe Interuniversitaire d'Etudes sur la Postmodernité in Montreal. I would like to thank Danny Trom, Seyla Benhabib and Michel Freitag for their invitation in the first place. I am grateful to Bruno Karsenti, Hélène Colliot-Thélène, Heidrun Friese, Fernando Suárez-Müller, Jeffrey Alexander, Ron Eyerman, Nadya Jaworski, Andreas Glaeser and, last but not least, José Maurício Domingues for comments, suggestions, corrections and discussions.

2 Three remarks about collectivism and individualism. First, one should not confound collectivism or emergentism with holism. So-called primitive societies are holistic societies, turned towards the past with a low degree of historicity. Ideologically and normatively, they hardly leave any place for the individual. Collectivist visions of the social, like the one I will defend, are not holistic. They give ample space to the individual and even insist that the causal power of society is always mediated (in the last instance) by the causal power of individuals. Second, the opposition between nominalism and realism only partially overlaps with the one between individualism and collectivism. Ethnomethodology, for example, is collectivist without being realist; just like Tarde's sociology, ANT is nominalist without being individualist. Finally, a radical nominalist could easily argue that the individual is as abstract as society. One can no more observe a person than one can observe a society. Both are composite entities that do not exist as such. Conversely, the realist could conclude from it that both are real.

3 In spite of his Marxist credentials, John Elster (1989: 248), for one, affirms: 'There are no societies. There only individuals who interact with one another.'

4 The Anglo-Saxon debate of the 1960s between collectivists and individualists (O'Neill, 1973) ended with a truce: victory of ontological individualism, defeat of methodological individualism. A quarter of a century later, Ogien (2000: 236) confirms the diagnosis and renews the historical compromise:

> One is allowed to say, without exaggerating, that of all the social theories that have survived the debate, there is hardly one that has endorsed the position [of ontological collectivism] without radically amending it, while most of them have been constructed with the explicit aim of showing its absurdity (to save perhaps the basic propositions [of methodological collectivism].'

5 For an intriguing investigation of mutual constitution of the basic constituents of social life in and through action, see Glaeser's (2005) 'consequent processualism'.

6 Collectives are located and intervene in society; collective practices are mediated by society, reproducing or transforming it in the process. Following critical realism, I conceive of society as a complex system of relations between social positions and ideas that exists at the macro, meso and micro levels. In extended conversations with the author, Michel Freitag has argued that the realist conception of society is too formal and he has proposed to envelop it in a more encompassing dialectical theory of society which analyses the latter, synchronically, as a transcendental totality that a priori forms, informs and regulates the symbolic practices and, diachronically, as a historically evolving set of mediations that regulate practices and reproduce society (cf. Freitag, 1986; see also Vandenberghe, 2006).

7 Giddens' famous concept of 'structuration' finds its origin in the debate about class. Giddens coined the concept to connect Marxist and neo-Marxist theories of class, understood as an economic category that refers to a series of social positions that make up a social formation, to more Weberian analyses that conceive of classes as status groups of consumption that have differential access to the market. Before being

generalised, reformulated and inserted into an ontology of praxis that directly connects agency to structure (and indirectly agency to systems via the structures), the concept of structuration simply referred to 'processes by which "economic classes" become "social classes"' (Giddens, 1980: 105). In this chapter I focus on the structuration of collectives and do not pay much attention to the reverse process of their 'destructuration'.

8 My interest in class, social movements and humanity explains in part why my analysis is an upbeat one. Epistemological considerations cannot be disconnected from moral and political ones. If I were to focus on race, ethnicity and identity, I would take a more deconstructivist line and analyse, like Brubaker (2002), the 'declining curves of groupness'.

9 Bourdieu, who is otherwise a fine dialectician and a realist, becomes a nominalist when it comes to collectives. His enthusiastic review of Denis Zaslawsky's analytic decomposition of the category of Being makes clear that his nominalism owes more to the informal philosophical logic of Russell, Ryle and Strawson than to Hegel's *Science of Logic* (cf. Bourdieu, 1982; Zaslawsky, 1982).

10 The tourist who visits Cambridge and asks to see the University of Cambridge after having seen King's College, St. John's, Queens', the quads and the mathematical bridge, makes a category mistake according to Ryle – 'as if "the University" stood for an extra member of the class of which these other units are members' (Ryle, 1945: 16). Passing from the substantive to the substance, the poor fellow commits the fallacy of misplaced concreteness and does not understand that the university does not exist outside, next to or above its colleges, departments and libraries.

11 Today's standard mainstream sociology (SMS) is an assemblage of positivism, Boolean statistics and network analysis. The latter is a highly specialised form of structural analysis that gained prominence in the mid-1970s. The main figures in the network are Harrison White, Barry Wellman, Ronald Burt, Ronald Breiger, Mark Granovetter, Peter Marsden, Peter Bearman and Edward Laumann. The abstruse terminology (structural holes, structural equivalence, strong, weak and bridge ties, multiplex relations, etc.) and the heavy use of complicated mathematical models (graph theory, blockmodelling and matrix analysis) are rather off-putting for the non-initiated. For an excellent introduction to social network analysis that does not presuppose proficiency in mathematics, see Wellman (1988, 1999).

12 Articulation is a central category of poststructuralist theories of identity. Articulation takes place when two externally related elements are interconnected through communication into a new identity. To articulate means to utter, but also to connect two elements that do not necessarily belong together. Stuart Hall (1996c: 141) gives the example of the 'articulated truck': 'A lorry where the front (cab) and back (trailer) can, but need not necessarily, be connected to one another.'

13 For an analysis of different forms of collective action, from violence (the mobs) and conventional actions (strikes, marches and demonstrations) to symbolic disruptions (sit-ins and sit-down strikes), see Tarrow (1994: 100–117).

14 In the next section I will bring in the notion of 'imagined community'. We will see that the connection between souls can be either direct (mental connection) or indirect (spiritual connection). Making abstraction of the technological mediation, which I will bring in at a later stage, I will treat the symbolic community as an intentional group whose members are in direct contact with one another.

15 Although Husserl already mentions 'personalities of a higher order' in paragraph 58 of the *Cartesian Meditations* (Husserl, 1950), the idea will only be worked out in the phenomenology of intersubjectivity (Husserl, 1973; especially texts 9 and 10). To foreclose the drift towards an ultra-Durkheimian position that shamelessly hypostatises the objective spirit into a group mind, I will interpret Husserl's analysis from a micro- and meso-, but not from a macro-perspective. Such a micro-sociological inter-

pretation corresponds to an interactionist reformulation of the project of the Fifth Cartesian Meditation.

16 For a more fine-grained investigation that is more indebted to Schütz and Mead than to Husserl and analyses the passage from a two- to a threesome in terms of the institutionalisation of reciprocal typifications of habitual action, see Berger and Luckmann (1966: 53–67); for an application, see also Berger and Kellner (1964) on partnership, marriage and the family. Surely there are limits to social integration through collective intentionality. There are now six billion inhabitants of planet Earth, and their actions cannot possibly be coordinated by means of communication.

> Even if we take into account that conscious systems on the other side of the globe are sleeping and others do not participate for whatever reasons to communication, the numbers of systems that operate at the same time is so large that effective coordination (and thus also the constitution of a consensus in an empirical sense) is completely excluded.
>
> (Luhmann, 1997: I, 115)

Luhmann is right on this point, but if the social systems globalise (globalisation 'from without'), so do the psychic systems (globalisation 'from within'). The emergence of a planetary consciousness can be considered as the subjective counterpoint of systemic globalisation (from globalisation 'an sich' to globalisation 'für uns').

17 In analytic philosophy, the theme of collective intentionality and joint intentional action has also been taken up by John Searle (1995), Michael Bratman (1999), Raimo Tuomela and Kaarlo Miller (1988). If I focus on Gilbert, it is because she deals most explicitly with the authors of the sociological canon. I think, however, that the critique I address to Gilbert also applies to her colleagues. Even if they rightly insist that 'We intentionality' cannot be reduced to 'I intentionality', they all have a rather limited conception of society, which they tend to reduce to Lewisian conventions anyway. All of the authors eliminate the 'objective spirit' and forget that the symbolic mediations that allow for the coordination of action are not only intersubjective, but also properly social. Moreover, none of the authors take into account that institutions and conventions exist in society. Like all hermeneutic reductions, this one makes abstraction of the system of material social relations at the macro-level.

18 For a more complex analysis of formal sociology, I refer the reader to my book on Simmel (Vandenberghe, 2001).

19 The asterisk refers to the advanced analysis of the semantic 'conditions of felicity' that have to be satisfied for a collective to exist as a plural subject that corresponds to the strong sense of the first-person plural as a full-blooded 'we'.

20 Drawing on ethnomethodology, one of the anonymous referees of *Sociological Theory* questions this affirmation. She or he argues not only that there are social practices that endogenously create their unity from within, but also suggests that the analysis of groups can dispense with the symbolic altogether. 'Take Baseball for instance. The only thing required is that one could get it wrong.' This is right, but the reviewer forgets that the bat-and-ball game is a team sport in which a pitcher 'pitches' the leather-covered ball towards a batter on the opposing team. Moreover, the game actually has to be learned ('This is how we do it') before it can be played as a baseball game (as opposed to, say, a cricket game), and that learning presupposes a language, rules, symbols and membership categorisation devices (Sack's MCDs). Thus understood, pitching is a bodily symbol that directly performs membership *in actu*.

21 In the Nazified version of 1933, which is not the one that has been republished in German or English, Schmitt leaves no doubt that it is 'not the soldier but the politician who determines the foe' (Schmitt, 1933: 17). By designating the other as an alien enemy, the politician (the *Führer*) effectively transforms cultural (ethnic/racial/religious/linguistic) markers into mortal divisions between the ingroup and the outgroup.

For a bloody application of Schmitt's theory to the civil war in former Yugoslavia, see Vandenberghe (1996).

22 In his analysis of personal pronouns, Benvéniste (1966: 225–236, 251–257) confirms the universality of the personal pronoun. The first, second and third person occur in all 64 languages he has analysed. I and You form a couple. The fracture intervenes with the third person, which refers, as he says, to a 'non-person'. Interestingly, he suggests that the 'We' can be constructed in two ways: an inclusive one which refers to 'I + You' and an exclusive one which refers to 'I + Them'.

23 Even Habermas concedes that there's no democracy without citizenship and no citizenship without exclusion: 'Any political community that wants to understand itself as a democracy must at least distinguish between members and non-members' (Habermas, 1998: 161).

24 For a convergent analysis of the modalities of incorporation of the other into the societal community, see Alexander's (2006: 409–457) discussion of assimilation, hyphenation and multiculturalism.

25 The texts I mention propose different approaches that deal with different collectivities and different issues. Habermas and Benhabib are concerned about citizenship and civil rights. Laclau and Mouffe deal with class and new social movements, while Barth, an anthropologist, analyses ethnic groups in poly-ethnic communities that are not multicultural societies. In the following discussion, I make abstraction of the differences between the authors, and pretend that they all deal with the same question to which they offer complementary answers.

26 Thinking with Schmitt, the fascist philosopher, against Schmitt, the philosophical Nazi, is always a risky enterprise (see how *Telos*, the journal of the New Left got dangerously entangled via Schmitt with the New Right). Instead of thinking with Schmitt, I suggest we think with all the others (Habermas, Derrida, Althusser, even Lacan if necessary) against Schmitt.

27 The clash between Benhabib's 'cosmopolitanism' and Mouffe's 'cosmopolitics' may not be as radical as the one between Schmitt and Habermas – after all, 'left-wing schmittists' are 'left liberals' (Mouffe, 1999a: 4) – but it is nevertheless a serious one and concerns the place of humanity (or 'bestiality', as Schmitt would say), and thus of ethics, in politics. My own position is a humanist and cosmopolitan one: the boundaries between particular collectives have to be deconstructed and make way for the largest collective that we can possibly imagine. Through intercultural and intercivilisational communication, the articulation of differences is teleologically driven by the constitution of a larger collective subjectivity (humanity) of which every extant collective represents only a particular instantiation.

28 Collectives can be diluted (as classes) or centred (as groups). Domingues (1995: 110–126) distinguishes two dimensions of the process of centring that can vary independently: identity, which refers to the degree of self-awareness of the group, and organisation, which refers to its capacity of decision. Etzioni's (1968) theory of societal guidance remains the best account of collective subjectivity.

29 With some goodwill, one can consider the three moments of identification, mediation and delegation as three modalities of representation: symbolic representation (Hall, 1996a, 1996b), techno-scientific representation (Latour, 1987) and political representation (Pitkin, 1967).

30 Causal powers can be exercised without being realised. This is the case when other causal powers, such as the ones of the state, for instance, intervene and block the actualisation of the powers of the generative mechanism at hand. In the following I make abstraction of the external 'opportunity and liability structures' in the environment, such as massive political repression exercised by the state, that systematically block the actualisation of the causal powers of the collective.

31 I borrow the notion of 'quasi-group' from Lord Dahrendorf (1959: 179–182), who actually got it from Ginsberg, but I give it a slightly different meaning. Quasi-groups

are potential groups, midway between classes and interest groups. The members of the group are related to one another, but only potentially and indirectly, by virtue of their common appurtenance to a class and thanks to the media. To the extent that the quasi-groups do not yet possess an organisation or a centre of decision, their capacity of action is real, though still virtual. To actualise that capacity and transform the quasi-group into a mobilised group, an organisation and a spokesperson are needed.

32 When the members of a symbolic community are 'interspiritually' connected through the media, they form a public, as defined by Tarde (1901: VI and II):

> The public is a dispersed crowd, where the influence of the minds of the ones on the minds of the others has become an action at a distance.... The public is a purely spiritual community, a dissemination of physically separated individuals whose cohesion is entirely mental.

When they are interconnected by media that allow for one-to-one communication, publics become virtual networks.

33 For a mediological investigation of the cybersphere, see the work of Pierre Lévy (1997, 1998).

34 The mobilisation of a network is almost always accompanied by a countermobilisation. The antinomial dynamic (us/them) that we analysed earlier in terms of the opposition between identification and categorisation reappears here as antagonistic interlocking of movements and countermovements in the multiorganisational field of the social movement industry (Klandermans, 1992).

35 Different groups can be linked to each other through common members who act as spokespersons, mediators and translators of their respective groups. In his popular essay on the stranger, Georg Simmel (1995: 764–771) pointed to the fact that strangers often function as diplomats who establish 'foreign relations' between the different groups to which they belong. This insight has been worked out and formalised by social network analysis (Breiger, 1974).

36 Protesters at one of the countersummits against the G8 were carrying a banner with the slogan: 'You are 8, we are 6 billion'.

37 In spite of its promising title, *Silence and Voice in Contentious Politics* (Aminzade *et al.*, 2001) has not much to say about spokespersons. It aims to highlight the 'silences' in resonance mobilization theory and to give 'voice' to neglected topics in research on social movements, such as space, personality, emotions or religion.

38 The representative activities of the spokesperson and its multiple analogues (the actor, the factor, the agent, the trustee, the guardian, the procurator, the deputy, the attorney, the lieutenant, the vicar, the delegate, the ambassador, the commissioner) boil down to essentially two: delegated by the collective, the spokesperson 'acts for' the group and in its name; symbolising the group, she or he 'stands for' it and makes it present in its absence (Pitkin, 1967: 60–112).

39 Inspired by Goffman, frame analysis has brought back cultural analysis in resource mobilisation theory, but it still shares the latter's utilitarianism and mentalism (Cefaï and Trom, 2001). It sets forth a powerful conception of strategic interaction, but it tends to reduce frames to instrumental cultural tools, conceiving of the latter as cognitive representations and undervaluing their pragmatic and affective dimensions. Moreover, it often refers to a social psychology of internalised states of mind, while frames provide a 'vocabulary of motives' that are part of public cultures available in social situations.

40 Just a couple of examples from the anarchist toolbox:

> Spokescouncils are large assemblies that coordinate between smaller 'affinity groups'. Each affinity group (which might have between 4 and 20 people) selects a 'spoke', who is empowered to speak for them in the larger group. Only the spokes can take part in the actual process of finding consensus at the council, but

> before major decisions they break into affinity groups again and each group comes to consensus on what position they want their spoke to take.... You can ask for a brainstorming session, in which people are only allowed to present ideas but not to criticize other people's.... A fishbowl would only be used if there's a profound difference of opinion: you can take two representatives for each side – one man and one woman – and have the four of them sit in the middle, everyone else surrounding them silently, and see if the four can't work out a synthesis or compromise together, which they can then present as a proposal to the whole group.
>
> (Graeber, 2002: 71–72)

41 Following speech act theory, I stress the ontological effects of performances. For a more dramatic approach that stresses the histrionic aspects of performances that successfully 'fuse' the spokesman and the group he represents, see Alexander (2004, especially p. 549):

> Successful performances overcome the deferral of meaning that Derrida recognized as difference. In a successful performance, the signifiers seem actually to become what they signify.... The actor seems to be Hamlet; the man who takes the oath of office seems to be the president.... The performance achieves verisimilitude – the appearance of reality.

42 For a social constructivist analysis of socio-professional categories that is indebted to Bourdieu and Boltanski and emphasises the interplay of social, scientific and political representations, see Desrosières and Thévenot (1988).

43 As a spokesperson of the Proletariat, Marx perfectly illustrates the performative theory of political representation. Before Marx, there were exploited workers, but there was no Proletariat. Thanks to the work of representation of minor proletarian intellectuals and major organic intellectuals, Marxism spread among the working classes. When they became conscious of their interests and their power, they started to organise themselves in parties, unions, cells, etc., realising and confirming thereby Marx's theory.

44 The publication of the quasi-totality of Bourdieu's interventions in the public sphere, from the Algerian War to the strikes of 1995 and Bourdieu's consequent acceptance on both the national and international stage as a 'total intellectual' (Bourdieu, 2002a), shows that his mistrust of the political system as a self-enclosed system of politicians was a constant in his career. This mistrust also explains his support of the comic Michel Coluche in the presidential elections of 1981. All his interventions aim to give a voice to those who are speechless, do not count much for the politicians and are not represented by the system to wit:

> the lazy, the dirty, the drugged, the alcoholics, the homosexuals, the women, the parasites, the young, the elderly, the artists, the prisoners, the butches, the apprentices, the blacks, the pedestrians, the Arabs, the mad, the transvestites, the former commies, the convinced non voters.
>
> (Coluche, announcement of his candidature for the presidential elections, cited in Bourdieu, 2002a, p. 162).

45 Offe and Wiesenthal (1980) present a communicative analysis of the organisation of interest groups. In spite of its brilliance, this Habermasian analysis is rather partial and dated, however. The authors argue that communicative logic only applies to labour unions; in contrast, to realise its interests, the federation of employers can make do with a monological and strategic logic.

Bibliography

Alexander, J.C. 2004. 'Cultural pragmatics: social performance between ritual and strategy', *Sociological Theory*, 22, 4, pp. 527–573.

Alexander, J.C. 2006. *The Civil Sphere*. Oxford: Oxford university Press.

Althusser, L. 1974. *Philosophie et philosophie spontanée des savants*. Paris: Maspéro.

Aminzade, R. *et al.* 2001. *Silence and Voice in the Study of Contentious Politics*. Cambridge: Cambridge University Press.

Anderson, B. 1983. *Imagined Communities: Reflections on the Origin and Spread of Nationalism*. London: Verso.

Archer, M. 1995. *Realist Social Theory. The Morphogenetic Approach*. Cambridge: Cambridge University Press.

Barth, F. 1969. 'Introduction', pp. 9–38 in Barth, F. (ed.), *Ethnic Groups and Boundaries: The Social Organization of Cultural Difference*. Boston, MA: Little, Brown and Company.

Barth, F. 1994. 'Enduring and emerging issues in the analysis of ethnicity', pp. 11–32 in Vermeulen, H. and Govers, C. (eds), *The Anthropology of Ethnicity: Beyond 'Ethnic Groups and Boundaries'*. Amsterdam: Het Spinhuis.

Benhabib, S. 2004. *The Rights of Others: Aliens, Residents and Citizens*. Cambridge: Cambridge University Press.

Bennett, L. 2003. 'The new media power: the internet and global activism', pp. 17–37 in Couldry, N. and Curran, J. (eds), *Contesting Media Power: Alternative Media in a Networked World*. Lanham, MD: Rowman and Littlefield.

Bennett, L. 2005. 'Social movements beyond borders: understanding two eras of transnational activism', pp. 203–226 in della Porta, D. and Tarrow, S. (eds), *Transnational Protest and Global Activism*. Lanham, MD: Rowman & Littlefield.

Benvéniste, E. 1966. *Problèmes de linguistique générale*. Paris: Gallimard.

Berger, P.L. and Kellner, H. 1964. 'Marriage and the construction of reality', *Diogenes*, 46, pp. 1–23.

Berger, P.L. and Luckman, T. 1966. *The Social Construction of Reality: A Treatise in the Sociology of Knowledge*. New York: Anchor Books.

Boltanski, L. 1982. *Les cadres: La formation d'un groupe social*. Paris: Minuit.

Boltanski, L. 1984. 'How a social group objectified itself: "cadres" in France, 1936–1945', *Social Science Information*, 23, 3, pp. 469–491.

Bourdieu, P. 1982. 'Zaslawsky, contre la magie des mots', *Libération*, 7 December, p. 21.

Bourdieu, P. 1984a. 'Espace social et genèse des "classes"', *Actes de la recherche en sciences sociales*, 52–53, pp. 3–12.

Bourdieu, P. 1984b. 'La délégation et le fétichisme politique', *Actes de la recherche en sciences sociales*, 52–53, pp. 49–55.

Bourdieu, P. 1987. 'What makes a social class? On the theoretical and practical existence of groups', *Berkeley Journal of Sociology*, 32, pp. 1–17.

Bourdieu, P. 2002a. *Interventions, 1961–2001: Science sociale et action politique*. Marseilles: Agone.

Bourdieu, P. 2002b. 'Sur l'esprit de la recherche', pp. 175–239 in Delsault, Y. (ed.), *Bibliographie des travaux de Pierre Bourdieu*. Paris: Le Temps des Cérises.

Bourdieu, P., Chamboredon, J.Cl. and Passeron, J.Cl. 1973. *Le métier de sociologue: Préalables épistémologiques*. Paris: Mouton.

Bratman, M. 1999. *Faces of Intention*. Cambridge: Cambridge University Press.

Breiger, R. 1974. 'The duality of persons and groups', *Social Forces*, 53, pp. 181–190.

Brubaker, R. 2002. 'Ethnicity without groups', *Archives européennes de sociologie*, 43, 2, pp. 163–189.

Brubaker, R. and Cooper, F. 2000. 'Beyond "identity"', *Theory and Society*, 29, 1, pp. 1–47.

Brunkhorst, H. 2002. *Solidarität: Von der Bürgerfreundschaft zur globalen Rechtsgenossenschaft.* Frankfurt am Main: Suhrkamp.

Calhoun, C. 1991. 'Imagined communities and indirect relationships: large scale integration and the transformation of everyday life', pp. 95–120 in Bourdieu, P. and Coleman, J. (eds), *Social Theory for a Changing Society.* Boulder, CO: Westview Press.

Calhoun, C. 1992. 'The infrastructure of modernity: indirect social relationships, information technology and social integration', pp. 205–236 in Haferkamp, H. and Smelser, N. (eds), *Social Change and Modernity.* Berkeley, CA: University of California Press.

Cefaï, D. and Trom, D. (eds) 2001. *Les formes de l'action collective: Mobilisations dans des arènes publiques.* Paris: Editions de l'EHESS.

Collins, R. 2004. *Interaction Ritual Chains.* Princeton, NJ: Princeton University Press.

Dahrendorf, R. 1959. *Class and Class Conflict in Industrial Society.* London: Routledge.

Debray, R. 1991. *Cours de médiologie générale.* Paris: Gallimard.

Debray, R. 2000. *Introduction à la médiologie.* Paris: P.U.F.

de Libera, A. 1996. *La querelle des universaux: De Platon à la fin du Moyen Âge.* Paris: Seuil.

Desrosières, A. and Thévenot, L. 1988. *Les catégories socioprofessionnelles.* Paris: La Découverte.

Domingues, J.M. 1995. *Sociological Theory and Collective Subjectivity.* London: Macmillan.

Domingues, J.M. 2000. *Social Creativity, Collective Subjectivity and Contemporary Modernity.* London: Macmillan.

Durkheim, E. 1960. *Les formes élémentaires de la vie religieuse: Le système totémique en Australie.* Paris: P.U.F.

Durkheim, E. 1977. *Les règles de la méthode sociologique.* Paris: P.U.F.

Elster, J. 1989. *The Cement of Society: A Study of Social Order.* Cambridge: Cambridge University Press.

Emirbayer, M. and Goldberg, C. 2005. 'Pragmatism, Bourdieu, and collective emotions in contentious politics', *Theory and Society*, 34, pp. 469–518.

Emirbayer, M. and Goodwin, J. 1994. 'Network analysis, culture, and the problem of agency', *American Journal of Sociology*, 99, 6, pp. 1411–1454.

Etzioni, A. 1968. *The Active Society: A Theory of Societal and Political Processes.* New York: Free Press.

Eyerman, R. 2006. 'Performing opposition or, how social movements move', pp. 193–217 in Alexander, J., Giesen, B. and Mast, J. (eds), *Social Performance: Symbolic Action, Cultural Pragmatics and Ritual.* Cambridge: Cambridge University Press.

Freitag, M. 1986. *Dialectique et société*, 2 vols. Lausanne: L'âge d'homme.

Giddens, A. 1980. *The Class Structure of Advanced Societies.* London: Hutchinson.

Gilbert, M. 1989. *On Social Facts.* London: Routledge.

Gilbert, M. 1990. 'Walking together: a paradigmatic social phenomenon', *Midwest Studies in Philosophy*, 15, pp. 1–14.

Glaeser, A. 2005. 'An ontology for the ethnographic analysis of social processes: extending the extended case method', *Social Analysis*, 49, 3, pp. 16–45.

Graeber, D. 2002. 'The new anarchists', *New Left Review*, 13, pp. 61–73.

Gramsci, A. 1971. *Selections from the Prison Notebooks.* New York: International Publishers.

Granovetter, M. 1973. 'The strength of weak ties', *American Journal of Sociology*, 78, pp. 1360–1380.

Greenwood, J. 1997. 'Introduction: the mark of the social', pp. 1–16 in Greenwood, J. (ed.), *The Mark of the Social: Discovery or Invention?* Lanham, MD: Rowman and Littlefield.

Habermas, J. 1992. *Faktizität und Geltung: Beiträge zur Diskurstheorie des Rechts und des demokratischen Rechtsstaats*. Frankfurt am Main: Suhrkamp.

Habermas, J. 1997. *Die Einbeziehung des Anderen: Studien zur politischen Theorie*. Frankfurt am Main: Suhrkamp.

Habermas, J. 1998. *Die postnationale Konstellation: Politische Essays*. Frankfurt am Main: Suhrkamp.

Hall, S. 1996a. 'Introduction: Who needs "identity"?', pp. 1–17 in Hall, S. and du Gay, P. (eds), *Questions of Cultural Identity*. London: Sage.

Hall, S. 1996b. 'The question of cultural identity', pp. 595–634 in Hall, S., Held, D., Hubert, D. and Thompson, K. (eds), *Modernity: An Introduction to Modern Societies*. Oxford: Blackwell.

Hall, S. 1996c. 'On postmodernism and articulation: an interview with Stuart Hall', pp. 131–150 in Morley, D. and Kuan-Hsing, C. (eds), *Stuart Hall: Critical Dialogues in Cultural Studies*. London: Routledge.

Hardt, M. and Negri, T. 2004. *Multitude: War and Democracy in the Age of Empire*. New York: Penguin.

Harré, R. 1979. *Social Being: A Theory for Social Psychology*. Oxford: Blackwell.

Harré, R. 1981. 'Philosophical aspects of the macro-micro problem', pp. 139–160 in Cicourel, A. and Knorr-Cetina, K. (eds), *Advances in Social Theory and Methodology: Toward an Integration of Micro- and Macro-Sociologies*. London: Routledge.

Harré, R. 1997. 'Crews, clubs, crowds, and classes: 'the social' as a discursive category', pp. 199–212 in Greenwood, D. (ed.), *The Mark of the Social: Discovery or Invention?* Lanham, MD: Rowman and Littlefield.

Husserl, E. 1950. *Cartesianischer Meditationen und Pariser Vorträge*, in *Husserliana I*. The Hague: M. Nijhoff.

Husserl, E. 1973. *Zur Phänomenologie der Intersubjektivität: Texte aus dem Nachlass 1921–1928)*, in *Husserliana XIV*. The Hague: M. Nijhoff.

Jenkins, R. 2000. 'Categorization: identity, social process and epistemology', *Current Sociology*, 48, 3, pp. 7–25.

Keck, M. and Sikkink, K. 1998. *Activists Beyond Borders: Advocacy Networks in International Politics*. Ithaca, NY: Cornell University Press.

Klandermans, B. 1992. 'The social construction of protest and multiorganizational fields', pp. 77–103 in Morris, B. and Mueller, C. (eds), *Frontiers in Social Movement Theory*. New Haven, CT: Yale University Press.

Laclau, E. and Mouffe, C. 1985. *Hegemony and Socialist Strategy: Towards a Radical Democratic Politics*. London: Verso.

Langman, L. 2005. 'From virtual public spheres to global justice: a critical theory of internetworked social movements', *Sociological Theory*, 23, 1, pp. 42–74.

Latour, B. 1987. *Science in Action: How to Follow Scientists and Engineers through Society*. Milton Keynes: Open University Press.

Latour, B. 1998. 'La gauche a-t-elle besoin de Pierre Bourdieu?', *Libération*, 15 September.

Latour, B. 1999. *Politiques de la nature: Comment faire entrer les sciences en démocratie*. Paris: La Découverte.

Latour, B. 2002. *La fabrique du droit: Une ethnographie du Conseil d'Etat*. Paris: La Découverte.

Latour, B. 2005. *Reassembling the Social: An Introduction to Actor–Network Theory*. Oxford: Oxford University Press.

Lévy, P. 1997. *L'Intelligence Collective: Pour une Anthropologie du Cyberspace*. Paris: La Découverte.

Lévy, P. 1998. *Qu'est-ce que le Virtuel?* Paris: La Découverte.

Livet, P. 1994. *La communauté virtuelle: Action et communication*. Combas: Editions de l'éclat.

Lockwood, D. 1964. 'Social integration and system integration', pp. 244–257 in Ollschan, G. and Hirsch, W. (eds), *Explorations in Social Change*. London: Routledge.

Luhmann, N. 1997. *Die Gesellschaft der Gesellschaft*. Frankfurt am Main: Suhrkamp.

Marx, K. 1960. *Der achtzehnte Brumaire des Louis Bonaparte*, in *Marx-Engels Werke, Band 8*. Berlin: Dietz Verlag.

Marx, K. 1976. 'Zur Kritik der Hegelschen Rechtsphilosophie: Kritik des Hegelschen Staatsrechts', pp. 203–233 in *Marx-Engels Werke, Band 1*. Berlin: Dietz Verlag.

Mellucci, A. 1989. *Nomads of the Present: Social Movements and Individual Needs in Contemporary Society*. London: Hutchinson.

Milgram, S. 1967. 'The small-world problem', *Psychology Today*, 1, pp. 62–67.

Mitchell, C. 1969. *Social Networks in Urban Situations*. Manchester: Manchester University Press.

Mouffe, C. 1999a. 'Introduction: Schmitt's Challenge', pp. 1–6 in Mouffe, C. (ed.), *The Challenge of Carl Schmitt*. London: Verso.

Mouffe, C. 1999b. 'Carl Schmitt and the paradox of liberal democracy', pp. 38–53 in Mouffe, C. (ed.), *The Challenge of Carl Schmitt*. London: Verso.

Mouzelis, N. 1995. *Sociological Theory. What Went Wrong?* London: Routledge.

Offe, C. and Wiesenthal, H. 1980. 'Two logics of collective action: theoretical notes on social class and organizational form', *Political Power and Social Theory*, 1, pp. 67–115

Ogien, R. 2000. 'Pourquoi est-il si difficile d'être purement matérialiste?', *Raisons pratiques*, 11, pp. 231–249.

O'Neill, J. (ed.) 1973. *Modes of Individualism and Collectivism*. London: Heinemann.

Pels, D. 2000. *The Intellectual as Stranger: Studies in Spokespersonship*. London: Routledge.

Pitkin, H. 1967. *The Concept of Representation*. Berkeley, CA: University of California Press.

Ryle, G. 1945. *The Concept of Mind*. London: Hutchinson.

Sandelands, L. 1994. 'The sense of society', *Journal for the Theory of Social Behaviour*, 24, 4, pp. 305–338.

Sartre, J.P. 1960. *Critique de la raison dialectique*. Paris: Gallimard.

Sawyer, K. 2003. *Social Emergence: Societies as Complex Systems*. Cambridge: Cambridge University Press.

Schmitt, C. 1933. *Der Begriff des Politischen*. Hamburg: Hanseatische Verlag.

Searle, J. 1995. *The Construction of Social Reality*. New York: Free Press.

Simmel, G. 1995. *Soziologie: Untersuchungen über die Formen der Vergesellschaftung* in *Gesammelte Schriften, Band 11*. Frankfurt am Main: Suhrkamp.

Snow, D., Rochford, B., Worden, S. and Benford, R. 1986. 'Frame alignment processes, micromobilization and movement participation', *American Sociological Review*, 51, pp. 464–481.

Sorokin, P. 1957. *Social and Cultural Dynamics*. London: Peter Owen Ltd.

Tarde, G. 1901. *L'opinion et la foule*. Paris: Félix Alcan.

Tarrow, S. 1994. *Power in Movement: Social Movements, Collective Action and Politics*. Cambridge: Cambridge University Press.

Tarrow, S. 2005. *The New Transnational Activism*. Cambridge: Cambridge University Press.

Tilly, C. 1978. *From Mobilization to Revolution*. Englewood Cliffs, NJ: Prentice Hall.

Tuomela, R. and Miller, K. 1988. 'We-intentions', *Philosophical Studies*, 53, pp. 367–389.

Vandenberghe, F. 1996. 'La Légalité, la légitimité et la politique du "nettoyage ethnique": quelques considérations métajuridiques sur Max Weber, Carl Schmitt et Jürgen Habermas', *Mana: Revue de sociologie et d'anthropologie*, 2, 2, pp. 193–216.

Vandenberghe, F. 1997–1998. *Une histoire critique de la sociologie allemande. Aliénation et réification*, 2 vols. Paris: La Découverte/MAUSS.

Vandenberghe, F. 2001. *La sociologie de Georg Simmel*. Paris: La Découverte.

Vandenberghe, F. 2002. 'Reconstructing humants: a humanist critique of actant–network theory', *Theory, Culture and Society*, 19, 5–6, pp. 51–67.

Vandenberghe, F. 2006. 'L'École de Montréal: théorie critique ou critique théorique de l' "asociété"?', *Société*, 26, pp. 115–151.

Vandenberghe, F. 2007a. 'Une ontologie réaliste pour la sociologie: système, morphogénèse et collectifs', *Information sur les sciences sociales/Social Science Information*, 46, 3, pp. 487–542.

Vandenberghe, F. 2007b. 'Régis Debray and mediation studies, or how does an idea become a material force?', *Thesis Eleven*, 89, 1, pp. 23–42.

Weber, M. 1964. *Wirtschaft und Gesellschaft: Grundriss der Verstehenden Soziologie*. Tübingen: Mohr.

Wellman, B. 1988. 'Structural analysis: from method and metaphor to theory and substance', pp. 19–61 in Wellman, B. and Berkowitz, S. (eds), *Social Structures: A Network Approach*. Cambridge: Cambridge University Press.

Wellman, B. 1999. *Networks in the Global Village: Life in Contemporary Communities*. Boulder, CO: Westview Press.

Zald, M. and McCarthy, J. 1987. *Social Movements in an Organizational Society*. New Brunswick, NJ: Transaction Books.

Zaslawsky, D. 1982. *Analyse de l'être: Essai de philosophie analytique*. Paris: Minuit.

3 Generative structuralism of Pierre Bourdieu

By means of concepts and symbols we try to make a temporal order of words stand for a relational order of things.

S. Langer, *Philosophy in a New Key*

'Entities of the world – relate!' (Emirbayer, 1997: 312). This could be the motto of a relational sociology. Bourdieu has opted for another one, namely 'The real is relational', which contains an ironic reference to Hegel rather than to Marx. In *Méditations pascaliennes*, a sociological meditation on the philosophies of our time from Searle to Habermas and Rawls, Bourdieu has described himself as a *pascalien* (Bourdieu, 1997a: 9). But I think that in so far as his 'generative structuralism' (Harker *et al.*, 1991: 3) can best be understood as an attempt to systematically transpose the relational conception of the natural sciences to the social sciences – an attempt which takes the form of an original synthesis of sociology (Weber, Marx, Durkheim and Mauss (Brubaker, 1985: 747–749), but also Elias, Mannheim and Goffman), phenomenology (Husserl, Heidegger and Merleau-Ponty), linguistic philosophy (Wittgenstein and Austin) and, last but not least, neo-Kantian epistemology (Bachelard and Cassirer, but also Panofsky and Lévi-Strauss) – one could as well, and maybe even better, describe him as a '*bachelardien*'.[1] Although the influence of Gaston Bachelard on Bourdieu has often escaped the attention of Anglo-American scholars who are not well acquainted with the French tradition of the history and the philosophy of science, and who may have encountered the names of Bachelard, Koyré, Canguilhem, Meyerson or Cavaillès only indirectly via their interest in Althusser, Foucault or Kuhn, whose famous book on the *Structure of Scientific Revolutions* (Kuhn, [1962] 1970) is directly influenced by Bachelard, I want to go back to the formative years of the French sociologist (the late 1960s and the early 1970s, when all his seminal ideas were in gestation) to show that his social theory can best be understood when it is seen as an attempt to systematically transpose Bachelard's 'applied rationalism' from the realm of the natural sciences to the realm of the social sciences.[2]

However, the focus on Bachelard should not obscure what Bourdieu owes to Ernst Cassirer's protostructuralist analyses of the relational principle in the modern sciences, from mathematics to physics and linguistics.[3] Indeed, the unfalsifiable metascientific 'hard core' (Lakatos) of Bourdieu's progressive research programme is formed by a sophisticated synthesis of Bachelard's rationalism with Cassirer's relationism. Together, they form the metatheory of sociological knowledge that underlies and generates the sociological theory of the fields of the production, circulation and consumption of cultural goods. This structuralist metatheory of knowledge is naturalist, but it is not positivist. Like contemporary critical realists (Harré, Bhaskar, etc.), Bourdieu argues for a non-positivistic interpretation of the epistemology of the natural sciences and reformulates it systematically in such a way that the possibility of a naturalistic social science becomes possible. Notwithstanding his nominal attacks on realist (empiricist) and substantialist (non-relational) philosophies of science, which do not accomplish the epistemological rupture with the spontaneous conceptions of reality,[4] I would like to show that his sociological metascience represents a rationalist version of critical realism.

Although I am generally sympathetic to Bourdieu's approach, I would like to formulate a positive critique of rationalism and try to argue for the necessity of a philosophical conversion from rationalism to realism. Once the philosophical ground is cleared, I will move on to a systematic reconstruction of the relational conception that forms the core of genetic structuralism to investigate in more detail how, in the wake of Bachelard, Bourdieu says *adieu* to empiricist accounts of science and conquers, constructs and establishes the facts by means of a conceptual detour via a theory of fields. In that context I will also expound the famous concept of the habitus, which by realising structures relates fields to actions and mediates between both as a Bachelardian attempt to transcend philosophical antinomies, and try to push it in a volontaristic direction more in line with the moral and political intent that animates his critical theory. Moving from a metatheoretical analysis of the theory of sociological knowledge, I will next analyse Bourdieu's general theory of fields as a concrete application of the relational mode of thought and present a highly formalised account of the general principles and properties of fields and subfields. In order to illustrate how this theory of fields represents a sociological application of the conjunction of Bachelard's rationalist and Cassirer's relationalist metatheories of the natural sciences, I will reconstruct Bourdieu's first studies of the religious and the scientific fields and probe their Weberian and Mannheimian resonances. Finally, I will conclude with a general evaluation of the research programme and a final question about ethics.

The possibility of naturalism

To what extent can society be studied in the same way as nature? Without exaggerating, one could call this question concerning the possibility of naturalism in the social sciences the primal problem of the philosophy of the social sciences (Bhaskar, 1989a). For, since the double foundation of sociology by Auguste Comte and Wilhelm Dilthey, the history of that subject has been polarised around a dispute between two traditions, affording rival answers to this conundrum. A naturalist tradition, whose immediate philosophical antecedents lay in the work of Hume, Comte, Mill, Mach and the Vienna Circle, has claimed that the sciences are (actually or ideally) unified in their concordance with positivist principles, based in the last instance on the Humean notion of law as the regular succession of two observable events. In opposition to positivism, an anti-naturalist tradition, which finds its philosophical ancestry in Vico, Kant, Hegel, Dilthey, Husserl and Wittgenstein, has posited a cleavage in method between the natural and the social sciences, grounded in a differentiation of their subject matters. For this hermeneutic tradition, the subject matter of the social sciences consists essentially of meaningful objects, and their aim is the elucidation of the meaning of these objects. Now, the great error that unites these disputants is, as Bourdieu says, their 'false representation of the epistemology of the natural sciences' (Bourdieu *et al.*, 1973: 18 – here and below all translations from cited works are mine), and the concomitant acceptance of an essentially positivist account of natural science, or at least of an empiricist ontology. Indeed, recent developments in the philosophy of science, and in particular those that are exemplified in the work of Rom Harré (1970) and that Roy Bhaskar has systematised under the title of 'transcendental realism' ([1975] 1978), have convincingly shown that science as it is actually practised by practising scientists and reflexively reconstructed by epistemology does not conform to the positivist canon.[5]

The sciences do not so much aim to arrive by inductive generalisation of the regular succession of observable phenomena at universal laws as they attempt to get 'behind' or 'beyond' the phenomena revealed to us by sensory experience, to give us knowledge of unobservable 'noumenal structures' (Bachelard) or 'generative mechanisms' (Harré) that somehow necessitate these phenomena. In this anti-Humean perspective, laws no longer refer to regular conjunctions of events, but are analysed in dispositional terms as the causal powers, or more precisely tendencies, of the underlying generative mechanisms. The combined tendencies of these 'deep' structures and transfactual mechanisms may generate events that may be observed, but the events may take place whether or not there is anyone around to observe them, and the tendencies of the noumenal structures remain the same even when they counteract each other in such a way as to produce no observable change in reality. In place of the ontology of experience and atomistic events constantly conjoined, transcendental realism thus establishes an ontology of unobservable causal powers and mechanisms. And in place of an analysis of laws as constant conjunctions of events, it analyses laws in terms of the tendencies of the underlying mechanisms that generate the events that may or may not be perceived: 'Tendencies may be possessed unexercised, exercised unrealized, and realized unperceived (or undetected) by men' (Bhaskar, [1975] 1978: 184).[6]

In order to 'exhume' the sciences and to overcome their empiricist fixation on perception and sense data, Bhaskar ([1975] 1978: 56–62) proposes to replace the 'flat ontology' of the empiricists with a more stratified vision of reality that distinguishes the overlapping domains of the real, the actual and the empirical. If the domain of the real is composed of transfactual generative mechanisms and structures that usually escape direct observation, the domains of the actual and the empirical, respectively, comprise patterns of events that are generated by these mechanisms and structures and the experiences in which they are apprehended. Given that the domain of the real cannot be reduced to and confounded with the domain of the empirical, Bishop Berkeley and the empirical realists are thus simply wrong: to be is *not* to be perceived. That reality exists independently of the observations and the descriptions we may have of it does not mean, however, that we can know reality independently of those observations and (re) descriptions. Reality can only be known thanks to the intervention of categories, theories and conceptual frameworks, but – *pace* Kuhn, Foucault and Rorty – they do not determine the structure of the world. Observations are always overdetermined by theory and theories are always underdetermined by observations, but if we want to avoid the 'epistemic fallacy' (Bhaskar, [1975] 1978: 36–38), which consists in the reduction of ontological questions to epistemological ones, we have to categorically distinguish between the 'transitive' and the 'intransitive objects of science' (Bhaskar, [1975] 1978: 17): between our categories, theories and conceptual frameworks, on the one hand, and the real entities, mechanisms, structures, and relations that make up the natural and the social world, on the other. Without this distinction between the epistemic or transitive and the ontic or intransitive level of knowledge, we risk projecting our socio-historically determined knowledge of the objects on the objects of knowledge themselves, substituting the one for the other, and taking the projected object for the thing itself, with the result that the world literally becomes (the reification of) my will and representation.[7]

Once the essentially positivist account of the natural sciences, which is shared by both the positivist defenders of naturalism and its hermeneutic critics, has been thus overhauled, the question concerning the possibility of naturalism in the social sciences can be raised in a refreshingly new way. Now that positivism is refused and refuted, the contributions of the phenomenological and hermeneutic traditions can be taken on board and the possibility of a third position, or (with due apologies to Giddens) a 'third way', explored, namely that of a qualified, phenomenologically informed and hermeneutically sensitive non-positivist naturalism.[8] Like other French sociologists and philosophers of his generation who studied at the 'Ecole Normale Sup' on the Rue d'Ulm (e.g. Desanti, Macherey, Badiou, etc.), Bourdieu is a product of the philosophical tradition of 'historical epistemology' that engenders what he refers to as 'an almost obsessional preoccupation with epistemological problems' (Bourdieu and Passeron, 1967: 197–198). Consequently, it comes as no surprise that Bourdieu has developed a theory of sociological knowledge that systematically explores the possibility of social naturalism. I now proceed to an analysis of his structuralist epistemology, showing its indebtedness to Bachelard's rationalism and critically comparing it to Bhaskar's critical realism. Needless to say, Bourdieu cannot be considered a mere 'executor' of Bachelard or Cassirer. Neither of them has made any direct contributions to sociology. The author of *Distinction* has, and that is, without doubt, his distinctive contribution to our disciplinary field.

The theory of sociological knowledge

Realism versus rationalism

In *Le Métier de Sociologue* (*The Craft of Sociology*), a handbook in epistemology he now describes as 'almost scholastic', but which contains the basic epistemological and methodological principles on which his whole structural sociology rests, Bourdieu sets forth the 'theory of sociological knowledge', comprising the 'system of principles that define the conditions of possibility of all the acts and all the discourses that are properly sociological, and only those' (Bourdieu *et al.*, 1973: 15–16, 48; see also Bourdieu, 1968: 681–682). He specifies that the epistemological and logical principles of the theory of sociological knowledge are metascientific in so far as they are simply sociological particularisations of the principles upon which all science is founded. Once interiorised, the principles of the theory of sociological knowledge form the 'sociological habitus' (Bourdieu *et al.*, 1973: 16; see also Brubaker, 1993), understood as the operational disposition of the practising sociologist to apply abstract principles in concrete empirical research.

Bachelard, the postal clerk turned philosopher who was one of Bourdieu's teachers at the prestigious École Normale Supérieure, is quoted almost as often as Durkheim in his early epistemological reflections on the logic of the discovery of the social sciences. A closer look at the theory of sociological knowledge reveals that the French sociologist has borrowed its main principles from Bachelard's rationalist reconstruction of the theoretical practices in the natural sciences. Bachelard offers, above all, a reconstruction of the 'everyday' philosophy of the scientists, that is the philosophy implicit in their spontaneous practice, which he critically opposes to the 'nocturnal' philosophy of the philosophers, forged in the schools of empirical positivism, to which scientists tend to return when they reflect on their practice (Bachelard, [1940] 1988: 13; [1953] 1990: 19). Probing the epistemological implications of the scientific revolutions in chemistry, biology and, above all, physics (relativity theory and quantum physics), he concluded that those breakthroughs undermined both the a priorism of the idealistic accounts of scientific reason and the naive empiricism of the positivist accounts of the sciences. Bachelard's epistemology is synthetic, or, as he says himself, 'dialectic' and 'discursive'. It is dialectic, not because it proceeds in a Hegelian fashion towards a closed and all-encompassing totality, but because the movement of thought is seen as a never-ending 'pincer movement' (*mouvement d'enveloppement*; Bachelard, [1940] 1988: 137) in which the limitations of a particular conceptual framework are discovered, overcome and integrated into a broader framework that includes the previously excluded aspect.

In the same dialectical vein, Bachelard attempts to show that the practical logic of the working scientist naturally transcends the philosophical oppositions of idealist rationalism and empiricist realism.[9] Practising scientists are not bothered by philosophical disputes and antinomies. Spontaneously and eclectically they combine the constructive imagination of the idealists (rationalism) with the instructed experience of the empiricists (realism), which philosophers tend to separate and to declare incompatible. Thus, the synthetic philosophy they act on, and which combines abstract theory (rationalism) and concrete research (empiricism), is the one which Bachelard calls 'applied rationalism' (Bachelard, [1940] 1986) or 'rational materialism' (Bachelard, [1953] 1990). They do not simply gather facts, but they construct elaborate abstract theoretical models of noumenal structures that necessitate the phenomenal facts, and they set up experiments that technically 'realise' and make concretely manifest the phenomenon that the theory has hypothetically posed as a possible effect of the noumenal structures. Instructed by the abstract theory, the scientist thus technically creates or 'realises' the phenomenon. In order to stress the break with the naive realism of the empiricists, however, it is essential to stress that Bachelard leaves no doubt about the 'direction of the epistemological vector': it is the one that goes 'from the rational to the real' and 'not from the real to the general' (Bachelard, [1934] 1991: 8), as has been professed by all philosophers from Aristotle to Bacon. Primacy is clearly conceded to theoretical reflection and to the construction of the theoretical object, and not to the 'immaculate perception' (Nietzsche) of the empiricists. Being the 'realisation' of the theory (Bachelard, [1934] 1991: 98), the real is thus, in effect, rationalised. Paradoxically, it is to render the contact with reality more precise and more penetrating that science is forced to carry out, as Gilles-Gaston Granger beautifully says, 'a detour via the realm of abstraction' (Granger, quoted in Hamel 1997: 16). In so far as the facts are not immediately given, but are properly speaking the mediated result of the technical realisation of the theory, Bachelard's realism can be characterised as a 'realism of the second position, a realism that reacts against usual reality, a realism made of realised and experienced reason' (Bachelard, [1934] 1991: 9).

If this realism of the second position is compared with Bhaskar's transcendental realism (for a comparison, see Bhaskar (1989b: 41–48)), we can clearly see that both react against and reject the standard positivist account of the natural sciences. Over and against empiricism both stress the theory-ladenness of facts and the importance of transfactual noumenal structures and generative mechanisms that necessitate and explain the phenomena. However, from the vantage point of Bhaskar's transcendental realism, which tries to sustain a clear concept of the independent reality of being (of the intransitive or ontological dimension) in the face of the relativity of knowledge (in the transitive or epistemological dimension), Bachelard's realism appears to be essentially a form of sophisticated neo-Kantian transcendental idealism that somehow reverses the real nature of the dependency of science and being.[10] Whereas for critical realism ontology is simply irreducible to epistemology, Bachelard equivocates and suggests at times not only that the world can only be known to be what it is thanks to science, which is unproblematic, but also – which is more controversial – that the world is what it is thanks to science. For, in Bachelard's opinion, it is the fact that science occurs that gives the world a structure such that it can be known by men, whereas in Bhaskar's opinion it is the fact the world has such a structure that makes science possible. From Bhaskar's perspective, the French historian of scientific ideas thus commits the 'epistemic fallacy', because assuming that statements about being can be reduced to statements about knowledge, he wrongly concludes from the fact that the world can only be known from science that its nature is determined by science. The idea that being can be analysed in terms of knowledge of being, that it is sufficient for philosophy to 'treat only the network and not what the network describes' (Wittgenstein, 1961: 6, 35), results in the dissolution of a world independent of but investigated by science, as can be gathered, for instance, from Kuhn's problematic statement that 'when paradigms change, the world itself changes with them' (Kuhn, [1962] 1970: 111).

Notwithstanding Bourdieu's heavy investment in empirical research and the fact that social objects do not exist independently of, and may be causally affected by, social science, I think that he commits the same epistemic fallacy. Like his structuralist predecessors (Lévi-Strauss, Althusser and Foucault), however, he tends to equivocate between a realist and conventionalist interpretation of science.[11] Although Bourdieu suggests at times that scientific representations of reality have their *fundamentum in re*, the main drift of his epistemological arguments points to the adoption of a more rationalist position in which scientific representations are not so much founded in reality as 'reality' is founded in them (as indicated by the fact that words like 'real', 'reality', and 'realisation' are always put between quotation marks). At this point I would like to note that my critique of Bourdieu's rationalism is not intended as a final indictment of his metascience, but as an invitation to resume the dialectical 'pincer movement' of thought in the direction of critical realism. In other words, I would like Bourdieu to abandon his scepticism about the existence of a theory-independent world and accept the idea that the world, which can indeed only be known under different (re)descriptions, actually exists independently of those (re)descriptions, or even better, that those alternative (re)descriptions of the world actually offer alternative accounts of the *same* world. This invitation is more than a philosophical skirmish. Given that the realist assumption that the (re)descriptions of reality refer to the same world is a necessary precondition for the rational comparison of theories and thus for a rational theory choice, the idea of scientific development over time depends on the overhaul of scientific rationalism. In a somewhat paradoxical formulation, we could say that the rationality of science presupposes the abandonment of scientific 'surrationalism' (Bachelard, [1940] 1988: 28).

In *Structuralism and the Theory of Sociological Knowledge*, Bourdieu develops a structuralist theory of the social in which empirical reality is conceived as an analogical reflection of the relations between elements which the theoretical model posits as a hypothetical but invisible structure: 'Theory as a system of signs organized to represent, through their own relations, the relations among the objects is a translation or, better, a symbol linked to what it symbolizes by a law of analogy' (Bourdieu 1968: 689). Thus, in so far as the real relations between the elements are somehow reduced to an analogical reflection of the theoretical relations that obtain between the elements of the theoretical structure, the ontology of the world is indeed induced by a structural epistemology of the world. However, aware as he is of the risk of ontologising epistemological propositions, he veers away at the last moment and has recourse to the neo-Kantian strategy of the immunisation of analytical fictionalism: 'All the propositions of the sociological discourse should be preceded by a sign which could be read as "everything happens as if…"' (Bourdieu, 1972: 173; 1980: 49).[12] As a result of this conventionalist stratagem, sociological propositions are no longer supposed to capture the world as it is, but are sceptically downgraded to the status of (re)descriptions of 'reality' that can never be more than heuristic devices to analogically represent or 'save' the phenomena.

Thanks to this epistemological vigilance, Bourdieu avoids the risk of the reification of the theory, but only at the price of ontological cowardice, if I dare say. The reifying move from the model of reality to the reality of the model is indeed averted, but as a result of this conventionalist twist the referential relation between the model and reality becomes ontologically obscure. When the referential move from the model of reality to the reality of the model, and from the signifier to the signified, is a priori rejected and denounced as a reifying move from the hypothesis of the model to its hypostasis, it is no longer possible to rationally test the ontological pretentions of the model. In the name of an 'ontophobic' fear for the 'fallacy of misplaced concreteness' (Whitehead, 1930: 65), one is thus no longer allowed to investigate whether the model actually refers to and captures reality, or whether it merely leads to its reification. In this sense, a realist interpretation puts more at stake than does a conventionalist one, because if the scientist possesses the concept of an ontological realm, distinct from his current claims to knowledge, his or her research can actually show that his or her hypothesis about the real thing was, in fact, only a real hypostasis of the thing. Epistemological pragmatism, on the other hand, avoids the risk of reification, but only at the price of epistemic relativism, because if the link between the epistemological and the ontological level is elastic, that is if we use analogical models of reality without making ontological claims about reality, we logically arrive at the situation where 'anything goes'. With Bhaskar, I think that a theory has to be ontologically bold rather than epistemologically cautious (Outhwaite, 1987: 19–44).[13] Rather than making conventionalist claims about conceptual necessities about the characteristics we must necessarily attribute to things, we should use real definitions of the things and try to capture their real structure. It is a (Quinian) fact that reality can be known under different descriptions, but in the absence of a correspondence theory between the model and reality, we cannot ascertain what reality is, and we end up in the absurd situation where there are as many worlds as descriptions under which reality can be known. With critical realism, we can thus conclude that it is only if we possess the concept of an ontological realm, distinct from our current claims to knowledge, that we can think out the possibility of a rational criticism of our claims.

Removing epistemological obstacles

Moving back from the lofty heights of philosophical criticism, we can proceed to an analysis of Bourdieu's transposition of Bachelardian epistemology to the realm of the social. Like Bachelard, Bourdieu calls for 'epistemological vigilance'. Science proceeds only by means of errors, by correcting errors. The first error is the empiricist error of the naive realist who takes facts as given and not as a result, as something to be conquered and systematically constructed. With Bachelard, Bourdieu states in his 'epistemological preliminaries' to sociology that the scientific fact is 'conquered, constructed [and] established' (*conquis, construit, constaté*; Bourdieu *et al.*, 1973: 24, 81). Consequently, the epistemological hierarchy of the scientific act subordinates the establishment of the fact to its construction, and its construction to the break with spontaneous conceptions of the social.

The 'first epistemological obstacle' (Bachelard, [1938] 1993: 23–54) to be overcome if sociology is to be a rigorous science is the spontaneous adherence of the sociologist to the immediate 'doxic experience' of the common sense and common sensical explanations of the social by traditional sociological theories.[14] In so far as scientific objectivity is only possible if one has first broken with the immediate object, the first imperative of sociology is to accomplish an 'epistemological rupture' (Bachelard, [1949] 1986: 104) between the common sense conception (*doxa*) and the scientific conception of the social (*episteme*).[15] From this perspective, Schütz's 'postulate of adequacy', which stipulates that scientific concepts (of the second order) should always remain tied to and translatable into common sense concepts (of the first order) (Schütz, [1932] 1974: 289, 324ff.; 1962: 44), has to be rejected categorically.[16] In Bourdieu's opinion, a science can only be scientific if it applies throughout the determinist principle of 'sufficient reason'. Transposed to the domain of sociology, the principle of determinism takes the form of the Durkheimian 'principle of nonconsciousness' (Bourdieu *et al.*, 1973: 31): Social life has to be explained not by the conceptions of its participants, but by structural causes that escape consciousness and explain and necessitate the observed phenomena. Every time one refers to psychological or interactional explanations of social facts, one can be sure of inverting the causes and the effects. Bourdieu leaves no doubt about that: 'It is the structure of relations which constitutes the space of the field, which commands the form which the visible relations of interaction and the content itself which agents have of it take on' (Bourdieu, 1982a: 42).[17]

Social facts can thus only be explained by social facts (Durkheim, [1895] 1986: 109), and those have to be systematically constructed against common sense and objectivated into a system of relations in such a way that the objective structural relations between the phenomenal elements necessitate and explain the behaviour of the elements of the constructed relation between the elements.[18] Statistical analysis of the numerical relations between elements are useful in so far as they allow the sociologist to break the illusory network of relations that are spontaneously spun in ordinary life, but they are only a first step and have to be inserted themselves in a relational network of a higher order that gives a rational account of the observed statistical relations.[19] The resistance that the science of sociology rouses when it strips immediate experience of its gnoseological privilege is inspired by a humanist philosophy of social action that takes the subject as the ultimate ontological reference without seeing that the objective but invisible system of the relations of the relations between the individuals has 'more reality' than the subjects it binds. Or, to say the same in the scholastic language of which Bourdieu is so fond: not the visible individuals but the invisible space of relations between individuals is the *ens realissimum* (Bourdieu, 1994: 53). However, this real but invisible system of relations does not simply hang in the thin air of Platonic ideas. It does not exist in itself, but similar to Popper's 'inmates' of 'world 3' (the 'world of theoretical systems'), it only manifests itself empirically in the real world ('world 1', the world of observable events, whose objective regularities are systematically captured by statistical data) thanks to the intervention of the habitus (see below), which belongs itself to 'world 2' ('the world of states of consciousness, or of mental states, or perhaps of behavioral dispositions'), but which mediates between world 3 and world 1 and thus 'realises' the theoretical system of constructed relations (see Popper, 1979: 106–190).

The primacy of relations

According to Bachelard and Bourdieu, who follows his mentor on this point, research is only scientific because and in so far as it effects an epistemological rupture between *doxa* and *episteme*. The move from the doxic realm of mere 'opinion' to the scientific realm of 'knowledge' presupposes a theoretical 'detour via the infinitely open realm of abstractions in order to render contact with experience more penetrating, powerful and precise' (Granger quoted by Hamel, 1997: 31). In so far as this theoretical detour aims to break (and to break with) 'everyday essentialism', which naturally reifies what are really relations into substances, the rationalist (or realist) construction of the theoretical objects as 'bundles' of relations is inherently linked to a relational mode of intellectual production. The conquest of the scientific fact against the spontaneous and preconstructed perception of the 'real object' is inseparable from its systematic construction as a 'theoretical object' by means of its objectivation as a coherent system of constructed relations. If common sense spontaneously adheres to a substantialist philosophy, science reflexively and methodically deconstructs phenomenal substances in order to reconstruct the phenomenon as a tangled tissue of relations – that is, as a rational or second-order configuration of relational attributes.[20]

Although Bachelard has clearly perceived the primacy of relations over substances that characterises the modern natural sciences, and maybe even the logic of modern worldviews in general (Dux, 1982) – as can be gathered from his motto: 'In the beginning is the relation' (Bachelard, 1929: 65)[21] – Bourdieu turns to Ernst Cassirer who, in his seminal book *Substance and Function*, has masterfully analysed the displacement of the Aristotelian logic of substances by a functional logic of generating relations which can be found in modern mathematics and physics, and also in geometry and chemistry.[22] Cassirer's neo-Kantian analysis of the concept of function is directed towards the elaboration of a transcendental logic in which the object is no longer presupposed by logic but is, so to speak, generated by it. Scientific concepts do not stand unrelated to each other, but are organised into coherent conceptual 'fields' or 'figurations' or, to use Cassirer's preferred language, into a 'lawful series of progressions' (*Reichenfolge*) that discloses and constitutes an analytical region of reality in a systematic way. In this relational conception the particular is no longer subsumed under the general, as is the case in the Aristotelian syllogism, but a functional or dialectical interrelation is established between both in such a way that the particular, which is overdetermined by theory, appears as the concrete synthesis of a bunch of general relations:

> The concept no longer disdainfully discards the particulars which specify the contents that it subsumes but, to the contrary, it attempts to disclose the necessity of the manifestation and the connection of the particulars themselves. What it thus proposes is a universal rule which allows us to compose and to combine the particular element in person.
>
> (Cassirer, [1910] 1994: 25)[23]

For instance, to take an example from the field of geometry, starting from a general mathematical formula, we can generate the particular geometrical figures of the circle, the ellipse, and so forth, just by changing the parameter that constitutes the figure in such a way that it describes and passes through a continuous series of values. Or, to take a more sociological example, which is consistently developed in *Distinction* (Bourdieu, 1979a), Bourdieu's masterpiece which is already a classic in sociology, starting from a particular volume and a particular structure of capital, we can vary the parameter and proceed continuously from the upper region of the constructed space of social positions, constituted by the dominant fraction of the dominant class (the industrial bourgeoisie), to the middle region, constituted by the dominated fraction of the dominant class (liberal professions and academics) and the dominant fraction of the dominated class (the shopkeepers and the handicraftsmen), to its lowest region, constituted by the dominated fraction of the dominated class (peasants and the unskilled manual workers). As a result of the application of the relational mode of thinking, 'the scientific concepts no longer appear as imitations of thing-like existences, but as symbols representing orders and functional links within reality' (Cassirer, [1906] 1971: 3). In so far as the reality of the objects has dissolved itself in a world of rational relations, we can indeed say with Bachelard and Hegel that 'the real is rational' (Hegel, [1821] 1971: 24), and with Cassirer and Bourdieu that 'the real is relational' (Bourdieu, 1987b: 3; Bourdieu and Wacquant, 1992: 72, 203; Bourdieu, 1994: 17).

Applied relationalism

Although the object seems to precede the point of view, Bourdieu shares Saussure's constructivist assumption that, in fact, it is 'the point of view [which] creates the object' (Saussure, [1916] 1985: 23). The delimitation of the field is thus an analytical one.[24] Thanks to the methodological construction of an autonomous and self-referentially closed system of internal relations between concepts, a coherent model of reality can be created that is supposed to be structurally homologous with reality. As we have seen above, however, Bourdieu does not wish to make an ontological argument about reality; stating that 'social functions are fictions' (Bourdieu, 1982a: 49), he resorts in the last instance to the conventionalist gesture of the 'as if'. To construct the system of entangled relations two things are important: first, the system has to be complete – that is the whole population of relevant elements has to be taken into account; and second, the elements have to be linked to each other by means of internal relations – that is, in such a way that they cannot be defined apart from each other, thus in such a way that they are mutually and conceptually implicated in each other. The musical scale and melodies offer good examples of paradigmatic and syntagmatic systems of internal relations or, to speak like Saussure, of internally related but arbitrary differences: the notes form a complete paradigmatic system, the value of each being rigorously determined by the position of all the others; and the melody, which syntagmatically reorders the notes, is nothing but the contingent realisation of an internally related series of musical possibilities. So does Marx's account of the economic cycle (Marx, [1857] 1973: 81–111): the production, consumption, distribution and exchange of economic goods are mutually implicated in a dialectical syllogism; as 'members of totality' they only represent 'distinctions within a unity' and, as such, they are 'in their one-sided form determined by the other moments'; even more, they are identical processes, but analysed from a different angle.[25] The same could be said not only of the positions that make up a field but of Bourdieu's main categories as well: the notions of field, capital and habitus cannot be defined separately; in fact, the field is identical to the distribution of capital and the habitus is identical to the field, but analysed from a different perspective.

Although Bachelard and Bourdieu do not use the distinction between essences and appearances, they certainly would agree with Marx that science always aims at knowledge of the hidden (Bachelard, [1949] 1986: 38; Bourdieu, 1996: 16). In order to uncover the hidden, science has to construct 'analogical models' of the social world, or maybe better, of the social space, which 'recover the hidden principles of the realities they interpret' (Bourdieu *et al.*, 1973: 76). The construction of an ideal-typical model of the space of structural relations among the phenomenal relations allows one to treat the different social forms as so many different realisations of the same (symbolic) function. In this perspective, 'the real' appears, as Bachelard says and Bourdieu likes to repeat after him, as 'a particular case of the possible' (Bachelard, [1934] 1991: 62), which presupposes, of course, that the particular case is related to the more general properties of which it is a function. Thus, to take an example from the academic field, when one knows the exact position of an 'epistemic individual' (Bourdieu, 1984a: 36), defined by the totality of the relevant properties like trajectory, volume and structure of the different sorts of capital (economic, cultural, social, symbolic, etc.) which can be assigned to it and which are taken to be efficacious in explaining the variation of the positions in the field, it does not really matter whether one considers different 'empirical individuals' like Lévi-Strauss, Braudel or Foucault, because from the point of view of the analyst, who considers them as 'realisations of the possible' or, as Marx would say, as 'personifications' of structures, they only represent 'similar cases of the possible' and as such, they are almost indiscriminable. Once the invariant properties (*illusio*, interests, struggle for monopoly of authority, volume and structure of capital, opposition between dominant and dominated fractions of the different classes, strategies of conservation and subversion, etc.) of a given field of practices are known, once the generative and unifying principles of a system of relations are codified and formalised in the theoretical model, this model can be transposed to, and compared with, other fields of practices so as to uncover functional and structural homologies.

This transposition of models of one field to another does not imply, however, that Bourdieu does not recognise the functional differentiation that characterises modern societies (Bohn, 1991: 133–139; Alexander, 1995: 157–164). Although fields have emerged historically and acquired a certain autonomy, they are interlocked in complex ways, and the comparative application of the generative formula of their structure and function shows precisely how 'formal' or structural invariance and 'material' or empirical variation can be thought together in such a way that the tendency towards reduction of one field to another, in this case the economic one, can be avoided.[26] However, even if the reductionism of the infamous 'last instance' is avoided in this way, the problem of reductionism reemerges in another way as a 'kind of field reductionism' (Swartz, 1997: 293) in which the producers of cultural products tend to be seen as emanations of the logic of the intellectual field and their products as so many epiphenomena of the respective positions they occupy in the field. As a theoretical fieldworker, Bourdieu has multiplied comparative research on different fields of practice (haute couture, literature, art, sport, philosophy, politics, housing markets and, last but not least, the media (Bourdieu, 1996) and the economy (Bourdieu, 1997b)).

Applied rationalism

Now that we have analysed how the scientific fact is conquered against common sense and systematically constructed as a relational effect of the theory, we can proceed to an analysis of the process of verification of the theory. Against the empiricist dogma of immaculate perception, Bourdieu stresses once more that facts are always and necessarily overdetermined by theory. In so far as empirical research techniques and instruments are, as Bachelard once said, 'really reified theorems' (Bachelard, 1971: 137), all the operations of sociological research, from the formulation of a questionnaire to its coding and its statistical analysis, have to be considered as 'so many theories in action' (Bourdieu *et al.*, 1973: 59). An accurate knowledge of what one does to and with the facts, and of what the facts can and cannot do, is thus the first requirement of sociological research. For instance, the technique of multivariate analysis, which seems applicable to all types of quantifiable relations, presupposes the independence of the dependent and the independent variables, and the sociologists, who by routine apply this linear mode of thought without much thought, are not even aware that the variables are internally linked and that they only take on their numerical value and are what they are thanks to their position and their function within a structural figuration (Elias, [1965] 1985: 234). And given that they don't think in terms of structural causality, they cling to the nominal identity of their variables, assuming that their effects are purely linear, and do not see that in each of the variables the network of entangled relations exercises its efficacy through all the others (Bourdieu, 1979a: 113–122, 512–514).[27] The result of the standard application of the technique of multivariate analysis is an ontological confusion between the method and the 'thing in itself' (*Ding an sich*), leading to a situation where the method is simply reified into a 'general linear reality' (Abott, 1988).[28] In order to avoid this risk of reification, any statistical correlation between variables obtained by multivariate analysis has to be systematically reinterpreted as a function of the system of the relations of relations that give meaning to the observed statistical relation. With the descriptive statistical technique of correspondence analysis, an advanced variant of factor analysis that is, obviously, Bourdieu's favourite technique, this is not necessary because it is, so to speak, nothing else but the operational materialisation of the relational mode of thinking which characterises his generative structuralism.

In so far as every fact implies the whole theory and the whole theory is implicated in every fact, Popperians consider the structural mode of verification, which relies not on a correspondence but on a coherence theory of truth, as unscientific, or even worse, as 'dogmatic' and 'intrinsically terrorist' (Ferry and Renaut, 1988: 259–268).[29] However, against Popper's falsification of ad-hoc hypotheses, one should stress with Duhem that 'one experiment can never falsify an isolated hypothesis but only a theoretical totality' (Duhem, quoted in Bourdieu *et al.*, 1973: 89–90).[30] Moreover, against Popper and with Lakatos (1970), who should be read as a Hegelian and thus as an intellectual cousin of Bachelard, one should consider that Bourdieu's generative structuralism does not represent a single isolated theory, which may or may not be refutable, but a thriving and well-integrated research programme that incorporates or 'envelops' a multiplicity of other theories from Garfinkel to Elias. Admittedly, the 'hard core' of the research programme is very hard. However, if we go along with Lakatos and accept that a discipline is scientific so long as 'progressive' research programmes triumph over 'degenerating' ones, then *mutatis mutandis* there is no reason to consider the project of the 'scientific collective' that Bourdieu is directing from Paris as pseudo- or unscientific. Stretching this point a bit and willingly forsaking the 'scientistic' posture of the 'happy structuralist', I would even be inclined to relax the criteria of scientificity and consider his research programme in more aesthetic terms. Embellished as it is by its Proustian tonality, Bourdieu's structural-relational mode of analysis offers a coherent and systematic 'picture' of the social world. In this respect, it resembles a painting which, thanks to constant retouching, becomes more unified, whereas each detail, detached from the whole, loses meaning and ends up representing nothing at all.[31] For Bourdieu, the world is not only his presentation but, ultimately, it is also his construction and his verification, made up of realised conceptual constructs and verified ideas.

Habitus, or the occasional realisation of the real

According to Bourdieu's mentor, thought progresses dialectically by means of a pincer movement that encircles limited positions and tries to incorporate them into a larger conceptual framework that successfully overcomes the former limitations. This dialectical movement of enlargement operates by a mediation through (but *pace* Adorno not 'in') the extremes. 'One could speak of a psychological law of the bipolarity of errors. As soon as a difficulty turns out to be important, one can be sure that by averting it, one will hit an opposed obstacle' (Bachelard, [1938] 1993: 20). Thus, to take the post-war history of our field as an example, when the one-dimensionality of Parsonsian structural functionalism (and related objectivist positions such as structuralism, Marxism, etc.) became increasingly manifest in the late 1960s, a micro-reaction ensued which, by the end of the 1970s, had shifted the metatheoretical balance to the other extreme of one-dimensional subjectivism, represented (for pedagogical reasons) by Schütz, Blumer, Garfinkel and others. It is only when the limitations of both objectivism and subjectivism were underscored that the possibility of a synthetic micro–macro link eventually emerged in the 1980s (Alexander *et al.*, 1987). Although our philosopher-turned-anthropologist had already developed the main outline of his attempt to transcend the 'bipolarity' of the subjectivist and the objectivist errors in the early 1970s (Bourdieu, 1972), his theory of practice is very much part of a larger 'structurist' movement in social theory which takes its inspiration from Marx's *Theses on Feuerbach*, and of which Sartre, Berger and Luckmann, Habermas, Giddens, Bhaskar, or the late Castoriadis are probably the best known representatives (Vandenberghe, 1998: 322–339).

Moving from epistemological considerations to more metatheoretical ones, we can now present Bourdieu's attempt to overcome the opposition between subjectivism and objectivism by introducing a supplementary relation: a vertical one that mediates between the system of objective positions and subjective dispositions. This is, of course, the point where the old and venerable Aristotelian concept of *hexis*, which Boetius and Thomas Aquinas translated as *habitus* and which the French ethnophilosopher has transformed into one of his central concepts, comes in.[32] As is well known by now, Bourdieu uses the concept of habitus, always understood as class habitus and defined as 'systems of durable and transposable dispositions, structured structures which are predisposed to function as structuring structures' (Bourdieu, 1972: 155; 1980: 88–89), as a kind of 'theoretical operator' which, by giving a formal coherence to actions that are materially extremely different, mediates between the invisible system of structured relations (by which actions are shaped) and the visible actions of the actors (which structure relations). As a logical construct, 'irreducible to its manifestations'

(Bourdieu, 1974: 31), the habitus itself cannot be observed; but like the practical instantiations of Giddens' virtual structures (Giddens, 1979: 53–76; 1984: 16–28), it can be observed in its actualisations, when a 'permissive condition' (the state of the field, of the market, etc.) furnishes the appropriate occasion for the virtual disposition to manifest itself in its actuality in relation with a particular situation (Bourdieu, 1979a: 112; 1984b: 135; 1997a: 178).[33] Thus, as a mediator of *energeia* and *actus* (Aristotle), the habitus (or its more corporeal variant, *hexis*) also mediates between the structures and the actions, solving thus the antinomy of objectivism and subjectivism:

> One should not forget that, ultimately, objective relations do not exist and do not really realize themselves except in and through the system of dispositions of the agents, produced by the internalization of objective conditions. Between the system of objective regularities and the system of directly observable conducts a mediation always intervenes which is nothing else but the habitus, geometrical locus of determinisms and of an individual determination.
>
> (Bourdieu, 1965: 22; 1968: 705)

Between the habitus and the field there is an 'ontological complicity' (Bourdieu, 1982a: 47; 1994: 154): when the habitus enters into relation with the social world of which it is the product, the habitus feels at home – 'like a fish in the water'. The habitus is internally linked to the field, even to the point that they refer to the same thing, but considered from a different angle: either as *ergon* (*opus operatum*) or as *energeia* (*modus operandi*).[34] The habitus is the internalisation or incorporation of the social structures, whereas the field is the exteriorisation or objectivation of the habitus. However, one should not conceive the relation between the two as a purely circular one, whereby the habitus, 'product of the structures and producer of the practices and reproducer of the structures' (Bourdieu and Passeron, 1970: 244), simply reproduces the structures.[35] Indeed, as Chairman Mao used to say, one should 'twist the stick in the other direction', read Bourdieu with the spectacles of Giddens, see his work as a run-up to Habermas and insist on the transformative capacities of the habitus.[36] Notwithstanding Bourdieu's self-censorship,[27] I think he would encourage such a transformative reading.[38] Even more, I think that he should, if he wants to bring his theory in line with his political intentions, which are now no longer repressed but openly declared (Bourdieu, 1998a; see below).

For sure, the habitus is the product of the social structures, but if one stops there, one falls into the trap of pure determinist reading and forgets that, as the generative principle of actions, evaluations and perceptions, the habitus also structures the social world.[39] The habitus reproduces the social world but, given that a process of 'selection' (Bourdieu, 1997b: 63) – or 'self-interaction' (Blumer, 1969: 15, 50) or (why not?) 'rational communication' (Habermas, 1981: 69, 212) – always intervenes between the stimulus and the response, 'one cannot mechanically infer the knowledge of the products from the knowledge of the conditions of production' (Bourdieu, 1984b: 135). The habitus transforms that by which it is determined, and even if the principle of transformation is to be found in the rift between structure and habitus, there is no reason not to suppose that the depth of this rift and its meaning depends on the habitus (Bourdieu, 1997a: 177–178). After all, the agents are determined, but only to the extent that they determine themselves. If 'there's always space for a cognitive struggle concerning the meaning of the things of the world' (Bourdieu, 1998b: 19), nothing excludes thus the potential of the agent to transform the world in a non-predictable way. Moreover, the open recognition of the creativity of the habitus and of its possibility to reflect on its own determinations has the non-negligible advantage of bringing the metatheoretical presuppositions of his theory of action, which is, after all, conceived as a theory which emphasises 'the primacy of practical reason' (Bourdieu, 1987a: 23), in line with the critical intention that animates his theory.[40] I think that his moral indignation, which is sublimated in 'theoretical hyperviolence' (Caro, 1980: 1175), would fare better if the hyperdeterminism were weakened so that voluntarism finally would get its due. As Sartre used to say, 'what really matters is not what one has made of man but what he does with what one has done to him' (quoted in Terrail 1992: 229).

The theory of fields

The field of cultural production

In the same way as the notion of the habitus was conceived with the intent to break away from the structuralist paradigm without falling back into the old philosophy of the subject or of consciousness, thus to 'get out of the philosophy of consciousness without doing away with the agent in its truth as a practical operator of constructions of reality' (Bourdieu, 1992: 253), the notion of the field (*champ*) was conceived from the very beginning as a way to 'reject the alternative between an internal interpretation and an external explanation' (Bourdieu, 1992: 254) before which all the cultural sciences (religious sciences, art history or literary history, sociology of religion, law or science) were placed. In cultural matters the opposition between formalist analysis, which offers an immanent (or 'tautegorical') interpretation of meaning (e.g. semiotics, archaeology, grammatology, postmodernism, etc.), and reductionist analysis, which presents an external (or 'allegorical') reading that directly relates meaning to social forms (e.g. Marxism),[41] can be overcome by showing that the external influences and constraints (economic and political ones, for instance) are always mediated and 'refracted' by the structure of the particular cultural field (literature, art, science, etc.), which intervenes between the social positions of the producer and his postures (*prises de positions*) in which they are expressed and whose principle lies in the structure and the functioning of the field of positions.[42]

The theory of the field is the concrete realisation of relational thought in a particular sphere of action (on fields, see Bourdieu, 1983a: 311–356; 1984b: 113–120; Bourdieu and Wacquant, 1992: 71–91). The guiding principle of all field theories has been formulated by Kurt Lewin, one of Cassirer's pupils: 'Instead of abstracting one or another isolated element from a situation, the meaning of which cannot be understood without reference to the total situation, the theory of the field starts with a characterization of the whole situation' (Lewin, 1963: 104). Unlike Lewin, however, Bourdieu gives an agonistic twist to his theory of fields. Although it is perfectly conceivable that the internally related elements would peacefully 'con-spire' to form an organic whole, Bourdieu has always thought of the field as a field of struggle or, as Elias says, as a 'field of tension' (Elias, [1970] 1984: 127). From the beginning, his relational conception of the field was mingled with a highly conflictual vision of the world as a battlefield for power, prestige and all sorts of capital in which competitive distinction, domination and misrecognition prevail over cooperation, disinterest and recognition (Swartz, 1997: 63). In any case, whether the field is conceived in a conflictual way or not, given that the relations between the individual elements are the result of all factors that constitute the 'figuration', when analysing the field one always has to 'start with the relations and think from there towards the related' (Elias, [1970] 1984: 127).

Analysing the whole of the relations that structure the field does not mean, however, that one has to investigate all the events that take place in the field. 'It means rather to reveal the fundamental structures which give a specific imprint to the orientation and the morphology of the singular events within the field' (Elias, 1976: 393). Bourdieu – who has borrowed the notion from Lewin, who explicitly refers to Cassirer, and from Elias, who was a distant cousin of Cassirer[43] – has systematically linked the notion of 'field' to the one of 'capital', with the result that he can define the field – he also uses the notions of 'market' and 'game' – as a structured space of social positions in which the positions and their interrelations are determined by the distribution of different kinds of capital (economic capital – i.e. material wealth, in the form of money, stocks and shares, etc.; cultural capital – i.e. knowledge, skills and other cultural acquisitions; symbolic capital – i.e. accumulated prestige and honour; and social capital – i.e. relations and networks of influence). Fields are to be viewed as systems of dominant and subordinated positions in which each epistemic position, which is contingently and empirically realised in the form of a concrete institution, organisation, group or individual, derives its distinctive properties from its internal relationship to all other epistemic positions. Given that the concrete positions, which represent so many realisations of the possible, are internally related, a change in one of them will necessarily have repercussions for all the others (e.g. when two giant firms merge the structure of the whole economic subfield is affected in the same way as Einstein's theory of relativity changed the whole subfield of physics). One of the most important properties of fields is the way in which they allow one form of capital (e.g. economic capital) to be transformed into another form of capital (for example, cultural capital, which can exist in three different states: embodied in their owner – e.g. language skills and personal familiarity with works of art; objectified – e.g. in books, paintings, etc.; and certified, as with diplomas and formal credentials (Bourdieu, 1979b)).

In so far as the relational conception is inseparable for Bourdieu from a conflictual *Weltanschauung*, the field is always a field of forces and of struggles in which individuals seek to maintain or to alter the relations of forces and the distribution of the forms of capital specific to it. Although the competing parties are opposed to each other (dissensus), they all share in common some fundamental presuppositions ('consensus in the dissensus' (Bourdieu, 1966: 902)), which are constitutive of the functioning of the field itself.[44] They believe in the game they are playing and in the value of what is at stake in the struggles they are waging (*illusio*). At any given moment in time the structure of the field, i.e. the space of social positions, can be determined by the structure of the distribution of the different species of capital between the groups or classes. Bourdieu characterises classes of social positions along three dimensions (Bourdieu, 1979a: 128–144), two of which are spatial and one of which is temporal: (1) volume of capital possessed; (2) structure of capital, i.e. composition of global capital according to the specific weight of the different species of capital relative to the global capital; and (3) objective social trajectory, past, present and potential, as indicated by movements along the spatial axes.

The analysis of culture in terms of the field proceeds in three stages (Bourdieu and Wacquant, 1992: 80). First, although the cultural (artistic, literary, juridical, philosophical, etc.) field is relatively autonomous, one should nevertheless place it within the field of power on which it is relatively dependent, because the struggle that goes on in the field of power determines whether the principle of the hierarchisation of the field of class relations is of an economic or of a cultural nature.[45] In our societies, economic capital is the dominant principle of domination and cultural capital is the dominated one. Thus, the intellectual field, for instance, occupies a dominated position in the field of power, which is itself situated at the dominant pole of the field of class relations. At any moment in time, the field is the locus of struggle between two principles of hierarchisation: a heteronomous criterion (success, as measured by book sales) that works to the benefit of those who dominate the field economically and politically (the people in 'suits' who distribute the resources, sit on committees, and decide on the marketability of books), and an autonomous criterion (quality, as measured by the recognition by peers) that favours the 'true scholars'. Second, one should uncover the objective structure of the relations between the positions occupied in the field by the agents or the institutions which are in competition with each other in the field. Here the point is to reveal the hierarchy of the products and the producers, which is based on the opposition between the 'field of restricted production', in which the producers produce for other producers, and the 'field of mass-audience production', which is symbolically excluded and discredited (Bourdieu, 1971c: 54–55). Finally, the analysis of the field should also include the detailed analysis of the trajectories and the dispositions of the producers who are in competition with each other within the field. To understand the practices of the producers and their products entails understanding that they are the result of the history of the positions they occupy and the history of their dispositions. Once the agent is introduced into the field, one can then dynamise the picture and analyse the interplay of objective positions and subjective dispositions and thus explain the postures (*prises de positions*) of the producers of a given field.

The generalised model of the field of cultural production presented above is the result of a long series of studies of particular fields that Bourdieu started in the 1960s with an analysis of the intellectual field, from Flaubert and the 'nouveau roman' to jazz and cinema (Bourdieu, 1966),[46] the conceptual framework of which is largely derived from and inspired by a brilliant and original reinterpretation of Weber's chapter on religion in *Economy and Society* (Weber, [1921] 1972: 245–381) in terms of his general theory of sociological knowledge (Bourdieu, 1971a, 1971b).[47] In so far as this interpretation gives a Marxian twist to Weber's notion of ideal goods and ideal interests, it also lays the groundwork for a general theory of the economy of symbolic goods which, by extending the logic of economic calculation to all goods, material as well as symbolic, without distinction, aims to demonstrate that there is a political economy of cultural goods. As a result of this thoroughly materialist reading of Weber, which outmarxes Marx and was anticipated by Mannheim (see below), an economic interpretation of non- and even anti-economic sectors, such as the religious one, becomes possible, which consistently shows that a well-intended and conspicuous disinterest in material rewards always pays in one way or another, even if this interest (in the sense of dividends) is not consciously intended by the agent. When 'strategic action' without strategising or 'traditional action' with a rational purpose is uncovered everywhere, the suspicion arises of economic reductionism and hyperutilitarianism à la Gary Becker, which detects unconscious egoism in conscious altruism, leading thus to the oxymoron of 'unconscious calculation', inevitably and to a certain extent justifiably (see Joppke, 1986; Honneth, 1990; Caillé, 1992; Alexander, 1995).

The central axis of variation of the fields is their degree of autonomy. Highly autonomous fields, like the scientific field, follow the binary code of true and false; highly heteronomous fields, like the political field, the Schmittian code of friend and foe (Bourdieu, 1986: 10). First, we will consider the religious field, which is open to external determinations and whose 'truth' is nothing else but the legitimate imposition of a cultural arbitrary that expresses mainly the interests of the dominant. The penultimate section will analyse the scientific field, which is more autonomous and in which the producers produce for other producers and not for a mass audience, as is the case in the religious field.

The religious field

In so far as Weber's theory of religion systematically relates the religious discourses of the sorcerer, the prophet and the priest to the larger social interests of its carrier strata (Weber, [1922] 1966: 237–268; [1921] 1972: 259–279), he has, in principle at least, developed a theory of the relative autonomy of the religious field, which allows him to transcend the opposition between a (structuralist) theory that interprets the changing content of religious messages in terms of the immanent laws of the mind and a (Marxist) theory that conceives them as a direct reflection of the material infrastructure of society, committing thus the error of the short-circuit. The problem with Weber is twofold: first, he remained caught in the substantialist mode of thought. Rather than systematically relating the protagonists of religious action (prophet, sorcerer and priest) to each other, he developed an ideal-type of each of them that searched for their general characteristics in the protagonists themselves, arriving thus at a 'mosaic theory' of reality (Parsons, [1937] 1949: 621). Second, Weber also remained entangled in the 'occasionalist illusion' (Bourdieu, 1972: 184). Rather than constructing the structure of objective relations between the positions which the religious agents occupy in the religious field, he reduced the 'objective structure', which determines interpersonal relations, to the 'conjunctural structure' of their interactions in particular groups and situations.

Those two problems can, however, easily be overcome according to Bourdieu. To bring home the harvest of Weber's rich analysis of the interactions between the religious specialists on the one hand and the lay population on the other, it is sufficient to construct the complete system of objective relations among the prophets, the priests, the sorcerers, and their secular followers, and to reinsert Weber's analysis in this structural scheme. Once this is done, the dynamic of the religious field, and the transformation of the religious contents themselves, can then be explained in terms of an analysis of 'the transactions between the specialists and the laypeople which are established on the basis of different interests and relations of competition which oppose the different specialists within the religious field' (Bourdieu, 1971b: 313). Indeed, in order to decipher the sociological meaning and functions of religious actions, it is necessary to consider the religious interests of those who produce, diffuse and receive religious messages. Whereas the religious specialists have an interest in the accumulation of 'religious capital' and compete therefore for the monopoly of the administration of the goods of salvation and the legitimate exercise of religious power over the laypeople, understood as the power to durably impress a religious habitus on them, the lay population has an interest in their messages in so far as, according to their respective position in the field of classes, they need either justification for their social privileges (dominant class) or compensation for their relative deprivation (dominated class). The offer of 'theodicies' (Leibniz) by the specialists finds thus its complement in the demand of 'sociodicies' (Bourdieu) of the masses. Depending on the demand of one, the offers of the others fluctuate. If the popular classes, and especially the peasants, pressed by economic urgency, look above all for immediate gratification, which they find in the profane and profaning magical manipulation of demons by the sorcerers, the other classes, less pressed by economic urgency, which explains why they can distance themselves from their immediate situation, have a need for the systematisation of religious representations and the moralisation of religious practices (Weber, [1922] 1966: 252–256; [1921] 1972: 259). They address themselves either to the Church and their priests or to the prophets and their sects.

At any time, the structure of the religious field is determined by the balance of power, which is the result of former struggles for the monopoly on the administration of religious goods, between the priests, the prophets and the sorcerers, which is itself a function of the extent to which they can mobilise the masses and satisfy their demands. The Church, which claims a monopoly on the legitimate interpretation of the world, is always confronted with the possibility of competition from the prophet, who offers an alternative systematic interpretation of the world, and from the sorcerer, who responds to punctual pragmatic demands. The prophet, a heretic producer of a systematic vision of the world, is opposed to the Church, this instance of reproduction of 'routinized charisma' (Weber, [1921] 1972: 142–148), and its orthodoxy. Engaged in strategies to subvert the reigning orthodoxy, the prophet tries to convince the masses of his or her rival interpretation of the world. Whether this succeeds or not does not so much depend on his or her personal charisma, as Weber thought, but on the demand of the masses, especially the proletaroid intellectuals, and the social tensions which reign within the Church and the larger world. In so far as prophets and heretics tend to appear at times of social crises and to preach to those who are already converted, their appearance has to be explained in relation to the particular figuration formed by the priests, the laypeople, and the prophet. To counter the subversion strategies of the prophet and competition with the sorcerer, the Church responds with two typical conservation strategies. On the one hand, it imposes a growing ritualisation of the religious practices that accompanies the annexation of magical beliefs; on the other hand, it adapts its original message and reinterprets it to appeal to the largest audience, introducing thereby a fundamental ambiguity wherein, thanks to the 'selective reception' (Bourdieu, 1971b: 315) that is relative to the position occupied in the social structure, all categories of the population can find themselves. Given that the religious authority and the secular power that the religious instances can mobilise in their struggle for religious legitimacy is never independent from the weight of the lay population which they mobilise, the struggles that are waged in the religious field are not only overdetermined by the structure of power relations between the classes in the field of power, but also inevitably have implications for this field. This structural homology between the two fields explains why the struggle in the religious produces 'euphemised forms' (Bourdieu, 1977b: 410) of the economic and political struggle between the classes and how the strategies for the conservation of the symbolic order contribute directly to the conservation of the political order, whereas the strategies of subversion of the symbolic order can only affect the political order when they are accompanied by the political subversion of this order. Thus, as the person of extraordinary situations, the prophet can only be a revolutionary if the political situation itself is in a revolutionary state.

The scientific field

One could plausibly argue that the hub of the new 'radical' sociologies of science consists of an ongoing 'correction and expansion' (Lynch, 1993: 42) of Mannheim's *Wissenssoziologie*, so as to include the exact sciences, which Mannheim explicitly exempted from the purview of his sociology (Mannheim, 1936: 43, 179, 272; 1952: 170). And indeed, in the same way as the so-called 'Strong

Program' (Bloor, 1991: 3–23) in the sociology of scientific knowledge only makes sense against the background of Mannheim's sociology of knowledge, Bourdieu's ongoing interest in the sociology of the scientific field (Bourdieu, 1976, 1990, 1997c) should be seen as an attempt to generalise Mannheim's thesis of the social determination of ideas. In a prize-winning essay of 1928, entitled 'Competition as a Cultural Phenomenon' (Mannheim, 1952: 191–229), which largely anticipates Bourdieu's sociology of science, the young Mannheim defends the thesis of the 'existential relativity of knowledge'.[48] This thesis does not stipulate that all knowledge can simply be reduced to the social circumstances of its production (the error of epiphenomenalism), but it does stipulate that both the production and the reception of socio-historical scientific knowledge is socially and historically determined. In the same way as the production of knowledge is a function of the particular social positions various groups occupy in the social structure, its reception (selection) is a function of a certain formation of the mind (categorical structure included), which is itself linked to a particular social position.[49] More particularly, Mannheim wants to show that the 'general sociological phenomenon of competition' (Mannheim, 1952: 195–196), of which economic competition is only a particular case, can and does explain the dynamics of the social production of cultural knowledge. In so far as the movement of thought depends in the last analysis upon the tensions that dominate the social sphere, theoretical conflict is always related to, and overdetermined by, social conflict:

> From the point of view of the social sciences, every historical, ideological, sociological piece of knowledge (even should it prove to be Absolute Truth itself), is clearly rooted in and carried by the desire for power and recognition of particular social groups who want to make their interpretation of the world the universal one.
>
> (Mannheim, 1952: 196–197)

The struggle for the public interpretation of reality, or at least for the prestige that goes with it, is thus the stake for which people fight, and the different interpretations of the world generally correspond to the particular positions they occupy in their struggle for power. Paraphrasing Clausewitz, we could thus say that science is politics pursued by other means (Latour, 1984: 257).

It is against this Mannheimian background of the general social relation of competition that we can best appreciate Bourdieu's enormous talent to concretise abstract ideas. Like Mannheim, Bourdieu starts his analysis of the field of scientific practices with the proposition that it is the arena of a competitive struggle, the particular stake (*enjeu*) of which is the monopoly on scientific authority. The relative indifference of scientists towards money and power should not hide the fact that all their practices are oriented towards the acquisition and accumulation of scientific capital (authority, prestige, recognition, celebrity, etc.), which is only a particular instance of social capital, which can then, of course, at a later stage be converted into other forms of capital (e.g. economic capital). The scientific field is highly autonomous ('restricted field of cultural production'). It is only because it follows its own immanent laws (the laws of the academic marketplace are irreducible to the laws of the market) and generates its own values and imperatives (universalism, communism, disinterestedness and organised scepticism (Merton, 1968: 604–615)) that the interests of scientists appear as disinterested. Once it is understood, however, that the interests in knowledge (*Erkenntnisinteressen*) of the scientists are strictly internal to the field, where they play a quasi-economic and quasi-political role, we can also understand that scientists have an 'interest in disinterestedness' (Bourdieu, 1976: 94; see also Bourdieu, 1994: 149–167) and that they can reap the profit of seeing themselves, and being seen by others, as not being interested in vulgar profit making (see also Mulkay, 1976). Their strategies of apparent disinvestment are strategies of the second order, which dissimulate the strategies of investment of the first order by which the scientists aim, consciously or not, 'to make a name for themselves', to make their own name (and for some even their first name) known in the field of their competing colleagues.

The struggle that scientists wage within the field is always a struggle for the power to define the definition of science which is best suited to their specific interests and which, if accepted as the legitimate definition, would allow them to occupy with legitimacy the dominant position in the field. And given that there is no external and impartial arbiter, the scientific-cum-political legitimacy claims are always a function of the relative power of the competing groups. From this conflictual perspective on the field of scientific production, which systematically relates the struggle over the 'relations of definitions' (Beck, 1988: 211–226) to the 'relations of production' that structure the positions in the field, even 'epistemological conflicts' (e.g. realism versus empiricism versus rationalism, etc.) can be analysed as 'political conflicts' (Bourdieu, 1976: 90). Depending on the state of competition in the academic marketplace, which can vary, as Mannheim has shown, from the monopoly position of one particular group to atomistic competition among a multiplicity of competing groups (Mannheim, 1952: 207–210), the opposition between the 'priestly' strategies of conservation and the 'prophetic' strategies of subversion of the structure of the field take on different meanings and functions.

The monopoly situation is characterised by a permanent conflict between the established, who in an attempt to defend the reigning orthodoxy and maintain their monopoly on the means of intellectual production (control over educational training, instances of consecration and scientific journals) carefully select their successors and try to keep heretical newcomers from entering the game, and 'heretics' like Einstein, Marx or Bourdieu himself, who enter into revolt not only against the scientific establishment but also against the social establishment as such. As accumulated scientific resources increase, the incorporated scientific capital needed in order to appropriate them and thereby gain access to scientific problems and tools increases as well, and the cost of entering the field becomes greater and greater. As a result, the degree of homogeneity between the competitors increases and the opposition between the succession strategies of the dominant fraction and the subversion strategies of the dominated fraction tends to lose its meaning. Even the outsiders are now somehow established, and the disputes that take place between the competitors take place against the background of undisputed *doxa* ('consensus in the dissensus'), which is taken for granted by all the parties of the struggle and which is thus never put into question by them.

As competition becomes institutionalised and as the accumulation of capital needed to accomplish scientific revolutions tends increasingly to occur in accordance with regulated procedures, the great periodic revolutions are replaced by a multiplicity of small, permanent revolutions that are increasingly devoid of political effects. In brief, the scientific field becomes more autonomous, and as it becomes more autonomous and self-regulating, scientific reason progresses and, eventually, the 'force of reason' (Kant), becomes the only form of force that is recognised and legitimately utilised in the field. At this point, Bourdieu joins Apel and Habermas, but with this notable difference: reason is no longer considered as a transhistorical universal but as the historical result of the progressive institutionalisation of rational discussions in the field of science (Bourdieu, 1997a: 111–151),[50] and possibly and hopefully also – but this depends on the institutionalisation of the conditions of rational discussion in other highly autonomous fields of cultural production – in the larger world as well (Bourdieu 1989: 548–559; 1992: 459–473; 1993b; 1994: 164–167, 239–244).[51]

According to Bourdieu, the social sciences have not yet reached this autonomy. Unlike the scientific fields, capable of producing and satisfying a strictly scientific interest and thus of maintaining a dialectical process of mutual and rational critique out of which reason ensues, 'the fields of production of learned discourses' (Bourdieu, 1976: 100) are highly dependent on external instances, and the apparent esoterism of the 'doxosophers' should not hide the exoteric dependence that they maintain with social demands. 'Falsely autonomous' and operating with a 'false rupture' with common sense and the real interests of the dominant classes, the social sciences are 'false sciences', doomed to produce and to maintain 'false consciousness' (Bourdieu, 1976: 100–103). Parading with the technological appearances of scientificity (e.g. log-linear modelling, path analysis, etc.) and the rhetoric of cumulativity (e.g. neo-Marxism, neofunctionalism, etc.), the social sciences do not aim to realise themselves as real sciences, but only to realise the official image of science. And even the radical sociologists, those of the Frankfurt School included, who contest the 'orthodox consensus' and ally themselves with the dominated classes, remain negatively but necessarily trapped within the presuppositions of the false science of their colleagues from the mainstream: 'The manifest conflicts between the tendencies and doctrines mask, from the participants themselves, the underlying complicity which they presuppose and which strikes the observer from outside the system' (Bourdieu, 1966: 902). Rather than reflexively uncovering the presuppositions of their opponents, they take them over, and the oppositions they set up (consensus versus conflict, quantitative versus qualitative analysis, objectivism versus subjectivism, etc.) function as so many 'mirror-traps' (Bourdieu, 1991: 383). Only the signs are thus reversed, and at the end of the day, the mutual opposition shows that the same game has been played over (and over) again.

Bourdieu claims that a 'reflexive sociology' (Bourdieu *et al.*, 1973: 95–106; 1982a; 1984a: 9–51; Bourdieu and Wacquant, 1992: 45–70), a sociology of sociology that objectivates the complete system of positions that engenders the rival strategies, allows him to transcend the 'mimetic rivalry' (Girard, 1982) that opposes the objective allies. Rhetorically, this move relies on the Mannheimian distinction between the 'particular special' and the 'total general' conception of ideology (Mannheim, 1936: 55–88, 264–286), which Bourdieu now reformulates in terms of a radical distinction between the 'polemical' and the 'reflexive' use of the sociology of knowledge (Bourdieu, 1983b: 51): in the first case, the sociology of knowledge is used to disqualify the strategies of one's opponents ('*x* is a petty bourgeois' – the sociologist is always the best critique of his or her opponents); in the second case, it is used to objectify the whole field, one's own position included (autoreflexive sociology by means of 'participant objectivation' (Bourdieu and Wacquant, 1992: 48)), i.e. self-observation through objectification of the objectivating subject and of its relation to the object). According to Bourdieu, the systematic objectivation of the field as the totality of the possible standpoints (*positions*) and their corresponding viewpoints (*prises de positions*), which he opposes to the partial and interested objectivations of the agents involved in the field, 'allows one to establish the truth of the different positions and the limits of validity of the different standpoints' (Bourdieu, 1997c: 38–39).

This Bachelardian move by which the author of *Homo Academicus* attempts to create a third position for himself is, however, problematic, first because he himself has clearly stated that there is and can be no independent position on the field within the field itself and, second, because the reflexive application of his own sociology to his own sociology unmasks his epistemological position as an ideological position and, thus, as a move within the field itself. And indeed, everything happens as if Bourdieu is only introducing a revamped version of Althusser's ideological distinction between science and ideology in the field of sociology to transcend the opposition between mainstream and radical sociology. And even more problematic, if his move is not a polemic but a reflexive one, not a 'cynical' but a 'clinical' one (Bourdieu, 1996: 68), then the question still remains how he can have access to the position of the 'impartial spectator', observing his own observations and those of the others, seeing what they don't see and maybe even what he doesn't see.[52] And indeed, this seems to be the point where Bourdieusian sociology turns into something godlike – into 'Bourdivine sociology'.

Although Bourdieu is tempted at times to totalise and close his own totalising scheme, he should know better, and he does indeed know better, as can be gathered from his highly reflexive inaugural lecture on the lecture at the Collège de France, where he warns explicitly against the Platonic and Hegelian temptations of the 'free floating intelligentsia' by noting that 'one should not expect of a thought on the limits that it will give access to a thought without limits' (Bourdieu, 1982a: 23). Although Bourdieu maintained some residual separation between science and politics till the mid-1990s, the political nature of his scientific endeavours has become clearer as times has passed. In the true spirit of the Enlightenment, advancing science in the name of emancipation and emancipation in the name of science, the most famous sociologist of France has chosen to intervene as a political agitator in the public sphere to give a voice to the excluded (the unemployed and the new poor, the gays and the lesbians, the Algerian intellectuals and the illegal immigrants in France, etc.) and to undermine the neoliberal hegemony. Indeed, since the December 1995 strike (see Duval, 1998), he has multiplied his interventions 'for a left on the left' (Bourdieu, 1998c) – and not for a 'left of the left', as his enemies like to misread him – critically analysed and attacked the media intellectuals and other 'fast thinkers' for their complicity with the dominant classes (Bourdieu, 1996), proposed a series of powerful arguments aimed to counter the onslaught of the welfare state and the global politics of 'flexploitation' with a proposal for a European social state (Bourdieu 1998a) and, last but not least, launched a very successful series of affordable, well-documented and readable booklets, whose format reminds one of Habermas' *Kleine politische Schriften* and which are 'animated by the militant will to diffuse the knowledge which is indispensable for political reflection and action in a democracy' ('Preamble' to Halimi, 1997).

Conclusion: from critique to reconstruction

At the end of the day, Bourdieu's generative structuralism may be seen as an ongoing socio-philosophical reflection and empirico-theoretical variation on the relational theme of thought, which allows him 'to let the categories dance', as Marx said in another context, 'to their own political melody'. Indeed, moving progressively downward along the continuum of scientific abstractions, from the philosophical, epistemological and metatheoretical reflections on a relational social theory to their theoretical, methodological and empirical implementations in a sociology of fields, we have seen how Bourdieu's argument can be internally reconstructed as a systematic transposition of Bachelard's and Cassirer's reformulation of Hegel's outrageous statement that the 'real is rational' and the 'rational real' from the natural to the social sciences. That the relational mode of thought is central to Bourdieu's project is proved by the fact that the two central metasociological concerns that have driven his research programme for 40 years, namely the substitution of a relational for a substantialist conception of social reality and the transcendence of the fundamental antinomy of subjectivist and objectivist approaches to the study of social life, can respectively be interpreted as a horizontal and vertical application of this relational mode of intellectual production. If the first metasociological concern has found its sociological way in a conflict theory of the general properties of social fields and an impressive series of empirical investigations of the different fields of cultural production, distribution and consumption, the second one has led to the sociological recovery of the phenomenological descriptions of the habitus in a sophisticated theory of practices and their role in the reproduction of structures. Together the theory of fields and the theory of the habitus (with their theoretical paraphernalia: *illusio*, capital, etc.), which are internally related in such a way that the one appears either as a practical medium (*modus operandi*) or as the consequence (*opus operatum*) of the other, form the 'hard core' of Bourdieu's progressive research programme.

If my internal reconstruction of 'genetic structuralism' has consistently shown what Bourdieu owes to other theories (of Bachelard, Cassirer, etc.), how it overlaps with other theories (of Elias, Mannheim, etc.), or even how it could benefit from other theories (of Critical Realism, Giddens, Habermas, etc.), this was not done to detract from his originality, let alone to depreciate his sheer talent, but with an eye to explore the possibility of (meta)theoretical alliances and knowledge–political coalitions between different intellectual strands. The internal reconstruction of Bourdieu's system of theories that I have proposed has all along been inspired by the dialectical motif of 'immanent critique' (Benhabib, 1986: 19–43). Refusing the use of elements and criteria of judgement that are external to the theory, an immanent critique closely follows the curvatures of the theory and attempts to judge it according to its own criteria, arguing thus from within the theory against it, not to undermine it, but in order to uncover and ultimately to recover its tensions and limits, so as to make the theory stronger and more coherent.

In this dialectical vein, I have advanced two main critiques of Bourdieu. First, an epistemological one. In order to avoid the 'epistemic fallacy', which reduces ontological questions to epistemological ones, he should avoid all equivocations between rationalist and realist interpretations of his work, abandon the conventionalist stratagem of the 'as if', and put his theory on the solid ontological foundations that critical realism is only too happy to provide. The social world is not an analogical reflection of the relations that the theory depicts (rationalism), but it is the other way around (realism). If Bourdieu wants his critical theory of the social to be critically assessed so that it can in turn critically assess the social, if he wants his theory to come to grips with and to have an effect on the social world, then he ultimately has to presuppose that the social world is more than an epistemic effect of his theory. Second, I have also advanced a metatheoretical critique. If Bourdieu wants to bring his sociological theory in line with his political intentions, he should open up his system, avoid deterministic descriptions of stable reproduction, and give voluntarism its due. This presupposes that the creativity of the habitus is openly recognised and that culture is not only seen as symbolically sublimated violence, not only as an instrument of domination, but also as an instrument of liberation. After all, a critical theory is not only a theory that uncovers the arbitrary nature of social necessity (domination), but also one that is able to reveal the possibility of the improbable (emancipation). It certainly describes reproductive practices, but only to stimulate praxis; and if it analyses the mechanisms by which actors are reduced to agents (not to say to mere carriers of structures), it is only to contribute to the construction of 'something like a subject' (Bourdieu, 1980: 41). In his more militant moods and political appeals for a *Realpolitik* of Reason (Bourdieu, 1992, 1994, 1997a), Bourdieu has recognised the spontaneity of action and the efficacy of ideas.

And, finally, a question: why not go further, all the way from a critical theory of domination to a political theory of emancipation, and from there to a normative theory of ethics? If a critical sociology presupposes not only an analysis of the forces of social domination, but also an analysis of the social forces of emancipation and the possibility of a transformative politics, then it also presupposes an ethics, or at least some formulation of normative criteria of moral judgement and some indication of the 'good life'. Bourdieu has already given us his critique of pure reason and his critique of judgement; what we now would like to see is his critique of practical reason.[53]

Note on the posthumous publications of Pierre Bourdieu

Some people are forgotten before they die, others, like Pierre Bourdieu (1930–2002), expire under the glare of publicity. Although the publication of the quasi-totality of his interventions in the public sphere – from the war of Algeria to the one in Bosnia and from the reform of the universities to his scathing attack on the media (Bourdieu, 2002a) – show that he was always a 'political animal', it is only in the last decade of his life that he willingly assumed the role of the 'total intellectual' à la Sartre and became a national celebrity. In *La sociologie est un sport de combat*, a documentary film made by Pierre Carles (2001), one sees the leading sociologist touring the country to criticise the neoliberal politics of globalisation, giving a voice to the 'no-nos' ('*les sans*'), those who have no voice, no job, no papers, no nothing.

A few months after his death, Bourdieu's autobiography was published, not in French, but in German (Bourdieu, 2002b). *Outline for a self-analysis* extends the final lecture of the course on the reflexive sociology of science that he gave at the Collège de France (Bourdieu, 2001) with a protracted socio-analysis of his intellectual journey. His ambivalence towards the intellectual world, which expresses itself in a strange but comprehensible mixture of intellectual arrogance and self-deprecation, appears as a psychic sedimentation of the years of lonely suffering he spent at the boarding school, a 'total institution' that almost broke him. Following his studies in philosophy at the *Ecole normale supérieure*, where he came under the influence of the 'historical epistemology' of Gaston Bachelard and Georges Canguilhem, the young philosopher from the province went to Algeria to fulfil his military service. During the war of independence, he did extensive fieldwork and became an anthropologist. The catalogue of the exhibition of the pictures he took in Algeria show that he had not only a sharp mind, but also a good eye for the details of everyday life (Bourdieu, 2003). Having moved in the 1950s from philosophy to ethnology, the young anthropologist 'converted' in the mid-1960s to sociology. Throwing himself frenetically into all kinds of sociological research on all kinds of objects and subjects (photography, comic strips, cultural taste, Heidegger, etc.), the sociological genius developed in the span of a few years (1966–1972) a total theory of the social world. Bourdieu was only in his mid-thirties when he formulated, at the highest level of abstraction and with the greatest conceptual precision, the interrelated theories of 'fields', 'the habitus' and 'symbolic violence' that form the backbone of his progressive research programme into the reproduction of the structures of domination.

The posthumous publication of three texts (Bourdieu, 2002c) written at different times, in which he analyses the progressive exclusion of peasants from the matrimonial market, allows one to follow in detail how he successively developed and integrated his main concepts in a grand theory of social reproduction. In the first text, Bourdieu presents a total description of his native village in the south of France. He explains the celibacy of the peasant through a masterful description of his habitus – 'he drags his big wooden shoes or his heavy boots even though he's wearing his Sunday shoes' (Bourdieu, 2002b: 114) – that can compare with Heidegger's. In the second text, the same problematic is treated once again, but this time the matrimonial practices are explained in terms of unconscious strategies of reproduction. In the third text, the symbolic dimension of the economic exclusion of peasants is covered through an analysis of the modernisation of rural regions. The book concludes with a violent postscript in which Bourdieu slams the urban representations of the rural and attacks Foucault in a footnote. Like Foucault's lectures at the College de France, Bourdieu's will also be published. The first volume is on the state (Bourdieu, 2012) and was published to mark the tenth anniversary of his death.

Notes

* A shorter version of this chapter was presented at a conference on Bourdieu's cultural theory at the University of Glasgow in September 1997. I would like to thank Craig Calhoun, Loïc J.D. Wacquant, Nathalie Heinich, J.C. Alexander, Saa Meroe, Bridget Fowler, Frank Papon, Peter Wagner, Steve Woolgar, Mike Lynch, Dick Pels, David Oswell and José Maurício Domingues for their useful comments and constructive criticisms.

1 Bourdieu is not a syncretic but a synthetic and heretical thinker. He draws on Durkheim, Marx, Weber and others, but in so far as he critically corrects them one could as well describe him as an anti-Durkheimian Durkheimian, an anti-Weberian Weberian or an anti-Marxist Marxist. One could even say that he thinks with Althusser against Althusser and against Habermas with Habermas, but not – and this is probably the only exception – that he thinks with Bachelard against Bachelard.

2 Until recently, most commentators have missed the important input of the French tradition of the history and philosophy of science in general and of Bachelard in particular. Wacquant has noted it (1996b: 152) and in the meantime Swartz (1997: 31–36) has corrected the oversight. In *Culture and Power*, he introduces his analysis of the influence of Bachelard on Bourdieu by noting that 'many of Bourdieu's central theoretical concerns remain somewhat elusive to much British and American sociology unless they are understood in light of this philosophical tradition' (Swartz, 1997: 31). Before Swartz and Wacquant, Raynaud had noted it, but unfortunately he ended up with the reductive characterisation of Bourdieu's sociology as the 'distinguished form of vulgar materialism' (Raynaud, 1980: 93). Alexander (1995), for his part, has taken over this partial characterisation, but without noticing the Bachelardian strand in Bourdieu's thought. Otherwise, I am sure, he could not have chastised Bourdieu for ignoring the postpositivist philosophy of science. Leaving aside the highly polemical form and some misgivings – which are due to his superficial

knowledge of the philosophical and political intricacies of the French field of cultural production (for an extremely violent critique of Alexander, see Wacquant, 1996c) – Alexander's metacritique of Bourdieu can be justified. That said, I want to add that although his 'symptomatic' reading is a possible one, it is certainly not the one I would favour – although I have presented a metacritique of Adorno's critical theory that is inspired by a Habermasian reading of Alexander's *Theoretical Logic in Sociology* (Alexander, 1982–1983) and, thus, is somewhat similar to his critique of Bourdieu (Vandenberghe, 1998: 55–103). But Bourdieu is not Adorno. If Adorno can be read as a hyperdeterministic Bourdieu (without theological overtones), reading Bourdieu as if one were reading the *Dialectic of Enlightenment* is rather reductionistic. In fact, I read Bourdieu in a voluntaristic way as the sociological counterpart of, and prelude to, Habermas' normative theory of communicative action.

3 More than any other sociologist, Bourdieu, who published Cassirer in the collection which he directed at the Editions de Minuit, is influenced by Cassirer – in two ways. First, the influence of Cassirer's philosophy of symbolic forms on the theory of symbolic violence is openly acknowledged and discussed by Bourdieu in his major statement on this central theme of his work (Bourdieu, 1977b: 405–411). I will not discuss this part of the Cassirerian heritage here, but will concentrate my exegesis on Cassirer's relational conception of knowledge and show how Bourdieu develops it into a full-blown theory of the properties of the field. It would also be interesting to explore Bourdieu's indebtedness to Panofsky, who was Cassirer's colleague at the Warburg Institute in Hamburg; unfortunately this analysis will have to be postponed till another time.

4 In his earlier works, Bourdieu always used the term 'realism' as a *Kampfwort* to attack the naive realism of the empiricists. Lately, however, the adjective realist has taken on more positive connotations that hint at a possible acquaintance with the realist movement in the Anglo-Saxon philosophy of the natural and the social sciences. See, for instance, *La noblesse d'Etat*, where Bourdieu describes his epistemology as 'inseparably constructivist and realist' (1989: 186) or *La misère du monde*, undoubtedly the book which seems the furthest removed from his earlier insistence on the necessary break with spontaneous conceptions and prenotions of the social, where he speaks of a 'realist construction' (Bourdieu, 1993a: 915–916).

5 Critical realism is the final nail in the coffin of positivism – which does not exclude, of course, that the deceased may reappear for a second time, 'like in a farce', as Marx would say. The strength of positivist accounts of the natural sciences can be gauged by the fact that even such a clear-sighted critique of positivist scientism as Habermas has taken the erroneous self-interpretations of positivists like Comte, Mach and even Popper at face value (see Habermas, 1971).

6 The fact that the noumenal structures and the generative mechanisms are only observable via their consequences raises the problem of their representation: How do we know that those transfactual structures exist? Who has accorded primacy of the unobservable over the observable? Who speaks for those structures? Who speaks in their name? Thanks to such critical questions about the representation of transfactual mechanisms and the role of spokespersons in science (Latour, 1984), we gain access to a reflexive sociology of intellectuals (Pels, 1999). At this point, a junction and (who knows?) maybe even a fruitful cooperation can be established between realist and rationalist forms of constructivism and their nominalist counterparts, as represented by the radical constructivism of 'Ants' (Actor–Network Theorists) like Callon (1986), Latour (1987) and Law (1994). Such a cooperation would, however, require that the radical constructivists abandon their ontological nihilism and make only methodological use of the 'anti-essentialist nexus (relativism, constructivism, reflexivity)' (Grint and Woolgar, 1997: 5) to show us how 'reality' – that is, the descriptions, redescriptions, and constructions of reality, but not reality itself, of course, which exists independently of those descriptions in the same way as the dog barks whether we

have a concept of it or not – is 'performatively' constructed as a matter of course by their spokespersons. Such a move from ontological to methodological nominalism implies a consequent switch from a 'deconstructivist' to a genuinely 'constructivist' posture, from construction to something more akin to phenomenological constitution (Lynch, 1993) – but that may be asking too much of the 'metareflexivists' who are convinced, like Derrida, that there is no '*hors texte*'.

7 That the scientists themselves sometimes think that by describing the world they constitute it, that they may be sceptical and even share the conventionalist agnosticism of the sociologists who observe their laboratory life (Latour and Woolgar, 1979; Knorr-Cetina, 1983) and try to efface the distinction between the representation and the object (Woolgar, 1991: 21–22) does not detract, and should not distract, from the importance of the distinction between the transitive and the intransitive dimensions of knowledge. SSK, the sociology of scientific knowledge, is only concerned with the study of the transitive, not with the intransitive dimensions of knowledge. It is thus epistemologically relativist and ontologically realist. Once this is granted, we can even accept the most provocative conclusions of Latour and Woolgar:

> By observing artefact construction, we showed that 'reality' [quotes added] is the consequence of the settlement of a dispute rather than its cause. If 'reality' [quotes added] is the consequence rather than the cause of this construction, this means that a scientist's activity is directed not toward reality [quotes removed], but toward these operations on statements.
>
> (Latour and Woolgar, 1979: 236–237)

8 Bhaskar's exploration of the ontological limits, such as concept-dependence, activity-dependence and greater time-space specificity of social structures, which the social realm imposes on naturalist research and which preclude the wholesale and unqualified transposition of the methods of the natural sciences to the social sciences, has given rise to a transformational model of social action that is, to a certain extent at least, remarkably similar to Giddens' structuration theory (see Bhaskar, 1989a; and for a critical comparison of Giddens and Bhaskar, see Archer, 1988: 72–100; 1995: 87–134).

9 Is it necessary to mention that Bourdieu, like his mentor, cannot recognise an antinomy without trying to transcend it? In this respect, errors and limits of thought seem to be very useful. They are there to be corrected, to be overcome and thus they are the medium of truth, the way to come closer to the truth, which is always conceived in properly fallibilist fashion as 'truth for the time being'.

10 The field of world-sociology is not a unified field yet. It remains fractured along national lines. This probably explains why Anglo-Saxon commentators, who are unfamiliar with the rationalist tradition of French *épistémologie* (Bachelard, Koyré, Canguilhem, Duhem, Cavaillès) or with the German neo-Kantian tradition of *Wissenschaftslehre* (Lask, Cassirer, Panofsky), project their own brand of the philosophy of science (Bhaskar) on Bourdieu's position, describing him as a 'critical realist' (e.g. Harker *et al.*, 1991: 201; Jenkins, 1992: 95–96; Fowler, 1997: 6, 17, 82). This erroneous attribution is, however, easily understandable, as it results from the confusion between the epistemological and the metatheoretical levels of analysis. In epistemological terms, Bourdieu is a neo-Kantian, and thus an idealist; in metatheoretical terms, he is a Marxist-Weberian, and thus a materialist; the conflation of both levels of analysis leads to the label 'realist', which is the materialist brand of epistemology. Needless to say, my critique aims only at the epistemological idealism, not at the metatheoretical one. Unlike Bourdieu's most vociferous critics, I am not claiming that Bourdieu's structuralism represents a sophisticated version of vulgar (or reductionistic) materialism but that (at worst) he reduces ontology to epistemology and (at best) he avoids making ontological commitments by resorting to a conventionalist wink to Vaihinger's neo-Kantian 'philosophy of the as if'.

11 For a discussion of this issue in relation to Althusser, see Benton (1984: 179–199). This reference to Althusser shows that it is not enough to draw on the late Marx to become a realist. What really matters is whether one interprets Marx in rationalist or in realist terms. That Althusser himself was clearly drifting in the direction of rationalism is revealed by his apparently insignificant remark, which echoes a famous line of Derrida, that 'we never get out of the concept' (Althusser *et al.* 1970: II, 67; see also pp. 20ff.).

12 Here Bourdieu seems to follow Lévi-Strauss, when he states that 'the fundamental principle is that the notion of social structure does not refer to empirical reality, but to the models which are constructed according to it' (Lévi-Strauss, 1958: 331). The break with Lévi-Strauss's objectivism comes at a later stage, when Bourdieu is going to criticise the 'scholastic fallacy' that consists in the intellectualistic transposition of the theoretical models in the head of the actors, enthroning metadiscourses and metapractices as the principle of discourses and practices, suggesting that actors act according to the model, which is a bit like assuming that we constantly walk around like tourists in a foreign city with a map in our hands. As we will see later, in discussing the notion of habitus, the invisible structure of differences takes on real existence and is 'occasionally' revealed in ordinary existence, veiled in the lived form of keeping distances, of affinities and incompatibilities, sympathies and rejections, etc.

13 By saying that science has to be ontologically bold (or even 'presumptuous') rather than epistemologically cautious (or 'modest'), I am explicitly contesting Kant's famous programmatic call for the dissolution of ontology – 'The proud name of an ontology that presumptuously claims to supply, in systematic doctrinal form, synthetic a priori knowledge of things in general … has to make place modestly for a mere analytic of understanding' (Kant, 1983: B, 884). However, in so far as critical realism claims that knowledge is ultimately grounded a posteriori, it does not simply reverse Kant's programme. Realism establishes, by means of a transcendental argument, that science necessarily presupposes an ontology of complex generative mechanisms, but it wisely leaves it to science to empirically investigate what those mechanisms are and how they function.

14 Here Bourdieu polemically draws on Husserl's phenomenology of the lifeworld. According to Husserl, the common sense world, our ordinary, everyday lifeworld, is a domain of 'passive doxa', i.e. a domain in which the real is taken for granted and not reflexively questioned as to the intentional acts of consciousness that constitute it. In the doxic experience of the world, the world is always there, passively and immediately given to consciousness as the unquestioned foundation of all the constitutive acts of consciousness and of the actions themselves: 'In passive doxa, being is not just pre-given as the substrate of all possible accomplishments of knowledge which actively contribute to it, but also as a substrate for all evaluations, practical determinations of ends and actions' (Husserl, [1938] 1985: 53). The epistemological rupture with the doxic experience of the lifeworld in order to construct the object as a scientific object of analysis is only a first moment of the research process, however. Eventually, the doxic experiences of the world will be reintegrated into the analysis as a scientifically objectivated experience that is theoretically understood as an experience that is 'functionally' determined by the relationally reconstructed structures. Then it will appear that those structured doxic experiences actively contribute to the stable reproduction of those structuring structures that ultimately depend upon the recurrent practices and experiences of the agents.

15 The 'hard' version of the break with 'portable sociology' (Javeau) is exposed in the epistemological handbook (Bourdieu *et al.*, 1973); the 'soft' version is presented in *La misère du monde*. In this beautiful book, which consists mainly of transcribed interviews with the excluded of this world (the racist shopkeeper, the hustler from the ghetto, the disillusioned syndicalist, the depressed teacher, the Algerian woman, etc.) that are preceded by little sociological *mises en perspective* by Bourdieu and his collaborators, the main concept ('misère de position', ordinary misery as linked to

social position) is not even defined sociologically, but the spontaneous prenotions of ordinary everyday life are inserted in a larger scheme of sociological constructions of the object, which Bourdieu has elaborated elsewhere but which remains largely implicit in this book. The main message is in fact a political one: if the politicians don't intervene to improve the social conditions of the little people, the excluded and the marginal, they will be considered as 'guilty for non assistance to persons in danger' (Bourdieu, 1993a: 944).

16 This radical disjuncture with the common sense conceptions of the social world does, of course, not exclude that the scientific concepts of the sociologist are afterwards disseminated to, and picked up by ordinary people (or 'lay sociologists' as the ethnomethodologists call them – Garfinkel and his colleagues do not hesitate to playfully 'respecify' chimpanzees as 'animal colleagues' (Lynch *et al.*, 1983: 213)). If anything, Bourdieu's social theory, which is after all intended as a critical theory, presupposes this kind of 'institutional reflexivity' (Giddens, 1990: 15–16), where knowledge 'spirals in and out' of the contexts it describes, thus performatively reconstituting both itself and its context. For a superb analysis of this 'double hermeneutic', which draws on Bourdieu's praxaeology, see Taylor (1985: 91–115).

17 The inevitable consequence of this theoretical move is, of course, that Bourdieu cannot take into account or account for the autonomy of the interaction order (cf. Luhmann, 1975: 9–20; Goffman, 1983).

18 Unlike most of the Anglo-Saxon *lectores* of Durkheim (with the notable exception of Johnson *et al.,* 1984), Bourdieu has always conceived of Durkheim as a rationalist and a structuralist and not as a positivist.

19 For a clarifying analytical discussion of relations of a higher order (relations of relations of relations), which is somewhat similar to Bourdieu, see Archer (1995: part II).

20 Although I won't say much here about 'symbolic violence', this is the point where Bourdieu inserts Marx's classic analysis of the ideological effects of the fetishistic illusion, which consists of the reifying inversion of things and relations in such a way that 'the social relation between men assumes, in their eyes, the fantastic form of a relation between things' (Marx, [1868] 1970: 72).

21 Or, perhaps, it's the other way round: 'In the relation is the beginning.' Donati's neofunctionalist exploration of a relational theory, which takes it lead from Alexander and Luhmann, also starts with the (Catholic) slogan 'In the beginning is the relation' (Donati, 1991: 80). Yet, his theory of relations is systemist, functionalist and ultimately interactionist, but not structuralist.

22 For an analysis of Cassirer's thought, which shows the continuity between *Substance and Form* and the philosophy of symbolic forms, see Vandenberghe (2001).

23 This Leibnizian idea of the relational (over)determination of the concrete particular by a multiplicity of variables, which can be expressed by means of a mathematical function, is neatly formulated by Bachelard in the following terms: 'Taken as a complex of relations a particular phenomenon is a genuine function of several variables. The mathematical expression analyzes it most thoroughly' (Bachelard, 1929: 209). Marx expressed the same idea in the 1857 'Introduction' to the *Grundrisse*, where he states:

> The concrete is concrete because it is the concentration of many determinations, hence unity of the diverse. It appears in the process of thinking, therefore, as a process of concentration, as a result, not as a point of departure, even though it is the point of departure in reality and hence also the point of departure for observation and conception
>
> (Marx, [1857] 1973: 101)

However, against Marx and with Sayer (1995: 18–42), who analyses the relation between private property, the market and the division of labour, one should stress that if the concrete is indeed a concentration or a function of several necessary relationships, the form of the concentration is contingent, and therefore only determinable through empirical research.

24 This is an absolutely non-Durkheimian move. As Durkheim has made it clear in his inaugural speech (Durkheim, [1888] 1970: especially pp. 78–85), the project of establishing sociology as an autonomous discipline is analytically linked to and dependent on the autonomy of its object. It should also be noted in this context that this analytical definition of the field is in conflict with Bourdieu's genetic analysis of the field, according to which fields are not a historical invariant but only emerge in modern times as self-referential systems, 'outdifferentiated from their environment' (Luhmann) or 'uncoupled from the life-world' (Habermas). For an exploration of the tension between the historical specificity and the transhistorical validity of Bourdieu's analytic apparatus, see Calhoun (1995: 132–161).

25 This 'overdetermination' (Althusser) is what distinguishes dialectical theories of (lateral) totalities from more functional analyses of systems (see Habermas, 1969). The dialectical inter-, or more precisely, intrarelations between the elements of an organic totality are hard to understand for more analytically inclined minds, like Pareto, for instance, who complained that Marx's concepts are 'like bats: one can see in them mice and birds at the same time' (quoted in Ollman, 1971: 3).

26 This combination of formal invariance and material variation is what makes successful cross-national comparisons of field research possible. Thus, to take the example of the educational field, even if outside of France there is no exact equivalent of, say, the Ecole Nationale d'Administration or the Collège de France (although Oxford's All Souls College comes quite close to it), it is enough to apply the relational grid, to transpose it to a new context and structural equivalents will undoubtedly be found.

27 The linear mode of thought thus violates what a network analyst has aptly called 'the anticategorical imperative' (Emirbayer, 1994: 1414). This imperative rejects explanations that conceive social behaviour as the result of individuals' common possession of categorical attributes and stipulates that those categorical attributes take on their meaning only when they are inserted in a structural system of internal relations.

28 Charting the hidden linear assumptions of multivariate analysis, Abott describes the reification-effect in the following terms:

> Many sociologists treat the world as if social causality actually obeyed the rules of linear transformations. They do this by assuming, in the theories that open their empirical articles, that the social world consists of fixed entities with variable attributes; that these attributes have only one causal meaning at a time; that this causal meaning does not depend on other attributes, on the past sequence of attributes, or on the context of other entities.
>
> (Abott, 1988: 181)

29 From a Popperian perspective, historical materialism, psychoanalysis and so-called 'individual psychology' appear as 'pseudo-sciences'. They are unscientific because they cannot be falsified. Their strength is their weakness. There is no doubt that the critique which Sir Karl addresses to Marx, Freud and Adler (but never to his own theory) applies to Bourdieu's theory of fields:

> These theories appeared to be able to explain practically everything that happened within the fields to which they referred. The study of any of them seemed to have the effect of an intellectual conversion or revelation, opening your eyes to a new truth hidden from those not yet initiated. Once your eyes were thus opened you saw confirming instances everywhere: the world was full of verifications of the theory. Whatever happened always confirmed it.
>
> (Popper, 1989: 34–35)

30 Caillé considers Bourdieu's work as the sociological pendant of Balzac's *Comédie humaine* and concludes that it belongs to the realm of 'conceptualized literature'

(Caillé, 1992: 113), without, however – and this is important – attaching overly negative connotations to this aesthetic characterisation. For my part, I find Bourdieu's work more Proustian, filled as it is with the subtleties of his observation, the innovative drift of his associations and the minutely detailed reflections on everyday life thanks to which life and blood is pumped into what otherwise would be a highly formalistic system. And although his 'long heavily articulated sentences, which one practically has to reconstruct as Latin sentences' (Bourdieu 1987a: 66) may remind one at times of Parsons' 'elephantine style', I must say – or, should I say, confess? – that I quite like his German-styled sentences with an overflow of commas, semicolons and hyphens, phrases embedded in one another, reflexive loops, literary plays on words, scholarly references to scholasticism, oblique polemical shots at unquoted adversaries and an almost Adornian predilection for chiasmatic inversions, negations and paradoxes.

31 The coherence of the theory, and thus of its 'truth', also finds expression in Bourdieu's 'methodological polytheism':

> Not only does he often triangulate or validate his results *ex post* with different methods – the fit between the various outcomes thus generated replacing the technical discussion of confidence intervals and the like – he also reads quantitative data 'ethnographically', that is as exploratory or confirmatory means of locating underlying patterns while, conversely, he often interprets field observations 'statistically', that is, with the aim of drawing inferences and to elaborate relations between variables.
>
> (Wacquant, 1990: 683)

32 For the intellectual history of the concept (Aristotle, Boetius, Averroes, Thomas Aquinas, Hegel, Husserl, Heidegger, Merleau-Ponty, Mauss and Panofsky), see Bourdieu (1985: 14), Funke (1974), Rist (1984) and Héran (1987). Notwithstanding the long standing of the concept, the influence of the phenomenological movement is really decisive in my opinion but, unfortunately, due to lack of space, I cannot explore the phenomenological link here. Although Husserl uses the concept quite regularly, Bourdieu is more influenced by Heidegger, his 'first love', who uses the concept less frequently. Notwithstanding the significant influence of *Ideen II* (Husserl, 1952) on Bourdieu (and Merleau-Ponty), it is clear that he has not much sympathy for the radical Cartesianism of Husserl's transcendental phenomenology and is only too happy to follow Heidegger's turn away from the transcendental phenomenology of the 'master' to an existential analytics of *Dasein*. Seen against this background, Bourdieu's critique of the philosophy of consciousness, which manifests itself in his insistence on the infra-reflexive and routinised nature of our practices, starts to make sense. Like Heidegger and against Husserl, Bourdieu is simply convinced that 'knowledge is a founded [or derivated] mode of being-in-the world of Dasein' (Heidegger, [1927] 1993: part I, 62). However, when it comes to the concept of habitus, it is clear that Merleau-Ponty's analysis of 'habit' comes closest to Bourdieu's. Having read Bourdieu before Merleau-Ponty, I really had the impression of reading Bourdieu when I was reading the phenomenological descriptions of the acts of 'writing on the typewriter' and 'playing the organ' (Merleau-Ponty, 1945: 166–172). For a fine exploration of the praxaeological workings of the habitus through the analysis of the pugilistic hexis, see Wacquant (1995) and for a self-presentation of the work and the variegated interests of Bourdieu's designated transatlantic interpreter, see Wacquant (1996d).

33 In this sense, one can describe the virtual powers of the habitus as 'passive powers' or 'liabilities', and liabilities as the dispositions of the agent to act in virtue of its essential nature, whereby the stimulus which activates the disposition of the agent is part of the extrinsic circumstances (Harré, 1970: 272). Just as the disposition to steal manifests itself only when an appropriate situation presents itself, the habitus only becomes actualised and manifest in certain concrete circumstances that trigger its powers.

34 The distinction between *ergon* and *energeia* comes from von Humboldt; it corresponds to the distinction between *opus operatum* and *modus operandi*, which comes from Panofsky. Cassirer, who worked with Panofsky at the Warburg Institute in Hamburg, is the mediator between the two.

35 Moreover, it is only in exceptional circumstances, if ever, that the habitus functions as the *malin génie* of perfect reproduction. The model is ideal-typical, which means according to Weber that it never occurs in reality, and thus is purely heuristic. One should remember that the limit situation of perfect reproduction is only a 'particular case of the possible' and avoid to 'universalize unconsciously the model of the quasi-circular relation of quasi-perfect reproduction which is only valid in the case where the conditions of the production of the habitus and the conditions of its functioning are identical or homothetical' (Bourdieu, 1974: 5). Notwithstanding the fact that Bourdieu also analyses situations where the 'ontological complicity' (Heidegger) between the habitus and the field is disrupted (the so-called *hysteresis*-effect; see Bourdieu, 1977a; 1984a: 207–250), it should, however, be noted that so far the situation of perfect complicity has been systematically privileged. In this respect, Bourdieu involuntarily reminds one of Parsons. And indeed, it is enough to fiddle a bit with a couple of key sentences of *The Social System* to obtain possible extracts from *Reproduction*:

> It will be assumed that the maintenance of the complementarity of role-expectations [of habitus and field], once established, is not problematical, in other words that the 'tendency' to maintain the interaction process is the first law of social process. This is clearly an assumption.
>
> (Parsons, 1951: 205)

> Theory, relative to such systems, is directed to the analysis of the conditions under which such a given constant system pattern will be maintained and conversely, the conditions under which it will be altered in determinate ways. This, we may surmise, is the fundamental basis of the assumption of our 'law of inertia' of social processes
>
> (Parsons, 1951: 482)

and last but not least, 'If theory is good theory, whichever type of problem it tackles most directly, there's no reason whatever to believe that it will not be equally applicable to the problems of change' (Parsons, 1951: 435). And indeed, being not only 'grand' but also 'great' and 'good' theory, there's no reason whatever not to read Bourdieu's system of theory against the grain as a systematic theory of the conditions of possibility of social change.

36 I always had the impression that Bourdieu's metatheoretical topology of the space of possibilities was perfect. Like Bachelard's in his 'epistemological profile' (Bachelard, [1940] 1988: 41–51), Bourdieu has systematically mapped the epistemological and metatheoretical oppositions that structure the sociological discipline:

> The opposition between Marx, Weber, and Durkheim, as it is ritually invoked in courses and dissertations, hides that the unity of sociology is maybe located in the space of possible positions. The antagonism, when it is understood as such, proposes the possibility of its own overcoming.
>
> (Bourdieu, 1987a: 49; see also 1971b: 295)

And even if, at the end of the day, in his attempt to transcend the ritual oppositions between objectivism and subjectivism, determinism and voluntarism, materialism and idealism, externalism and internalism, etc., he always ends up at the same pole of the polarity, 'transcending, for instance, the objectivist-subjectivist dualism while remaining firmly rooted in objectivism' or 'vociferously rejecting determinism while persistently producing deterministic models of social process' (Jenkins, 1992: 175), in principle, nothing should stop us from trying to bend the stick in the other direction. By arguing this way, I am trying to rejoin the celebrated 'return of the subject' and the pragmatic, descriptive and interpretative inflection that characterises French post-Bourdieusian social theory and manifests itself in the greater emphasis that the 'Habermasso-Ricoeurdian' praxis axis and the 'ethno-Boltanskian' action fraction place on the reflexive nature of action (see Gauchet, 1988; Dosse, 1995). If, for personal reasons, Boltanski and other ex-Bourdieusians had to break with Bourdieu's critical social theory as such to develop a 'theory of social critique' (Boltanski and Thévenot, 1991), I am seeking to arrive at the same position by means of an 'immanent critique'. Arguing with Bourdieu against Bourdieu, I am trying to open up the system from within and to loosen the grip of its tightly constructed *problématique*. This does not mean that I am not interested in the limits of the system, but only that I restrain myself from straying outside of the confines of the system. Just like Bourdieu himself, I am fascinated by what falls outside the system: the true gift, true communication, true friendship, true love, in brief the Maussian 'miracle' of 'symbolic exchange' that escapes domination, calculation, manipulation, etc. Thus, to take his most recent book on male domination, which offers a 'feminist' reinterpretation of his early anthropological research on traditional classification systems in Kabylia (Bourdieu, 1972) and uses it as an ideal-type to uncover the omnipresence of symbolic male domination in the West, what really interests me is the (unscientific?) 'Post-scriptum on Love and Domination' (Bourdieu, 1998b: 116–119) where Bourdieu talks openly, probably for the first time, about the limits of his system, in the case of the miraculous cease-fire, the end of war and fights, the end of strategic exchange or, more positively, non-violence, mutual recognition, full reciprocity, disinterest, trust, wonder, happiness or 'peace', to speak like Adorno.

37 Just one example: At the end of *La noblesse d'Etat*, Bourdieu sketches a model of the historical progression of the universal. In an interview with Wacquant (1993b: 35–36), he confesses that, when he was reading the proofs of the book, he decided to cut it out but that the production manager at Editions de Minuit inadvertently left it in the volume.

38 Comparing his earlier work, even a more praxaeological one like *Esquisse d'une théorie de la pratique*, where Bourdieu explicitly states that practices 'always tend to reproduce the objective structures of which they are in the last analysis the product' (Bourdieu, 1972: 175) with his later work (especially Bourdieu, 1997a), we can notice that a progressive weakening of the hyperdeterminism has taken place. Although the Chomskyan accents of the 'generative capacity' of the habitus have been present from the very beginning (Bourdieu and Passeron, 1967: 151–164), the stress on the active, improvisatory, inventive and even creative nature of the habitus is relatively new (Bourdieu, 1984b: 134–135; 1987a: 23; 1997a: 170–193).

39 It is enough to compare Ravaisson's metaphysical booklet on the habitus, which Heidegger liked so much, where habit is characterised as the transformation of Freedom into Nature and of the Will into Instincts (Ravaisson, [1838] 1997: 82–103), to see that Bourdieu has given an activist twist to the concept of 'second nature'.

40 In a superb critique of Bourdieu's reflexive sociology, Kögler (1997a) shows that although Bourdieu presupposes in principle the possibility of a reflexive reshaping or restructuring of the habitus, he is in fact unable to bridge the gap between intellectual and lay discourse and to link the reflexivity of the sociologist to the reflexivity of the agents. Drawing on Gadamer, Kögler (1997b) tries to solve the problem by hermeneutically explicating the habitus in such a way that the theoretical reconstruction of the habitus by the sociologist is reconnected to the critical self-understanding of the habitus of the agents.

41 The reductionist nature of historical materialist analyses of culture is well caught in Sartre's punching and widely quoted passage on Valéry: 'Valéry is a petit bourgeois intellectual, no doubt about it. But not every petit bourgeois intellectual is Valéry. The

heuristic inadequacy of contemporary Marxism is contained in these two sentences' (Sartre, 1963: 56). To understand why Valéry, or Flaubert for that matter, writes as he writes and perhaps even what he writes, one has to re-open the short-circuit and insert the field as an autonomous mediator between the basis and the superstructure.

42 By saying that external influences are 'refracted' by the structure of fields, Bourdieu seems to follow and accept one of Luhmann's central claims, namely that fields are self-referentially closed systems that can only communicate, or more precisely, 'resonate' with each other if the coded messages coming from other systems in their environment are somehow retranslated into the binary code of the receiving system (for the clearest outline of the self-regulation of systems through a selective opening up of closed systems to their environment, see Luhmann, 1986).

43 Personal discussion with Stephen Mennell, Toronto, August 1997. For a well-informed analysis of the relation between Cassirer and Elias, see Maso (1995). At this point, it should be noted that Bourdieu does not define the field as a structure of relations between people, as Elias does, but as a structure of relations between positions or, as Bhaskar would say, as a 'position-practice system' (Bhaskar, 1989a: 41). This difference, which can be formulated as a difference between institutional and figurational conceptions of structure (Mouzelis 1995: 69–80), explains why, notwithstanding all similarities, Elias' figurational sociology still has an empiricist ring to it which Bourdieu has completely rationalised away.

44 This idea of the 'consensus in the dissensus', according to which the dissensus not only presupposes but also reinforces the consensus or, to say the same somewhat differently, according to which conflict actually contributes to the emergence of a shared understanding and thus to the integration of the opponents in a community, is typically French. One finds it not only in Bourdieu, but also in Touraine's analytics of social movements as triangular reaction-formations of Identity, Opposition and Totality (Touraine, 1978: 103–133) and in Lefort's concept of politics ('le politique') as the generative and foundational form of social division and integration (Lefort, 1986: 1–27).

45 Some analytical clarification might be useful at this point to unpack the concepts, which are nested like Russian dolls. (1) A space is anything that is topologically constructed as a relational structure of differences, generated by a principle, or, as Cassirer would say, by a 'lawful progression' or 'mathematical function' that discloses and constitutes a region of reality. (2) All societies are social spaces, i.e. structures of relational differences, generated by the principle of the distribution of the different species of capital in currency in a given society. (3) Social spaces are fields, that is fields of forces and fields of struggle in which social classes try to transform the structure of the field. (4) The structure of forces of the field of power determines at any given moment the principle of the hierarchisation of the positions in the field: either economic capital or cultural capital is the dominant principle. Classes struggle for the determination of the dominant principle of the hierarchical dispersion of positions in the field. The dominant classes are only dominant if they successfully impose their sort of capital as the dominant principle of hierarchisation. (5) The field of power should not be confounded with the political field, which is a subfield like any other. The field of power is a sort of 'metafield' that regulates the struggles for power throughout all fields. Its determinate configuration at any moment in time has implications for the struggles for the imposition of the principle of hierarchisation that go on in the subfields of cultural production, because the configuration of the field of power overdetermines the configuration of the subfields. The state of the structure of the field of power determines the structure of oppositions of the subfield and thus also the possible alliances that can be formed in the subfield, and also between the members of the subfield and those of their environment. Moreover, the structural homology that exists between the field of power and the subfields of cultural production means that cultural productions can and do offer an ideological legitimisation of

the status quo in so far as the conservation of the symbolic order contributes to the conservation of the political order. On the other hand, one should also note that the subversion of the symbolic order can have effects on the political order, but only if the symbolical subversion is accompanied by a social subversion of the field of political power.

46 Verdès-Leroux, who has 'read and re-read 10,000 pages' of Bourdieu's 'dry, artificial, immensely repetitive and unscientific' prose without finding anything worth preserving, has compiled an impressive but incomplete list of fields (and their corresponding species of capital) that indirectly indicates the plurality of his interests, the power of his theoretical tools and the fertility of his prolific production:

> Scientific field, literary field, field of power, religious field, juridical field, field of constructors, field of the production of houses, field of territorial powers, political field, economic field, field of journalism, field of ideological production, field of cultural production, field of painting, field of the institutions of higher education, field of the political sciences, field of political marketing, field of universities, field of the *grandes écoles*, field of *haute couture*, field of comic strips, field of pop art, field of publishing houses, field of contemporary physics, field of galleries, etc. (and don't forget the subfields).
>
> (Verdès-Leroux, 1998: 199)

47 Although both articles overlap, the second article (Bourdieu, 1971b) is much more complex than the first (Bourdieu, 1971a) in so far as Bourdieu systematically intermingles Marx, Weber and Durkheim (and a few others) in the picture and introduces his highly sophisticated and synthetic theory of symbolic power (Bourdieu, 1977b) in his analysis of the religious field in order to unveil the ideological contribution of religion to the maintenance of the social order. Although the theory of symbolic violence occupies a central place in Bourdieu's project (see Wacquant, 1987, 1996a, and especially 1993a: 1, where he states that 'Bourdieu's entire oeuvre may be read as a quest to explicate the specificity and potency of symbolic power'), I will leave it out of my analysis and concentrate on the relational aspects of the theory of fields.

48 Although Bourdieu's ideas largely echo those of the young Mannheim, which echo those of Carl Schmitt (Pels 1988: 229–231), I have never seen a reference to the 1928 essay. It is not even clear whether Bourdieu has actually read it.

49 In terms that remind us of Bourdieu's analysis of the relation between the field and the habitus, Mannheim writes that

> certain qualitative features of an object encountered in the living process of history are accessible only to minds of a certain structure. There are certain qualitatively distinguished features of historically existing objects that are open to perception only by a consciousness as formed and devised by particular historical circumstances.
>
> (Mannheim, 1952: 194)

For a further exploration of affinities, see Kögler (1997a).

50 In a thoughtful article, Pels (1995) has shown that universalism does not arise from the internalisation of a normative 'culture of critical discourse' (Gouldner's CCD), but from a set of social constraints that forces the rivals in the field to a cross-checking of their mutual products that unintentionally turns the pursuit of self-interest into a motor of the progress of reason ('private vices, public virtues').

51 Just like Foucault, Bourdieu shares Habermas' concern with communication, even if he analyses it from a different angle. For Habermas, the ideal speech situation is characterised by the absence of power, whereas for Bourdieu and Foucault it is the absence of communication without symbolic violence that characterises power. This shared emphasis on communication (with and without constraints) is what allows a

Habermasian reading of Bourdieu (and, possibly, of Foucault as well) and a Bourdieusian (or Foucaldian) reading of Habermas. Rather than simply opposing the one to the other, one should see that their politics of knowledge are perfectly complementary. For Bourdieu, power always comes first (power as *arche*). The task of politics consists in the creation of an egalitarian social universe that would render a discussion without symbolic constraints possible (discussion as *telos*). For Habermas, on the other hand, the ideal speech situation is always already given, or at least counterfactually anticipated as given (communication as *arche*). The task of a radical reformist politics consists in its institutionalisation in a democratic system. Although Bourdieu rightly claims that the ideal speech situation does not exist, he would certainly not want to conclude from this that the ideal of the speech situation does not exist either!

52 Observations of observations may allow one to relativise one's observations of the first order, but in so far as they remain observations, the 'blind spot' of their own observations always perdures. Or, as Luhmann says, 'even the observation of the second order cannot see what it cannot see. At best it can see that it cannot see what it cannot see' (Luhmann, 1989: 333).

53 In the meantime Bourdieu has honoured me with some 'frank and perhaps somewhat brutal remarks' on this article. He confirms that the 'hard core' of his theory is formed by a synthesis of Bachelard's rationalism and Cassirer's relationalism, rejects my insinuations that he might be a crypto-rationalist and declares that, like Bhaskar, whose work he has recently discovered, he has been a realist all along, and finally complains that I have made abstraction of the empirical content of his work, which explains why I have not only committed what one could call a scholastic fallacy of the second power (my term) but also why my interpretation of his political interventions in the public sphere does not rise far above the level of journalism (letter to the author 26 November 1998).

Bibliography

Abott, A. 1988. 'Transcending general linear reality'. *Sociological Theory*, 6, 2, pp. 169–186.

Alexander, J.C. 1982–1983. *Theoretical Logic in Sociology*, 4 vols. Berkeley, CA: University of California Press.

Alexander, J.C.. 1995. 'The reality of reduction: the failed synthesis of Pierre Bourdieu'. In *Fin de Siècle Social Theory*. London: Verso.

Alexander, J.C., Giesen, B., Münch, R. and Smelser, N. (eds.). 1987. *The Micro-Macro Link*. Berkeley, CA: University of California Press.

Althusser, L., *et al.* 1970. *Lire Le Capital*, 2 vols. Paris: Maspéro.

Archer, M. 1988. *Culture and Agency: The Place of Culture in Social Theory*. Cambridge: Cambridge University Press.

Archer, M. 1995. *Realist Social Theory: The Morphogenetic Approach*. Cambridge: Cambridge University Press.

Archer, M., Bhaskar, R., Collier, A., Lawson, T. and Norrie, A (eds.). 1998. *Critical Realism: Essential Readings*. London: Routledge.

Bachelard, G. 1929. *La valeur inductive de la relativité*. Paris: Vrin.

Bachelard, G. [1934] 1991. *Le nouvel esprit scientifique*. Paris: P.U.F.

Bachelard, G. [1938] 1993. *La formation de l'esprit scientifique: Contribution à une psychanalyse de la connaissance*. Paris: Vrin.

Bachelard, G. [1940] 1988. *La philosophie du non*. Paris: P.U.F.

Bachelard, G. [1949] 1986. *Le rationalisme appliqué*. Paris: P.U.F.

Bachelard, G. [1953] 1990. *Le matérialisme rationnel*. Paris: P.U.F.

Bachelard, G. 1971. *Epistémologie: Textes choisies*. Paris: P.U.F.

Beck, U. 1988. *Gegengifte: Die organisierte Unerantwortlichkeit*. Frankfurt am Main: Suhrkamp.

Benhabib, S. 1986. *Critique, Norm and Utopia: A Study of the Foundations of Critical Theory*. New York: Columbia University Press.

Benton, T. 1977. *Philosophical Foundations of the Three Sociologies*. London: Routledge.

Benton, T. 1984. *The Rise and Fall of Structural Marxism: Althusser and His Influence*. London: Macmillan.

Bhaskar, R. [1975] 1978. *A Realist Theory of Science*. Hemel Hempstead: Harvester Wheatsheaf.

Bhaskar, R. 1989a. *The Possibility of Naturalism: A Philosophical Critique of the Contemporary Human Sciences*. Hemel Hempstead: Harvester Wheatsheaf.

Bhaskar, R. 1989b. *Reclaiming Reality: A Critical Introduction to Contemporary Philosophy*. London: Verso.

Bloor, D. 1991. *Knowledge and Social Imagery*. Chicago, IL: University of Chicago Press.

Blumer, H. 1969. *Symbolic Interaction: Perspective and Method*. Berkeley, CA: University of California Press.

Bohn, C. 1991. *Habitus und Kontext: Ein kritischer Beitrag zur Sozialtheorie Bourdieus*. Opladen: Westdeutscher Verlag.

Boltanski, L. and Thévenot, L. 1991. *De la justification: Les économies de la grandeur*. Paris: Gallimard.

Bourdieu, P. 1966. 'Champ intellectuel et projet créateur'. *Les Temps Modernes*, 246, pp. 865–906.

Bourdieu, P. 1967. 'Postface', pp. 137–167 in E. Panofsky, *Architecture gothique et pensée scolastique*. Paris: Minuit. Translated by Pierre Bourdieu.

Bourdieu, P. 1968. 'Structuralism and theory of sociological knowledge'. *Social Research*, 35, 4, pp. 681–706.

Bourdieu, P. 1971a. 'Une interprétation de la théorie de la religion selon Max Weber'. *Archives européennes de sociologie*, 12, 1, pp. 3–21.

Bourdieu, P. 1971b. 'Genèse et structure du champ religieux'. *Revue française de sociologie*, 12, pp. 295–334.

Bourdieu, P. 1971c. 'Le marché des biens symboliques'. *Année sociologique*, 22, pp. 49–126.

Bourdieu, P. 1972. *Esquisse d'une théorie de la pratique: Précédée de trois études d'etnologie kabyle*. Genève: Droz.

Bourdieu, P. 1974. 'Avenir de classe et causalité du probable'. *Revue française de sociologie*, 15, 1, pp. 3–42.

Bourdieu, P. 1976. 'Le champ scientifique'. *Actes de la recherche en sciences sociales*, 2–3, pp. 88–104.

Bourdieu, P. 1977a. *Algérie 60: Structures économiques et structures temporelles*. Paris: Minuit.

Bourdieu, P. 1977b. 'Sur le pouvoir symbolique'. *Annales*, 3, 405–411.

Bourdieu, P. 1979a. *La distinction: Critique sociale du jugement*. Paris: Minuit.

Bourdieu, P. 1979b. 'Les trois états du capital culturel'. *Actes de la recherche en sciences sociales*, 30, pp. 3–6.

Bourdieu, P. 1980. *Le sens pratique*. Paris: Minuit.

Bourdieu, P. 1982a. *Leçon sur la leçon*. Paris: Minuit.

Bourdieu, P. 1982b. *Ce que parler veut dire: L'économie des échanges linguistiques*. Paris: Fayard.

Bourdieu, P. 1983a. 'The field of cultural production, or: the economic world reversed'. *Poetics*, 12, pp. 311–356.

Bourdieu, P. 1983b. 'Les sciences sociales et la philosophie'. *Actes de la recherche en sciences sociales*, 47048, pp. 45–52.

Bourdieu, P. 1984a. *Homo academicus*. Paris: Minuit.

Bourdieu, P. 1984b. *Questions de sociologie*. Paris: Minuit.

Bourdieu, P. 1984c. 'Espace social et genèse de classes'. *Actes de la recherche en sciences sociales*, 52053, pp. 3–15.

Bourdieu, P. 1985. 'The genesis of the concepts of habitus and of field'. *Sociocriticism*, 2, 24, pp. 11–24.

Bourdieu, P. 1986. 'La force du droit: eléments pour une théorie du champ juridique'. *Actes de la recherche en sciences sociales*, 64, pp. 3–19.

Bourdieu, P. 1987a. *Choses dites*. Paris: Minuit.

Bourdieu, P. 1987b. 'What makes a social class? On the theoretical and practical existence of groups'. *Berkeley Journal of Sociology*, 32, pp. 1–17.

Bourdieu, P. 1989. *La noblesse d'Etat: Grandes écoles et esprit de corps*. Paris: Minuit.

Bourdieu, P. 1990. 'Animadversiones in Mertonem', pp. 297–301 in J. Clark, C. Modgil, and S. Modgil (eds), *Robert K. Merton: Consensus and Controversy*. London: Falmer Press.

Bourdieu, P. 1991. 'Epilogue: on the possibility of a field of world sociology', pp. 373–387 in P. Bourdieu and J. Coleman (eds), *Social Theory for a Changing Society*. Boulder, CO: Westview Press.

Bourdieu, P. 1992. *Les règles de l'art: Genèse et structure du champ littéraire*. Paris: Seuil.

Bourdieu, P. (ed.). 1993a. *La misère du monde*. Paris: Seuil.

Bourdieu, P. 1993b. 'Un entretien avec Pierre Bourdieu'. *Le Monde*, 7 December.

Bourdieu, P. 1994. *Raisons pratiques: Sur la théorie de l'action*. Paris: Seuil.

Bourdieu, P. 1996. *Sur la télévision, suivi de L'emprise du journalisme*. Paris: Liber éditions.

Bourdieu, P. 1997a. *Méditations pascaliennes*. Paris: Seuil.

Bourdieu, P. 1997b. 'Le champ économique'. *Actes de la recherche en sciences sociales* 119: 48–66.

Bourdieu, P. 1997c. *Les usages sociaux de la science: Pour une sociologie clinique du champ scientifique*. Paris: Inra.

Bourdieu, P. 1998a. *Contre-feux: Propos pour servir à la résistance contre l'invasion néo-libérale*. Paris: Liber-Raisons d'agir.

Bourdieu, P. 1998b. *La domination masculine*. Paris: Seuil.

Bourdieu, P. 1998c. 'Pour une gauche de gauche'. *Le Monde*, 8 April.

Bourdieu, P. 2001. *Science de la science et réflexivité*. Paris: Raisons d'agir.

Bourdieu, P. 2002a. *Interventions politiques, 1961–2001 : Sciences sociales et action politique*. Marseille: Agone.

Bourdieu, P. 2002b. *Ein soziologischer Selbstversuch*. Frankfurt am Main: Suhrkamp.

Bourdieu, P. 2002c. *Le bal des célibataires : Crise de la société paysanne en Béarn*. Paris: Seuil.

Bourdieu, P. 2002d. *Bibliographie des travaux de Pierre Bourdieu*. Paris: Le Temps des Cérises.

Bourdieu, P. 2003. *Images d'Algérie : Une affinité élective*. Paris: Actes Sud.

Bourdieu, P. 2012. Sur l'Etat : *Cours au Collège de France 1989–1992*. Paris: Raisons d'agir/Seuil.

Bourdieu, P. and J.C. Passeron. 1967. 'Sociology and philosophy in France since 1945: death and resurrection of a philosophy without subject'. *Social Research*, 34, 1, pp. 162–212.

Bourdieu, P. and J.C. Passeron. 1970. *La reproduction: Eléments pour une théorie du système de l'enseignement*. Paris: Minuit.

Bourdieu, P. and L.J.D. Wacquant. 1992. *Réponses: Pour une anthropologie réflexive*. Paris: Seuil.

Bourdieu, P., *et al.* 1965. *Un art moyen: Essai sur les usages sociaux de la photographie*. Paris: Minuit.

Bourdieu, P., Chamboredon, J.-C. and Passeron, J.-C. 1973. *Le métier de sociologue. Préalables épistémologiques*. Paris: Mouton.

Brubaker, R. 1985. 'Rethinking classical theory: the sociological vision of Pierre Bourdieu'. *Theory and Society*, 14, pp. 745–775.

Brubaker, R. 1993. 'Social theory as habitus'. In C. Calhoun, E. Lipuma, and M. Postone (eds), *Bourdieu: Critical Perspectives*. Cambridge: Polity Press.

Caillé, A. 1992. 'Esquisse d'une critique de l'économie générale de la pratique'. *Cahiers du LASA*, 12–13, pp. 109–220. (Reprinted in A. Caillé, *Don, intérêt et désintéressement. Bourdieu, Mauss, Platon et quelques autres* [Paris: La Décourte]).

Calhoun, C. 1995. *Critical Social Theory: Culture, History, and the Challenge of Difference*. Oxford: Blackwell.

Callon, M. 1986. 'Eléments pour une sociologie de la traduction: La domestication des coquilles Saint-Jacques et des martins pêcheurs en baie de Saint-Brieuc'. *L'Année Sociologique* 36: 169–208.

Caro, J.Y. 1980. 'La sociologie de Pierre Bourdieu: eléments pour une théorie du champ politique'. *Revue française de sciences politiques* 30: 6: 1171–1197.

Cassirer, E. [1906] 1971. *Das Erkenntnisproblem in der Philosophie und Wissenschaft der neuere Zeit, Band 1*. Darmstadt: Wissenschaftliche Buchgesellschaft.

Cassirer, E. [1910] 1994. *Substanzbegriff und Funktionsbegriff: Untersuchungen über die Grundfragen der Erkenntniskritiek*. Darmstadt: Wissenschaftliche Buchgesellschaft.

Collins, H.M. 1992. *Changing Order: Replication and Induction in Scientific Practice*. Chicago, IL: University of Chicago Press.

Donati, P. 1991. *Teoria relazionale della Società*. Milano: Franco Angeli.

Dosse, F. 1995. *L'empire du sens: L'humanisation des sciences humaines*. Paris: La Découverte.

Durkheim, E. [1888] 1970. 'Cours de science sociale', pp. 77–110 in J. Filloux (ed.) *La science sociale et l'action*. Paris: P.U.F.

Durkheim, E. [1895] 1986. *Les règles de la méthode sociologique*. Paris: P.U.F.

Duval, J. *et al.* 1998. *Le 'décembre' des intellectuels français*. Paris: Liber-Raisons d'agir.

Dux, G. 1982. *Die Logik der Weltbilder: Sinnstrukturen im Wandel der Geschichte*. Frankfurt am Main: Suhrkamp.

Elias, N. [1965] 1985. *De gevestigden en de buitenstaanders: Een studie van de spanningen en machtsverhoudingen tussen twee arbeidsbuurten*. s'GravenhaGe: Ruward.

Elias, N. [1970] 1984. *Wat is sociologie?* Utrecht: Spectrum.

Elias, N. 1976. *Über den Prozeß der Zivilisation: Soziogenetische und psychogenetische Untersuchungen. Zweiter Band: Wandlungen der Gesellschaft. Entwurf zu einder Theorie der Zivilisation*. Frankfurt am Main: Suhrkamp.

Emirbayer, M. 1994. 'Network analysis, culture, and the problem of agency'. *American Journal of Sociology*, 99, 6, pp. 1411–1454.
Emirbayer, M. 1997. 'Manifesto for a relational sociology'. *American Journal of Sociology*, 103, pp. 281–317.
Ferry, L. and Renaut, A. 1988. *La pensée 68: Essai sur l'antihumanisme contemporain*. Paris: Gallimard.
Fowler, B. 1997. *Pierre Bourdieu and Cultural Theory: Critical Investigations*. London: Sage.
Funke, G. 1974. 'Hexis (habitus)', pp. 1120–1124 J. Ritter (ed.) in *Historisches Wörterbuch der Philosophie, Band 3*: Schwabe and Co.
Gauchet, M. 1988. 'Changement de paradigme en sciences sociales'. *Le Débat*, 50, pp. 165–170.
Giddens, A. 1979. *Central Problems in Social Theory: Action, Structure and Contradiction in Social Analysis*. London: Macmillan.
Giddens, A. 1984. *The Constitution of Society: Outline of the Theory of Structuration*. Cambridge: Polity Press.
Giddens, A. 1990. *The Consequences of Modernity*. Cambridge: Polity Press.
Girard, R. 1982. *Le bouc émissaire*. Paris: Grasset.
Goffman, E. 1983. 'The interaction order'. *American Sociological Review*, 48, pp. 1–17.
Grint, K. and Woolgar, S. 1997. *The Machine at Work: Technology, Work and Organization*. Cambridge: Polity Press.
Habermas, J. 1969. 'Analytische wissenschaftstheorie und dialektik', in T.W. Adorno *et al. Der Positivismusstreit in der deutschen Soziologie*. Neuwied: Luchterland Verlag.
Habermas, J. 1971. *Knowledge and Human Interests*. Boston, MA: Beacon Press.
Habermas, J. 1981. *Theorie des kommunikativen Handelns. Band 2: Zur kritik der Funktionalistischen Verunft*. Frankfurt am Main: Suhrkamp.
Habermas, J. 1998. *Die postnationale Konstellation: Politische Essays*. Frankfurt am Main: Suhrkamp.
Halimi, S. 1997. *Les nouveaux chiens de garde*. Paris: Liber-Raisons d'agir.
Hamel, J. 1997. *Précis d'épistémologie de la sociologie*. Paris: L'Harmattan.
Harker, R., Mahar, C. and Wilkes, C. 1991. *An Introduction to the Work of Pierre Bourdieu: The Practice of Theory*. London: Macmillan.
Harré, R. 1970. *The Principles of Scientific Thinking*. London: Macmillan.
Hegel, G.W.F. [1821] 1971. *Grundlinien der Philosophie des Rechts oder Naturrecht und Staatwissenschaft im Grundrisse*, in *Werke in 20 Bänden*. Frankfurt am Main: Suhrkamp.
Heidegger, M. [1927] 1993. *Sein und Zeit*. Tübingen: Max Niemeyer Verlag.
Héran, F. 1987. 'La seconde nature de l'habitus: Tradition philosophique et sens commun dans le langage sociologique'. *Revue française de sociologie* 37: 385–416.
Honneth, A. 1990. 'Die zerrissene Welt der symbolischen Formen. Zum kultursoziologischen Werk Pierre Bourdieus'. *Die zerrissene Welt des Sozialen. Sozialphilosophische Aufsätze*. Frankfurt am Main: Suhrkamp.
Husserl, E. [1938] 1985. *Erfahrung und Urteil: Untersuchungen zur Genealogie der Logik*. Hamburg: Felix Meiner Verlag.
Husserl, E. 1952. *Ideen zu einer reinen Phänomenologie und phänomenologischen Philosophie. Zweites Buch: Phänomenologische Untersuchungen zur Konstitution*, in *Husserliana, Band 4*. The Hague: Martinus Nijhoff.
Jenkins, R. 1992. *Pierre Bourdieu*. London: Routledge.
Johnson, T., Dandeker, C. and Ashworth, C. 1984. *The Structure of Social Theory: Dilemmas and Strategies*. London: Macmillan.

Joppke, C. 1986. 'The cultural dimensions of class formation and class struggle: on the social theory of Pierre Bourdieu'. *Berkeley Journal of Sociology*, 31, pp. 53–78.

Kant, I. 1983. *Kritik der Reinen Vernunft*, in *Werke, Band 4*. Darmstadt: Wissenschaftliche Buchgesellschaft.

Keat, R. and Urry, J. 1982. *Social Theory as Science*. London: Routledge.

Knorr-Cetina, K. 1983. 'The ethnographic study of scientific work: toward a constructivist interpretation of science', pp. 115–140 in K. Knorr-Cetina and M. Mulkay (eds), *Science Observed: Perspectives on the Social Study of Science*. London: Sage.

Kögler, Id. 1997a. 'Alienation as Epistemological source: reflexivity and social background after Mannheim and Bourdieu', *Social Epistemology*, 11, 2, pp. 141–164.

Kögler, Id. 1997b. 'Reconceptualizing reflexive sociology'. *Social Epistemology*, 11, 2, pp. 223–250.

Kuhn, T. [1962] 1970. *The Structure of Scientific Revolutions*. Chicago, IL: University of Chicago Press.

Lakatos, I. 1970. 'Falsification and the methodology of scientific research programmes', pp. 91–196 in I. Lakatos and A. Musgrave (eds), *Criticism and the Growth of Knowledge*. Cambridge: Cambridge University Press.

Latour, B. 1984. *Les Microbes: Guerre et paix*. Paris: Métailié.

Latour, B. 1987. *Science in Action: How to Follow Scientists and Engineers through Society*. Cambridge, MA: Harvard University Press.

Latour, B. and Woolgar, S. 1979. *Laboratory Life: The Social Construction of Scientific Facts*. London: Sage.

Law, J. 1994. *Organizing Modernity*. Oxford: Blackwell.

Layder, D. 1990. *The Realist Image in Social Science*. London: Macmillan.

Lefort, C. 1986. *Essais sur le politique*. Paris: Gallimand.

Lévi-Strauss, C. 1958. 'La notion de structure en ethnologie'. *Anthropologie structurale*. Paris: Plon.

Lewin, K. 1963. *Feldtheorie in den Sozialwissenschaften: Ausgewählte theoretische Schriften*. Bern: Verlag Hans Huber.

Luhmann, N. 1975. *Soziologische Auf klärung 2: Aufsätze zur Theorie der Gesellschaft*. Opladen: Westdeutscher Verlag.

Luhmann, N. 1986. *Ökologische Kommunikation*. Opladen: Westdeutscher Verlag.

Luhmann, N. 1989. *Gesellschaftsstruktur und Semantik: Studien zur Wissenssoziologie der modernen Gesellschaft, Band 3*. Frankfurt am Main: Suhrkamp.

Lynch, M. 1993. *Scientific Practice and Ordinary Action: Ethnomethodology and Social Studies of Science*. Cambridge: Cambridge University Press.

Lynch, M., Livingston, E. and Garfinkel, H. 1983. 'Temporal order in laboratory work', pp. 205–237 in K. Knorr-Cetina and M. Mulkay (eds), *Science Observed: Perspectives on the Social Study of Science*. London: Sage.

Mannheim, K. 1936. *Ideology and Utopia: An Introduction to the Sociology of Knowledge*. New York: Harcourt, Brace & World.

Mannheim, K. 1952. *Essays on the Sociology of Knowledge*. London: Routledge.

Marx, K. [1857] 1973. *Grundrisse: Foundations of the Critique of Political Economy*. Harmondsworth: Penguin Books.

Marx, K. [1868] 1970. *Capital: A Critique of Political Economy, Vol. 1*. London: Lawrence & Wishart.

Maso, B. 1995. 'Elias and the Neo-Kantians: intellectual backgrounds of the *civilizing process*'. *Theory, Culture and Society*, 12, pp. 43–79.

Merleau-Ponty, M. 1945. *Phénoménologie de la perception*. Paris: Gallimard.

Merton, R.K. 1968. *Social Theory and Social Structure*. New York: Free Press.
Mouzelis, N. 1995. *Sociological Theory: What Went Wrong? Diagnosis and Remedies*. London: Routledge.
Mulkay, M. 1976. 'Norms and ideology in science'. *Social Science Information*, 15, 4, pp. 637–656.
Ollman, B. 1971. *Marx's Conception of Man in Capitalist Society*. Cambridge: Cambridge University Press.
Outhwaite, W. 1987. *New Philosophies of Social Science: Realism, Hermeneutics and Critical Theory*. London: Macmillan.
Parsons, T. [1937] 1949. *The Structure of Social Action*. Glencoe, NY: Free Press.
Parsons, T. 1951. *The Social System*. New York: Free Press.
Pels, D. 1988. *Property and Power in Social Theory: A Study in Intellectual Rivalry*. London: Routledge
Pels, D. 1995. 'Knowledge politics and anti-politics: towards a critical appraisal of Bourdieu's concept of intellectual autonomy'. *Theory and Society*, 24, pp. 79–104.
Pels, D. 1999. *The Intellectual as Stranger: Studies in Spokespersonship*. London: Routledge.
Popper, K.R. 1979. *Objective Knowledge: An Evolutionary Approach*. Oxford: Clarendon Press.
Popper, K.R. 1989. *Conjectures and Refutations: The Growth of Scientific Knowledge*. London: Routledge.
Ravaisson, F. [1838] 1997. *De l'habitude*. Paris: Payot & Rivages.
Raynaud, P. 1980. 'Le sociologue contre le droit'. *Esprit*, 3, pp. 82–93.
Rist, G. 1984. 'La notion médiévale d' "habitus" dans la sociologie de Pierre Bourdieu'. *Cahiers Vilfredo Pareto*, 22, 67, pp. 201–212.
Sartre, J.P. 1963. *Search for a Method*. New York: Vintage Books.
Saussure, F. de. [1916] 1985. *Cours de linguistique générale*. Paris: Payot.
Sayer, A. 1995. *Radical Political Economy: A Critique*. Oxford: Blackwell.
Schütz, A. [1932] 1974. *Der Sinnhafte Aufbau der sozialen Welt: Eine Einleitung in die verstehende Soziologie*. Frankfurt am Main: Suhrkamp.
Schütz, A. 1962. 'Common-sense and scientific interpretation of human action', pp. 3–47, in *Collected Papers I: The Problem of Social Reality*. The Hague: Nijhoff.
Swartz, D. 1997. *Culture and Power: The Sociology of Pierre Bourdieu*. Chicago, IL: University of Chicago Press.
Taylor, C. 1985. *Philosophy and the Human Sciences: Philosophical Papers 2*. Cambridge: Cambridge University Press.
Terrail, J.P. 1992. 'Les vertus de la nécessité: Sujet objet en sociologie'. *Cahiers du LASA*, 12–13, pp. 221–262.
Touraine, A. 1978. La voix et le regard: Sociologie des mouvements sociaux. Paris, Seuil.
Vandenberghe, F. 1997. *Une histoire critique de la sociologie allemande. Aliénation et réification. Vol. 1: Marx, Simmel, Weber, Lukács*. Paris: La Découverte.
Vandenberghe, F. 1998. *Une histoire critique de la sociologie allemande. Aliénation et réification. Vol. 2: Horkheimer, Adorno, Marcuse et Habermas*. Paris: La Découverte.
Vandenberghe, F. 2001. 'From structuralism to culturalism: Ernst Cassirer's Philosophy of Symbolic Forms', *European Journal of Social Theory*, 4, 4, pp. 479–497.
Verdès-Leroux, J. 1998. *Le savant et le politique: Essai sur le terrorisme sociologique de Pierre Bourdieu*. Paris: Grasset.
Wacquant, L.J.D. 1987. 'Symbolic violence and the making of the French agriculturalist:

an enquiry into Pierre Bourdieu's sociology'. *Australian and New Zealand Journal of Sociology*, 23, 1, pp. 65–88.

Wacquant, L.J.D. 1990. 'Sociology as socioanalysis: tales of *Homo academicus*'. *Sociological Forum*, 5, 4, pp. 677–689.

Wacquant, L.J.D. 1993a. 'On the tracks of symbolic power: prefatory notes to Bourdieu's "state nobility"'. *Theory, Culture & Society*, 10, pp. 1–17.

Wacquant, L.J.D. 1993b. 'From ruling class to field of power: an interview with Pierre Bourdieu on "La noblesse d'Etat"'. *Theory, Culture & Society*, 10, pp. 19–44.

Wacquant, L.J.D. 1995. 'The pugilistic point of view: how boxers think and feel about their trade'. *Theory and Society*, 24, pp. 489–535.

Wacquant, L.J.D. 1996a. 'De l'idéologie à la violence symbolique: culture, classe et conscience chez Marx et Bourdieu'. *Actuel Marx*, 20, 2, pp. 65–82.

Wacquant, L.J.D. 1996b. 'Reading Bourdieu's "capital"'. *International Journal of Contemporary* Sociology, 33, 2, 151–169. (Reprinted as Preface to the English translation of Bourdieu 1989).

Wacquant, L.J.D. 1996c. 'Notes tardives sur le "marxisme" de Bourdieu'. *Actuel Marx* 83–90.

Wacquant, L.J.D. 1996d. 'Violences, corps et sciences: remarques transatlantiques. Entretien avec Loïc J.D. Wacquant'. *Prétentaine*, 5, pp. 211–221.

Weber, M. [1921] 1972. *Wirtschaft und Gesellschaft: Grundriss der verstehenden Soziologie*. Tübingen: J.C.B. Mohr.

Weber, M. [1922] 1966. 'Die Wirtschaftsethik der Weltreligionen', pp. 1–237 in *Gesammelte Aufsätze zur Religionsoziologie, Band 1*. Tübingen: Mohr.

Wittgenstein, L. 1961. *Tractatus Logico-Philosophicus*. London: Routledge.

Whitehead, A. 1930. *Science and the Modern World*. Cambridge: Cambridge University Press.

Woolgar, S. 1988. *Science: The Very Idea*. London: Ellis Harwood.

Woolgar, S. 1991. 'Reflexivity is the ethnographer of the text', pp. 14–39 in S. Woolgar (ed.) *Knowledge and Reflexivity: New Frontiers in the Sociology of Knowledge*. London: Sage.

4 Posthumanism, or the cultural logic of global neo-capitalism[1]

> Philosophy is a long footnote at the bottom of this declaration, uttered with fear and trembling: 'Nous voici, nous les humains, nous les mortels!'
>
> Ricoeur, 1989: 101

Revolutions and reifications

The heated discourse on globalisation (and its globalisation) and the rise of a powerful anti-globalisation movement might be indicative of the fact that post-industrial neo-capitalist societies are slowly but surely nearing the threshold of a new civilisational shift. In the next 20 or 30 years or so, societies within the North Atlantic rim will undergo a 'transformation of their material bases' and enter what Gramsci (1971: 316–318) called 'a new epoch of civilization' within advanced capitalism. This new epoch builds further on the capitalism, industrialism, surveillance and consumerism of today and radicalises some of its features (accumulation of capital, centralisation of power, dematerialisation of production, individualisation of consumption, etc.), yet is radically different from the one that emerged after the Second World War. The contours of this knowledge-based capitalist techno-civilisation are still vague. Sociologists who analyse the global transformations of late modernity in the domains of economics, politics, technology, ecology, law, culture, war, etc., don't know how to refer to the newly emerging form of society: late modern (Giddens), late capitalist (Mandel), post-Fordist (Coriat), postmodern (Lyotard), post-industrial (Bell), informational (Castells), programmed (Touraine), liquid (Bauman) and risk (Beck) have all been proposed as adjectival labels for the new times, but apart from the terms of postmodernity and its successor, globalisation, none of them has really stuck. Perhaps it's still too early and it's only with hindsight, after dusk, that historians will be able to formulate the ontology of our present. Meanwhile the proverbial man on the street wonders 'what else, what more' the future will bring. Even if he's a happy consumer and is not averse to technological change, he's anxious about the future. At his most philosophical moments, he may voice his complaints about the destruction of nature, the commercialisation of society and the spiritual decline of humanity. Speculating about the next 50 or 100 years, his wife is pessimistic about the future and fears for the future of their children and grandchildren. 'What will the human be in one, ten or a hundred million years?' (Hottois, 2001: 35) falls beyond their purview, though I suspect that, like most people, our couple would answer like Lord Keynes: 'In the long run, we are all dead.'

Three revolutions into one

Globalisation is a container term. Although it predominantly refers to a global 'change of scale' that is arguably triggered by the restructurations of the economic realm (unification of financial markets, liberalisation of world trade, internationalisation of the division of labour, global spread of consumerism, declining costs of transportation and communications, etc.), it is important not to reduce globalisation to its economic dimension and to adopt an interdisciplinary approach that is able to take into account the economic as well as the political, technological, ecological, social, moral and cultural dimensions of the accelerated 'time-space compression' we are witnessing today (Vandenberghe, 1999). As a catchword of our time, globalisation does not only refer to economic transformations across the globe, but to the conjunction and integration of the economic, digital and biotechnological revolutions in a single revolution that is triggering an epochal civilisational shift. Together, those three simultaneous revolutions are radically transforming the parameters of human existence and, uncontrolled, they may even put the survival of humanity at risk (Guillebaud, 2001: 36–40).[2]

First, there is, of course, the global economic revolution. Since the fall of the Berlin Wall, capitalism has become the only game in town. It's not the end of history, but with the spread of the neoliberal ideology through the globe, there seems to be no alternative to the market and hardly any limits to its operations. As flows of capital, money, goods, services, people, information, technologies, policies, ideas, images and regulations transcend individual nation-states and dissolve their borders, the regulating power of the State is being curtailed. Everywhere, the welfare state is under attack and the question remains if, once destroyed, it will ever be reconstructed. The power of the State is waning when it is most needed to domesticate capitalism and restrain the immense power of transnational corporations. If the State is not reorganised from within into a federation of cosmopolitan states that can successfully re-regulate the market, the global economy might well be able to submit all other subsystems to its imperatives and to transform the world into a single, unified economic world system. Braudel's *économie-monde* might be looming at the horizon, not as a rigid and well-integrated system, but as a global meshwork. The second revolution is the digital or cyber revolution. The first computers were invented in the 1940s; by the 1980s the first personal computers became available for use in the office and household; during the 1990s virtually all offices in the West had switched from typewriters to computers; today the occasional colleague (like Axel Honneth) who still writes his text by hand is an oddity. In 1990 Tim Berners-Lee invented the World Wide Web. Nowadays, virtually everybody in the West has access to the internet. The globetrotter won't have much of a problem finding an internet café anywhere in India, China or Mozambique, though the connections might be excruciatingly slow. It is estimated that by 2035 five billion people will be online worldwide. All spheres of life are progressively integrated into the cyberworld. One after the other, economy, finance, commerce, culture, science, education, communication, leisure and pleasure go virtual. The third revolution, the one I will talk about in this final chapter, is the genetic revolution or the revolution in molecular biology and its bio-industrial applications.

The three revolutions are not unlinked. They interact, interfere and strengthen each other; together they revolutionise existing societies and prepare their entry into a techno-capitalistic civilisation. Capitalism, informatics and the biosciences cannot be separated; together they form a complex and highly dynamic techno-industrial system that undermines traditional conceptions of the human. For the first time in history, human evolution can be accelerated and steered. This may be a blessing, but it can also lead to the self-destruction of humanity. Technology in itself is innocent, as Weber rightly said, but capitalism is not.[3] Incorporated and driven by the neo-capitalist logics of accumulation, the techno-sciences may become dangerous, perhaps even lethal, if they are not kept in check.

The thesis I want to defend in this chapter is that the conjunction of capitalism, informatics and genetics might be paving the way to the technological modification and commodification of human nature and, thereby, to a new kind of reification (*Verdinglichung*) that neither Marx nor Lukács had foreseen when they coined the concept.[4] The old concept of reification was forged to analyse the transformation of labour power into a commodity and to criticise the degradation of human beings into things. Reformulating the concept of reification, Habermas actualised it in the 1980s to investigate the invasion of the life-world by the objectifying logic of the market and the administration. The colonisation of the life-world undermines its communicative infrastructure and leads to the generalised diffusion of strategic behaviour through all the realms of life. The new reification goes further. As the techno-sciences scientifically deconstruct and technologically overcome the ontological distinctions between the human, the animal and the thing, human life itself is objectivated, patented, modified and commodified. Neo-capitalism knows no limits – apart from the ones that it is wont to transgress – and speculates on life itself. The new developments in the biosciences and the attempts of the techno-industry to transform life itself into a commodity show that global neo-capitalism does not only colonise the life-world, but that it is intent on reifying and colonising life itself for the sake of profit.

The old reification transformed humans into things. The new one is more radical and simply scrambles the old ontological distinctions between the human, the animal and the thing. As the dividing lines between entities become fluid, complex and porous, human beings lose their distinctiveness:

> Does genetics not bring us back in fact to an undifferentiated community of the human and the animal? Do cognitive sciences not suggest the hypothesis

> of a brain computer or a possible artificial intelligence and do they thereby not establish the proximity between man and machine? Do molecular physics not postulate a principled continuity of matter, living matter and man included?
>
> (Guillebaud, 2001: 17)

Once the human is downgraded to the animal and nature upgraded to the human, the distinctions between the ontological regions are bound to disappear. Reduced to genes, molecules and machines, everything can be mixed and recombined in a monstrous living artefact that is neither fish, flesh nor good red herring.

With Habermas (2001b: 51), we can distinguish three ways to destroy civilisation. The first way is cultural. Looking back at a tradition of its own making and desperately searching for some kind of stability, different forms of fundamentalism – from the ecological to the theological – are willing to pay the price of the cultural and structural de-differentiation of modern societies to obtain some illusory security. The second way to destroy civilisation is systemic. Modern societies can not only destroy themselves through de-differentiation, but also through the exacerbation of the differentiation of its subsystems. Systematically uncoupled from the communicative structures of the life-world, the reifying logic of the economic, administrative, legal, scientific and technological subsystems can enter the life-world, with the result that the subjects start to behave as if they and the others in their environment were some kind of mini-systems themselves. According to Luhmann, this has already happened. The future lies behind us. Radicalising the reifying logic of the second way of destruction, the third way (sic) relates to the risks of a technological modification and commodification of human nature itself. Driven forward by the thirst of profit, the techno-scientific advances in the contemporary bio-, cyber- and nano-industries steadily undermine the moral limits of anthropic production and open up the post-human perspective of the *Übermensch*, of the technological unmaking of the human through the genetic (com)modification of human nature.

To understand the perspective of the technological destruction of the human, one might follow the paradoxical reversals of G.B. Vico's principle of the *verum factum*, which, supposedly, founds the human sciences as hermeneutic sciences, into the engineering principle of universal 'factibility' (Heidegger's *Machenschaft*). In an indirect polemics with Descartes' theory of innate ideas, Vico stated in his *Scienza nuova* that we can understand history, because we have made it.[5] However, we cannot understand nature: only God, who has made it, can understand it. As soon as the principle was formulated in 1744, Feuerbach and Marx creatively reformulated it. We have made God; therefore, we can understand Him. Theology thus turns into anthropology. And we have also made nature, not just the urban environment and the countryside, but as the French wave in the social studies of science has taught us, also nature as such, nature as it is studied by the natural sciences. Anthropology thus turns into technology. And now that technology also makes the human, the circle is closed and technology reverts back to theology. At this point everything is made, but there is hardly anything left to understand, apart perhaps from the non-culture of disenchantment that has brought us there.

New reactionaries, new ideologies

In this chapter I want to present a *critical analysis of post-humanism from a humanist perspective*. The contemporary developments in the fields of bio-, cyber- and nano-technology that reinvent nature and reconstruct the human will not be welcomed here as the latest move in the 'pomo-debate' that finishes off the human by deconstructing the 'phallogoanthropocentrism' of Western thought, but rather as one more nail in the coffin of humanity. What I present is a 'heuristics of fear' (Jonas, 1984: 385) at the beginning of the third millennium. If I extrapolate and exaggerate the extent of the risk, it is only for strategic reasons, and not because I believe that after the end of God, history, grand narratives, philosophy, art, nature, etc. we have already reached the end of Man, though if we are not careful, the end might well be nigh. My catastrophism is not naive, but like Dupuy's (2002), it is enlightened, reflexive and relatively controlled; it calls for prudence, not despair. Similarly, if I adopt a conservative posture in epistemo-ontological matters and unashamedly try to rehabilitate humanism – 'a term used to signify all that is bad in traditional theorizing: universalism, rationalism and essentialism' (Stavro-Pearce, 1994: 217) – it is only for moral and political reasons. I want to vouchsafe the normative position that is necessary to criticise universal commodification and to politically combat the new reifications of our time. That the epistemological radicalism of deconstruction ends up deconstructing itself is only consequent, but that in spite of all its intentions, declarations and gesticulations it accompanies the 'creative-destruction' of the world by the global entrepreneurs of today as its soundtrack is more worrying.[6] What we need after postmodernism and deconstruction is critique and reconstruction.

In France and elsewhere a revamped vitalism is now spreading like a virus through academia and beyond. It attracts the more radicalised students and, of late, the apolitical Deleuze who never travelled, has even become the hero of the wandering anarcho-communistic factions of the anti-globalisation movement. *La pensée 68*, the old structuralism of the 1960s, is now definitively *passé*. Structures are out of fashion, networks and rhizomes are in. As the structural relations between the positions that make up the system are backgrounded, the intersubjective relations between actors who perform networks gain prominence in intellectual discourses. In the same way as markets are opposed to the State, networks are pitched against structures and introduced into systems in order to make them more fluid and flexible, more agile and nimble, better adapted for survival in a rapidly changing market environment. Bourdieu, Lacan, Foucault, Derrida, Levi-Strauss are dead. As to the old revolutionaries of yore, they have now become 'new reactionaries' (Lindenberg, 2001). I will not go into such cheap polemics. Instead, I will propose an *Ideologiekritik* of the new vitalism, as it is expressed in a whole range of posthumanist theories of complexity, connectivity, non-linearity, fluidity, etc. that consider the opposition between the human and the non-human as another superfluous distinction that needs to be philosophically, scientifically and technologically deconstructed. I will not say that the neo-Nietzschean vitalists of today are reactionaries. As a matter of fact, they are not, but in so far as the contemporary fascination for networks tunes in all too well with the neo-capitalist politics of global flexibilisation, they find a willing ear with shareholders and new actionaries. Taking a critical look at Deleuze, Serres, Simondon and other posthumanists who have inspired the seminal formulation of actor–network theory of Latour and Callon, I will present the fascination for networks and rhizomes as a 'retiology' (Musso, 2003: 233, 326) – that is, as an ideology of networks for the newly emerging transnational ruling class. Looking at posthumanist philosophies and sociologies of technology against the background of the contemporary developments in the biosciences, molecular biology and genetics in particular, I will read them as ideological expressions of the cultural logic of neo-capitalism and use them as a springboard to develop a neo-Marxist critique of bio-political economy.

In the 'untimely considerations' that follow on the deconstruction of the categories of the human and the non-human by posthumanist theories and late-capitalist practices, the theoretical-critical, and at times polemical, mode of presentation of ideas has been chosen. The chapter is divided into four parts. The first part is more epistemological and deals with the concepts of nature and culture. Drawing on critical realism and transcendental phenomenology, I try to outline the contours of a realist phenomenology of human, animal and spiritual nature. This phenomenology of nature forms, however, only the background from which the critical analysis of the experimental scrambling of the regional ontologies that characterises posthumanism will depart. In the second part I will introduce the main tenets of posthumanism through an analysis of the co-evolution of technology and humanity. That human beings exteriorise their organs into technology and that the artificial organism modifies in turn the make-up of human beings is the basic insight that underlies posthumanist philosophies of technology. In more detail, I will look at the work of André Leroi-Gourhan, Gilles Deleuze and Félix Guattari, Michel Serres and Gilbert Simondon. In the third part, which is more sociological, I will connect posthumanism to neo-capitalism and argue that the latter is, in effect if not in intent, Deleuzian. As a network of networks, it is rhizomatic, flexible, chaosmotic, evolving, expanding. In the negativist spirit that characterises the work of the Frankfurt School, I will show via an analysis of government of the self, the commodification of culture and the modification of nature, how contemporary capitalism does not only colonise the life-world but also life itself. Finally, in the last part, I will take up the issue of nature again, but from a more normative perspective, and conclude with an appeal to ethics: instead of changing nature, should we not rather change culture?

I The nature of culture

The nice thing about culture is that everyone has it. The Bororo, the Mekeo, the Baktaman, the Katchin, the Nuer and the Taliban have it, but so do IBM,

McDonald's and the IACR (the International Association for Critical Realism). Culture has become a global phenomenon. By this Marilyn Strathern (1995) means that the Euro-American perception of the ubiquitous role of culture in human affairs, which is typical of cultural anthropology, postcolonial and cultural studies, can be summoned in almost any context and at almost any level of human interaction. To the extent that anthropology puts things in contexts and conceives of culture both as a particularising context and as a generalising meta-context of contexts, anthropology can be understood as an analytical machine for creating and comparing differences, for making incommensurables and providing at the same time a comparative framework for making them commensurable.

The culture of modernity

Travelling to exotic countries and coming back to their homes and universities, anthropologists import cultures and export culture. Culture may now be everywhere – in the streets and the universities, but also on the shelves of your local supermarket – but the fact remains that this double conception of culture as a singular *plurale tantum* is in itself most singular.[7] It is a relatively recent European invention. As a concept of philosophical significance, it emerged in Germany in the eighteenth century as a romantic reaction to the universalism of the Enlightenment. Like its conceptual counterpart, nature, and like alienation, which dialectically thematises the ontological degradation of culture into (second) nature, culture is, as Raymond Williams (1976: 76) has remarked, 'one of the two or three most complicated words of the language'.

In European languages, the word culture is used in at least three different senses: a more philosophical one, an anthropological one and a common sense one (Schnädelbach, 2000: 10–19).[8] As opposed to nature (*phusis* in Greek, referring to that which grows by itself and exists independently of humans – Aristotle, *Physis*, II, 1), culture in the broadest sense refers, first of all, to everything that has been created by humans and is socially transmitted and reproduced. Culture, one could say, is everything human, everything which is produced by humans and which cannot be understood by itself. Without humans there is no culture, but without culture there are no humans either, as human beings are by nature cultural beings. Culture in this encompassing sense refers to the totality of human products that produce human beings.

Moving from culture in the singular to cultures in plural, we arrive at the second meaning: culture as a symbolic expression and emanation of the 'soul' of a collectivity that differentiates that collectivity from other collectivities and determines their 'whole way of life, from birth to the grave, from morning to night and even in sleep' (Eliot, 1948: 31). Babylonian, Egyptian, Hindu, Arabic, Chinese, European and (why not?) Brazilian, Carioca and Bororo cultures represent so many cultures, so many different ways of world-making, so many different ways of life. Speaking of English culture, the American essayist and poet T.S. Eliot lists Derby Day, Henley Regatta, the Twelfth of August, a cup final, the dog races, the dartboard, Wensleydale cheese, boiled cabbage cut into sections, beetroot in vinegar, nineteenth-century Gothic churches and the music of Elgar. Third, within each of the cultures, of which English culture represents only a particular, so to say, provincial example among others, culture can refer to a social subsystem, differentiated among others from the political, economic and juridical subsystems – that is, internally differentiated into several fields and subfields of cultural production, from museums, arts and literature to comics and haute couture, to mention only a few which Bourdieu has investigated.

Culture in singular, as opposed and yet internally related to nature, exists only in plural. The conception of culture as a *plurale tantum*, as one among other cultures and as a subsystem of the social system is typically modern. Herodotos, Protagoras and other sophists were obviously aware of the existence of other cultures, but they nevertheless remained ethnocentric and conceived of the non-Greeks as barbarians. Although modern cultures have also been prone to exclude the 'Other', to phrase it mildly, they were also able and willing to consider themselves as barbarians and to question their own superiority:[9]

> The extent to which Western society has historically constituted itself through the denial of the 'other' and violent oppression of whole constituencies of the human species is indisputable and today increasingly well documented. So, too, is the process through which it began to question these exclusions, and to open itself to the possibility that these 'others' had been illegitimately excluded
>
> (Soper, 1995: 66)

In modernity, the recognition of cultures other than one's own and the understanding of one's own culture as one culture among others are correlative processes that trigger the reflexivity of culture as such. If there is culture, it is first of all between those that do not share the same culture.

Taking the attitude of the exotic other, seeing one's own culture through the eyes of the culture of the other leads not only to a relativisation of one's own culture and a concomitant opening up to the other cultures in and through a progressive 'fusion of horizons', as Gadamer says, but also, and perhaps more interestingly, to a methodological self-objectification that estranges and thereby makes one aware of one's own culture. This methodological self-alienation paves the way to a critical hermeneutics that is able to uncover and make conscious the culturally and historically determined deep symbolic forms that prestructure our vision of the world, others and ourselves, and thereby mediate and make possible our being-in-the-world (Kögler, 1992). In any case, awareness and acceptance of multiple cultures induce reflexive processes of cultural self-relativisation and self-objectification that make one become aware of culture as such, and correlatively, of nature as such. This reflexive emergence of the distinction between nature and culture is an epochal cultural event. It grounds the human sciences in general and anthropology in particular, or at least that branch of anthropology that defines itself by its subject matter and proceeds by way of a comparative analysis of culture.[10]

Although pre-modern and modern cultures are both equally caught up in 'the symbolical nets that they have spun themselves' (Cassirer-Geertz), the difference between 'us' and 'them' is that 'we' are able reflexively to know that we are spinning the threads of reality, whereas 'they' are not aware of what they do, or at least not on this metalevel. Modern cultures are by definition reflexive cultures. They do not simply live in cultural worlds like fish in water, but they know that they do so. They not only know that the world they live in is their own product, but they also know that it is a contingent and conventional world that could be different and is amenable to change. In so far as this self-awareness of cultures proceeds from and presupposes a demarcation from nature (*phusis*), we can presume that 'the concepts of nature and culture are co-original' (Schnädelbach, 2000: 16) and that they are thus constitutive of each other.[11] Indeed, if we follow the speculative historians, from Hegel and Cassirer to Castoriadis and Gauchet, and link the de-differentiation of nature and culture to the epochal transition from *mythos* to *logos* that marks the coming of age of humanity, we can see that the emergence of the concept of nature is itself a moment in the 'disenchantment' of the natural world and the advent of modernity. Nature only comes into existence as an autonomous domain when it is no longer conceived of as a 'magical garden', filled with demons, spirits and other anthropomorphisms, but objectified as an impersonal 'mechanism that is submitted to the laws of causality' (Weber, 1922: 564). This scientific objectification of nature is inseparable from the progressive denaturalisation of culture. As a matter of fact, the objectification of nature is itself an important stage in the grand Weberian narrative of the rationalisation of culture and society that characterises the world-historical advent of modernity. In modernity, culture is no longer alienated as 'second nature', created and instituted by the finger of God, but is thoroughly demystified and recognised as a human product. Conceived of as *nomos*, culture appears to the modern mind as a conventional order of reality that is, in principle, malleable by humans. Unlike pre-modern cultures that occlude their creative potential by positing a metasocial or divine foundation of their own constitution, modern cultures are thoroughly reflexive and autonomous. They give themselves their own laws, and to the extent that they know and accept that they do so, they are able to understand the cultural processes of 'imaginary institutions' that constitute them as socio-cultural historical institutions. History and culture have always existed, but it is only in modern societies that they exist in the reflexive form of 'historicity' and 'culturicity' (to coin a new term).

The difference between nature and culture is not completely unknown to pre-modern cultures, however. According to Lévi-Strauss (1968), this distinction is as universal as the incest taboo. All cultures make a demarcation between nature and culture, the wild and the domestic, or the raw and the cooked, even if their demarcation does not necessarily correspond to ours (Strathern, 1980). But to the extent that pre-modern cultures lack reflexivity and are not aware of the distinction itself, we can paraphrase Bruno Latour (1991) and conclude with some irony that 'they have never been modern'.[12]

Towards a realist phenomenology of nature

What is at issue in the contemporary debates on nature that oppose the realism of the 'nature-endorsing' approach of the ecologists to the constructivism of the 'nature-sceptical' perspectives of third-wave feminists (Soper, 1995) is not the nature–culture distinction itself, but the way it is to be drawn, and whether it is to be conceptualised as one of kind or degree. Are we thinking of an absolute distinction between the 'ontological regions' of the material world of things and the cultural world of humans, or should we rather conceive of them as 'typological regions'? Should we think of an opposition between absolute realms, or of a continuum in which no hard and fast distinctions can be drawn between nature and culture, between things and humans? Or should we perhaps follow the radicalisation of postmodernism-turned-posthumanism and ignore the distinction altogether, happily mixing humans and non-humans in a heterogeneous network?

A realist theory of nature

In an attempt to answer those (admittedly) difficult philosophical questions and to overcome the stalemate of the opposition between naturalists and culturalists, I will seek guidance and inspiration in critical realism. With Bhaskar and the realist movement, I start from the distinction between the 'transitive' (or epistemic) and the 'intransitive' (or ontological) dimension of knowledge (Bhaskar, 1978: 17). Applied to nature, the principle of the existential intransitivity of the objects of knowledge simply states that nature exists independently of our observations and descriptions of it. Assuming for a moment that all human beings were to disappear, nature would presumably still exist. The principle of the socio-historical transitivity of the knowledge of the objects recognises that nature can only be known under certain descriptions and that those are socially and historically variable.

The whole point of this somewhat scholastic distinction is to foreclose the 'epistemic fallacy' which, assuming that statements about being can be reduced to statements about knowledge, erroneously concludes from the fact that nature can only be known under certain descriptions that those descriptions constitute nature (without quotation marks). Collapsed into 'nature', nature becomes culture, while the intransitive or extra-discursive existence of nature is simply elided. The signifier 'nature' performatively constructs 'nature', and at the end of the day the signified is deferred and the referent 'exterminated' by discourse. To counter the preposterous 'de-ontological' claims of radical constructivism and to bring their practitioners back to their senses (and to common sense), one should, however, take the risk of being a pedant and remind them of the elementary lessons of realist epistemology. Even if objects can only be known 'to us' under certain descriptions, one is nevertheless not allowed to conclude that the descriptions actually construct the objects themselves. Régis Debray (1998: 267), the self-proclaimed founder of 'mediation studies', has correctly remarked that

> it does not follow from the fact that the objective world is inseparable from the practical representations that a society has of it that the latter can construct all its objective references. That a map contributes to the formation of a territory does not mean that the territory is the invention of the cartographer.

Indeed, even if mapping and map-making exemplify the ways in which spaces are made presentable and re-presentable in maps, charts, pictures and other inscription devices so that they become available for further exploration, specification, sale, contract, management or any other form of 'government' (Rose, 1999: 30–37), the defetishisation of the map should not overstep its boundaries. To shore up its political arguments, it should rather recognise the existence of a mapable substrate and analyse how the techniques of mapping construct a political space of government through the enclosure of entities (land, estates, populations, constituencies, etc.).[13]

Once the independent, extra-discursive existence of nature 'out there' is recognised and accepted, we can grant the constructivist that there is, and can be, no reference to nature that is independent of discourse – except in discourse.[14] Provided that we do not interpret the discursive mediation and construction of nature as 'nature' (*Natur für uns*) as an epistemological licence for the erasure of nature (*Natur an sich*), we can even accept Judith Butler's most provocative thesis that the 'construction of "sex" as the radically unconstructed' (Butler, 1990: 7) is itself a discursive construction. Sex is indeed constructed as 'prediscursive', as nature, prior to culture, but precisely through discourse. Discourses of bodies and bodies of discourse intersect in and through reiterative and citational practices that construct what appears as an unconstructed 'outside'. Given that this outside is 'not an "absolute" outside, an ontological thereness that exceeds or counters the boundaries of discourse', but a 'constitutive "outside" which can only be thought – when it can – in relation to that discourse' (Butler, 1993: 8), the body doesn't really matter for Butler, except of course as the unmarked body that makes the cultural distinction between nature and culture, sex and gender possible.[15]

Moreover, to avoid further misunderstandings, it should also be stressed that the distinction between the transitive and the intransitive dimensions of knowledge does not aim to deny the social construction of nature, or its social destruction for that matter. The realist conception of nature only aims to posit the existence of a natural substrate in the physical world that is always already presupposed by the natural sciences and that functions as a transcendental condition of the possible forms of human intervention in nature, from those of the engineer and the transsexual to the lyrical poet and the sociologist of science. With Kate Soper (1995: 155–160), we can indeed distinguish between the realist or 'deep' concept of nature and the lay or 'surface' concept of nature. The latter is used to refer to empirical nature, i.e. to the ordinary observable features and the directly tangible forms in the environment: the fauna and the flora, the countryside, the landscape, 'the nature we have destroyed and polluted and are asked to conserve and preserve' (Soper, 1995: 156). As an object of human destruction or of human appreciation, nature is always a human construction.

Provided that we distinguish between deep and surface nature, we can easily accept Beck and Giddens' thesis of the 'end of nature'. Sociologists and anthropologists of science have convincingly demonstrated in the last decade that the nature on which the scientists are working in their labs, the brains of the rats they are chopping into slices, the genes they are manipulating, are effectively and literally social constructions (Latour and Woolgar, 1978). And so is the landscape we admire. The nature and countryside we love and drive to in our cars on sunny Sunday afternoons is mostly a cultural landscape. In the countryside, nature is mostly agriculture, and quite often the 'pure nature' we crave is a nature that has been artificially reconstructed as nature by bulldozers (Keulartz, 1998).

Regional ontologies

Can we conceive of nature as something that exists independently of culture and at the same time as something that is always subsumed under culture? Can we combine the insight that the nature–culture distinction is universal with the fact that not all cultures draw it exactly in the same way? To answer that question, let us move from the transcendental realism of Roy Bhaskar to the transcendental phenomenology of Edmund Husserl. Although the idealism of Husserl might at first seem incompatible with the materialism of Bhaskar, one should nevertheless remember that both of them are concerned with a transcendental inquiry into the conditions of possibility of knowledge. Taking the epistemic practices of the natural scientists as the starting point of their epistemological research, Husserl and Bhaskar each attempt in their own way to answer the Kantian question – 'How is nature possible?' – by reflexively uncovering the a-priori conditions of knowledge. If Bhaskar demonstrates that the natural sciences always already and necessarily presuppose the intransitive existence of nature as an incontrovertible fact, Husserl insists for his part that this nature can only be grasped if it is categorically constituted as nature (of a certain kind) in and through the epistemic practices of the scientists.[16] By proposing a theory, or perhaps better, a method to describe and analyse the 'marvellous correlation between the object of knowledge and the phenomenon of knowledge' (Husserl, 1958: 12), that is the object as it appears to consciousness, Husserl goes further than Bhaskar.[17] Unlike Bhaskar, he not only shows that knowledge of nature necessarily presupposes *that* there is indeed something like nature 'out there' (nature as transcendent object of knowledge), but he also analyses in detail *how* this nature can be grasped as nature (of a certain kind), that is how the epistemic activities of the subjects constitute nature as an intentional object of a certain kind (nature as phenomenon or immanent object of knowledge). By offering a method for describing in minute detail how the mind can grasp something that exists outside of the mind by constituting it inside the mind as an object of a certain kind, he thereby solves an epistemological problem that Bhaskar does not really touch.

Inversely, by insisting on the intransitive or transcendent properties of the objects of knowledge, Bhaskar can offer a transcendental index or guideline for the constitutive activities of the mind and act as a safeguard so that the mind cannot constitute the object of knowledge as it pleases, but has to take into account the essential properties of the objects of knowledge. What I want to suggest is that a 'cross-reading' of Husserl and Bhaskar indicates the way of a realist phenomenology of nature that is able to describe and account for the correlation between the object and the phenomenon of knowledge.

In an earlier article (Vandenberghe, 2002a) I drew on Husserl's complicated analysis of the structures of constitution of the material world (the thing-world), the animated world (the animal world) and the spiritual world (the human world) to contest the ontological confusion of things and humans that has become the trademark of actor–network theory.[18] Going 'back to the things themselves' in order to analyse how different phenomena give themselves to consciousness and are intentionally constituted as givens of consciousness, I was claiming that all phenomena, human and non-human, have an essence (*eidos*) that predetermines what they necessarily must be when they are to be things of a certain kind. This essence can be a priori determined through the procedure of 'eidetic variation' (Husserl, 1952: III).[19] By submitting a given phenomenon, say a book, to a process of imaginative variation, we can freely vary the perspectives on the book, introduce other books that are different from the first one in terms of colour, size, shape, texture, etc., and gain insight into the materially determinate essence of the book that remains invariant and of which any variation represents only a particular instance and possibility. Once grasped intuitively, an essence can be compared and contrasted with other essences at varying levels of generalisation and specification. At the highest level of generalisation, we can distinguish the three ontological regions of material, animate and spiritual nature that found, respectively, the physical sciences, the biological and psychophysical sciences, and the human sciences. Convincing ourselves that they are essentially different, we can arrive at a categorical determination of the essence of the thing, the soul and the spirit. Simplifying the long and important but complicated eidetic analyses of *Ideen II* (Husserl, 1952) on the constitution of the world that were so important for Merleau-Ponty, we can say that a thing belongs to the material world by virtue of the fact that it is causally related to other things in a unified spatial-temporal context. The spirit belongs to a human world by virtue of the fact that it is endowed with meaning and intentionally constituted as a cultural world. The transition from the first region to the latter is made possible through the body, which is both an object of nature and an organ of the will, something that can touch, but also something that is touched. Although Husserl distinguishes between three ontological regions, he is, in fact, mainly concerned with the a-priori establishment of a categorical distinction between the regions of nature and culture, and with the relation between the natural world and the spiritual, whereby the latter is granted priority over the former.

Regional typologies

Assuming for the sake of argument that the distinction between the ontological regions of nature and culture could be established on secure transcendental-eidetic foundations, we can now reinterpret those regional ontologies as 'regional typologies of the historical life-world' (Luckmann, 1970) and combine the transivity of nature with the intransitivity of the nature–culture divide.[20] This move from a transcendental to an empirical phenomenology of the constitution of the regions of reality recodes the opposition between nature and culture, which corresponds to an objective order of the world, into an 'artificial creation of culture' (Lévi-Strauss, 1967: xvii). This cultural recoding of the universal divide allows us to make sense of the fact that even if all cultures draw a line between nature and culture, they nevertheless draw it differently.[21]

Without falling into the evolutionist traps of the early anthropologists, I think, however, that we can generally differentiate the typologies of the pre-modern and the modern life-worlds by saying that the former are holistic societies with gift economies that tend to interpret things within a anthropomorphic frame as if they were human, whereas the latter are individualistic societies with commodity economies that tend to interpret humans in a fetishistic frame as if they were things.[22] By insisting on the *as if* character of those typifications, their conventionalist or imaginary status is recognised: things are things and humans are humans *by nature*, but that does not mean that humans cannot be conceived and treated as animals or things, things as animals or humans. It is enough to swap the perspectives, seeing ourselves and the 'others' through the estranging eye of the anthropologist, to obtain a perspective on the perspective that allows for a systematic relativisation or 'symmetrisation' (à la Bloor) of both of the regional typifications. What seems strange to 'us' is familiar and ordinary to 'them', and *vice versa*, but there's no reason to assume that either of the miscategorisations is superior to the other. As Castoriadis (1975: 221) rightly says, 'Treating a human as a thing is not less but more imaginary than seeing a human as an owl.'

In the realm of the imaginary, one is no longer dealing with differences in kinds or realms, but with a continuum and fluid transitions between the extremities. In a world in which nature can become culture and culture can become second nature, things, animals and humans can be more or less natural, more or less human, and shift from one end of the continuum to the other, as can be gathered from the fact that the Greeks considered slaves as things, that the colonial masters considered negroes as animals and that there are still too many husbands who consider their spouses as pets. In the meantime, blacks, women and pets have jumped the ditch between humans and non-humans, while at the same time everything, or almost everything, from body parts, babies and football players to audiences and human capacities, can be alienated and reified into a commodity (Radin, 1996). Notwithstanding the fetishism that is attached to commodities, they don't grow on trees but are eminently cultural. Like slaves, goods have a trajectory or a biography (Appadurai, 1986). In the same way as slaves are dehumanised when they are sold as things and forced to work (the slave as 'thing in the field') and rehumanised in a new setting (the slave as 'person in bed' – Patterson, quoted by Kopytoff, 1982: 220), goods are reified into commodities when they enter the market and decommodified and repersonalised as they leave the sphere of circulation to enter the sphere of consumption.

By allowing for a cultural recoding of the ontological divide through regional typologies, the 'interpretative flexibility' of the world is foregrounded. The regional ontologies of the world do no more determine the interpretations of the world than the base determines the superstructure, though the latter are obviously conditioned by the former. Nevertheless, if we want to conceive of some kind of progress through 'epistemic gain' (Taylor, 1989), we have to assume as a regulative ideal that in the very long run the regional typologies of the life-world will come to overlap and coincide with the regional ontologies.[23] When appearances and essences are identical, humans, animals and things will be considered as what they really *are*. This asymptotical overlap (or *Deckung*, in Husserlian parlance) of the ontological and the epistemological, of words and things, can be expected on the grounds of the self-corrective mechanism that is built in human cognition. Nothing forbids us to conceive of human beings as baboons, baboons as cauliflowers, cauliflowers as stones and stones as persons, but the imaginary transfer of the project on the object is nevertheless restricted by the fact that the meanings that are intentionally transferred and projected from the subject onto the object will eventually be confirmed, modified or discomfirmed by the objects themselves. Thus, when I intentionally represent the stone as a person, the noematic meaning of the stone which I constitute in my present experience of the stone and automatically transfer to the next phase of the experience will be partially or totally confirmed or disconfirmed, depending on whether the stone walks, talks, etc., or not. When the projected meaning is totally confirmed and the object fills and fulfils each and every one of the expectations, then the object and the project perfectly overlap.

> Then the real *adequatio rei et intellectus* is produced. The object is really 'present' or 'given', exactly as the object is intended and as the object that it is intended to be; there is no longer a partial intention that lacks fulfillment.
>
> (Husserl, 1980: II, 118)

This is the noetic experience of evidence, and when it is continuously repeated and sediments into a relatively natural worldview, we can presume – for the time being and until further notice – that we have arrived at the truth and that the object really is as it is and as it gives itself to consciousness. 'The objective correlate [of noetic experience of evidence] is called Being, or also Truth' (Husserl, 1980: II, 122). Truth may be an artefact, but when the artifice is intersubjectively validated and the relation between culture and nature is continuously confirmed in and through discursive practices, the ontology and the typology of the natural, the animal and the human world naturally overlap. When the congruence between them is given with evidence, we can counterfactually presume that the regional typology is grounded in reality as such. When it speaks the language of reality, reason presumably cannot be wrong – or can it?[24]

So far so good, were it not that since the Second World War the stable ontologies of yore have become subject to epochal technological inventions and reinventions of nature that are so revolutionary that they may well undermine any attempt to maintain a-priori distinctions between humans, animals and things. As a result of the recent developments in bio-, nano- and cybertechnology, my archaeo-modernist refusal to treat ontologies as simple ways of speaking that can be changed at will seems quaint and outmoded. That humans and non-humans can be assembled and interconnected in heterogeneous networks is nothing new. If we may believe Latour and the other members of his expanding actor–network network (Latour, Callon, Akrich, Law, Mol, etc.), the fact that societies are stabilised through quasi-objects (aka 'hairy' objects), that objects are, so to speak, the 'cement' that keeps human collectives together, is the *differentia specifica* that distinguishes human beings from baboons (Strum and Latour, 1988). In this respect pre-modern cultures are not that different from modern cultures. 'We' may have 'couch-potatoes', electronic cars and nuclear power stations, but the fact that we have more and longer socio-technical networks in which humans and non-humans are chained to each other only shows that we are not really modern and that, like 'them', we don't really make a-priori distinctions between nature and culture (Latour, 1991). In so far as actor–network theory teaches us a postmodern way of telling semiotic stories about technology and about how it 'redistributes' the actions of humans and non-humans over syntagmatic chains, it represents a most innovative, provocative and interesting take on the sociology of science and technology that projects and presents itself as an experimental ontology. The problem with this and similar socio-philosophical attempts to develop an experimental ontology that wilfully scrambles the demarcations between the material, the animal and the human world lies not with those attempts themselves, but with the fact that their joyous anti-humanism may well offer an ideological countenance to the socio-technical practices of the engineers of the contemporary bio- and cybertech industries of late capitalism that make tons of money by artificially producing a monstrous nature that transforms the nature of the human itself.[25]

As far as I'm concerned, postmodernists and their radical cousins, the posthumanists, can 'cyborg anything – mix and juxtapose elements that are thereby made compatible in so far as their combination creates a workable circuit of ideas' (Strathern, 1995: 165). But when I read in the newspaper that sheep are cloned and that it soon will be our turn, when I hear on the radio that pigs' genes are modified and patented so that their hearts can be transplanted into human bodies, when I'm told that the world champion of chess has been beaten by 'Deep Blue' and that some people are dreaming of 'downloading' the entire human brain into an artificial, immortal body or to upgrade it periodically with new software programs available from the market, I start worrying about the future of 'really existing humanity'. I start wondering about the innocence of the posthumanist celebrations of the new 'meat and metal symbiosis' that allows us finally to overcome our philosophical anthropocentrism and to become the monstrous *Übermensch* that Nietzsche and the neo-Nietzschians want us to become: 'The organic can rise to yet higher levels. Our eagerness to know nature is a means to perfect the body.... In the long run, it is not a question of Man at all: he is to be overcome' (Nietzsche, quoted by Deleuze, 1965: 59).

II We have never been human

This is a story about organised complexity, technological mediation and human alienation. Looking for a third position that polemically overcomes the ancient 'conflict of the faculties', postmodern philosophers, historians and sociologists of science and technology set sail for the Canadian High North. Tracking through the icy waters and the immense arctic archipelagos, they search for the epistemic equivalent of 'the Northwest Passage' between Alaska and Greenland that connects the Atlantic and Pacific Oceans.[26] The passage that connects the natural and the human sciences is a complex unfolding topological network of mutual translations between theories and practices, forms and forces, words and things, that performatively co-construct and co-produce the long winding road that connects nature and culture, base and superstructure. At the end of the journey, the passage appears at the misty horizons:

> [It is] the passage that one didn't hope to find anymore between two types of knowledge, each of which always deals with humans and the world, but separated by a bar, as if there were two worlds, the one of those who are awake and the other of those who are asleep, as if there were two humanities, the one that is busy transforming things, and the one that delights in its own relations.
>
> (Serres, 1980a: 60)

At the intersection of the natural and the human sciences, mediating between both, stands *techno-logy* (among other things and other sciences), understood as the science of the productive forces that socially transform nature and naturally make society.

Reconnecting the two humanities, 'technology' acts as double mediation between nature and society that performatively co-constructs the objects and the subjects as it interconnects them into a 'seamless web'. Humans make artefacts and the artefacts they make organise and fix them into human collectives. Socially constructed by humans, technology constructs society (Akrich, 1994) – that is how one could neatly summarise the constructivist position of contemporary social studies of science and technology. Having supplemented the mantra of the action sociologists 'no humans – no society' ('intersubjectivity') with its inversion 'no objects – no society' ('interobjectivity') (Latour, 1994), the postmodern investigators of science and technology go on, however, and tell us that without objects there would not only be no society, but there would be no human beings either.[27] By means of a posthumanist gloss, Mike Michael (2000: 1) eloquently summarises the main tenets of actor–network theory:

> There are no humans in the world. Or rather, humans are fabricated – in language, through discursive formations, in their various liaisons with technological and natural actors, across networks that are heterogeneously comprised of humans and non-humans who are themselves so comprised.

The exteriorisation of the organs

To make hard the claim that human beings would not be human without non-human beings, French anthropologists, sociologists and mediologists of a post-humanist bent draw on the seminal work of André Leroi-Gourhan, the palaeo-anthropologist and prehistorian who deciphered the 'mythogrammes' of the grottes of Lascaux and who can be considered as the antipode of Lévi-Strauss.[28] As a student of the prehistory of humanity, Leroi-Gourhan has analysed the process of humanisation in terms of the progressive specialisation of the two corporeal zones of the face and the hand, which, once liberated by the upward posture of humans, have made possible the exteriorisation of the brain and the body into the extra-organic realms of symbolical institutions and material technology, both of which have led to a better grip on reality.[29] Putting man thus 'back on his feet', Leroi-Gourhan pithily summarised his conclusion in *Le geste et la parole*, his masterwork in two volumes, by saying that 'humanisation begins with the feet' (Leroi-Gourhan, 1964: I, 211). Indeed, the vertical locomotion of the 'Zinjanthrope' has liberated the hand from the constraints of locomotion, which is a precondition for the development of tools, and the liberation of the hand has in turn liberated the mouth from the tasks that are related to food and thus made speech possible.

In this grand narrative of the process of humanisation, which started two and a half million years ago, the development of the brain appears only as a secondary process that follows the general one, though once developed, it will take a decisive role in the evolution of mankind. Once the double capacity of the fabrication of tools and symbolic expression is functionally acquired, the process of humanisation and civilisation can begin and be understood as an ongoing process of progressive *exteriorisation of the operational programmes* that allow human beings to successfully adapt to their environment. At first, a piece of technology is a prosthetic extension of the hand that is exteriorised, but then it becomes independent of the hand and starts to follow its own laws. The same holds for language. At first, memory is the extension and exteriorisation of speech, but then, with the invention of writing, memory can be stored in archives, knowledge can evolve according to its own laws and be accessed at any time or consumed anywhere, thanks to the mass media. With the total exteriorisation of the organs in autonomous socio-cultural and socio-technical institutions and organisations, the evolution of humans is 'liberated' or 'unballasted' from its biological substrate and comes to its term:

> Liberated from his gestures, his muscles, the programmation of his actions, his memory, liberated from his imagination by the perfection of the means of tele-diffusion, liberated from the animal and the vegetal world, from the wind, the cold, the microbes, the unknown of the mountains and the seas, the *homo sapiens* of zoology is probably close to reach the end of its career.
> (Leroi-Gourhan, 1964: II, 266)

Having found its origin in the materiality of the human constitution, the 'replacement of the organs' (*Organersatz*) by technology has led, as Gehlen (1957: 10) says, to 'the replacement of the organic as such' (*Ersatz des Organischen überhaupt*). From the hand to the brain and beyond, the process of extension, 'exsudation' and exteriorisation of the organs has found its provisional point of culmination in the substitution of the functions of the brain (information, computation, decision) by the computer.

Human evolution seems to be characterised by a tendency towards increasing spiritualisation. If we may believe Leroi-Gourhan, everything happens as if the evolution of the species were geared to converge and culminate in the Supreme Consciousness of the divine 'point Omega' – as theorised by his friend and co-religionist Teilhard de Chardin. Steered by a tendency towards enlightenment and dematerialisation, and a correlative affirmation of the Spirit that culminates in the emergence of a 'collective intelligence' (as theorised by Pierre Lévy) that is able to steer evolution, human genesis is conceived by Leroi-Gourhan as a form of 'orthogenesis', that is a kind of Lamarckian evolution in which the variations onto-theo-teleologically lead to the end of supreme mastery (Groenen, 1996: 61–90).

The specialisation and exteriorisation of the human organs in a socio-technical super-organ – society – that allows the humans to intervene more successfully than ever in their external environment and to adapt it to their own ends appears as the end product of biological evolution. The zoo-technological story of Leroi-Gourhan is not a happy one, however. Far from leading to the perfection of the individual as such, the exteriorisation of the human faculties eventually leads to a progressive integration of the individual as 'a piece of the indefinitely perfectible mechanism of a totally socialised society' (Leroi-Gourhan, 1964: II, 199). After a couple of million years of evolution, we may ask ourselves if human societies are not at the point of regressing into societies of ants and bees in which the individual element is almost cybernetically programmed to be part and parcel of the social organism. In this new fable of the bees, reason is once again cunning. Everything happens as if the human–machine complex needed individual freedom only during a couple of millennia to integrate the individual into a supra-individual organism that functions like a beehive in which the behaviour of each is synchronised through cybernetic tele-guidance with the behaviour of all. Writing in the 1960s, Leroi-Gourhan had already clearly understood the technocratic and consumerist trend of late capitalism: 'A restricted elite will not only work out programmes of life, politics, administration, techniques, but also emotional relations, epic evasions and the image of a life that is totally imagined' (Leroi-Gourhan, 1964: II, 203). His vision of the future of humankind was rather bleak. Anticipating the times in which humans would be interconnected with computers, he predicted that the process of humanisation would end in a 'terminal cyberworld' (to borrow a phrase from Virilio), which he envisioned in the most horrific terms as 'a humanity without teeth that would live and lie down using what remains of its anterior members to push buttons' (Leroi-Gourhan, 1964: I, 183).

The apotheosis of humanity coincides thus with its apocalypse. In one of those dramatic reversals, to which dialecticians are accustomed, the liberation of human beings through technology turns out to coincide with their alienation by technology. Consequently, the exteriorisation of organs of the humans reverses into their reification by a super-organ that follows its own inhuman laws, while imposing them on its elements. Once again, as in the story of the Golem, the human becomes the creature of its own creation. Leroi-Gourhan warned us: Unless we keep our technology in check, 'we may have only a couple of thousand years left, if not a couple of centuries' (Leroi-Gourhan, 1982: 242).

A theory of alienation without alienation

As a Catholic and a convinced humanist, Leroi-Gourhan was not really a posthumanist. I suspect that he would have had little sympathy for the wacky projects of the transhumanists and ectropians who want to 'employ technology in the near-term for the purpose of attempting to perfect ourselves' (see www.transhumanism.org).[30] In so far as his theory of socio-technological evolution offers the perfect platform for the development of a coherent post- or even anti-humanist position, it should nevertheless be taken seriously.[31]

By conceiving of the anthropogenesis as a 'technogenesis' (Stiegler, 1994: 58), Leroi-Gourhan has systematically extended the theory of the techniques of the body to technology as such. Inspired by Marcel Mauss (1950), his mentor, who has shown that even our seemingly most natural ways of behaving such as walking or swimming presuppose the learning of a technique, the French prehistorian has shown that technology is the exteriorisation of operational chains of behaviour that forms the human being in its totality (*l'homme total*) – in its biological, psychological as well as social dimensions. In order to be able to use a piece of technology, say a car or a computer, human beings have to learn a series of habits, gestures, reactions and other schemes of action that get progressively sedimented into a stable *habitus*. Through the formation of the habitus, the individual incorporates the technology at the same time as she or he is incorporated in it. Through this mutual incorporation of human and machine, an integrated operational technological apparatus is built up that not only mediates between the human and the environment, but that co-constructs both at the same time.[32]

Contemporary posthumanism builds further on the theory of humanisation through the exteriorisation of organs into an integrated technological apparatus, but while it maintains it as an accurate description of the becoming other than human – 'technogenesis as heterogenesis' – it divests it of its essentialist assumptions and normative overtones.[33] Although the notion of exteriorisation sounds vaguely similar to Hegel and Marx's notion of *Entaüsserung* (extraneation or alienation), the posthumanist reappropriation of it is highly selective. The 'expressivist' idea that there might be something 'inside' of humans that they exteriorise in and through their *praxis* and that this *praxis* is precisely what distinguishes them from animals is ditched. The interior does not exist prior to its exteriorisation; the interior emerges at the same time as the exterior and is constituted by it. Both are co-original and emerge at the same time. The essence of the human is to have no essence. Given that humans have no essence, they cannot express their 'species being' (*Gattungswesen*) in their work and, as a result, they cannot be alienated from it either. In so far as posthumanism accepts the theory of the 'exteriorisation of organs' while refusing to interpret its dialectical reversal in terms of dehumanisation, it can be described as a theory of alienation without alienation – '*Entfremdung* to be understood by philosophers', as Marx (1972: III, 34) once said, attacking the beautiful soul of the German literati.[34]

Like post-modernism, post-humanism wholeheartedly says 'yea' to life and wants to be affirmative. Refusing to consider the negativity of alienation in the dialectical light of its *Aufhebung*, it dismisses the old humanist notions of Man, alienation and reification. Following Nietzsche's (fourth) Prologue to *Zarathustra*, posthumanists celebrate the negativity of dehumanisation as a constructive step in the unfinished overcoming of the limits of the human, thanks to which the human becomes other than human, and creatively redefine alienation as 'alteration'.[35] The human is no longer a being, but a becoming, a being that becomes other through the exteriorisation of its organs in a plethora of extraorganic mediations. Paraphrasing de Beauvoir, we could say that for the posthumanist man is not but that he becomes what he is and what he is not, by overcoming himself, thanks to technology.

'Technology is the invention of man' (Stiegler, 1994: 145–187). The phrase is necessarily ambiguous, undecidable even. Who invents what? Is technology a human invention or is the human a technological invention? The paradox of humanisation through exteriorisation is that technology and humanity emerge at the same time. As the human is inseparable from the protheses that supplement it, the 'what' gives birth to the 'who'. Having ditched every form of essentialism, posthumanists adopt a performative vision of anthropology in which human beings are literally made by what they have made, by culture, but also and above all by technology. By means of technology, nature is humanised. Seen from another angle, the humanisation of nature appears, however, as the naturalisation of humans. The technological mediation that intervenes between humans and nature establishes a performative or 'transductive' relation between them. Co-constructed or performed by the relation, the human can no more exist outside of its relation with the non-human than the non-human can exist outside of its relation with the human. 'Pro-jected' and 'pro-duced' by humans, technologies, techniques, instruments and tools in turn act back on humans and modify them. Altering inner and external nature, material practices, bodies, language, habits, percepts, affects, etc., the naturalisation of the human has opened the way to the artificial evolution of mankind.

This is nothing new. In the overture of his philosophical soap opera, Sloterdijk revisits the creation myth (*Genesis* (2, 4–7)) and presents the first human being as an artefact – as living earthenware. Created by God out of the earth, Adam appears as a theo-technological product of his time: 'Android figures are made according to routines of ceramics: the biblical genesis reflects the state of the art of earthmaking at the time.... Metaphysics begins as metaceramics' (Sloterdijk, 2000: 33). From Adam and the Man of the Caverns to the *Homo sapiens*, the human being is made by what he makes. The silexes, pebbles and bones made and transformed the Man of Cro Magnon. Today, it is the spectacles, the pacemakers and the laptops that make *Homo sapiens*. We have never been human. Having estranged the human, nothing human is strange to the posthumanist. Once we understand that we are made by the technologies that we make and that we become human through our implants, transplants and prostheses, we can even appreciate the intelligence of a stupid statement like this one: 'For a humanist, the best friend of man is man himself. For a non-humanist, it is his gun, his car or his mobile phone' (Tisseron, 1998: 273). Indeed, the heterogeneous assemblages of humans and non-humans that transform, fix and stabilise the social, cultural and political networks also make, transform and modify human ways of acting, thinking, feeling, seeing and being. Inverting the classic tenets of humanism, the posthumanists not only affirm that it is the objects that make humans (like when we say that it is 'the suit that makes the man'), they also insist that technologies follow their own laws (techno-logics) and have a mind of their own, that they have unintended and unexpected consequences, both happy and perverse, that no one – no individual, no society, no politics – can control. Like language in Saussure, technology forms an autonomous self-evolving system that cannot be controlled by those who use it. Where humanists cry 'wolf' and see only a sign of dehumanisation, alienation and reification, posthumanists see only a normal, 'human, inhuman, all too human' process of humanisation through exteriorisation, reification and alienation.

Machinic heterogenesis

Human nature has a history (Moscovici, 1977). Thanks to their diligence, human beings create technology and intervene in nature, but this intervention transforms human nature at the same time. As far as we can go back in history, we never encounter pristine human nature. The oppositions between nature and culture, nature and technology, technology and society, do simply not hold. Nature is not static, neither is technology, nor are the results of their interaction. As a product of history, nature is always 'second nature'. From its origins, human nature has been 'fabricated' by technical evolution. Although technogenesis significantly relativises the place of humanity in the greater scheme of things, it still has not broken completely with the anthropocentric mode of thinking. This only happens when we give up our ingrained resistance to fluxes of becoming and accept the experimental production of creative ontologies in which all the boundaries between the human, the animal and the material are wilfully transgressed, pragmatically blurred and, finally, technologically overcome. Rejecting the distinction between the posthuman and the inhuman as a mere survival of 'old European thought' (Luhmann-Rumsfeld), contemporary anti-humanism links up with vitalism. Joyously celebrating the becoming of Life, it seeks to conceptualise the death of Man free of anthropocentric conceits.

The most radical and influential attempt to theorise the posthuman condition in non-anthropocentric terms has been 'composed' as an esoteric, vitalist, orgiastic, vibrating 'machinic opera' by Gilles Deleuze, a philosopher, and Félix Guattari, a practising psychoanalyst and lifelong political activist, in *A Thousand Plateaus* (Deleuze and Guattari, 1980).[36] The 1,000 plateaus of the vitalists do not form a mountain, but open up 1,000 ways that, unlike those of Heidegger, lead everywhere. Displacing the 'question concerning technology' by the 'question concerning the machine', Deleuze and Guattari present the genesis of the human not only as a technogenesis but, extending and radicalising it, dissolving *anthropos* into *bios*, equally as a 'bio-technogenesis' (Ansell Pearson, 1997: 124) – that is, as a machinic production that plunges the human species back into the magma of the becoming of life.

The machinic conception of evolution conceives of the human as a component of a heterogeneous assemblage that cuts across all lineages of different kinds and re-arranges them in 'monstrous couplings' and 'anomalous becomings'. To the extent that the technological approach still suggests that the machine is a complex tool and, thus, an extension or exteriorisation of the human that fabricates the human, it still maintains the idea of human evolution. The machinic approach is more radical. It replaces the idea of evolution with the idea of 'involution' (Deleuze and Guattari, 1980: 292), understood not as a form of regression, but of 'creative evolution' that brings heterogeneous populations into symbiosis, creating thereby 'counter-natural alliances' between different species, such as the monkey and the human, the tree trunk and the crocodile, or the wasp and the orchid, to take Deleuze and Guattari's favourite example.[37]

Moving away from the genealogical or filiative conception of evolution, represented by the model of the tree or the root, involution allows for a 'rhizomatic' becoming whereby humans can creatively-destructively enter into the most monstrous of couplings with Gods, humans, animals, plants, things, tools, machines, etc. Although a rhizome can grow on roots, it is not a root itself, but a subterranean stem or underground sprout, such as a bulb or a tuber, with multiple branching roots and shoots that go off and proliferate in all directions, break off at a certain point and form a rhizome with other offshoots or something else – 'with the wind, an animal, human beings' (Deleuze and Guattari, 1980: 18).[38]

A rhizome is a meshwork in which each and every point can in principle be connected, one way or another, with any another point.[39] By entering into 'transversal communication' with different lines of descent, rhizomatic offshoots scramble the genealogical trees. They have neither a beginning nor an end, but start, so to say, in the middle. Unlike the model of the tree, which reduces the multiplicity to the One, the rhizome eliminates every possible reference to a possible substance or substantive, synthesis or dialectics that leads back to the One in order to stimulate the proliferation of the Multiple and celebrate the virulence of Life. Multiplicity is more than a matter of logic, however. It is something one must make or do – 'le multiple, *il faut le faire*' (Deleuze and Guattari, 1980: 13).[40] We must always make connections, ever more connections, between points, offshoots and lines of flight, since they are not given, cross the boundaries and experimentally realise other possibilities than the ones that are given. As the rhizome grows and proliferates by making always new connections, it becomes more complex, always more complex, and transgresses all the boundaries till there is only one single, but always expanding and deterritorialising machinic flux – the *phylum* – of unformed materiality that fills the entire space with the most disparate things and ends up covering the whole earth.

The plane of immanence

The machinic assemblage that is always in the making, always becoming, is a potentially infinite open system. It knows no limits and no boundaries. Without temporal or spatial limits, it transgresses the boundaries between the ontological regions, and levels all that exists to a single ontological plane, the so-called 'plane of immanence' or 'plane of nature' (Deleuze, 1981: 164–175) – though nature has nothing to do with it as it eschews all distinctions between natural and artificial kinds and includes bodies and souls, spirits and things. Opposed to the plane of transcendence, in which the multiplicity is always captured and organised by a hidden subject, form or force that cannot be seen, but that has to be inferred, deduced or transduced from the given, the common plane of immanence has no supplementary or 'intransitive' dimension. There's no depth, only a surface; there's nothing hidden, no God, no Master, no Man, no Plan that steers and organises from above the becoming of the world.[41] On the one-dimensional plane of immanence, there is no dialectical synthesis of heterogeneous and disparate elements; there's only, as Leibniz said, the becoming of 'a continuous becoming like an ocean' (Serres, 1972: 10), the division of which into Ethiopian, Caledonian or any other sea is arbitrary.[42] Everything is loosely connected with everything into a heterogeneous assemblage of sorts, and immediately given, levelled, reduced to relations of speed:

> In any case, there is pure plane of immanence upon which everything is given, upon which unformed elements and materials dance that are distinguished from one another only by their speed and that enter into that individuated arrangement depending on their connections, their relations of movement. A fixed plane of life upon which everything stirs, slows down or accelerates.
>
> (Deleuze and Guattari, 1980: 312)

Speed and slowness do not refer to quantitative degrees of movement, however, but to qualitatively different types of movements of bodies through space, to two different ways of making space; namely, the geometrical way and the topological-energetic one. Whereas the former analytically carves up space and organises it by means of walls, pillars and closings, the latter opens up space and 'performs' it as it follows the flux of unformed materiality that moves along rhizomatically, shooting off in all directions, making connections, 'occupying or filling a smooth space in the manner of a vortex, with the possibility of springing up at any point' (Deleuze and Guattari, 1980: 473).

Whatever moves on the plane of immanence is taken up in the vortex of becoming and consummated by it. Whatever enters the energetic flux is dissolved into a 'dance of unformed elements and materials'. The becoming of life that dissolves all forms of being into a pure magma of energetic, immaterial forces, this cosmic soup of free-floating submolecular, subatomic particles out of which organisms and beings emerge and in which they are sunk – this is the *ultimate reality*.[43]

On the plane of immanence, there's life – just as we say that there is water or sand – and all beings, without distinction, partake of it. 'Of pure immance, we shall say that is A LIFE, and nothing else' (Deleuze, 1995: 4). Life knows no distinctions or boundaries between genera, species, subjects, substances or organs. As it flows underneath, above, in and through everything and everywhere, it 'disindividuates', disintegrates and annihilates all beings and all entities into an anonymous flux of becoming. Needless to say that, swamped by life, the human also disappears – 'like a face in the sand at the edge of the sea' (Foucault) – in this orgiastic night of becomings and begoings.[44]

Homo homini parasitus

This vitalist 'ontology of the annihilation of beings' (Foucault, 1966: 291) forms the background of the biophilosophy of 'germinal' or 'viroid' life that is put forward in the 'Becoming-Animal' plateau of the book.[45] Like Othello, Deleuze would be only too happy to 'change my humanity with a Baboon'. Breaking with the evolutionist models of descent, they conceptualise the becoming-animal (vegetal, mineral, etc.) of the human as a becoming 'anomal', i.e. anomalous and monstrous, through a machinic process whereby the human enters into symbiosis with heterogeneous populations. In biology, symbiosis refers to the process whereby genetic material is transmitted between populations of different species, such as baboon and cat or wasp and orchid, for example, through bacterial contamination and viral infection, and *not* through sex:

> Propagation by epidemic, by contagion, has nothing to do with filiation by heredity. The vampire does not filiate, it infects. The difference is that contagion and epidemic involve terms that are entirely heterogeneous: for example, a human being, an animal, a bacterium, a virus, a molecule, a micro-organism.
>
> (Deleuze and Guattari, 1980: 295)

Symbiotic exchange through infection, contagion, mutation or genetic drift does not happen at the 'molar level' of the organism or the species but underneath it, at the 'molecular level' of the bacterial micro-organisms (microbe, virus, bacillus, worm, phagocyte) that enter the organism and spread from within as they mingle with the micro-organisms of the host. The lesson that Deleuze and Guattari have to teach us is ultimately a filthy one: 'The human is an integrated colony of amoeboid beings, just as these amoeboid beings (prococtists) are integrated colonies of bacteria. Like it or not, our origins are in slime' (Ansell Pearson, 1997: 124). Dust to dust, slime to slime, *Homo sapiens* dissolves into a sticky substance. Degraded and debased, the species regresses to the sorry state of '*parasitus sapiens*' (Serres, 1980b: 143).

Feeding onto each other, growing on and into each other, the symbiotic populations transgress the boundaries and form heterogeneous 'blocks' of machinic becoming through a cascade of supermolecular differentiations. Those blocks are not simply hybrids. Whereas hybridisation brings together elements that are pure and uncontaminated before they are mixed, machinic symbiosis infects and fuses them in a new living synthesis that ignores the ontological boundaries to such an extent that it becomes hard to say who is host and who is parasite. In symbiotic becoming, the distinction between the inside and the outside is fluid. This holds not only for the heterogeneous organisms, but also for their relation with the environment. Both are linked through a porous intermediary environment, such as the membrane, that mediates between them. The opposition between the organism and the environment is dissolved into a heterogenetic flow that interconnects the organism and the environment, co-constructing both at the same time. 'An animal, a thing can thus never be separated from its relations with the environment: the interior is only a selected exterior, the exterior, a projected interior' (Deleuze, 1981: 168). But if the organism 'selects' its environment, rather then the other way round, if the organism does not adapt to the environment, but creates its environment by 'deterritorialising [fluidifying] itself with respect to the exterior and reterritorialising [reorganising] itself with respect to its internal environment' (Deleuze and Guattari, 1980: 71), then we are done with the principles of Darwinian evolution. A new 'Copernican revolution' takes place, but this time in biology.[46] Indeed, it is no longer the living being which adapts itself to its environment, but it is now the environment which adapts itself to the living being. Through internal differentiation and self-organisation, the environment is identified and assimilated by the organism; through self-closure, the irritable organism surveys, selects and regulates the stimuli of the environment that are going to affect it.

In terms of systems theory, one would say that machinic organisms are self-organising, self-regulating or autopoietic systems. Using the reflexive lingo of contemporary 'radical constructivism',[47] we can define autopoietic systems with Maturana, Varela, and Luhmann (1987: 30–70) as networks that produce and maintain themselves by producing out of the elements of which they are composed the network that produces the elements of which they are composed. Autopoietic systems are by definition self-referentially or organisationally closed systems. They recursively constitute the basic elements of which they are made up by circular reference to their own self-reproduction as autonomous systems of communications. This self-reference allows the system to maintain its structure invariant, while each of its vanishing elements is continuously replaced by new, different ones. Paradoxically, this self-closure of the system is a precondition for its opening to the environment. Concretely, this means that as an autonomous and self-determining unity, the system can only react to the 'provocations' of the environment in accordance with its own mode or code of operation. The environment cannot influence the system directly but only indirectly in so far as the self-referentially closed system opens itself up to the environment and allows it from within to selectively influence the system from without. In other words, the system can only communicate about the environment within itself. It cannot communicate with the environment without disintegrating.

On this crucial point, machinic heterogenesis differs from autopoiesis (Ansell Pearson, 1997: 140–142; 1999: 168–170). Less concerned with the maintenance of their own stability, machinic assemblages do not maintain the organisation of their structure invariant. As they cross techno-ontological thresholds between regions, they enter into a genuinely dynamic, open and transgressive relation with their environments, which are after all not that different from what they are, and allow for the punctual emergence of flexible, mutable, variable modes of organisation. At this point, where the 'necessary disequilibrium and far-from equilibrium conditions' (Kauffman) required for a truly creative model of evolution are introduced into the system, machinic autopoiesis mutates into machinic heterogenesis. Linking up machinic heterogenesis with complexity theory, fusing Deleuze with Serres, we could say with the latter that when order is created out of chaos, islands emerge out of a disorderly sea: 'Order is an uncommon island. It is an archipelago. Disorder is the common ocean out of which those islands emerge' (Serres, 1977: backflap).

Intermezzo: living machines

Schematically speaking, one can conceive of technological development through the ages – 'from prehistory to ballistic missiles' (Latour and Lemonnier, 1994) – in terms of a quatriphasic process of exteriorisation or objectivation of the human capacities, activities and organs in machinic organisms that 'liberate' (Leroi-Gourhan), ameliorate and 'unballast' (Gehlen) the human capacities, activities and organs. In the first phase, the organ is removed from the body and exteriorised in the tool, while manual and intellectual work is still being done by the human. In the second phase, the physical force of the human is objectivated in the machine that now works for and in place of the human. In the third phase, it is not just the physical force that is exteriorised in the machine. With the automatisation of the machines, the psychic capacities and activities of the human are also 'unballasted' as the functions of the brain (consciousness, computation and decision) are exteriorised and incorporated in the machine. In the fourth phase, the integration of machines into a living whole, life as such, is finally exteriorised into a complex *anorganic living organ.*

Since the natural sciences, technology and the capitalist system of industrial production became systematically coupled in the late eighteenth century, the pace and the reach of the correlative process of the humanisation of machines and the machinisation of humans has been accelerated and intensified, first with the industrial revolution and, now, with the post-industrial one, to such an extent that, today, life itself can be explained scientifically and produced technologically. From the hand to the mind to life as such, we see a progressive movement from the internal to the external – and back. As the internal workings of the organism are analysed and properly understood by the sciences, they are exteriorised and constructed by technologies as an artificial organism that functions like a natural one. Arnold Gehlen (1957: 21) has aptly summarised the process in the following terms: 'As technology progresses, man brings into unanimated nature a principle of organisation that is already operative inside the organism at multiple locations.' Scientific progress consists in the 'explicitation' of the hidden, 'making it explicit' through research, while technological evolution consists in the exteriorisation, materialisation and reification of the explicit. If science is indeed 'phenomenological' as Sloterdijk (2004: 74–79) says, in the sense that it makes the invisible visible and brings the phenomenon into 'existence' as an object of perception, then technology is a phenomeno-technique that reifies and thereby realises the object as an object of manipulation. From the perception of the interior to the manipulation of the exterior, there's no solution of continuity, but unremitting 'e-volution' (from *e-volvere*), 'ex-plication' (from *ex-plicare*) or 'un-winding' (as in *ent-wicklung*) of the interior into phenomenal 'ex-posure' and control.

Incidentally, the history of the concept of the network confirms this analysis of the process of the exteriorisation of the internal workings of the organism into a non-organic but organised and evolving social body (Musso, 2003). From biology to philosophy, engineering and sociology, the root metaphor of the network always associates images of the body and of techniques to suggest the existence of a living tissue. Originally, the network refers to a woven net (*retis*). Hippocrates, Herophiles and Galienus used it in medicine to study the tissue of canals, ways and vessels like the veins, muscles and nerves that cover the human body, but also the brain, described by Galienus as *rete mirabili*. Later on, in the seventeenth century, Descartes and especially Leibniz transformed the 'percept' into a 'concept' and formalised the network in mathematical terms. With the industrial revolution, the concept leaves the body to become a 'construct'. The reticular image of the body is taken up by engineers and becomes the template for the technological construction of the great artificial territorial networks like the rail, the telephone or the electricity network: 'The natural network becomes artificial. From a given it becomes a construct. From a tool, it becomes a machine. The engineer conceives and constructs it, while the doctor observed it' (Musso, 2003: 146). When Saint-Simon and Proudhon borrow the concept of the network from the engineers to theorise social relations and develop utopian models of society, the technical network becomes the template for the political construction of social networks. Today, with the development of the internet, which interconnects machines (and persons) into a worldwide web, the concept is popularised and commercialised and becomes a 'decept', which can refer to almost anything that is interconnected – from spiderwebs, crystals, roots of trees and the cerebral cortex to waterworks, telephones, computers and transnational terrorist NGOs like Al-Qaeda. Through complexity theory, the socio-political conception of the network is once again linked to biology and neurology. Vitalist conceptions of technology abound and merge with technological conceptions of society. Eventually, sociology itself becomes a kind of 'baroque social physiology' of which all the other sciences can be considered as branches. As Tarde (1999: 58) said: 'Every thing is a society, every phenomenon is a social fact.... All sciences seem destined to become branches of sociology.'

Moving back from sociology to technology, I now want to take a closer look at molecular biology and present it as an *anthropic technology of communication*.[48] What the sciences can theoretically conceive of is now on the verge of being artificially conceived and technologically produced as a living system, whether this system is a virtual organism (artificial life), a virtual mind (artificial intelligence), or a mixture of both (cyborg). Cyber- and biotechnologies converge asymptotically in the 'rewriting' of the human code, mostly for commercial purposes.[49] From this perspective, the postmodern infatuation with complexity theory does not so much represent a break with cybernetics, the 'science of communication and control' (Wiener), as its ominous continuation as thermodynamics of the umpteenth generation. Symbiosis may have appeared at first as a clear break with the determinism of the grand narrative of DNA, but today the living organism is understood as a hypercomplex, open, self-organising system. Complexity theory generally analyses open systems as unstable, self-organising 'dissipative structures'. When such dissipative structures reach points of bifurcation, their behaviour and future pathways become unpredictable. Higher-order, more differentiated structures may emerge as a result.[50] Dissipative systems are regulated by the thermodynamics of open systems and can be analysed, described and formalised, at least in simple cases, as a mathematical model of differential equations. In the meantime powerful computer programs have been developed that are able to simulate the evolution of life (Hayles, 1999: 222–246). Through recursive looping of the computing operations, small deviations become quickly magnified, leading to complex interactions that generate unpredictable evolutions.[51] In such a synthesis of artificial life, the becoming of life over a couple of million generations is effectively replicated in the span of a few days by intelligent machines.

It is true that cybertechnologies abstract from the body and reduce the human to an intelligent machine that processes information. When the biological sciences reduce in turn the human to DNA, to a complex string of information that can be cybernetically decoded, recoded and recombined,[52] then it is not clear how complexity theory can help the human to escape unscathed from the digital pincer movement that reduces everything to the bits and bytes of the barcode. The universality of cybernetics realises the project of the *mathesis universalis* (Leibniz). When everything, life included, can potentially be levelled and reduced to information and the communication of modularised information, the effective techno-industrial realisation of the one-dimensional plane of immanence may be just around the corner. I bet that all that is possible can and will eventually be realised.

Inscribing every phenomenon and every event that cybernetics describes as a transitory moment of a global moment of 'trans-lation', everything can be 'transformed' into anything else, according to some algorithm. 'In principle, there's no naturally occurring genome that cannot be experimentally redesigned' (Haraway, 1997: 246). In theory, theory becomes virtually practical and the sciences become techno-sciences, to use a term coined by Jacques Ellul. Cybernetics is not just produced as a universal theory and epistemology, but also and already as a universal *praxis*, *techne* and technology. When scientific mastery is immediately coupled to the virtual mastery of its application, 'theory does no longer disclose anything (*épistémè*), but makes virtually everything (*technè*)' (Freitag, 2002: 291).

In spite of all the hype about genetic engineering and genetic therapies, one should, however, note that the biosciences do not really know how genes really function or how to explain their causal connection with illnesses. All they know is what the right and what the wrong sequences of nucleotides are, and how the genotypical variation is correlated with the phenotypical one. Wilfully confounding statistical correlation with causal explanation, they logically and pragmatically conclude that the wrong sequences have to be replaced by the right ones and, leaving aside all so-called epigenetic factors (everything besides the genes) as well as the complex interactions between genes, they simply explain the illness in terms of a wrong sequence of nucleotides. From the perspective of critical realism, which considers that an explanation is only given when the 'constant conjunction' (Hume) between genotype and phenotype is explained by a generative mechanism that actually produces the conjunction in question, the market-driven search for applications of molecular biology in the form of genetic tests and therapies can be interpreted as a practical strategy that aims to hide the deep theoretical and moral crisis of the new discipline of genomics.

The order of things

In his theory of translation, which has obviously inspired Latour and Woolgar's (1978) brilliant ethno-philosophical analysis of the laboratory life at the Salk Institute in California, Michel Serres (1974: 15–72), the French philosopher who translates science into poetry and poetry into science, presents a Leibnizian analysis of genetics as a progressive translation of the idea of biological generation into a calculus of bio-chemical reproduction: 'The history of genetics consists of a slow passage from the reproduction of animals to the production of texts' (Serres, 1974: 20). On the one hand, there are qualitative, observable phenotypical differences between living beings; on the other hand, there is an underlying, invisible genotypical code made up of letters, ciphers and characters. The passage, or translation, between the visible and the readable characters – *le visible et le lisible* – is effectuated when the phenomenal variety between the living beings is projected onto a single topological-energetic plane and deciphered as a continuous variation of the DNA-code through differential combination of the biochemical letters of which it is made up. Combining identity with difference into a heterogeneous network of relations between words and things that is able to explain the generation of the phenomenal variety of organs and organisms, including the most anomalous ones, in terms of the infinite possibility of combinations of the code, contemporary biology finds the traces of its code everywhere, precisely because it decodes the totality of nature by projecting the variations of its code onto a stable referent. 'When the reference is a plan, and the plan a collection of projected traces, every decomposition (*découpage*) of the real is like a book: Notification of the resolution of things into words, of the predominance of language' (Serres, 1977: 28).[53]

If the world of yesterday was a text, the world of today and tomorrow is a hypertext. Thanks to hyperlinks, texts can be interconnected so as to form one single, giant deterritorialised hypertext that is continuously evolving and expanding without any foreseeable limits (Lévy, 1998: 33–48). With the hypertext, there is no longer *a* text, but only text – just as we say that there is water or sand. The page we see on the screen of our computer is not really a text, but a small window that gives us a view on (though never an overview of) a potentially endless reserve of text. The hypertext is a rhizome in which 'any point can be and should be connected with any other point' (Deleuze and Guattari, 1980: 13). Paraphrasing the topological language of the theory of organised complexity, we could say that the hypertext is a complex network of overlapping and interconnected lines, ways and roads that meet at the summit or at the cross-roads, where they bifurcate again and go off in multiple directions. Given that any point or summit is virtually connected with any other summit in the network, 'there are as many ways as one wants to go from one summit to the other, or at least a very large number, as long as the number of summits is finite' (Serres, 1968: 12).

If the network is like a 'crumpled space' that can be folded, unfolded and refolded like a handkerchief, the global network itself is, in turn, made up of local networks of overlapping and interconnected ways that co-exist in the network and interfere in complex ways with one another.[54] Although the way to the summit cannot be predicted in a network of networks of overlapping and interconnected ways, the movement through space can very well be followed and traced mathematically, graphically and topographically on the plane of immanence.

One way or many, the progression to the summits can easily be traced and recoded in the binary terms of informatics. Life itself is nothing but a network, nothing but a hypertext, nothing but a microbacterial flux that can be traced and captured by the informatics of life. Nature is a hypertext and so is life itself. Life is a mess, a viral network, in which 'all bacteria may be seen as nodes in one great web of interconnectivity' (Clark, 2000: 26). Nature is no more than the provisional outcome of local processes; it is a complex dynamical system that plays across all distinctions of kinds. Scientifically understood, life can now be technologically rewritten. Genetics as bio-informatics is applied information technology. Four hundred years after Galileo Galilei famously pronounced that nature is written in the language of mathematics, the sciences of biology and communication are integrated into a unified cybernetic science of information that translates the totality of the world, life included, into a digital code – the code of the 'informatics of domination' (Haraway, 1991: 161–167) that underlies the rewriting of nature by the cyber- and biotechnologies of late industrial capitalism.

Mechanology as vitalist technology

Cybernetics teaches us that the organism is a living, self-organising system that reproduces itself (like a dictionary) through the self-referential production of the elements (words) out of which it is made up. But if the organism functions as a self-organising system, then the converse is also true: the self-organising system functions like an organism. It follows, not so much logically as techno-logically, that the scientific analysis of life can thus also become the template for the technological production of artificial systems as living systems, with the result that the age-old dividing line between mechanism and vitalism, technology and biology, simply vanishes. When the (Kantian) distinction between machine and organism is effectively overcome, the production of a vitalist technology or mechanology that studies inorganic living beings becomes possible – as a preamble and propedeutics to a mechanological sociology and a machinic society?

According to Gilbert Simondon (1969), who has developed the mechanological perspective, technology progresses and becomes progressively more 'concrete' as its starts to function as an artificial organism that has successfully integrated the elements as organs of a self-organising whole. The concrete technical object is in symbiosis with its environment. It has not only attained an internal coherence through the relative closure that allows for the recursivity of the internal operations as well as the circularity of causes and effects, but, by incorporating a part of the environment as an 'associated environment', it has also transformed the latter into a condition of its own functioning, integrating it thus as part of a self-organising system of causes and effects. 'Through technical concretisation', writes Simondon (1969: 46), 'the object that was at first artificial becomes more and more like a natural object.' Although the machinery functions like an organism that is in symbiosis with its environment – humans and the other machines with which it is interlinked – so as to form a single smoothly functioning machine, the symbiotic integration of the system and its environment can obviously not be accomplished by the machines themselves. On this point, cybernetics is plainly wrong, according to Simondon. Reducing the system to an organism, it forgets that the integration of the humans and the non-humans into a self-regulating machinery necessarily presupposes human intervention:

> Self-regulating machines need the human as a technician, i.e. as an associate.... This aspect of self-regulation through which the environment in its totality

> has to be taken into account cannot be accomplished by the machine on its own, however perfectly automated.… There's something living in a technical whole and the function of the integration of life can only be secured by human beings.
>
> (Simondon, 1969: 125)

Thanks to the technical intervention of human beings, the ontological hiatus between life and mechanism and, thus, also between human and machine, can finally and successfully be overcome in a living, self-regulating machine in which humans and machines are symbiotically integrated. Coupled to each other, humans and machines form an 'associated milieu' that is fully individualised and conditions itself through a multiplicity of recursive processes and feedback loops. Human beings may appear as servants of the machine, but in so far as their integration into the machine is in the last instance effectuated by human beings who understand how machines function, Simondon chastises theories of alienation for 'misunderstanding of the machine' (Simondon, 1969: 9). To overcome the alienation of human beings by the machine, we should understand that human beings are not opposed to machines, but among them. Machines are the 'associates' of humans, whereas humans are the 'shepherds' of the machines. It is only if we accept to become mediators and partners (or interpreters) of machines, rather than dominators (or legislators), that 'mediocracy' and democracy can coincide and that we shall eventually be able to move beyond alienation.

Speaking for the machines, Simondon may be right, but in his enthusiasm for the machine, he unfortunately has forgotten to relocate the shepherd and his machines into the socio-economic context that mediates their relation and to ask the crucial questions: Who mediates the mediators? Who educates the educators? And how can one be sure that the mediators of the machine are not themselves integrated into a megasystem as one of its living parts? After all, the essence of technology is nothing technological in itself. A machine is always social before it is technical, even if the social is invariably co-constructed by the technological. The windmill may well be linked to the feudal society, as Marx said in a famous passage, but the windmill does no more produce the feudal society than the steam machine produces the industrial society, or the computer the post-industrial one. Technological determinism is the ideology of technocracy, and technocracy is anti-democracy. What a machine is and what it does to humans depends on the humans that make it. But what they make and why they make it, depends in turn on the social machinery in which they are integrated. And today, the social machine in which they are integrated is the capitalist megamachine. To understand it and to understand what it does to human beings, we now turn to an analysis of global neo-capitalism that produces the producers, the consumers and life itself as a commodity.

III Neo-capitalism and the colonisation of life

'One day, perhaps, the century will be Deleuzian' (Foucault, 1994: II, 76). What was supposed to be an anti-platonic compliment by Foucault to his friend and philosophical companion can be interpreted with hindsight as a sociological statement about the state of the world. Continuing and radicalising the global trend of the late modern capitalism of the twentieth century, everything seems to indicate that the twenty-first century will not be spiritual and dialectical, but empiricist and materialist, pragmatic and performative, heterogeneous and machinic, chaosmotic and rhizomatic, hypercomplex and hypercapitalist. 'Pluralism = Monism' (Deleuze and Guattari, 1980: 31) – the magic formula of the becoming without end that Deleuze and Guattari were searching for on a thousand plateaus has been found, and almost realised, on a global scale and a single plane by contemporary neo-imperial capitalism.

Deleuzian capitalism

The machinic *phylum* that animates capitalism and flows through its unified body without organs is money. Money is always in flux and never rests. It is, as Simmel (1989) says in his *Philosophy of Money*, the objectivation of economic circulation in a symbol without substance that represents all possible goods and that, by substituting itself to them, speeds up the circulation of goods. Flowing through the subsystems of society, invading them from underneath, vivifying them from within, money is the blood that flows through the veins of capitalism and unifies the subsystems into the single market of the integrated world-system of the world economy (Braudel's *économie-monde*). Marx famously likened capital to a vampire. 'Capital is dead labour which, like a vampire, only becomes alive by sucking out living labour, and the more it sucks, the more it is lively' (Marx, 1968: 247). Marx had obviously understood the internal connection between labour and capital when he predicted its enlarged reproduction on a global scale, but fixed as he was on the category of work, he could not foresee that production would become post-industrial and that capital could exist and reproduce itself without labour (Vandenberghe, 2002b). But neo-Mancunian capitalism is inventive and productive, and to capitalise, it progressively leaves the factory and invades, like a parasite, all spheres of life and the life-world itself. At the end, it ends up, as we shall see, producing and consuming life itself.

The basic principle of rhizomatic sociology is that society is always *en fuite*, always leaking and fleeing, and may be understood in terms of the manner in which it deals with its lines of flight. There is always something that flees and escapes the system, something that is not controllable, or at least not yet controlled. With their machinic analysis of becoming, Deleuze and Guattari want to encourage leakages and 'cause a run off – *faire fuire* – as when you drill a hole in the pipe or open up the abscess' (Guattari, 1977: 120; Deleuze and Guattari, 1980: 249; Deleuze, 1990: 32). The intention is obviously anti-systemic – draining the system, digging holes, continuing the work of the old mole. Yet, today, the capitalistic system itself thrives on anti-systematicity, 'artificial negativity' (Adorno), or 'repetition and difference' (Deleuze). It feeds, as it were, on its own problems and in the process it changes itself and mutates. The 'repetition of the same' eventually leads to 'difference', which is tantamount to saying that the survival of capitalism means 'continuity with difference'. Capitalism explores and anticipates the deterritorialising lines of flight to capture them from without, enter into symbiosis with them, and redirect them from within, like a parasite, towards its own ends. Capitalism is inventive; its creativity knows no limits – 'it is of the viral type' (Deleuze and Guattari, 1980: 580).

Deleuze and Guattari put their anti-capitalist hopes in the guerrilla tactics of the schizoid minority that refuses to play the game of the self-content majority. Although they know that the skirmishes of the dispersed minority accompany the war machine of the entrepreneurial companies like their 'supplement', although they realise that capitalism advances like a war machine that feeds on the lines of flight and indicated that capitalism knows no internal limits, they nevertheless believed that capitalism would find its logical conclusion in the schizophrenic production of a free flow of desire: 'Schizophrenia is the external limit of capitalism itself' (Deleuze and Guattari, 1972: 292). What they apparently meant by that mad statement is that the final crisis of capitalism would eventually be generated not by the regulation or domestication of capitalism, but by the complete commodification of the desiring machines that we are. Only by accelerating the decadence of the present system, only through some kind of self-commodification in a consumerist potlatch would the capitalist system be beaten by its own game:

> Which is the revolutionary path, if there's one? To withdraw from the world market.... in a curious renewal of the 'economic solution' of the fascists? Or might it go in the opposite direction? To go still further in the movement of the market, of decoding and territorialisation? ... Not withdraw from the process, but going further, 'accelerating the process', as Nietzsche said. As a matter of fact, we ain't seen nothing yet.
>
> (Deleuze and Guattari, 1972: 285)[55]

The new spirit of capitalism

A quarter of a century later, the process of accumulation has accelerated to the point that *capitalism itself has become Deleuzian in form, in style and in content*. This junction is not accidental. As usual, an ironic and profoundly perverse relationship exists between the romantic ethic and the spirit of capitalism (Campbell, 1987: 202–227). Needless to say that I am not claiming that Deleuze's libertarian critique of capitalism was anti-critical or phoney from the start and that Deleuze is somehow the Giddens of the 1970s: a neo-liberal disguised as a libertarian, or Thatcher on LSD. What I am claiming is, rather, that capitalism has progressively integrated the critique of capitalism into its mode of functioning, with the result that capitalism appears stronger than ever, whereas the critique of capitalism seems rather disarmed.

In their magistral analysis of the new spirit of capitalism, Boltanski and Chiapello (1999: 241–290) have convincingly demonstrated that capitalism has co-opted the post-modernising critique of the 1960s and 1970s and used it as a way to reorganise itself and expand infinitely. The industrially organised capitalism of the 'golden thirties' (1945–1973) was essentially Fordist. Bureaucratic, hierarchical, pyramidal and centrally controlled, planified and Taylorised, oriented to the mass production of standardised goods, it was elephantine, rigid and alienating. The neo-corporatist arrangement between the government, the employers and the unions guaranteed job security, an indexed income, a steady career track and a pension, but this security hardly compensated for the employees' lack of autonomy. Attacking the dehumanising and disciplining, massifying and standardising nature of the 'capitalist-bureaucratic-technical-totalitarian society of planned exploitation and directed consumption' (Lefebvre) in the name of spontaneity, creativity and authenticity, the libertarian left took over the 'artistic critique' of capitalism of the bohemians and translated their grievances in a language that was inspired by surrealism and the 'masters of suspicion' (Marx, Freud and Nietzsche).

At first, the capitalists reacted to the 'artistic critique' of the *soixante-huitards* in a traditional way. They negotiated with the unions about 'quantitative demands' and granted a pay-rise but, realising that the critique did not abate in spite of the concessions, they opened discussions with the unions about the 'qualitative demands'. To solve the motivational crisis among the ranks of the disenchanted workers, they started introducing changes in the workplace that granted more autonomy to the workers. As the increase of freedom was being paid by a decrease in security, the result was most ambivalent. 'Through this change of politics, autonomy was somehow exchanged against security' (Boltanski and Chiapello, 1999: 274).

In the wake of the crisis of accumulation of the 1970s, the capitalists proceeded to a neo-liberal reinterpretation of the libertarian critique of capitalism of the radical left. Transforming the cultural contradiction into a sociological compatibility, they progressively introduced more and more flexibility in the organisation via the application of market principles. The old bureaucratic elephant of Fordism started to dance to the neoliberal tune, but the elephants' keepers had to hold on firmly if they didn't want to lose their jobs. As the Fordist regime of 'heavy' accumulation was supplanted by the post-Fordist regime of 'flexible accumulation', the organisation became not only 'leaner' (decentralisation of management, flattening of the pyramid, flexible specialisation and orientation to niche markets, rotation of tasks, life-long learning, outsourcing and subcontracting, etc.), it also became 'meaner'. The principles of the market were progressively introduced in the organisation, unions were sidelined, wages were individualised, contracts liberalised and labour time flexibilised, with the result that, 30 years later, the individualised, casualised and contractualised flexi-worker is confronted with insecurity and delivered to a completely restructured, radically flexibilised labour market on which he has not only to sell his labour force, but also his personality, his self and ultimately perhaps also his soul.

Together with the decline of the welfare state, the flexibilisation, casualisation and informalisation of labour might well lead in the near future to a dualisation of society and a 'Brazilianisation' of the world (Beck, 1999: 93–110).[56] Insecurity and vulnerability are no longer seen as a perverse effect of the dismantling of rigidities, but welcomed, valued and used to increase competitivity among the workers. Using old-fashioned language, we could say that insecurity is now 'functional'. Disorganising time as well as the career-track, flexible capitalism does not only apply the JIT (or just-in-time) approach to the punctual delivery of goods, but also to the workers and management itself. Conceived as some kind of 'standing reserve' that can be hired and fired at will, managers and workers alike have to become flexible, adaptable and multi-skilled, disposable and at the disposition of a new employer, available and 'at hand', ready for the spot market and prepared to seize any job that might improve their situation. The emphasis that is put on adaptability and availability for the market transforms the worker into a performing 'actor-networker' who behaves strategically and constantly looks out for opportunities to enhance his social capital by making connections, always more connections, on which he can market his human capital, his connections and his personality. The good networker who treats his or her person as a marketable asset is a master in self-presentation and decorum. Promising to give himself entirely in any project, he remains in fact unattached to the job and to his self in order to remain at the disposition for any other project that might come up. Redefining his self as the opportunity may require, the actor-networker treats his personality as a mask, reverting thereby to the original meaning of the term *persona* as the-one-who-speaks-through-the-mask.

Coincidence or not, the fact that the identity of the networker is variable and performed in and through the relations that he enters into chimes all too well with the contemporary discourses on performativity, mobility, fluidity, complexity, topology, relations, networks, performances, displacements, multiple selves, etc. that follow the 'postmodern flip' in the human sciences.[57] In the meantime, those fashionable discourses have also been introduced in the 'cultural circuit of capitalism' and discovered by the consultant gurus and hero-managers of the business schools (Thrift, 1999). Transposing metaphors of the body from biology and physics to economics and psychology, the post-Darwinian message of complexity theory is relatively straightforward: corporations, groups and individuals must become flexible and fluid, transformative and innovative, agile and nimble like complex biological systems that successfully survive in nature (Martin, 1994).[58] Displacing the politics of distribution by a politics of identity, those discourses have started to infiltrate and infect society at large – like a virus.

With hindsight, we can now see that the hatred of the collective and transcendence, the pragmatism of connections and the disindividuation of the self that is the trademark of Deleuze & Co. is not accidental; it anticipates, expresses, accompanies and helps to perform the subject as actor-networker and to transform society into a network of transient associations. Chaos and disorder used to be enemies that had to be weeded out. With the transition from 'heavy' and 'solid' to 'light' and 'liquid' modernity (Bauman, 2000), order as such is devalued, while chaos becomes the norm and the means to rationalise and flexibilise the enterprise. Were it not for its celebratory tone, we might even have welcomed

Deleuze and Guattari's borderline description of schizophrenia as a more or less adequate expression of the disorganisation of time, the fracturing of life-narratives and the superficiality of relations that characterises the corrosion of character of the networkers of the new economy (Sennett, 1998). As it stands, I am more tempted, however, to see the 'Deleuze-effect' as a syndrome and symptom of a countercultural 'bad trip' – or 'the sixties gone toxic', to borrow a phrase from Jameson's (1991: 117) justly celebrated essay on the cultural logic of late capitalism.

Colonisation, commodification and reification

From a systemic point of view, the flexible rationalisation of the organisation that transforms the worker into an actor-networker can best be understood in terms of the generalised introduction of market principles in the organisation, with the result that the boundaries between the organisation and its environment (markets and other organisations) are eroded and that the relations between the inside and the outside are radically transformed. Decentralisation and segmentation of the organisation itself, autonomisation of its unities and marketisation of their internal relations, increased self-organisation of the unities and of the sub-unities, introduction of modes of financial calculation and budgetary obligations, translation of programmes into costs and benefits that can be given an accounting value, orientation towards shareholders' value, all those structural transformations that accompany the introduction of the principles of exchange, competition and calculation in what was heretofore a hierarchical-monocratic-bureaucratic organisation effectively convert the organisation into a flexible and profitable network of enterprises pursuing a common project of sustainable capitalisation. When intra-organisational networks are interconnected in inter-organisational networks that cut across sectors and when those start to network and become interconnected on a global scale in a machinic network of sorts, we become the involuntary witnesses of the rhizomatic spreading of networks across sectors and frontiers that marks the passage from the network enterprise to the global network society of late capitalism. The global economy is not made up of nations, but of transnational networks of companies that spread through the world in search of cheap labour and a quick buck. 'Networks, not firms, have become the actual operating unit' (Castells, 1996: 171).

Although the spread of networks might appear anarchic at first, it should be noted that the centrifugal process of decentralisation is balanced by a centripetal process of concentration and command. In the archipelago of networks, there is a mainland of power that commands the 'decentralised concentration' of capital. In his trilogy on the rise of the network society, Manuel Castells has drawn attention to the fact that the global network is geared to the extraction of profit and enframed by a 'meta-network of financial flows' that is operated by electronic networks: 'Networks converge toward a meta-network of capital that integrates capitalists interests at the global level and across sectors and realms of activity' (Castells, 1996: 506), and 'Thus, global financial markets, and their networks of management, are the actual collective capitalist, the mother of all accumulations' (Castells, 1998: 343).[59]

The virtual integration of regional, national, multinational and transnational corporations into a global network of networks is not only driven by the introduction of market principles (marketisation as input); the thirst for profit is also what drives the expansion of the networks through the globe and triggers the colonising process of universal commodification (commodification as output) that characterises contemporary neo-capitalism.[60]

Unlike the imperial capitalism of yesteryear, which had to expand through space and integrate its non-capitalist environment in a colonial system of exploitation to guarantee the continuous extraction and accumulation of surplus value, contemporary network capitalism no longer colonises the world. It colonises the life-world instead and introduces the calculating and objectifying logic of the economy and the administration into everyday-life, threatening thereby the communicative structure of society (Habermas, 1981: I, ch. 4). Having progressively integrated the markets of the periphery and the semi-periphery into a single world market, the logic of the market-society progressively invades and colonises the life-world 'like the masters of colonisation in tribal societies' by commodifying culture, the mind, the person and, ultimately, life itself.[61]

Once capitalism has conquered the whole world and covered it with a financial network that eludes control by the states and captures the heterogeneous totality of monetary fluxes, capital starts to operate like a Deleuzian machine with a 'general axiomatic of decoded flows' (Deleuze and Guattari, 1980: 567) that functions on a single plane. This axiomatic is general because it transvalues all possible goods into commodities and recodes all possible values into determinate prices,[62] and it is global because it deterritorialises the flows and operates in the smooth space of world-capitalism. Saying that capital operates as a general and global axiomatic system that functions on the plane of immanence is a convoluted way of saying that it rules the whole world and forms an empire that no longer has an outside and that can thus no longer be criticised from without, but only from within, through a subversion of the axiomatics of capital.[63] When the lines of flight are sealed or, what amounts to the same, captured and co-opted by the axiomatics of capital, there is nothing that is not enframed by capitalism, nothing that escapes the global flows of capital, though that does not mean that there is no alternative. Only that the alternative has to come from within capitalism.

To survive and further expand, capital had to shift from colonisation in the strict sense to colonisation in a more encompassing sense. To overcome its dependency on labour, it had to shift from an extensive to a more intensive form of production and integrate the other spheres of life and, ultimately, the production of life itself, into its axiomatics. Indeed, having reached the limits of the exploitation of labour, capital transgresses them and starts to exploit *'immaterial labour'* – that is, intellectual, communicative, symbolic or emotional labour that is produced outside of the sphere of production.[64] To continue the process of accumulation and overcome its dependency on labour, capitalism had to exploit the life-world and extract value from communicative processes that are not productive in the strict sense and that it cannot produce itself, but on which it is nevertheless dependent. The exploitation of material labour is no longer sufficient; intellectual labour has now to be exploited as well.

Capitalism is innovative. To innovate continuously it constantly draws on knowledge that it does not produce itself, but that is the result of individual and collective processes of communication, cooperation and learning that take place in the life-world. With the privatisation of the commons, the boundaries between production and communication, production and consumption, labour and leisure, paid and unpaid work disappear. As the consumption of services, cultural goods and information during leisure time produces the knowledge and skills that capitalism needs to constantly innovate, the distinction between production and consumption collapses. When free time becomes productive, everything becomes work. By becoming the source of the production of values through communication, innovation and continuous improvisation, 'immaterial labour eventually merges with the work of the production of the self' (Gorz, 2003: 20).

With the exploitation of immaterial labour, capitalism takes a 'linguistic turn' and extends its reach into the lifeworld. A double extension of capital takes place, which is both quantitative and qualitative. Echoing the Marxist distinction between the 'formal' and the 'real' subordination of labour under capital, i.e. between the extraction of surplus value that operates by means of an extension of the workday and accumulation by means of the technological rationalisation of the production process, cognitive capitalism accumulates not only more, but also differently. With Deleuze and Guattari, we can conceptualise the colonisation of the life-world in terms of a progressive generalisation of machinic control beyond the sphere of production and a concomitant interiorisation of domination by the subject. When the machinic production of capital captures the subjects to control them from within, 'enslavement by the machine' mutates into 'subjection to the machine'.

Since the machinic production of capital has left the factory and spread to the whole of society, the capitalist machine reproduces itself on an enlarged scale by producing the subjects that produce and consume the products they have produced. Deleuze and Guattari suggest that modern technology has successfully overcome the opposition between enslavement and subjection, domination and submission or alienation and subjectification. In the cybernetic 'human–machine systems' of advanced liberal capitalism, humans and machines have been coupled through a multiplicity of recursive processes and feedback loops and integrated in some kind of a living, self-regulating megamachine that operates globally on a single plane. Having incorporated the humans as components of its own machinery, humans have become the living medium and mediation of the system: 'A small amount of subjectification took us away from machinic enslavement, but a large amount brings us back to it' (Deleuze and Guattari, 1980: 572).

Using language that posthumanists self-consciously avoid, we could say with Adorno (1975: I, 391) – but against Simondon (see above) – that 'reification reaches its limits with the reification of humans'. When the constraints of the system are no longer imposed on humans from without, but alienation is mediated through them, alienation is introjected and reaches its very limits. Overdramatising a bit, we could say that the end of alienation coincides asymptotically with the end of Man. Indeed, when enslavement by the machine is no longer opposed to machinic, but both tend to coincide with the 'becoming-machine' of Man, subjection becomes the mode of alienation. Subjected to a capitalist megamachine that produces willing subjects, the latter have been fully integrated into a living machine that functions not against their will, their thoughts, their desire, their body, etc., but *through* those.

Deleuze and Guattari's dialectics of subjectification remind me of Adorno and Horkheimer's dialectic of the enlightenment. Although I have always opposed their bleak depiction of late capitalist society as a 'totally administered world' (*total verwaltete Welt*) on metatheoretical and social-theoretical, as well methodological and empirical grounds (Vandenberghe, 1997–1998, 2009), I am now tempted to consider their analysis as a brilliant anticipation of what was to come. At this point, I must confess that I am slightly afraid that the contemporary conjunction and co-evolution of science, technology and neo-capitalism might well offer a belated confirmation of some of the most radical theses on reification, alienation and commodification that have been propounded by the first generation of the Frankfurt School.[65] To flesh out my worries, I will analyse the structural transformations of contemporary capitalism and underline their alienating consequences. More particularly, I will present the '*government of the subject*', the '*commercialisation of experience*' and the '*commodification of life*' as three overlapping processes that undergird the current forms of societal rationalisation and reification. Progressively invading the domains of *the person, culture and nature* in order to control and commodify them, advanced liberal capitalism colonises the life-world and life itself. It not only threatens the communicative infrastructure of the life-world, which is bad enough, but worse: the conjunction and integration of capital, science and technology potentially puts the human race itself at risk and opens thereby, though probably not in the way that the structuralists had expected it, the perspective of the end of the human sciences.[66]

Governing the self

Capitalism not only produces objects, but also subjects and subjectivities. To assure the conditions of its own enlarged reproduction, it has not only to produce goods and services, but also the producers and consumers of those products and services. Those processes of the production and reproduction do not remain constant, however, but are historically variable, as Michel Foucault has amply shown in his genealogical studies of the mid-1970s, from *Discipline and Punish* to *The History of Sexuality*. Analysing the epochal changes in the epistemic, normative and institutional constellations through the ages (Suárez Müller, 2004), Foucault used his study of the changes in the penal regime of the eighteenth and nineteenth centuries to theorise the different forms of production of subjects and subjectivities – from the 'sovereign power' of the Ancien Régime to the 'disciplinary power' of modernity and from there perhaps also, as Deleuze (1986, 1990: 229–247) suggests, to the regulatory power of the emerging 'society of control'.

In the society of control, which regulates conduct through the continuous modulation of affects, disciplinary power is more economic and liberal, more subtle and indirect, more decentralised and capillary, micro and molecular, diffused and individualised, though not less pervasive and effective than the forms of power that preceded it. Unlike sovereign power, which is exercised through corporal punishments and decisions about life and death, disciplinary power is not repressive but democratic and productive:

> It is a power that aims to produce forces, to make them grow and regulate them rather than block, submit or destroy them.... It is a power that is positively exercised over life, that attempts to administer, raise, multiply and exercise precise controls and global regulations over it.
>
> (Foucault, 1976: 179–180)[67]

Targeting the self of the subjects through a host of panoptic and confessional technologies, the former operating through the external, the latter through the internal environment of the individual, it aims to produce docile bodies and responsible subjects. Disciplinary power does not destroy the subject: it produces it as one of its effects. In the original project of the *History of Sexuality*, which was initially to count six volumes and not just three or four, Foucault wanted to enlarge his genealogy of ethico-political subjectification, from the Greeks to the Middle Ages and beyond, by illustrating how responsible, autonomous, free subjects are produced, not just in prisons, factories, schools and hospitals, but continuously and throughout society. Looking at his last investigations on the 'care of the self' from the perspective of his middle, more sociological period, we come to realise that what he was really after was a genealogy of the present society of control that shows, through a careful analysis of the technologies of subjectification and other techniques of the self, how disciplinary power produces subjects not against their will, but by adopting and co-opting their will, thus precisely *through* their will. There are thus not two Foucaults, the one of the analytics of power and the other of the problematics of the subject, but only one, who analyses power in terms of the government of the self and the others. As Foucault (1994: 223) himself says: 'It is thus not power, but the subject that constitutes the general theme of my research.'[68]

Systematically extending the scattered remarks of the last Foucault on pastoral power, the police and government into a sociological theory of power, knowledge and subjectivity in advanced liberal societies, Nikolas Rose (1999a, 1999b), the animator and instigator of the Anglo-Australian school of 'governmentality-studies', has forcefully introduced the notion of 'government' over and against the notion of domination to theorise and analyse the multiplicity of theories and vocabularies, methodologies and technologies, instruments and techniques of rule (from the layout of buildings and the structures of timetables to the statistical methods of calculation and the psychoanalytic ones of interpretation) through which a heterogeneous network of governmental and non-governmental authorities and agencies (from the Ministry of Economic Affairs all the way down to the economist, the manager, the journalist, the teacher, the priest, the doctor, the counsellor and the psychoanalyst) seek to control and regulate, shape and modulate the conduct of individuals that constitute a population by working on and through their aspiration and intentions.[69]

Government is a form of power referring to the 'conduct of conduct' (Foucault, 1994: IV, 237). To govern is not to impose directly a certain action, but to control it indirectly through the structuration of the possible field of options and actions of individuals. In so far as governing means governing through the freedom, aspirations and beliefs of the individuals rather than in spite of them, government does not annul the capacity of individuals as agents, but presupposes it and draws on it to further its own ends: 'Personal autonomy is not the antithesis of political power, but a key term in its exercise, the more so because most individuals are not merely the subjects of power but play a part in its operations' (Rose and Miller, 1992: 174). Appealing to the aspirations of self-determination and self-realisation, the government of subjects passes through the personal strivings of each and every individual for self-fulfilment. Power does not crush aspirations, but acknowledges and adjusts itself to them, while instrumentalising and utilising them for its own objectives.

In the same way as one should not identify government and domination, one should not identify government with the State and avoid the paranoiac prism of conspiracy theories that seek the 'interpelating' hand of the State in any of its ideological apparatuses. Rather than thinking of the State extending its power through its apparatuses, the analytics of power 'decapitates' the State and concentrates its analysis of the powers of freedom on the proliferation of a heterogeneous multiplicity of governmental and non governmental, public and private, legal, scientific, economic, religious, educational, therapeutic and other organisations and institutions, authorities and agencies that seek to regulate, modulate and influence the internal worlds of organisations, institutions, families and individuals by shaping them in desired directions. Among the plurality of mediating instances that intervene between the State and the individuals while interconnecting, intentionally or unintentionally, the aspirations of the authorities and the activities of individuals, one finds, among others, bureaucrats and experts, philosophers and philanthropists, sociologists and psychologists, doctors and hygienists, managers and planners, priests and parents. Although all those different actors follow their own interests, confront their own problems and look for their own solutions, each and any of them can potentially be 'enrolled' by other actors who 'translate' their interests and bring them thereby into a loose alignment of sorts, forming a governmental 'dispositif' (Foucault), 'assemblage' (Deleuze) or 'actor-network' (Latour) of sorts:[70]

> Each of these diverse forces can be enrolled in a governmental network to the extent that it can translate the objectives and values of others into its

> own terms, to the extent the arguments of another become consonant with and provide norms for its own ambitions and actions.
>
> (Rose and Miller, 1992: 10)

Thanks to the continuous translations of the respective epistemologies, moralities and ideologies into common visions of the 'good life' and their materialisation into concrete programmes of action, white papers, reports, books, plans, etc., flexible and loose associations are established between a variety of agents that come to share a common language and common interests and that seek to shape, each in its own way, the practices of individuals by summoning them to become loving parents, ardent consumers, active citizens and enthusiastic employees. As networks form and relays, translations and connections are established to the mutual benefit of those who govern and those who are governed, power is disseminated through the whole of society and a machinic assemblage without exterior is performatively constructed that couples from within the political aspirations of the authorities to the individual motivations of the subjects.

Drawing attention to the fundamental role that theories, technologies, techniques, methodologies and methods of government play in rendering the practices of individuals, groups, organisations and populations thinkable, representable, calculable and administrable, or in short: *governable*, genealogists of the present insist on the importance of studying empirically the humble and mundane technologies, instruments and 'inscription devices' (Latour) by which all kind of authorities seek to instantiate government and rule 'at a distance':

> Techniques of notation, computation and calculation; procedures of examination and assessment; the invention of devices such as surveys and presentational forms such as tables; the standardisation of systems of training and the inculcation of habits; the inauguration of professional specialisms and vocabularies; building design and architectural forms – the list is heterogeneous and is, in principle, unlimited.
>
> (Miller and Rose, 1990: 8)

In their detailed studies of the variegated techniques of social regulation, governmentality studies draws on several specialised subdisciplines like science studies, economics, accounting or architecture, but reconfigures their materials within the framework of a political sociology of power.

Against this background we can now analyse some of the major transformations of the mode of social regulation that have intervened in the last quarter of a century and that characterise 'advanced liberalism' (Rose, 1993, 1999b: 137–166). We have already seen that capitalism has been able to restructure itself and expand in the 1970s and 1980s through a neoliberal co-optation of the libertarian aspirations to autonomy and authenticity that were voiced by the new left in the 1960s and the 1970s and the new right in the 1970s and the 1980s. Translating and displacing the aspirations of autonomy, freedom, initiative, creativity, spontaneity, originality and responsibility of the individual into a political programme that aims to roll back the State and to 'govern without governing society' (Rose, 1993: 298), neo-liberalism has succeeded in turning the critique of alienation, domination and bureaucracy to the advantage of the market. Thatcherism, Reaganism and, in its wake, also 'Third Way-ism', have reactivated the anti-statism of classical liberalism and linked it up with a series of techniques that has rendered the criticism of welfare and bureaucracy 'governmental' and, thus, implementable. Through liberalisation, privatisation and budgetary restraint, it has paved the way to a system of 'governance without government'.

Compared with the old labourist, Keynesian and Fordist mode of social regulation of the 'golden thirties', the new liberal mode is much more global though dispersed and multi-layered, much more marketised and consumerist, and also much more accountable and controllable. Four aspects stand out: *globalisation, marketisation, privatisation* and *control*. First, social regulation is now on the verge of becoming a global affair (Bayart, 2004). Globalisation introduces a major change of scale of government. Although local and national regulations are obviously still important, a whole series of governmental agencies are now operating not only below, but also, as the phrase goes, above and across states. Local, regional, national and international agencies and authorities, like the EU or the GATT, for instance, as well transnational non- and quasi-governmental organisations, like the ILO or Greenpeace, are now increasingly coordinating their policies in the domain of health and labour standards, economical and ecological regulation or anti-terrorism, to name a few examples, and exerting sophisticated and effective pressures on states, organisations and individuals. Government is increasingly privatised (e.g. privatisation of public services, but also of war – mercenaries making up 10 per cent of the 'coalition of the willing' in the second Gulf War) while, conversely, private instances are publicised (e.g. creation of public law through contractual agreements, such as the multilateral agreement on investments (MAI) that spanned the battle of Seattle). What is emerging, therefore, is a decentred, dispersed and multi-layered system of government at the global level. Second, a whole range of marketised mechanisms (contracts and subcontracting, public–private partnerships, quasi-markets, internal, budgeting, end-user empowerment, etc.) have been introduced into economic life to replace the rigidities of central planning and stimulate competition not only among private firms, but also among the public services. Through the introduction of competition in social services, the privatisation of public services and the generalised transformation of clients into customers, the scope of economic rationality has vastly expanded. Third, the productivistic logic of the enterprise and the consumerist language of choice have spread from the economic to the individual sphere. Through techniques of market research, advertisement, designing, branding, life-styling and, not to forget, credit, individuals are seduced into consumption and summoned to become entrepreneurs of their own life, as it were, through the acquisition of goods and services. As Zygmunt Bauman (1995: 270) pithily remarks: 'It is thus not only the gas industry but life in general that has been privatised.' This 'privatisation of life' has now invaded all spheres of life: production, consumption, education, leisure, health and even death. Fourth, to render organisations accountable, transparent and controllable, audits are now regularly used (as British academics trying to cope with the constraints of the Research Assessment Exercises (RAE) and the Teaching Quality Assessments (TQA) no doubt have noticed). If individuals are controlled through the 'conduct of conduct', organisations are for their part regulated through auditing, or the 'control of control', as Power has aptly called it (Power, 1994). Transforming organisations in order to make them conform to ideals of auditability, auditing attempts to act indirectly upon systems of control rather than directly upon first-order activities. In so far as the technologies of government of advanced liberalism embody new receptivities to private sectors of management, we can conclude by saying that they are political technologies that 'enterprise up' individuals and organisations alike.

The commodification of culture

It has become commonplace to note that late capitalism has taken a 'cultural turn'. This cultural turn in the economy should be understood in the context of the more general de-differentiation of the social subsystems that characterises postmodern societies (Crook *et al.*, 1992). The collapse of the boundaries between culture and the economy works in two ways: the economy interpenetrates culture and transforms it into a commodity (economisation of culture), while culture is coupled in return to the economy, losing its autonomy in the process (culturalisation of the economy). The dissolution of the autonomy of the domain of culture does not mean that culture loses its importance. To the contrary, it gains in importance and effectiveness. Conceiving of the dissolution of culture as an 'explosion', an astute observer of the postmodern scene has noticed 'a prodigious expansion of culture throughout the social realm, to the point at which everything in our social life – from economic value and state power to practices and the very structure of the psyche itself – can be said to have become cultural' (Jameson, 1991: 48).

As a result of this 'shifting out' of culture through the social realm, culture assumes the role that was once imparted to the material forces of production. In so far as the whole production process has shifted from the production of goods to the production of signs, this shifting out is in line with the shift from an industrial to a post-industrial and post-Fordist mode of capitalist production. What is increasingly being produced and consumed nowadays are not material objects but semiotic objects or signs. As the aesthetisation of commodities progresses, the design and branding of consumer products become more and more important. Objects are increasingly aestheticised and emptied of their material content, with the aesthetic form trumping the latter. Use value becomes secondary, and at the end, everything happens as if it is now the exchange value that induces the use value. Even more, according to Baudrillard, the exchange value simply absorbs the latter, becomes self-referential and turns into a simulacrum, that is, into a copy without an original. Although Baudrillard's influential theory of 'hyperreality' playfully, and at times, cynically exaggerates the extent of the dematerialisation of reality, there can be no doubt about the fact that the 'spectacularisation' (Debord) of commodities indeed characterises contemporary consumer culture.

Contemporary mass culture is more and more commodified, but that does not mean that it is standardised and homogenised. To the contrary, commodification leads to diversification and heterogenisation. Today's mass culture is pluralist, heterogeneous, fragmented and diversified, or postmodernist, to use a vague word which summarises it all. Diversity sells, and to guarantee a constant access to diversity, the margins of the sub- and countercultures of rebellious youth are constantly inspected for novelty. Counterculture aims to subvert the mainstream, while the mainstream attempts to co-opt the subculture. The idea that consumer culture is a form of conformism has become a commonplace of anti-consumerism. It obscures the fact that capitalism feeds on 'negativity' and 'difference' and that rebellion is actually fuelling the carousel of fashion and, thus, is implicitly complicit in the making of 'fashion victims'. Consumer culture is hip. Advertising tells us that we are unique and different, non-conformist and not part of the masses, and sells us what we need to become what we are – a nose ring, a tattoo, the latest double CD of Paul Oakenfold or whatever else might be needed to distinguish oneself from one's fellow punters and to make an 'artwork of one's self'. The idea of conspicuous consumption has been outmoded by hip consumerism: 'It's no longer about keeping up with the Joneses, it's about being different from them' (Rutherford, quoted by Ray and Sayer, 1999: 11).

In the new age of cultural capitalism, it is not only popular culture – 'folklore and proletarian art, plus sports' (Kuper, 1999: 229) – that is commodified. Since high culture is no longer exempted from the free market, but considered as an upmarket niche on the high street, we can say that culture as such, understood as the totality of symbolic expressions that determines 'the whole way of life, from birth to the grave, from morning to night and even in sleep' (Eliot), has become colonised and integrated as a profitable province of the economic system. Culture, which was once considered in opposition to the vulgar interests of the economic sphere, has become a commodity – and 'nothing else but a commodity' (Adorno, 1977: 338).

The 'webs of significance' that human beings spin around themselves to make sense of the world have been systematically raided by the culture industries. This was already the case when Adorno and Horkheimer coined the phrase to refer to the American mass culture of the 1940s and 1950s but, following the digital revolution, the commercialisation of culture has progressed to the point that experience itself is now on the verge of becoming a commodity, and nothing else but a commodity. The integration of computers, telecommunications, cable television, consumer electronics, broadcasting, publishing and entertainment in an integrated communications network that is largely controlled by a few global corporations (Disney, Time Warner, Bertelsmann and Vivendi Universal) has given commercial enterprises unprecedented control over human experiences. With the transformation of the culture industry into an 'industry of programmes', human experience has become the consummate commodity of the new capitalist economy. The mind is more or less directly plugged into the terminals of the multi-media: 'The technical system that was up to now essentially a dispositif to transform material has become a system to transform spirit, operated by a whole network that transmits programmes' (Stiegler, Bernard, 2001: 136).

Integrating Leroi-Gourhan, Derrida and Husserl into a theory of external memory, Bernard Stiegler has argued that the transmission of television programmes leads to a massive synchronisation of the individual consciences for the sake of profit. 'When millions, perhaps hundred millions of people watch the same event on television, at the same time, live, consciences all over the world interiorise, adopt and live the same temporal objects at the same time' (Stiegler, 2004: 51). This synchronisation of consciousness is at the same time a programmation of the mind. What is at stake is the control of the time of attention in order to control the information, the cognition, the volition, the affects, the pulsions – in short, the mind and the body of the consumer. In order to sell soap, sweets, laptops, mobile phones, plane tickets or dreams, one has to address consciences, and those consciences are markets, or perhaps even a 'meta-market' (Stiegler, 2004: 46, 125) that grants potential access to all the other markets.

Jeremy Rifkin (2001) analyses the long-term shift from industrial to cultural production. He contends that hypercapitalism is entering a new phase, the 'age of access', in which markets are giving way to networks and ownership of goods is steadily replaced by paid access to interconnected supplier–user networks. Whether it is music, games or films, cuisine, travel or theme parks, sports or gambling, what one pays for and what is marketed is not so much the goods and the services as the cultural experiences one consumes. By connecting the mind to the market and selling lived experiences, capitalism has commodified time and culture. Slowly but surely it comes to resemble the 'context of total blindness' (*totaler Verblendungszusammenhang*) that Adorno had anticipated by exaggerating and extrapolating the dumbing impact of the culture industries: 'Capitalism is making its final transition into full-blown cultural capitalism, appropriating not only the signifiers of cultural life and the artistic forms of communication that interpret those signifiers but lived experience as well' (Rifkin, 2001: 144). As the culture industry gives way to the 'experience industry', there is hardly a sphere of life that escapes the reach of capitalism. By paying for access to experiences and for the experiences themselves, we become, so to speak, the consumers of our own lives.[71]

The colonisation of life

Having colonised the life-world, capitalism turns its attention to nature and invades life itself to modify and commodify it. Since the late 1970s, the large multinational corporations, which had closely observed the developments in molecular biology and genetic engineering, began to invest substantially in biotechnology. Dependent on the universities for their expertise and on oil, chemical and pharmaceutical corporations for capital, the biotech industry rapidly enrolled the biosciences to redesign, patent and re-engineer life itself for commercial purposes. The first transgenic organisms appeared in the 1980s and by 1988 Oncomouse™, a transgenic mouse, designed for research in cancer and marketed by Du Pont at $50–75 per piece, became the first patented animal in the world (Haraway, 1997: 49–118). Since then, the biosciences have made great progress and, using viruses as vectors for transmitting DNA between different species, they have fabricated and patented some of the most monstrous creatures for the sake of profit: tobacco plants with firefly genes; fish and tomatoes with anti-freeze genes; headless embryos of mice and frogs, dispensing with their superfluous heads so that they can harvest their organs; monkeys with jellyfish genes and human embryo cells merged with enucleated cows' eggs; cloned calves and sheep carrying human genes, cows producing lactoferrin, a human protein useful for treating infections; and not to forget, Dollies, sheep that are cloned, and Pollies, sheep that are both cloned and genetically engineered (Best and Kellner, 2001: 171–175).

Involved in a highly competitive race for the human race, the private corporation Celera Genomics and the publicly funded Human Genome Project announced in 2000 that they had completed a rough draft of the entire human genome. While the atlas of the genome can be consulted for payment, the question about the ownership of the human genome remains unsolved: does the human genome belong to the individual person with a particular genome, to the scientist or the company who has identified particular genes or nucleotide sequences, or is it the common heritage of mankind? The question is momentous: if the human genome is the collective property of humanity, deliberative intervention should never occur without collective deliberation. If it is not, then the genome can be patented, privatised and subjected to monopolistic control.[72] Observing the 'gene rush', NGOs predict that in less than 25 years, much of the 'genetic commons' – the legacy of millions of years of biological and cultural evolution – will have been isolated, identified and enclosed in the form of intellectual property, controlled, for the most part, by a handful of biotechnological corporations without frontiers (or scruples) like Monsanto, Novartis, Du Pont or Aventis. What is seen as intellectual property is often, as Vandana Shiva says in her critical analysis of property rights, TRIPs and patents, 'information "pirated" from non-western societies and indigenous communities' (Shiva, 2001: 33).

Moving from the molecular to the molar body, we can now proceed with our analysis of the colonisation of life and further inspect the commodification of the body and its parts.[73] Enslavement, exploitation, prostitution, body trafficking and other practices that reduce human bodies to a pair of hands, a pair of breasts or a vagina are only some examples of the commodification of the body that precede the systematic objectification, fragmentation, modification and commodification of the body by modern medicine. Driven by a highly technocratic ethos, the medical sciences drive out the common sense conceptions of the body as a unitary object, as something that we 'are' rather than as something that we 'have'. Abstracting the body from the human being that is embodied (dualism of body and mind), as well as from the other human beings (individualism) and the cosmos to which it was once intimately tied through a cascade of homologies (disenchantment of the world), the medical sciences consider the body as something that exists in itself and functions like a machine, or, to quote Descartes, like a 'watch composed of wheels and counterweights' (Le Breton, 1990: 61–82; see also Leder, 1992). Objectivating the body by means of sophisticated visual techniques (such as X-rays, sonography, endoscopy, magnetic resonance imaging) that render the body transparent and thus also permeable, the medical sciences increasingly conceive the body as an array of parts, organs and tissues that can be repaired or, if needed, replaced by other parts, organs and tissues. Like the global economy, the body is now an open, complex, flexible machine, with spares and parts available from the 'body shop' (Kimbrell, 1993).

The market of transplants (organs, tissues, or fluids from other bodies, living or dead) and implants (artificial organs or body parts made of plastic, metal, nylon, or other synthetic materials) has led to the fragmentation of the body and the breaching of its boundaries. In an interesting article on 'spare part surgery', Cecil Helman notes that the body has been reconceptualised as a 'machine' (and 'machines' reconceptualised as 'people'): 'The body is now a collection of 'parts' or 'pieces', for which 'spares' are available when they finally wear out' (Helman, 1988: 15). Through transplants and implants, the individual is permanently linked to the world of the market, industry and science and transformed into a 'potential prosthesis' for another individual (Le Breton, 1990: 234; 1993: 296). Whereas the implants and prostheses are mass-produced by the industry, the transplants and organs are available on the world market[74] – or on the black market, as the bodies of innocents and poor people are now raided once again by organised body snatchers with links to the underworld.[75]

Through the implantation of mass-produced heart valves, pace makers, artificial hip joints, prosthetic arms and legs and synthetic lenses, the patient becomes effectively a 'cyborg'. Through the transplantation of mass-marketed hearts, kidneys, lungs, lymph nodes, nerves, bone marrow and the infusion of blood and plasma, she or he becomes – like Frankenstein – a living patchwork of foreign bodies. Through implants and transplants, the cybernetic organisms become a living node in the medical network of commercial relations between producers, suppliers, doctors and nurses. 'Overall, it is the older members of this society who, as they emerge from the workforce, will be reincorporated into the world of industry through the ageing of the bodies' (Helman, 1988: 15). Ageing, they become consumers of implants and transplants; sick, they become cyborgs, attached to a complex array of machines that keep them alive; dying, they become potential donors of organs. In all cases, the bodies have been invaded by the medical industry and linked to a complex, evolving transnational network of corporate actors and commodified actants.

The commodification of the human body transforms the body into capital. When the medical industry proposes the patient a transplant or an implant, it modifies and commodifies the body and transforms it into human capital. When the bio-industry proposes genetic tests and promises genetic cures, it speculates on life itself and accumulates capital within us. While posthumanists enthusiastically welcome the new bio-, cyber- and nano-technologies that could modify our inherited genetics, physiology, neurophysiology and neurochemistry, they forget the social relations in which those technologies are embedded and avoid the problem of capital in their grandiose projections of humanity. 'Capital R us': capital is within us and we are within capital. In this very specific sense, we can indeed say with Rikowski (2003: 143) that 'we are already transhuman as a life-form within the social universe of capital: We are capital, human capital, humanity capitalised.'

Although capitalism tends to invade the totality of existence, one should not conclude too quickly, however, that reification has become total, that everything is commodified and that there is no way out. If capital is already in us, then the class struggle can be waged in us and the body becomes the site of resistance and struggle. Even if our body has been objectivated as a material anatomo-physiological body (*Körper*) among bodies, the fact remains that for the time being, we still experience our body as a living body (*Leib*), that is, to use the phenomenological terms of Marcel, Plessner and Merleau-Ponty, as something that we *are* and not only a something that we *have*. Although we are always already caught in the tentacular grips of an integrated and integrating machinic capitalism, the omnipresence of commodification does not mean that in our everyday life we have become mere appendices of the capitalist megamachine and thus, so to say, executors of our own life. In spite of everything and for the time being, we remain human. We communicate, empathise, rationalise, moralise and criticise. To avoid the totalising closure of its critical analysis of the processes of reification, commodification and alienation, a critical theory of contemporary society has to take those anthropological constants into account. Having presented elsewhere a metacritical analysis of critical theory (Vandenberghe, 1997–1998, 2009), I am only too aware that a critique of domination presupposes a theory of emancipation to be effective. Yet, if I have insisted in this lengthy chapter on the colonising and totalising logic of capitalism, it is to flag the danger involved and in the hope of contributing thereby to an active critique and passive resistance to the imperial tendencies of the neo-capitalist system. There is hope. While capital goes transnational, resistance is globalising as well. From Chiappas to Seattle and Bombay to Porto Alegre, the resistance against universal commodification is gathering momentum. All over the place, people are resisting the new world order that is emerging, and screaming for global justice. Naomi Klein (2001: 82), the Canadian activist and spokesperson of the anti-globalisation movement, bears testimony to the dispersed actions of the multitude:

> Thousands of groups today are all working against forces whose common threat is what might broadly be described as the privatization of every aspect of life, and the transformation of every activity and value into a commodity.... American students are kicking ads out of the classroom. European environmentalists and ravers are throwing parties at busy intersections. Landless Thai peasants are planting organic vegetables on over-irrigated golf courses. Bolivian workers are reversing the privatization of water supply....

> Typically these anti-privatization campaigns get under way on their own. But they also periodically converge – that's what happened in Seattle, Prague, Washington, Davos, Porto Alegre and Quebec.

In all its extraordinary and contradictory diversity, the anti-globalisation movement unifies the different new social movements of the last century (anti-capitalist, anarchist, ecopax, feminist, gay and lesbian, etc.) into a single social movement that counterfactually represents humanity and defends the general interest through advocacy. As such, it can be considered as the legitimate heir of the working-class movement of the nineteenth century. When activists and citizens manifest in the streets to protest and contest the hegemonic project of the leaders of the world, the spirit of the world manifests itself once again. Another world is possible…

IV Gen-ethical considerations on the reinvention of nature

Now that we have arrived at the point where, driven forward by the 'werewolf hunger for profit' (Marx, 1968: 280) and the unrelenting search for new niches and markets, the expanding neo-capitalist network of networks has colonised the whole universe (or almost) and melted everything that is solid into fluxes of pure becoming, I would like to return to the initial discussion about nature and culture. This time, however, I will not reflect on the distinction between nature and culture from an epistemo-ontological angle. Instead I will treat the question of the future of human nature from a more normative perspective and inquire if we could perhaps set ethical limits to the colonisation of life by the techno-sciences in general and the bio-industry in particular. Taking up the suggestion of Gilbert Simondon (1969: 102) that 'each epoch has to reinvent its humanism by orienting it to the principal danger of alienation', I will look more closely at the slippery slopes of genomics that might put the future of humankind at risk and suggest that, in order to impose normative limits to human engineering, we should reinvent and reintroduce nature as a conventional and consensual marker.

The end of nature

The experimental scrambling of the ontological regions of material, animal and human nature by the bio-, cyber- and nano-scientific industries has given rise to the emergence of strange nether lands in which cyborgs, chimeras and other monstrous couplings are experimentally produced and fabricated for the sake of profit. It would be convenient if we could still appeal to nature as a meta-social order that grounds society and culture to set moral limits to what human beings in general and the techno-sciences in particular can do. Unfortunately, nature has been modified, 'demoralised' and commodified by human intervention to the point that one can no longer rely on it to impose normative limits to the colonisation of life by the scientific–industrial complex of late capitalism. To understand how 'we', moderns, 'progressed' to the 'extermination' of nature, we have to go back once again to the reflexive emergence of the nature–culture distinction in the sixteenth and seventeenth centuries but, this time, the story needs to be told from the point of view of the invention of nature.[76]

The rationalising processes of the objectivation of nature and the self-objectivation of culture that are the harbingers of modernity have dispensed with the hypothesis of the divine.[77] Just as God has been demystified and uncovered as a human invention, so, too, nature has been defetishised and apprehended as a social construction. The humanisation of God and the objectivation of nature are internally related processes in the secular process of the disenchantment of the world. Remember Swammerdam, the Dutch entomologist of the seventeenth century? He opened his course on zoological anatomy with a divine promise: 'With the anatomy of the louse, I'll bring you a proof of God's providence' (cited in Weber, 1992a: 91). Apart from a few well-meaning scientists and credulous New Age acolytes, 'we moderns' no longer believe that science and theology are compatible. Although scientism has become a religion in itself and scientists seem to have arrogated the divine power of conception to themselves, science is the secular power *par excellence* that eradicates the infamous superstition at its very root.

The scientific objectivation of nature secularises the order of being and transmutes nature into a cultural construct. No longer God-given, detranscendentalised and secularised, nature becomes a contingent, meaningless order of regularity, subject to the laws of causality. Since Galileo, the natural sciences no longer deal with nature, but with a theoretical-mathematical conception of possible nature of which the phenomenal nature only represents and realises a particular instance (Cassirer, 1994: I, 314–318, 377ff.). Instead of understanding nature as some kind of a substance that is a given to the senses, it is theoretically constructed as a theoretical contexture of functional relations of causal determination that can be disclosed in and through scientific experiments. Together, the epistemological disconnection of scientific experience from its pre-scientific origins and the mathematisation of mechanics have allowed the modern sciences to break with the traditional metaphysics of substance and to effectuate the transition to a constructivist, functional or relational and experimental conception of nature (Böhme *et al.*, 1977: 7–10).

Once the laws of nature are known, experimental knowledge can be systematically applied and used to control and manipulate, transform and fabricate nature. Knowledge is power, as Bacon famously said, and power is the will to dominate nature and harness it to serve human purposes. What he did not say, but what is also sociologically implied in the linkage of science and technology, is that knowledge does not only increase the power of human beings over nature, but also over people.

Recoding the distinction between nature and culture as a cultural distinction, modernity has introduced the reflexivity it has about its own culture into the realm of nature. With Latour (1991), we could even say that the separation of nature and culture is a precondition for the scientific analysis and the technological transformation of nature. Unable to separate out nature as an independent realm, differentiated from culture, pre-modern cultures could not experiment on the modern scale. 'We', moderns, can, and this cultural difference explains in part why we have become the 'masters and possessors of nature', to use Descartes' consecrated phrase, and colonised, exploited and dominated nature on an unprecedented scale. While the modern separation of nature from culture has allowed for the scientific investigation and technological transformation of nature, the techno-scientific successes of late capitalist modernity have, paradoxically and rather perversely, resulted in the 'end of nature', which raises, of course, the timely metascientific question of the 'mastery of the mastery' of nature.

Indeed, three or four centuries after the techno-scientific revolution, modernity has so thoroughly modified and commodified the natural environment that nature itself appears now as an artefact and an artifice of human enterprise. Radically reshaping the connections between social life and the material world, industrial capitalism's culture of mastery has transformed the natural environment into a created environment. As a result, nature is no longer 'given' as something that exists outside of society (and culture), as a kind of self-evidential ground and background of society, but rather as something that can be transformed, manufactured and changed at will. Modifiable, modified and manufactured, nature has become as contingent as culture. Neither necessary, nor impossible, it is no longer perceived as something that exists outside of society and that we can take for granted, but as something that is increasingly threatened by the modern culture of mastery that characterises industrial capitalism. From this vanishing perspective, we can even understand the emergence of the ecological movement in terms of the disappearance of nature. It is because nature is disappearing that it is so central and that everybody talks about nature, whether it is to preserve, to further exploit or to deconstruct it. In any case, when nature is threatened by human enterprise, we end up discovering that it was never autonomous: 'The distinction between the natural and the cultural is revealed for the construction it always was' (Strathern, 1992b: 55).

Of course, nature does not really disappear. Rather, what disappears and implodes is the distinction between nature and culture (Lau and Keller, 2001), or nature and society for that matter, as society and culture are not distinct entities, but different aspects of the same socio-cultural reality. The implosion of the distinction between nature and culture not only means that nature is recognised as a cultural artefact and a social construction, but also, and, perhaps above all, that the natural sciences that socially construct nature are now themselves explicitly recognised as cultural artefacts and social constructions. Attacking the 'culture of no culture' of the natural sciences, exposing the social relations of production and definition that are responsible for the scientific objectivation and technological exploitation of nature, the constructivist turns, twists and returns in the social studies of science and technology have demolished the firewall that separated science and technology from politics and radically politicised the production of knowledge in the natural and social sciences.

The politicisation of the sciences adds the contingency of culture to the contingency of nature. When both nature and the scientific production of nature are susceptible to all kinds of transformations and redefinitions, nature becomes optional and, so to say, optical. Depending on the perspective one takes on nature, it can either be considered as a social construct or as a natural given, as *thesei* or *phusei*, with the result that what is natural ensues from a decision. The hole in the ozone-layer, global warming and BSE can all be analysed, for example, as a natural state of affairs or as a social construction. When macro-sociologists (like Beck) show that natural states of affairs are, in fact, non-intended consequences of human action and decision; when micro-sociologists (like Latour and Woolgar) next demonstrate that scientific facts are literally constructed in the lab; and when critical scholars (like Haraway) finally uncover the racist, capitalist and gendered subtexts of the micro-sociologists, no layer of scientific practice remains outside the reach of the sociological techniques of interpretation, defetishisation and politicisation of natural facts.

The reinvention of nature

Until recently, human beings lacked the knowledge and the capacity to transform and reconstruct human nature. They could therefore take it for granted and consider it as a basic precondition beyond our purposes and outside of our responsibility. But now that human nature itself has become malleable and optional, they come to realise that there are no longer any natural barriers to artificial intervention and technological engineering. Thanks to the revolution in the techno-sciences, humans can now control human evolution, alter the biological make up of humans and their offspring, and literally create new species that scramble the lines and the times of spontaneous evolution. As creators of humans, humans have become gods, or at least god-like, not in their wisdom, though, but in their knowledge and transformative power. Humans have always made history, but not under conditions of their own choosing. Now they also make biology. By altering human nature for the sake of profit, the techno-sciences short-circuit history, speed up evolution and court the risk of destroying humanity in the name of health. One thing is clear, however: 'Biology under control is no longer nature' (Strathern, 1992b: 35).

Since nature is no longer a symbol for the given parameters of human existence, nature, human or otherwise, we can no more rely on it to impose limits on human enterprise. And yet, if we want to ensure that humanity does not destroy the biological foundations of civilisation, if we want to hold fast to the idea of *humanitas* and the future of humanity, it seems to me that we have to reinvent nature and reintroduce it as a normative convention that sets limits to its reconstruction. Now that the natural and the social sciences have technologically reconstructed nature and discursively deconstructed essences, it may seem a bit quaint and queer, however, to want to introduce nature, albeit as a convention. Now that the boundaries between nature and culture, between humans, animals and machines, and also between life and death, have been eroded, it may seem unreasonable and unseasonable to want to reintroduce the distinction between nature and culture as a conventional context that grounds society and culture. And yet, to be on the safe side and to avoid the modification of human nature beyond recognition, I would like to suggest that instead of changing nature, we start to change culture.

Since nature has become optional, we need a conscious decision to moralise human nature and not to reconstruct it – one we take knowing that we could also act otherwise. To reduce the contingency of nature I would like to propose a conventional redefinition of human nature as something 'sacred', or, at least, as something that inspires awe and deserves respect and should therefore not be experimented or tampered with without precaution.[78] Or, as Hans Jonas (1987: 218) says in a quasi-theological vein: 'We should learn again to fear and tremble and, even without God, learn to fear the sacred.'

Although I have intentionally used the term 'sacred', the strategy I want to pursue is not the theo-conservative one of the sacralisation of nature, however, but the neo-humanist one of the moralisation of nature. Divested from its mystical envelope, the rational core of the religious intuition can be redeemed, I think, through a consequent linguistification, immanentisation and secularisation of the sacred. Unlike the sacralisation of nature, which presupposes somehow that human nature is divine and that only God has the right to reconstruct human nature, the moralisation of nature is humanist in intent and purpose. It accepts that humans have the right to reconstruct nature, but stresses that this right has to be balanced by a duty to preserve human nature and to defend it against arbitrary control. Using Weberian terms (Weber, 1992b), we could say that the moralisation of nature is first and foremost intended and understood as an 'ethics of responsibility' and not simply as an 'ethics of conviction'. If it accepts in principle the transformability of human nature, it is only to open up the ends and the means of the techno-sciences to public discussion and scrutiny. Given that it most emphatically subscribes to the 'precautionary principle', it does not absolve politicians and scientists of their responsibilities, but urges them instead to take explicitly into account the unintended, unforeseeable and potentially uncontrollable consequences of technological decisions in their prudent decisions.

In the age of high reflexivity, the traditional conceptions of nature can obviously not simply be restored. Defending a traditional conception of nature in a traditional way would be tantamount to ecological fundamentalism.[79] And it would bring us dangerously close to the reactionary romanticism of (some versions of) 'deep ecology'. What we need is not 'second nature', but, I contend, 'third nature', i.e. nature self-consciously posited by spirit as a highly reflexive, consciously formulated conventional and consensual, nomic and normic conception of nature. What I am thinking of is some kind of a communicative update of the Kantian theory of the postulates of practical reason for the age of genetics (cf. Kant, 1956b: A215–241). For Kant, the postulates of practical reason are not theoretical dogmas but rather necessary conditions for obedience of a finite being to the moral laws which determines its will in general and the categorical imperative in particular. As is well known, the (second) formulation of the categorical imperative stipulates that one should always act 'so as to treat the humanity, in your own person or in the person of another, as an end-in-itself and never simply as a means' (Kant, 1956a: BA67), always as a person and never as a mere thing. This imperative remains valid, of course, for humans in the age of technical reproducibility, but instead of postulating the existence of god, freedom and immortality, I would like to suggest that we introduce human nature as a theoretical postulate of practical reason and a normative presupposition of 'gen-ethics'.

Gen-ethics is understood here with Habermas (2001a) as the bio-ethical division of the 'species-ethics' (*Gattungsethik*) that conventionally and consensually defines the nature of the human and thereby sets normative limits to the human freedom to technologically alter human nature and change it beyond recognition.[80] The intent of a modern and modernist gen-ethics is obviously not to forbid once and for all genetic engineering or other human experiments in bio-, cyber- and nano-technology, but to regulate them. As Wolfgang van den Daele (2000: 24) rightly says: 'What has become technically at our disposition through the sciences, should again be made unavailable (*unverfügbar*) through normative control.'[81] From this gen-ethical perspective, a definition of 'third nature' that is counterfactually valid for the whole of humanity should be consensually formulated and validated in an 'ideal speech situation' and consciously introduced as a necessary precondition of practical reason and as a guarantee that humans do not treat human beings and their genes as simple means for one's own ends or the ends of others, but that they pay due respect to the dignity (*Menschenwürde*) of the human person.[82] Of course, we cannot pre-empt what the outcome of such counterfactual discussions would be, but we can nevertheless safely presume that the participants will, for instance, consensually decide that genetic engineering with eugenic intent, human cloning and breeding between animals and humans enter into conflict with the commonly accepted ideas about the identity and the dignity of human beings. Be that as it may, the intent of a discourse-ethical redefinition of human nature is not so much to define once and for all what it means to be human as to decide about the techno-scientific interventions in human nature that are incompatible with the 'humanity of humanity' (Morin, 2001) – that is, with the self-identity of a humanity that defines itself by distinguishing the human both from nature and from the animal, while recognising that the human has emerged out of nature and remains an animal.

Knowing that we could reconstruct human nature and consciously deciding not to do so on the basis of scientifically informed normatively oriented discussions between scientists, citizens and politicians about the unintended, unforeseeable and uncontrollable consequences and risks that humanity would be confronted with if it were to authorise the cloning of humans or genetic engineering without restrictions, this is the prospect of a gen-ethical politics that takes the precautionary principle seriously. What is needed is not simply a survey about what the citizens think about the biosciences – 44 per cent of the French confuse the latter with phytotherapy anyway, according to a recent survey – but a roundtable discussion in which citizens, scientists and politicians take part (Habermas, 1971: 104–145). Having been informed by the scientists about what is possible from a techno-scientific point of view, the citizens and the politicians tell the scientists what is desirable from a normative point of view and together they take a well-informed and well-founded decision to act or not to act. Reformulating Beck's gloss on the precautionary principle, we obtain the following gen-ethic device:

> Even when we don't know what we have to know [about the possible consequences of techno-scientific reconstruction of human nature], we have nevertheless to decide [on the basis of a conventionally defined and consensually validated concept of human nature] that we will not decide and to take a decision when we will decide [not to allow the reconstruction of human nature].
>
> (Beck *et al.*, 2001: 40)

Sub-politics and the technological performance of morality

To learn? Or not to learn? That is the gen-ethical question of the age. Should we adapt our norms to the world or the world to our norms? Should we adopt a cognitive attitude to norms, pragmatically revise them when the circumstances demand it and opportunistically redefine our vision of humanity as human nature is occasionally reconstructed by the techno-sciences (Luhmann, 1969)?[83] Or should we perhaps stubbornly stick to our norms, maintain our normative intuitions against all odds, and insist on the dignity of the person to normatively re-regulate the techno-sciences (Habermas, 1998: 243–256)?

I must confess that I am internally split. Looking at the future and the unprecedented risks that humanity is confronted with, I feel inclined to stress the unconditional validity of our norms, normative intuitions and visions of humanity. Looking at the past, however, I observe how our norms and normative intuitions have been periodically revised as techno-scientific advances required it and how, by manipulating the bodies, scientists have also been manipulating our norms and performatively redefining our visions of humanity. Initially, the dissection of corpses by Mondino and Vesalius was condemned by the Church as a clear-cut case of profanation that would thwart the resurrection of the body, but by the end of the seventeenth century the opening of the body had become generally accepted by the educated factions of the population who attended *en masse* the anatomical theatres and cabinets of curiosity (Le Breton, 1993: 169–219). Moving closer to us, the transplantation of organs, which was also originally attacked as morally unacceptable, became quickly established as a revered practice, even if it redefined our visions of life and revised our definitions of death (Kimbrell, 1993: 36–44; Sharp, 1995: 361–362). Prior to 1968, death was recognised by the absence of easily detectable signs, such as pulse and respiration. To facilitate the acquisition of viable organs from potential donors, death was redefined in 1968 in terms of irreversible coma. Of late, new definitions of death have been proposed so that babies and neo-morts ('faux vivants') with lower, but without higher, brain function can be declared officially brain-dead before they die. The implication of this new 'performance' of death implies that, legally and technically speaking, a brain-dead, heart-beating, breathing cadaver is considered alive till the organs are 'harvested' and the plug is finally pulled.

In-vitro fertilisation (IVF) is another good case that instructs us about the inbuilt obsolescence of our visions of the human and of our normative resistance to changing human nature. In 1978, the first test-tube baby, Louise Brown, was born in Great Britain. Until then, it was considered unthinkable that a human being could be conceived without sexual intercourse and regarded as normatively unacceptable that a human being could be fabricated in a Petri dish and implanted in a surrogate mother. Having sex, transmitting genes and giving birth indicated a natural sequence that could and *a fortiori* should not be changed. But what was unthinkable and unacceptable until yesterday has become almost generally accepted today, as can be gathered from the fact that since 1978 some five million test-tube babies have been born around the world. Included in the right of self-determination of childless couples, IVF and other baby-making techniques, such as DI (donor insemination), GIFT and ZIFT (gamete and zygote introfallopian transfer), have now become an option for childless couples and, increasingly, for single mothers and homosexual couples as well.

The speed with which the transplantation of organs and artificial insemination have been diffused through society and accepted by the population at large shows that the half life of our norms is steadily declining. What is considered as unacceptable and intolerable today may very well appear as normal and beneficial tomorrow. Leaving aside techno-industrialists, Raelians and mutants,[84] I presume that today most, if not all of us, are against human cloning, and yet I can almost predict that in ten or twenty years' time human beings will be cloned for therapeutic reasons and that cloning will be a most profitable industry. Or, in the words of an Indian doctor: 'Ten years from now, I will be able to grow you foetuses like popcorn' (quoted in Cohen, 2001: 23).

Although the philosopher in me is tempted by the Kantian perspective of Habermas and I am inclined to start preaching like an unreconstructed humanist about the inviolability (*Unantastbarkeit*) of human dignity, the sociologist in me wants to correct the naïveté of the philosopher and to enlighten him or her sociologically about the limits of the Enlightenment. Such a sociological analysis of the limits of philosophical Enlightenment does not aim to undermine its premises, but to strengthen its promises: emancipation of and through reason (*Aufklärung*) rather than from it (*Abklärung*), as Luhmann (1992: 42) maliciously suggests[85] – that remains the perspective of a critical social theory that presents a philosophically informed and normatively oriented analysis of the techno-scientific risks of dehumanisation and alienation in late capitalist, post-industrial consumerist societies. That a critique of alienation is only possible if and as long as the alienation of human beings is not total is self-evident. As long as humans are human and resist the total self-objectivation, they can in principle criticise the system, change it from within, and practically reorient its course. Nuclear power, germ line engineering and cloning cannot be disinvented, but confronted with the 'manufactured uncertainties' and dangers of the global risk society, citizens can still exert pressure on the politicians they have elected and democratically press for a political domestication of capitalism, as well as a normative regulation of the techno-sciences.

Personal reflection and resistance are always possible and always necessary, but not sufficient. What is needed is not only ethical behaviour, but also sociological insight into the 'sub-politics' of the bio-technological sciences that technologically push through fundamental decisions that concern every individual without any legitimation, without any control and without any consultation of parliament. Exposing the political power and the bio-politics of the medical-industrial complex, Ulrich Beck (1986: 335–336) compares the politics of the *fait accompli* of medicine with a silent and undemocratic social revolution:

> Despite all the criticism and scepticism, what continues to be possible, even taken for granted, in the area of medicine would, if transferred to official politics, be equivalent to the scandal of simply implementing epoch-making fundamental decisions on the social future, while bypassing the parliament and the public sphere, and making debate on the consequences unreal by virtue of their realisation in practice.

To normatively regulate and socially domesticate the techno-sciences, the sociological analysis of the depoliticising mechanisms and the sub-political processes that bypass the checks and balances of parliamentary democracy has to be supplemented by social critique and political reform. Given that the political demands of a moral regulation of the techno-sciences will be formulated and worked out in the medium of the law, the political reform will in any case be implemented through the formulation of juridically binding norms. Although the struggle is ultimately a spiritual one, it will first be waged as a legal one.

The slippery slopes of liberal eugenics

Although we can counterfactually presume that a normative consensus exists about bio-ethical norms of decency and that such a virtual consensus is sufficiently solid and universal to justify a ban on germ line engineering with eugenic intent or human cloning for reproductive purposes, a sociological analysis of the limits of the moralisation of nature informs us that we cannot rely on this consensus to regulate the biosciences and to assure that humans will not be genetically engineered and cloned in the next decade or so. Norms are only constraining and binding as long as the technical projects remain in the realm of science fiction. Once the technological development turns the fiction into a fact, moral judgements tend to become ambiguous and the taboo on the reconstruction of human nature quickly vanishes among large parts of the population. Usually, medical purposes have spearheaded technological interventions in human nature. Using military language to describe the demoralising effects of medicine, Wolfgang van den Daele (2000: 25), a former member of the

Starnberg-Group and now a distinguished member of the bio-ethical committee of the German Bundestag, considers 'the medical intervention [a]s the open flank of all taboos concerning human nature'. Indeed, the history of the medical sciences and the bio-medical industry in the last quarter of a century shows that medical interventions and therapies – from the transplantation of human organs and the implantation of artificial ones via IVF to somatic and possibly also cell line engineering – have always provided the initial justification for the technical transgression of sacrosanct boundaries.

The reason for the regular transgressions of binding norms by bio-medical technologies is to be found in the fact that good health generally trumps all other values. As a result, 'an ethics of rigorous respect for the naturalness of human nature cannot be defended against people's interests in life and good health' (van den Daele, 1992: 551). The valuation of good health and the promises of the medical industry to cure illnesses explain why normative regulations are always provisional and why technological prohibitions, such as the current ones on PGD (pre-implantation genetic diagnosis) and somatic cell engineering should rather be read and understood as 'moratoria' (van den Daele, 2000: 27) that can and will be lifted when and as soon as a medical therapy for a cure becomes available. On this basis, we can not only expect that some of our normative resistances to genomics are going to vanish in the near future, but we can also almost predict that the interest in reducing suffering and the promise of a cure for a whole spate of illnesses will lead us down the slippery slope of 'liberal' or 'pastoral' eugenics (Agar, 2000; Rose, 2001).[86]

Unlike the authoritarian eugenics of the past, which was state-driven and aimed to improve the genetic stock of the population, the new eugenics is market-driven.[87] On the basis of access to information about the full range of genetic tests and therapies, prospective parents will use all the new genetic technologies on offer to select a desirable genotype for their future children. Although the prospective parents do not directly aim to improve the genotype of future generations, the aggregated demand for corrections and enhancements of the genome of their offspring will nevertheless undercut the distinction between 'positive' (or ameliorative) and 'negative' (or defensive) eugenics. Indirectly, but almost inescapably, the individual demand for 'biologically correct' children will pave the way for a return to eugenics that is no longer imposed by an authoritarian state, but driven by the market and freely chosen by the parents: 'The distinguishing mark of the new liberal eugenics is state neutrality.... Authoritarian eugenicists would do away with ordinary procreative freedoms. Liberals instead propose radical extensions of them' (Agar, 2000: 171).

Although the technologies of somatic and cell line engineering that promise a cure for diseases that arise from single genes, such as Huntington's disease, sickle-cell anaemia and haemophilia are more spectacular, and therefore more likely to receive attention in the media, most of the diseases that can be cured through genetic engineering are in fact rather rare.[88] Although the bio-medical industry will undoubtedly search to explore the commercial possibilities of therapies that correct genetic defects ('a cure in search of a disease'), they will more likely invest in all kinds of genetic screenings that can be offered and sold to the families 'at risk' ('a test in search of a disease'). Given that the diagnosis technologically precedes the cure, it is in any case more logical and profitable to start with the development of genetic tests that screen the genetic material of the parents for defects and risks. Moreover, unlike the cure, which concerns only the sick, diagnosis interests all prospective parents, or initially at least those who are 'at risk', and obviously their children as well.

Initially introduced to screen the genetic material for specific diseases, the genetic tests will, however, quickly be proposed to all parents. After all, parents do not simply desire children; they desire healthy children.[89] Once again, the alleviation of suffering and the promise of health will act as a spearhead for the generalisation of genetic 'quality controls'. The scenario for the marketisation of genetic tests is always the same. Looking back at how the reach of IVF was extended over the years, Elisabeth Beck-Gernsheim (1991: 42) has already described the typical pattern of generalised diffusion of medical innovations:

> New biomedical help is first introduced to prevent or alleviate suffering for a narrowly defined catalogue of unambiguous problematic cases. Next comes a transitional phase of habituation during which the domain of application is extended further and further. Eventually, the final stage is reached: all women and men are defined as clients.

Although genetic screening is not compulsory, there's nevertheless a strong social pressure to act responsibly and undergo a test, if only to be informed about the medical risks and to be able to prevent predictable illnesses. Talk about prevention and prophylaxis should not hide, however, what is really being proposed:

> More is at stake than oral hygiene. What is really meant is the prevention of the birth of genetically damaged children through renunciation of the desire for children or (and this is the most likely option) through 'experimental' pregnancy and abortion in case of an unfavourable diagnosis.
>
> (Beck-Gernsheim, 1994: 326–327)

What is really being proposed, if not imposed, is not so much the prevention of illnesses, as the existence of an ailing individual. Following the lead of Agamben's (1998) terrific book on bio- and thanatopolitics, we could describe the life that does not pass the test and that, as a result, is deemed not to deserve to live as 'sacred life' – life that can be eliminated without punishment.

Moving from genetic testing to genetic engineering, the prospects for avoiding the slippery slope of eugenics do not look much better. Some 'scientific tourism' has taught me that, when talking about genetic engineering, one should carefully distinguish between 'germ line' and 'somatic cell engineering'. Using viral vectors to transmit genetic material into cells, somatic cell engineering aims to replace sick cells with healthy ones. Genetically engineered cells have, like normal cells, only a limited life-span. This means that the somatic genetherapy has to be periodically renewed and that the genetic information is not transmitted to the next generation, at least if the viruses do not spread and accidentally introduce the engineered gene in the cell lines of the patient. From a bio-ethical point of view, somatic engineering, which is still in an experimental stage, can be compared to organ transplantation: 'Whether organs or single cells are transplanted does not make for a moral difference'(Zoglauer, 2002: 98). Unlike somatic engineering, germ line engineering permits the alteration of genetic material such that genetic changes become permanently encoded in the sex cells of the resulting adult. While techniques of germ line engineering have already been successfully used in animals to accelerate the genetic improvement of livestock, the technical feasability of germ line engineering of the human genome remains so far only theoretical. Notwithstanding all their disagreements, bioethicists seem to agree that germ line engineering that directly attempts to change the genotype of future generations amounts to eugenics and cannot be ethically justified. 'However, when such changes arise as an indirect and otherwise unavailable consequence of an approved form of somatic cell line engineering, they are morally acceptable' (Lappé, 2000: 164).[90]

Morally acceptable or not, through appeals to health and promises of a therapy, the commercialisation of technological advances in medicine point almost inescapably to the liberal application and market-driven implementation of a non-authoritarian and humane form of eugenic politics that risks destroying the dignity of humanity while advancing under the cover of human progress. The sociological prognosis that humanity will soon go down the slippery slope of 'consumer eugenics' may seem demoralising, but one never knows; perhaps this prediction might actually function as a warning and help to prevent us from the worst. 'Catastrophy remains a possibility', says Dupuy (2002: 82), 'but only the inevitability of its future realisation can lead to prudence.'

Posthuman humanist postscript

Nothing is certain, however, not even the worst. But to avoid the self-destruction of the human, we have to invent a new humanism that is able to distinguish between the inhuman and the posthuman and can combat the new forms of domination, alienation and reification. Edgar Morin (2001: 242) is right when he says that 'the battles of tomorrow will be waged in the spiritual domain' – the domain of the *Geist*, not the one of the mind. In the name of the human, humanists of all sorts and all continents have to track and unrelentlessly criticise the categorical mistakes of those who willingly confuse the worst with the millennial advent of the best. Celebrating the overcoming of the human as the 'ecstatic clearing in which the human responds to Being' (Sloterdijk, 1999: 32), posthumanists philosophically rationalise and ideologically legitimise the progress and progression of the inhuman. Although the end of the human might be looming and the future of humanity is not assured, we have only started the human adventure. We may have lost the confidence in the future, but we have not lost the battle yet. The posthuman is our destiny, the inhuman is not our fate. Although and precisely because the coming century will most likely be Deleuzian, we have no choice. In the name of humanity and in the hope that the era of the posthuman will not be inhuman, we have to reject the anti-humanism of the neo-Nietzscheans and try to define a new humanism for the coming age. Against Foucault, but with Malraux, I thus conclude with a warning: the twenty-first century will be spiritual, or it won't be.

Notes

1 A French translation of this chapter on posthumanism has appeared in *Complexités du posthumanisme: Trois essais dialectiques sur la sociologie de Bruno Latour*. I would like to thank Christina Toren, Ruth McNally, Wolfgang van den Daele, Harry Kunneman and Marc de Leeuw for incisive comments and probing questions. In spite of some of their warnings, I remain solely responsible for all problematic affirmations, rhetorical exaggerations and polemic sleights of hand.

2 I'll leave aside terrorism and nuclear catastrophes, possibly induced by terrorist networks, and concentrate my attention on the risks of the techno-sciences in general and the biosciences in particular. I intend to explore the advances in bio- and neurochemistry, from Prozac and Viagra to MDMA, in another paper at another time. For a courageous exploration of the imminent risks of 'knowledge-enabled mass destruction' through destructive self-replication in genetics, nanotechnology and robotics, see the highly publicised exercise in whistle-blowing by Bill Joy (2000).

3 The term neo-liberalism is problematic. This ideology of shopkeepers aims to introduce the competitive logics of the market in all spheres of life and thereby forgets that the introduction of the free market has, historically and politically, always depended on the State. The free market was, as Polanyi famously said, 'planned' from the very beginning. To emphasise that contemporary capitalism enrols the State as one of its agents of globalisation, I use the term neo- (or neo-Mancunian) capitalism to refer to all the transformations and restructurations of global capitalism. Since the crisis of 2007, neoliberalism has been discredited as an ideology, though not as a practice. The austerity measures of the last five years have been more ruthless in the unwinding of the welfare state than 30 years of exuberant neoliberalism.

4 For the history of the concept of reification, see my entry in the *International Encyclopaedia of the Social and Behavioral Sciences* (Vandenberghe, 2001).

5 In a beautiful and famous passage of his *New Science*, Vico boldly stated his thesis of the *verum factum*:

> In the night of thick darkness enveloping the earliest antiquities, so remote from ourselves, there shines the eternal and never failing light of a truth beyond all question: that the world of civil society has certainly been made by men, and that its principles are, therefore, to be found within modifications of our human mind. Whoever reflects on this cannot but marvel that the philosophers should have bent all their energies to the study of the world of nature, which, since God made it, He alone knows: and that they should have neglected the study of the world of nations or civil world, which since men had made it, men could come to know.
>
> (paragraph 331, quoted in Berlin, 1976: 27).

6 Postmodernism was supposed to open up new ways of thinking. What we witness, however, 20 years after its inception, is the return to and re-establishment of all kinds of old things: religion (Catholicism for Vattimo, Judaism for Derrida), ethics (of proximity for Levinas and of hospitality for Derrida), metaphysics (of process for Stengers and of complexity for de Landa) and even revolutionary politics (see Zizek on Lenin, forget Mouffe on Carl Schmitt).

7 The interconnections between the singularity and the plurality of culture (culture as being both a *singulare tantum* and a *plurale tantum*) are of a 'mereographic' nature. Culture can be part of different systems that are internally related to each other via part–whole relations that can be described differently from different angles and thereby redescribed as something else (Strathern, 1991). Following the connections and shifting perspectives on the connections, so that what looks as a part can also be seen as a whole of which it is part, we can return to the example of culture and say with Marilyn Strathern, whose work has inspired my approach to culture:

> Culture belongs to the domain of human activity, and in that sense is universally part of it; but as an idea it may also be claimed as the specific construct of a specific era and is thus (and to the contrary) also part of particular culture at one point in time.
>
> (Strathern, 1992a: 73)

8 This classification is obviously a simplification. Anthropologists will no doubt remember that Kroeber and Kluckhohn had already collected 164 definitions of culture in 1952, when the semi-autonomous discipline of cultural studies still had to be invented and the *Anthropological Abstracts* did not have the oversized format of an antiquated telephone book.

9 As Lévi-Strauss (1969: 22) said: 'The barbarian is first of all the man who believes in barbarism.'

10 Speaking for the American school of cultural anthropology, Robert Lowie proclaimed in 1917 that 'culture is, indeed, the sole and exclusive subject-matter of ethnology, as consciousness is the subject-matter of psychology, life of biology, electricity as a branch of physics' (quoted in Kuper, 1999: ix). In European anthropology, culture is not opposed to society, but considered as an aspect of society: the cultural is the social viewed from another perspective, not a distinct analytic entity.

11 Unfortunately, the history of ideas does not confirm the thesis of the co-originality of the concepts of nature and culture. The concept of nature as an inanimated causal mechanism is linked to the scientific revolution of the sixteenth and seventeenth centuries, which is itself linked to the emergence of enterpreneurial capitalism. The concept of culture comes later in the seventeenth and eighteenth centuries and is linked to the colonial expansion of the great powers. Here I am not so much concerned, however, with a Weberian genealogy of modernity as with a socio-epistemological analysis of the conditions of possibility of anthropology. For a similar attempt to account for the emergence of sociology, see Vandenberghe (1997–1998: I, 9–24).

12 Jack Goody contests the universality of the distinction between nature and culture, but by contesting it, he affirms its artificiality as 'our' ethnocentric particularity:

> The division between nature and culture is in some ways rather artificial. I would claim that there's no such pair in either of the two African languages known personally to me (LoDagaa and Gonja). Though there's a certain 'opposition' of 'bush' and 'house', 'cultivated' and 'uncultivated', there's nothing that would correspond to the highly abstract and rather eighteenth century dichotomy that is current in western intellectual circles.
>
> (Goody, quoted in Horigan, 1988: 40–41)

13 For a documentation of several 'cartocontroversies' (the Peters projection controversy, the Vinland map, etc.) that show how one can lie with maps and how maps continue politics on paper, see Monmonier (1995).

14 After all, Derrida's famous statement that we never get out of discourses and texts ('Il n'y a pas d'hors texte') is not meant to deny that he is writing his text with a pen on a piece of paper, that the trains in the underground in Paris are riding or that the overground ones in London have once again collided. Inversely, my critique of the cultural

deconstruction of nature does not aim to deny that texts can change nature. The example of the Shakespeare Society in Connecticut, which imported from England all the birds that occurred in the texts of the great bard to set them free, proves that culture can, literally, change nature. More generally, but less literary, culture 'leaks' into nature and effectively helps to construct it in the same way as the indications of the architect direct the performances of the house-builders, though with non-intended perverse effects in the long run and on a grand scale.

15 Judith Butler is the theorist of transsexualism. But in so far as one will hardly find any references in her texts to silicone injections, aesthetic operations or other material practices that subvert the naturality of the distinctions between the sexes, one might as well say that her theory of transsexualism is really a theory of transtextualism. Always wrapped up in language, the body is as unfathomable as the Kantian Thing-in-itself.

16 With Kern (1962), we can distinguish three ways to explore the 'infinite continent' of phenomenology that Husserl has opened up for analysis, namely the Cartesian way, the way via intentional psychology and the ontological way. The latter is the one that interests me: it does not annihilate the world as object but takes it as an index for the analysis of the constitution of the world as phenomenon. When phenomenology is entered via the ontological way, the dead end of the transcendental ego is avoided so that the realism of Bhaskar and the phenomenology of Husserl are no longer incompatible, but rather complementary. One might thus as well describe the ontological way to phenomenology as a phenomenological way to ontology.

17 The method in question is the so-called 'transcendental reduction' which 'brackets' the real world in order to reflexively analyse the constitutive activities of the mind. By suspending temporarily the ontological question of the existence of the world 'out there', the latter is no longer treated as a resource but as a topic in its own right. After analysis, the world is not only entirely regained, but also entirely understood in its objectivity as the intentional correlate of the epistemic acts of the inhabitants of the world.

18 I was only interested in establishing the ontological difference between the natural world and the social world, not the one between the animal and the human world. Humans are animals. We share 99.4 per cent of our genes with chimpanzees (and 52 per cent with potatoes and 48 per cent with bananas). On this basis, American scientists have recently proposed reclassifying the chimpanzee as *Homo (pan) troglodytes* and the bonobo as *Homo (pan) paniscus*. Unlike Peter Singer, I would not use a genetic argument to extend human rights to our brothers and sisters in the forest (and *a fortiori* to those in the zoo), but a pathocentric one. There's one book that convinced me to enlarge my humanism. It is *Our Inner Ape* in which the Dutch primatologist Frans de Waal (2005) describes the moral sentiments of chimpanzees and bonobos. Like us, animals suffer, and like us, they are oftentimes other-directed and moved by empathy, forgiveness, care, etc.

19 For an excellent analysis of eidetic variation and regional ontologies by one of Husserl's former assistants, see Landgrebe (1963).

20 Luckmann opens his culturalist attack on Husserl's realism by exposing the tacit assumption that the transcendental ego is somehow human. Following the phenomenological sociology of Alfred Schütz, he argues that the human being is not constitutive, but socially constituted as human through the application of the typifications of the life-world. Instead of conceiving those views as exclusive of each other, I try to integrate them by conceiving of the regional typologies as differential or transitive interpretations of one single reality, differentiated into different regional ontologies.

21 Just one example, which I borrow from Viveiros de Castro (2002), but anthropologists and historians could easily bring in other ones. According to the Araweté, who assume a basic continuity between all animate beings, people share with animals the same kind of soul and thus the same identities and indeed mental constructs. What differentiates them are their bodies. It is bodies which see and which determine what

is seen. From out of their human body, human beings can only 'see' animals as non-human; but when the animals' point of view is imagined, these creatures do not see human beings as human beings – to them people appear as animals, and the animals appear to one another as people.

22 This distinction between animated things and reified persons corresponds to the one between gifts (Mauss) and commodities (Marx). In the same way as the distinction between nature and culture can only be made within culture, the distinction between gifts and commodities only makes sense from the point of view of the commodity economy.

23 The notion of epistemic gain is post-metaphysical:

> It aims to establish, not that some position is correct absolutely, but rather that some position is superior to some other. It is concerned, covertly or openly, implicitly or explicitly, with comparative propositions. We show one of those comparative claims to be well founded when we can show that the move from A to B contains a gain epistemically.
>
> (Taylor, 1989: 72)

In spite of all the epistemic gain, the assumption of a perfect onto-typological overlap is introduced here as a mere 'regulatory ideal' (Kant). Even in the very long run, there still will be a penumbra of meanings that is not shared.

24 At the end of this chapter I will come back to the complex interrelations of nature and culture in order to analyse them not from an epistemological but from an ethical perspective.

25 For a catalogue of the contemporary cabinet of techno-scientific curiosities – from pharming, cloning, xenotransplantation, bionics, biomimicry and biopiracy to nanotubes, humanimals, wearable computers, DNA chips, botox injections, neurochips and penis pumps, see Best and Kellner (2001: 149–204).

26 Update: as a result of global warming, the Arctic ice has started to melt and opened up the Northwest Passage to commercial maritime transport and oil prospection. The United States, Canada, Russia, Denmark and Norway are disputing the territory.

27 For excellent overviews of the different theories that have brought in objects and technology to solve the Hobbesian problem of the social order, see Blandin (2002) and Barber and Trepos (2007).

28 Although Leroi-Gourhan remains relatively unknown inside and outside of France, one should not underestimate his importance. His work has significantly influenced Derrida's grammatological analysis of the difference between writing and speech, Deleuze and Guattari's double articulation of expression and content, Latour and Callon's co-construction of society and technology, Stiegler's investigations of the exteriorisation of memory and Debray's formulation of mediation studies.

29 Adumbrations of Leroi-Gourhan's thesis of the 'exsudation' of organs can already be found in Leibniz and the philosophy of technologies of Ernst Kapp. Among the contemporaries of Leroi-Gourhan, one finds similar conceptions of technology in the work of Arnold Gehlen (1957), Helmut Plessner (1965, especially pp. 309–321, where he exposes his 'law of natural artificialism') and Marshall McLuhan (1964), who conceives of the media as extensions of man, as is indicated in the subtitle of his book. Without reference to Leroi-Gourhan, Sloterdijk (2004, 748–756, 803–805) has expanded the theory of the exteriorisation of organs by conceiving of the welfare state and social services as an exteriorisation of the uterus.

30 Transhumanists start from the assumption that the human is a 'deficient animal' (Nietzsche) that is unable to cope with the complexity of the techo-scientific environment. On the webpage of Stellarc, a posthumanist net-artist, the latter affirms peremptorily that

> it is time to question whether a bipedal, breathing body with binocular vision and a 1400cc brain is an adequate biological form. It cannot cope with the quantity, complexity and quality of information it has accumulated; it is intimidated by the

precision, speed, and power of technology and is biologically ill-equipped to cope with its new extraterrestrial environment.

(www.stelarc.va.com.au)

To improve the human stock and overcome the biological limitations of the human condition, transhumanists and ectropians have singled out three 'person engineering technologies' (PETs): genetic engineering, artificial intelligence and nanotechnology.

31 In the same way as postmodernism can be said to extend modernism, posthumanism can be seen as a radicalisation of humanism. From the point of view of the history of ideas, Pico della Mirandolla can be considered as a precursor. His famous invocation: 'O man, model and sculptor of yourself (tu ipsius arbitrarius plastes et fictor), may you give to yourself the form that pleases you!' sounds eerily contemporary. Like the humanism that it supersedes, posthumanism values instrumental rationality, progress and humanity; it denies and actively combats all supernatural forces that are supposed to control our destiny. It simply goes further by urging that we should push beyond the human stage of evolution and take human destiny in our hand.

32 Text programs, karaoke machines and Stephen Hawkins offer three contemporary examples of such an accomplished man–machine integration. A text program like Word proposes synonyms, translations, spell checks and grammatical corrections. While the text is being written, it offers cognitive assistance and intervenes both on the writing and the writer. Consequently, the ensuing text can be considered as a genuine 'co-production' of the writer and the text program. Karaoke machines, which one can now find in virtually all Japanese hotels and inns, integrate the singer into the machine and use the human voice to 'play-back' pre-programmed sounds and images. Stephen Hawkins, the famous physicist and successor of Newton in Cambridge, is permanently attached to an automatic wheelchair and a sophisticated computer that allows him to communicate through a vocoder with the outside world. Integrated into a functioning techno-scientific unit, the wheelchair, the vocoder and Stephen himself form a living and thinking cyborg.

33 The idea that the human is constructed by technology is a common trope of posthumanism. Peter Sloterdijk, for example, uses it in his controversial *Rules for the Human Parc* when he presents Man as the being that dwells not only in language, but also in houses, and thus as the being that makes houses that make Man and has to be domesticated politically, and also genetically, through prenatal selection (Sloterdijk, 1999: 35–47). In Germany this anthropo-technological proposal has sparked off a huge and rather nasty controversy between Habermas and Sloterdijk. See the weekly interventions by proxy in *Die Zeit* from September 1999 onwards.

34 Deleuze and Guattari do not even aim to hide that they have no truck with the Hegelo-Marxian theory of alienation: 'We denounce all the oppositions of man and machine, of man alienated by the machine, etc.' (Deleuze, 1990: 32).

35 'Slightly alienated, or better: alterated' (Latour, 2002: 16). Fascinated by the in-between of the *Aufhebung*, Nietzsche, and the neo-Nietzscheans with him, love danger and welcome the *Untergang* of the human as a sign of its overcoming:

> The greatness of Man is that he is a bridge and not an end; what is lovely in man is that he is a transition and a decline.... I love the one who only lives to know and who wants to know so that one day the *Übermensch* will live. And so he wants his own decline. I love the one who works and invents so that one day he will build the house of the *Übermensch* and prepare the soil, the animals and the plant for his return; after all he wants his decline.
>
> (Nietzsche, 1988: 16–17)

36 The terminology of Deleuze and Guattari is esoteric and makes understanding difficult for the non-initiated. On the very first page of the book, the book itself is presented as a machinic assemblage or *agencement*:

> In a book, as in all things, there are lines of articulation or segmentarity, stata and territories, but also lines of flight, movements of deterritorialisation and destratification. Comparative rates of flow on these lines produce rates of relative slowness and viscosity, or on the contrary, of acceleration and rupture. All this, lines and measurable speeds, constitutes an assemblage.
>
> (Deleuze and Guattari, 1980: 9–10)

This seems obscure but, strangely enough, it is by reading faster rather than slower that Deleuzian texts slowly start to make sense.

37 Deleuze and Guattari (1972: 47, 339, 385; 1980: 20, 89, 360) have furtively borrowed the example of the unnatural coupling of the wasp and the orchid from Darwin. The wasp is an integral part of the orchid's reproductive system and morphology. The wasp uses the orchid for food whereas the orchid uses the wasp for fertilisation.

38 Although the image of the rhizome comes from the vegetal kingdom, colonies of ants offer perhaps a better example:

> A rhizome may be broken, shattered at a given spot, but it will start up again on one of its old lines, or new lines. You can never get rid of ants because they form an animal rhizome that can rebound time and again after most of it has been destroyed.
>
> (Deleuze and Guattari, 1980: 16)

39 A rhizome is a network: 'In a network there always exists at least one way from one given point to another one, or from one given point to any other point; quite often, to many points; at the limit, to all the points' (Serres, 1974: 27).

40 The connection between Latour and Deleuze is direct. Faint echoes and after-images of Deleuze and Guattari's pragmaticism can be found in John Law's Franco-British translations of actor–network theory as a business ontology:

> Perhaps there's nothing more than stories performing themselves and seeking to make connections, practical and local connections, specific links. In which case? In which case, we are no longer in the business of epistemology.... Instead we are in the business of creating links, of making them, of bringing them more or less successfully into being.... We are in the business of ontology.
>
> (Law, 1997: 8–9)

41 The radical empiricism of Deleuze and the critical realism of Bhaskar form the extremities of the epistemo-ontological continuum. Whereas Deleuze aims to systematically destroy any and every transcendence in the bud, even to the point of evacuating the emergence of a possible collective, Bhaskar (2000) has recently added a supplementary transcendental turn to his dialectical critical realism and introduced God as the real, total and enduring ultimatum of reality.

42 Although Deleuze has found the model and the inspiration for his plane of immanence as heterogeneous space of becoming through continuous variation in Spinoza (Deleuze, 1981), one might as well follow Michel Serres (1968, 1974) and conceptualise it in the Leibnizian tradition as a 'topological-energetic space'.

43 Deleuze and Guattari's *Lebensphilosophie* has clear affinities with the Buddhist view of the world as a cosmic dance of particles. In a passage on meditation, Guattari makes the link with Buddhism explicit:

> Solitude, meditation, desiring contemplation pushed to its term and the loss of individuation to the profit of cosmical arrangements all lead to a paradoxical conjunction of individuated hypersubjectivation and radical abandonment of the subject to collective arrangements.
>
> (Guattari, 1977: 327)

For a phenomenological analysis of the dissolution of reality in Theravada Buddhism, allow me to refer to my 'Uncartesian meditations on the phenomenology of the nostril' (Vandenberghe, 2002c).

44 Having lost the boundaries that separate persons, animals and things, individuals are no longer conceived of as indivisible, bounded units, but as 'dividuals' (Deleuze, 1990: 244) that absorb or transmit heterogeneous material influences, reproducing thereby the anonymous flux from which they originated and to which they will ultimately revert.

45 For a comprehensive exploration of the bio-philosophical aspects of Deleuze and Guattari's vitalism, see Ansell Pearson (1997, 1999). In his *User's Guide to Capitalism and Schizophrenia*, Massumi (1992: 93–141) covers the same ground, but is more inspired by the recent developments in physics than in biology.

46 In her remarkable book on the influence of the biology of his time (Rolf, Virchow, Haeckel) on Nietzsche, Barbara Stiegler (2001) interprets Nietzsche's philosophy of life as a biologisation of Kant's epistemology in which the living body takes the place of the transcendental subject. The body synthetically constitutes the environment as a unity, but this unification through assimilation and incorporation of the environment is haunted by the memory of the alterity, which enhances the internal complexity of the subject and drives its individualisation forward.

47 Like a train can hide another train, a constructivism can hide another one. Unlike the empiricist constructivism of the fourth wave of the sociology of science (after Mannheim, Merton and the Strong Programme) and the linguistic deconstructivism of third-wave feminism (after liberalism and socialism), the radical constructivism of the second-order cyberneticians, neurologists, biologists, anthropologists and sociologists like von Foerster, Maturana, Varela, Bateson, Morin and Luhmann offers a non-reductionist theory of cognition that analyses the construction of reality as a reflexive, self-organising and self-referential construction of the experience of reality. On radical constructivism, see Schmidt (1991).

48 Like Castells (1996: 30), I include not only informatics and electronics, but also genetic engineering in the realm of information technologies.

49 For a history of cybernetics and its influence on structuralism, systems theory, post-structuralism and postmodern philosophy, see Lafontaine (2004); for a history of the developments of biotechnology that analyses the integration of informatics, biologics and economics, see Haraway (1997: 49–101, 244–265).

50 DeLanda (1992) uses the lingo of complexity theory (bifurcations, bistability, attractors, repellors, catastrophe, chaos, dissipative structures and emergence), to theorise the evolution of the vital phylum, from the hypothetical emergence of a crystal planet to cell differentiation and from human speciation to social formations.

51 It may be of interest to note that the programs that simulate the evolutionary process use symbiosis to introduce mutations:

> Among the mutants were parasites that had lost their own copying instructions but developed the ability to invade a host and hijack its copying procedure.... Later runs of the programme saw the development of hyperparasites.... Hyperparasites wait for parasites to invade them.
>
> (Hayles, 1999: 227).

52 Joshua Lederberg, Nobel-prize winner and participant of the famous Ciba-Symposion on the Future of Man, soberly redescribed the human in terms of a sequence of paired nucleotides:

> Now we can define man. Genotypically at least, he is six feet of a particular molecular sequence of carbon, hydrogen, oxygen, nitrogen and phosphorous atoms – the length of DNA tightly coiled in the nucleus of his provenient egg and in the nucleus of every adult cell, 5 thousand million paired nucleotide units long.
>
> (Lederberg, 1963: 263–264)

Given that all genetic information is located in the nucleus of the cell and that the technique of recombinant DNA aims to alter or, in the case of cloning, to fix the genetic material that is contained in the nucleus, Hans Jonas (1987: 102, 171, 207) has proposed to rename molecular biology – in analogy with nuclear physics – as 'nuclear biology'.

53 Extending the metaphor of the text, a popularising textbook on the genome describes the latter as a book:

> Imagine that the genome is a book. There are twenty three chapters, called chromosomes. Each chapter contains several thousand stories, called genes. Each story is made up of paragraphs, called exons, which are interrupted by advertisements called introns. Each paragraph is made up of words, called codons. Each word is written in letters, called bases.
>
> (Ridley, 2000: 7)

In passing I note that the preceding quotation of Michel Serres does not come from a text on biology, but from a text on the episteme of the sciences of the nineteenth century. Given that the episteme of the classic epoch is written like a language and that all the sciences of the encyclopaedia can be translated in the universal language of structuralism, the language of biology represents only an example of a more general case that characterises all the sciences – and, *pace* Foucault, not just the sciences of economics, linguistics and life. For a systematic exploration of the role of writing technologies and inscription devices that translate all kind of possible objects and things into the language of science by projecting their form onto a one-dimensional plane, see the masterful article of Bruno Latour (1985) on 'mutable mobiles' and 'centres of calculation'.

54 To make things even more complex, reflexive and fluid: the description of the network is itself a network, with the result that it becomes undecidable if the hypertext of the network offers a complex description of the network, or a recursive projection of the network on a complex state of affairs. Not only are the phenomena to be described complex, but in complexity theory, scientific practice itself is a phenomenon of organised complexity. For a complex description of the history of mathematics in terms of networks, bifurcations, ways, etc., see Serres (1968: 78–112).

55 This is not an aberration, but a reiteration – as if we would get to the truth if only we would keep on lying through our teeth: 'There has never been a struggle against the society of consumption, this idiotic notion. To the contrary, we say that there has never been enough consumption' (Deleuze, 1990: 32).

56 Brazilianisation is a synonym for the deterioration of labour conditions and the informalisation of labour. From experience, I know that Brazil is not a developing country, but a rich, unequal and unjust society. Half Belgium, half India ('Belindia'), it is at the same time part of the First and the Third World. In any case, Beck's theories of the risk society and second modernity do not apply to Brazil, not because there's no risk, but because in the absence of ecological consciousness among the masses, one arrives at the paradoxical conclusion that one has to build the risk society.

57 For a general analysis of the many parallels between postmodernism and the more political-economic discourse of neoliberalism, see Ray and Sayer (1999).

58 Under the auspices of the Institute of Sante Fe, complexity theory is simplified and offered as one more strategy of innovation to business people. Here's an example of how the idea of the emergent order is sold to managers who are 'living on the edge':

> The suggestions of complexity theory for business practice are a flattening of the management hierarchy, distribution of control through the system with fluid networks of interaction between the parts, and the necessity of periods of chaos for the emergence of appropriate new order. The move towards a more anarchic, spontaneous dynamic is clearly threatening to the controlling managers, but it appears to be the path to creativity and diversification.... All the participants in this sector of social organisation can then experience a higher quality of life, since

> they have greater freedom, more opportunities for creative play, and richer interactions – good for them and good for the organisation.
>
> (Goodwin, quoted in Thrift, 1999: 47).

59 The transnational streams of money that irrigate the global financial system are muddy and bloody waters. The 'mother of accumulation' does not discriminate between her legitimate and illegitimate sons and daughters. The global network of networks also includes transnational networks of crime, like the Sicilian Cosa Nostra, the Colombian cartels, the Japanese Yakuza, the Chinese Triads or the Russian Mafias. Adepts of dependency theory will appreciate that the *favelas* of Latin America are integrated into the global economy through the *narcotrafico*. While drugs traffic is the most important segment of this worldwide industry, trade in weapons, radioactive materials, human beings, organs, etc. is also highly profitable. At the heart of the system is money laundering, 'the mother of all crimes' (Castells, 1997: 260, see also Castells, 1998: 166–205), which connects the criminal economy to the global financial markets.

60 Radin (1996) reminds us that universal commodification is an ideal-type that can be understood in a literal or in a metaphorical sense. Although metaphorical commodification sets the scene for literal commodification, I am not interested here in the market rhetoric of a Gary Becker or a Judge Posner who apply the reductionist model of neoclassic economy to the whole world. Conceiving of everything (babies, body parts, etc.) as fungible objects and of every social interaction (love, marriage, even rape) as a market transaction, they know the value of nothing and attribute a price to everything, even where no money changes hands and no real markets are involved – as yet.

61 Habermas' theory of the colonisation of the life-world by the subsystems of the economy and the state was meant as a reformulation of the Frankfurt School's theory of reification in the language of the communicative paradigm. The original formulation hardly contained a word on colonisation in the strict sense or on colonisation in the broad sense. In fact, it is only as an unintended consequence of the so-called Sloterdijk-debates on posthumanism that he has recently analysed the colonisation of life under the heading of 'liberal eugenics' (Habermas, 2001a, see below).

62 *Non olet* – in a more scatological vein, Guattari (1977: 17) compares the axiomatic reduction of all values to the lowest common denominator to shit:

> When I talk about shit, it is hardly a metaphor: Capitalism reduces everything to shit, that is to say to the state of undifferentiated and decoded streams out of which everyone has to take its part in a private mode and with a sense of culpability.

63 Integrating Marx's analysis of capital with Deleuze and Guattari's analysis of machinic production, Hardt and Negri (2000) have systematically developed a few pages from *A Thousand Plateaus* on the imperial war machine and the axiomatics of capital (cf. Deleuze and Guattari, 1980, 525–527, 566–568, 584–588, 613–614) into a full-blown theory of the global rise and the violent demise of the neo-capitalist empire.

64 Italian activists like Toni Negri, Maurizio Lazaratto and Paolo Virno, who were linked in the 1970s to the 'operaist movement' (*autonomia operaia*), have worked out the notion of 'immaterial labour' and integrated it in a systematic theory of cognitive capitalism. In the following I am drawing on Negri *et al.* (1998) as well as Azaïs *et al.* (2001).

65 The apocalyptic tone, especially when I deal with genetics, may suggest proximity to the first generation of the Frankfurt School (Adorno, Horkheimer, Marcuse). As my analysis is much more indebted to the second generation for its normative underpinnings (Habermas), it has, in fact, much more affinity with the more sociological research of the third generation of the *Institut für Sozialforschung* on the paradoxes of formal and communicative rationalisation of late capitalism (cf. Honneth, 2002).

66 The end of the human sciences has been most crisply and brutally formulated by Claude Lévi-Strauss (1962: 326): 'We believe that the ultimate end of the human sciences is not to constitute, but to dissolve the human.'

67 To stress that power produces and regulates life by targeting the body, Foucault has introduced the notions of 'bio-power' and 'bio-politics'. Although he explicitly mentions that biology is inflected by politics – 'le biologique se réfléchit dans le politique' (Foucault, 1976: 187) – bio-politics is more concerned with the political administration of the life of populations than with the bio-technological production of life. Neo-Foucaldians like Rose, Rabinow and Agamben have now revised and updated the concept of bio-power so as to include the genetic modification of organisms and the commodification of the body.

68 Even if there's only one Foucault, there have been shifts in his analysis of power (Lazaratto, 2000). In the 1970s modern, disciplinary or bio-power was analysed in the quasi-military terms of war and struggles as politics by other means, its aims consisting in the weakening of the resistances of the enemy; in the 1980s the notion of government displaces the one of power and is internally linked to freedom, which is integral to the operation of power. Instead of the strategies of the battlefield, it's the communicative relations between the parent and the child or the teacher and the pupil that become the ideal-typical loci of the exercise of power.

69 Foucault analysed 'governmentality' in 1978 in his lectures at the Collège de France. Meanwhile, the main texts on 'government' have been posthumously republished in volume 3 and 4 of the *Dits et écrits* (Foucault, 1994: III, 635–657, 719–723; IV, 134–161, 222–243). The journal *Economy and Society* offers concrete examples of the theoretically informed sociological and historical research that is the hallmark of neo-Foucaldian studies. In his introduction to the new subdiscipline of governmentality studies, Mitchell Dean (1999: 11) defines government as

> any more or less calculated and rational activity, undertaken by a multiplicity of authorities and agencies, employing a variety of techniques and forms of knowledge, that seeks to shape conduct by working through our desires, aspirations, interests and beliefs, for definite but shifting ends and with a diverse set of relatively unpredictable consequences, effects and outcomes.
>
> (Dean, 1999: 11)

70 Funnily enough, the convergence of the theories of Foucault, Deleuze, Latour and Rose can also be analysed as an assemblage. Enrolling and incorporating some of the main concepts of actor–network theory (e.g. translations, interessement, inscription devices, centres of calculation, etc.) into governmentality studies, Nikolas Rose, the spokesperson of the defunct History of the Present Research Network, has brought ANT to a new captive audience of Francophile political scientists and forged a loose theoretical alliance between Foucauldians (Ewald, Donzelot, Rose, Osborne, etc. – see the journal *Economy and Society*), Deleuzians (Negri, Alliez, Hardt, etc. – see the journal *Multitudes*) and Latourians (Hennion, Law, Stengers, etc. – see the journal *Cosmopolitiques*) on both sides of the channel.

71 For an affirmative, enthusiastic and almost chiliastic interpretation of the interconnection of markets and minds by a convinced Deleuzian, see Lévy (2000).

72 Since the 1980s patents have become the oil of the bio-industry. To procure a patent on genetic material it must be shown that, through the process of research, development and production, the 'natural product' has been transformed into an 'invention'. Anything can be patented, as the Indians found out with horror when they were informed in 1997 that the American company RiceTec had reinvented, patented and thus appropriated their Basmati rice. Another US company, Myriad Pharmaceuticals, has patented the breast cancer gene and has a monopoly on all diagnostic use of this patented gene. In 2001 the US patent and trademark office extended the boundaries of

what can be patented to include single nucleotide polymorphisms (SNPs or 'snips') – the smallest unit of genetic variability.

73 For an exhaustive overview of the literature on the commodification of the body, see Sharp (2000).

74 Although the organs and human tissues that are 'harvested' are mostly 'given' and described as 'gifts of life', observers of the business have noticed that recipients are usually shown a price sheet which reveals that the procuration of organs is paid for. The business of transplantation is, in fact, 'a multi-million dollar medical industry where clients in need pay steep fees for the procurement, preparation, transportation, and surgical replacement of body parts' (Sharp, 2000: 303–304). For a subtle critique of the 'gift of life', see Lock (2001: 65–73) and Scheper-Hughes (2007).

75 The contemporary traffic in organs reminds us eerily of the theft of bodies from hospitals, the buying of cadavers from the hangmen and the profanation of tombs for the sake of anatomical dissection that Le Breton (1993: 113–168) has described in detail in his 'nocturnal history' of Western medicine. Although there is now a global economy in body parts that flow from poor to rich countries and from the young to the elderly, a good deal of the macabre stories about cannibalism, vampirism and the theft of bodies and body parts are often nothing but rumours. Reconnecting the occult economies of the postcolonial countries to the global market, Comaroff and Comaroff (1999) suggest in a nicely crafted article that the urban legends should be read as so many symptoms of a fear of the creeping commodification of life itself that reflect on the level of the imaginary the violent abstractions of real capitalism.

76 In order to avoid the impression that the realist theory of nature has been rendered superficial by the extermination of nature, I would like to remind the reader of the distinction between 'deep' and 'surface' nature. When I speak about the extermination of nature, I obviously aim to refer to the latter. Even if humans were to destroy themselves and their environment, deep nature would still remain and retain its essential properties, though there would be no scientists left to investigate them, no sociologists to investigate and deconstruct the investigations of their colleagues, and no meta-sociologists either to criticise the irresponsibility of those deconstructions.

77 Latour (1991: 23) also defines modernity in terms of the co-emergence of nature, culture or society, and the disappearance of God: 'Modernity arises first from the conjoined creation of those three entities: [humans, non-humans and a crossed-out God]'. But whereas he contends that modernity has obscured the continuing proliferation of hybrids, I would like to propose instead that the hybridisation of humans and non-humans characterises late modernity and that the post-humanist indistinction between humans and non-humans obscures and obliterates the experimental machinations and colonisations of the capitalist megamachine.

78 If the attempt to technologically reconstruct nature is modern, the attempt to redefine the human in terms of human nature is not, as Gernot Böhme (2001: 65–66) has correctly noted:

> In the past, one could leave aside what human nature is. In modernity, humans have in fact not defined themselves in terms of nature, but in terms of rationality, reason and mind, because those are the faculties in which they recognised self-determination. Today, however, nature has to be explicitly brought in and related to the self-understanding of humans.

79 Giddens (1994: 100) defines fundamentalism as the attempt to defend tradition in a traditional way.

80 Species-ethics represents, in fact, the normative-evaluative branch of philosophical anthropology that seeks to answer the metaphysical question: 'If and why humanity should be; why the human should be maintained as evolution has produced it and why its genetic material should be respected; or, in short, why there should be life in the first place?' (Jonas, 1987: 48). Habermas (2001a: 70–80) has introduced species-ethics

as an anthropological 'embedding' of his discourse ethics. If discourse ethics deals with 'moral questions', that is with questions that pertain to justice and are universally valid, ethics deals in his vocabulary with 'ethical questions' that pertain to the 'good life' of an individual or a community. Unlike norms, visions of the good life are not universally valid, but hold only for particular individuals and communities. Although species-ethics deals with ethical questions, those questions are relevant for the universal community of human beings. Technically speaking, species ethics deals thus with the ethical value of a moral form of life.

81 This line echoes another one: what has been deregulated by the market should be re-regulated by government. In the same way as the political regulation of the market does not mean to eliminate the market, the normative regulation of the techno-sciences does not mean to abolish the autonomy of scientific research, but to force scientists to take into account the unintended and unacceptable consequences of scientific experimentation with humans. The call for a normative regulation of the techno-sciences is not anti-science: 'It is something else than the expression of musty anti-modernist resistance.... The perspective is not the one of re-enchantment, but of a becoming reflexive of modernity that becomes enlightened about its own limits' (Habermas, 2001a: 49–51).

82 In the *Foundations of the Fundamental Principles of the Metaphysics of Morals*, Kant opposes value to dignity and defines the dignity of the human person as an absolute value that cannot be compared to any other value and is therefore above all value (*über allen Preis erhaben*):

> In the kingdom of ends everything has either value or dignity. Whatever has a value can be replaced by something else which is equivalent; whatever, on the other hand, is above all value, and therefore admits of no equivalent has a dignity.
>
> (Kant, 1956a: A93)

83

> Expectations that are adapted to reality in case of disappointment are experienced and treated as cognitive. The opposite holds for normative expectations: one doesn't drop them when someone acts against them.... Normative expectations are characterised by a determination not to learn in case of disappointment.
>
> (Luhmann, 1972: I, 42–43).

84 In the *Manifesto of the Mutants*, the principle of non-precaution is explicitly defended:

> We want to create new species, use human clones, choose our genes, shape our minds and bodies, control germs, devour transgenic feasts, donate our extra cells, see in infrared, hear ultrasound, feel pheromones, cultivate our genes, replace our neurones, make love in space, converse with robots, test modified cerebral states, add new senses, last twenty years or two centuries, live on the Moon, settle on Mars, become familiar with the galaxies.
>
> (www.ifrance.com/mutation)

85 *Aufklärung, not Abklärung* – reconstruction, not deconstruction. The pun could be liberally translated into another one: ReKanting, not recanting of the Enlightenment.

86 The best warrant against eugenic temptations is to be found in the acceptance of the handicapped child as 'one of us' (Nussbaum, 2001). Postmodern ethics wants to cultivate a sense of otherness and defend the other. To the extent that the critique of Kantian morality is accomplished through a systematic deconstruction of universal categories and distinctions, postmodernism ends up, however, with a strange tension between philosophy and technology: on the one hand, it wants to preserve difference, on the other hand, it deconstructs the category of the human and thereby opens up the way to experiments with otherness.

87

> Man is gifted with pity and other kindly feelings; he has also the power of preventing many kinds of suffering. I conceive it to fall well within his province to replace Natural Selection by other processes that are more merciful and not less effective. This precisely is the aim of Eugenics.
>
> (Galton, quoted by McNally, 1995: 141)

In the following pages I use the term eugenics in accordance with the classic definition of Sir Francis Galton, the cousin of Darwin who coined the term in 1883 to refer to proposals, policies or practices that aim to modify natural selection in a humane way and lead to genetic improvement of the human species. Whereas the inhumane practices of Nazi Germany fail both criteria, the bio-capitalist proposals and practices satisfy the criteria and can thus properly be called eugenic.

88 The illnesses may be rare, the cures are even rarer. The asymmetry between genetic diagnosis and therapy may be hard to bear for the patients: they are diagnosed as 'virtually ill', even if no cure is in sight. Promising health, the medical profession all too often tends to underemphasise the extent to which health and well-being may be incompatible and prefers to ignore or minimise the existential anguish and the moral pain that inevitably accompany the 'limit situation' (Jaspers) that unhinge the life-stories of the patients when they are confronted with the collateral effects of medical treatment. In a moving testimony of his own heart transplantation and of the cancer that broke out eight years later as a result of the medical treatment, Jean-Luc Nancy (2000: 40–41) evokes, for instance, how he (it) went from pain to pain and estrangement to estrangement as he submitted himself to a permanent regime of medical intrusion:

> To the more than daily intake of drugs and the controls in the hospital were added the dental sequels of radiotherapy, as well as the loss of saliva, the control of food and contagious contacts, the weakening of the muscles and of the kidneys, the fading of memory and of the force to work, the reading of the analyses, the insidious return of mucitis, candidose or polyneuritis, and the general sentiment of no longer being dissociated from a network of measures, observations, chemical, institutional and symbolic connections that cannot be ignored.

89 Parents do not only desire healthy children, but they also wish and dream of beautiful, creative, original, sensitive and intelligent ones. Although genes for Einsteinian intelligence, Habermasian morality and Latourian wit may be impossible to find – though they might possibly be cloned – the move from a desire for children to a desire for dreamchildren explains why some rich parents would be only too willing to follow up the proposals for 'designer children' that the market already has on offer – which raises the prospect of an impending genetic divide between the poor and the rich.

90 Coming back from the United States, Habermas (2002: 283–285) has noticed a discrepancy between the perspectives on bio-technology of his European and American colleagues. Whereas the Germans are still debating if further developments in genomics should take place, the Americans seem as confident about scientific progress as the Europeans were at the beginning of the twentieth century and no longer question the advance of genomics. Instead, they simply accept the therapeutic implementation of genetic therapies and wonder how the 'shopping in the genetic supermarket' should be regulated. Comparing the French with the American views on bio-ethics, Rabinow (1999: 71–111) notes that the Americans allow for more latitude for commercial relations concerning the body and the person than the French, who follow a more Kantian line and privilege dignity over value and autonomy. Deconstructing and ridiculing the French attempts to protect the dignity of the person ('ritualistic safeguards', 'this-worldly mysticism', 'commitment to fixed (if empty) concepts of the human person'), the American anthropologist has nothing else to offer *in fine* but a Foucaldian 'ethic of experimentation'.

Bibliography

Adorno, T.W. 1975. *Soziologische Schriften I*, in *Gesammelte Schriften, Band 8.1*. Frankfurt am Main: Suhrkamp.

Adorno, T.W. 1977. *Ohne Leitbild. Parva Aesthetica*, in *Gesammelte Schriften, Band 10.1*. Frankfurt am Main: Suhrkamp.

Agamben, G. 1998. *Homo Sacer: Sovereignty and Bare Life*. Stanford, CA: Stanford University Press.

Agar, N. 2000. 'Liberal eugenics', pp. 171–181 in H. Kuhse and P. Singer (eds), *Bioethics*. London: Blackwell.

Akrich, M. 1994. 'Comment sortir de la dichotomie technique/société. Présentation des diverses sociologies de la technique', pp. 105–131 in B. Latour and P. Lemonnier (eds), *De la préhistoire aux missiles balistiques: L'intelligence sociale des techniques*. Paris: Editions la découverte.

Ansell Pearson, K. 1997. *Viroid Life: Perspectives on Nietzsche and the Transhuman Condition*. London: Routledge.

Ansell Pearson, K. 1999. *Germinal Life: The Difference and Repetition of Deleuze*. London: Routledge.

Appadurai, A. (ed.) 1986. *The Social Life of Things: Commodities in Cultural Perspective*. Cambridge: Cambridge University Press.

Azaïs, C., Corsani, A. and Dieuaide, P. (eds) 2001. *Vers un capitalisme cognitif. Entre mutations du travail et territoires*. Paris: L'Harmattan.

Barber, R. and Trepos, J.-Y. 2007. 'Humains et non-humains: un bilan d'etape de la sociologie des collectifs', *Revue d'Anthropologie des Connaissances*, 2007, 1, pp. 35–58.

Bauman, Z. 1995. *Life in Fragments: Essays in Postmodern Morality*. Oxford: Blackwell.

Bauman, Z. 2000. *Liquid Modernity*. Oxford: Blackwell.

Bayart, J.F. 2004. *Le gouvernement du monde: Une critique politique de la globalisation*. Paris. Fayard.

Beck, U. 1986. *Risikogesellschaft: Auf dem Weg in eine andere Moderne*. Frankfurt am Main: Suhrkamp.

Beck, U. 1999. *Schöne neue Arbeitswelt. Vision: Weltbürgergesellschaft*. Frankfurt am Main: Campus.

Beck, U, Bonβ, W. and Lau, C. 2001. 'Theorie reflexiver Modernisierung – Fragestellungen, Hypothesen, Forschungsprogramme', pp. 11–59 in U. Beck and W. Bonβ (eds), *Die Modernisierung der Moderne*. Frankfurt am Main: Suhrkamp.

Beck-Gernsheim, E. 1991. *Technik, Markt und Moral: Über Reproduktionsmedizin und Gentechnologie*. Frankfurt am Main: Fisher.

Beck-Gernsheim, E. 1994. 'Gesundheit und Verantwortung im Zeitalter der Technologie', pp. 316–335 in U. Beck and E. Beck-Gernsheim (eds), *Riskante Freiheiten*. Frankfurt am Main: Suhrkamp.

Berlin, I. 1976. *Vico and Herder: Two Studies in the History of Ideas*. London: Hogarth Press.

Best, S. and Kellner, D. 2001. *The Postmodern Adventure: Science, Technology and Cultural Studies at the Third Millenium*. London: Routledge.

Bhaskar, R. 1978. *A Realist Theory of Science*. Brighton: Harvester Press.

Bhaskar, R. 2000. *From East to West: Odyssey of a Soul*. London: Routledge.

Blandin, B. 2002. *La construction du social par les objets*, Paris: P.U.F.

Böhme, G. 2001. 'Kritische Theorie der Natur', *Zeitschrift für kritische Theorie*, 12, pp. 59–71.

Böhme, G., van den Daele, W. and Krohn, W. 1977. *Experimentelle Philosophie: Ursprünge autonomer Wissenschaftsentwicklung*. Frankfurt am Main: Suhrkamp.
Boltanki, L. and Chiapello, E. 1999. *Le nouvel esprit du capitalisme*. Paris: Gallimard.
Butler, J. 1990. *Gender Trouble: Feminism and the Subversion of Identity*. London: Routledge.
Butler, J. 1993. *Bodies That Matter: On the Discursive Limits of 'Sex'*. London: Routledge.
Campbell, C. 1987. *The Romantic Ethic and the Spirit of Modern Consumerism*. Oxford: Blackwell.
Cassirer, E. 1994. *Das Erkenntnisproblem in der Philosophie und Wissenschaft der neueren Zeit*, 3 vols. Darmstadt: Wissenschaftliche Buchgesellschaft.
Castells, M. 1996. *The Rise of the Network Society*. Oxford: Basil Blackwell.
Castells, M. 1997. *The Power of Identity*. Oxford: Basil Blackwell.
Castells, M. 1998. *End of Millenium*. Oxford: Basil Blackwell.
Castoriadis, C. 1975. *L'institution imaginaire de la société*. Paris: Seuil.
Clark, N. 2000. 'Botanizing on the asphalt? The complex life of cosmopolitan bodies', *Body and Society*, 6, 3–4, pp. 12–33.
Cohen, L. 2001. 'The other kidney: biopolitics beyond recognition', *Body & Society*, 7, 2–3, pp. 9–29.
Comaroff, J. and Comaroff, J.L. 1999. 'Occult economies and the violence of abstraction: notes from the South African postcolony', *American Ethnologist*, 26, 2, pp. 279–303.
Crook, S., Pakulski, J. and Waters, M. 1992. *Postmodernization: Change in Advanced Societies*. London: Sage.
Dean, M. 1999. *Governmentality: Power and Rule in Modern Society*. London: Sage.
Debray, R. 1998. 'Abécédaire et parti-pris', *Cahiers de médiologie*, 6, 2, pp. 263–283.
DeLanda, M. 1992. 'Nonorganic life', pp. 129–167 in J. Crary and S. Kwinter (eds), *Incorporations*. New York: Zone Books.
Deleuze, G. 1965. *Nietzsche*. Paris: P.U.F.
Deleuze, G. 1981. *Spinoza: Philosophie pratique*. Paris: Minuit.
Deleuze, G. 1986. *Foucault*. Paris: Minuit.
Deleuze, G. 1990. *Pourparlers: 1972–1990*. Paris: Minuit.
Deleuze, G. 1995. 'L'immanence: Une vie..', *Philosophie*, 47, 1, pp. 3–7.
Deleuze, G. and Guattari, F. 1972. *L'anti-Oedipe: Capitalisme et schizophrénie*. Paris: Minuit.
Deleuze, G. and Guattari, F. 1980. *Mille plateaux: Capitalisme et schizophrénie 2*. Paris: Minuit.
de Waal, F. 2005. *Our Inner Ape*. New York: Penguin.
Dupuy, J.P. 2002. *Pour un catastrophisme éclairé: Quand l'impossible est certain*. Paris: Seuil.
Eliot, T.S. 1948. *Notes Towards the Definition of Culture*. London: Faber.
Escobar, A. 1999. 'After nature: steps to an antiessentialist political ecology', *Current Anthropology*, 40, 1, pp. 1–16.
Foucault, M. 1966. *Les mots et les choses*. Paris: Gallimard.
Foucault, M. 1976. *Histoire de la sexualité I: La volonté de savoir*. Paris: Gallimard.
Foucault, M. 1994. *Dits et écrits 1954–1988*, I–IV. Paris: Gallimard.
Freitag, M. 2002. 'La nature de la technique', pp. 245–313 in *L'oubli de la société. Pour une théorie critique de la postmodernité*. Rennes: Presses universitaires de Rennes.
Gehlen, A. 1957. *Die Seele im technischen Zeitalter: Sozialpsychologische Probleme in der industriellen Gesellschaft*. Hamburg: Rowohlt.

Giddens, A. 1994. 'Living in a post-traditional society', pp. 56–109 in U. Beck A. Giddens and S. Lash, *Reflexive Modernization*. Cambridge: Polity Press.

Gorz, A. 2003. *L'immatériel: Connaissance, valeur et capital*. Paris: Galilée.

Gramsci, A. 1971. 'Americanism and Fordism', pp. 279–318 in *Selections from the Prison Notebooks*. London: Lawrence & Wishart.

Groenen, M. 1996. *Leroi-Gourhan: Essence et contingence dans la destinée humaine*. Bruxelles: De Boeck.

Guattari, F. 1977. *La révolution moléculaire*. Fontenay-sous-Bois: Editions Recherches.

Guillebaud, J.C. 2001. *Le principe d'humanité*. Paris: Seuil.

Habermas, J. 1971. *Technik und Wissenschaft als Ideologie*. Frankfurt am Main: Suhrkamp.

Habermas, J. 1981. *Theorie des kommunikativen Handelns*. Frankfurt am Main: Suhrkamp.

Habermas, J. 1998. *Die postnationale Konstellation: Politische Essays*. Frankfurt am Main: Suhrkamp.

Habermas, J. 2001a. *Die Zukunft der menschlichen Natur: Auf dem Weg zu einer liberalen Eugenik?* Frankfurt am Main: Suhrkamp.

Habermas, J. 2001b. *Glauben und Wissen*. Frankfurt am Main: Suhrkamp.

Habermas, J. 2002. 'Replik auf Einwande', *Deutsche Zeitschrift für Philosophie*, 50, 2, pp. 283–298.

Haraway, D. 1991. *Simians, Cyborgs and Women: The Reinvention of Nature*. New York: Routledge.

Haraway, D. 1997. *Modest_Witness@Second_Millenium. FemaleMan© _Meets_Oncomouse™*. London: Routledge.

Hardt, M. and Negri, A. 2000. *Empire*. Cambridge, MA: Harvard University Press.

Hayles, C. 1999. *How We became Posthuman: Virtual Bodies in Cybernetics, Literature and Informatics*. Chicago, IL: University of Chicago Press.

Helman, C. 1998. 'Dr. Frankenstein and the industrial body: reflections on "spare part" surgery', *Anthropology Today*, 4, 3, pp. 14–15.

Honneth, A. (ed.) 2002. *Befreiung aus der Mündigkeit: Paradoxien der Gegenwärtigen Kapitalismus*. Frankfurt am Main: Institut für Sozialforschung/Campus.

Horigan, S. 1988. *Nature and Culture in Western Discourses*. London: Routledge.

Horkheimer, M. and Adorno, T.W. 1969. *Dialektik der Aufklärung: Philosophische Fragmente*. Frankfurt am Main: Fisher.

Hottois, G. 2001. 'Y a-t-il une philosophie de la technique?', pp. 27–45 in T. Ferenczi (ed.), *Penser la technique*. Bruxelles: Editions Complexe.

Husserl, E. 1952. *Ideen zu einer reinen Phänomenologie und phänomenologischen Philosophie*. Zweites Buch: *Phänomenologische Untersuchungen zur Konstitution* (Ideen II) – Drittes Buch: *Die Phänomenologie und die Fundamente der Wissenschaften* (Ideen III) in *Husserliana*, Bd. IV & V. The Hague: Martinus Nijhoff.

Husserl, E. 1958. *Die Idee der Phänomenologie: Fünf Vorlesungen* in *Husserliana*, Bd. II. The Hague: Martinus Nijhoff.

Husserl, E. 1980. *Logische Untersuchungen*. Zweiter Band: *Elemente einer phänomenologischen Aufklärung der Erkenntnis*, Zweiter Teil. Tübingen: Max Niemeyer Verlag.

Jameson, F. 1991. *Postmodernism, or the Cultural Logic of Late Capitalism*. London: Verso.

Jonas, H. 1984. *Das Prinzip Verantwortung: Versuch einer Ethik fur die technologische Zivilisation*. Frankfurt am Main: Suhrkamp.

Jonas, H. 1987. *Technik, Medizin und Ethik: Zur Praxis des Prinzips Verantwortung*. Frankfurt am Main: Suhrkamp.

Joy, B. 2000. 'Why the future doesn't need us', *Wired*, 8, 4, pp. 238–264.

Kant, I. 1785/1956a. *Grundlegung zur Metaphysik der Sitten*, in *Werke, Band IV*. Wiesbaden: Insel Verlag.

Kant, I. 1788/1956b. *Kritik der praktischen Vernunft*, in *Werke, Band IV*. Wiesbaden: Insel Verlag.

Kern, I. 1962. 'Die Drei Wege zur transzendental-phänomenologischen Reduktion in der Philosophie E. Husserls', *Tijdschrift voor Filosofie*, 24, pp. 303–349.

Keulartz, J. 1998. *Struggle for Nature: A Critique of Radical Ecology*. London: Routledge.

Kimbrell, A. 1993. *The Human Body Shop: The Engineering and Marketing of Life*. New York: Harper Collins.

Klein, N. 2001. 'Reclaiming the commons', *New Left Review*, 9, pp. 81–89.

Kögler, H. 1992. *Die Macht des Dialogs: Kritische Hermeneutik nach Gadamer, Foucault und Rorty*. Stuttgart: J.B. Metzler.

Kopytoff, I. 1982. 'Slavery', *Annual Review of Anthropology*, 11, pp. 207–230.

Kuper, A. 1999. *Culture: The Anthropologist's Account*. Cambridge, MA: Harvard University Press.

Lafontaine, C. 2004. *L'empire cybernétique: Des machines à penser à la pensée machine*. Paris: Seuil.

Lappé, M. 2000. 'Ethical issues in manipulating the human germ line', pp. 155–164 in H. Kuhse and P. Singer (eds), *Bioethics*. Oxford: Blackwell.

Landgrebe, L. 1963. 'Seinsregionen und regionale Ontologien in Husserls Phänomenologie', pp. 143–162 in *Der Weg der Phänomenologie*. Gütersloh: G. Mohn.

Latour, B. 1985. 'Les "vues" de l'esprit: une introduction à l'anthropologie des sciences et des techniques', *Culture technique*, 14, pp. 4–30.

Latour, B. 1991. *Nous n'avons jamais été modernes: Essai d'anthropologie symétrique*. Paris: La Découverte.

Latour, B. 1994. 'Une sociologie sans objets? Remarques sur l'interobjectivité', *Sociologie du travail*, 4, pp. 587–607.

Latour, B. 1999. *Politiques de la nature: Comment faire entrer les sciences en démocratie*. Paris: La Découverte.

Latour, B. 2002. *Jubiler: ou les tourments de la parole religieuse*. Paris: Les empêcheurs de penser en rond.

Latour, B. and Lemonnier, P. (eds) 1994. *De la préhistoire aux missiles balistiques. L'intelligence sociale des techniques*. Paris: La Découverte.

Latour, B. and Woolgar, S. 1978. *Laboratory Life: The Social Construction of Scientific Facts*. London: Sage.

Lau, C. and Keller, R. 2001. 'Zur Politisierung gesellschaftlicher Naturabgrenzungen', pp. 82–95 in U. Beck and W. Bonss (eds), *Die Modernisierung der Moderne*. Frankfurt am Main: Suhrkamp.

Law, J. 1997. 'Traduction/trahison', *Sociology*, 56, pp. 1–20.

Lazaratto, M. 2000. 'Du biopouvoir à la biopolitique', *Multitudes*, 1, pp. 45–57.

Le Breton, D. 1990. *Anthropologie du corps et modernité*. Paris: P.U.F.

Le Breton, D. 1993. *La chair à vif: Usages médicaux et mondains du corps humain*. Paris: Métailié.

Leder, D. 1992. 'A tale of two bodies: the cartesian corpse and the lived body', pp. 17–35 in D. Leder (ed.), *The Body in Medical Thought and Practice*. Dordrecht: Kluwer Academic Publishing.

Lederberg, J. 1963. 'Biological future of man', pp. 263–273 in Wolstenholme, G. (ed.), *Man and his Future*. London: Churchill.

Leroi-Gourhan, A. 1964. *Le geste et la parole*. Vol. 1: *Technique et language*, Vol. 2: *La mémoire et les rythmes*. Paris: Albin Michel.

Leroi-Gourhan, A. 1982. *Les racines du monde*. Paris: Belfond.

Lévi-Strauss, C. 1962. *La pensée* sauvage. Paris: Plon.

Lévi-Strauss, C. 1968. *Les structures élémentaires de la parenté*. Paris: Mouton.

Lévi-Strauss, C. 1969. *Race et histoire*. Paris: Mouton.

Lévy, P. 1998. *Qu'est-ce que le virtuel?* Paris: La Découverte.

Lévy, P. 2000. *World Philosophie. Le marché, le cyberespace, la conscience*. Paris: Odile Jacob.

Lindenberg, D. 2001. *Le rappel à l'ordre: Enquête sur les nouveaux réactionnaires*. Paris: Seuil.

Lock, M. 2001. 'The alienation of body tissue and the biopolitics of immortalised cell lines', *Body & Society*, 7, 2–3, pp. 63–91.

Luckmann, T. 1970. 'On the boundaries of the social world', pp. 73–100 in M. Natanson (ed.), *Phenomenology and Social Reality: Essays in Memory of Alfred Schutz*. The Hague: Martinus Nijhoff.

Luhmann, N. 1969. 'Normen in soziologischer Perspektive', *Soziale Welt*, 20, pp. 28–48.

Luhmann, N. 1972. *Rechtssoziologie 1*. Reinbeck: Rowohlt.

Luhmann, N. 1987. *Soziale Systeme: Grundriss einder Allgemeinen Theorie*. Frankfut am Main: Suhrkamp.

Luhmann, N. 1992. *Beobachtungen der Moderne*. Opladen: Westdeutscher Verlag.

McLuhan, M. 1964. *Understanding Media: Extensions of Man*. Bergenfield: New American Library.

McNally, R. 1995. 'Eugenics here and now', *The Genetic Engineer and Biotechnologist*, 15, 2–3, pp. 135–144.

Martin, E. 1994. *Flexible Bodies: Tracking Immunity in American Culture – From the Days of Polio to the Age of Aids*. Boston, MA: Beacon Press.

Marx, K. 1848/1972. 'Das kommunistische Manifest', in *Marx/Engles Werke, Band III*. Berlin: Dietz Verlag.

Marx, K. 1887/1968. *Das Kapital, Band 1*, in *Marx/Engels Werke, Band XXIII*. Berlin: Dietz Verlag.

Massumi, B. 1992. *A User's Guide to Capitalism and Schizophrenia: Deviations from Deleuze and Guattari*. Cambridge, MA: MIT Press.

Mauss, M. 1950. Les techniques du corps', pp. 363–386 in *Sociologie et anthropologie*. Paris: Presses universitaires de France.

Michael, M. 2000. *Reconnecting Culture, Technology and Nature: From Society to Heterogeneity*. London: Routledge.

Miller, P. and Rose, N. 1990. 'Governing economic life', *Economy and Society*, 19, 1, pp. 1–31.

Monmonier, M. 1995. *Drawing the Line: Tales of Maps and Cartocontroversy*. New York: Henry Holt and Company.

Morin, E. 2001. *La méthode. Vol. 5: L'humanité de l'humanité. L'identité humaine*. Paris: Seuil.

Moscovici, P. 1977. *Essai sur l'histoire humaine de la nature*. Paris: Flammarion.

Musso, P. 2003. *Critique des réseaux*. Paris: P.U.F.

Nancy, J.-L. 2000. *L'intrus*. Paris: Galilée.

Negri, T., Lazzarato, M. and Virno, P. 1998. *Immaterielle Arbeit und Subversion*. Berlin: ID-Verlag.

Nietzsche, F. 1885/1988. *Also sprach Zarathustra*, in *Kritische Studienausgabe (Colli & Montinari), Band 4*. München/Berlin: DTV-de Gruyter.

Nussbaum, M. 2001. 'Disbled lives: who cares?', *The New York Review of Books*, 11 January.

Pels, D., Hetherington, K. and Vandenberghe, F. 2002. *Sociality and Materiality: The Status of the Object in Social Science*, Special edition of *Theory, Culture and Society*, 19, 5–6.

Plessner, H. 1965. *Die Stufen des Organischen und der Mensch: Einleitung in die philosophische Anthropologie*. Berlin: de Gruyter.

Power, M. 1994. 'The audit society', pp. 299–316 in A. Hopwood and P. Miller (eds), *Accounting as Social and Institutional Practice*. Cambridge: Cambridge University Press.

Rabinow, P. 1999. *French DNA: Trouble in Purgatory*. Chicago, IL: Chicago University Press.

Radin, M. 1996. *Contested Commodities: The Trouble with Trade in Sex, Children, Body Parts, and other Things*. Cambridge, MA: Harvard University Press.

Ray, L. and Sayer, A. (eds) 1999. *Culture and Economy After the Cultural Turn*. London: Sage.

Ricoeur, P. 1989. 'Humans as the subject matter of philosophy', pp. 89–101 in P. Kemp and D. Rasmussen (eds), *The Narrative Path: The Late Work of Paul Ricoeur*. Cambridge, MA: MIT Press.

Ridley, M. 2000. *Genome: The Autobiography of a Species in 23 Chapters*. New York: Harper Collins.

Rifkin, J. 2001. *The Age of Access*. New York: Penguin Putnam.

Rikowski, G. 2003. 'Alien life: Marx and the future of the human', *Historical Materialism*, 11, 2, pp. 121–164.

Rose, N. 1993. 'Government, authority and expertise in advanced liberalism', *Economy and Society*, 22, 3, pp. 283–299.

Rose, N. 1999a. *Governing the Soul: The Shaping of the Private Self* (second edition). London: Free Association Books.

Rose, N. 1999b. *Powers of Freedom: Reframing Political Thought*. Cambridge: Cambridge University Press.

Rose, N. 2001. 'The politics of life itself', *Theory, Culture and Society*, 18, 6, pp. 1–30.

Rose, N. and Miller, P. 1992. 'Political power beyond the state: problematics of government', *British Journal of Sociology*, 43, 2, pp. 173–205.

Scheper-Hughes, N. 2007. 'The tyranny of the gift: sacrificial violence in living donor transplants', *American Journal of Transplantation*, 7, 3, pp. 507–511.

Schmidt, S. 1991. 'Der radikalen Konstruktivismus: Ein neues Paradigma im interdisziplinaren Diskurs', pp. 11–88 in S. Schmidt (ed.), *Der Diskurs der Radikalen Konstruktivismus*. Frankfurt am Main: Suhrkamp.

Schnädelbach, H. 2000. *Philosophie in der modernen Kultur*. Frankfurt am Main: Suhrkamp.

Sennett, R. 1998. *The Corrosion of Character: The Personal Consequences of Work in the New Capitalism*. New York: Norton.

Serres, M. 1968. *Hermès I: La communication*. Paris: Minuit.

Serres, M. 1972. *Hermès II: L'interférence*. Paris: Minuit.

Serres, M. 1974. *Hermès III: La traduction*. Paris: Minuit.

Serres, M. 1977. *Hermès IV: La distribution*. Paris: Minuit.

Serres, M. 1980a. *Hermès V: Le passage du Nord-Ouest*. Paris: Minuit.

Serres, M. 1980b. *Le parasite*. Paris: Grasset.

Sharp, L. 1995. 'Organ transplantation as a transformative experience: anthropological insights into the restructuring of the self', *Medical Anthropology Quarterly*, 9, 3, pp. 357–389.

Sharp, L. 2000. 'The commodification of the body and its parts', *Annual Revue of Anthropology*, 29, pp. 287–328.

Shiva, V. 2001. *Protect or Plunder? Understanding Intellectual Property Rights*. London: Zed Books.

Simmel, G. 1989. *Philosophie des Geldes*, in *Simmel Gesamtausgabe, Band 6*. Frankfurt am Main: Suhrkamp.

Simondon, G. 1969. *Du mode d'existence des objets techniques*. Paris: Aubier.

Sloterdijk, P. 1999. *Regeln für den Menschenpark: Ein Antwortschreiben zu Heideggers Brief über den Humanismus*. Frankfurt am Main: Suhrkamp.

Sloterdijk, P. 2000. *Sphären: Mikrospärologie. Band I: Blasen*. Frankfurt am Main: Suhrkamp.

Sloterdijk, P. 2004. *Sphären. Plurale Sphärologie. Band III. Schäume*. Frankfurt am Main: Suhrkamp.

Soper, K. 1995. *What is Nature? Culture, Politics and the non-Human*. Oxford: Blackwell.

Stavro-Pearce, E. 1994. 'Towards a posthumanist feminism', *Economy and Society*, 23, 2, pp. 217–245.

Stiegler, Barbara. 2001. *Nietzsche et la biologie*. Paris: P.U.F.

Stiegler, Bernard. 1994. *La technique et le temps. 1. La faute d'Épiméthée*. Paris: Galilée.

Stiegler, Bernard. 2001. 'Hypostases, phantasmes, désincarnations', pp. 136–148 in D. Parrochia (ed.), *Penser les réseaux*. Seyssel: Champ Vallon.

Stiegler, Bernard. 2004. *De la misère symbolique. 1. L'époque hyperindustrielle*. Paris: Galilée.

Strathern, M. 1980. 'No nature, no culture: the Hagen case', pp. 174–222 in C. MacCormack and M. Strathern (eds), *Nature, Culture and Gender*. Cambridge: Cambridge University Press.

Strathern, M. 1991. *Partial Connections*. London: Rowman and Littlefield.

Strathern, M. 1992a. *After Nature: English Kinship in the Late Twentieth Century*. Cambridge: Cambridge University Press.

Strathern, M. 1992b. *Reproducing the Future: Essays on Anthropology, Kinship and the New Technologies*. Manchester: Manchester University Press.

Strathern, M. (ed.) 1995. *Shifting Contexts: Transformations in Anthropological Knowledge*. London: Routledge.

Strathern, M. 1999. *Property, Substance and Effect: Anthropological Essays on Persons and Things*. London: Athlone Press.

Strum, S. and Latour, B. 1988. 'Redefining the social link: from baboons to humans', *Social Science Information*, 26, pp. 783–802.

Suárez Müller, F. 2004. *Skepsis und Geschichte. Das Werk Michel Foucaults im Lichte des absoluten Idealismus*. Berlin: Königshausen.

Suárez Müller, F. 2005. 'Die Wiederaufstehung des Neffen Rameaus im Sphärenprojekt Sloterdijks', Ms.

Tarde, G. 1999. *Monadologie et sociologie*. Paris: Les empêcheurs de penser en rond.

Taylor, C. 1989. *Sources of the Self: The Making of the Modern Identity*. Cambridge, MA: Harvard University Press.

Thrift, N. 1999. 'The place of complexity', *Theory, Culture and Society*, 16, 3, pp. 31–69.

Tisseron, S. 1998. 'Abécédaire et parti-pris', *Cahiers de médiologie*, 6, 2, pp. 263–283.

Vandenberghe, F. 1997–1998. *Une histoire critique de la sociologie allemande. Aliénation et réification*, 2 vols. Paris: Editions la Découverte.

Vandenberghe, F. 1999. 'Globalizzazione e individualizatione nella tarda modernità. Un'introduzione teoretica alla sociologia della condizione giovanile', pp. 3–68 in G. Bettin (ed.), *Giovani e democrazia in Europa*, Tomo I: Cedam, Padova.

Vandenberghe, F. 2001. 'Reification, history of the concept', pp. 12993–12996 in D. Smelser and P. Baltes (eds), *International Encyclopaedia of the Social and Behavioral Sciences*, Vol. 19. Oxford: Pergamon Press.

Vandenberghe, F. 2002a. 'Reconstructing humants: a humanist critique of actor–network theory', *Theory, Culture and Society*, 19, 5–6.

Vandenberghe, F. 2002b. 'Working out Marx: Marxism and the end of the work society', *Thesis Eleven*, 69, pp. 21–46.

Vandenberghe, F. 2002c. 'Uncartesian meditations on the phenomenology of the nostril and the dissolution of the self', *Psychological Foundations* (New Delhi), 1, 2, pp. 48–62.

Vandenberghe, F. 2009. *A Philosophical History of German Sociology*. London: Routledge.

van den Daele, W. 1992. 'Concepts of nature in modern societies and nature as a theme in sociology', pp. 526–560 in M. Dierkes and B. Biervert (eds), *European Social Science in Transition*. Boulder, CO: Westview Press.

van den Daele, W. 2000. 'Die Natürlichkeit des Menschen als Kriterium und Schranke technischer Eingriffe', *WechselWirkung*, 21, 103–104, pp. 24–31.

Viveiros de Castro, E. 2002. *A inconstância da alma selvagem*. São Paulo: Cosacnaify.

Weber, M. 1922. *Gesammelte Aufsätze zur Religionssoziologie I*. Tübingen: Mohr.

Weber, M. 1917/1992a. *Wissenschaft als Beruf* in *Max Weber Gesamtausgabe, I/17*. Tübingen: Mohr.

Weber, M. 1919/1992b. *Politik als Beruf* in *Max Weber Gesamtausgabe, I/17*. Tübingen: Mohr.

Williams, R. 1976. *Keywords: A Vocabulary of Culture and Society*. London: Fontana.

Zoglauer, T. 2002. *Konstruiertes Leben. Ethische Probleme der Humangentechnik*. Darmstadt: Wissenschaftliche Buchgesellschaft.

Index